BPP UNIVERSITY
LIBRARY AND
INFORMATION SERVICES

D0519695

Iss
Ma

This book is due back on or before
the date stamped below.

BPP Business School Library, 2 St.
Mary Axe, London. EC3A 8BF.
Tel. 0207 025 0486

library@bpp.com

BPP
UNIVERSITY

BPP University

108920

We work with leading authors to develop the strongest
educational materials in accounting, bringing cutting-edge
thinking and best learning practice to a global market.

Under a range of well-known imprints, including
Financial Times Prentice Hall, we craft high quality print
and electronic publications which help readers
to understand and apply their content, whether
studying or at work.

To find out more about the complete range of our
publishing, please visit us on the World Wide Web at:
www.pearsoned.co.uk

Issues in Management Accounting

Third Edition

Edited by
**Trevor Hopper, Deryl Northcott
and Robert Scapens**

FT Prentice Hall
FINANCIAL TIMES

An imprint of **Pearson Education**
Harlow, England • London • New York • Boston • San Francisco • Toronto • Sydney • Singapore • Hong Kong
Tokyo • Seoul • Taipei • New Delhi • Cape Town • Madrid • Mexico City • Amsterdam • Munich • Paris • Milan

Pearson Education Limited

Edinburgh Gate
Harlow
Essex CM20 2JE
England

and Associated Companies throughout the world

Visit us on the World Wide Web at:
www.pearsoned.co.uk

First published 1991
Second edition published 1995
Third edition published 2007

© Pearson Education Limited 1991, 1995, 2007

All rights reserved. No part of this publication may be reproduced, stored in
a retrieval system, or transmitted in any form or by any means, electronic,
mechanical, photocopying, recording or otherwise, without either the prior
written permission of the publisher or a licence permitting restricted copying
in the United Kingdom issued by the Copyright Licensing Agency Ltd,
Saffron House, 6–10 Kirby Street, London ECIN 8TS.

All trademarks used herein are the property of their respective owners. The use of any
trademark in this text does not vest in the author or publisher any trademark ownership
rights in such trademarks, nor does the use of such trademarks imply any affiliation with
or endorsement of this book by such owners.

ISBN 978-0-273-70257-3

British Library Cataloguing-in-Publication Data
A catalogue record for this book is available from the British Library

ARP Impression 98

Typeset in 9.5/12.5pt Palatino by 35

The publisher's policy is to use paper manufactured from sustainable forests.
Printed in Great Britain by Clays Ltd, St Ives plc

Contents

Contents

Part 2
'New' management accounting techniques

Part 3
'New' applications of management accounting

Part 4
Understanding management accounting change

List of contributors

Fadi Alkaraan is Assistant Professor of Management Accounting at the University of Aleppo, Syria. He received his PhD from Manchester Business School, UK, and has since held positions at Abu Dhabi University and United Arab Emirates University. His research interests include strategic management accounting, management accounting change, and strategic investment appraisal and decision-making in the UK.

Christian Ax is Associate Professor at the School of Business, Economics and Law at Göteborg University, Sweden. His current research interests include studying the diffusion of management accounting innovations, the design and use of management control systems, and the relationship between financial accounting and management accounting.

Gudrun Baldvinsdottir has been a Lecturer at the University of Dundee, UK, since 2005, having previously held academic positions at the University of Göteborg in Sweden. Her main research interests are the relationships between management accounting and such concepts as trust, accountability and communication.

Trond Bjørnenak is Professor of Management Accounting at the Norwegian School of Economics and Business Administration Bergen. His research interests include conceptual modelling of management accounting systems, diffusion of management accounting innovations, and the design and use of costing systems in practice. He is on the editorial boards of *Management Accounting Research* and various practitioner-oriented Scandinavian journals.

Jan Bouwens is Professor of Accounting at Tilburg University in the Netherlands and holds a research fellow position at Melbourne University Australin. His research is in performance measurement systems design. He is mainly interested in how organisations structure their activities and put performance measures in place so as to explore and exploit the firm's synergy potentials.

John Burns is Professor of Management and Accountancy at the University of Dundee, UK. He has also previously held academic positions at the University of Manchester and the University of Colorado. He is an Associate Editor for *Management Accounting Research*, and co-founder of the European Network for Research of Organisational and Accounting Change (ENROAC). His main research interests are management accounting and organisational change, and institutional theory.

Cristiano Busco is Associate Professor of Management Accounting at the University of Siena, Italy and a part-time Senior Lecturer at Manchester Business School, UK. He has also held a visiting position at the University of Southern California, Los Angeles. He has published in academic and professional journals including *Management Accounting Research* and *Strategic Finance*. His research interests include aspects of management accounting theory and practice, as well as accounting interplays with processes of organisational change.

Niels Dechow is a Lecturer of Management Studies at SAID Business School at the University of Oxford, UK. With a background in management accounting and control, his main research focus is on the implications of new technologies and modern control concepts for corporate information management.

Lin Fitzgerald is Professor of Management Accounting at Loughborough University Business School, UK, where she is currently Head of the Accounting and Finance Department. Lin is a member of CIMA's Research Board and her research interests and publications are in the areas of performance measurement and cost information for decision-making in service organisations. Much of her research is inter-disciplinary and case based.

Richard Fleischman is a Professor of Accountancy at the Boler School of Business, John Carroll University, USA. He is the editor of the *Accounting Historians Journal* and has written extensively on the cost accounting of the British Industrial Revolution, US standard costing, and the complicity of accountants in support of the racism reflected in Anglo-American slave regimes.

Warwick Funnell is currently a Professor of Accounting in the School of Accounting and Finance at the University of Wollongong, Australia and at the University of Kent, UK. His main research interests are the history of public sector audit and contemporary reforms to public sector accountability and management. He is the author of six books, the most recent of which is *Accounting for War*.

Elena Giovannoni is a Lecturer in Business Administration at the Faculty of Engineering, University of Siena, Italy. She was a Marie Curie Research Fellow at the Manchester School of Accounting and Finance and has held a visiting position at Manchester Business School, UK. She has published in academic and professional journals including *Accounting History* and *Strategic Finance.*

Robert F. Göx is Professor of Management Accounting and Control, and President of the Department of Business Administration at the University of Fribourg, Switzerland. He is a member of the editorial board of the *European Accounting Review*. He also served on the board of the *Journal of Management Accounting Research* (2002–2006). His research interests include management accounting and the design of compensation systems.

Markus Granlund is Professor of Management Accounting at Turku School of Economics, Finland. His research interests cover a wide range of technical and behavioural issues in the fields of management accounting and information systems. He is also an Associate Editor of *European Accounting Review.*

Allan Hansen is Associate Professor of Management Accounting at Copenhagen Business School, Denmark. His research interests cover a wide range of issues related to cost accounting and performance measurement in new product development, manufacturing and inter-organisational relations. Currently, he is exploring the role of practice-based research strategies in management accounting.

Graeme Harrison is Professor of Accounting in the Department of Accounting and Finance at Macquarie University in Sydney, Australia. His research interests are management accounting and international accounting, particularly national and organisational cultural influences on management control systems.

Trevor Hopper is a part-time Professor of Management Accounting at the Manchester Business School, UK, visiting professor at Stockholm School of Economics, Sweden and adjunct professor at Victoria University of Wellington, New Zealand. He has held visiting positions at Griffith University – Gold Coast, Australia; University of Michigan, USA; Queen's University, Canada; and the Universities of Kyushu and Fukuoka, Japan. His major research interests lie in the areas of management accounting and control, especially from organisational perspectives.

Christopher Humphrey is a Professor of Accounting and Head of the Manchester Accounting and Finance Group at Manchester Business School, UK. His research interests include auditing, public sector financial management, accounting education and qualitative research methodology. He is an associate editor of the *European Accounting Review* and is on the editorial advisory boards of several other international journals. He is currently a co-opted academic member of the Council of the Institute of Chartered Accountants in England and Wales (ICAEW).

Ingrid Jeacle is a Senior Lecturer in Accounting at the Management School and Economics, University of Edinburgh, UK. Her research interests include both historical and contemporary management accounting practices. She has a particular interest in the role of accounting in everyday life, encompassing such issues as consumerism, fashion, architecture and interior design.

Kalle Kraus is a PhD student in the Department of Accounting and Business Law at the Stockholm School of Economics, Sweden. His research interest lies primarily in the area of inter-organisational control in public sector organisations.

Johnny Lind is Associate Professor at the Department of Accounting and Business Law at the Stockholm School of Economics, Sweden. His main research interests are in the areas of inter-organisational control, strategy and management control, and accounting in the manufacturing sector.

Beverley R. Lord is a Senior Lecturer in the Department of Accountancy, Finance and Information Systems at the University of Canterbury, New Zealand. Her major research interest is management accounting innovation, particularly in small and medium enterprises.

Maria Major is Assistant Professor of Management Accounting at ISCTE Business School in Lisbon, Portugal. Her PhD from the University of Manchester, UK, was on ABC and regulation in the telecommunications sector. Maria's current research interests lie in management accounting change in private and public organisations and she is on the editorial board of *Journal of Accounting & Organizational Change*. She is currently conducting a research project funded by the Portuguese Government on management control in the healthcare sector.

Jill McKinnon is Associate Professor of Accounting and Assistant Director of the Graduate Accounting and Commerce Centre at Macquarie University in Sydney, Australia. Her research interests include international accounting, cultural influences on accounting, financial accounting and local government audit tendering.

Falconer Mitchell is Professor of Management Accounting at the University of Edinburgh, UK. He is also Chairman of the Research Board of the Chartered Institute of Management Accountants, UK. His research interests lie in cost management and the development of management accounting.

Sven Modell is Professor of Accounting at the Manchester Business School, UK. His research interests pivot around the social, political and institutional aspects of management accounting and control, especially in a public sector context. He has conducted extensive research into changing performance management, costing and resource allocation practices. His current research targets performance management issues in central government.

Jodie Moll is a Lecturer in Accounting at the Manchester Business School, UK. Her main research interests are in the areas of management control and public sector accounting. She gained her PhD degree at Griffith University, Australia, studying higher education reform and the budgetary effects on universities. Jodie is an associate editor for the *Journal of Accounting & Organizational Change*.

Jan Mouritsen is Professor of Management Control at Copenhagen Business School, Denmark. His research is oriented towards understanding the role of management techniques in various organisational contexts. This research includes topics such as intellectual capital and knowledge management, technology management, management control and operations management, new accounting and management control. He is on the editorial board of 17 journals and has published more than 190 articles and books.

Hanne Nørreklit is Professor of International Management Control at Aarhus School of Business, University of Aarhus, Denmark and part-time Professor at the Manchester Business School. Her research areas include international management control, management rhetoric and validity issues in management control.

Deryl Northcott is Professor of Management Accounting at the Auckland University of Technology, New Zealand. She is co-editor of *Qualitative Research in Accounting & Management* and an editorial board member for the *Journal of Accounting & Organizational Change*. Her research interests include capital investment decision-making and health sector costing, benchmarking and performance management.

Angelo Riccaboni is Professor of Accounting and Dean of the Faculty of Economics at the University of Siena, Italy. Angelo is also the chairman of CRESCO, the Centre for Evaluation and Control of the University of Siena. His research interests include various aspects of management control theory and practice.

Hanno Roberts is Professor of Management Accounting and Control at the Norwegian School of Management in Oslo, Norway. He has held visiting positions in Finland, France, Germany, Spain and Sweden, and is an editorial board member of several international and national research journals. His research interests lie in the areas of management accounting and control for the knowledge-intensive firm, and of local information systems and organisational change.

Robert W. Scapens is an Emeritus Professor at the Manchester Business School, UK, and Professor of Management Accounting at the University of Groningen in the Netherlands. Together with Michael Bromwich, he co-founded *Management Accounting Research* and he is now the Editor-in-Chief. He is recognised as a leading international researcher in the management accounting field. He has used both quantitative and qualitative research methods, and has written extensively on research methodology and the methods of case research. His recent research has included major projects on management accounting change (for CIMA and ESRC) and on performance measurement systems in multinational corporations (for ICAEW).

Roland Speklé is Professor of Management Accounting and Control at Nyenrode Business University in Breukelen, the Netherlands. His main research interests concern the economics of organisational control. Primarily working from a comparative contracting perspective, his research focuses on understanding differences in management control structures within and between firms.

Juhani Vaivio is Acting Professor of Management Accounting at the Helsinki School of Economics (HSE), Finland. His research has investigated strategic non-financial measurement, the logic of management accounting change, changing roles of business controllers, accounting and culture, and methodological issues. Besides scholarly duties and executive training, Juhani is Director of HSE MBA Programs and Head of the HSE International Center.

Alfred Wagenhofer is a Professor of Management Accounting and Control and Head of the Center for Accounting Research at the University of Graz in Austria, and is a Professor at the European Institute for Advanced Studies in Management, Belgium. He is co-editor of the *Zeitschrift für betriebswirtschaftliche Forschung/Schmalenbach Business Review*. His research interests include financial as well as management accounting and international accounting.

Introduction

Trevor Hopper, Deryl Northcott and Bob Scapens

The aims of this third edition of *Issues in Management Accounting* remain unchanged from previous editions. Our intention is to produce a collection of articles on cutting edge research topics, written by leading researchers in a style accessible to managers, students and academics who are not necessarily specialists in the area. The motivation is our belief that conventional management accounting textbooks are invariably weak on theory, neglect contemporary research, and are unduly conservative and professionally and technically oriented. Nevertheless, this book does not seek to replace such textbooks, but rather to complement and extend them so readers can gain a broader insight into current management accounting issues by incorporating material from recent research.

Eleven years have elapsed since the second edition, and 15 since the first. Both were adopted on many courses worldwide. Given this passage of time, rather than adapting and updating material from previous editions we decided to start with a clean slate. Consequently, no chapters from previous editions were retained or updated. This is no reflection on their quality: many remain definitive and valid today, and readers would benefit from reading them alongside contributions in this edition. However, we decided to review the field of management accounting research afresh in order to ascertain key topics deserving of a chapter in this new edition, and to decide who might effectively write on them. We were fortunate that each author first approached responded positively, and on reflection we realised that the choice of contributors had become more international. Not only has management accounting practice become more global, so has the academic research community.

The contributions are organised in four parts that develop and advance important management accounting research themes. Part 1 examines the changing nature of management accounting, providing the context for Part 2's focus on 'new' management accounting techniques and Part 3's discussions of 'new' applications of management accounting. Part 4 presents contributions to understanding contemporary management accounting change and how the developments in management accounting theory and practice can be seen as a response to such change. However, the parts are not mutually exclusive – inevitably and rightly they overlap considerably.

The topics within these four parts are not dramatically different to those in the first edition, although research advances offer greater insights. For example, history remains central for explaining not only the past but also the present; behavioural issues surrounding control and change continue to be vital and perplexing; accounting's role in public sector transformation persists and remains contentious; information technology developments increasingly transform the role of accountants and their control systems; consultants continue to offer 'new' (or repackaged old) techniques accompanied by frenetic rhetoric on the deleterious consequences of not adopting them; researchers remain divided theoretically, especially between the social theory and economic camps. In addition, management accounting continues to extend beyond issues of internal control, which emphasises manufacturing cost efficiency and stability. Now, it embraces wider strategic, inter-organisational, global and cross-cultural issues and it focuses on change and adaptation, value creation through knowledge production and innovation, and how new organisational forms pose challenges for conventional management accounting.

The part on the changing nature of management accounting pursues some themes contained in previous editions, most notably the effects of new philosophies of operations management and the rapidly changing information and communications technology. Chapter 1 by Hansen and Mouritsen and Chapter 3 by Dechow, Granlund and Mouritsen discuss these developments and note their often unexpected and dramatic effects, although readers are counselled against too readily assuming the demise of conventional management accounting. Chapter 2 by Jeacle examines the implications for management accounting of the growth of consumerism and the shift from standardised mass production to the niche retailing of fashion items in the face of the more variegated and fickle life-styles of consumers. This is an international phenomenon, certainly in richer societies, and mirrors how firms and markets are becoming more international.

Chapter 4 by Busco, Giovannoni and Riccaboni examines the effects of globalisation on the control structures of international organisations and considers whether a worldwide convergence of management accounting knowledge and practices is occurring. Chapter 5 by Harrison and McKinnon, which traces the effects of different national cultures on the efficacy of different types of management control, addresses practical concerns about how to manage the growing globalisation of business, the rapid diffusion of ideas internationally, and geographically dispersed organisations containing divergent cultures. In Chapter 6, Burns and Baldvinsdottir reflect on how change is impacting the role of management accountants. They argue that the major debate resides in whether the management accountant's job is disappearing or merely being reconstituted, as new technologies and flatter, less functional organisational structures diminish the accountants' ownership and control of organisational data. It may be that everyone is capable of becoming their own management accountant and consequently the role of management accountants (if that is what they will be called in the future) will be that of analysts serving multi-functional teams.

The first edition of this book noted how management accounting is subject to a stream of innovative new practices, often justified by berating the conventional practices, and equally often marketed by large, international firms of consultants. This remains so today. Hence, Part 2 examines the allegedly 'new' management accounting techniques; namely strategic management accounting, activity-based costing/management, balanced scorecards, strategic investment appraisal, and performance measurement systems. All the chapters in Part 2 note how the growth of strategic concerns has extended the management accounting domain. This is attributed to the growing sensitivity of businesses to heightened environmental threats and opportunities and the imperative to anticipate change and respond quickly. The growth of strategic management accounting issues is reviewed by Lord in Chapter 7, while more specific techniques are examined in the other chapters in this part.

Balanced scorecards, examined by Nørreklit and Mitchell in Chapter 9, are seen as an attempt to link strategic concerns to operational systems by identifying and controlling key factors that go beyond financial variables. Its antecedents lie in activity-based costing/management (ABC/M), which is examined by Major in Chapter 8. Retrospectively, ABC/M may be seen as an attempt to extend and improve control over the growing proportion of overheads in modern businesses. Moreover, value now accrues not only from production efficiency, but also from less tangible activities such as design, product development, product innovation and marketing. Hence the desire to measure and evaluate activities that were previously treated as an inevitable 'burden' and beyond detailed management accounting control. Chapter 10, in which Northcott and Alkaraan review developments in capital investment appraisal, extends this theme by noting how investment evaluation techniques can go beyond the financial and easily measurable factors to incorporate less tangible but vital elements of investment.

In Chapter 11 Fitzgerald picks up on the tension between, on the one hand, the 'financialisation' of measurement and control, wrought partly by greater short-termism induced by capital market pressures and, on the other hand, the need to identify, measure and monitor non-financial factors, and to reinforce them with appropriate performance evaluation and rewards. This chapter compares and contrasts such performance measurement systems as economic value added and the balanced scorecard, and examines their behavioural consequences. None of the contributions in this second part actually rejects the new techniques, but all show how research has revealed problems requiring consideration and/or resolution; thereby adding a note of caution to temper the claims of uncritical advocates of these new techniques.

While Part 2 focuses on techniques that seek to address emerging issues in contemporary organisations using a largely accounting-centric approach (albeit reformulated to incorporate other factors), Part 3 explores the challenges presented by the growing scope of management accounting and describes some of the new approaches being developed to meet them. Chapter 12 by Bouwens and Speklé links Parts 2 and 3 through an analysis of EVA (economic value added). Here, the possibilities of evaluating and rewarding activities using modern economic approaches are examined. The authors explore the desirable characteristics of performance measurement systems, and assess whether EVA adds value; concluding that it is no panacea. In Chapter 13 Kraus and Lind broaden the discussion to explore issues of management control in inter-organisational relationships, defined as various forms of cooperation between independent organisations; for example, joint ventures, strategic alliances, technology licensing, research consortia, strategic partnerships, supply chain relationships, business relationships, and outsourcing relationships. The chapter indicates some of the tools that can be used for inter-organisational control, but it is stressed that the appropriate tools will depend on the nature of the relationship.

The discussion is broadened further in Chapter 14 by Moll and Humphrey, who examine management accounting issues in the public sector; with a particular focus on the challenges presented by the Public Finance Initiative and Public–Private Partnerships (PFI and PPP). The chapter explores the role of, and key matters confronting, public sector management accountants in an era where considerable attention is devoted to matters of public sector financial management and the soundness of public finance and capital investment decisions. The final chapter in Part 3, Chapter 15 by Roberts, examines the role of management accounting in knowledge-based organisations. In modern advanced economies knowledge resources are an extremely important source of value and competitive advantage. The chapter argues that management accounting for knowledge resources does not require a radical overhaul of existing management accounting practices, but it does require a long and hard look at how they are used.

Having considered the broadening scope of management accounting in Part 3, Part 4 explores issues concerned with management accounting change. Chapter 16 by Modell reviews a number of influential strands within the growing research literature on management accounting change and assesses the relative merits and limitations of each. In particular, it discusses the factor studies that focus on the implementation of new 'advanced' management accounting techniques, as well as the more process-oriented research based on institutional theories which provide examples of both management accounting change and resistance to change. Continuing the theme of management accounting change, Chapter 17 by Ax and Bjørnenak examines a fundamental, but as yet poorly understood, phenomenon; namely, the origins of management accounting innovations and how are they diffused. Why is there a constant stream of new techniques, why do they wax and wane, how do they move to new locations, what drives this process, and who is involved? The chapter explores both the demand side (based on efficient choice theory) and the supply side (based on both the management fashion perspective and the market and infrastructure perspective).

We take a much longer time perspective on change by looking at the past in Chapter 18. In that chapter Fleischman and Funnell remind us not to be so preoccupied by novelty and newness that we neglect the relevance of the past for understanding contemporary problems. Their articulation of what history has to contribute to those wishing to understand the present should be read alongside the review of management accounting history by Ann Loft in the previous edition, for it presumes some knowledge of management accounting history on the part of the reader.

Finally, we come to the question of how to best study and theorise about management accounting practices. The last two contributions examine this issue with respect to economics (Chapter 19) and qualitative research (Chapter 20). In Chapter 19, Göx and Wagenhofer argue that from the perspective of economic research, management accounting provides information that is useful to decision-makers within the firm. The chapter presents some of the economic models that can be used to explore the decision-making role of management accounting information. The authors conclude that economic research complements other research methods to help us better understand management accounting practices. In Chapter 20, Vaivio provides an overview of some of these other research methods. The aim of the chapter is to build an understanding of qualitative research to enable the reader to appreciate the theoretical significance of fieldwork and case studies. The chapter presents a broad panorama of ideas about qualitative research in management accounting, and seeks to act as a counterweight to textbook idealisations, formalised economic models and consultancy products.

To summarise, whilst this new edition updates developments in ongoing research themes that were described in previous editions, it also contains new trends which have become more prominent in recent years. First, management accounting knowledge has become more global, as is reflected in the greater international diversity of the authors in this third edition. Today the management accounting research community transcends national boundaries, and changes in management accounting practice are linked to the rapid transfer of ideas across national borders. Also, the focus of management accounting is increasingly on managing transactions and organisations globally rather than nationally, as noted in the chapters dealing with cultural differences, change, control in multinational firms, and the diffusion of accounting innovations.

A second trend concerns the increasingly porous boundaries of organisations and the broadening scope of management accounting. The latter is marked by the changing composition of the costs that need to be controlled, the extension of KPIs and critical performance measurement variables (beyond the merely financial), the incorporation of external factors, and the changing role of the management accounting function (from scorekeeping to business analysis). Increasingly, competitive advantage and value added stem from non-manufacturing activities, which consequently are becoming major objects of management scrutiny and the focus of management accounting practices. The relative decline of manufacturing in advanced economies, or at least its export to cheaper developing countries, has prompted the growth of allegedly 'new' accounting techniques which offer the prospect of dissecting what was previously dismissed as an inscrutable 'overhead burden'.

Third, changes in the global business environment have prompted an increasing interest in the role, if any, that management accounting can play in this new world. Many of these changes are reflected in this new edition, including the 'hollowing out' of manufacturing organisations in richer countries, whereby many manufacturing and service activities are sub-contracted offshore to lower cost countries, the recognition that competitiveness and value added lie in intelligent organisations and knowledge-based systems, and the social shift from production to consumerism, with shopping and retailing its apotheosis.

Fourth, a persistent undercurrent in many of the contributions is concern about the transformation and possible disappearance of the management accounting function. The automation of many of its routine activities, the greater integration of controls, and the growing need for advice and problem-solving, rather than routine reporting, are raising profound issues about the changing role of management accountants. Rather than relying on traditional techniques and tasks, the professional management accountant of the future will need new skills and training. The requirement to embrace broader roles will call for constantly updated management accounting knowledge, including the ability to access, generate and interpret research in its widest sense.

To conclude, the contributions assembled in this third edition describe advances across a broad range of contemporary management accounting topics. Their exposition of enduring research concerns and new, emergent themes offers fresh insights into many important topics and questions occupying contemporary management accounting researchers and practitioners. The resultant themes of change, adaptation and under-standing combine to make this third edition of *Issues in Management Accounting* a significant advance on what has gone before and, we hope, a useful signpost for what is to come.

Acknowledgements

We are grateful to the following for permission to reproduce copyright material:

Chapter 1, Table 1.1 from Slack, N., Chambers, S., Johnston, R. (2004) *Operations Management*. FT Prentice-Hall/Pearson Education, Harlow; Chapter 3, Figures 3.1 & 3.4 from SAP AG (1999c) *Tools and Accelerators Turbo Charging Your Installation*. Walldorf, Germany, SAP AG; Chapter 3, Tables 3.2 & 3.3 from Dechow, N. (2001) SAPiens perspectives on Enterprise Resource Planning. Copenhagen Business School. PHD Series 11.2001 © Niels Dechow; Chapter 3, Figure 3.3 from Keller, G., Teufel, T. (1999) SAP R/3 Process-oriented Implementation: Iterative Process Prototyping; Chapter 4, Figure 4.4 from http://www.ge.com/en/ge/contact.htm, General Electric; Chapter 9, Figure 9.1 and Appendix 9.1(1) from Kaplan, R.S. and Norton, D.P. (1996) The Balanced Scorecard, p. 9 & p.155. Harvard Business School Press, Boston; Chapter 9, Appendix 9.1(1) from The University of Edinburgh Balanced Scorecard for 2005/2006 as at December 2006 (as published at http://www.PLANNING.AC.ED.UK/BSC/0506BSC.htm). Material reproduced with the permission of the University of Edinburgh. Please see website www/planning.ed.ac.uk/BSC.htm for current information; Chapter 10, Figures 10.1 and 10.2 Reprinted from *British Accounting Review* 38 Alkaraan, F., Northcott, D. Strategic capital investment decision-making: A role for emergent analysis tools? 1–25 Copyright 2006 with permission from Elsevier; Chapter 10, Figure 10.3 Reprinted from King, P. (1975) Is the emphasis of capital budgeting theory misplaced? *Journal of Business Finance and Accounting* 2(1): 69–82, with permission from Blackwell Publishing.

In some instances we have been unable to trace the owners of copyright material, and we would appreciate any information that would enable us to do so.

Part I

The changing nature
of management accounting

1

Management accounting and changing operations management

Allan Hansen and Jan Mouritsen

Introduction

Management accounting calculates organisational performance for decision-making, coordination and motivation using techniques such as cost allocation, responsibility centres, transfer prices, product costing, performance measurement and budgeting. All are expected to contribute to increased firm value. Operations management has a parallel agenda, but has other techniques. These specify flows of materials, resources and products, outline layout in manufacturing and service settings and are concerned with non-financial aspects of performance such as time, quality, flexibility and innovation, which are steps in a chain leading to increased firm value.

Whereas management accounting typically focuses on performance numbers that managers use 'at a distance' for control or decision-making, operations management primarily focuses on 'hands-on' technological, organisational and architectural dimensions of operations. These differences are often described as creating a tension between the two disciplines, and accounting is often portrayed as a problem for operations management due to its hierarchical and financial focus and its orientation towards standards and control. These characteristics of accounting are said to fit poorly with changing operations practices that emphasise lateral relations, learning, continuous improvement, empowerment and non-financial performance. These tensions have led some to argue that accounting should be disconnected from operational control.

In this chapter we critically examine this claim, arguing that there are several connections between accounting and operations controls. In particular, hierarchy, financial criteria, standards and control still play significant roles in operations management, even though they may seem provocative to the operations management rhetoric of laterality, empowerment, learning and non-financial success. However, in discussing these concerns, we intend to develop a new understanding of the interrelationship between operations management and management accounting to learn more about the role of accounting and the characteristics of operations management. There are many connections between management accounting and operations management; the remainder of this chapter discusses these.

The chapter is organised as follows. The next section outlines central issues in new operations management practices. Then, we describe how operations management research depicts the 'problem of accounting' and follow this with an outline of how management accounting research has responded to the challenges from new operations management principles. The chapter ends with concluding remarks.

Operations management: central issues

Skinner (1974) argued that the role of manufacturing or operations is strategic. Several commentators, researchers and others have followed his suggestions for increasing a company's competitive advantage through manufacturing (Hayes and Wheelwright, 1984; Schonberger, 1986; Womack et al., 1991). Numerous complex management concepts have been introduced to delineate better ways to manage modern operations. Total quality management (TQM), just in time (JIT), lean manufacturing, agile manufacturing, time-based management, world class manufacturing and flexible manufacturing are just a few examples.

Operations management books say that operations management is about the frictions posed by time and space on organisations and beyond. It requires time and energy to transport things from one location to another; movements of parts to and along assembly lines can be cumbersome; and coordinating people around a product, process or service raises complex temporal and locational challenges. Therefore, a central concern is how people, technology and materials should be organised given different production characteristics such as volume, variety, variation in demand, and types of customer contact. Operations management is concerned with how production processes, both within and beyond organisational boundaries, meet external demands for the firm's products or services. It is possible to identify two extreme types of manufacturing systems. One combines high volume, low product variety, low variation in demand and low customer contact. The other is the opposite, namely low volume and high product variety, high variation in demand and high customer contact. The first represents a manufacturing system run for maximum efficiency, whereas the other concentrates on flexibility.

Figure 1.1 shows how four key dimensions of a manufacturing system differ between two alternative approaches to designing operations to accommodate changes in the environment. One design produces at a low cost and the other, whilst more costly, can produce more differentiated products that sell at relatively higher prices. The system on the right of Figure 1.1 is a mass-producer with high routine and predictability, while the system on the left is flexible and complex. Actual designs implement these principles in some form. But, before illustrating this, it is useful to introduce the opposing ideas about factory and operations organisation that are inherent in materials' requirement planning (MRP) systems and just in time (JIT) principles, since they illustrate the control problems encountered in such production systems.

Material requirement planning and just in time systems

The 1980s was an important period for operations management because two directly opposing systems of manufacture stood face to face: the American and the Japanese. Previously, the superiority of the American system was taken for granted in most of the modern world, but Japanese manufacturing success challenged it. The discussion revolved around the relative merits of a production organisation based on hierarchical intervention using MRP systems and a lateral view of production organisation based on JIT (see Table 1.1).

Low Low repetition Each staff member performs Several jobs Less systemisation High unit cost	**Volume**	*High* High repeatability Specialisation Systemisation Capital intensive Low unit cost
High Flexible Complex Match customer needs Irregular High unit cost	**Variety**	*Low* Well defined Routine Standardised Regular Low unit cost
High Changing capacity Anticipation Flexibility Demand driven High unit cost	**Variation in demand**	*Low* Stable Routine Predictable High utilisation Low unit cost
High Short waiting tolerance Customer satisfaction Customer contact skills necessary High received variety Decentralisation High unit cost	**Customer contact**	*Low* Time lag between production and consumption Standardised Low contact skills necessary High staff utilisation Centralisation Low unit cost

Figure 1.1 Sources of differentiation in operations
Source: Slack *et al.*, 2004.

As Table 1.1 illustrates, MRP and JIT provide distinct and opposing principles for designing manufacturing systems and associated planning and control techniques. The MRP system is largely hierarchical while JIT is largely lateral. MRP principles emphasise corporate planning, whereas JIT emphasises adaptation between sequentially connected stations. MRP tries to maximise productivity and capacity utilisation, whereas JIT stresses throughput and quality.

MRP uses a master plan to identify demands for raw materials, intermediate products and finished products over the relevant planning horizon. The breakdown of this is done by a planning department, using bills of materials that detail how products are built from various components. This is done for each product and each station that produces and assembles components. The aim is to determine economically optimal production batches by minimising set-up costs, inventory holdings and handling within each process. Inventory levels are a function of optimal batch size. Hence, MRP is a *push-system*: production planning pushes products through the system based on detailed plans of what each station should produce and when.

JIT is different as it attempts to eliminate inventories rather than use them as management levers. JIT reduces inventory by reducing batch sizes, the throughput time of products, and set-up times, and by eliminating redundant components and products.

Table 1.1 **Differences between MRP and JIT**

	MRP	JIT
Success criteria	• The ambition is to maximise capacity utilisation at every station in a production system.	• The ambition is to maximise throughput and quality for the production space.
Work organisation	• Sequentially dependent stations disrupt each other.	• Each station is a small part of a larger process of production which has primacy relative to the station.
Coordination mechanism	• MRP systems plan for activities and inventories for and around each station. • Based on forecast information, the MRP system breaks down required production for each station per period, and it builds necessary inventories based on knowledge about fluctuations in and uncertainty about demand and production efficiency.	• KanBans are small items of information which inform a previous station that a later station needs inputs. • The KanBans, which are simple requests, relate stations to each other through concrete requirements derived from actual production. There are no inventories because KanBans refer to actual demand for products.
The planning process	• From a master plan about demand for products, the MRP principle is to break down operations so that activities are organised in time and space through a centralised planning effort.	• The production of each station is determined by actual production orders, which respond immediately to foreseen production schedules.
Handling of uncertainty	• Inventories before and after each station reduce interdependencies because they buffer against unplanned shortfalls for preceding stations.	• Zero defect strategies and multi-skilled workers reduce uncertainty. Each station only produces items explicitly demanded from a station located later in the production process. This eliminates inventories and reduces waste.

JIT's imperatives are to eliminate: (i) work-in-progress inventories by reducing batch size, (ii) raw material inventories by making suppliers deliver directly to the production line at the right time (just before use), (iii) errors by emphasising total quality management, (iv) finished-good inventories by only producing to order, and (v) costs of handling materials by designing the factory layout to minimise the movement of components. JIT is a *pull-system:* demand based on the KanBan, a production order that travels upstream and pulls production through the manufacturing system. Detailed production planning is thus lateral; central production planning is primarily concerned with capacity planning and investments. Figure 1.2 details the different flows of information within MRP and JIT systems.

The arrows in bold from left to right show movements of materials and goods. The two-way arrows illustrate links between central planning and the work of stations. The dotted lines illustrate KanBan information going from right to left.

The principles of each system are very different. Increasingly, MRP principles are ridiculed for being traditional and in conflict with world class manufacturing practices.

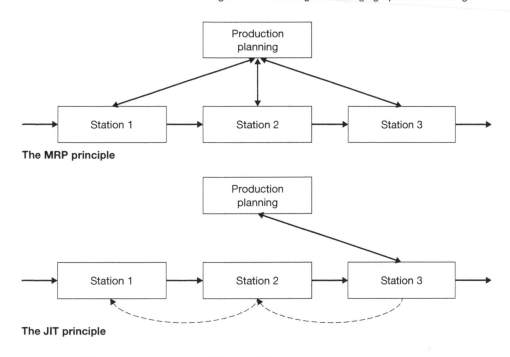

Figure 1.2 Differences between MRP and JIT principles of manufacturing

However, before examining this claim, it is useful to consider *how* both approaches can provide productive principles for operations management. Both try to do the same thing: to organise production by aligning consumer demand with the assembly of components within and outside the firm. MRP is driven by a master schedule based on estimated future customer demand and derives a production schedule by modelling lead time. The production schedule, a time-phased plan for making parts available when and where they are used, is an ideal however, because disturbances like quality problems or breakdowns confuse the plan and increase inventories. The MRP master plan can thus become unworkable locally. In contrast, JIT attempts to meet customer demand directly, since KanBans ensure that the immediate customer (often an internal station) is served according to actual demand. This works well if throughput time is less than demand lead time (i.e. production exceeds the demand time constraints). If this is not the case, some feed-forward planning and inventory building may occur even in JIT settings. This may be effective when disturbances are low – i.e. when demand has been levelled – which makes JIT good for control, but less useful for planning. Such complexity is dealt with more easily by MRP because, in principle, detailed parts requirements and special features can be entered into the planning system. JIT has problems aligning different volumes and variability, and handling instantaneous change. Over the last two decades, the operations management debate has favoured JIT, which has evolved into world class manufacturing and lean manufacturing approaches.

Lean manufacturing

Today, lean or world class manufacturing is considered best practice. Karlsson and Åhlström (1996) illustrate how lean manufacturing integrates a firm's development, procurement, manufacturing and distribution activities. They suggest that the firm should be understood in lateral terms, arguing that assembling and moving a product or a service into, through and beyond the firm is fundamental to understanding value creation. Hierarchical activities are seen to be non-value adding and to violate lean manufacturing principles that 'specify value by specific product, identify the value stream for each product, make value flow without interruptions, let the customer pull value from the producer and pursue perfection' (Womack *et al.* 1991, p. 5).

In the lean firm, the product rather than the organisation is central. Production technologies are developed around the product, and the value chain constitutes the processes that support the product – i.e. functions and entities exist to provide services to the product. The value chain provides a perspective on the firm but is also a performance criterion: everything that can or does impede progression to this end is non value adding. Therefore, time and waste are central concerns. Waste can have many forms – superfluous materials, time spent on activities that add no value to the customer, idle equipment and inventories are examples – and it is claimed that many companies waste 70–90% of their resources. Lean manufacturing attempts to eliminate waste through techniques such as cellular manufacturing, pull scheduling/just in time (KanBan), Six-sigma/total quality management, rapid set-up, and team development. Cellular manufacturing is an example of how attention is directed to the flow of products between production locations. To enable this to happen quickly, blockages are erased through attention to waste and failure. To foster productivity and cost considerations, the firm must be flexible and dependable, which requires speedy response times and quality to be in place. This has been summarised as: quality → speed → dependability → flexibility → cost-reduction (e.g. Slack *et al.*, 2004, p. 680).

Lind (2001) demonstrates that lean manufacturing (or world class manufacturing) differs from traditional manufacturing in several respects (see Table 1.2). He identifies two extreme approaches to organising manufacturing operations. Lean or world class manufacturing is portrayed as fast, flow orientated, responsive, decentralised and customer orientated, whereas traditional manufacturing is depicted as slow, hierarchical, bureaucratic, centralised and production oriented. There is little doubt which is preferred: lean or world class manufacturing claims to benchmark best practice whilst the traditional form is considered too rigid and ineffective. Lean manufacturing is more than a practice – it is an aspiration portrayed in positive terms that implies all organisational ills can be resolved by the one remedy. Proponents of lean manufacturing have no hesitation in advocating it. The best model is said to be in place, now practice should follow suit. No serious alternative is given and therefore there are no 'pros and cons' – only 'pros'. If lean manufacturing does not work it is often attributed to mistaken implementation.

Table 1.2 accords hardly any role to management accounting in lean manufacturing. Accounting calculation is not mentioned and how management control should take place is not specified. Rather, it is assumed to emerge if the structural conditions of lean manufacturing are in place. Management accounting, it appears, has no input to

Table 1.2 Differences between lean and traditional production

	Lean production	Traditional production
Product structure		
Customisation	High degree of product differentiation and fast response to customer demand.	Low degree of product differentiation and slow response to customer demand.
New products	New products are a significant part of the total volume of production. Time to market is important.	New products are not a significant part of the volume of production. Time to market is not so important.
Production technology		
Automation	High degree of automation in both machinery and administrative routines.	Low degree of automation in both machinery and administrative routines.
Quality control	High degree of quality control in the machines.	Low degree of quality control in the machines.
Planning system	JIT based upon KanBans.	MRP system.
Batch size	Small batch size.	Large batch size.
Production layout		
Physical grouping of the machines	Flow-based layout. Short throughput time.	Functional layout. Long throughput time.
Organisational structure		
Company level		
Differentiation-integration	Less need for integration functions.	Several functions such as production planning, budgeting, etc.
Centralisation	Responsibility and authority are delegated within the company.	Responsibility and authority are concentrated with the senior managers.
Specialisation	Less need for specialised functions.	Several functions are specialised within a particular area.
Hierarchy	There are few organisational levels and few managers.	There are several organisational levels and several managers.
Work level		
Differentiation-integration	Activities are combined into complex tasks. Work group organisation. The wage system is group based.	Activities are combined into simple tasks. Individual piecework organisation. The wage system is individual piece rate.
Centralisation	Delegation of responsibility and authority. For example, the workers are responsible for product quality.	Concentration of responsibility and authority. For example, specialised workers are responsible for inspecting quality.
Specialisation	Mastery of multiple skills through training.	Labour is semi-skilled and specialised.
Hierarchy	Coordination and advice.	Instructions.

Source: Based on Lind (2001).

operations management activities. This is noteworthy because operations management texts exhibit no shortage of ambitions to reduce cost. Cost is a common performance criterion in operations management, but cost accounting is frowned upon. There presents an interesting paradox – costs are important, but the techniques that visualise them are seemingly not.

Management accounting – a problem for operations management

Operations management is often quite hostile to management accounting, as the following quotes from Schonberger (1990) show:

> Controlling what causes costs is logical, direct, and effective. It replaces the ineffective conventional approach to cost control, which is the carrot and the stick: a limp carrot and a thin stick. The cost-variance report was the stick. It said, Cut your costs, or else. But it offered no specific hints as to how. The limp carrot was the pay and reward systems – again not tied to much that was specific and clearly worthy of reward. (p. 188)

> Don't try to pin down all costs . . . Instead, drive costs down and quality, response time, and flexibility up by plotting quality, cycle time, set up time etc. on large visible screens on the wall. This is the most cost effective way there is for upper managers and line employees alike to size up results and take pride in accomplishments. (p. 113).

Schonberger attacks accounting for its ambiguities and lack of answers on what to do. The 'non-monetary process data are the lifeblood of improvement projects . . . [They] tell what needs to be done and, to a very large extent, prioritize those needs. Cost data are not part of that improvement methodology' (Schonberger, 1996, p. 104). Here, accounting is a problem rather than a solution. It brings the carrot and the stick but no remedies for solving problems. It mystifies organisational arrangements through allocation mechanisms; consequently nobody understands what goes on. Even 'modern' accounting such as activity based costing is a problem. Its attention to activities and causation is fine, but the bureaucracy associated with the production and use of this information is problematic; and information is still too cursory: 'One reason is the ABC paradox. If the method employs few cost drivers, the cost data may be too imprecise to be useful at the level of an improvement project . . . Cost analysis will want to employ many cost drivers for greater precision. Then, however, the ABC methods become too complex to be understood, believed in, and willingly and confidently used by the improvement team' (ibid., pp. 105–6). Accounting is seen as a misspecification, and 'we can agree at least that the conventional accounting system with its overhead allocation does not tell a straight story. What it does, at the operational level, is process data' (ibid., p. 106). Operational data are claimed to be superior because they are clearer, but also because they incorporate a more valid theory of business behaviour, e.g. total quality management:

> TQM clarifies objectives and restates them as universal principles of good business practice. Less rework, flow distance, setup time, throughput time, process variation – the common stuff of continuous improvement – *always* are cost-beneficial. (Schonberger, 1996, p. 104; emphasis in original)

The critique of accounting is sweeping and fundamental: accounting misrepresents and distorts; it creates carrots and sticks but gives no indication of how things can be improved; and it develops bureaucracy. Operations, on the other hand, develop 'universal principles of good business practice' and create preferable actions through process-oriented information and actions. Accounting hinders important improvement activities by producing dysfunctional incentives and delaying information.

One possible solution offered is to redesign management accounting to make it lean. Maskell (1996, 2000) and others reappraise extant management accounting to make it relevant for lean operations. Maskell, for example, claims that lean manufacturing needs lean accounting. The central concern is to transform the accounting focus from the scrutiny of those in remote places to providing local accounting information needed by managers such as cell leaders and process managers:

> Value-stream cost management [is] a simplified form of activity cost analysis [which] provides cost information in a focused manner . . . Traditional companies focus on optimizing departmental effectiveness. Lean companies focus on perfecting the value-stream process. (Maskell, 2000, p. 47)

Cost information is presumed to be simple; the lean firm does not need much information since variances are rare. Rather than building a complex costing system, lean accounting recommends simpler systems. For example, instead of advocating a complete variance reporting system, lean accounting suggests implementing back-flush accounting which assumes that operations have been carried out correctly and thus detailed evaluation procedures are redundant.

Lean accounting sees accounting transactions as potential waste. Instead, accounting techniques should also be developed just in time, i.e. when needed. Consequently, lean accounting has few standardised procedures; it is built around the needs of local users who seek adequate rather than perfect accounting information. Lean accounting would eliminate heavy support processes, reduce bureaucracies of 'number crunching', and deliver information just in time.

Table 1.3 illustrates how lean accounting is simple accounting and uses variants of target costing and activity analyses to help these activities to be executed efficiently. Maskell (1996, pp. 8–9) provides a list of techniques that can be applied locally to enable lean accounting to aid lean manufacturing: activity-based costing/management, customer profitability, non-financial performance measurements, value-added analysis, process mapping, target costing, value engineering, life-cycle costing, quality function deployment, and competitive benchmarking. All these techniques could be used, not as a grand system of calculation, but as possible bases for ad hoc analyses. These analyses should be situational and not driven by abstract concerns for control. And how could this happen? Maskell advocates simplifying accounting in the following sequence (1996, pp. 73ff):

1 Stage one: the object of reporting systems
    (a) Eliminate labour reporting
    (b) Eliminate variance reporting
    (c) Reduce cost centres

2 Stage two: inventories

   (a) Eliminate detailed job-step reporting

   (b) Eliminate WIP inventory reporting

   (c) Establish backflushing

3 Stage three: structure of accounting processes

   (a) Eliminate work orders

   (b) Eliminate month-end reporting

   (c) Eliminate integration with financial accounts

   (d) Eliminate budgeting

4 Stage four: new accounting

   (a) Eliminate cost accounting

   (b) Install backflush accounts payable

   (c) Use electronic funds transfer and EDI

After this, not much is left for conventional accounting to do, at least according to arguments mobilised in operations management. But, what is the response of management accounting researchers?

Table 1.3 Distinctions between traditional accounting and lean accounting

	Traditional accounting	Lean accounting
Budgeting	• There is extensive and detailed budgeting for every department and cost centre, and for every cost account and sub-account. • There is a formal budget development approach, and every department manager develops budgets that are submitted to senior management for approval. • Budgets versus actual reports are printed monthly and reviewed in budget meetings.	• There are only high-level budgets for planning purposes. • Firms are controlled primarily through non-financial measures and the continuous improvement process within the value-stream organisation. • Monthly sales and operations planning are used to update plans and monitor progress.
Performance measurement	• The primary performance measurement is done by the accounting department. There is extensive use of variance analysis, financial ratios, and other financially based measures. • There is concern about productivity. Measures of direct labour productivity and equipment utilisation are used. • The primary performance measures are available monthly as part of the month-end reports and many other reports are used for reporting local performance.	• There is a lot of statistical analysis of performance measurements and the measures are used by finance people and other specialists to understand risk and capability within the value stream and processes. • All targets for the performance measurement system are driven by customer-focused target cost and performance objectives. • Measurement systems are used to highlight drivers of waste.

Source: Based on Maskell (2000, p. 50).

Critical reflections on 'the problem of accounting' – a management accounting perspective

Both operations management and management accounting researchers say that changing operations environments are related to changing roles and functions of management accounting (Kaplan, 1983; Johnson and Kaplan, 1987; Womack and Jones, 1991). In this section we discuss the alleged problems of accounting put forward by operations management commentators and critically assess responses from management accounting scholars. The critique against accounting can be summarised in the following four concerns:

1 Accounting promotes financial performance measures rather than non-financial ones.
2 Accounting promotes hierarchical rather than lateral relations.
3 Accounting promotes standard (status quo) situation rather than improvement.
4 Accounting promotes control rather than empowerment.

Even if management accounting can be described as financial and hierarchical, and concerned with standards and control, it may well have a role in the new manufacturing setting. In the following we explore why.

Claim 1: Relevance is lost because accounting promotes financial performance measures rather than non-financial ones

The reason why non-financial performance measures are more important in modern manufacturing is explained in two different ways. The first argument is that manufacturing strategy has changed (Hayes and Wheelwright, 1984). It is claimed that strategies focussing on cost efficiency are being challenged by differentiation strategies focused on flexibility, speed and quality (Porter, 1980), and that lean manufacturing can combine both strategies. Thus, cost efficiency, flexibility, quality and speed can be obtained at the same time. This implies that the critical success factors for winning the new competitive battle are non-financial measures, such as speed, quality and flexibility. Leading (non-financial) indicators are what should be accounted for.

The second argument is that financial performance measures are too abstract and non-operational to inform empowered workers in the new manufacturing systems. When workers are empowered they need detailed information about operational concerns to make the right decisions. Financial accounting measures are presumed to be too aggregated to be useful for workers, whereas non-financial performance measures are perceived as more real and more useful for informing operational decision-making.

Response 1: Financial information is useful at the shop floor

Although financial accounting information is often portrayed as irrelevant and too aggregated for decision-makers at the operational level of the organisation, management accounting researchers have shown that financial performance measures are often used at the shop floor (Preston, 1986; Jönsson and Grönlund, 1988). For example, Jönsson and Grönlund (1988) illustrate how financial performance measures play a significant role in operational improvement processes in a flow-based production layout. They describe how operators and a foreman together conducted a follow-up investigation on tool consumption, based on a deviation found via a standard cost system. The team scrutinised the operation in a shaft-line step by step. Finally they discovered the reason for the deviation. The part that was processed consisted of a shaft with a disc at one end. The joint material between the two parts was too hard for the tool used. Either the material had to be softer, or a harder tool had to be used. They contacted the supplier of the raw material for the part and learnt that the joint could not be softened without losing quality. Since quality is the prime objective, the only thing to do was to get a harder, more expensive tool. After two months both operations and tool consumption were back in balance (Jönsson and Grönlund, 1988, p. 526). Similarly, Kaplan and Cooper (1998) argue that activity-based cost calculations are useful for operational decisions even if considerable resources are needed to develop accurate cost driver rates. Thus, financial information seems to be useful and meaningful at the shop floor. If disaggregated or reorganised, it can be a stimulus for learning and improvement of the manufacturing system.

Management accounting research also argues that a focus on cost does not necessarily neglect the importance of flexibility, speed and quality. On the contrary, cost information is important for understanding the economic consequences of, and providing incentives for, flexibility, quality and speed. Flexibility is often defined as the ability to produce a wide range of continually changing products with a minimal degradation of performance. The ability to produce diverse products at low cost is critical in integrated manufacturing systems (Schonberger, 1986; Womack *et al.*, 1991). Cost allocation has been widely researched, and it is concluded that traditional absorption cost systems using volume-based allocation bases for indirect costs are obsolete in modern manufacturing settings (Kaplan, 1983). Overhead costs do not correlate significantly with production volume in manufacturing system that pursue flexibility (Miller and Vollmann, 1985). Activity-based costing (ABC) has been offered as a solution to this problem (Kaplan, 1988), hence providing more accurate cost information that is aligned to the new operational reality – not least by revealing the cost of flexibility.

The cost of quality, often defined as 'all expenditures associated with ensuring that products conform to specifications or with producing products that do not conform' (Ittner, 1996, pp. 114–15), has been addressed in the management accounting literature. Concerns with the cost of quality originated in the early 1950s in the quality control literature (Juran, 1979/1951). This introduced the economic conformance level (ECL) model as a primary tool for exploring dimensions of quality costs. This model is now included in numerous management accounting textbooks, and it helps conceptualise quality cost by dividing it into appraisal and prevention costs (conformance costs), and internal and external failure costs (non-conformance costs). This provides insight into the economics of quality and provides a framework for discussing an optimal level of quality.

Finally, cost accounting has also been related to concerns about production time. JIT (Schonberger, 1986) and time-based management (Stalk, 1988) mobilise throughput as a key strategic parameter, and Eliyahu Goldratt's theory of constraints (TOC) addresses the relationship between cost accounting and throughput (Goldratt, 1990). The theory of constraints sees throughput as being in opposition to inventory. Excess inventories can: increase cycle time, decrease due date performance, increase defect rates, increase operating expenses, reduce the ability to plan, and ultimately reduce sales and profits. Since excess inventories can create so many problems, Goldratt is critical of accounting practices that are said to provide artificial incentives to build inventories.

Interest in throughput and TOC is reflected in management accounting research (Noreen *et al.*, 1995; Dugdale and Jones, 1996). TOC prefers a minimal variable costing system, where only three variables are relevant: (1) throughput – measured as cash received from sales less material costs; (2) operating expenses – all organisational expenses other than material costs; and (3) inventory – measured as assets acquired (facilities, equipment and materials) but not yet converted to cash. The goal is to maximise throughput while keeping steady, or preferably reducing, operating expenses and inventory. Under the TOC, direct materials are treated as a variable cost, while direct labour and all other costs are treated as fixed. This minimises incentives to overproduce, and maximises incentives to focus on throughput subject to the capacity of the individual production activities of the firm.

Therefore, management accounting seem to be crucial in lean manufacturing systems because it provides information for operators for local decision-making and learning, contributes to understanding the economics of the new manufacturing strategy, and creates incentives according to the goals of lean manufacturing systems.

Response 2: Non-financial information and the problem of the real

Non-financial information may be more tangible or 'real', as operations management writers point out. However, this does not preclude lean manufacturing companies from having cost accounting systems and overhead allocations. In any case, non-financial information may not necessarily be more 'real'. Are common sense understandings of quality, speed, flexibility etc. as unproblematic as operations management assumes? For example, does the concept of quality have a clear and robust common sense status? Looking into practice, both financial and non-financial criteria have a *problem of representation*. Flexibility, innovation and quality, which all are important success criteria in lean production, can be represented in measurements in many different ways. For instance, product quality can be accounted for by customer satisfaction measured among first year users of a company's products. But there are other equally defensible possibilities, such as the satisfaction of second year users with experience of the product. Or, it is possible to say that satisfaction measures are really not about quality, which is more of an engineering concept established through measures of incorrect parts per million. These are different measures of the same concept. They mean different things. It is not obvious that non-financial data are as unambiguous and real as operations management writers claim.

Disagreements over what quality and customer value are, or what flexibility may mean, reveal doubts about the extent to which non-financial data are real and whether they relate to people's intuitive feelings and experiences. As a result, financial systems may persist despite their difficulties, since information about the economics of flexibility, quality and innovation is important for understanding the effects of various non-financial measurements.

There is, therefore, ambiguity in the translations from quality to dependability to speed to flexibility to cost-reduction suggested by lean management and other conceptualisations of modern manufacturing. Each element in the sequence is a problem, and the sequence is unstable because each element is ambiguous and its impact on later concepts is uncertain. Consider the following sequence:

$$\text{Quality} \rightarrow \text{Customer satisfaction} \rightarrow \text{High demand} \tag{1}$$

This sequence says that a quality product leads to customer satisfaction, which in turn leads to high demand for the product. This is plausible and it follows the logic often associated with non-financial information; it leads from one concept into another. However, the logic is not universal. It is equally possible to outline the following sequence:

$$\text{Quality} \rightarrow \text{High cost} \rightarrow \text{High price} \rightarrow \text{Low demand} \tag{2}$$

Sequence 2 starts in the same place as sequence 1 but takes another route. Quality may also lead to high cost because it requires expensive production methods, costly materials, or sophisticated monitoring systems. High cost may in turn lead to high price and thus to low demand. Sequence 2 is no truer than sequence 1, but it is equally probable. This illustrates that non-financial data may be no easier to understand than financial data. It too carries ambiguity and must be interpreted; hence it is not self-evident common sense as operations management writers often claim.

Claim 2: Relevance is lost because accounting promotes hierarchical rather than lateral relations

The presumption that modern manufacturing is characterised by uncertainty and dynamic relations implies that planning is no longer possible through hierarchies – including management accounting – and it should be replaced by mechanisms of mutual adjustment. Management accounting, understood as a hierarchical planning tool based on standards, forecasts and variance analysis, is accused of producing planning errors and dysfunctional consequences in complex and uncertain organisational settings. In this respect, management accounting is seen as parallel to MRP (see above). The complexities and dynamics often present in new operational settings are presumed to be better accommodated by lateral rather than hierarchical coordination to ensure quality, flexibility, innovation and productivity. New organisational devices, such as multi-skilled workers, cross-functional teams, self-management principles and liaison roles, are proposed as answers to complex and dynamic environments that require fast and innovative responses.

Thus, hierarchical planning is replaced by other means like KanBans, cross-functional meetings and automation that diffuse production scheduling and information across organisational units and individuals in manufacturing systems. In this situation, the accounting system is presumed to be interactive (Simons, 1995) where workers are expected to be self-managing, planning and learning about operations through customised information.

Response 1: If only information sharing was unproblematic

If coordination involved only cross-functional meetings and liaison roles to share information, it would not be so troublesome. Cross-functional teams and liaison roles are central in the new manufacturing setting, but what incentives and abilities to share information exist in such arrangements? Several accounting researchers argue that to facilitate cross-functional coordination it is necessary to establish incentives, clarify organisational goals and report performance results. Cost accounting and performance measurement may play an important role here.

The non-insulated allocation scheme, in which the allocated costs of one organisational department depend on another department's operating performance, creates incentives for mutual monitoring, information sharing and cooperation by managers in different organisational units. For example, two departments in a high-tech firm share the same factory building and both are profit centres. Assume that the common costs of the shared factory space are $1 million per month. In January and February, the computer modem department has profits of $8 million before allocations. The disk drive department has profits of $8 million in January and $2 million in February. If common costs are allocated on the basis of actual profits, then profits-after-cost-allocations for one department depend on the performance of the other department (Zimmerman, 2006, p. 360).

Also, performance measures concerning inventory levels, quality, sales, etc., may be important information either for building incentives, or for directing attention to problems and challenges. If for instance a purchasing manager is responsible for inventory levels and quality in the production department, this may affect his or her purchasing behaviour and provide incentives for a lateral view of the organisation. And, even if there are no incentive problems (as some operations management commentators argue), this information may still be useful because there are limits to information sharing in lateral relations. The individual decision-makers in the value chain do not necessarily have knowledge of the whole value chain, even when there is mutual integration with the decision-makers further upstream and downstream. In order to disseminate this insight, information and accounting may be needed. Thus, opportunism and bounded rationality challenge the stability, or even the possibility, of information sharing and decision-making in a lateral perspective. Here, a hierarchy may create incentives or provide information that enables the lateral orientation.

Response 2: Accounting as prior to operations management

Operations management's critique of accounting may also be due to it looking in the wrong places for accounting. It may be that operation management's attention to non-financial measures does not recognise how accounting sometimes creates the space within which non-financial measures are used.

Mouritsen and Bekke (1999) discuss how time – whether lead time, throughput time, speed or punctuality – is a one-dimensional performance indicator. To make this one-dimensional measure work, the production space is designed by forcing other criteria out. Certain mechanisms to simplify production are developed before time can function as a management tool. One mechanism is to develop a group of mobile workers who go to the place in the factory where there is a bottleneck. Rather than making

17

complex decisions about how to use scarce capacity, which would require more than time information to execute, capacity is made variable. Another mechanism is to place component inventories with suppliers and thus simply eliminate raw material inventories from the factory. A third mechanism is to turn finished goods into marketing devices in sales companies, which removes finished goods from the factory and makes them the responsibility of others; again the 'waste' of inventories has been erased. These three mechanisms all, in their different ways, take financial decisions about capacity and levels of inventories out of the hands of production managers. They do not face decisions involving conflicting tradeoffs between different financial and economic effects. All three mechanisms mediate between productivity and flexibility, or between inventories versus capacity utilisation. They all help to produce the situation where time can become the singular decision parameter.

Even more radical is Miller and O'Leary's (1993, 1994) discussions of modern manufacturing, where they find accounting to be several things. Miller and O'Leary show linkages between accounting calculation, the development of the product, manufacturing systems, the person and national aspirations for productivity. They show how strategic and competitor accounting, capacity cost analyses, and investment bundles showing the constellation of investments in new production technology needed, were introduced to shape manufacturing systems. Accounting develops debates about competitiveness and relates this to how different types of manufacturing systems are possible. To Miller and O'Leary, accounting calculations are used to justify a manufacturing system that is lean or modern rather than based on a hierarchical view of the factory. Here, management accounting calculations help managers to develop a programme of advanced management. This takes shape prior to manufacturing and influences the form of the manufacturing system, which may then be governable more by non-financial means.

Both sets of authors claim that accounting calculations push decision-making criteria that are at odds with lean management away from the factory, which makes lean manufacturing possible. Accounting calculations (about supplier costs, inventory costs and capacity constraints) promote factory design decisions that reduce the need for operations managers to make decisions about tradeoffs between flexibility, productivity, investment in inventories, cost arrangements with suppliers, etc. Accounting calculations are invisible to operations because they externally control the boundaries of the factory; they are not visible inside because the debates surrounding such choices are insulated from operations.

Claim 3: Relevance is lost because accounting promotes standardisation rather than learning and continuous improvements

Standard cost systems and variance analysis are criticised for providing incentives that conflict with aspirations for 'zero defect' strategies and lateral relations emphasised in lean and world class manufacturing. Standard cost systems and variance analyses have been criticised for promoting the 'status quo', i.e. standards provide incentives to accept a given level of production defects in the production system rather than to find the cause of the defects. Standards do not stimulate individuals to exceed standards. Furthermore, standards are often considered as mechanisms that lead to sub-optimisation in organisations. Johnson (1992 p. 49) argues that 'achieving standard direct cost "efficiency" targets leads to larger batches, longer production runs, more scrap, more rework, and less communication across processes. Ironically, managers' efforts to achieve high standard cost efficiency ratings have tended over time to increase a company's total costs and to impair competitiveness, especially by increasing lead times . . . Indeed, motivating people to act in response to standard cost variances will, in most cases, throw processes further and further out of control.'

Response 1: Understanding the motivational consequences of standards

One concern with standards in the operations management literature is that they normalise defects and waste in the production system. Waste and defects are included in the product cost calculations and thereby accepted. Workers get used to them rather than chasing and eliminating them, which would be the obvious thing to do in a zero defect strategy embedded in lean and world class manufacturing. Many management accounting researchers respond that this is really not a problem, because standards can easily be adjusted and updated in today's management accounting systems. Targets for improvement can also be included in standards and thereby motivate higher performance. The problem is that standards may not be updated or are not challenging.

Problems with standard setting may affect employees' performance due to the challenge of asymmetric information. Managers and supervisors do not necessarily know the job or process that they evaluate and employees may exploit that for their own benefit. In these cases, games may arise around standard setting. For instance, 'quota restrictions' may be practiced by employees to hide their abilities to perform. They may consciously under-perform in order not to improve the standard, which may mean that performance standards decrease or at least do not increase. The solution is often described in terms of trust between managers and supervisors on the one side and employees on the other. Can employees trust that they will benefit from their improvement of manufacturing performance? Mistrust may promote dysfunctional behaviour in regard to standard setting.

A standard can have different properties and there may be a discrepancy between motivational and planning purposes. If improvement targets are included in the standard, these may challenge the coordination of planning activities. Effective motivation often requires standards that are higher than what is normally achievable (Locke, 2000) and frequent adjustment is necessary. In contrast, standards for planning must be achievable (i.e. accurately reflect the estimated performance of the system) and only adjusted for changes in the planning schedule. In the management accounting literature this problem has been examined either through discussions on how standard setting represents a trade-off between planning and motivation, or how accounting systems should incorporate multiple standards – some for planning and others for motivation. Lean management has a tendency to ignore such concerns and assumes that obtained standards are the relevant ones.

Response 2: Standard setting and lateral relations

As Johnson claimed, management accounting would argue that standard setting and lateral relations do not necessarily have to conflict. It depends upon what standards are set for – what is the object for the standard? Is it for a machine, an individual task, a group activity or a value chain? If standards are set for individuals or groups and related to the incentive system this may lead to sub-optimisation, as the individuals or groups will improve their own performance measures at the expense of the whole process or the lateral relations. These issues concern how the performance measures conflict with or support a lateral view of the organisation. As described above (see discussion of claim number 2), performance measures may produce 'corridor thinking', but they may also support a lateral view by tying individuals' or groups' performance evaluation to performance in organisational entities further upstream or downstream. This has consequences for the extent to which the individual or group is oriented towards their own or others' performance and incentives for integration and lateral thinking.

Claim 4: Relevance is lost because accounting promotes top-down control rather than empowerment

In lean manufacturing employees are presumed to be well-informed, aligned with corporate goals and competent, which implies that employees should no longer be controlled by accounting, but should manage themselves. The notions of self-management and empowerment, essential in lean manufacturing systems, run counter to accounting numbers that are diagnostic levers of control whereby operations are planned, monitored and evaluated by upper-level managers.

Response 1: The replacements of accounting – yes, there are alternatives, but still . . .

Management accounting research tends to agree: the limitation of accounting or diagnostic control in the age of empowerment is recognised (Simons, 1995). The replacement of accounting has various justifications. Some argue that when there is high uncertainty over means and ends, clan control should replace bureaucratic (accounting) control (Ouchi, 1980). Employees are presumed to internalise norms and values consistent with behaviour that enhances organisational value. In these settings trust, socialisation and social sanctions are crucial for explaining how well norms and values will direct behaviour in a way valued by an organisation.

It is debatable to what extent uncertainty over means and ends exists in lean and world class manufacturing. Nevertheless team spirit is often presumed to be an important ingredient in the empowered lean and world class manufacturing system. Norms and values, rather than diagnostic control mechanisms, are thought to influence employees' aspirations. However, even if the scope of the accounting system is different this does not mean that hierarchical accountability is eliminated. Accounting no longer accounts for individual performance, but for team performance. Measuring the team rather than the individual may lead to the creation of team norms or rules, because team members become a new entity that is collectively held accountable. This implies that members monitor and correct each other. Therefore, it is not a replacement of accounting, but rather a change in the role of measurement.

Sometimes employees are not only disciplined by norms, but also by technology or physical architecture. For instance, Alles *et al.* (1995) argued that monitoring by numbers is less important in modern manufacturing than in traditional systems, because low inventory levels stop employees hiding or shirking. Alles *et al.* analysed worker motivation, inventory level decisions and incentive systems when firms change to JIT and found that reduced WIP (work in progress) buffers improved information available to managers. It facilitated their identification of bottlenecks in the line, process flaws and improvements made by workers, which improved their insight into the production process. Direct observation of JIT production processes provided effective visibility, so workers could not shirk or hide. Technology ousted opportunism.

Self-management implies that authority for decision-making and control are given to employees. Here, accounting numbers are interactive levers of control used for individual learning and decision-making rather than top-down monitoring and performance evaluation. However, inter-active accounting numbers may, paradoxically, not only guide individual decision-making and planning. They may also have a disciplinary effect, as workers cannot control how these numbers are used for surveillance by others. Thus, local, operational data is not only useful locally; it can become part of wider systems of accountability. Paradoxically, self-management and lean manufacturing can bring stronger hierarchical systems of accountability.

Response 2: Responsibility centres are still in demand but with different scope

Management accounting will still be used for control and monitoring because responsibility centres are still in place in modern manufacturing settings, though several accounting researchers illustrate how the number and shape of cost centres change in JIT settings. Foster and Horngren (1987) remind us that any significant change in operations is likely to justify a corresponding change towards a smaller number of cost centres when JIT is implemented.

Other types of responsibility centres, like 'pseudo profit centres', are also promoted by management accounting as relevant in changing operations management practices. Kaplan and Cooper (1998) observe that some companies motivate their employees by providing them with profit information about operations. Profit is a more comprehensive financial signal than cost, and profit enhancement a more powerful impetus for improvement than cost reduction it is argued. These systems provide psychological benefits by focusing teams on actions directed at increasing profits, rather than emphasising the negative action of decreasing or avoiding costs. In addition, having measures of team profitability encourages the team to align its actions with overall firm performance (ibid. p. 65). They provide incentives for continuous improvement even when employee work teams are not organised as 'real' profit centres. Employees do not have the authority to decide pricing, product mix or output; these decisions remain with higher management. Thus, hierarchical systems of accountability still play a significant role in modern manufacturing settings – however, their scope may have changed.

Conclusion

Operations management stresses lateral rather than hierarchical relations in organisations. Accounting calculations are dismissed as a servant of hierarchy that fails to trace the flow of products and cannot satisfactorily help improve operations. Accounting calculations are presented as enemies of quality, flexibility and even cost reduction because they mystify the affairs of the firm. Instead, non-financial operating data and empowered, competent and self-managing employees are advocated, as they can identify how to improve the business.

Management accounting research has responded to challenges posed by manufacturing by analysing its claims on the relevance of non-financial information, flattening the organisational structure, supporting local decision-making and motivating continuous improvement. Accounting research challenges the claims made by lean thinking, especially its ideas of information sharing, motivation, trust and learning in organisations.

However, management accounting and operations management have much to say to each other because, as Bromwich and Bhimani (1994) note, many challenges facing modern management accounting come from an operations environment. Our analysis corroborates this view: new ways to conceive of management accounting emerge from studying its interaction with operations management. Both have similar concerns and conclusions about the importance of non-financial information in modern manufacturing environments. However, our analysis challenges the caricature of accounting often made in debates about operations management and more generally.

We suggest that the language of operations is not a purely non-financial one. Employees do understand financial language to some degree. Standard cost systems are used as a catalyst for improvement processes and 'pseudo profit centres' provide incentives for continuous improvement. Furthermore, management accounting is important as it describes the economics of flexibility, speed and innovation. Management accounting also has a role in illuminating and analysing the structure of the factory. The abstraction of financial data cannot systematically be avoided by introducing non-financial performance measures. Flexibility, quality, speed and customer orientation can be represented in many ways, which makes both financial and non-financial measures abstract and incomplete.

In order to realise lateral relations, there is an impact of hierarchy. Also lateral relations require incentives, organisational goals and reporting of performance results. Opportunism, as well as bounded rationality, means that information sharing and decision-making in a lateral perspective is not without challenges. Hierarchy may provide incentives and information used to facilitate a lateral orientation. Management accounting plays a role here.

We also argue that standard cost systems and variance analysis do not necessarily conflict with aspirations for 'zero defect' strategies and lateral relations as is suggested by many operations management commentators. Many management accounting researchers respond that this may not be a problem because standards can be adjusted and updated in today's management accounting systems. This adjustment has to be careful though, because optimistic standards may be more relevant for motivation purposes than for coordination.

The limitations of accounting or diagnostic control in the age of empowerment are recognised. Other means of control exist and are applied in the new operational setting. For instance, in lean manufacturing norms and values, rather than diagnostic control mechanisms, often discipline employees. This does not mean that hierarchical accountability is eliminated; rather the scope of responsibility centres changes. Management accounting does not only account for individual performance, but also for team process and value chain performance.

Operations management has challenged management accounting for some time. However, management accounting may equally be a challenge for operations management, as the boundaries around and within operations depend upon calculations that connect flows of products and services, individuals with organisational goals, and ideas of competitiveness to profitability and control. Operations management and management accounting can learn from each other. As Bromwich and Bhimani (1994, p. 248) argue: '[w]ithin a context of dynamic change, management accounting cannot afford to be inward oriented. Its continued development must rest on its rich history side by side with an appreciation of pressures, constraints and opportunities that enable it to maintain a proactive edge.' Operations management can enable management accounting to develop and vice versa.

References

Alles, M., Datar, S.M. and Lambert, R.A. (1995) 'Moral hazard and management control in just-in-time settings', *Journal of Accounting Research*, **33**, supplement, 177–204.

Bromwich, M. and Bhimani, A. (1994) *Management Accounting: Pathways to Progress*, London: Chartered Institute of Management Accountants.

Dugdale, D. and Jones, T.C. (1996) *Accounting for Throughput*, London: The Chartered Institute of Management Accountants.

Foster, G. and Horngren, C.T. (1987) 'JIT: cost accounting and cost management issues', *Management Accounting*, **68**(12), 19–25.

Goldratt, E.M. (1990) *Theory of Constraints*, Croton-on-Hudson, NY: North River Press.

Hayes, R.H. and Wheelwright, S.C. (1984) *Restoring our Competitive Edge*, New York: John Wiley & Sons.

Ittner, C.D. (1996) 'Exploratory evidence on the behavior of quality costs', *Operations Research*, **44**(1), 114–30.

Johnson, H.T. (1992) *Relevance Regained – From Top-down Control to Bottom-up Empowerment*, New York: The Free Press.

Johnson, H.T. and Kaplan, R.S. (1987) *Relevance Lost – The Rise and Fall of Management Accounting*, Boston, MA: Harvard University Press.

Jönsson, S. and Grönlund, A. (1988) 'Life with a subcontractor: new technology and management accounting', *Accounting, Organizations and Society*, **13**(5), 512–32.

Juran, J.M. (1979/1951) *The Quality Control Handbook*, New York: McGraw-Hill.

Kaplan, R.S. (1983) 'Measuring manufacturing performance: a new challenge for managerial accounting research', *The Accounting Review*, **58**(4), 686–705.

Kaplan, R.S. (1988) 'One cost system isn't enough', *Harvard Business Review*, **66**(1), 61–6.

Kaplan, R.S. and Cooper, R. (1998) *Cost and Effect: Using Integrated Cost Systems to Drive Profitability and Performance*, Boston, MA: Harvard Business School Press.

Karlsson, C. and Åhlström, P. (1996) 'Assessing changes towards lean production', *International Journal of Operations and Production Management*, **16**(2), 24–41.

Lind, J. (2001) 'Control in world class manufacturing – a longitudinal case study', *Management Accounting Research*, **12**(1), 41–74.

Locke, E.A. (2000) 'Motivation by goal setting', In R. Golembiewski (ed.), *Handbook of Organizational Behavior*, New York: Marcel Dekker.

Maskell, B.H (1996) *Making the Numbers Count*. Portland, OR: Productivity Press.

Maskell, B.H. (2000) *Lean Accounting for Lean Manufacturers*, Dearborn, MI: Society for Manufacturing Engineers.

Miller, P. and O'Leary, T. (1993) 'Accounting expertise and the politics of the product: economic citizenship and modes of corporate governance', *Accounting, Organizations and Society,* **18**(2/3), 187–206.

Miller, P. and O'Leary, T. (1994) 'Accounting, "economic citizenship" and the spatial reordering of manufacture', *Accounting, Organizations and Society,* **19**(1), 15–43.

Miller, J. G. and Vollmann, T.E. (1985) 'The hidden factory', *Harvard Business Review,* **63**(5), 142–50.

Mouritsen, J. and Bekke, A. (1999) 'A space for time: accounting and time based management in a high technology company', *Management Accounting Research,* **10**, 159–80.

Noreen, E.W., Smith, D. and Mackey, J.T. (1995) *The Theory of Constraints and its Implications for Management Accounting,* Great Barrington, MA: The North River Press.

Ouchi, W.G. (1980) 'Markets, bureaucracies, and clans', *Administrative Science Quarterly,* **25**(1), 129–41.

Porter, M.E. (1980) *Competitive Strategy,* New York: The Free Press.

Preston, A. (1986) 'Interactions and arrangements in the process of informing', *Accounting, Organizations and Society,* **11**(6), 521–40.

Schonberger, R.J. (1986) *World Class Manufacturing – The Lessons of Simplicity Applied,* New York: The Free Press.

Schonberger, R.J. (1990) *Building a Chain of Customers: Linking Business Functions to Create the World Class Company,* New York: Hutchinson Business Books.

Schonberger, R.J. (1996) *World Class Manufacturing – The Next Decade,* New York: The Free Press.

Simons, R. (1995) 'Control in an age of empowerment', *Harvard Business Review,* **73**(2), 80–8.

Skinner, W. (1974) 'The focused factory', *Harvard Business Review,* **52**(3), 113–21.

Slack, N., Chambers, S. and Johnston, R. (2004) *Operations Management,* Harlow, England: Prentice Hall.

Stalk, G. (1988) 'Time – the next source of competitive advantage', *Harvard Business Review,* **66**(4), 41–51.

Womack, J., Jones, D. T. and Roos, D. (1991) *The Machine that Changed the World,* New York: HarperCollins.

Zimmerman, J.L. (2006) *Accounting for Decision Making and Control,* New York: McGraw-Hill Irwin.

Further reading

Berliner, C. and Brimson, J.A. (1988) *Cost Management for Today's Advanced Manufacturing,* Boston, MA: Harvard Business School Press. One of the first management accounting books to describe the cost management challenge from changing manufacturing practices.

Bromwich, M. and Bhimani, A. (1989) *Management Accounting: Evolution not Revolution,* London: Chartered Institute of Management Accountants.

Bromwich, M. and Bhimani, A. (1994) *Management Accounting: Pathways to Progress,* London: Chartered Institute of Management Accountants. These two books map the development of accounting thought over time and across the world. An important driver of these changes is said to be changes in operations management.

Jazayeri, M. and Hopper, T. (1999) 'Management accounting within world class manufacturing: a case study', *Management Accounting Research,* **10**(3), 263–301. A critical and reflective field study of the role of accounting in a changed operations management practice.

Kaplan, R.S. (1990) *Measures for Manufacturing Excellence,* Boston, MA: Harvard Business School Press. One of the seminal academic books that frames the relationship between management accounting and operations management (contains contributions from several authors).

Maskell, B.H. and Baggaley, B. (2003) *Practical Lean Accounting: A Proven System for Measuring and Managing the Lean Enterprise,* New York: Productivity Press. A very practical book that introduces the principles of lean accounting.

Slack, N., Chambers, S. and Johnston, R. (2004) *Operations Management,* Harlow, England: Prentice Hall. A popular textbook on operations management. Introduces and describes current principles and tools within the operations management disciplines.

Womack, J., Jones, D.T. and Roos, D. (1991) *The Machine that Changed the World,* New York: HarperCollins. One of the founding books on lean production. Describes and reflects upon the Toyota production system.

2

Management accounting for consumerism

Ingrid Jeacle

Introduction

This chapter seeks to shed light on a topic which, not withstanding its centrality to everyday life in twenty-first century society, has until recently suffered from severe academic neglect within accounting research. Shopping is a seemingly trivial activity. It pales into insignificance when compared with serious social concerns such as the state of economic growth, political unrest and environmentalism. Yet consumption, as a research topic, has become increasingly popular across the social sciences during recent years. One rationale for this arises from an increasing recognition of the importance of consumption in contemporary society. The image of the modern citizen is frequently characterised as that of consumer rather than producer. The rhetoric of the consumer has even penetrated and colonised domains beyond those of private consumption. For example, one is no longer a patient, student, museum visitor or public transport user, but rather a consumer of these services. Certainly, terms such as 'consumer society' and 'consumer culture' have become synonymous with the characterisation of late twentieth/early twenty-first century Western society.

However, despite a burgeoning interest in consumption as a field of academic inquiry the accounting discipline has remained relatively isolated from the world of the consumer. This chapter attempts to redress this neglect by examining the role of accounting in the management of two significant retail organisations. First, management accounting practice within the department store, one of the most pivotal sites in the development of contemporary consumer culture, is explored. This discussion, whilst historically based, is nonetheless a prerequisite to a fuller understanding of existing managerial practices in retailing generally. The second type of retailing institution considered is the twenty-first century fashion chain. Engaged in a fast and dynamic marketplace, this organisational form relies on a flexible and efficient supply chain to gain competitive advantage. The role of accounting in facilitating this advantage is the focus of later sections. However, before such investigations commence, it is useful to first consider the broader question of why the role of management accounting in consumerism warrants examination at all. One answer, as the following section argues, lies with the centrality consumption has come to occupy in contemporary everyday life.

Consumerism as a research agenda

Consumption rose to prominence as a serious topic of scholarly inquiry only in recent decades (Campbell, 1995). It was traditionally viewed by sociologists as relatively marginal in comparison with such concerns as class and religion. However, there was gradually an increasing awareness that an understanding of society required equal attention to both low and high culture. In other words, seemingly mundane everyday practices such as shopping were as important as lofty debates on religion and gender. Consumption could no longer be viewed as simply the satisfaction of basic food/clothing needs, but rather an important practice in shaping everyday existence. For example, the relationship between shopping and recreation was increasingly acknowledged. Shopping has become a leisure activity. An obvious example of this unity of the consumption and leisure experience is the trip to the shopping mall. Indeed, sociologists argue that the shopping experience is now a fundamental component in identity construction and the sense of self (Bocock, 1993). It is not surprising, therefore, that sociologists have increasingly turned their attention to consumption practices to understand contemporary society.

This new interest in consumption is not restricted to contemporary practices, but extends to understanding consumer society within a historical perspective (Laermans, 1993). Consequently, a number of researchers have attempted to trace the exact location and timing of the emergence of consumer culture; suggestions include nineteenth century France, early twentieth century USA or post Second World War Britain. More importantly perhaps, the increasing attention accorded to consumption has resulted in a significant shift in academic focus, away from the world of work towards the world of the consumer (Lancaster, 1995). As Campbell (1995, p. 100) observes:

> Increasingly that which was formerly considered central is now viewed as marginal (most noticeably the world of work and employment, but also and more controversially, the phenomenon of social class itself), whilst topics long regarded as insignificant, if not actually trivial and frivolous, such as fashion, advertising and shopping, are now considered critical to an understanding of contemporary 'post modern' society. Clearly, the later change should be welcomed, for these phenomena have been neglected for too long.

It is not surprising, therefore, that traditional models for explaining consumer behaviour increasingly appear inadequate for understanding the centrality of consumption within contemporary society. Economic theory has been the dominant means by which such behaviour was traditionally explained. However, the deficiencies of traditional marginal utility theory in explaining consumer behaviour have been gradually exposed. For example, it is silent on the origins of consumer tastes and wants. In essence, economics has been characterised by an absorption with the production domain at the expense of its demand side equivalent. Consumption, the critics argue, cannot be captured within a simplistic economic model; rather it is a complex process with numerous interdisciplinary strands (Bocock, 1993).

Consequently, attention has shifted to a new wave of theorists in attempting to understand the significance of consumption to everyday life. Laermans (1993) provides a useful overview of the perspectives of two such social theorists. The work of

Bourdieu is one prominent example. It is often viewed as an extension of Veblen's theory of conspicuous consumption, which proposes that individuals consume in order to exhibit their wealth. Bourdieu, however, adopts a broader definition of social status than one based on the mere display of pecuniary wealth. The consumption of cultural capital, such as higher level education, he argues, is a key determinant in social enhancement. The extent of one's cultural capital, Bourdieu claims, symbolises one's taste, which in turn distinguishes each individual. Another notable scholar in the field is Baudrillard, who explains consumption practices in terms of the creation of signs. By consuming certain products the consumer, he argues, engages in signifying practices. Acting as signs, commodities, he claims, provide a medium of communication rather than the satisfaction of any real need. The purchase of designer brands, for example, communicates a strong message to one's fellow consumers.

From the above it is evident that the world of consumption, in all its manifestations, is now a legitimate source of interest to an array of disciplines. However, scholarly attention to apparently frivolous subjects, such as shopping, fashion and body shape, is still only evolving hesitantly within accounting research. This is unfortunate as consumption provides an interesting alternative to production, the traditional site of accounting research. Accounting scholars have comprehensively investigated and documented the role of accounting in the factory. For example, how the dominance of the scientific management movement led to a preoccupation with standard costing and variance analysis. By extending their vista beyond the walls of the manufactory to the vast array of consumer sites, accounting researchers will achieve a broader contextual understanding of the accounting craft. This is particularly important given the growing realisation that accounting has relevance beyond the narrow confines of its own discipline, perhaps best crystallised in Hopwood's (1983) call to situate accounting research within a much broader context than it had previously occupied. The complex network of interrelations between an accounting practice and its social and organisational context, it was argued, was not adequately explored by conventional accounting research, which was characterised by a preoccupation with the technical. Capturing the spirit of this transformation, Miller (1994, p. 1) observes:

> In the space of little more than a decade, there has been a profound transformation in the understanding of accounting. Accounting has come to be regarded as a *social and institutional practice*, one that is intrinsic to, and constitutive of social relations, rather than derivative or secondary . . . accounting is no longer to be regarded as a neutral device that merely documents and reports 'the facts' of economic activity. Accounting can now be seen as a set of practices that affects the type of world we live in, the type of social reality we inhabit, the way in which we understand the choices open to business undertakings and individuals, the way in which we manage and organize activities and processes of diverse types, and the way in which we administer the lives of others and ourselves.

Further, given an increasing awareness of the importance of understanding the role of accounting in everyday life (Hopwood, 1994), mundane practices such as shopping should not be seen as too lowly a subject of serious scholarly inquiry for the accounting researcher.

To summarise, consuming is a central component of everyday life. Its influence extends from the purchase of necessities through to leisure activity and identity construction. Whilst the shopping experience may be equally adored and hated, it has become an inescapable reality of most societies. Academic inquiry has only recently awakened to this significant transformation. Histories of the consumer revolution in alternate sites have attempted to redress a serious neglect in historical knowledge, whilst new sociological theories of consumption have sought to shed greater insights into a complex practice which can no longer be explained by traditional modes. In an attempt to study accounting in the context in which it operates, it is important to venture into new territory: the world of the consumer. As a consequence, a broader conception of 'the social' evolves. To view the social as the realm of production alone is a narrow and confining framework. This chapter seeks to augment existing understanding of accounting by adopting an approach which incorporates the two faces of generic man – man as producer and consumer.

Management accounting in an icon of consumer culture: the department store

It is impossible to consider the issue of management accounting and consumerism without reference to one of the great bastions of consumer culture: the department store. Whilst perhaps today the shopping mall or high street store has taken the lead in retailing, old departmental establishments such as Macys (New York) and Harrods (London) still manage to draw the crowds. The department store is generally regarded as one of the cornerstones in the emergence of contemporary consumer culture. We noted in the previous section how historians and sociologists have investigated the birthplace of consumerism. Although each scholar might differ with regard to the exact time and place of this occurrence, all would acknowledge the leading role of the department store in the creation of contemporary consumer society (Laermans, 1993).

We take for granted today the freedom to enter a store and browse freely amongst the goods. However, this was a novelty to the nineteenth century shopper; entering a shop automatically implied an obligation to buy. In addition, goods were generally held hidden behind counters and unavailable for casual inspection without the assistance of the sales staff. The department store, which emerged in the late nineteenth century, was therefore an innovative establishment for customers to engage freely and unhindered with the commodities (Lancaster, 1995). It was pioneering in many other ways too. The idea of bringing together a vast range of differentiated products under one roof was novel. Previously, establishments specialised in product categories (e.g. linens, clothing, shoes or hats). The department store also originated many of the marketing devices commonly used today such as large plate glass windows for display purposes and promotional campaigns based around the seasons. Hosting a lavish array of customer services such as fashion shows and coffee salons, by its golden age, at the turn of the twentieth century, the department store became one of the few public spaces where respectable women could socialise outside the home.

In the following section we will explore the role accounting plays in managing these large retail organisations.

Management accounting and departmental inventory control

A department store consists in many regards of numerous independent entities all gathered under the one roof. Although store policies apply equally across departments, each unit normally has considerable autonomy, with decision-making power delegated to the departmental head who, together with his/her assistants, is responsible for buying all products sold within the department. The head of a department is therefore also the senior buyer of that department. Buying is crucial to successful retailing. A poor buying decision can result in vast quantities of unsold inventory and a significant monetary loss on that product line. Consequently, as with all organisations that have an autonomous divisionalised structure, the management of department stores need some means to measure the performance of each unit. Given the objective of retailing is to turn over inventory at the best possible profit, measurement of departmental profitability is an obvious performance indicator. This information then allows management to identify poor buying within departments and examine each department's performance relative to others. With only a fixed selling floor area available, such information may prompt management to expand the trading space of more profitable departments at the expense of lesser performing ones, or even close down certain departments altogether. Therefore, the ability to regularly measure the gross and net profitability of each department is an essential element of department store management.

However, the calculation of such a simple measure of profitability has not always been readily available to department store management. Given the diverse range of products held by the department store, it is inevitable that its inventory is vast. Before the advent of computerised automated inventory systems, each department had to conduct a manual count of all goods before a figure for closing inventory, and hence gross profit, could become available. Such was the sheer scale of this task, often requiring closure of the store, it was carried out only every six months. The information potential of the departmental profitability measures at this late stage was obviously limited; a more regular means of measuring departmental performance was needed. Consequently, from the 1920s, a new method of inventory measurement became popular. In particular, a growing number of US stores, including such famous names as Macys New York, quickly adopted the new practice known as the retail price inventory method (RPIM). It is now an established method of inventory valuation in departmental retailing.

The RPIM operates on a very simple premise. Rather than valuing goods at cost price within the accounting records, goods are instead entered at their retail/selling price. Then whenever a product is sold for a price other than the original recorded selling price, for example if it is discounted due to obsolescence or sales promotion, the accounting records are amended to reflect this adjustment. A markdown adjusts the records for a selling price lower than expected, whilst a markup reflects the adjustment necessary when the actual selling price is higher than originally expected. It is vital to the accuracy of the method that all such price adjustments are completely recorded. It is then a simple operation to determine an estimated closing inventory. At any point in time, the deduction of purchases (valued at retail price and adjusted for markups/downs) from actual sales will yield a closing inventory at retail price. Using the average departmental profit markup, an estimated inventory at cost price can therefore be easily determined. In this manner, each department's gross profit can be calculated and performance measured without the need for a time-consuming physical inventory count. The following example illustrates the above points.

Consider a store in its first month of operations that has purchased 1,000 shirts at €10 each. These shirts were marked up by 100% on cost (i.e. the selling price was €20 per shirt). By the second week of the month, some patterns appeared especially popular and this prompted the store to markup 200 shirts by €3. Other patterns appeared to be moving very slowly and this gave rise to a markdown of 200 shirts by €4 each. Sales for the month were €16,000. A computation of ending inventory at selling prices is given below:

	At cost	At retail
	€	€
Beginning inventory	0	0
Purchases	10,000	20,000
Add: markups		600
Less: markdowns		(800)
Sub-total	10,000	19,800
Less: sales		(16,000)
Ending inventory at retail		3,800

Ending inventory at cost is established by calculating a markup percentage to adjust ending inventory at retail. In the example above, one possible variant involves calculating the average markup on cost as 98% ((19,800/10,000) − 1) resulting in an ending inventory at cost of €1,919 (3,800/1.98).

In addition to the ability to regularly calculate a department's profitability, once implemented the RPIM provides store management with a greater degree of control over inventory as buying errors become instantly highlighted within the markdown total. This was found to be a significant benefit of the method when it was first initiated in US stores (Walsh and Jeacle, 2003). Previously, under the cost method, a departmental buyer could simply offset major markdowns, arising from poor buying decisions, against profits on more successful purchases. Store management were ignorant of the extent of such practices until the RPIM revealed a more detailed analysis of total departmental profits. The method is also useful in the determination of inventory loss arising from theft or obsolescence, commonly referred to as shrinkage. Assuming that all price revisions have been accurately recorded, the difference between the estimated inventory book value at retail and the retail value of a physical inventory represents the extent of shrinkage. The RPIM therefore is not simply a means of inventory valuation, but also a valuable tool for managerial control.

What is interesting about the RPIM is that, despite the arrival in recent decades of software accounting packages which perpetually update inventory records and yield instantaneous departmental closing inventory data, the method is still widely used in contemporary department stores. In other words, even though technological advances have removed the requirement for its original use, the easy estimation of closing inventory without a physical count using the RPIM is still institutionalised. US stores in particular still retain the practice and it is a common feature of US university accounting curricula. Indeed, a chapter devoted to the topic is often found within North American management accounting student textbooks. Another point worth noting is that the RPIM is in essence a very simple method of accounting for inventory. Yet, as we have seen, once implemented it can provide highly useful information on departmental performance which forms the basis of management decision-making. Accounting techniques do not have to be highly complex in order to be effective: some of the most potent management tools are often the simplest. In the following section another simple management accounting technique is examined, which also had important control implications for department store management. Perhaps more importantly, however, this particular accounting practice played a significant role in a defining moment in consumerism.

Management accounting and departmental overhead control

Clothes shopping is a significant component of contemporary consumerism. Trips to the shopping mall or high street frequently incorporate the purchase of new clothes. Later in this chapter, the role of accounting in the management of fashion retail organisations will be more fully examined. At this juncture, however, it is useful to consider how the introduction of a simple accounting practice within department stores facilitated the establishment of an inherent aspect of clothes consumption today: a system of standardised clothes sizing.

Each country/continent has its own clothes sizing system. For example, within women's clothing, the US industry uses a system centred on values such as 8, 10, 12, etc., whilst in continental Europe, the sizing system consists of the numbers 34, 36, 38 and so on. However, regardless of the differing values used, the common aim of sizing systems is to allow the consumer to select the appropriately sized garment in the knowledge that it will fit reasonably well. Indeed, an accurate standardised clothes sizing system is an essential element to consumer self-selection, as it facilitates the freedom to browse, select and purchase clothes without the assistance of sales staff. Mail order and Internet shopping in particular, where no facility exists to try the garment before purchase, relies heavily on such a system.

The advent of a clothes sizing system was a consequence of the shift from made-to-measure garments, tailored to the needs of the individual, to ready-to-wear styles for the masses. The department store was the first retailing establishment to launch ready-to-wear styles during the early years of the twentieth century. However, in these pioneering days the garments were not always immediately ready-to-wear; some alteration was generally necessary to ensure a proper fit. All department stores therefore had garment alteration workrooms for such purposes. The alteration service was usually free to the customer (or subject to a token charge) and therefore the monetary cost to the store of running these workshops could be considerable. Traditionally this cost was treated as a general store overhead and not charged back to departments. This strategy often resulted in the costly overuse of the alteration room's facilities. There was scope, for example, for a departmental buyer to buy cheap but poorly fitting garments which required significant alteration time. The profit from their sale boosted departmental performance whilst the costs of alteration were borne by the alteration workroom. However, from the 1920s onward, in an attempt to exert some control over this workroom overhead, US stores decided to introduce an overhead allocation method based on departmental usage (Jeacle, 2003). In other words, if say 20 per cent of the garment alteration room services were used by the women's dress department, then this department would be allocated 20 per cent of the cost of running the garment alteration room. This charge-back to each department impacted on departmental profits and hence adversely affected the perceived performance of the buyer/head of that department.

The solution to the departmental buyer's dilemma was relatively simple. In order to minimise the charge-back to their departments, buyers increasingly sought to buy only garments that fitted well and therefore would require little use of the alteration workroom. This strategy, however, necessitated close cooperation with garment manufacturers to establish correctly sized garments. Some stores even developed their own standardised sizing models which they then used to check the quality of fit of their purchases. Incorrectly sized garments were sent straight back to the supplier. So the introduction of a simple overhead allocation method, based on usage of the alteration workroom, produced a strong incentive for buyers to encourage the establishment of a system of standardised clothes sizing. Such informal initiatives were later formalised with government sponsorship of national body size surveys and the publication of official sizing measurements. This occurred in the 1940s in the US and the early 1950s in Britain. However, department stores were the real pioneers and management accounting played a significant role in the unfolding drama.

Similar to the RPIM, the above case is another example of the potentially potent influence of accounting practice. Once again, the accounting technique introduced was exceptionally simple. The allocation of overheads to departments or products based on some measure of usage is an elementary lesson in management accounting. However, when implemented within this organisational context we see its far-reaching repercussions, giving credence to the earlier claim that accounting is not the neutral and objective technique it is often cast as. In this instance, the buyers keenly felt the adverse profit ramifications of the introduction of the charge and this provided them with a strong impetus to initiate a process which culminated in the standardised clothes sizes that are an inherent component of contemporary consumer culture. It is vital, therefore, to recognise the social and organisational context of even the most seemingly innocuous accounting technique.

Before concluding this section it is worth mentioning the revolution in clothes sizing which lies in the near future. No longer may it be necessary to categorise the population into somewhat crude classes of bodily size. The expansion of computer generated body scanning will ultimately provide a unique measure for all. This data will then be sent by the retailer to the manufacturing plant or e-mailed by the Internet consumer to online shopping sites. The result will be made-to-measure clothes for the masses. Mass customisation, as the concept is termed within the clothing industry, is already available in a limited capacity. The menswear retailer Brooks Brothers provides a full three-dimensional body scan for suit purchasers in its New York store. The consumer's quest for the perfect individual clothing fit will no doubt ensure that body scanning becomes a key trend in clothes retailing more generally.

Management accounting and 'fast fashion': the twenty-first century fashion chain

If it has been easy in the past to dismiss shopping as a trivial activity unworthy of serious scholarly inquiry, then it is all too tempting to ignore that most seemingly fickle aspect of retailing: fashion shopping. Fashion is often portrayed as something frivolous, a practice engaged in by silly teenagers or women (mostly) with more money than sense. Why would accounting researchers, or any scholars for that matter, wish to investigate such an inconsequential activity? However, like consumption generally, fashion has become a topic of recent academic debate. Social scientists have explored how clothing generally, and fashion clothing in particular, is an important component of self-expression and identity construction in contemporary society (Crane, 2000).

As accountants, used to dealing with the so-called cold hard facts of business, we may be tempted to dismiss such musings as irrelevant to our immediate concerns. However, we cannot ignore the sheer scale of the retail giants that distribute these fashion garments to the masses. For example the Swedish fashion organisation H&M has a presence in 21 countries and employs over 45,000 staff. Another popular fashion chain, Zara, a member of the Spanish Inditec group, one of the world's largest fashion groups, has approximately 2,000 stores in more than 50 countries. Finally, the US fashion retailer Gap manages a staff base of 150,000 and reported revenues of over 16 billion US dollars for 2004.

It is this type of fashion organisation, rather than the haute couture end of the market, which is the focus of this chapter. The fashion chain stores provide inexpensive fashion to the mass market. They are the face of contemporary consumer culture; they are scattered throughout every shopping mall and littered along every high street. As an inherent feature of everyday life, it is important for accounting researchers to acknowledge their presence and investigate their practices. Indeed their practices should be particularly interesting to the management accounting researcher as these organisations operate in a fast moving and competitive environment. Fashion styles change at an incredibly fast pace today. No longer do we have traditional autumn/winter and spring/summer season collections – a contemporary fashion garment can have a life of only a few weeks (Jackson and Shaw, 2001). The terms 'disposable fashion' and 'fast fashion' (drawing parallels with the fast food industry) are commonly used to describe the situation. This inevitably creates a high degree of business risk in fashion retailing (Abernathy et al., 1999). If a retailer makes an erroneous forecast on a particular fashion trend, the result is a vast inventory of unwanted clothes which must be sold at discounted prices. In order to limit this risk, the best strategy is to delay buying decisions as long as possible to enable the retailer to more accurately predict new fashion trends. However, such a delayed purchasing strategy carries the risk that the retailer will receive the goods from the wholesalers too late, and the optimum time for selling these particular fashion garments will have passed.

The key to this dilemma is therefore to cut the lead time between the placement of an order with the clothing manufacture and the product's arrival into the store. A short lead time allows the fashion retailer to be more responsive to sudden changes in styles.

The fashion retail chains Zara and H&M, for instance, have lead times as low as two to three weeks on their high fashion garments. Within the fashion industry this flexibility is termed quick response (QR). The QR strategy involves the adoption of a range of lean retailing practices (Abernathy *et al.*, 1999) and the development of strong supply chain partnerships between retailers and manufacturers. The core tenets of QR and its implications for management accounting will be discussed in the following section.

Management accounting and the quick response initiative in fashion retailing

QR can be broken into two distinct elements. First, QR demands that products move forward along the supply chain (from manufacturer to retailer) as quickly as possible. Therefore, when a retailer places an order for garments, QR requires these items to be manufactured and distributed to stores within as short a time frame as possible. This is the *physical* side to the QR initiative. However, QR has a second strand; it also requires the fast movement of *information* back along the supply chain (from retailer to manufacturer). Information on customer preferences is essential to identify and appropriately respond to trends within the market. Let us consider each of these two elements in turn.

The physical movement of product along the supply chain can be influenced by several factors. At the garment's design stage, the use of computer technology has greatly facilitated the speed at which designs can be implemented and modified (Blackburn, 1991). Computer-aided design (CAD) systems can be electronically linked to software for cutting and sizing the garment fabric (this is known as computer integrated manufacturing (CIM)). Another means of speeding up response time is batch or modular manufacturing, where small batches of diversified garments are manufactured rather than the traditional long production runs of one garment type. The advantage of this strategy is that it provides the manufacturer with a greater degree of flexibility. If one particular garment style fails to sell, manufacture can respond swiftly by diverting resources from this batch into more popular lines. There is no need to halt the entire production run and suffer the consequent delays of establishing a new one. Increasingly the traditional emphasis on economies of scale is being replaced with attention to economies of scope; manufacturers need to exhibit a broad scope in order to respond to fast changing product demands. Consequently, flexibility is as important as speed in achieving a quick response within the fashion market.

Once manufactured, the product needs to arrive in stores as speedily as possible. This prompted a number of retailers to shift their manufacturing sources from distant locations to more proximate facilities (Jackson and Shaw, 2001). A prime example of this strategy is the retail giant Zara, which sources 50 per cent of its fast fashion garments from its own, locally situated, manufacturing plants. The Swedish retail chain H&M similarly sources approximately half of all purchases from within Europe. Even when the manufacturing source is nearby it is still a significant logistical operation to distribute the garments amongst all store branches on a timely basis. The importance of logistics within the fashion industry is evident in that over 3,000 individuals are employed by the latter organisation within its logistics function alone.

The above initiatives facilitate the movement of garments forward along the supply chain at reduced lead times. The second strand to QR is the movement of sales information back along the supply chain from retailer to manufacturer. The content of this information reveals customer preferences on each product line. Consequently, it is easy to identify the fast versus slow selling garments and hence to take appropriate action. Manufacturing resources can then quickly be diverted away from these slow selling lines in favour of the more popular items (Blackburn, 1991). Once again, advances in computer technology have facilitated this process. The initial sales information is captured within the store at the time of garment purchase. Every garment (or stock keeping unit (SKU) as it is known in the industry) carries a barcode (usually appearing on the price ticket) which carries detailed information such as garment supplier, colour and size. Laser scanning of a garment's barcode using electronic point of sale (EPOS) technology allows a comprehensive array of data on inventory movements to be collected: essentially barcoding facilitates the tracking of every SKU. This vital information can then be instantaneously sent to clothing manufacturers with the aid of electronic data interchange (EDI). Automatic inventory replenishment can therefore take place without waiting for direct purchase orders from the retailer (Abernathy *et al.*, 1999). Close working relationships with a number of trusted suppliers is essential before retailers can implement the sharing of such trading information. However, even if a retailer does not automatically share this information externally, an internal analysis of the data collected at point of sale effectively informs buying decisions passed back to manufacturers and hence ensures a quick response to market conditions. It is in the reporting of such information that management accounting plays an essential role.

One of the most common reporting formats used in the fashion business for such an analysis is the weekly sales stock and intake plan, known within the retail trade as the WSSI. This is an important control tool in inventory management as it accumulates weekly data for sales, closing and opening inventories, markups and markdowns. Both actual and budgeted figures are incorporated into the plan. It may seem surprising to actually plan ahead for potential markdowns in price, but from experience management will expect a certain level of inventory to be discounted. This will therefore be built into the plan.

A WSSI is prepared for every product line. It provides an instant overview of performance, facilitating an easy identification of slow-moving versus fast-moving inventory lines. The decision as to whether orders need to be cancelled or placed with the manufacturer can then be made. The WSSI's incorporation of information on closing inventory holdings is also requisite to this process. In addition to aiding the buying decision, the WSSI is a useful tool for delivery scheduling, both external and internal scheduling. Deliveries from external suppliers need to be scheduled to arrive to meet anticipated demand, but scheduling is also necessary to ensure the timely delivery of goods from the retailer's central warehouse/distribution centres to branch stores. The WSSI's analysis of anticipated demand and inventory holdings is one important tool in this process.

Table 2.1 shows an example of a WSSI for women's T-shirts for a four-week period for one chain within a fashion group. The figures used are at retail rather than cost

Table 2.1 The WSSI

Week no.	Actual/ budgeted opening inventory	Actual/ budgeted weekly inventory intake	Actual/ budgeted markups	Actual/ budgeted mark-downs	Actual/ budgeted weekly sales	Actual/ budgeted closing Inventory	Budgeted weekly sales	Comments
1	805*	250*	–	–	824*	231*	750	Demand higher than anticipated
2	231*	675*	–	–	807*	99*	800	Product demand still high
3	99*	745*	–	–	504*	340*	775	Demand fallen off
4	340*	210	46	464	40	464	464	Plan markdowns

* = actual figures

price – a consequence of the shift in retail reporting that accompanied the widespread adoption of RPIM inventory valuation. Assume a new printed T-shirt is introduced in the first week of the month. Actual demand for this new style is as yet unknown so initial inventory holdings and the first week's delivery intake is based on fashion forecasts. The garment proves popular and, as can be seen from the weekly sales results, actual demand is higher than anticipated. The budgeted sales level for week 2 is duly increased to reflect this additional demand and inventory purchases increase significantly from weeks 1 to 2. Demand for the garment remains high in week 2. However, given the small decrease in actual sales (824 to 807) from week 1 to week 2, the budgeted sales level for week 3 is reduced accordingly. Sales actually fall well below budgeted levels in week 3 reflecting the speed of contemporary fashion fads. Consequently, in week 4 planned purchases of the product are scaled back and markdowns (based on 10 per cent sales discount) are built into the budget. This is a simple example of the application of the WSSI. In a large retail organisation this process is carried out for every product across every branch. Management accounting information is at the heart of retail decision-making, hence the QR initiative.

Nevertheless, it would be erroneous to regard this plan as belonging only to the narrow preserve of the accounting office. As discussed in the earlier section on department store retailing, the buyer plays a key role within retailing. Within a large fashion organisation there are buyers for every product range: for example, casual wear, formal wear, accessories. Fashion buying is a highly demanding job, which entails travelling around the world in a constant search for the most competitive and efficient suppliers. The buyer must also exhibit an astute awareness of fashion trends, for they carry the burden if their garment selection fails to sell. Consequently, the WSSI is an important source of information for the buyer who will examine it in minute detail to detect changes in the popularity of each line. Another key player in retail operations to which the WSSI is an indispensable aid is the merchandiser. Whilst the buyer might traditionally be regarded as the fountain of artistic flair, the merchandiser is generally perceived as a more analytical character. Highly numerate, the merchandiser helps prepare and analyse sales forecasts and is responsible for control of the buyer's budget. The merchandiser also monitors inventory levels and oversees the distribution of inventory to branches. The WSSI is the basis of communications between the merchandiser and logistics personnel. Its revelations are also vital to the fashion retailer's creative in-house design teams as it indicates the popularity of styles. All of these non-accounting/finance related functions rely heavily on management accounting information in their daily activities and, as will be discussed in the conclusion, the interaction between the accounting team and these functions provides rich insights into the role of management accounting in consumerism.

To summarise, the fashion business shares a strong similarity with the food industry, where QR initiatives also play a crucial role. Time is of the essence in both markets. Whilst fashion garments may not be quite as perishable as foodstuffs, the increasing pace of change in fashion has prompted commentators to draw analogies between the concept of fast food and fast fashion. To successfully implement a QR strategy it is not sufficient for the fashion retailer to implement time-saving initiatives in isolation; the key to success is to be part of a highly efficient supply network. It is important therefore that management accounting systems are designed and adapted to support this process. This necessitates mechanisms to facilitate the accumulation and sharing of data on sales and inventory movements with supply partners to implement appropriate responses on a timely basis. Indeed, the demands on the accounting system may extend beyond this; the next stage is collaborative design of management accounting systems. Collaborative planning, forecasting and replenishment (CPFR) initiatives between supply partners are viewed as likely future means of improving responsiveness within the network (Rosenau and Wilson, 2001). QR requires the management accounting system to encompass a performance measurement system with a strong emphasis on time-based measures, but it is not the traditional labour-based garment assembly time measures which are important. Rather a broader perspective on time, which encompasses the entire supply network from garment sale to replenishment on store shelves, is required. The role of accounting in managing the supply chain has already been advocated within the accounting literature (Shank and Govindarajan, 1992), but accounting researchers have yet to examine its full potential within consumerism generally and the fashion industry in particular.

However, time is only one factor, albeit an important one, in the successful management of fashion. Price competitiveness is equally important to operators at the more inexpensive end of the fashion market. Consequently, rigorous cost control is essential. Like the management of time, the management of costs requires an extended focus beyond the immediate legal boundaries of the organisation. This process is the subject of the following section.

Inter-organisational cost management and the fashion business

Unlike the haute couture designer end of the market, the fashion chain store business is extremely price sensitive. Competition between the key high street/shopping mall fashion retailers is based not only on getting the latest trend onto the shelves as fast as possible, but also on achieving this as inexpensively as possible. Cost reductions at the garment design and manufacture stages are therefore paramount. The design of any product can have significant ramifications for future production costs: costs become committed at the design stage. It is important, therefore, that the design of the high street garment pays attention to both the requisites of fashion and cost effective production runs (Jackson and Shaw, 2001). The location of a garment's seams, for example, can have repercussions for the efficient use of fabric. Marker planning attempts to plan the cutting of fabric to ensure minimum wastage. Careful consideration of this at the design stage can help achieve lower levels of fabric usage. Also, design decisions influence the degree of complexity inherent in the production process. For example, the fewer buttons and pockets a garment design has, the simpler will be its assembly. There is, therefore, a constant dilemma at the heart of high street fashion: the satisfaction of fashion's latest dictates whilst maintaining price advantage.

Management accounting can play an important role in resolving this conflict. Typically within the fashion industry, the design and manufacturing processes are carried out at independent sites. Whilst the main fashion retailers employ their own inhouse design teams, they rarely have their own manufacturing facilities. With the exception of the Spanish chain Zara, most high street fashion retailers outsource their production requirements, often to sites in Asia. Inter-organisational cost management (IOCM) can prove particularly effective within this context for it tries to maximise cost reduction opportunities through initiatives between supply chain partners (Cooper and Slagmulder, 1999). Target costing lies at the heart of IOCM, for it is an effective method of cost control which takes the competitive selling price for the organisation's product as its starting point. All efforts are then directed at achieving the target cost that, in association with this sales price, achieves the required profit level (Ansari and Bell, 1997). Implementing target costing within a single organisation generally entails coordinating cross-functional teams (design, production, finance) throughout the organisation, but within IOCM it also involves coordination of teams across organisational boundaries, for a significant component of cost becomes committed at the design stage. As Cooper and Slagmulder (1999, p. 2) advocate:

> The first way to reduce costs across organizational boundaries is during product design. Here, interorganizational cost management is a structured approach to coordinating the product development activities of firms in supplier networks so that the products and components those firms produce can be manufactured at their target costs. It is of particular importance to lean enterprises because usually they outsource as much as 70% of the value-added of their products. With such a high degree of outsourced value, coordinating product development throughout the supplier network is critical to the firm's success.

In the fashion industry, coordinating the retailer's design team with the supplier's production team is particularly effective as it can result in a garment design which encompasses fashion's latest trends whilst simultaneously ensuring appropriate management of costs. Open-book accounting can facilitate this process, being useful for achieving target costs across organisational boundaries (Mouritsen et al., 2001) for it provides cost transparency throughout the supply chain and it can help the retailer's design team to better understand and appreciate the supplier's manufacturing costs. Thus the cost impact of design modifications can be considered to appropriately balance fashion's dictates and the pressure for cost control.

IOCM practices like open-book accounting also have significant ramifications for the design of management accounting systems. It is essential for lean retailers who outsource their manufacturing requirements to modify their systems to facilitate the sharing of design and cost information with supply partners (Tomkins, 2001).

Conclusion

It is no longer credible to dismiss shopping as a trivial activity and too lowly a subject of scholarly inquiry. Sociologists have been quick to realise the potential of investigating consumer habits for furthering our comprehension of contemporary society. However, it is only in recent years that the accounting researcher has recognised the scale and significance of consumerism and has acknowledged that a fuller understanding of the role of accounting within everyday life necessitates embracing this alternate world. Perhaps one rationale for such past neglect is the traditional male dominance of the accounting academia, the members of which have been oblivious to the transformations on the high street. These transformations are now manifest not only physically but also electronically. For example, the Internet shopping site eBay has over 100 million registered members worldwide and reported revenues of over 3 billion US dollars in 2004. Electronic commerce generally has rapidly become an integral feature of contemporary life. Access to Internet facilities has opened up an infinite array of consuming possibilities from grocery shopping at 2.00 a.m. to property purchase on the other side of the world. University degree programme have responded to this new phenomenon by incorporating courses on e-commerce and e-business as standard components of the curriculum. Yet, the subject remains a relative black hole in terms of management accounting research.

This chapter has highlighted the valuable role of accounting in two significant organisational forms of consumerism: the department store and fashion chain store. A number of insights can be drawn from this analysis with regard to the role of management accountants and management accounting in consumer organisations generally.

First, some observations on the role of the management accountant in retailing can be posited. The management accountant operating in a retail environment interacts with a host of organisational actors beyond the confines of the counting house. The creative character of the fashion designer may seem initially far removed from the number crunching of the bookkeeper, but in the dynamic and competitive world of contemporary consumerism these two roles have more in common than may be instantly apparent. A drive for cost efficiency entails a tight coordination of these two functions and, as we have noted, accounting information can play a crucial role in identifying cost-reduction opportunities at the design stage. The management of inventory is at the heart of retail operations; consequently store buyers and merchandisers need regular inventory information to assist purchase and distribution decisions. These are two further organisational characters with whom the management accountant needs to engage in order to fully reveal the vital assistance of accounting data in retail management.

This first observation is in line with the recent recognition that the role of management accountants has evolved. The scope of their work and influence has gradually expanded into new territories. This can be seen in several ways. For example, the traditional focus on the preparation of the monthly profit and loss account and the annual statutory report is now only a small component of their repertoire. The work of management accountants has expanded to encompass the planning, and indeed shaping, of an organisation's strategic direction. The domain of their activities has moved beyond the limits of the finance function to actively embrace the more operational aspects of the business; we see accountants physically situated across business units. Their titles too reflect their new, more business oriented roles; the term analyst, for instance, has gained momentum. Management accountants working within consumer organisations are not immune to this trend; they must be familiar with all aspects of retail operations, including sourcing, distribution and merchandising decisions.

The second observation that can be drawn from the chapter's earlier discussion relates to the issue of strategic management accounting. The increasing recent attention to this concept within the accounting discipline has already noted the importance of adopting a broader perspective on the scope of accounting. Liaising with parties beyond the immediate legal boundaries of the organisation in order, for example, to implement cost-reduction initiatives along the supply chain is now a recognised function of the management accountant. This is no less important a role in the case of consumerism, where the intensive nature of competition makes all cost-reduction efforts imperative. Therefore, it is important that attention is devoted to the interactions between the retail management accountant and the designers/production engineers within any outsourced facility. In addition, given the sheer pace of change in consumer preferences, particularly within the fashion clothing arena, the speed and efficiency of the supply chain network is an essential element of retail success. This places importance on establishing clear lines of communication between the retail accountant and supply chain manager.

A third and related observation concerns the design of management accounting systems and performance measures. The context in which consumer organisations operate is highly dynamic and consequently their management accounting systems cannot afford to operate in a vacuum. Given the importance of the supply network to retailing, the accounting system must exhibit a sufficient degree of openness and flexibility in order to assimilate the two-directional flow of information between retailer and manufacturer. The ultimate conclusion to this process would involve the collaborative design of management accounting systems between retailer and key supply partners. The design of performance measurement systems also needs to acknowledge the environment in which retailers operate. For example, time-based measures that capture the responsiveness of the organisation's supply chain and track lead times are essential. In addition, given the importance of cross-functional teams when implementing IOCM, performance measures need to be team rather than individual based.

In conclusion, there is still a great deal more to be learnt about the role of management accounting in consumerism. Over a decade ago, Otley (1994) remarked that our understanding of management accounting could be enriched with insights from those dynamic organisations operating at the leading edge of fast moving markets. This observation still holds true today and retail organisations generally, and fashion retailers in particular, are positioned within such an environment. If twenty-first century accounting scholars devote as much time to unravelling consumption practices as their twentieth century counterparts devoted to production, then this gap in our knowledge should hopefully be quickly addressed.

References

Abernathy, F., Dunlop, J., Hammond, J. and Weil, D. (1999) *A Stitch in Time: Lean Retailing and the Transformation of Manufacturing – Lessons from the Apparel and Textile Industries,* Oxford: Oxford University Press.

Ansari, S.L. and Bell, J.E. (1997) *Target Costing: The New Frontier in Strategic Cost Management,* Chicago, IL: Irwin.

Blackburn, J. (1991) 'The Quick-Response movement in the apparel industry: a case study in time-compressing supply chain', in J. Blackburn (ed.), *Time-based Competition: The Next Battleground in American Manufacturing,* Homewood, IL: Irwin, pp. 246–67.

Bocock, R. (1993) *Consumption.* London: Routledge.

Campbell, C. (1995). 'The sociology of consumption', in D. Miller (ed.), *Acknowledging Consumption,* London: Routledge, pp. 96–126.

Cooper, R. and Slagmulder, R. (1999) *Supply Chain Development for the Lean Enterprise,* Portland, OH: Productivity Press.

Crane, D. (2000) *Fashion and its Social Agendas: Class, Gender, and Identity in Clothing,* Chicago, IL: University of Chicago Press.

Hopwood, A. (1983) 'On trying to study accounting in the contexts in which it operates', *Accounting, Organizations and Society,* **8**, 287–305.

Hopwood, A. (1994) 'Accounting and everyday life: an introduction', *Accounting, Organizations and Society,* **19**, 299–301.

Jackson, T. and Shaw, D. (2001) *Fashion Buying and Merchandise Management,* London: Macmillan.

Jeacle, I. (2003) 'Accounting and the construction of the standard body', *Accounting Organizations and Society,* **28**, 357–77.

Laermans, R. (1993) 'Learning to consume: early department stores and the shaping of the modern consumer culture (1860–1914)', *Theory, Culture & Society,* **10**, 79–102.

Lancaster, B. (1995) *The Department Store: A Social History,* Leicester: Leicester University Press.

Miller, P. (1994) 'Accounting as social and institutional practice: an introduction', in A. Hopwood and P. Miller (eds.), *Accounting as Social and Institutional Practice,* Cambridge: Cambridge University Press, pp. 1–39.

Mouritsen, J., Hansen, A. and Hansen, C. (2001) 'Inter-organizational controls and organizational competencies: episodes around target cost management/functional analysis and open book accounting', *Management Accounting Research,* **12**, 221–44.

Otley, D. (1994) 'Management control in contemporary organizations: towards a wider framework', *Management Accounting Research,* **5**, 289–99.

Rosenau, J. and Wilson, D. (2001) *Apparel Merchandising: The Line Starts Here,* New York: Fairchild.

Shank, J. and Govindarajan, V. (1992) 'Strategic cost management: the value chain perspective', *Journal of Management Accounting Research,* **4**, 179–97.

Tomkins, C. (2001) 'Interdependencies, trust and information in relationships, alliances and networks', *Accounting, Organizations and Society,* **26**, 161–91.

Walsh, E. and Jeacle, I. (2003) 'The taming of the buyer: the retail inventory method and the early 20th century department store', *Accounting Organizations and Society,* **28**, 773–91.

Further reading

Consumption

Featherstone, M. (1991) *Consumer Culture and Postmodernism,* London: Sage.

Mackay, H. (ed.) (1997) *Consumption and Everyday Life,* London: Sage. Both texts provide thoughtful insights into understanding the role of consumption in contemporary society.

Department store

Jeacle, I. and Walsh, E. (2002) 'From moral evaluation to rationalization: accounting and the shifting technologies of credit', *Accounting, Organizations and Society,* **27,** 737–61. This article examines the role of management accounting, in particular aged debtors ledger analysis, in the management of consumer credit.

Leach, W. (1984) 'Transformations in a culture of consumption: women and department stores, 1890–1925', *Journal of American History,* **71,** 319–42. This article provides a comprehensive history of the innovative marketing practices initiated in US department stores at the turn of the twentieth century.

Fashion

Brydon, A. and Niessen, S. (eds) (1998) *Consuming Fashion: Adorning the Transnational Body,* Oxford: Berg. This book is a useful source for further theoretical insights on the role of fashion in contemporary everyday life.

The following texts provide a comprehensive analysis of the more practical issues surrounding the business of fashion.

Davis Burns, L. and Bryant, N. (1997) *The Business of Fashion: Design, Manufacturing, and Marketing,* New York: Fairchild Publications.

Jones, R. (2002) *The Apparel Industry,* Oxford: Blackwell Science.

Supply chain management

Christopher, M. (1992) *Logistics and Supply Chain Management: Strategies for Reducing Costs and Improving Services,* London: Pitman Publishing. This book provides a useful analysis of the various dilemmas surrounding the management of the supply chain with some insightful references to the fashion industry.

3

Interactions between modern information technology and management control

Niels Dechow, Markus Granlund and Jan Mouritsen

Introduction

The pace of development in information technology (IT), which comprises all technologies used to create, store, exchange and use information in its various forms, has been dramatic over the last ten years. The use of IT to support business processes has increased considerably with the advent of the Internet, communication software and database technologies (see the glossary in the Appendix to this chapter). These developments have enhanced the possibility of globally integrating business processes, as local and disparate information systems become supplanted by global databases and corporate computing (enterprise resource planning systems or ERPS; see Davenport, 1998). Data input and informationoutput become flexible, hence many employees in the firm can draw on the same database and, in principle, calculate profitability, costs and productivity across organisational entities. These developments are accompanied by software rental (application service providing/provider or ASP) and developments of standard models for electronic data representation (XML/XBRL; see Debreceny and Gray, 2001). Programming work has changed, so firms increasingly purchase software packages instead of developing programs in-house. This has arguably led to faster and less expensive information system development life cycles.

The challenge for management accounting is to analyse how new technological possibilities can enhance the relevance, quality, speed and dependability of information stored, produced and disseminated through IT. This chapter analyses this relationship and in particular examines how increasingly integrated IT systems, such as ERP systems, challenge management accounting practices.

The development of IT for management accounting purposes

A common objective behind most information technologies used in modern organisations is to create an infrastructure (including hardware, software and data transmission networks) that supports the development of new applications based on business and consumer needs rather than what is merely possible technologically and financially (Moschella, 1997). The interface between IT and accounting is complex, but management control is becoming increasingly involved with managing technology.

The relationship between IT and accounting-based management control systems is characterised by Boland (1999, p. 239) as follows:

> Whereas accounting is concerned with specific types of representations and the ways to 'get them right', information systems is concerned with representation in general. Information systems professionals are concerned with constructing representations, but they tend to be one-off, ad-hoc responses to requests of the managers or staff being served by a system.

For accounting, the stability of representations lies in economic categories and key ratios that integrate the balance sheet and the income statement. Accounting seeks visibility and transparency of organisational entities, products and processes. For IT, connectivity is at stake. While accounting focuses on 'getting things right' in relation to visibility and transparency, IT is concerned with 'getting users connected' via requirements analysis, system-building and project management. This distinction can be developed along several dimensions as illustrated in Figure 3.1.

Figure 3.1 defines accounting and IT as distinct areas of expertise. This is an exaggeration, but it helps point out differences easily overlooked when new information technologies capture the interest of users, designers, implementers, researchers and sometimes even students (Weber, 1987). For IT researchers and practitioners, accounting information systems are rarely seen as critical. The IT interest is in e-business solutions, information system implementation processes, and information system security.

Management accounting is typically not a central challenge here, but it is important for IT because rapid changes in information technology can distribute accounting data within firms in new, faster, more effective and secure ways. This becomes more important the more integrated IT becomes, for example as ERP systems replace ledger systems and standalone applications with integrated databases.

Ledger systems and ERP systems

In the era of ledger systems, no one paid much attention to the relationship between IT and management. However, the advent of ERP systems integrates data between areas

Accounting defines representations for visibility and transparency in firms and for capital markets	←→	Information technology creates virtual networks and connections between people inside and outside the firm
Capital markets and management control concerns	**Environment**	Possible virtual networks within and beyond the enterprise
Balance sheet, income statement, management accounting reports	**Context**	Requirements analysis, systems design, project management
'Getting them right'	**Purpose**	'Getting them connected'
Form and function of analysis	**Focus**	Implementations design
Transparency of organisational spaces and products	**Ideal**	Alignment of people and technology
Activity based costing, balanced scorecards, value based management	**Recent applications**	Object-oriented approaches, corporate infrastructure modelling tools, distributed architectures

Figure 3.1 **Accounting and IT representations**

such as accounting, production and sales, making it up-to-date and available to all in real time, even to remote organisational functions. ERP systems packages provide solutions that only require configuration of functionalities (e.g. selecting from a menu by ticking a box indicating, for example, which method should be used for stock valuation) rather than requiring cumbersome language code writing. This does not mean that technological integration of data is simple. Often when firms embark on integrating many standalone systems into one database, they find that they cannot integrate all the data. Some has to be thrown away. The introduction of centralised databases brings new dilemmas because choices must be made about their content. Organisations cannot know everything in an integrated database, and new struggles emerge about what information should be put there. Hence, accounting is challenged on what are the real needs for information (Dechow and Mouritsen, 2005).

Each generation of information technology changes the focus of organisational information. Ledger systems, ERP systems, data-warehouses, XBRL and 'best-of-breed' systems (where each function may have its own independent system) suggest that technology can be related to management in different ways, as we will discuss. In principle, with ERP systems the management problem is more one of *producing* information by configuring software packages than of *using* information from an established system. With ERP, IT helps to shape organisational arrangements. People depend on IT and IT is conditioned by people (Orlikowski, 1992). Relationships between accounting and IT are intense because, in the modern firm, accounting is impossible without IT (Granlund and Mouritsen, 2003).

ERP promises a platform for managing the whole business, not merely certain parts of it. ERP systems develop an agenda about integration, standardisation and centralisation (Granlund and Malmi, 2002; Chapman and Chua, 2003; Scapens and Jazayeri, 2003). When it is possible to assemble and report information about all organisational entities and processes in integrated ways, this has implications for management control (Dechow and Mouritsen, 2005).

ERP systems see the relationship between information systems and management control through a 'business information model', which is used to extract reports. One does not have to be a 'management accountant' to perform these tasks. Indeed, management accountants may increasingly focus on how others produce reports, rather than producing the reports themselves. They are likely to focus more on technological possibilities for information production than reporting. Although in principle new technologies can present data in many ways, in practice they can do so only through design, which happens prior to data entering the databases. Technology is rigid. It compels us to do certain things in a certain sequence to get our reports out.

The content of this chapter

This chapter illustrates how the management of IT involves developing interfaces between management and information technology. There is an important distinction between the *project-mode* of the IT system during its implementation and the *practice-mode* when it is used and mobilised routinely. In the practice-mode the system's infrastructure is incomplete (unlike the tasks of everyday practice), because typically it is difficult to foresee all possible uses and concerns that the system should address. There are two reasons for this. First, as they engage with the system, users discover new, relevant applications for it. Second, the system's procedures may not work as expected and may consequently debar information-processing activities that were previously taken for granted.

New, sophisticated information technologies do not merely automate certain information production activities, therefore. They also define where automation ends, i.e. where other, sometimes manual, ways to account for and control organisational resources and performance are necessary. Because system infrastructure is never perfect and never perfectly integrated, organisations in practice often have to develop add-on procedures and support systems to supplement a core system infrastructure that has limitations to its information-processing capabilities. We can refer to such procedures and systems as *'extrastructure'*. In various, highly context specific ways they help the infrastructure to handle the information processing needs of the firm.

The following three sections use ERP systems to illustrate how management control is involved with managing technology. The first examines integration and elimination of data, and illustrates how modern technologies are, paradoxically, poor in organising themselves. They may offer choices about data structures, but they cannot identify the logic of these choices. They establish linear, step-by-step propositions that project implementers can use. However, linear explanations can postpone management control problems or hide them under the cloak of technological solutions. Modern project management helps to organise information technologies, but it is less concerned with the details of how it can support organisational decision-making.

The second section illustrates the challenge of making modern technologies relevant to management. It illustrates how ERP systems acquire purposes through the management control techniques they adopt. This is a circular movement. These purposes help IT to perform, but at the same time they can also develop informational 'blind spots' because, when constructed, information is rigid rather than flexible.

The third section argues that the properties of technology and management are unstable. The challenge is to find users who can stabilise and promote the technology and make it relevant to organisational decision-making. Although new information technologies often create attention in surprising ways, they need users to articulate them. State-of-the-art technologies pose important questions about management control during the project and practice stages, but they rarely function as 'complete calculation machines' (as claimed by Cooper and Kaplan, 1998). They are incomplete.

The fourth section argues that management control must be concerned with the management of technology. Contemporary information technologies bring managers new control problems involving two related questions. The first concerns what to do in *projects* and in *practice*. The second concerns how information technology operates through the system infrastructure designed at the project stage, or through the 'extrastructure' of supplements to the (imperfect) IT infrastructure. These questions render control relative; it becomes less about roles and responsibilities, and more about connecting technological design and developing support for it in many organisational places. Technological data hierarchies replace classical organisational definitions of hierarchy and disperse management control.

Integration and elimination

Modern information technologies are complex if measured by the number and comprehensiveness of the integrative functions they provide. But, they rarely provide explanations of how functionalities work, i.e. *how* they are important to, for example, management accounting. The IT perspective often promotes the structure of meta-data, the configuration of transaction processes and matching managerial responsibility structure with the technological infrastructure. For example, the structure of data influences how a user can track customer information throughout a system, when the fiscal year begins and ends, and the currencies through which the firm can transact. This structure conditions how data can describe organisational processes and functions, and how it can track responsibilities and thus attach costs and revenues to organisational entities. This is a management control problem, but is rarely defined as such; often it is seen more as technological cost/benefit decisions, implementation methods, and milestones that organise the technology development process. As Figure 3.2 from the German system vendor SAP AG illustrates, a process can be a roadmap.

The map has headlines for each implementation stage. It suggests that organisations can implement an ERP system if they (i) have a planning phase, (ii) develop a business blueprint, (iii) design the configuration, (iv) conduct final testing and (v) undertake ongoing maintenance. Each step makes a statement about organisation; for example, the explanation of the first step is:

> The secret to a smooth ride is proper planning and organizational readiness . . . All company decision-makers should be behind the project. Get them to agree up front that R/3 will support the bulk of your business. Acceptance is key to the acceleration of your implementation . . . (SAP AG, 1999a, p. 6)

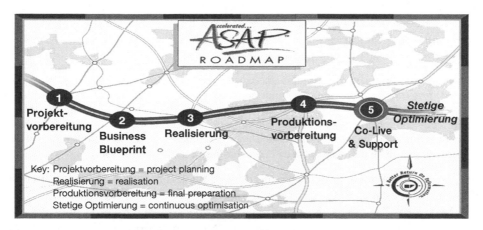

Figure 3.2 Illustration of the development roadmap
Source: SAP, 1999a, p. 6.

The claim is that top management support is required to implement technology. Then, other elements explain how implementation, albeit comprehensive, is not cumbersome:

> A seasoned travel agent knows the right questions to ask to make sure that your trip is a success. The Question and Answer Database acts as your implementation travel agent, reducing implementation time by asking the right questions, helping you to accurately define your enterprise areas, organizational structure, and technical requirements. (SAP AG, 1999b, p. 6)

This statement outlines what integrated systems may deliver, what modern technology offers, and how an organisation will 'come out in better shape' if it follows the specified sequence of activities involved in its implementation. It is a significant challenge, but the process secures relevant solutions and marginalises problems. The system emerges at the end of the implementation, when IT 'goes live' as an integrated information system. This project-based narrative rarely debates the end product. It may make IT difficult, but it rarely allows IT to become very complex.

Configuration begins with a question and answer database to establish the technical parameters of the system. An illustration is given below:

---

*A company code is an independent accounting unit for which a balanced set of books is produced. It is a **legal entity**. Balance sheets and profit and loss statements are required at the company code level. What are the legal entities that constitute your business?* _____
Do you produce a profit and loss statement and a complete balance sheet with retained earnings for each legal entity? (If a complete balance sheet including an equity section is not produced, then it is not a company.) ☐ Yes / ☐ No
Source: SAP America Inc, FI questionaire, 1997

The question and answer database develops a model of the business in non-technical language and helps to implement the roadmap shown in Figure 3.2. This step-by-step procedure develops general propositions on what the systems should achieve, without recourse to technical language. It presents a simple picture devoid of technology choices and resplendent with management objectives:

> Business people benefit from business objects as a means of abstraction. They are not at all interested in the details of a 'purchase requisition' programming code, for example. Much more important is the fact that business people can continue to use their own language in order to efficiently communicate their business needs. Therefore, business and IT people can both talk about identical business objects from two completely different points of view. Business objects close the communication gap between IT and business . . . (SAP AG, 1999c, pp. 3–4)

This assumes that managers need not know about technology and the architecture of integrated systems. Rather, IT people translate between technological and managerial concerns. However, this is problematical because the relation between data integration, strategy and control is complex. Modern information systems require management input into decisions about the interface between management and technology, since management concerns such as strategy and control must be represented

Table 3.1 **Management control premises/scenarios**

Operational control	Scenario 1	Scenario 2
Strategic control	Strategic business units repr. as business areas	Strategic business units repr. as company codes
Markets	Uniform by structure	Varying by structure
Technologies and process	Standardised to a large degree	Different in various business units
Logistical integration	Within location of business	Within SBU across legal entities
Internal supply chain transactions	No internal pricing	Transfer pricing
Plant coordination	Specific/non-specific to business area	Always business unit specific
Inventory	Specific/non-specific to business units	Always business unit specific
Purchasing	Plant/cross-plant/cross company code	Plant/cross-plant/cross company code
Sales	Specific/non-specific to business units	Always business unit specific
Consolidation	N/A on business unit level	Unconsolidated/consolidated year end/business unit
Profitability analysis	Central/local	Cross enterprise, central and local specific per business unit
Cost accounting	Central/local	Central/local

Source: Dechow (2001), based on SAP (1997a).

or modelled differently in a systems architecture. For example, SAP AG presents two scenarios:

> Scenario 1 is characterised by large support for the operative goals . . . Scenario 2, on the other hand, supports more the strategic goals of the enterprise. Depending on which of the goals, that is, strategic or operative, are given higher priority, scenario 1 or 2 can be selected. (SAP AG, 1997a, pp. 3–12)

Table 3.1 lists characteristics of both scenarios. It illustrates how modern IT becomes complex because of the sheer volume of management and organisational concerns it addresses and the questions it raises about the role of technology for control processes.

The two scenario columns in Table 3.1 illustrate that the association of IT and management is not given, but requires choice. The strategic business unit can be configured as a 'business area' or as a 'company code'. Each configuration defines different options. For example, only a company code configuration allows a system to execute transfer pricing routines and allows the entity to produce consolidated accounts. The company code configuration provides a corporation with more flexibility in defining profit and cost centres, but its price is either a less agile system or a significantly more expensive hardware set-up.

In principle a corporation will choose between a 'business area' and 'company code' configuration according to its control needs. The 'company code' configuration produces a more expensive and more data-heavy system (leading to reduced data response rates), while the 'business area' configuration shown to the left of Table 3.1 supports operative goals, is a more data-lean system, and costs less to implement and use. Table 3.1 illustrates how a technology configuration choice also entails choices about configuring control and strategy.

In addition to the long list of technical implementation activities, there are also numerous non-technical activities such as reviewing strategic vision and mission, core capabilities, transaction processes and, last but not least, the control model – for example, whether or not to establish a system of internal transfer prices. These management concerns, which are connected with decisions about IT, affect the attributes of the system infrastructure as listed in the first column of Table 3.1. Therefore, there is more to the implementation of information systems than what is apparent from implementation methodologies used by vendors.

Every configuration choice has opportunity costs, since the system could have been set up to do things other than those actually established in the technical configuration (Chapman, 2005). Whilst sophisticated ERP systems in principle can do everything, in practice the technological configuration sets limits that prevent the system from serving certain possible uses. One question in relation to Table 3.1 is whether the information system can be adapted if the business context changes, for example if a firm needs to add a new business unit or wants to adopt a new strategy for transfer pricing. In an integrated systems environment, such changes can weaken the system because they require a different kind of data-integration from the one originally configured into the system.

The following section examines how the interface between technology and management can be accomplished. Technology is difficult to explain to management, and so is often translated into various known management control tools to give meaning to the notion of integration that databases make possible (Bloomfield and Vurdubakis, 1997; Dechow and Mouritsen, 2004).

Calculation and configuration

Modern information systems refer to various management tools or concepts. For example, the SAP R/3 system (currently SAP Solutions, which includes the R/3 system, a business information warehouse and a SEM package) embraces several management concepts (see Figure 3.3). Dechow (2001) illustrates how they identify alternatives for modelling an organisation. Technology can use either financial or operations-based data to focus integration on how we work (W), how we measure performance (P), how we identify and maintain corporate boundaries (B), or how we develop corporate resources (R). Each concept gives a voice to technology and identifies how technology can be a solution to a management problem.

Figure 3.3 presents possible purposes of information systems, but how are the relevant purposes identified? Surveys (e.g. Booth et al., 2000), cross-sectional field studies (Granlund and Malmi, 2002) and case studies (e.g. Ribeiro and Scapens, 2004) indicate that new IT does not dramatically improve or change accounting *techniques* (e.g. the methods of cost allocation or budgeting, etc.) It appears that the huge potential for new management information is not currently developed in

Management Concepts							
KM	SVA	BSC	ABC	BPR	TQM	SCM	CRM
Royalty Maximisation	Navigation	Segmentation		Cooperation	Conforrmation	Regulation	Loyalty
With activity based costing, integration relates strategy design and business workflow				With business process re-engineering, integration aligns the organisation with a customer			
With balanced scorecards, integration relates the horizontal and the vertical organisation				With total quality management, integration takes place in episodes based on the notification of the 'right' people			
With shareholder value analysis, integration aligns management by means of a calculation				With supply chain management, integration allocates global process-ownership			
With knowledge management, integration is about the cost-oriented exploitation of data				With customer relationship management, integration is about the capability-oriented exploration of data			
R	B	P	W	W	P	B	R

Figure 3.3 **Management concepts serving technology**

Source: Dechow, 2001.

practice. The discovery of new relevant information is an open process which does not guarantee a useful solution.

Figures 3.4, 3.5 and 3.6 illustrate three different representations of a process: a role activity diagram (Figure 3.4), an event-driven process chain (Figure 3.5) and relations between databases (Figure 3.6). The graphics, which are again borrowed from SAP, mediate management and technology in different ways. Even if in principle all three graphics illustrate a business process, they describe managerial concerns in different ways.

The 'role-activity diagram' (RAD) focuses on the organisation of roles and activities. It draws attention to flows of activities and work, and thus prompts a concern about workflow efficiency. The event-driven process chain (EPC) diagram in Figure 3.5 is also a workflow diagram, but this diagram includes different details when depicting each operation of the process as a function. It shows which organisational unit is responsible for each function/operation, what information is necessary to carry out the function, and when sub-functions of the operation are required. In this way, the event-driven process chain (Figure 3.5) not only visualises certain parts of the sequence of operations as a control flow from left to right (as in Figure 3.4), but it also shows a flow of data from top to bottom through which the architecture of a process is translated into an object-oriented data model.

The EPC diagram (Figure 3.5) is concerned with how events trigger *logical relations* of different sets of data to each other. It differs from the RAD (Figure 3.4) where management is primarily concerned with the *strategic relation* of roles and activities in the conduct of business. The RAD suggests that management need not be concerned with the operations of the data screen and the operative effectiveness of the system in general, which is the concern of the EPC.

The two diagrams frame managerial focus differently. Moving between the diagrams, it appears there is ample space for misunderstandings. Figure 3.4 suggests that management should be concerned only with the complexity of the process

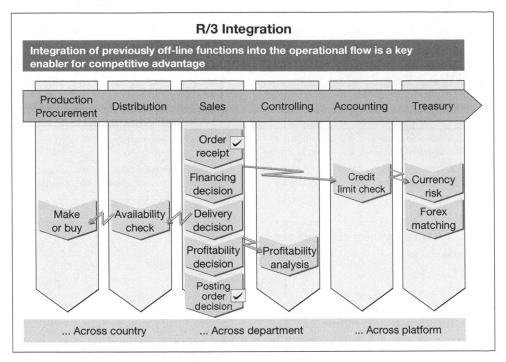

Figure 3.4   Process as Role-Activity Diagram (RAD)

Source: www.sapfans.com – R/3.

flow; e.g. management is interested in the sequence of activities of an invoice process. When Figure 3.4 is related to Figure 3.5 there are suddenly numerous other concerns, e.g. the number of users and the number of data screens a user has to operate to create the invoice.

Given the differences in focus and framing between (i) the strategic managerial concern with workflow promoted by the RAD diagram and (ii) the logical association of data in the EPC diagram, there is a risk that translations from one to the other frame will not be efficient. The challenge is that, technologically, business processes operate through neither RADs (Figure 3.4) nor EPCs (Figure 3.5), although both are used to frame the development of the system architecture. From a technological point of view, business processes operate via relational database tables as illustrated in Figure 3.6.

Figure 3.6 shows that processes are managerial constructs. We can talk about processes, but very few processes are directly observable. They can only be visualised through a (graphical) representation such as Figure 3.4. Whilst IT can visualise lateral processes, it is itself based on hierarchical data tables.

The visualisation of process happens through the structuring of identifiers in the technological structure. The markers create links between hierarchies of data and

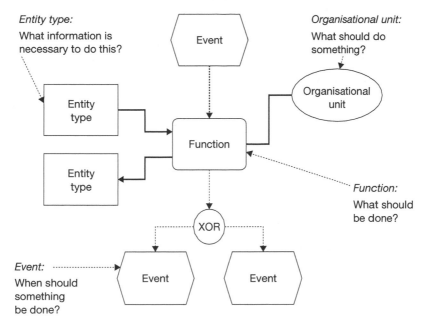

Figure 3.5 Process as event-driven process chain (EPC)
Source: Keller and Teufel, 1999, p. 159.

make it possible to analyse certain things across these hierarchies. This will be important when a financial controller wants to analyse certain things, such as customer profitability, where some information comes from a cost hierarchy and other information comes from the customer relationship information. If, for example, customers are identified by name and address in the system, analysts will only be able to perform a coherent profitability analysis on the basis of individual addresses. If a customer moves and is listed under a new address, this will create two customers and lead to uncertainty about the allocation of costs and calculation of profitability. If the old address is deleted, so is the customer's history.

Thus, the technological design of relational databases influences the coherence of management processes. The complexity of the relation between technology and management is not easy for a company to predict during the early phases of an implementation, when it is busy developing role-activity diagrams. Choices about these drawings develop technical properties of accounting and management concepts that SAP refer to as choices between 'organisational structure' and 'process structure':

> Many of the common management theories developed in recent years (Business Process Reengineering, Total Quality Management, Lean Management, and so on) have as their goal the optimization of the business system within an enterprise. . . *To optimize the business system, you must take into account the mutual dependence between the organizational structure and the process structure of the enterprise.* 'Reengineering' the business processes of a company can require the adjustment of the organizational structures. (SAP AG, 1997a, pp. 2–6: emphasis added)

55

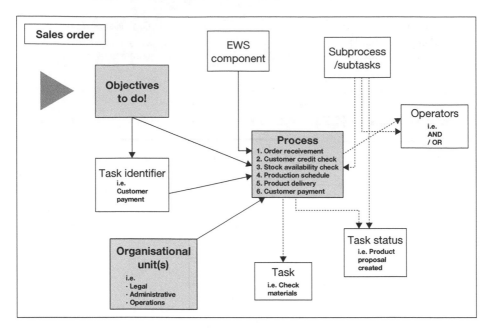

Figure 3.6 **Process as relational database**
Source: SAP, 1997b.

The organisational structure and the process structure are mutually dependent, but they do not tell the same story about the firm and its central problems (see Figure 3.3). Both stories derive from, and refer back to, the relational database. Management concepts and IT vocabularies are difficult to reconcile because, for example, a managerial focus on process re-engineering often requires technical adjustments to the organisational structure represented by the system. Concepts and ideas from process re-engineering must be organised through the design of data-tables at the technological level. The challenge lies in vocabulary, because lateral processes implied in a management language are not lateral in information systems – the latter are programmed to run up and down the steps of hierarchical data-tables. Whereas the commercial language is decidedly lateral, the technological language is hierarchical. Through numerous representations, not least graphical ones, the technical language is accommodated to simulate a lateral flow.

Technology needs management concepts to explain how it can provide integration and be useful. SAP AG distinguishes between three different technology scenarios, depicted in Table 3.2 as management holdings, financial holding companies and strategic alliances (Dechow, 2001).

The left-hand column in Table 3.2 lists dimensions that differentiate the three different system set-ups. The table suggests that each configuration entails a choice between managing the corporation as a 'management holding', a 'financial holding' or a 'strategic alliance'. Technology promises to integrate corporations, but it requires management to specify the level and characteristics of integration. As the bottom row of Table 3.2 suggests, for example, the configuration choice influences

Table 3.2 Three technology scenarios at the first of five ERP configuration levels

Technology Scenario	Basic 1 system set up for 1 company	Advanced 1 system set up for X companies	Multiple systems 1 enterprise with X company systems
Logistical integration	Within location of business	Focused at the level of Strategic Business Units across legal entities	Only to a limited extent across business units and enterprise
Technologies and process	Standardised to a large degree	Different in various business units	Different in various business units
Markets	Uniform by structure	Varying by structure	Varying by structure
Internal transactions	No internal pricing	Transfer pricing	Market-based customer/vendor relationships
Operational control	Standard reporting	Independent operative and strategic control	Full B.U. autonomy: system master data, open items management and controlling
General reporting	Reports for external rendering of accounts	Autonomous SBUs in relation to profitability and cost reporting	Independent
New business	Legal entities should not be planned in short term	Legal entities planable in medium term	Legal entities planable 'anytime'

Source: Dechow (2001), based on SAP (1997a).

how a corporation can add new business units to an existing information system structure. If a corporation has invested in a basic system it may be unable to incorporate a new business unit as a legal entity. Integration can have various possible objectives and the choice of system can frustrate corporate ambitions for expansion. Technology can thus become a hindrance.

Technology has many options, but it cannot deliver integration until management delineates the purposes of integration. The extent to which technology will be useful depends on the number of tools involved in making information available. Given that technology only responds to managers when they want a management report, there is often a considerable time lag before organisations realise how successfully they specified their requirements. The critical success factor is whether the information technology's purpose is defined according to management concerns.

Recent studies indicate how difficult it is to define the purpose of technology once and for all. It changes and develops over time. Planning and implementing a state-of-the-art management control system may differ from realising it in the long run (Granlund and Malmi, 2002) because many users of the technology and management agenda are typically unknown during implementation. This is not due to any lack of preparation, but is because opportunities are identified through developing and using the system (Dechow and Mouritsen, 2005). Once something is done, new things are learnt and then new purposes emerge. Thus, design often reflects how things were *meant* to work rather than how they *will* work.

This argument is developed in the following section, which argues that realising management control by using state-of-the-art technologies is more uncertain than expected. First, it is not certain who the users of sophisticated control systems will be, since score-keeping, attention-direction and problem-solving are often done outside the accounting function. Second, the role of technology and the organisational purposes in using technology are not static even when implementation is completed.

Organising and realising management control systems

Various studies suggest that ERP systems have little impact on the development of management control techniques, and that their overall impact remains moderate compared to expectations (e.g. Sutton, 1999). Often the accounting parts of ERP systems are replicated and transferred from the old system, so change is not typically part of the design. Granlund and Malmi (2002) traced the moderate impact of ERP systems on management accounting systems and speculated on their design limitations. They noted that firms had little experience with new technology, there was often a time lag between efforts and effects, and many struggled with project modes of systems design. Information systems were perceived as cumbersome or non-supportive of some modern management accounting techniques, though future developments may change this. Some problems arose from systems not being well understood even by implementation consultants, so some potentially supportive functions were not considered. Since technology constantly develops, this is important – we cannot assume that installed technologies are optimal or even relevant compared to their possibilities. Configuration choices can add to the confusion by rendering some desired functionalities impossible.

Another strand of literature argues that firms implementing ERP systems will experience a learning curve before benefiting from the investment (e.g. Ross and Vitale, 2000). This literature develops the stage-maturity model (Nolan, 1979), which is often used to guide ERP implementation (e.g. KPMG Consulting, 1997). This model hypothesises that firms undergo a series of stages when developing and using ERP systems (Holland and Light, 2001). However, this can be a problematical model of development, as it may not represent what actually happens (Benbassat *et al.*, 1984).

A third and emerging strand of literature examines how ERP technologies work as systems in the context of organisational concerns and conditions. These studies illustrate how ERP systems enable actors to solve problems and create solutions. Despite massive investments in ERP it is still fragile, and it remains cumbersome to integrate management control through technology. These studies find little support for the idea of learning curves. Instead, they illustrate how people address the deficiencies of ERP systems and find alternative, complementary ways to make integration work (Quattrone and Hopper, 2001, 2005; Chapman, 2005; Dechow and Mouritsen, 2005).

Other studies claim that the role of accountants changes when new technology is implemented. Accounting tasks become dispersed and not confined to the accounting department (Caglio, 2003; Scapens and Jazayeri, 2003; see also Granlund and Malmi, 2002; Quattrone and Hopper, 2005). Some organisational members become 'hybrid-accountants' and analytical accounting work shifts away from the accounting function. Some studies argue that ERP systems may render the accounting function largely redundant for information production, though this is an extreme view (Granlund and Malmi, 2002; Chapman and Chua, 2003).

In this literature, accounting cannot be distinguished from technology because control stems from management interfaces with technology. However, technology and management are difficult to reconcile because, despite the properties of technology being open during implementation, they are rarely flexible after implementation. Before IT is configured it can potentially do many things for management. Yet, many options are not investigated systematically, and they remain unclear to the organisations. This is important because, once choices are made, other configuration options/paths disappear or remain unknown and are thus denied further consideration.

Once implementation is completed and the idealised infrastructure becomes manifest in IT, the properties of technology are closed. Hence the infrastructure can handle some transactions and analyses, but others become difficult. Consequently, organisational actors create supplements and develop local information (Dechow and Mouritsen, 2005). They shape technology to make solutions despite the technology being cumbersome, for example by adding new information systems or developing ad hoc, personalised procedures that are modelled in local spreadsheets, independent of the integrated database.

The technology implementation model does not produce a stable system. It only becomes stabilised in use, even in combination with supplementary local information systems and technologies (e.g. spreadsheet files or manual tables of information) that rectify deficiencies of the technology installed. Users solve problems and create solutions that stabilise technology and technology can interact with management in multiple ways.

Management of technology

With new technologies such as ERP systems, management control becomes increasingly concerned with managing technologies rather than controlling budgets, accounting reports, and variance analyses. Integrated technologies bring new management control problems because they enable some information production to be automated and some calculations to be performed locally. Consequently, management control becomes increasingly involved with configuring information technology and shaping which calculations can be made locally.

Technology mobilises problems and issues in organisationally diverse places. Users can take responsibility for information technology, in the sense that they decide when it works and when it needs repair. Management control becomes concerned with developing technology to inform various organisational questions, rather than just specifying organisational responsibilities once and for all. Organisational roles, responsibilities and problems can be defined from anywhere. Technology becomes no one's property, but can potentially be mobilised by anybody. No longer can only management accountants produce profitability reports; these reports can also be generated in production, marketing or other places with access to the ERP system. Since modern information technology is integrated, it covers many aspects of organisational entities and enables, in principle, anybody to draw on information pertaining to others.

Conclusion

This chapter has analysed the interfaces between IT and management control. We suggest that management control is increasingly concerned with managing technologies. With the introduction of advanced IT like ERP systems, management control can be expressed from diverse parts of the firm because this technology is integrated. Hence, the exercise of management controls changes.

Some studies have analysed this interface. Some focus on the effects of IT on management accounting systems, while others examine how technologies are made to work in practice. New and sophisticated management tools automate information production, but they also make organisations define where automation ends and hence where alternative (even manual) ways to account for organisational work, performance, boundaries between entities, and resources become important.

Information systems rarely work as predicted in implementation projects. They need project management, but practices of managing identify their possible uses. Modern information systems pose many questions about the interface between management and technology. There are different ways of doing this; each facilitates some forms of integration, but makes others difficult or even impossible. Each configuration of technology involves an opportunity cost, therefore.

Properties of technology and management are rarely stable across time and space, and modern technologies need users who work at the centre of the system as well as others who work at the periphery. The latter operate distantly from system development and implementation, creating local remedies for emergent technological problems and helping the system work to deliver desired outcomes. Control practices are becoming less about executing organisational roles and responsibilities and more about integrating technological design and its mobilisation in many locations simultaneously. Strong organisational hierarchies come under attack after system integration. This disperses control throughout the organisation and produces hierarchies that function for a time but crumble when interest in their work fades.

References

Benbassat, I., Dexter, A.S., Drury, D.H. and Goldstein, R.C. (1984) 'A critique of the stage hypothesis: theory and empirical evidence', *Communications of the Association for Computing Machinery*, **27**(5), 476–85.

Bloomfield, B.P. and Vurdubakis, T. (1997) 'Visions of organisation and organisations of vision: the representational practices of information systems development', *Accounting, Organizations and Society*, **22**(7), 639–68.

Boland, R. (1999) 'Accounting as a representational craft: lessons for research on information systems' in W.L. Currie and B. Galliers (eds), *Rethinking Management Information Systems*, Oxford: Oxford University Press, pp. 229–45.

Booth, P., Matolcsy, Z. and Wieder, B. (2000) 'Integrated information systems (ERP-systems) and accounting practice – the Australian experience', Paper presented at the 3rd European Conference on Accounting and Information Systems, 27–28 March 2000, Munich, Germany.

Caglio, A. (2003) 'Enterprise Resource Planning systems and accountants: towards hybridization?' *European Accounting Review,* **12**, 123–53.

Chapman, C. (2005) 'Not because they are new: developing the contribution of enterprise resource planning systems to management control research', *Accounting, Organizations and Society,* **30**(7/8), 685–9.

Chapman, C. and Chua, W.F. (2003) 'Technology-driven integration, automation, and standardization of business processes: implications for accounting', in A. Bhimani (ed.), *Management Accounting in the Digital Economy,* Oxford: Oxford University Press, pp. 74–94.

Cooper, R. and Kaplan, R.S. (1998) 'The promise – and peril – of integrated cost systems', *Harvard Business Review,* **76**, 109–19.

Davenport, T. (1998) 'Putting the enterprise in enterprise system', *Harvard Business Review,* July–August, reprint 98401, 3–10.

Debreceny, R. and Gray, G.L. (2001) 'The production and use of semantically rich accounting reports on the Internet: XML and XBRL', *International Journal of Accounting Information Systems,* **2**, 47–74.

Dechow, N. (2001) *SAPiens perspectives on Enterprise Resource Planning.* Copenhagen Business School, PhD Series, 11.2001.

Dechow, N. and Mouritsen, J. (2004) 'ERP manuscripts of accounting and information systems: learning from SAP AG's presentation of Enterprise Resource Planning systems', in K.W. Andersen and M. Thanning Vendelø (eds.), *The Past and Future of Information Systems,* Edinburgh: Butterworth-Heinemann.

Dechow, N. and Mouritsen, J. (2005) 'The quest for integration, management control and Enterprise Resource Planning systems', *Accounting, Organizations and Society,* **30**(7/8), 691–733.

Granlund, M. and Malmi, T. (2002) 'Moderate impact of ERPS on management accounting: a lag or permanent outcome?' *Management Accounting Research,* **13**, 299–321.

Granlund, M. and Mouritsen, J. (2003) 'Problematizing the relationship between management control and information technology' [introduction to the Special section on 'Management control and new information technologies'], *European Accounting Review,* **12**, 77–83.

Holland, C.P. and Light, B. (2001) 'A stage maturity model for Enterprise Resource Planning Systems use', *The DATA BASE for Advances in Information Systems,* **32**(2), 34–45.

Keller, G. and Teufel, T. (1999) *SAP R/3 Prozessorientiert Anwenden* (3. erweiterte Auflage), Bonn: Addison-Wesley.

KPMG Consulting (1997) 'Profit-focused software package implementation'. *Research Report,* London: KPMG Management Consulting.

Moschella, D. (1997) *Waves of Power: Dynamics of Global Technology Leadership 1964–2010,* New York: Amacom.

Nolan, L.R. (1979) 'Managing the crisis in data processing', *Harvard Business Review,* **57**(2), 115–26.

Orlikowski, W.J. (1992) 'The duality of technology: rethinking the concept of technology in organizations', *Organization Science,* **3**, 398–427.

Quattrone, P. and Hopper, T. (2001) 'What does organizational change mean? Speculations on a taken for granted category', *Management Accounting Research,* **12**, 403–35.

Quattrone, P. and Hopper, T. (2005) 'A "time–space odyssey": management control systems in two multinational organizations', *Accounting, Organizations and Society,* **30**(7/8), 735–64.

Ribeiro, J.A. and Scapens, R.W. (2004) 'Power, institutionalism, ERP systems and resistance to management accounting: a case study', Paper presented at the 27th Annual Congress of the EAA, Prague.

Ross, J. and Vitale, M.R. (2000) 'The ERP revolution: surviving vs thriving', *Information Systems Frontiers,* **2**(2), 233–40.

SAP AG (1997a) *Consultant's Handbook,* Walldorf, Germany: SAP AG.

SAP AG (1997b) *Objects in the R/3 Process Model,* Walldorf, Germany: SAP AG.

SAP AG (1999a) *Tools and Accelerators Turbo Charging Your Installation,* Walldorf, Germany: SAP AG.

SAP AG (1999b) *Accelerated SAP–Driving Rapid Implementation,* Walldorf, Germany: SAP AG.

SAP AG (1999c) *R/3 System–SAP Business Objects,* Walldorf, Germany: SAP AG.

Scapens, R. and Jazayeri, M. (2003) 'ERP systems and management accounting change: opportunities or impacts? A research note', *European Accounting Review,* **12**, 201–33.

Sutton, S.G. (1999) 'The changing face of accounting and the driving force of advanced information technologies', *International Journal of Accounting Information Systems,* Sampler paper, 2–6.

Weber, R. (1987) 'Toward a theory of artifacts: a paradigmatic base for information systems research', *Journal of Information Systems,* **1**, 3–19.

www.sapfans.com, R/3 Sapfans – the SAP fan club. (Page currently unavailable.)

Further reading

Bhimani, A. (ed.) (2003) *Management Accounting in the Digital Economy,* Oxford: Oxford University Press. A book with many chapters analysing issues of IT and management control in the current global knowledge society.

Cooper, R. and Kaplan, R.S. (1998) 'The promise – and peril – of integrated cost systems', *Harvard Business Review,* **76**, 109–19. One of the first studies to analyse how integration (ERP systems) may affect management accounting calculations.

Dechow, N. and Mouritsen, J. (2005) 'The quest for integration, management control and Enterprise Resource Planning systems', *Accounting, Organizations and Society,* **30**(7/8), 691–733. An original contribution analysing the complex relations between ERP systems and management control in two case companies.

Granlund, M. and Malmi, T. (2002) 'Moderate impact of ERPS on management accounting: a lag or permanent outcome?' *Management Accounting Research,* **13**, 299–321. One of the first empirical studies to map the effects of ERP systems on management accounting practice.

Quattrone, P. and Hopper, T. (2005) 'A "time–space odyssey": management control systems in two multinational organizations', *Accounting, Organizations and Society,* **30**(7/8), 735–64. An original contribution focusing on how ERP systems affect management control, especially how time and space tend to lose importance in the ERP system environment.

Appendix: Glossary

ASP, application service provider A form of outsourcing. A company that offers access over the Internet to applications and related services that would otherwise be located in personal or enterprise computers. ASP technology promises to significantly reduce the total cost of ownership of IT.

BoB, best of the breed Best software in a certain functional area, like product costing or budgeting (best in regard to user perceptions: flexibility, functionality, user friendliness, etc.).

BI, business intelligence Analytic tools–sometimes designed as web portals–using data mining and other techniques for analysing not only company internal data-sources, but also external ones.

Data mining software Software sorting through data to identify patterns and establish relationships.

DW, data warehousing In this model selected data is copied (and simultaneously extracted and cleaned) from operative and other massive databases (DB) to data warehouses for user-friendly analysis and reporting.

EAI, enterprise application integration Plans, methods and tools aimed at modernising, consolidating and coordinating the computer applications in an enterprise.

ERPS, enterprise resource planning system An integrated information system taking care of all information flows of an organisation that operates on a centralised database where data is entered once at the point of transaction.

Legacy systems Applications and data inherited from languages, platforms and techniques that predate current technology.

Middleware General term for any programming that serves to glue together or mediate two separate and often already existing programs.

Object-oriented modelling (programming) A modelling approach organised around 'objects' rather than 'actions', and data rather than logic. Historically, software has been viewed as a logical procedure that takes input data, processes it, and produces output data. The programming challenge was seen as how to write the logic, not how to define the data. Object-oriented programming assumes that what we really care about are objects we want to manage rather than the logic to manage them. Examples of objects range from customers (described by data elements such as name, address, etc.) to assets (whose properties can be described and managed) down to product components.

OLAP, online analytical processing User-friendly multidimensional analysis software.

SEM, strategic enterprise management CPM, corporate performance management BPM, business performance management Software families for managerial analysis and reporting (names vary by vendor, but contents are very similar). Such software typically include functionality for key performance indicator systems, EVA calculations, balanced scorecards, various risk management tools, activity-based costing, and/or various other operational and financial planning tools. Such software is provided both by ERPS vendors and other software companies.

(Continued)

Appendix: Glossary (*Continued*)

SOA, service-oriented architecture A new platform for application, process management, and integration sectors of the software industry consisting of loosely coupled software parts. SOA promises higher flexibility and lower total cost of ownership than client-server solutions (e.g. ERP solutions).

XBRL, eXtensible Business Reporting Language XML-based (eXtensible Mark-up Language) language developed specifically for automating business information requirements, such as the preparation, sharing and analysis of financial reports. HTML (Hypertext Markup Language) only defines the appearance of web pages, whereas XML and thus XBRL also define document contents.

4

Globalisation and the international convergence of management accounting

Cristiano Busco, Elena Giovannoni and Angelo Riccaboni

Introduction

The last 20 years have witnessed a major transformation in business corporations, which have been forced to re-define their strategies, structures and processes in light of the changing business arena. Market globalisation has led to strategies of merger and acquisition, and has encouraged organisations to secure competitive advantage through process standardisation and world-scale efficiency, as well as flexibility and local responsiveness. In the resulting uncertain market environment, the challenge facing global organisations is the ongoing alignment of *local* business processes with *global* corporate strategies as they continuously adapt how they do things to compete successfully.

Executives seeking integration in a global organisation face a difficult task. Integrating widespread sub-units and operations requires managing and coordinating several intra-organisational relationships – vertical and hierarchical ties between the headquarters and subsidiaries, as well as horizontal and lateral ties between subsidiaries within the same organisation. The business literature has elaborated various theoretical frameworks to capture the evolution of global organisations (see Govindarajan and Gupta, 2000; Bartlett *et al.*, 2004). For example, scholars have distinguished between 'ethnocentric', 'polycentric' and 'geocentric' organisations (Perlmutter, 1969), as well as 'multinational', 'global' and 'transnational' mentality at work (see Bartlett and Ghoshal, 1989, 1993). Governing global organisations requires managing several tensions – centralisation versus decentralisation; standardisation versus differentiation; strategy integration versus local responsiveness – which raise questions about the roles of management accounting systems as key governance mechanisms (Catturi, 2003; Quattrone and Hopper, 2005; Busco *et al.*, 2006a).

Aligning *local* business processes with *global* corporate strategies requires organisational resources to be organised and monitored to achieve the goals underpinning the corporate vision. Organisational leaders must translate their mission and strategies into specific objectives and measures, and communicate them across the organisation increasingly often relying on comprehensive, organisation-wide management accounting systems. Within global organisations such systems integrate organisational resources, which (i) are spread across the world, often in varied business environments, and (ii) cannot always be measured in purely financial terms. Thus, systems of control and accountability that comprise, but also extend, traditional financial measures are an integral part of adapting to changing market conditions and integrating the different functions, businesses and subsidiaries that characterise managing global organisations.

Accounting and management control researchers have attempted to explain how these organisational systems create a global–local dialectic between the headquarters and 'distant' peripheries (Dent, 1996; Catturi and Riccaboni, 1996; Arnold and Sikka, 2001; Barrett *et al.*, 2005; Busco *et al.*, 2006a, 2006b; Quattrone and Hopper, 2006). This literature addresses issues of centralisation versus decentralisation by examining how processes of authority allocation, information processing, performance measurement and control construct physical and virtual distances that characterise the structure of global organisations (see Robson, 1992; McNamara *et al.*, 2004; Quattrone and Hopper, 2005). In this context, integration and coordination have often been linked to the existence of a superordinate centre (generally the headquarters) from which subordinate processes and activities are judged (Egelhoff, 1984; Mouritsen, 1995). Additionally, advances in information technology, such as enterprise resource planning systems and other integrated information systems, have shaped convergence and standardisation (see Granlund and Malmi, 2002; Quattrone and Hopper, 2005).

This chapter explores management accounting practices in the context of growing globalisation. It focuses on global organisations as privileged venues whereby globalisation is produced and reproduced on a daily basis through organisational practices. Drawing on a series of illustrative case studies, we examine the role of management accounting as a key governance mechanism to align *local* practices to the *global* strategies, and whether this results in increasing homogenisation and convergence of accounting practices. In particular, the following issues will be addressed:

- The way in which broad-based, financial and non-financial systems of measurement and accountability are used by organisational leaders to create, develop and maintain a common organisational language, and how this language becomes embedded in corporate culture. We rely on the case of General Electric (GE), which is an example of a company that has grown globally by acquisition through the so-called 'GE Way'. This leads us to explore how performance measurement systems are drawn upon to coordinate the diverse elements of a global organisation.

- The use of management accounting systems to manage patterns of vertical (between corporate, divisional, subsidiary and unit levels) and lateral (among divisions and units) information flows within global organisations. Insights from the case of Nestlé Waters are offered to illustrate how integration can be achieved by shifting from a geographic to a product view of the business, and the role of management accounting practices in coordinating distant markets within the same business unit.

- The role of accounting in managing 'distances' between the centre and the peripheries of global organisations, and how this role can be mediated through advances in information technologies. We rely on two cases from one American and one Japanese corporation to debate the assertions that ERPs (enterprise resource planning systems) inevitably enhance integration by centralising accounting and control systems. In particular, we explore how ERPs may create different forms of distance and relations between headquarters and geographically dispersed subsidiaries.

- The governance mechanisms that global organisations are relying upon, and their extended understanding of 'accountability'. Issues of governance are increasingly perceived as going beyond the ownership structure and the composition of the board of directors, to encompass performance measurement and the coordination of widely distributed human resources within an integrated framework. Such a broadened perspective suggests a need to investigate the challenges that the finance organisation may face in providing organisational leaders and front-line managers with increasingly heterogeneous and complex information flows. We draw on evidence from GE to illustrate how this broader approach to governance and accountability has been deployed in that context, and the role played by the finance organisation.

Next, before addressing the different issues listed above, we review the literature on the evolution of global organisations and illustrate different integrating strategies including centralisation versus decentralisation, standardisation versus differentiation, and changing vertical and lateral relations. Finally, the relationships between globalisation and management accounting practices are summarised in the conclusion.

Governing global organisations: changing strategies and emerging needs

During the last twenty years, the number, size, nationality and geographical spread of global organisations have increased enormously. Market globalisation has encouraged the establishment of inter-firm relationships across countries, involving cross-national agreements, partnerships, alliances, joint ventures or business groups. Cross-border agreements have tried to create value by combining resources, sharing knowledge and risk, and gaining access to markets, technologies and complementary skills. In this context, coordinating and integrating cross-border activities become crucial.

Within global organisations, corporate headquarters' control over the subsidiaries has traditionally been regarded as a central integrating function (Chang and Taylor, 1999; Gupta and Govindarajan, 1991). Research on integration and coordination within global organisations has traditionally assumed the existence of a superior authority (the headquarters) that judges subordinate activities (see Mouritsen, 1995). Thus, considerable attention has been paid to the headquarters–subsidiary relationship (*vertical relation*) and the governance mechanisms used by headquarters to regulate transactions with subsidiaries (Doz and Prahalad, 1984; Gupta and Govindarajan, 1991).

More recently, it has been recognised that market globalisation has increased environmental turbulence, and desires for greater flexibility are spawning new organisational forms. Hierarchical vertical relations, with centralised power and authority, are increasingly being replaced by more complex integration mechanisms with different patterns of centralisation and decentralisation. *Lateral relations* (i.e. relations between subsidiaries) become more relevant, and power and authority are more dispersed (Martinez and Jarillo, 1989, 1991; Meer-Kooistra and Scapens, 2002; Quattrone and Hopper, 2005).

Research on the evolution of global organisations has identified their strategies and structures within the last 30 years. The literature has distinguished between 'ethnocentric', 'polycentric' and 'geocentric' organisations (Perlmutter, 1969); 'multinational', 'global' and 'transnational' strategies (Bartlett and Ghoshal, 1989, 1993); 'multi-domestic', 'global' and 'network' firms (Harzing, 2000; Forsgren, 2002); 'decentred' and 'multi-focal' organisations (Doz, 1986; Ghoshal and Barlett, 1990); and 'heterarchical' and 'hierarchical' structures (Hedlund, 1986).

In the rest of this section, the main features of these categories are reviewed and summarised to distinguish three approaches – multinational, global, and transnational – that embrace the changing strategies and emerging needs for governing activities across borders (Perlmutter, 1969; Martinez and Jarillo, 1989; Bartlett and Ghoshal, 1993; Dent, 1996). In particular, these approaches imply different degrees of:

- centralisation versus decentralisation
- standardisation versus differentiation
- strategy integration versus local responsiveness
- vertical versus lateral relations.

It is important to highlight that, even if one approach may be prevailing, the integrating strategies implemented by global organisations often combine elements of the multinational, global and transnational approaches and in some cases alternative approaches may also emerge.

The multinational approach

The *multinational approach* recognises that the company's worldwide subsidiaries have different and nationally responsive strategies. Multinationals: are characterised by a variety of domestic organisation structures; attempt little integration of activities across geographically scattered units; grant subsidiaries considerable autonomy and decentralisation; have high levels of differentiation and local responsiveness (high localisation). Here, vertical relationships are largely administrative and financial. Lateral exchanges are limited and national – rather than international – and competition is the primary concern (see Figure 4.1).

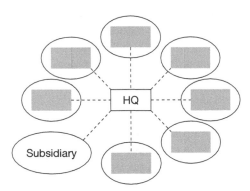

- High subsidiary autonomy and decentralisation (*as illustrated by the dotted lines that connect the HQ with subsidiaries*).
- Little integration of activities.
- High product differentiation and local adaptation.
- Multiple and nationally responsive strategies.
- Polycentric attitudes (local practices are preserved).

Figure 4.1 **The multinational approach**

Within companies with a multinational mentality, subsidiary managers tend to be nationals of the host country. Relying on their local market knowledge and the parent company's willingness to invest in foreign operations, these managers can often build up significant local growth and autonomy from the headquarters. However, local adaptations can also lessen efficiency in design, production, logistics, distribution and other functional tasks for economies of scale and benefits of knowledge sharing are not secured.

The multinational approach produces a *polycentric* (i.e. host-country oriented) attitude, which implies that the local culture is optimal and should be adopted. It assumes that host-country cultures are different, and foreigners are difficult to understand, that local people know what is best for themselves, that subsidiaries should have as local an identity as possible, and that financial control binds the company together. *Local practices are preserved and given a pivotal role.*

The global approach

In many organisations operating worldwide, nationally differentiated products and practices have been increasingly standardised alongside an increased centralisation of functions and decision-making authority. This has been labelled the *global approach*, where global strategies incorporate worldwide marketing, world-scale efficiencies (through integrated research and development, manufacturing and distribution) and product cross-subsidisation for international market penetration.

Rather than being nationally responsive, subsidiaries must implement functional strategies set at headquarters. The assumption is that cross-national tastes and preferences are similar and can be satisfied by standardised (rather than locally differentiated) products. Centralising strategic decisions and worldwide responsibility requires more central coordination and control than other strategies (see Figure 4.2).

The global approach is often associated with an *ethnocentric* attitude (i.e. it reproduces the culture of the country that is host to the headquarters). Ethnocentrism assumes that the company's host country culture (ways of analysing problems, values, beliefs, language, non-verbal communication) is universally applicable. The assumption is 'this works at home; therefore it must work in your country'. Executives in both the headquarters and subsidiaries express the national identity of the firm by associating the company with the nationality of the headquarters.

In ethnocentric organisations 'global' practices prevail and parent company culture is normally imposed. This assumes that core elements of the headquarters' business model must be transplanted to subsidiaries. Transplanting core beliefs and attitudes to a subsidiary often requires particular individuals and mechanisms to act as translators and value carriers. However, several critical issues, such as local resistance to global strategies, responsiveness to local customers and adaptation to local regulations, need to be properly addressed if a global approach is adopted.

The transnational approach

Sometimes the need for greater flexibility and decentralisation has led to even more complex governance structures, whereby national responsiveness and worldwide

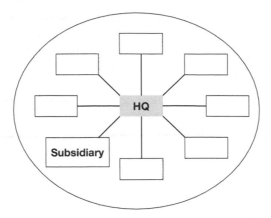

- High centralisation of decision-making authority and control (*as illustrated by the bold lines that connect the HQ with subsidiaries*).
- High centralisation of activities, cross-subsidisation and world-scale efficiency.
- High product standardisation and global marketing.
- Implementation of global strategies, centrally set.
- Ethnocentric attitudes (global practices prevail).

Figure 4.2 **The global approach**

learning are managed simultaneously. This has been labelled a *transnational approach,* where local units are integrated in a complex network of products, financial resources, technology, skills, knowledge, ideas and people.

Resources and activities are neither centralised nor decentralised. They are dispersed and specialised simultaneously, and are integrated into an interdependent network. Innovations and knowledge are shared across operations organisation-wide (see Figure 4.3). Moreover, within this network relationships and information flows are not only between the headquarters and local subsidiaries (vertical relations), but also are among different local subsidiaries (lateral relations). In contrast to the global model, the transnational approach emphasises national responsiveness and flexibility while, compared to the multinational approach, it recognises the need for intense coordination and knowledge sharing.

The transnational approach is often associated with *geocentric attitudes* (i.e. world oriented). Geocentricism assumes that a synergy of ideas from different countries should prevail. Its ultimate goal is a worldwide approach in both headquarters and subsidiaries. The corporate culture is developed by integrating *local* and *global* practices, through both vertical and lateral interaction.

Within the transnational model, national subsidiaries form the basic building blocks of the distributed network. Whilst decentralisation can create strong centrifugal forces, knowledge exchange and integration become crucial to bind the organisation

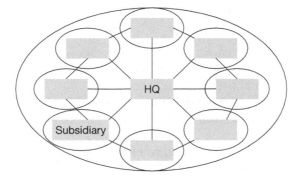

- Not centralisation, nor decentralisation (*as illustrated by the lines that connect both the HQ and the subsidiaries*).
- High integration into a worldwide network.
- High specialisation, diffusion of resources and lateral interaction.
- Merging national responsiveness and worldwide learning.
- Geocentric attitudes (local and global practices are integrated).

Figure 4.3 **The transnational approach**

together, managing consensus around a shared strategic intent, resolving tensions between global and local practices, and reconciling standardisation and differentiation of product distribution.

This section has outlined different approaches for governing globally operating organisations. Each approach discussed – multinational, global and transnational – implies different strategies of centralisation versus decentralisation, standardisation versus differentiation, and global integration versus local responsiveness, and suggests different patterns of vertical and lateral relations. This raises questions about the roles of management accounting under growing globalisation.

Next, we draw on some illustrative examples to offer a snapshot of the extent to which systems of performance measurement and management accounting participate in such processes of governance and global integration. Particular attention will be given to how accounting practices reproduce global tendencies versus local understandings, support vertical versus lateral relations, and collapse versus reinforce distance between the centre and the peripheries.

We begin with the case of General Electric (GE), which is an example of a company that has grown globally by acquisition through the so-called 'GE Way'. GE's acquisition of an Italian company, Nuovo Pignone (NP), describes how accounting and performance measurement systems help integrate local cultures within a global organisation. The case of Nuovo Pignone's acquisition illustrates a global strategy at work, where integration took place through the diffusion of a global culture of measurement infused by the parent company (see Busco *et al.*, 2006b).

Growing global by acquisition: when the GE Way met a local culture

General Electric is a large corporation managed through a shared organisational language, commonly referred to as the 'GE Way'. Over the past 20 years GE has grown globally by acquisition and has employed a common culture to align the strategies of its heterogeneous businesses. The GE Way, or 'the social architecture of the company' as GE's top management often call it, is built around the *GE Operating System*, and the language of measurement and accountability. During the 1990s, initiatives such as *work-out, change acceleration programs* and *best practice sharing* sustained GE's policy of growing global by creating a shared business language. In particular, the 'work-out' process involves identifying an area in need of improvement and bringing together people from all sides of the process (design, marketing, production, sales, etc.) to identify a better method and to solve potential problems.

The GE Operating System represents the 'GE Way' in action (see Figure 4.4). This involves continual, intense learning sessions where Business CEOs, top executives and managers responsible for major corporate initiatives share views and best practices from across the company. For newly acquired companies, the GE Operating System often represents a major challenge. With no chance to escape or postpone processes of integration, they are urged to adapt very quickly through leadership meetings such as the Operating Managers Meetings, Corporate Executive Councils and Quarterly Business Reviews, as well as intense business processes like Sessions I (strategy review), Sessions II (budgeting), Sessions C (individual appraisal) and Sessions D (compliance).

GE's acquisition of Nuovo Pignone illustrates how the American corporation used accounting and performance measurement systems to deploy the 'GE Way' within its global organisation. This provides an example of a *global approach* to integration.

Breaking the 'local culture' through systems of measurement and accountability

Originally established as Pignone in 1842 in Florence, Italy, Nuovo [New] Pignone (NP) was established in 1954 following its acquisition by ENI, a state-owned holding company, and in 1994 it was acquired by GE. Initially set up as a cast-iron foundry, NP grew and prospered through the design and manufacture of specialised equipment, such as electrical turbines, compressors and pumps. Its technical achievements included the world's first gas-powered internal combustion engine. Given NP's reputation for the quality of its engineering and products and its extensive market portfolio, GE decided to acquire this major competitor. Today, NP is the core division of GE Oil & Gas, with headquarters in Florence.

The process of integration with GE was grounded in major changes to the role of *measurement*, especially performance measurement, within NP. The culture of NP was so different to that of GE that a massive cultural change was required. NP had no tradition of using performance measurement systems, whereas GE's management relied extensively on them for communication and control. Before the acquisition, NP was

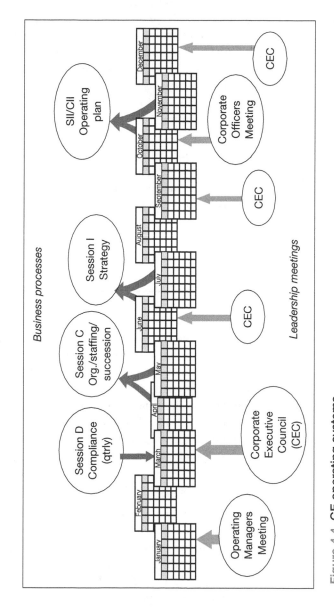

Figure 4.4 GE operating systems

Source: GE.

state-owned and very bureaucratic. It had to produce budgets and reports for head office and state departments, but these were largely ceremonial and not integrated into management processes. However, NP was reasonably profitable due to its excellent products and production systems. Following its acquisition by GE, significant changes took place: the redesign of its accountability system, and the implementation of a Six-sigma initiative – a measurement-based quality improvement programme.

When the integration process began, the first three GE managers to arrive at NP were the new chief financial officer, the financial planning and analysis manager, and the corporate auditor. GE knew it was buying a company with good product technology but poor performance measurement systems and little financial management. Within the first six months, NP underwent a metrics revolution. Significant effort was made to create a measurement system that aligned NP's strategy and business goals to the GE's operating system, as well as providing timely and accurate information.

Redesigning accountability involved major restructuring of the accounting and finance function and its systems. Manufacturing Finance, the department traditionally responsible for cost accounting, was strengthened and new departments were established, namely Financial Planning and Analysis, and Commercial Finance. In addition, GE assigned a new taskforce of finance managers to individual divisions to give finance advice. Restructuring the finance function reflected GE's view that accountants' talents should include, but transcend, traditional controllership. They should be fully fledged participants in driving the business to win in the marketplace – 'a role far bigger than the dreary and wasteful budget "drills" and bean counting that once defined and limited the job', suggested the CEO's letter to shareholders within GE's 1997 Annual Report.

Managers at all levels were given intensive training in the new systems and were encouraged to translate their business operations into financial terms. The language of measurement became an important component of learning. For example, sales personnel were encouraged to see their customers as financial entities and to look for every opportunity to improve customers' financial condition by selling General Electric solutions that truly affect their bottom line. Thus, as declared by an internal booklet, sales and sales support professionals were urged to 'wear the hat of finance', and act as *financial consultants* in assisting their accounts.

Towards a 'redefined culture' as NP reproduces the GE Way

Along with such restructuring of the accounting and finance function and systems of accountability, the Six-sigma initiative played the major role in integrating NP with the GE organisation. Six-sigma is a quality improvement philosophy, which has had a major impact in several large businesses over the past decade. Following its development by Motorola (in 1987), many companies (e.g. Texas Instruments, Asea Brown Boveri and AlliedSignal) have implemented Six-sigma. Six-sigma became a major initiative within GE in the mid-1990s, when GE globally was, on average, operating at three and a half to four sigma, which implied waste of $8–12 billion per year, or 10–15 per cent of total revenues.

Six-sigma consists of a range of tools, techniques and processes for achieving tight quality targets (sigma measures the number of mistakes per million discrete operations).

However, successful implementation of Six-sigma requires numerous financial and non-financial measures to be integrated into a holistic performance measurement and accountability systems. This had not traditionally been a strength of NP.

Each Six-sigma project starts from an *a priori,* customer-driven identification of 'macro' critical-to-quality (CTQ) issues. These CTQs are then broken down into multiple critical processes, which need to be investigated in order to reduce defects and increase profitability. Therefore, within a continuous improvement programme, these critical processes are examined by specific 'micro' projects. These projects involve five separate steps, which are referred to by the acronym D-MAIC:

1 Define – a preliminary phase where the key characteristics of the process are identified.
2 Measure – where CTQ defects and non-conformity are measured in sigma terms.
3 Analyse – where the fundamental causes of the defects are analysed using a wide variety of tools, ranging from brainstorming to statistical techniques.
4 Improve – where the processes are re-engineered through redesign, modification, etc., to bring the number of defects within the desired limits.
5 Control – where the ongoing activities are controlled through monitoring techniques, such as statistical process control, to ensure that the improvements are maintained.

The achievements of the individual projects are constantly monitored both in financial terms (including cost of quality) and according to a wide range of non-financial indicators (numbers of defects, customer satisfaction, supplier quality, etc.). Thus, since the introduction of Six-sigma in GE, there has been a major expansion in the measures used to monitor performance at all levels in the businesses, and particularly at the level of the individual projects. Such measures are designed to take the 'temperature of every single business process or project'.

Due largely to its organisational-wide diffusion, Six-sigma has come to comprise shared operational and managerial knowledge, both internationally across GE's global subsidiaries and intra-organisationally across its businesses and functions. In many GE companies, such as Nuovo Pignone, the introduction of Six-sigma has served an important role in extending the culture of measurement across all areas of the business. Six-sigma was crucial in enabling new knowledge to be validated and, eventually, to become crystallised in a set of common (best) practices. The language of Six-sigma is used to spread stories of operational successes, as well as the financial benefits achieved. Six-sigma is a way of thinking that is now embedded in the culture of GE.

Within NP the *local* – technical – culture was not repudiated but became framed and complemented by the GE Way characterised by a *global* culture of measurement and accountability (see Figure 4.5). Few managers and employees left the company; rather they participated in the transformation that merged the engineering-oriented capabilities of NP with GE's obsessive attention to bottom-line results. During this process, management accounting systems converged to enable the dialectic between the dominant culture of the organisation and the local understandings. Importantly, finance managers and the finance experts within Six-sigma projects helped translate operational matters into financial terms, and humanised the unfamiliar jargon of the 'GE Way' through a series of shared organisational practices and processes of interaction.

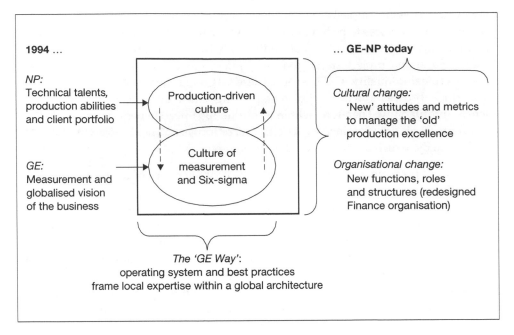

1994 ...

NP:
Technical talents,
production abilities
and client portfolio

GE:
Measurement and
globalised vision
of the business

Production-driven
culture

Culture of
measurement
and Six-sigma

... GE-NP today

Cultural change:
'New' attitudes and metrics
to manage the 'old'
production excellence

Organisational change:
New functions, roles
and structures (redesigned
Finance organisation)

The 'GE Way':
operating system and best practices
frame local expertise within a global architecture

Figure 4.5 **The integration process at GE-Nuovo Pignone**

Next, the case of Nestlé Waters shows how integration can be achieved by shifting from a geographic to a product view of the business. In particular, we explore the role of management accounting practices in coordinating distant markets within the same business unit. This integrating strategy involves new patterns of vertical and lateral interactions, which rely on performance measurement systems, and a shift from a multinational to a transnational approach (see Busco *et al.,* 2006a).

Vertical and lateral relations within Nestlé Waters

For many decades Nestlé's strategy has been to decentralise its products, brands and communications to be responsive to local consumers. This involved granting autonomy to each business and low integration of activities across different subsidiaries.

Nestlé had five e-mail systems and 20 versions of accounting and planning software. This created serious coordination problems as most employees could not access production and sales figures from units other than their own. Nestlé America, for example, paid more than 20 different prices for vanilla from the same supplier because each factory gave vanilla a different code and local managers could not compare what other factories were charging.

Until the early 1990s Nestlé's organisational structure focused mainly on distinct, autonomous geographic areas. Recently, as market turbulence and competition increased, Nestlé recognised that greater integration was needed to obtain the benefits of global learning, synergies and cost reduction. Following its acquisition of new businesses, which increased the heterogeneity and complexity of Nestlé's product portfolio, the company started to change its strategy by structuring some businesses not only by geography, but also by product category. This was the case in the mineral water business: Nestlé Waters was Nestlé's first management structure based on product categories rather than geography. This change in the water business provides an example of a shift from a multinational strategy (i.e. high decentralisation and high local responsiveness) to a transnational strategy (i.e. greater integration and high local responsiveness).

The development of the mineral water business, and its growth through acquisition, meant Nestlé Waters had to redefine its approach to the market. In 2000, Nestlé Waters was restructured with the introduction of two business units (BUs). Each coordinates, and makes decisions about, the international brand strategy and profitability (see Figure 4.6):

● The French BU (headed by Perrier-Vittel – PV) manages all activities from production to distribution of the French international brands (Perrier, Vittel and Contrex, bottled in France by Perrier-Vittel and sold in French and international markets).

● The Italian BU (headed by Sanpellegrino – SP) manages all activities of the Italian international brands (S.Pellegrino and Acqua Panna, bottled in Italy by Sanpellegrino and sold in the Italian and international markets).

As illustrated in Figure 4.6, the new BUs link different legal entities (such as Sanpellegrino, Perrier-Vittel, NW North America, NW UK) belonging to Nestlé Waters: the producer of the international brands (i.e. Sanpellegrino for the Italian BU and Perrier-Vittel for the French BU) and the internal distributors (i.e. NW North America, NW UK, etc.). The new structure emphasises lateral relations for coordinating activities within the same BU. As illustrated earlier, intense lateral relations characterise the transnational approach.

How management accounting practices enable lateral relations

With the introduction of the two BUs within Nestlé Waters, the management accounting system was restructured to fulfil new information and control requirements. New accounting practices were implemented to support 'lateral' relations between producers and distributors of international brands. These centred around a profit and loss account that consolidated information from producers and distributors ('End-to-End' Profit and Loss account – 'end-to-end' means 'from the producer to the distributor').

Currently, each BU's planning processes follow a common calendar. The main steps are:

1 Development of the global brand strategy.
2 Budget preparation.
3 Binding contract between the producer and its distributors.
4 Implementation and control.
5 Reporting and feedback.

The planning and budgeting for the international water brands starts with the development of the global brand strategy, which concerns brand positioning, pricing

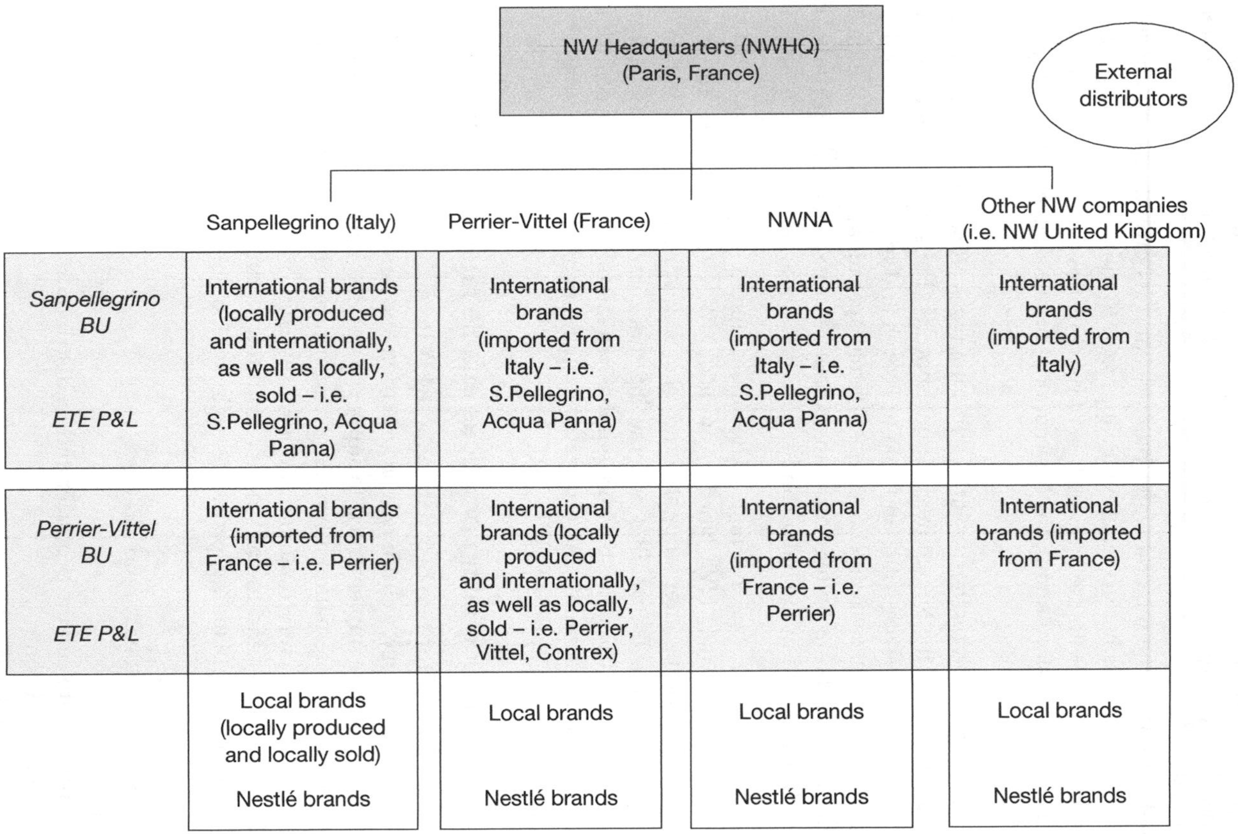

Figure 4.6 The introduction of the business units in NW's organisational structure

External distributors

NW Headquarters (NWHQ) (Paris, France)

	Sanpellegrino (Italy)	Perrier-Vittel (France)	NWNA	Other NW companies (i.e. NW United Kingdom)
Sanpellegrino BU	International brands (locally produced and internationally, as well as locally, sold – i.e. S.Pellegrino, Acqua Panna)	International brands (imported from Italy – i.e. S.Pellegrino, Acqua Panna)	International brands (imported from Italy – i.e. S.Pellegrino, Acqua Panna)	International brands (imported from Italy)
Perrier-Vittel BU	International brands (imported from France – i.e. Perrier)	International brands (locally produced and internationally, as well as locally, sold – i.e. Perrier, Vittel, Contrex)	International brands (imported from France – i.e. Perrier)	International brands (imported from France)
	Local brands (locally produced and locally sold)	Local brands	Local brands	Local brands
ETE P&L	Nestlé brands	Nestlé brands	Nestlé brands	Nestlé brands

strategy, brand development, and the volume strategy. According to the internal procedures set by NWHQ, this document is initially drafted by the BU managers, then discussed with distributors and eventually approved by NWHQ.

The global brand strategy is then translated into a plan (a market development programme) for each distributor, defining market priorities, volumes and price targets, and resources to be committed. The programme is drawn up by each distributor and discussed with the producer until mutual agreement is reached. The programme provides the basis for the long-term plan (LTP). Once approved by producers and distributors, the first year of the LTP is the basis for the operating plan.

The 'End-to-End' Profit and Loss account (ETE P&L) is then obtained by consolidating data obtained from both the producer and the distributors. It shows the international brand profitability in terms of end-to-end profitability, which is the joint profitability of the producer and distributors. The budget preparation entails vertical and lateral relations during the following phases:

1 Definition of the international brand profitability and the profit rate set for distributors by NWHQ (vertical relations).
2 Preparation of the budgets by distributors – i.e. the distributors' proposed market prices and volume targets – and expenditures for marketing, sales force and merchandising, storage and distribution, and administration (lateral relations).
3 Discussion between the BUs and the distributors (lateral relations) until agreement on the previous parameters (see phase 2) is reached.
4 Determination of transfer prices based on resale price less an agreed percentage (the 'resale less' method) using the parameters defined in the first three phases.
5 Production of the international brand's ETE P&L (by each BU finance manager), followed by a discussion between the producer and the distributors until a revised ETE P&L is agreed (lateral relations).
6 Definition and validation of the budgeted ETE P&L by the finance department of the BU (lateral relations).
7 Final approval of the budgeted ETE P&L by NWHQ (vertical relations).

Importantly, the budgeting procedures were defined and agreed by the two BUs according to guidelines from NWHQ. Implementing the new planning and budgeting process required considerable lateral communication and information exchange among the producers and distributors. Currently, the reporting requirements from the distributors to the BUs include:

● monthly – actual sales statistics; specific comments on international brands' trends;
● quarterly – P&L by brand;
● annually – actual P&L by brand, budget monthly sales by format, budget P&L by brand and format.

Conversely, reporting requirements from the BUs to the distributors include:

● monthly – general comments on international brands' sales performance globally; specific comments on international brands;
● quarterly – P&L end-to-end by brand and market;
● annually – actual end-to-end P&L by brand, format and market.

Before the BUs were created, lateral information exchanges between the different NW companies was limited. No attempts were made to integrate the international brand strategy and calculate international brand profitability worldwide. With the introduction of BUs and the implementation of the ETE P&L, Nestlé Water's producers and distributors had to think strategically in terms of joint profitability as equal partners belonging to the same global organisation. As a Sanpellegrino finance manager observed:

> The new performance measurement and accountability centred around the ETE P&L has brought a new end-to-end mentality, fostering the BU integration through shared goals between the producer and the distributor. On the one hand it improved the producer's control over the distributors' activities. On the other hand it links the distributors and the producer to a common faith as they have a shared goal to achieve and, in so doing, it favours identification around a global brand commitment.

Convergence and differentiation of management accounting practices in NW

The need to redefine its business not only geographically but also around product categories made NW reinforce the means of coordinating local markets with global strategies. Such mechanisms extended beyond just formally creating the BUs to internal structures of governance, including accounting techniques such as the ETE P&L. Thus, shared accounting practices, organisational knowledge and business rationales were diffused across different legal entities and within each BU. The new system fostered horizontal information exchange and communication around brand categories, thereby fostering lateral relations (see Figure 4.6).

The ETE P&L, built around the information needs of the BUs, integrated NW laterally by providing different subsidiaries with a homogeneous accounting platform for sharing information on international brands. The need to track legal entities' (subsidiaries') profitabilities requires additional systems to consolidate financial results from their international brands business with local brands' P&Ls. Therefore, within each subsidiary two different management accounting systems coexist (see Figure 4.6):

- a system that integrates international brands' data across legal entities (lateral integration within the BUs);
- a system that consolidates financial data within each legal entity (integration within the subsidiaries).

Within NW, management accounting systems were crafted to reinforce the new patterns of organisational integration: lateral and vertical integration is achieved through convergence (within the business unit) and differentiation (between the business unit and the legal entities) of accounting practices.

In the following discussion we draw on Quattrone and Hopper (2003) to illustrate how accounting and information systems can 'manage' distances between the centre and the peripheries of global organisations. Several studies show how information and communication technologies (such as computer-supported cooperative work systems, intranets, enterprise resource planning systems, etc.) help to achieve greater integration and control (see Bloomfield and Combs, 1992). Shared databases, simultaneously accessible from many locations, fulfil the dream of remote and instantaneous control by real-time performance information. This belief is often taken for granted (Granlund and Malmi, 2002; Quattrone and Hopper, 2005) but, as will be demonstrated, implementing organisation-wide resource planning systems is unpredictable and implies learning, mediation and customisation. The end point of this, if it is ever reached, may differ substantially from initial plans and expectations (Quattrone and Hopper, 2003).

IT and 'a-centred' corporations: evidence from two globally operating organisations

Quattrone and Hopper (2003, 2005) illustrate how ERP implementation may have different repercussions on management accounting and control systems, and integration. Based on information from one American and one Japanese corporation (anonymised respectively as 'Think Pink' and 'Sister Act'), they challenge assertions that ERPs inevitably enhance integration by centralising accounting and control systems. In particular, they suggest that ERPs may create different forms of distance and relations between headquarters and geographically dispersed subsidiaries. A summary of the two case studies follows.

The case of Think Pink (American corporation)

Think Pink manufactures and supplies home building products and composite materials worldwide. This global organisation saw implementing ERPs as an important opportunity to deploy an organisation-wide accounting and control system. The main purpose was to improve communication and coordination between headquarters and subsidiaries by fully integrating business areas and functions. This had consequences for accounting systems. Data was now stored centrally in a common database and in real time. However, the widespread access to the systems enabled business areas' functional managers to input or elaborate data in real time without the intervention of the accountants (e.g. the purchase department made entries for raw materials). In this new picture, accounting lost the ability to exercise centralised control.

Posting accounts at different points of the organisation meant that local managers could arrive at work and face headquarters' questions based on accounts different from those that existed when the manager left work the previous evening. Overall, managers felt a loss of control. Now business activities could access data immediately from different locations (the collapse of space) and controllers could access business results simultaneously with, or sometimes before, those responsible for them (the collapse of time). The diffusion of responsibilities and data inputs made it difficult to hold employees and segments accountable for their actions, which left the organisation in a state of continuous flux. Paradoxically, although ERPs accumulated accounting data centrally, the collapse of distance ruptured traditional boundaries between departments, functions, geographical areas and hierarchical levels, and reduced personal feelings of 'being in control'. The ERP introduction created different loci of discretion by decentralising centralisation.

An example lay in the relationship between the European headquarters in Belgium and a UK subsidiary. Prior to deploying an ERP, the subsidiary's performance was evaluated centrally from regional European headquarters. The accountants and the analysts located within the subsidiary had to wait for data from the centre to know how the plant was performing compared to other similar plants across Europe. Such data were provided by the centre together with instructions for performance and profitability improvements. Following the ERP implementation, all plants and regions started internal benchmarking with others in real time, and seeking advice from each other and taking remedial measures without mediation from the former centre of control.

The case of Sister Act (Japanese corporation)

Sister Act is a manufacturing company that markets office automation products, and industrial and domestic sewing machines. Its organisational structure separates manufacturing, and sales and distribution into different companies, with manufacturing directly controlled by the headquarters in Japan. The headquarters is the centre of the corporation, and it integrates the functional and spatial divisions between manufacturing and sales companies hierarchically. Importantly, accounting transactions define the organisational structure of Sister Act and reproduce distinct geographical, hierarchical and functional responsibilities.

Within Sister Act, the ERP implementation did not mark a discontinuity in information systems development. Rather, it extended a project on group integrated accounts started in the early 1990s prompted by changed legal regulations on group consolidation. A Microsoft Excel template was created for all subsidiaries. This offered a simple but effective way of consolidating that was consistent with accepted accounting principles. Each subsidiary used the same template, shaped by accounting categories within profit and loss accounts and balance sheets. As the project unrolled it was gradually transformed from facilitating consolidation for external reporting to the global provision of an integrated database for management information.

When managers realised the organisational disruption that a fully integrated ERP application might cause, the project was restricted and confined to speeding up existing transactions, so that traditional organisation structures, power relations and methods of control were retained. Thus, the ERP project replicated existing spatial and functional differentiations between the headquarters and subsidiaries as it mirrored prevailing organisational relationships. The customisation of the ERP maintained distance between the centre and the periphery, and retained traditional notions of control, contrary to the initial rationale for the ERP implementation.

Construction of distance and a-centred organisations

Drawing on recent studies by Quattrone and Hopper (2003, 2005) the previous discussion illustrated how ERP implementations impact on management accounting and control practices. Two global organisations during the late 1990s purchased and implemented the same ERP system. Both initially wanted to implement global systems to achieve instantaneous and centralised control by real-time information, but they ended up with very different systems.

Within Think Pink, an integrated, centralised, real-time database offered the possibility of increased central control and coordination by collapsing distances between different units. However, a multitude of centres of control emerged. It became difficult to trace where the centre of the global organisations lay: points of control and decision-making became multiple, unstable, shifting and constantly interacting. This organisation became neither centralised nor decentralised but 'a-centred'.

The case of Sister Act shows contrasting results. The implementation of an ERP maintained the spatio-temporal gaps between geographical and functional areas, and between the centre and the periphery. The reproduction of existing boundaries permitted information delays between entities and existing control methods to remain in place. Rather than redefining relations between hierarchical levels, functional areas and operational activities, ERP reinforced the status quo. Its configuration created a unitary notion of space and time enabling action at a distance to continue (Quattrone and Hopper, 2005). While the case of Sister Act shows that accounting systems can support multinational strategies (keeping the distance between the centre and the peripheries), the case of Think Pink illustrates that different strategies (neither centralised nor decentralised) may emerge.

Beyond compliance: the role of the finance organisation within integrated governance

The previous sections have illustrated how management accounting systems address (and are influenced by) the tensions between global tendencies and local practices, vertical and lateral relations, and centralisation and decentralisation of decision-making within global organisations. These tensions need to be balanced and managed through the most appropriate governance system. Issues of governance are becoming increasingly important within global organisations and the meaning of 'governance' has now extended far beyond the ownership structure and the composition of the board of directors to encompass performance measurement and the coordination of widely distributed human resources. Such a broadened perspective to governance brings challenges to the finance organisation when providing organisational leaders and front-line managers with increasingly heterogeneous and complex information flows (see Busco *et al.*, 2006a).

Towards integrated governance: the three sides of accountability

Over the past ten years several high profile incidents of corporate failure and managerial misconduct have put the mechanisms for governing complex organisations under scrutiny. In an attempt to regulate such key organisational issues, a number of reports, codes and laws have been introduced worldwide, focusing on the legal and regulatory framework for managing and supervising a company. Among others, the publication of the Cadbury Report in 1992 represented a milestone in setting out measures to enhance corporate integrity based on improved information, continued self-regulation, more independent boards and greater auditor independence.

Although the Cadbury Report broadly defines corporate governance as *the system by which companies are directed and controlled*, it presents a rather narrow view of the concept of governance, focusing only on the financial aspects of accountability. In 1999, the Turnbull Report provided guidelines for boards of directors on risk management and internal control, including not only financial risks, but also operational, technological, reputational and environmental risks. Accordingly, managerial accountability has been mainly discussed in terms of compliance with internal and external rules, contractual agreements, codes and principles, and in terms of oversight through internal control and financial reporting systems. This view is reinforced by the Sarbanes–Oxley Act of 2002 and by the SEC rules that define a set of standards for corporate accountability, according to which corporate leaders are required to behave.

The increasing complexity of the market environment and of stakeholders' requirements has changed the need for, and the nature of, organisational governance quite significantly. Effective corporate governance is not limited to compliance risks. The governance system can no longer be regarded as something that happens at the top of the organisation. It has to be deeply embedded in day-to-day operations and activities and in how those activities are coordinated and aligned with strategic decision-making, objectives and rules set at the senior management level. Corporate leaders are increasingly required to take into account the different typologies of risks that may compromise organisational performance and the achievement of planned objectives.

The performance dimension of governance has often been neglected within current debates. However, the need to fill such a gap has recently begun to be recognised by the professional accounting bodies. In a recent document, the Chartered Institute of Management Accountants and the International Federation of Accountants (CIMA and IFAC, 2004) emphasised that corporate governance (i.e. conformance and accountability – assurance) represents only one element of overall enterprise governance. Another element is represented by 'business governance', based on performance and value creation. These two dimensions of governance are deeply related to each other and both must be considered when designing an enterprise governance framework. A past president of the Institute of Chartered Accountants in England and Wales emphasised that in defining the concept of corporate governance a distinction should be made between conformance and performance: governance should be regarded not only in terms of shareholder protection, but also has to include business performance (see Ward, 2002). This requires broadening the concept of 'accountability'.

Accountability cannot be read only in terms of compliance with a set of principles according to which managers are required to behave in fulfilling the expectations of the stakeholders. Accountability has to be grounded in individuals' day-to-day ways of thinking and behaving within the organisation and in the set of values, beliefs and attitudes that shape organisational activities and interactions. In this context, knowledge management and organisational culture can play a key role in promoting individual commitment to company goals and values, and in enhancing a sense of belonging to the whole organisation.

As illustrated in Figure 4.7, 'accountability' to stakeholders is a multidimensional phenomenon, which requires governance mechanisms to address and integrate the following issues (see Busco *et. al*, 2006a, 2006b):

Figure 4.7 **The three sides of accountability**

- *Compliance* – to ensure effective accountability to stakeholders, value creation has to be achieved in accordance with internal and external rules, codes and principles. The lack of compliance can damage organisational image and reputation, thereby affecting the creation of value. Accordingly, compliance risks within the organisation and across business units need to be identified, managed and minimised.
- *Performance* – managers are accountable to the stakeholders for the performance of the businesses. They are required to recognise the various typologies of risk involved in the business (financial, operational, reputational, environmental, etc.) as well as putting in place management systems to measure effectiveness and efficiency of current initiatives and programmes.
- *Knowledge* – the ability to create value affects and is affected by organisational culture. In particular, knowledge management and learning processes are capable of enhancing individual commitment to internal and external rules, organisational goals and strategies, thereby promoting compliance and performance.

The examples of Nestlé Waters and GE illustrate the role of management accounting in governing global organisation. Nestlé Waters' accounting tools, such as the 'end-to-end profit and loss statement' (ETE P&L), were used to link performance measurement and knowledge management. In NW, the new management accounting system facilitates lateral information and knowledge sharing between the producers and the distributors of international brands; at the same time, it promotes the integration of product strategies across different countries, and the achievement of joint goals (such as the EBITA of the international brands) among different subsidiaries belonging to NW group.

Similarly, the process of integration that followed GE's acquisition of Nuovo Pignone illustrates how management accounting systems can be used in managing performance and knowledge within a global organisation. The culture of measurement and the Six-sigma programme enabled GE leaders to create, develop and maintain a common organisational language which was used to communicate internally across the many different business units and to align local business processes with global corporate strategies. Finally, we draw from the case of GE to describe how the three sides of accountability shown in Figure 4.7 may be integrated through specific organisational-wide initiatives that combine compliance with performance measurement and knowledge management. This is the case of the Controllership initiative.

Aiming to ensure greater transparency and accuracy in financial management, as well as to enforce senior management accountability, the GE 'Controllership initiative' (the main principles of which are contained in the GE booklet titled *The Spirit & Letter*) has been implemented. This goes beyond the creation of an environment of corporate responsibility and seeks to foster a business culture which is nowadays fully engrained within GE operating systems. This culture relies on performance measurement practices which are shared across business areas and operating companies. It utilises a series of metrics drawn from statistics, finance and operations management to build a rigorous framework for tracking financial results and corporate governance. The main purposes of controllership within GE are:

- *integrity in communications,* which ensures timely, complete, fair, understandable and accurate reporting of actual and forecast financial and non-financial information within all GE reports;
- *compliance* with applicable laws, regulations and company policies;
- *rigorous business processes* to ensure that management decisions are based on accurate economic analysis (including a prudent consideration of risks), and that GE's physical, financial and intellectual assets are safeguarded and efficiently employed;
- *preservation* of required documents and records, including all documents that are known to be relevant to litigations, audits or investigations.

Besides *traditional compliance-related* requirements, such as the need to follow GE's General Accounting Procedures (GAP) and all Generally Accepted Accounting Principles (GAAP), *The Spirit & Letter* extends its requirements to strategic and operating decisions. In particular, the Controllership Initiative seeks to ensure that:

- financial and non-financial information and operating metrics are reported accurately and on a timely basis;
- economic and risk-based criteria are used to make business decisions;
- timely and accurate forecasts and assessments are provided to management;
- sound processes and controls are constantly maintained;
- financial results are consistent with actual underlying performances;
- physical assets or other resources are fully utilised, and eventually promptly reallocated;
- routines and controls in newly acquired businesses and at remote, thinly staffed sites are adequate.

The role of finance in integrated governance

The Sarbanes–Oxley Act in the US has directly impacted on the finance organisation and the Chief Financial Officer (CFO), introducing new responsibilities for the trustworthiness and reliability of financial reports (section 302) and new requirements for internal controls (section 404). These new responsibilities call for a redefinition of the role of the finance organisation and the CFO within the governance process. They are required to collect and deliver the stories behind the numbers to a large audience of increasingly financially literate stakeholders. In order to fulfil such expectations, the most difficult challenge for the finance function is to build an environment that allows internal stakeholders at every level to participate collaboratively and comprehensively in, and to take ownership of, the processes of compliance, the systems of strategic planning and budgeting, and the mechanisms (and especially language) of knowledge management.

Finance managers have to link strategic objectives, operational plans, and individual performance goals by leveraging the vision of top management and the ability of front-line managers whose expertise has to be integrated within streamlined communication channels. By linking corporate strategic imperatives with operational measures, the financial metrics and KPIs translate and drive strategy through the entire organisation by ensuring that business operations are aligned with the vision of the board. If communication channels are properly streamlined, operational managers, together with sales and commercial personnel, can provide timely information to keep senior managers fully informed about the changing conditions on the 'front-lines'. This process helps global organisations to act proactively, i.e. anticipating change and dealing promptly with critical situations as they occur, rather than waiting for the quarterly performance reports.

Within this process of interaction, coordination and knowledge sharing, the CFO and the entire finance function are required to: create and maintain a common language based on a culture of measurement, compliance and responsibility; manage promptly the cycles of internal and external communication; and deliver constructive advice to improve business performance in the face of changing opportunities for value creation.

In building and, more importantly, maintaining integrated governance over time, the finance function can play an important role in the processes of conformance, performance measurement and knowledge management. This role requires finance experts to be involved in a wide range of activities, including: (i) strategic planning and risk assessment, (ii) operational and financial budgeting, (iii) collection and timely reporting of the 'actual', (iv) consolidation and financial reporting, and (v) evaluating current performance for the analysis, interpretation and improvement of both short-term and long-term plans.

As mentioned above, the Sarbanes–Oxley Act places specific requirements on the CFO (as well as the Chief Executive Officer). The momentum generated by the Sarbanes–Oxley requirements, to go beyond compliance and to develop a more integrated approach to accountability and governance, can provide an important opportunity for a cultural shift in organisations. To that aim, finance experts must develop the following main skills:

● accounting skills (both general and specific);
● controlling/monitoring skills (auditing, assurance, knowledge of internal and external rules and codes) to improve both internal and external compliance;
● knowledge of the business to improve organisational performance;
● experience of supporting decision-making processes and team working abilities to improve performance and coordination;

- interpersonal and communication skills to improve knowledge sharing and team working.

For example, within GE the finance organisation includes a Financial Planning and Analysis (FP&A) department, as well as a group of finance managers who are located in the individual divisions, processes and functions. FP&A is characterised by three major functions:

- *Controllership* – through planning and reporting activities, FP&A managers are instrumental in ensuring that financial record-keeping is reliable, the procedures of financial reporting and disclosure are transparent, and resources are used efficiently and effectively.
- *Planning* – FP&A managers analyse the financial measures to provide CFOs and CEOs with accurate information about the current state of their businesses, to enable them to make the right decisions.
- *Communication* – the FP&A department is the main channel for the collection and distribution of financial information within the business.

The finance managers supervise the budgeting and reporting activities within specific divisions, processes and functions. They coordinate business opportunities, plans and performance measurements, as well as ensuring the consistency of financial information, compliance with statutory obligations, and the observance of common policies and processes. Given the responsibility for business forecasting and variance analysis, finance managers have to be physically located close to the business operations. On the one hand, they liaise with the FP&A department on such matters as financial closing, project reporting and ad hoc analyses while, on the other hand, they work closely with the operational managers to ensure that the financial and operating goals of the division/process/function are achieved.

In GE, finance experts are required to play a central role not only in managing financial measures (planning), but also in collecting and distributing information on the business (communication) and in ensuring conformance with internal and external rules and regulations (controllership). This example provides a snapshot of the fundamental role played by the finance organisation in linking the three sides of accountability shown in Figure 4.7.

Conclusion

This chapter discussed the role of management accounting systems given growing globalisation. Using a series of illustrative case studies, we explored the role of management accounting and performance measurement systems as key governance mechanisms to align *local* practices to *global* tendencies. In the beginning, we drew on the existing business literature (see, amongst others, Bartlett and Ghoshal, 1989, 1993) to identify three main tensions involved in managing global organisations: global tendencies versus local understandings; vertical versus lateral relations; centralisation versus decentralisation of decision-making. We suggested that those tensions represent crucial governance issues and need to be managed through the most appropriate mechanisms. Illustrative case studies

Table 4.1 The global–local dialectic and its implications for management accounting

Dimensions of the global–local dialectic	Implications for management accounting illustrated within the case studies
Global tendencies vs. local understandings	General Electric – Management accounting practices converged to resolve the dialectic tension between the dominant culture of the organisation (the GE Way) and the local (technical) understandings.
Vertical vs. lateral relations	Nestlé Waters – Lateral and vertical integration was achieved through convergence (within the business unit) and differentiation (between the business unit and the legal entities) of management accounting practices.
Centralisation vs. decentralisation	Sister Act (Japanese corporation) – Information technology and management accounting practices maintained the distance between the centre and the peripheries.
	Think Pink (American corporation) – Information technology and management accounting practices created multiple centres of control, making the organisations neither centralised nor decentralised but 'a-centred'.
Integrated governance and accountability	General Electric and Nestlé Waters – Management accounting systems play a central role, along with specific corporate initiatives, in integrating three important dimensions of accountability: compliance, performance and knowledge. Such a broadened perspective offers the finance organisation a key part in governing global organisations.

explored how management accounting systems participate – *in practice* – in the governance of global organisations (see Table 4.1).

The empirical evidence is that accounting and control systems both affect and are affected by processes of integration under growing globalisation. The case of GE-Nuovo Pignone illustrated how management accounting practices converged to resolve the dialectic tension between the dominant culture of the organisation (the GE Way) and the local (technical) understandings. Importantly, local culture was not repudiated but was framed and complemented by the GE Way, characterized by a *global* culture of measurement and accountability. These processes allowed the traditional technical competence of Nuovo Pignone to be translated in financial terms and diffused corporate-wide through a new organisational language.

The case of Nestlè Waters illustrated how accounting practices can be purposively crafted to facilitate new patterns of organisational integration. Here, lateral and vertical integration were achieved through convergence – within the business unit – and differentiation – between the business unit and the legal entities – of accounting practices. Within each subsidiary, a system of lateral integration of international brands (such as the End-to-End P&L) coexisted with practices that monitored the performance of the local brand.

Additionally, empirical evidence from Quattrone and Hopper (2003, 2005) illustrated how information technology and accounting practices help maintain or collapse distances between headquarters and peripheries. This influences processes of centralisation versus decentralisation of decision-making authority. Within Sister Act (a Japanese corporation), ERPs and management accounting practices maintained distances between the centre and the peripheries, contrary to the assertions that ERPs inevitably enhance integration and collapse distances. However, in Think Pink (an American corporation), although an integrated, central, real-time database offered the possibility of accumulating accounting data centrally to increase central control and coordination, many centres of control emerged, making the organisations neither centralised nor decentralised but 'a-centred'.

We have seen how the need to achieve greater integration by diffusing a global culture can result in an increasing convergence of management accounting practices. Such convergence can lead to the development of a common language of measurement that results from (and helps to shape) the dialectic between the dominant culture of the organization and local features. However, business strategies implemented by global organisations may lead to both convergence and differentiation of management accounting systems. Shared management accounting practices can be used as basic building blocks for communication and information exchange (both vertically and laterally). On the other hand, vertical and lateral coordination may be achieved by adapting and differentiating accounting practices to match different patterns of integration. This process can be mediated by information systems, whose implementation has an impact in maintaining or reducing the distance between the centre(s) and the peripheries.

Finally, we suggested that in governing global organisations, compliance with corporate rules and external regulations is not enough. Issues of governance are increasingly perceived as going beyond the ownership structure and the composition of the board of directors to encompass performance measurement and knowledge management within an integrated framework. Such a broadened perspective extends the concept of 'accountability', and offers to the finance organisation important roles and responsibilities for the governance of global organisations.

References

Arnold, P. and Sikka, P. (2001) 'Globalization and the state profession relationship: the case of the Bank of Credit and Commerce International', *Accounting, Organizations and Society*, **26**, 475–99.

Barrett, M., Cooper, D.J. and Jamal, K. (2005) 'Globalization and the coordinating of work in multinational audits', *Accounting, Organizations and Society*, **30**, 1–24.

Bartlett, C.A. and Ghoshal, S. (1989) *Managing Across Borders: The Transnational Solution*, Boston, MA: Harvard Business School Press.

Bartlett, C.A. and Ghoshal, S. (1993) 'Beyond the M-form: toward a managerial theory of the firm', *Strategic Management Journal*, **14**, 23–46.

Bartlett, C., Ghoshal, S.B. and Birkinshaw, J. (2004) *Transnational Management*, 4th edn, Boston, MA: McGraw-Hill.

Bloomfield, B.P. and Combs, R. (1992) 'Information technology, control and power: the centralization and decentralization debate revisited', *Journal of Management Studies*, **29**(4), 459–84.

Busco, C., Frigo, M., Giovannoni, E., Riccaboni, A. and Scapens, R.W. (2006a) *The Role of Performance Measurement Systems within Global Organizations*, London: ICAEW.

Busco, C., Riccaboni, A. and Scapens, R.W. (2006b) 'Trust for accounting, accounting for trust', *Management Accounting Research*, **17**, 11–41.

Catturi, G. (2003) *L'azienda Universale*, Padova, Italy: Cedam.

Catturi, G. and Riccaboni, A. (1996) 'Management control and national culture in Italy', in G. Catturi and A. Riccaboni (eds), *Management Control and National Culture: A Comparative Survey of the Mediterranean Area*, Padova, Italy: Cedam, pp. 77–134.

Chang, E. and Taylor, M.S. (1999) 'Control in multinational corporations (MNCs): the case of Korean manufacturing subsidiaries', *Journal of Management, 25,* 541–65.

CIMA and IFAC (2004) *Enterprise Governance. Getting the Balance Right,* report, Chartered Institute of Management Accountants and International Federation of Accountants.

Dent, J.F. (1996) 'Global competition: challanges for management accounting and control', *Management Accounting Research, 7,* 247–69.

Doz, Y. (1986) *Strategic Management in Multinational Companies,* Oxford: Pergamon Press.

Doz, Y. and Prahalad, C.K. (1984) 'Patterns of strategic control within multinational corporations', *Journal of International Business Studies, 15,* 55–72.

Egelhoff, W.J. (1984) 'Patterns of control in the US, UK, and European multinational corporations', *Journal of International Business Studies,* Fall, 73–83.

Forsgren, M. (2002) 'Are multinational firms good or bad?' in V. Havila, M. Forsgren and H. Håkansson (eds), *Critical Perspectives on Internationalisation,* Amsterdam: Pergamon, pp. 29–58.

Ghoshal, S. and Bartlett, C.A. (1990) 'The multinational corporation as an interorganizational network', *Academy of Management Review, 15*(4), 603–25.

Govindarajan, V. and Gupta, A. (2000) 'Analysis of the emerging global arena', *European Management Journal, 8*(3), 274–84.

Granlund, M. and Malmi, T. (2002) 'Moderate impact of ERPs on management accounting: a lag or permanent outcome?' *Management Accounting Research, 13,* 299–321.

Gupta, A.K. and Govindarajan, V. (1991) 'Knowledge flows and the structure of control within multinational corporations', *Academy of Management Review, 16*(4), 768–92.

Harzing, A.W. (2000) 'An empirical analysis and extension of the Bartlett and Ghoshal typology of multinational companies', *Journal of International Business Studies, 31,* 101–20.

Hedlund, G. (1986) 'The hypermodern MNC: a heterarchy?' *Human Resource Management, 25,* 9–36.

Martinez, J.I. and Jarillo, J.C. (1989) 'The evolution of research on coordination mechanisms in multinational corporations', *Journal of International Business Studies, 20*(3), 489–514.

Martinez, J.I. and Jarillo, J.C. (1991) 'Coordination demands of international strategies', *Journal of International Business Studies, 22*(3), 429–44.

McNamara, C., Baxter, J. and Chua, W.F. (2004) 'Making and managing organizational knowledge(s)', *Management Accounting Research, 15,* 53–76.

Meer-Kooistra, J. and Scapens, R.W. (2002) 'Lateral relations: management control of relationships *within* and *between* organisations', Working paper, University of Groningen.

Mouritsen, J. (1995) 'Management accounting in global firms', in D. Ashton, T. Hopper and R.W. Scapens (eds), *Issues in Management Accounting,* 2nd ed., London: Prentice Hall, pp. 299–320.

Perlmutter, H.V. (1969) 'The tortuous evolution of the multinational corporation', *Columbia Journal of World Business, 4,* 9–18.

Quattrone, P. and Hopper, T. (2003) 'Management control systems in multinational organizations: the effects of implementing ERP', briefing 09.03, September, ICAEW, London.

Quattrone, P. and Hopper, T. (2005) 'A "time-space odyssey": management control systems in two multinational organizations', *Accounting, Organizations and Society, 30,* 735–64.

Quattrone, P. and Hopper, T. (2006) 'What is IT? SAP, accounting and visibility in a multinational organisation', *Information and Organization, 16,* 212–50.

Robson, K. (1992) 'Accounting numbers as "inscription": action at a distance and the development of accounting', *Accounting, Organizations and Society, 17,* 685–708.

Ward, G. (2002) 'Corporate governance: why should companies care', briefing 03.02, March, ICAEW, London.

Further reading

Bartlett, G.S. and Ghoshal, S. (2000) *Transnational Management,* Boston, MA: McGraw Hill. This book focuses on developing strategies, designing organisations and managing operations across borders, by distinguishing between 'transnational' and 'international' or 'multinational' management.

COSO (2004*) Enterprise Risk Management – Integrated Framework,* September, Committee of Sponsoring Organisation of the Treadway Commission. This report extends and integrates the internal control framework with risk management systems and tools suggested to implement effective governance.

Fahi, M., Roche, J. and Weiner, A. (2005) *Beyond Governance. Creating Corporate Value Through Performance, Conformance, and Corporate Responsibility,* Chichester: John Wiley & Sons. This book outlines the potential role played by performance measurement in implementing the enterprise governance system. A 'strategic scorecard' is proposed as a governance tool for measuring and monitoring the strategic position, options and risks of the organisation.

Giddens, A. (1990) *The Consequences of Modernity,* Cambridge: Polity Press. This book provides a sociological perspective on globalisation and the institutional transformations associated with modernity.

Havila, V., Forsgren, M. and Håkansson, H. (eds) (2002) *Critical Perspectives on Internationalisation,* Amsterdam: Pergamon. This book provides different perspectives on processes, mechanisms and problems of internationalisation and management across borders.

Nohria, N. and Ghoshal, S. (1997) *The Differentiated Network. Organizing Multinational Corporations for Value Creation,* San Francisco, CA: Jossey-Bass Inc. This book provides an overview on value creation, knowledge flows, innovation and integration through interpersonal networks within multinational corporations.

PriceWaterhouseCoopers (2004) 'Integrity-driven performance. A New Strategy for Success Through Integrated governance, Risk and Compliance Management', White Paper, PriceWaterhouseCoopers. The paper proposes various sets of KPIs and scorecards as key tools to be used by corporate leaders for monitoring the governance system.

5

National culture and management control

Graeme Harrison and Jill McKinnon

Introduction

In this chapter, we examine the effect of culture on the design and operation of management control systems at the cross-national level. We do so in two overlapping contexts. The first is understanding differences (and similarities) in approaches to management control in different countries. For example, researchers have consistently observed greater degrees of centralisation (centralised control) in organisations in France and Chinese-based societies than in Great Britain and North America. Understanding these differences is important because, more than ever, people are moving across national borders to work and live parts of their lives in different companies in different countries. To function effectively in those different companies and countries, people need to understand the differences in the management practices they will encounter and be sensitive to the cultural underpinnings of those differences.

The second context is how a multinational company controls the operations of its global subsidiaries. A company may be based in Great Britain, where it has developed a set of management control practices that appear to work. If this company chooses to establish a subsidiary in Italy or Taiwan, can it transplant its home control practices to the overseas subsidiary, or must it change them to suit the cultural circumstances of the subsidiary's host country? This question is increasingly important given the rapid growth in global business and competitiveness that characterise contemporary times. Global competitiveness means that multinational firms must manage their cross-national operations effectively and efficiently. Transplanting the firm's domestic control system is efficient because it saves the costs of developing a new system. However, this may be ineffective if people in the subsidiary do not accept the system because it doesn't suit their cultural context.

The chapter is organised as follows. First, we discuss the concept of national culture, drawing on arguably the best-known (and equally controversial) taxonomy of Geert Hofstede. Second, we define and describe management control systems. We then review the research linking culture to control systems and examine its implications for managers and companies operating in cross-national situations. We draw on theoretical and empirical research published in leading accounting, management and international business journals – some is our own research conducted over the past two decades, but most is the work of more erudite others. We also identify the limitations of this research. One such limitation is the predomination of western (particularly Anglo-American) versus eastern (Chinese countries and Japan) comparisons. Hence, many of our illustrations relate to those comparisons.

National culture

Culture is one of the most contested concepts in the social sciences. Anthropologists, sociologists, psychologists and historians all stake claims to culture, and definitions of culture abound in their literatures; some 160-plus definitions by one early count (Kroeber and Kluckhohn, 1952). The only commonality among these disciplines and their practitioners is that each sees their own conceptions and definitions as correct and the others as wrong.

Most of the research linking national culture to management control systems, which, incidentally, is a recent phenomenon of the last 15–20 years, has used the conception of culture provided by Geert Hofstede (for many years Professor of Organizational Anthropology and International Management at Maastricht University in the Netherlands). Hofstede (2001, p. 9) defined culture as mental programming – 'the collective programming of the mind that distinguishes the members of one group of people from another'. He argued that the core of culture is values, with values being 'a broad tendency to prefer certain states of affairs over others'. As a psychologist with IBM in the late 1960s and early 1970s, Hofstede was associated with a survey of the work-related values of employees across IBM's worldwide subsidiaries. The survey involved some 116,000 questionnaires and, with a follow-up some years later, produced data on the values of IBM employees across 50 countries.

The original survey was not designed to compare across countries. However, when the data were analysed, they revealed substantial similarities in the values of people within countries and substantial differences across countries. Furthermore, the similarities and differences could be reduced using statistical data reduction techniques to four main dimensions of culture: power distance, individualism versus collectivism, uncertainty avoidance, and masculinity versus femininity. A subsequent study added a fifth dimension, long-term versus short-term orientation. Hofstede rated the 50 countries in his studies on each of these five dimensions. Ratings for 40 of the countries are reproduced in Table 5.1.

Table 5.1 Country index scores for Hofstede's cultural dimensions[a,b]

Country	Power distance	Individualism	Uncertainty avoidance	Masculinity	Long-term orientation [c]
Arab countries	**80**	38	**68**	**53**	
Argentina	**49**	46	**86**	**56**	
Australia	36	**90**	51	**61**	31
Belgium	**65**	**75**	**94**	**54**	
Brazil	**69**	38	**76**	49	**65**
Canada	39	**80**	48	**52**	23
Chile	**63**	23	**86**	28	
China	na	na	na	na	**118**
Colombia	**67**	13	**80**	**64**	
Costa Rica	35	15	**86**	21	

(Continued)

Denmark	18	**74**	23	16	
Ecuador	**78**	8	**67**	**63**	
Finland	33	**63**	**59**	26	
France	**68**	**71**	**86**	43	
Great Britain	35	**89**	35	**66**	25
Germany	35	**67**	**65**	**66**	31
Greece	**60**	35	**112**	**57**	
Hong Kong	**68**	25	29	**57**	**96**
Indonesia	**78**	14	48	46	
India	**77**	48	40	**56**	61
Ireland	28	**70**	35	**68**	
Italy	**50**	**76**	**75**	**70**	
Japan	**54**	46	**92**	**95**	80
Malaysia	**104**	26	36	**50**	
Mexico	**81**	30	**82**	**69**	
Netherlands	38	**80**	53	14	**44**
Norway	31	**69**	50	8	
New Zealand	22	**79**	49	**58**	30
Peru	**64**	16	**87**	42	
Philippines	**94**	32	44	**64**	19
South Africa	**49**	**65**	49	**66**	
Singapore	**74**	20	8	48	**48**
Spain	**57**	**51**	**86**	42	
Sweden	31	**71**	29	5	33
Switzerland	34	**68**	**58**	**70**	
Taiwan	**58**	17	**69**	45	**87**
Thailand	**64**	20	**64**	34	**56**
Uruguay	**61**	36	**100**	38	
USA	40	**91**	46	**62**	29
Venezuela	**81**	12	**76**	**73**	

Notes: a Higher numbers indicate higher scores on each cultural dimension.

b Numbers in bold (not bold) represent countries as high (low) on each dimension.

c Long-term orientation scores available for a sub-set of countries only.

Source: Hofstede (2001).

The second column in Table 5.1, *Power distance* (PD), refers to the extent to which people accept that power in institutions and organisations (political, social or business) is distributed unequally. People in high PD societies more readily accept power inequalities coming from wealth, status or position, and believe that powerful people have the right (and responsibility) to command, and are entitled to privileges and perquisites not available to less powerful people. By contrast, people in low PD societies believe in egalitarianism. Although there are hierarchies in institutions and organisations, these exist for administrative necessity and do not reflect existential inequality between people at different levels. Denmark is a low PD society. Anecdotes of members of the Danish royal family and senior politicians catching public transport when going about their business, rather than being chauffeur-driven in limousines, are consistent with a low PD society. Australia is also a low PD society. When the then Governor-General of Australia, Sir William Slim, visited a cattle station in outback Queensland, he is reported to have alighted from his official car and extended his hand to a weathered stockman on his horse. 'Good morning, I'm Slim,' said Sir William. 'How yer goin' mate,' replied the stockman, 'Slim who?' (Withers, 1989, p. 1).

Table 5.1 shows the ratings of countries on Hofstede's PD index. Scandinavian countries (Finland, Denmark, Norway, Sweden), Anglo-American countries (Australia, Canada, Great Britain, New Zealand, the USA) and some European countries (such as Germany and the Netherlands) are relatively low PD. South American (Argentina, Brazil, Chile, Colombia, Mexico, Peru, Venezuela), Chinese-based (Hong Kong, Malaysia, Singapore, Taiwan, Thailand) and Arab countries, plus some other European countries (notably Belgium and France) are relatively high PD.

Individualism versus collectivism (IDV) is defined best by Harry Triandis, an eminent professor of psychology at the University of Illinois:

> Collectivism (is) a social pattern consisting of closely linked individuals who see themselves as part of one or more collectives (family, co-workers, tribe, nation); are primarily motivated by the norms of, and duties imposed by, those collectives; are willing to give priority to the goals of these collectives over their own personal goals; and emphasize their connectedness to members of these collectives. Individualism is a social pattern that consists of loosely linked individuals who view themselves as independent of collectives; are primarily motivated by their own preferences, needs, rights, and the contracts they have established with others; give priority to their personal goals over the goals of others; and emphasize rational analyses of the advantages and disadvantages of associating with others. (Triandis, 1995, p. 2)

Triandis (1995, p. 1) contrasts an engineer in India offered 25 times his salary to move to New York and a Californian engineer offered a 50 per cent rise to make a similar move. The Indian declined, the Californian accepted. The USA is rated as the most individualist of cultures on Hofstede's index, while India is more collectivist. Triandis also contrasts a supervisor in Japan, who knows a lot about the personal life of a subordinate and arranges for her to meet a potential husband, with a subordinate in England who does not tell her supervisor that her father had just died. Great Britain is a highly individualist culture; Japan a more collectivist one.

Table 5.1 shows the ratings of countries on the *individualism versus collectivism* scale (the IDV index); with higher (lower) scores indicating higher (lower) levels of individualism. The ratings of countries on the IDV index appear to be a reverse of the PD scores. Scandinavian, Anglo-American and some European countries, again including Germany and the Netherlands, are relatively high IDV societies, while South American and Chinese-based countries are relatively low IDV (high collectivist). Hofstede (2001, p. 216) notes that there is a negative correlation between PD and IDV, but it is spurious and driven by a third factor, national wealth. Plus, some countries, particularly Belgium and France, go against the negative correlation and are both high PD and high IDV.

Uncertainty avoidance (UA) relates to how people react to the uncertainty of the future. People in high UA societies regard uncertainty as a threat, leading to stress and discomfort. They seek to reduce uncertainty through rules and regulations in legislative and institutional activities, adherence to religious beliefs, and investment in technology and nature-mastering research. People in low UA societies more readily accept life's uncertainties and spend less anxiety, time and money trying to reduce them. Table 5.1 shows that the Latin countries both in South America (Uruguay, Peru, Argentina, etc.) and southern Europe (Portugal, Spain and Italy) are scored as high UA. Japan is also high, while the Anglo-American, most northern European, and most Asia-Pacific and Chinese countries are low UA.

Hofstede (2001, p. 180) lists the following characteristics of legislation in a high UA society: 'many and precise laws and regulations', 'citizens negative towards legal system', 'laws should be broken if unjust', and 'higher speed limits on motorways'. While these may seem somewhat contradictory, they will be perfectly understandable to anyone who has lived and driven in Italy – a high UA society on Hofstede's measure. In an excellent British television programme on driver behaviour in Italy presented by Jeremy Clarkson, an Italian professor with a good sense of humour states that it is not difficult to make laws in Italy, just unnecessary.

Humour aside, UA is perhaps the most problematic of Hofstede's five dimensions. First, while Hofstede's study showed UA as a dimension on which countries differed, this has not been supported in two subsequent multi-country value surveys; Hofstede and Bond's (1988) Chinese Value Survey (CVS) across 23 countries and Smith *et al.*'s (1996) survey of 43 countries. Second, casual observation of the country ratings in Table 5.1 raises a number of questions. For example, if investment in technology and nature-mastering research is a characteristic of a high UA society, how does this fit with the US being low UA but making heavy investment in medical, information technology and space exploration research? Based on these concerns, some researchers question the coherence and relevance of the UA dimension.

Masculinity versus femininity (MAS) is the extent to which analogues of the stereotypical family roles of gender are found in societies. High MAS (masculine) societies value assertiveness, competitiveness and overt manifestation of achievement and success, including material success. Conversely, low MAS (feminine) societies value personal relationships, supportiveness, a non-material quality of life and modesty in achievement. Hofstede (2001, p. 300) gives the example that popular fiction characters in the USA (a relatively high MAS society) are often powerful and strong heroes (Superman and Batman, for example), while in the lower MAS societies of Denmark and the Netherlands, anti-heroes, comic characters and underdogs thrive.

Table 5.1 shows the *masculinity versus femininity* country ratings (the MAS index) with higher (lower) scores indicating higher (lower) levels of masculinity. Japan ranks as substantially the most masculine culture on Hofstede's measure. The Scandinavian countries cluster as the most feminine, but otherwise there is less clustering and greater spread among the countries comprising regional (Asia, Latin America, northern Europe) or historical (Anglo-American) groupings than for the other cultural dimensions. A Japanese accounting professor, when showing the authors around his campus, walked into a lift ahead of us. He then turned and said: 'When I'm in Australia, I'll let Jill go first.'

Table 5.1 shows the *long-term versus short-term orientation* country ratings (the LTO index), with higher (lower) scores indicating higher (lower) levels of long-term orientation. The Chinese-based societies (China, Hong Kong, Taiwan, for example) score high LTO, while Anglo-American countries (Great Britain, USA, Canada, Australia, New Zealand) score low LTO. Long-term versus short-term orientation (LTO) relates to the relative emphasis placed on the short-term compared to the long-term. Low LTO (or short-term oriented) societies expect immediate results and immediate gratification of needs, including social consumption and spending. High LTO societies are more prepared to defer need gratification, more prepared to save and invest for the future, and more oriented to perseverance (Hofstede, 2001, pp. 360 and 367).

There is a smaller set of countries in Table 5.1 for LTO compared to the other dimensions because, as noted earlier, LTO was not developed from Hofstede's original study. Rather, it was developed from a later study of a smaller number of countries, specifically Hofstede and Bond's (1988) Chinese Value Survey (CVS). The CVS study began with a set of work values developed by Chinese scholars, compared to Hofstede's original set of values developed by westerners. Therefore, it is not surprising that the Chinese (eastern) and Anglo-American (western) countries polarise on LTO, because the CVS tapped fundamental philosophical differences between eastern and western societies, arising in large part from the influence of the teachings of Confucius on Chinese values. Indeed, this cultural dimension was originally called Confucian Dynamism.

Cautions and criticisms of Hofstede's culture

Hofstede's approach to culture is not without critics (some quite vehement) and criticisms. Before moving to the research that has used Hofstede's taxonomy, we discuss these criticisms because they give rise to cautions in interpreting the research findings. One criticism is that equating culture with nation states ignores the multi-cultural composition of countries which have different ethnic regional groups such as Switzerland (with German, French and Italian enclaves), or different ethnic mixes such as Malaysia (with Chinese, Indian and indigenous Malay cultural groupings) and Australia (with a highly diverse ethnic mix of British, Chinese, sub-continental and Middle Eastern groups as a result of immigration over the past 50 years).

This is fair criticism. Hofstede went to considerable lengths to acknowledge regional, ethnic and 'religious' cultures existing within nation states, but argued that, often, the nation state is necessarily the focus. Anyone applying Hofstede's dimensions in management research or practice must be satisfied that the dimensions apply in the country of application. Researchers will typically do this by running Hofstede's cultural measures on the sample of people they are studying.

A related concern is the tendency to group countries together as culturally homogeneous. Lenartowicz and Johnson (2003), for example, research Latin American countries. They argue that people often think Latin America is culturally homogeneous; however, in reality it is diverse across ethnic, language and religious divides that have formed and been sustained by unique historical and geographical circumstances. Lenartowicz and Johnson divide Latin America into six cultural regions. They find some similarities across the regions, notably the importance of group interests, which is consistent with Hofstede's clustering of Latin American countries as collectivist. But, they also find considerable differences. Lenartowicz and Johnson's work demonstrates general support for Hofstede's dimensions; however, it also shows that those dimensions are broad-grained and, while countries can be roughly clustered on dimensions, finer distinctions and richer elaborations of national and regional cultures are always needed for greater depth of cultural understanding. We return to this issue later.

A second criticism of Hofstede's study is that it was restricted to middle level managers in city locations in one industry and firm and can, therefore, only describe the values of middle-class urbanites who work for IBM. Again, this is fair comment, although the restriction had the methodological strength of a closely matched sample. Hofstede was not comparing, say, Swedish nurses with German police. This would have introduced an occupational culture difference that would confound a national culture explanation of differences (the nursing occupation may be argued to be more caring and nurturing, i.e. more feminine, than policing). Holding many other factors constant and allowing only country to vary meant that Hofstede was able to assert that the differences in cultural dimensions were a function of country.

A third criticism is that Hofstede's measures were derived in the late 1960s and early 1970s and are, therefore, out of date. There is evidence that globalisation, technological and educational transfer, and movements in a country's collective and individual wealth can change a country's culture over time. Our own work, which has concentrated on Australia, the USA, Singapore, Taiwan and Hong Kong, has shown movements in Hofstede's scores for power distance and individualism from his original 1960/1970 studies to ours of the 1990s. We find, for example, that managers in Singapore (Australia) scored higher (lower) on individualism and lower (higher) on power distance than Hofstede's original ratings. However, even if these scores have come somewhat closer together, it is still the case that Singapore demonstrates higher levels of power distance and lower levels of individualism than Australia. Most writers on culture agree that cultures do change, but only slowly. And contemporary studies that have replicated or applied Hofstede's measures across varying countries conclude that the dimensions are as relevant in the early twenty-first century as they were when his original study was conducted.

Finally, Hofstede's approach is criticised as being too simplistic in reducing the rich complexity of culture to a limited set of aggregate dimensions. Culture cannot, it is argued, be reduced to five dimensions with labels attached. We return to this criticism in the next section. A related criticism is that conceptualising culture as the 'collective programming of the mind' implies that behaviour is conditioned and denies that individuals have the ability to think and act independently. Hofstede's approach is accused of treating individuals as 'cultural dopes'; i.e. reducing people's behaviour to a consequence of values and ignoring the complexity, eccentricities and other inputs to individual behaviour. One of the authors once took over an executive development class of accountants from several professional firms in a UK city. In the front row was a man dressed, from the spinning propeller on his cap through polka-dot balloon pants to his oversized shoes, as a circus clown. 'That's just Lawrence,' explained a member of the class afterwards. 'Last week, he turned up as an undertaker. Next week, who knows?' But the other 19 all wore dark suits.

Management control systems

There are many definitions of management control and multiple classifications of the components or elements of management control systems (MCS). We define management control as the set of mechanisms that assist an organisation to achieve its objectives. These may be formal, deliberately chosen, mechanisms – such as the extent to which an organisation prescribes or proscribes behaviour through written rules and procedures; or informal, naturally occurring, mechanisms – such as the extent to which information is shared between people in the organisation in a variety of settings.

With respect to the components of MCS, we draw first on Richard Whitley's (1999) characteristics of (1) the exercise of control through formal rules and procedures, (2) the exercise of control over how organisational unit activity is carried out, (3) the influence and involvement that organisational members have in exercising control, and (4) the scope and type of information used to evaluate and reward performance. These characteristics are synthesised from a broad literature on MCS.

The extent to which control is exercised through formal rules and procedures is also referred to as *formalisation*. It ranges from low, where there is little use of standardised rules and procedures, to high where the opposite situation pertains. Whitley (1999, p. 509) notes that a high degree of formalisation 'implies a strong institutionalization of impersonal regulations governing economic activities and their assessment'. The extent that control is exercised over how organisational units' activities are carried out is also referred to as *concentration of authority*, specifically whether authority is concentrated at corporate level management (centralisation), or is delegated to lower level managers in the organisational hierarchy (decentralisation). Formalisation and concentration of authority are often grouped together under the heading *organisational structure*, as they both reflect control consequences of prior organisational structural choices.

A large body of research has sought to determine the conditions under which different degrees of formalisation and (de)centralisation provide higher levels of control. It is not the purpose of this chapter to address this literature. Intuitively, however, factors such as the size of an organisation and the environment in which it operates are relevant. For example, the larger the organisation and the greater the number of markets and products it is involved in, the greater the need for decentralisation because central management will not have the local knowledge necessary for effective decisions at the local level. Also, the more uncertain and volatile the markets the organisation operates in, the greater the need for lower levels of formalisation because managers need to be able to make decisions without the shackles of many rules and procedures.

The third characteristic of Whitley's (1999) MCS is the influence and involvement that organisational members have in exercising control. This is also referred to as *participation* and includes the extent that people are involved in, and can influence, the setting of performance targets for which they are held responsible. Again, there is a large body of MCS literature linking participation to a range of individually and organisationally desired outcomes. For example, higher levels of participation are often effective in enhancing motivation and job satisfaction, leading to higher job commitment and performance.

Whitley's fourth characteristic is the scope and type of information used in the MCS to evaluate and reward performance. This characteristic is multi-faceted and includes choices such as: the time frame for evaluation (is performance measured against short-term or longer-term indicators?); the set of performance indicators to be used in evaluation (does it allow for multiple indicators, including financial and non-financial indicators, or is it concentrated on a single or restricted set of items such as bottom-line profit?); and the linkages between target performance indicators and evaluation and reward (are evaluation and reward tightly linked to target attainment, or only loosely linked?). These choices relate to control because decisions on the scope and type of information to be included in the performance measurement system determine the behaviours of organisational members – under the 'what gets measured gets managed' principle. And control is about the behaviour of people; control systems are directed at motivating and providing incentives for organisational members to act and make decisions congruent with the organisation's goals.

These four characteristics of MCS may be classified as formal controls because they typically result from decisions about MCS design. They may also be regarded as 'traditional' controls because they have developed in archetypical organisations of the twentieth century with relatively fixed organisational structures of the functional, product or divisional form, and with hierarchical authority lines. By contrast, *fluid workgroups and teams* and *informal information sharing* (which may be classified as informal controls) are becoming increasingly important in organisations facing a new millennium environment of rapid technological change, product and service innovation and intense global competition. In these conditions, traditional organisational forms, and the patterns of interaction they promote, can constrain creativity and response times. Hence, more flexible organisational forms and interaction patterns are necessary.

Fluid workgroups and teams constitute ad hoc and temporary task forces formed to solve specific problems, where solutions require inter-functional cooperation and expertise and need to be found quickly. The teams are fluid because they comprise people from different organisational specialisations, who move in and out of teams as problems demand. The teams also benefit from changing leaders, as different individuals, independent of status or hierarchical level, will have greater knowledge and capacity to lead depending on the problem at hand.

Informal information sharing is important because it provides a channel for transmitting information that should, if unimpeded, be faster and more directly relevant to action than information provided through formal organisational channels. Information provided through formal channels is often lagged and *ex post*, whereas informal information sharing is *ex ante*, and its control effect is also, therefore, *ex ante*. Additionally, Bruns and McKinnon (1993) argue that informal information, sourced through personal communications such as meetings and other naturally occurring interactions among organisational members, dominates other sources of information in directing day-to-day decisions and actions.

National culture and management control systems

In this section, we review the research linking national culture and management control systems (MCS). We do not discuss individual studies; rather we seek to synthesise the research findings and evaluate their cumulative impact on our understanding of the culture/MCS relationship. Harrison and McKinnon (1999) and Chow *et al.* (1999) provide detailed listings of individual studies until the mid-1990s. We draw on those papers plus relevant studies from the mid-1990s to date. We take each of the MCS characteristics and examine how observed variations in each characteristic across countries have been associated with cultural dimensions.

Organisational structure: formalisation and concentration of authority

As noted earlier, formalisation is the extent that control is exercised through formal rules and procedures, and concentration of authority is the degree that decision-making authority is concentrated at the top of the organisational hierarchy (centralisation) or devolved down the hierarchy (decentralisation). The cultural dimensions relevant to formalisation and concentration of authority are uncertainty avoidance and power distance respectively. Indeed, the definitions of uncertainty avoidance and power distance are almost synonymous with the MCS characteristics.

Uncertainty avoidance (UA) measures the degree to which people feel (un)comfortable with uncertainty and the extent that they seek to reduce it through rules and regulations. As a consequence, organisations in high UA cultures are likely to place greater emphasis on control through written rules, standardised operating procedures, and formalised planning. Empirical research generally supports this, although it is limited and is somewhat beset with contradictions. Studies that have compared Japan (a high UA culture) and the US (lower UA) show greater formalisation and structuring of activities in Japanese organisations and more formal use of budgets for communication and coordination of activities. Studies also show a greater use of quantitative analyses in planning and decision-making in Japan, a situation linked to UA because of the aura of certitude such analysis brings.

One of the strongest research findings is an association between power distance (PD) and concentration of authority. Theoretically, high PD cultures are characterised by a high regard for formally constituted hierarchies and an acceptance that authority and responsibility for leadership and decision-making are vested at the upper levels. Acceptance of this by both superiors and subordinates leads to the cultural consistency of high PD with an MCS characterised by centralisation. This, almost tautologous, theoretical association is supported by empirical research which has consistently found higher levels of centralised control in organisations in countries such as Japan, Hong Kong, China, Singapore, Taiwan and France, compared to organisations in countries such as the UK, USA and Australia. Table 5.1 shows the former group of countries to be higher PD than the latter.

However, the research also shows that while high PD is associated with taller hierarchies and centralised authority across a number of countries, how hierarchies and authority operate to affect control in those countries differs considerably. One of the earliest studies of culture and control, Lincoln *et al.* (1981), pointed out differences in how hierarchies operate in France compared to Japan. In France, the hierarchy operates in a highly bureaucratic manner and is designed to institutionalise authoritarian administration and control, but also to preserve the independence of individuals in the hierarchy. By contrast, the hierarchy in Japanese organisations operates paternalistically, reinforcing relationships of dependence and commitment between subordinates and superiors. This difference is also culturally explicable. As well as being high PD, France is also highly individualist on Hofstede's IDV scale, while Japan is more collectivist. The combination of high PD and high IDV in French organisations means that the hierarchy provides structural barriers between individuals at different levels and, as a consequence, renders information flows up and down the hierarchy more difficult. By contrast, the combination of high PD and low IDV (collectivism) in Japanese organisations means that the hierarchy does not create structural barriers between individuals, but serves as a vehicle for the reciprocal exchange of paternalism on the part of superiors and commitment on the part of dependent subordinates.

Other researchers have also identified differences in the effect of PD and hierarchical control within Asian nations. Studies comparing Japanese organisations with Chinese and Korean ones typically support the paternalistic, dependence basis of the Japanese hierarchy and argue that this gives rise to 'emotional' loyalty and trust among subordinates (Whitley, 1991). In contrast, Chinese and Korean hierarchies operate with more authoritarian superiors who are more remote from subordinates than their Japanese counterparts, giving rise to what Whitley (1991) called 'conditional loyalties' in these organisations. Michael Bond, Professor of Psychology at the Chinese University of Hong Kong and an expert on Chinese culture, contrasts the superior/subordinate relationships in Japanese and Chinese societies:

> [Chinese managers] spend less time consulting in large meetings, reasoning with peers, persuading subordinates, making concessions within the workplace . . . and more time making decisions alone, giving orders, supervising the execution of those orders personally. (Bond, 1991, p. 79)

Snodgrass and Grant (1986) have argued that the hierarchy is a strength of control in Japanese organisations because it encourages more open exchange of information. (We will return to information sharing later.) The argument is that the high degree of vertical differentiation, together with the associated personal relationships of interdependency and trust, 'eliminates the need to hoard information for one's own career or advancement'. By contrast, Bond (1991) argues that hierarchy can constitute an obstacle to information exchange in Chinese organisations. He notes that the authoritarian and remote nature of the superior/subordinate relationship, together with loyalties that are 'only as wide as the immediate boss's range of relationships . . . and hence . . . difficult to meld into an organization-wide affiliation' often results in 'interdepartmental indifference, stonewalling, and competitiveness in Chinese organizations' (Bond, 1991, p. 84).

We have gone into some detail about implications of the hierarchy for control in different high PD countries for two reasons. The first is the main purpose of this chapter; i.e. to enable managers brought up in, say, a low PD culture where societal and organisational institutions generally demonstrate decentralised authority, to understand and be sensitive to the more centralised control structures in higher PD societies. The second reason is to demonstrate that understanding control structures in different societies requires more than an unquestioned application of Hofstede's dimensions. The statement that we are likely to find centralised (decentralised) concentration of authority in high (low) PD societies is correct. However, understanding how PD affects authority and, in turn, how this and the hierarchy affect control, requires a deeper examination of the cultures of different societies.

Participation

Participation is the extent to which organisational members are involved in, and can influence, the setting of performance targets and budgets they will be held responsible for. Two texts used in teaching management accounting at the authors' university both argue that participation is 'good', and people at all management levels should have the opportunity to participate in setting their budgets. The reasons given are as follows: (i) lower-level managers have more task-specific knowledge and can provide better performance estimates; (ii) participation conveys a sense of individual responsibility and autonomy; (iii) it creates conditions under which targets are seen as fair by the individuals concerned; and (iv) it provides the mechanism whereby the budget goals become internalised as the individual's goals, thus producing goal congruence – a primary criterion for effective management control.

The first reason differs from the remaining three. It relates to the task and is, therefore, universal across organisations irrespective of country or culture. The other three reasons all relate to the person and, in particular, focus on the person as an individual. It is little surprise that both texts are by authors at US universities (and used in an Australian university). As shown in Table 5.1, the USA is the highest ranked country on the cultural dimension of individualism, with Australia a close second. Additionally, the USA and Australia are both relatively low on power distance. In low PD cultures, hierarchies do not imply intrinsic inequalities of power, and people at lower hierarchical levels want and expect to have input into decisions that affect them. By contrast, in high PD cultures superiors are expected to make decisions as a consequence of their hierarchical status, and subordinates are more accepting of a non-consultative, non-participative decision style.

Similarly, in highly individualist (high IDV) societies, people are motivated by individual responsibility and autonomy; they will defend their interests in ensuring the fairness of performance targets, and must be convinced that achieving the organisation's goals will also achieve their own goals. By contrast, in low IDV cultures there is a collectivist rather than self-orientation, and organisational members expect the organisation (and their superiors) to defend their interests in return for loyalty. There is less emphasis on individual responsibility and autonomy in motivation, and more on duty and responsibility to the organisation.

The cultural dimensions, therefore, suggest that individuals in low PD, high IDV cultures will seek and respond more favourably to opportunities for participation in performance-setting decisions than individuals in high PD, low IDV (more collectivist) cultures. This underpins the textbook assertion that participation is 'good', and is borne out in much empirical research that has explained the preference for participation in low PD, high IDV cultures in terms of both individually and organisationally desirable outcomes. However, the situation is more complex because positive responses to participation have also been found in countries with opposing cultural dimensions.

Our own research, for example, compared organisations in Australia (low PD, high IDV) and Singapore (higher PD, more collectivist) and found equally positive responses to participation in both countries. Our results have subsequently been corroborated by other studies. That is, participation appears to have positive control effects in both low PD, high IDV cultures, and in the reverse high PD, low IDV cultures. We attribute this to the fact that participation has two components, involvement and influence. The former can occur without the latter; subordinate managers can be involved in budget setting and can contribute knowledge to inform a decision, but the final decision might well remain with the superior, and be accepted as such by the subordinate. Consequently, while high IDV and low PD might create a preference for influence in the participative process, the opposite – low IDV and high PD – might create the preference for involvement. This is consistent with the belief in low IDV (collectivist) cultures that group decisions are better than individual decisions.

As new research emerges and older research findings are re-evaluated with new knowledge, this relationship between IDV, PD and participation appears to have support. A classic study of attitudes to budget development by US and Japanese managers (Daley et al., 1985) found that US managers agreed more with the statement that budgets should be developed from the 'bottom up', but Japanese managers agreed more with the statement that 'a manager should work with his superior in preparing his budget'. This study was atheoretic with respect to cultural dimensions, and the different findings for the two budget development attitudes were seen as problematic by Daley et al. However, they are consistent with the argument that higher individualism drives the influence component of participation, while lower individualism (higher collectivism) drives the involvement component.

For practising managers, the results for participation are helpful. They suggest that the positive effects of participation on control, argued typically from the Anglo-American perspective of manager motivation, are generalisable across cultures. Participation works. However, the manner in which it works is clearly different across cultures. We would expect to see positive reactions to participation in enhancing control in low PD, high IDV cultures when the influence component of participation is present, and in high PD, low IDV cultures when the involvement component is present. For researchers, these findings mean that future studies of culture and participation need to clearly disentangle the two components.

Scope and type of information

The fourth characteristic of MCS is the scope and type of information used to evaluate and reward performance. Research in this area has concentrated on the time frame for evaluation, the set of performance indicators used in evaluation, and the linkages between performance indicators and evaluation and reward. We discuss the first two together because they are interrelated.

Time frame and set of performance indicators

The time frame for evaluation relates to whether organisational members' performance is measured against short-term or longer-term indicators. The set of performance indicators relates to whether measurement is focused on a single or limited number of indicators (typically financial 'bottom-line' indicators), or includes multiple indicators (financial and non-financial). Intuitively, the cultural dimension of long-term versus short-term orientation (LTO) is relevant to the choice of time frame for evaluation. Although there is limited research, this expectation is generally borne out. Several studies of budgetary and strategic planning comparing Japan, Hong Kong, Singapore, the USA, the UK and Australia generally show longer planning horizons in the first three countries (longer-term oriented on Hofstede's index) compared to the latter three (shorter-term oriented). Studies of manager performance evaluation time frames show a similar dichotomy.

Additionally, Japan, Hong Kong and Singapore are low IDV (collectivist) cultures relative to the high IDV cultures of the USA, the UK and Australia. In a high IDV culture, the individual maintains a self-interested, calculative involvement with the organisation, while in a low IDV one the involvement of the individual with the organisation is group-interested, moral and duty-based. This is relevant to whether people are motivated to plan long-term, and whether they are prepared to take decisions that are in the long-term interest of the organisation. Many such decisions (introducing a new product or service, or entering a new market, for example), involve a sacrifice in short-term performance for longer-term benefits. A consequence is that a person who takes a longer-term decision might see their or their unit's performance decline in the short-term, and may have moved on from that unit before the benefits are captured. This will be more readily accepted by people in low IDV (collectivist) societies. In contrast, people in high IDV societies are likely to be more reluctant to take decisions that have long-term benefits if those decisions prejudice performance in the short-term.

As we will return to in the conclusion, although culture is the focus of this chapter, this does not imply that culture is the only or major determinant of control systems in organisations. Germany has typically been linked with Japan as being longer-term in organisations' control and strategic approaches, yet the two have little cultural commonality. They are, of course, similar in other factors affecting organisational behaviour, such as their greater dependence on financial institutions with which they maintain ongoing relationships and their lesser dependence on share markets and the associated pressures for short-term performance.

The cultural dimensions of masculinity versus femininity (MAS) and LTO are both relevant to the set of performance indicators used in evaluation. Van der Stede (2003, p. 267) argues that the emphasis on achievement and competition in high MAS societies produces greater focus on meeting a 'bottom-line' performance target, and less focus on the development and well-being of organisational members. He argues further that such a restricted focus 'is likely to be less accepted or even counterproductive' in low MAS countries, where preferred performance measures would include multiple and less financially oriented indicators. Similarly, Hofstede (2001, p. 383) observed that accounting systems in high MAS countries (such as the USA and Germany) place more emphasis on achieving purely financial targets than those in low MAS countries (such as the Netherlands or Sweden).

Van der Stede failed to find an association between MAS and management control systems (MCS) in his study of organisations in ten European and North American countries. However, there have been several studies of performance evaluation systems in companies in the USA, Canada, the UK, Germany and Japan. These studies have not been based on cultural hypotheses, but they have found consistent support for the importance of financially based performance measurement systems. Given that these countries are all relatively high MAS, they support Van der Stede's and Hofstede's hypothesis that high (low) MAS is associated with greater (lesser) emphasis on 'bottom-line' financial performance. More research is needed in this area.

Research has also found consistent differences in the emphasis placed on different financial performance measures across countries, which can be partly explained by the LTO cultural dimension. Borkowski (1999, p. 552) showed that: 'Net income is more important in countries with a longer-term outlook (Japan and Germany) than . . . in Canada, US and UK. Conversely, cost reduction is more important to Canadian, US and UK (companies) than to German and Japanese, particularly if the cost reductions that can be implemented yield immediate results.' Once again, the caveat applies that different pressures for short- versus long-term performance arise from different corporate financing choices. Nonetheless, the sharp distinction between Japan and the Anglo-American countries on Hofstede's LTO culture scale is relevant to the different focus on longer-term versus shorter-term performance evaluation criteria. Carr and Tomkins (1998, p. 213) go further to argue that: 'In many cases this (Anglo-American short-termism) has undermined commitment to international competitiveness and more proactive strategic decisions.'

Linkage between performance indicators and evaluation and reward

There has been considerable research into the control consequences of tight versus loose linkages between budget-based performance indicators and evaluation and reward. This research originally focussed on the reliance on budget-based accounting performance measures in the evaluation of subordinates by their superiors, and was given the acronym RAPM (reliance on accounting performance measures). In a non-cultural context, early RAPM research sought to identify conditions under which different levels of RAPM produce positive manager attitudes and performance-related behaviour. The theory is that positive outcomes will result if the subordinate perceives the evaluative style to be appropriate for the conditions under which he or she has to perform. For example, low RAPM is seen as appropriate in conditions of high environmental uncertainty where a manager's budget target can be rendered unachievable by unforeseeable events outside his or her control. Perceptions of evaluative style also depend on perceptions of superior/subordinate relationships generally, and the individual's relationship to the organisational collective. National culture becomes relevant because it addresses such relationships.

Theoretically, power distance, individualism versus collectivism, and uncertainty avoidance are relevant to subordinate responses to different evaluative styles. Subordinates in high PD, collectivist and high UA cultures are likely to respond more positively, *ceteris paribus,* to higher RAPM (or tighter linkages between budget targets and performance evaluation and reward), while those in low PD, individualist and low UA cultures are likely to respond more favourably to lower RAPM (or looser linkages). In a high PD culture, subordinates accept that their superiors have the prerogative to make decisions, including performance assessment decisions, unilaterally; in a low PD culture subordinates expect to be consulted on decisions that affect them. If subordinates in a low PD culture fail to attain budget targets, they expect an opportunity to represent themselves to explain the circumstances that produced the performance outcomes, and to negotiate a performance assessment based on those circumstances. Subordinates in a high PD culture do not have this expectation, are less likely to seek it, and are more likely to accept a rigid linkage between budget-based performance and evaluation and reward.

Individualism versus collectivism is relevant for two reasons. First, people in high IDV cultures are likely to respond unfavourably to tight linkages between budget targets and evaluation, because this rigidity runs counter to the individualist's desire for self-direction. The second argument is based on the concept of 'face'. Face has been described as 'the positive social value a person . . . claims for himself' (Goffman, 1955, p. 213). It is a human universal. However, people in collectivist societies, particularly Chinese ones, are more influenced by face than are people in individualist societies. In individualist societies, people can choose how, and to what degree, they engage in self-presentation. In collectivist societies, again particularly Chinese ones, face is an automatic consequence of an individual's status in the collective.

In an individualist society, self-respect can be maintained in the presence of an adverse evaluation by a superior, as long as the individual believes that he or she has done a good job. However, in a collectivist society, it is not the individual's assessment of his or her own performance that is important. Rather, it is the superior's evaluation because it is this evaluation that is visible to the subordinate's reference group and determines whether face in the group is maintained or lost. Where preservation of face is important, higher RAPM (or tighter linkages between budget targets and performance evaluation) is likely to be preferred by subordinates because they know what level of performance they have to achieve and that a satisfactory evaluation will follow achievement. Finally, uncertainty avoidance is relevant. Subordinates in high UA cultures are more likely to respond positively to tight linkages between budget-based targets and evaluation and reward as this reduces the uncertainty inherent in more loosely linked relationships.

Empirical research has generally supported these expectations. For example, Daley *et al.*'s (1985) study of Japanese and US managers found that the Japanese managers (in a higher PD, more collectivist and higher UA culture than the USA) believed more strongly that a manager who failed to attain budget should be replaced, and that top management should judge performance mainly on attainment of budget profit. The authors' own research found that Singaporean managers (in a higher PD and more collectivist culture than Australia) responded more positively (in terms of higher job satisfaction and lower job-related tension) when evaluated at higher levels of RAPM, while the Australian managers responded more positively to evaluation at lower levels.

Similarly, Van der Stede (2003), in his study of MCS design in subsidiaries of Belgian parent companies in ten European and North American countries (Belgium, Canada, Denmark, France, Great Britain, Germany, Greece, the Netherlands, Norway and Portugal), found that subsidiaries in countries with more individualist cultures generally have looser budgeting processes than those in more collectivist cultures. Additionally, managers in countries where the culture is higher PD and higher UA are subject to more tightly detailed budgeting processes than those in lower PD and UA countries. Van der Stede (2003, p. 279) concluded that the more intensive use of budgeting processes as a mechanism of 'interfering' in the affairs of the subsidiaries in high PD/high UA societies 'is either tolerated or honoured by the (subsidiary) manager out of respect for corporate management (high-power distance) and/or a desire to avoid uncertainty'. In contrast, 'budgeting processes appear to be more hands-off when dealing with managers in individualistic cultures.'

Fluid workgroups and teams

Fluid workgroups and teams are ad hoc task forces formed temporarily to solve specific problems requiring inter-functional, maybe inter-divisional, cooperation and expertise. With colleagues from the USA and Taiwan (Professors Chee Chow at San Diego State University and Anne Wu at National Chengchi University), we have been researching how culture can influence the effectiveness of such teams. Our research has centred on Australia and Taiwan as proxies for Anglo-American and Chinese-based societies.

The cultural dimensions theoretically most relevant are individualism versus collectivism, and power distance. These are also the dimensions on which Anglo-American and Chinese societies differ most, with the former characterised by high IDV and low PD and the latter by low IDV (high collectivism) and high PD. Individualism versus collectivism is relevant because it captures the emphasis that societal members place on self-interests relative to group interests. Collectivist societies are characterised by group orientation and willingness to subordinate individual interests to the interests of the group, while individualist societies are characterised by a self (or 'I') orientation and a lack of willingness to subjugate self-interests. On the surface, this suggests a comparative advantage of collectivist societies in group and teamwork.

However (and this reinforces the need for caution in the application of aggregate dimensions of culture), such a suggestion ignores that the locus of group orientation differs across collectivist societies, giving rise to a crucial distinction between in-groups and out-groups. The locus of group orientation in the collectivist society of Japan is the organisation, while in Chinese-based collectivist cultures in-groups and out-groups are largely defined at the level of smaller organisational units, such as established functional groups and departments. These may be based on friendships and associations built over a considerable period of time. People in collectivist cultures belong to only a few in-groups, which are stable over time. These groups are relatively rigid, making movement of individuals among groups difficult. In contrast, people in individualist societies tend to have many in-groups; they regard interactions with each group as restricted to a calculated purpose and time, and experience little difficulty in moving among groups on the basis of their ability to satisfy the individual's needs. Bond (1991) cites a study that found children in the high IDV culture of the US could easily shift their relations with others from cooperation to competition with a reward incentive, while children in the collectivist cultures of Taiwan and Hong Kong could not.

Our study in Australia and Taiwan supported this theoretical association. Using hypothetical work-related scenarios in interviews with managers in both countries, and using both quantitative and qualitative analysis, we found evidence of a greater ability to adapt to fluid workgroups and teams in the Australian sample than the Taiwanese one. The difference was highly statistically significant, and the qualitative analysis supported the underlying reasons for the differences. Taiwanese managers typically cited the importance of established groups and personal relationships, and the uncertainty that would be produced by their disruption. In contrast, the Australian managers saw few impediments to moving people in and out of temporary groups. (The Australian managers cited personality as a reason affecting individuals' abilities to move among groups, while no Taiwanese manager cited this individual-level factor.)

Our study also showed that people in the Taiwanese organisations had greater difficulty accepting different group leadership based on expertise or knowledge rather than on seniority. This is consistent with power distance differences. In high PD societies (Taiwan), authority and responsibility for leadership are vested in the formally constituted hierarchy. In contrast, in low PD societies, authority and responsibility are vested more easily in power arising from expertise and knowledge, irrespective of hierarchical status. The Taiwanese managers argued that reversing the hierarchical roles of 'leader' and 'led' would cause difficulties on both sides. Those in positions of authority would feel 'demoted' and suffer loss of face if 'relegated' to a member-only role, and those taking the leader role would feel tension in leading a team containing a hierarchical superior. (A caveat is that we did not investigate teamwork *per se*. While collectivist societies might have greater difficulty adapting to changing team members and leaders, they might, as noted earlier, have a comparative advantage in teamwork generally.)

Informal information sharing

Informal information sharing is an important source of rapid and decision-relevant information for organisational members. The information at issue is tacit knowledge – information about local markets and conditions acquired by individuals through personal experience. If informal information is to be shared, conditions and incentives must exist that facilitate and do not impede individuals' propensity to share. Informal information sharing is important in all organisational contexts. However, its importance is heightened where information exchange occurs across divisions and/or organisational units in different countries.

Our study of Australian and Taiwanese managers also included examination of how cultural factors might influence informal information sharing. We examined information sharing in face-to-face meetings, an important context for the transfer of tacit knowledge in modern organisations. We used three hypothetical scenarios involving information sharing, all of which carried some tension or conflict for the person with information to share. In one, a person needed information from others at the meeting but requesting it would expose ignorance. In the second, putting information forward would be seen as confrontational to other people. The third involved information that, if revealed, would expose a mistake they had previously made. We tested the scenarios in two forms: in the first we assumed that the focal person's superior was present, and in the second we assumed that the meeting was among peers only.

For all three scenarios in the first form (meeting with superior present), both sets of managers (Taiwanese and Australian) were found to share their information despite possible adverse consequences to them personally. However, we also found some differences in behaviour, which can be attributed to culture. In the first scenario, the Taiwanese managers were significantly more likely to seek information from others even if it meant exposing ignorance. This is consistent with collectivism, where the self-interest of the individual is subordinate to the collective and the individual sees a moral, or duty-based, involvement with the collective. Qualitative analysis of the interview responses supported this, with frequent reference being made to the interests of the company, and the importance of having the issue fully understood in order to support the best organisational decision. In contrast, the Australian managers were less likely to risk exposing their ignorance. This is consistent with the self-interest motive in individualist cultures, together with a more calculative, less duty-based, involvement with the collective. Factors most often cited in the Australian responses as affecting information sharing related to individual personality.

For the second scenario (the focal person had information which, if brought to the meeting, would be seen as confrontational), the tendency to share information was significantly greater for Australian managers than Taiwanese. This is consistent with the individualist nature of Australian society, where interactions among people are contextualised or compartmentalised. Direct confrontation can take place in one context without prejudicing ongoing interactions. By contrast, in collectivist societies such as Taiwan, the maintenance of harmony in interpersonal relationships is important, and there is less ability to disassociate an instance of confrontation from the ongoing relationship between the people concerned. The qualitative data again supported these influences. The Australian managers frequently referred to individual assertiveness as driving challenging statements made in the meeting. By contrast, the Taiwanese managers typically referred to 'righteous speaking', and 'solving a problem is everyone's responsibility'. The Taiwanese managers would put the information forward, but would do so 'diplomatically' and in a manner that avoided overt confrontation.

We then replicated the scenarios but removed the superiors from the meeting. Generally, we found an increase in the propensity of people to share information, not unsurprisingly because of the reduced pressure of exposing one's ignorance, acting confrontationally, or admitting a mistake in the absence of one's boss. However, the increase was smaller for the Taiwanese managers than the Australians. The qualitative data revealed that, for many of the Taiwanese managers, the removal of the superior from the meeting reduced its importance – the meeting had lost its decision-maker.

These managers saw little benefit in putting forward information that would carry adverse consequences for them, but would not carry the offsetting benefits of a better decision. Once again, we see the importance of the hierarchy and power distance in Chinese societies, and the role of culture in affecting organisational control processes.

Comparing the five national culture dimensions

The previous section shows that most of the culture and management control systems (MCS) studies have involved power distance (PD), individualism versus collectivism (IDV) and uncertainty avoidance (UA). Far fewer studies have involved masculinity versus femininity (MAS) and long-term versus short-term orientation (LTO).

There are several reasons for this. One is that researchers would probably rank PD, IDV and UA as theoretically more pervasive influences on organisational and management processes, including MCS design, than MAS and LTO. A second reason, as noted at the beginning, is that MCS research to date has been dominated by comparisons between western (particularly Anglo-American) and eastern (typically Chinese-based and Japanese) societies. In these comparisons, the dimensions of PD and IDV are particularly distinctive and important. Chow *et al.* (1999) reviewed nine studies examining a range of MCS components in Anglo-American versus Chinese-based countries. Eight involved PD, IDV and/or UA, while only two drew on LTO and only one on MAS. The results for the MAS hypothesis were contrary to the theoretical prediction. Even moving out of the east–west comparison, Van der Stede's (2003) study of MCS design in ten European and North American countries found some support for the influence of PD, IDV and UA on those systems, but not for MAS.

A third reason is that the research to date has typically focused on intra-organisational controls; that is, on controlling the activities and behaviour of people within the organisation. However, many organisations are now outsourcing non-core and, in an increasing number of cases, core activities. Research is following, theorising that control of outsourced activities can be approached through formal contracting or trust, and examining the circumstances when one or the other (or a combination of both) will yield effective control. Contracting places the parties (outsourcer and outsourcee) in an arm's-length, potentially adversarial, relationship, where obligations and standards for performance are specified and formalised *ex ante* by the outsourcer, and enforced through *ex post* penalties and other legal safeguards. In contrast, a trust approach places the parties in a mutually cooperative situation where risks are shared and control arises from the development of trust between the parties.

Non-cultural research into the conditions under which a contracting or trust-based approach to outsourcing control would be appropriate concentrates on economic and market-based characteristics of the transaction, such as the degree of specificity (or uniqueness) of the assets employed in the outsourced activity. However, there is considerable scope for culture to influence the choice of outsourcing controls, and, in this context, MAS would appear to become more important than it has been in MCS research to date. Research by Steensma *et al.* (2000), into whether entrepreneurs in different cultures approach cooperative relationships differently, has shown that entrepreneurs in high MAS cultures approach cooperative relationships with a 'win–lose, zero-sum gain ethos' (p. 595) and favour tight, formal contracting to ensure they do not lose should difficulties arise. Steensma *et al.* attribute this to the 'toughness' and competitiveness of a high MAS culture, and contrast it with low MAS or feminine cultures wherein trust and forbearance are more easily achieved.

Extrapolating this to control of outsourced activities suggests we would expect to find outsourcers placing greater emphasis on formal contracting and legal sanctions in high MAS countries, and more emphasis on trust in low MAS countries. For practising managers involved in controlling inter-country outsourcing activities (and other inter-organisational cooperative relationships such as alliances and joint ventures), the knowledge that 'some cultures are more trusting than others' is salutary.

Placing culture and cultural research in perspective

The aim of this chapter was to examine how national culture affects management control systems (MCS) in different countries. However, it is important we conclude by placing the role of culture in perspective and do not leave the impression that national culture determines MCS design or behavioural reactions to MCS, or that associations between culture and behaviour in organisational control are as clear-cut as our review of the studies may suggest. This means we also have to place cultural research and its typical methods and methodologies in perspective.

First, culture is neither impermeable nor superordinate in its affect on organisations and control systems within them. We have shown that organisations in high PD cultures are likely to demonstrate higher degrees of centralisation of authority than in low PD ones. Nonetheless, there are, of course, highly decentralised organisations functioning effectively in high PD countries, and highly centralised organisations in low PD ones. In these cases, the choice of (de)centralisation is strategic, based on non-cultural factors such as the diversity and volatility in an organisation's product or service markets.

Similarly, we have shown that people in high PD and collectivist cultures experience greater difficulty adapting to fluid workgroups and teams, and that people in individualist cultures exhibit more self-interested and opportunistic behaviour and may be motivated to retain and not share organisationally beneficial information that is individually prejudicial. But we also observed organisations in the high PD and collectivist culture of Taiwan using fluid workgroups and teams effectively, and organisations in the high IDV culture of Australia creating conditions that facilitated information sharing.

These organisations are using conscious intervention strategies of selection and socialisation. One of the Taiwanese organisations, whose strategic need for fluid workgroups is high, targets its recruitment at people who are quite comfortable moving in and out of newly formed groups and accepting or conceding group leadership as circumstances dictate. Classification of a country as high PD does not mean that everyone in the society exhibits personal traits analogous to high PD. Culture refers to the general expectations of interpersonal relations within society, as they tend to be institutionalised in social and organisational structures. It does not reflect the aggregate personality of individuals. With respect to socialisation, this company also employs a rotation system where people are regularly moved around departments to socialise them to accept moving in and out of newly formed groups.

Among our Australian companies were a number that consciously seek a climate (or micro-culture) that encourages information sharing. Team building exercises and programmes are part of this socialisation process. Other companies have switched their performance evaluation and reward systems to reflect group rather than individual performance. Profit-sharing schemes, based on profit at the divisional or corporate level, are also part of this socialisation process.

Our Taiwan versus Australia study also allows us to comment on cultural research and the methods it typically uses. Most cultural/MCS research to date has used the survey method. Surveys have advantages. They are cost efficient and can reveal aggregate associations between cultural dimensions and MCS characteristics and test the significance of those associations statistically. This chapter would not have been possible without such studies; the associations we have described among Hofstede's cultural dimensions and MCS characteristics have been found and supported by credible and rigorous research using the survey method.

However, survey research is also limited. First, it is arm's-length and abstracted from the organisational context in which control systems operate. Hence, it could not reveal the ways in which the Taiwanese and Australian companies in our study were using intervention strategies to accommodate cultural factors in control systems. We were able to gain this understanding because we used qualitative data drawn from in-depth interviews with practising managers, in which we were able to probe responses and elicit a richer understanding of the culture/MCS relationships in those companies.

Additionally, both culture and management control systems are holistic phenomena and greater than the sum of their component parts. Thus, while the cross-sectional survey-type studies can tell us something about linkages between individual cultural dimensions and MCS characteristics, they cannot tell us how those dimensions and characteristics operate in their complex totalities. They cannot tell us, for example, how different components in the MCS may serve as substitutes or complements for one another in an holistic MCS. Nor can they give us insight into the dynamic processes of control involving complex interactions among organisational actors and structures that arise from particular organisational histories and circumstances that constantly evolve over time. The next challenge for researchers of culture and MCS design is to get into the organisations themselves, and observe and learn from the actors *in situ* how they construct and enact control in their everyday organisational life and how culture is embedded in that life. Interestingly, this will involve the ethnographic method of living in, and with, the organisation and will take MCS researchers back to the anthropological origins of cultural research.

Conclusion

At the beginning of the chapter, we identified two contexts in which it is important to understand the effect of culture on management control systems (MCS) at the cross-national level. The first was the greater mobility of individuals in their working lives in the twenty-first century. Individuals crossing national and cultural borders (the two do not always coincide) to work require an understanding of the differences in management control practices they are likely to encounter, and sensitivity to the cultural underpinnings of those differences. In this chapter, we have sought to identify some of the differences in MCS that researchers have observed in empirical studies across different countries and cultures. We have also sought to give these differences a theoretical basis, using Hofstede's framework of cultural dimensions. Consequently, the differences do not stand isolated, country by country, but can be understood in terms of underlying cultural characteristics and can, therefore, be extrapolated to countries and cultures for which we have no empirical research.

The second context is how a multinational company controls the operations of its global subsidiaries. Here, we reinforce the comment that national culture is neither impermeable nor superordinate in its effect on organisations and their control systems by referring again to Van der Stede's (2003) research on the management control practices of subsidiaries of Belgian companies in European and North American countries. For each Belgian parent, Van der Stede found some differences in the budgetary control processes across subsidiaries in different countries. These differences were consistent with the cultural settings of the subsidiaries, suggesting that there is some divergence in MCS consistent with national culture differences.

However, Van der Stede also found that the MCS of the subsidiaries varied more by parent company than by country location. That is, there was greater evidence of parent company influence on the subsidiaries' MCS across countries than cultural influence. Van der Stede called this intra-corporate isomorphism, arising either from the parent coercing the subsidiary to adopt the control practices of the parent, or from the tendency of subsidiaries to imitate the parent's control practices. Van der Stede's findings suggest that multinational companies can make strategic decisions about preferred MCS and can operationalise them in different countries and cultures. However, managers in these companies still need to understand, and be sensitive to, the cultural dictates of personal and interpersonal behaviour of the countries in which they operate, because the strength of differences will determine the ease or difficulty the company will have in implementing its chosen management control practices.

References

Bond, M. H. (1991) *Beyond the Chinese Face: Insights from psychology,* Hong Kong: Oxford University Press.

Borkowski, S. (1999) 'International managerial performance evaluation: a five country comparison', *Journal of International Business Studies,* **39**, 533–55.

Bruns, W.J. Jr and McKinnon, S.M. (1993) 'Information and managers: a field study', *Journal of Management Accounting Research,* **5**, 84–108.

Carr, C. and Tomkins, C. (1998) 'Context, culture and the role of the finance function in strategic decisions. A comparative analysis of Britain, Germany, the U.S.A. and Japan', *Management Accounting Research,* **9**, 213–39.

Chow, C.W., Shields, M.D. and Wu, A. (1999) 'The importance of national culture in the design of and preference for management controls for multi-national operations', *Accounting, Organizations and Society,* **24**, 441–61.

Daley, L., Jiambalvo, J., Sundem, G.L. and Kondo, Y. (1985) 'Attitudes toward financial control systems in the United States and Japan', *Journal of International Business Studies,* **16**, 91–110.

Goffman, E. (1955) 'On face-work: an analysis of ritual elements in social interaction', *Psychiatry,* **18**, 213–31.

Harrison, G.L. and McKinnon, J.L. (1999) 'Cross-cultural research in management control systems design: a review of the current state', *Accounting, Organizations and Society,* **24**, 483–506.

Hofstede, G. (2001) *Culture's Consequences: Comparing Values, Behaviors, Institutions, and Organizations Across Nations,* 2nd edn., Thousand Oaks, CA: Sage Publications.

Hofstede, G. and Bond. M.H. (1988) 'The Confucius connection: from cultural roots to economic growth', *Organizational Dynamics,* **16,** 4–21.

Kroeber, A.L. and Kluckhohn, C. (1952) *Culture: A Critical Review of Concepts and Definitions,* Cambridge, MA: Peabody Museum of American Archaeology and Ethnology, Harvard University.

Lenartowicz, T. and Johnson, J.P. (2003) 'A cross-national assessment of the values of Latin American managers: contrasting hues or shades of gray?' *Journal of International Business Studies,* **34,** 266–81.

Lincoln, J.R., Hanada, M. and Olson, J. (1981) 'Cultural orientations and individual reactions to organizations: a study of employees of Japanese-owned firms', *Administrative Science Quarterly,* **26,** 93–115.

Smith, P.B., Dugan, S. and Trompenaars, F. (1996) 'National culture and the values of organizational employees', *Journal of Cross-Cultural Psychology,* **27,** 231–64.

Snodgrass, C. and Grant, J.H. (1986) 'Cultural influences on strategic planning and control systems', *Advances in Strategic Management,* **4,** 205–28.

Steensma, H.K., Marino, L. and Weaver, K.M. (2000) 'Attitudes toward cooperative strategies: a cross-cultural analysis of entrepreneurs', *Journal of International Business Studies,* **31,** 591–609.

Triandis, H.C. (1995) *Individualism and Collectivism,* Boulder, CO: Westview Press.

Van der Stede, W.A. (2003) 'The effect of national culture on management control and incentive system design in multi-business firms: evidence of intracorporate isomorphism', *European Accounting Review,* **2,** 263–285.

Whitley, R.D. (1991) 'The social construction of business systems in East Asia', *Organization Studies,* **12,** 1–28.

Whitley, R. (1999) 'Firms, institutions and management control: the comparative analysis of coordination and control systems', *Accounting, Organizations and Society,* **24,** 507–24.

Withers, G. (1989) 'Living and working in Australia', In K. Hancock (ed.), *Australian Society,* Sydney: Cambridge University Press, pp. 1–22.

Further reading

Chow, C.W., Shields, M.D. and Wu, A. (1999) 'The importance of national culture in the design of and preference for management controls for multi-national operations', *Accounting, Organizations and Society,* **24,** 441–61. This empirical cross-cultural study includes a good literature review and raises many issues for future cultural research in management control.

Harrison, G.L. and McKinnon, J.L. (1999) 'Cross-cultural research in management control systems design: a review of the current state', *Accounting, Organizations and Society,* **24,** 483–506. Reviews and critiques 15 years of cross-cultural research in management control, with particular emphasis on the conceptualisation and operationalisation of culture.

Hofstede, G. (1991) *Cultures and Organizations: Software of the Mind,* London: HarperCollins. A popular and highly readable version of Hofstede's work geared to organisations – useful for those who want a quickly accessible coverage of culture and its implications for organisations and management.

Hofstede, G. (2001) *Culture's Consequences: Comparing Values, Behavior, Institutions, and Organizations Across Nations,* 2nd edn, Thousand Oaks, CA: Sage Publications. This is the second edition of Hofstede's seminal work on national culture – very comprehensive and detailed and a must for cultural researchers and scholars.

Triandis, H. (1995) *Individualism and Collectivism,* Boulder, CO: Westview Press. An excellent coverage of individualism and collectivism, one of the most important cultural dimensions on which people and societies differ.

6

The changing role of management accountants

John Burns and Gudrun Baldvinsdottir

Introduction

The view of accountants in much of society has generally been negative. They have been on the receiving end of adverse publicity, even ridicule, in newspapers, business journals and films (Smith and Briggs, 1999; Dimnic and Felton, 2006). The words of a 'Vocational Guidance Counsellor' when discussing the job prospects of an accountant (Mr Anchovy) in an episode of TV's *Monty Python's Flying Circus* are typical:

> You see, our experts describe you as an appallingly dull fellow, unimaginative, timid, lacking in initiative, spineless, easily dominated, no sense of humour, tedious company and irrepressibly drab and awful. And whereas in most professions these would be considerable drawbacks, in chartered accountancy they are a positive boon (Flying Circus, Episode 10, first transmitted 21.12.69).

However, a perusal of recent commentaries (predominantly from developed countries and large, private organisations) indicates that management accountants are experiencing significant role changes, involving a decline in dull and tedious 'scorekeeping' roles and a corresponding increase in exciting and proactive 'business-consultancy' roles (IMA, 1999; IFAC, 2001).

This chapter reviews such developments. It is structured as follows. First, there is a brief discussion of traditional roles of management accountants. Next, we examine some commonly cited drivers of changes in management accounting practice – i.e. the backdrop to role changes. Following that, we draw on case study evidence to illustrate the new skills apparently required by reconstituted management accounting roles. Finally, the chapter considers possible opportunities and challenges in management accountants' future roles.

The traditional management accountant's role

Around twenty years ago, most organisations had an Accounting (or Finance) Department comprising financial accounting experts, management accountants (or controllers), financial ledger clerks, tax experts, internal auditors and more. Furthermore, the department would include a mix of qualified accountants, trainee accountants and non-qualified accounting clerks. Often, the accountants were isolated from the rest of the business, surfacing only to discuss the monthly accounting figures with business managers, if at all.

Management accountants were regarded as experts in the preparation and interpretation of business information for decision-making and control. Traditionally their roles involved undertaking routine 'scorekeeping' tasks – i.e. collating performance data and 'policing' business managers against predominantly financial targets (Jablonsky et al., 1993). A management accountant would produce and analyse reams of paper reports and calculations, culminating in a (normally) quite substantial set of management accounting reports. Applying techniques such as budgeting, product costing, capital appraisal methods, standard costing and variance analysis would be a commonplace day-to-day activity.

Traditionally, management accountants have also been viewed as independent and objective assessors of the financial performance of different business functions (Hopper, 1980). This role as a supplier of objective accounting figures to management implies a rather passive role for the management accountant, distanced from line activities with limited involvement in, for example, the performance assessment of individuals. The numbers are assumed to 'speak for themselves'. Individual responsibility has been taken as a precondition for the success of management control devices underpinned by various organisational structures and institutions, e.g. responsibility centres and responsibility accounting systems (Anthony and Govindarajan, 1998). To achieve the requisite financial responsibility, budgets are established for responsibility centres so that the performance of individual managers and departments can be monitored and rewarded. A crucial role of the management accountant was thus seen as being a monitor and controller of others' performance.

Responsibility, reinforced by incentives, is an essential feature of the traditional management accounting model (Scapens et al., 2003). It emphasises the role of business units, departments, sections and groups, as well individuals' responsibility for business activities. For example, the head of a business unit is made personally responsible for that unit's performance, and his/her subordinates are also individually responsible for the performance of their departments and/or functions, and so on down the hierarchy. Underpinning the traditional model is the principle that the performance of individuals or groups responsible for each business area can be quantified and an incentive system applied – i.e. incentives are linked to individual performance. Such incentives are external and tangible rewards for the desired performance. They constitute exchangeable merchandise with a market value, hence they are usually financial.

This approach is, however, premised on a narrow economic view of rationality and motivation. It ignores more subtle intrinsic incentives and rewards associated with personal growth, community and self-fulfilment. Moreover, this responsibility accounting has an individualising effect. The division of the business into separate areas of responsibility, each accountable for its own performance, is often supplemented by the creation of formal or informal competition between responsibility centres – using such tools as league tables and performance ladders.

Thus, the accountant's traditional 'controllership' role involved monitoring the performance of each area of responsibility and producing financial reports to be transmitted up the organisational hierarchy and, ultimately, consolidated into financial reports for the business as a whole. This encouraged a focus on external financial reporting requirements and a 'financial accounting mentality', as Johnson and Kaplan (1987) claimed in their book *Relevance Lost*.

Following this brief overview of traditional roles of management accountants, we explore claims that new roles, more akin to a 'business-orientation' (Granlund and Lukka, 1997, 1998), have emerged recently. But first, we must establish the context of such developments – i.e. what are the main drivers of role changes?

Background to the changing roles of management accountants

Numerous factors have driven business managers to seek new information, with consequences for the roles of management accountants. These are briefly discussed below, namely: globalisation, technology, accounting scandals and corporate trends.

Globalisation

The increasing globalisation of business over the last two decades (i.e. of product, service and capital markets) has had a significant impact on the management accountant's role. Because of global distribution networks, faster and cheaper transportation and real-time information (e.g. through the Internet), most organisations now face international, rather than local or national, competition.

Markets can be vast, with fewer and decreasing barriers to global trade, and much more can be instantaneously known about one's competitors. Products often have shorter life cycles and customer tastes are more ephemeral. Consequently, most organisations now face shorter periods of competitive advantage; any such potential must be exploited quickly and with vigour (i.e. via speedier reaction times). These developments have ramifications for management accountants because business managers in the twenty-first century demand faster, though still relevant and focused, information (i.e. real-time information for real-time decision-making), and wider access to the global information that today's information technology can provide.

Also, many organisations have become more explicitly focused on product quality and customer satisfaction. Customers are now often more choosy and discriminating. They take the availability of product variety as given and may not necessarily be loyal. Thus, customer satisfaction – keeping the customers you already have, as well as attracting new customers – is a priority for most businesses and customer management has become a central concern of today's management accountants.

Finally, there is also greater complexity and uncertainty associated with transactions. Consequently, many organisations now explicitly incorporate business risks as part of their management process, and future management accountants may become more involved in risk assessment.

Technology

The increasing speed of technological change has also profoundly affected the roles of management accountants. For instance, there has been significant impact from advances in production technologies, including advanced manufacturing technologies

(AMTs), computer-aided design and computer-aided manufacture (CAD/CAM), robotics (i.e. automation), and flexible manufacturing systems. Also, recent years have witnessed changes in how products and services are supplied and delivered to customers. Such changes demand new forms of information from the management accountant.

Crucially, there has also been considerable advance in information technology during recent decades. Information preparation and dissemination is becoming much easier and processing capacities are much greater. PCs are plentiful and it is easy for organisational staff to take their desktop PC for granted. However, this was not so 15–20 years ago, when a room-sized mainframe computer would produce the monthly management accounts, but often only if left to run overnight or even longer. Today, with appropriate software, a small laptop computer can produce these accounts in minutes and transmit them to the other side of the world in seconds.

The increased capacity of computing has profoundly affected organisational work and information flows, with consequences for the roles of management accountants. A plethora of business communication technologies – for instance, the Internet and the World Wide Web, e-mail, video-conferencing, 'virtual' (global) and real-time reporting mechanisms, and e-business tools – means information is now extremely portable and transparent. Moreover, tomorrow's management accountants can take for granted further advances in information technology.

Accounting scandals

The many financial scandals during recent years have raised questions about failings of the accounting and auditing profession. In popular opinion, accounting and accountants are now closely connected to ethical failures in the business community. The Enron-led wave of accounting scandals (which also included WorldCom, Tyco, Royal Ahold and Parmalat, to name only a few) shed billions in shareholder value, put thousands of people out of work and eroded confidence in the capital markets. Further, the trust placed in accountants and the information they produce has been seriously undermined (Copeland, 2005).

The seriousness of this weakened trust is encapsulated in recent increases in regulations, monitoring and sanctions, such as the Sarbane–Oxley Act in the USA (2002) and the 8th Company Law Directive in the European Union (2005). However, although these new regulations have made some contribution towards re-establishing trust within the business community, including the accounting profession, scandals continue to surface. The business community, and particularly the accounting profession, still has a long way to go to prove its trustworthiness.

The new regulations imply rigorous documenting and continuous evaluation of control effectiveness. Most of this relies on work undertaken by employees, not least because it is too costly to engage external auditors for this. Thus the role of management accountants as interpreters of overall performance in financial reports remains crucial.

Corporate trends

Corporate trends can also impact business information needs, and hence the roles of management accountants. For instance, during the 1970s much of the industrialised world experienced a wave of mergers and acquisitions, creating more and larger global conglomerates. This precipitated changes in how organisations collated and used information internally.

More recently during the 1990s, some organisations moved in the opposite direction by de-merging and focusing on the core competencies of their business. Resulting trends such as de-layering, de-skilling, downsizing, employee empowerment, team-orientation and business process re-engineering had important ramifications for management processes and changes to information needs, often involving faster response times to customer demands.

Privatisation of many government-controlled organisations and extensive deregulation measures, particularly in developed countries during the 1980s and 1990s, also had a significant impact on how service organisations are managed and, hence, their information needs. Organisations such as airlines, financial services and utilities (e.g. gas, electricity and water supplies) found cost management and profitability were more critical following increased competition. Many of these service industries adopted the management accounting practices of their private sector and commercial counterparts, with varying degrees of success.

Another recent trend is the establishment of business networks, alliances and relationships – shaping accounting for new organisational forms involving information sharing, cooperation and flexibility. Some organisations now pool costs, even with their competitors (e.g. airline companies), and collaborate in research and development. Others are linking up with suppliers in supply chain management and, increasingly, some organisations are establishing more formal links with customers. Indeed, customer relationship management has become particularly important – i.e. targeting market segments, tweaking product designs for customer-specific requirements, providing more flexible delivery methods, integrating information systems, and reshaping organisational structures and processes to better focus on key customers. All these developments have changed information needs and, hence, the roles of management accountants.

The last decade has also seen many medium-to-large organisations shifting from hierarchical structures to leaner and flatter structures that focus on entire business processes (or value chains) from an original customer order through to after-sales services. Aligned with this, many organisations are electing to outsource necessary, but non-value-adding, business activities and processes. Such reorganisation towards a process orientation demands different management information than is normally associated with a hierarchical/functional orientation, as will be illustrated below.

New and emerging roles

Having established the context to management accountants' changing roles we can better consider role changes during recent times. To illustrate this we draw from a case study of a multinational manufacturer of pharmaceutical products. Below is a brief introduction to this company.

Case illustration: Pharmaceuticals

Pharmaceuticals is the UK-based manufacturing arm of a multinational producer of pharmaceutical products such as tablets, inhalers and liquid medicines. (Note that the real name of this company is disguised. A more expansive commentary on this case study can be found in Burns and Baldvinsdottir, 2005). For the two decades leading up to the mid-1990s the company was very prosperous, particularly due to the success of two patented drugs, weak competition and benign pricing policies within the industry.

During this profitable period, the organisation was structured in a hierarchical and functional manner. Accounting was one organisational function and all accounting related tasks were housed there – i.e. financial reporting, transaction processing, taxation, management accounting and internal audit.

However, Pharmaceuticals underwent dramatic changes in the mid-1990s. The two successful products came to the end of their patent lives, global competition expanded, and governments worldwide began to impose stricter price restrictions on pharmaceutical products. This brought tougher economic times for the company and senior management realised that 'things had to change'.

A comprehensive programme of organisational change was instituted, which included a dismantling of many functional tasks. These were replaced by horizontal/process-oriented product teams. Now individual manufacturing sites dealt with specific products across their entire value chains – i.e. from the original product order, through engineering, operations, marketing, and eventually to the final delivery of goods, cash collection and after-sales service provision. The generic term adopted in the organisation for this was 'process ways of working' (PWW). The new ways of working brought the formation of newly powerful management teams comprising experts from different parts of the business, such as design, engineering, operations and marketing. Importantly, these teams also included management accountants more oriented to business analysis and consulting, following the implementation of PWW.

PWW thus reorganised and realigned products at individual sites, each under the control of an individual 'product stream leader'. As stated, Pharmaceuticals had previously been a functionally based organisation, with each function located at sites of operation spread across the UK. Following the introduction of PWW, however, many ex-functional departments were disbanded and their staff incorporated into the product streams. Only three functional departments retained their former independent status, namely Accounting, IT and Quality. All three made a monthly charge to individual product streams for their services.

We can now consider in more detail the role changes for management accountants, drawing on evidence from the Pharmaceuticals case.

Hybrid accountants

A perusal of recent practitioner-oriented literature gives a strong hint that the management accountant's vocation is transforming beyond the traditional scorekeeping/controllership role. There is evidence that today's roles are more 'exciting' and 'consulting-based', and involve minimal day-to-day accounting tasks:

> Growing numbers of management accountants spend the bulk of their time as internal consultants or business analysts [. . .] They spend less time preparing standardized reports and more time analyzing and interpreting information. Many have moved from the isolation of accounting departments to be physically positioned in the operating departments with which they work. Management accountants work on cross-functional teams, have extensive face-to-face communications with people throughout their organizations, and are actively involved in decision making (IMA, 1999, p. 3).

Increasingly, information systems perform routine accounting tasks automatically. For example, transaction processing, reconciliations and accounting reports can be handled by information systems on a largely automatic basis. Simultaneously, other accounting-related tasks, such as statutory reporting ('the financial accounts'), taxation and internal audit, are undertaken by smaller teams of specialists. That is, 'Centres of Excellence' are being established, involving fewer personnel than in the past, and normally taking full advantage of the increased capacity and speed of computer processing (Moore and Birkinshaw, 1998). Furthermore, some organisations have elected to outsource selected accounting processes to external providers such as independent accounting or taxation firms (Mirchandani and Ligget, 2002).

During the 1980s and early 1990s, Pharmaceuticals' accounting department was quite centralised, with most of its accountants performing duties such as transaction processing, statutory and/or group reporting, and clerical-type financial management. But, with the introduction of PWW, the nature of the accounting department and the role of accountants changed. Although the accounting department remained a separate functional area, there was a significant decline in accounting staff from 120 in 1990 to 60 in 1997 (and falling). This reduction was largely borne by people involved in transaction processing and statutory reporting. Apart from a small group responsible for statutory (and/or group) reporting, most accountants by the late 1990s worked within the product streams. They were expected to combine their accounting knowledge with a detailed understanding of the business process in which they worked. They were described by some company members as 'hybrid accountants' who advised product stream leaders on strategic issues as well as assisting other managers with day-to-day decisions and performance measurement.

In addition, for remaining routine management accounting tasks (e.g. basic budgeting and costing techniques) the evidence was that business managers increasingly bore many of these tasks themselves. Scapens *et al.* (2003, pp. 8–9) referred to this as the 'decentering' of accounting knowledge. Managers are increasingly commercially aware, and conscious of 'bottom-line' (profitability) implications of local business decisions rather than dismissing such concerns as the remit of accountants. Normally today's accountants must assist in any way they can, but will not necessarily be involved in day-to-day routine accounting tasks. This more proactive role of management accountants implies that they can promote the ethical values of a company. This can be achieved in many ways, including demonstrating why more expensive, environmentally friendly material may be beneficial to the company in the long run, or encouraging managers to evaluate subordinates on more than just financial criteria.

Technical and professional accounting expertise, however, remains fundamentally important for management accountants. Indeed, as mentioned above, following recent and much-publicised corporate collapses (e.g. Enron) and increased public interest in governance and social reporting, expertise in technical aspects of accounting (e.g. stewardship and controllership) is more critical than ever. However, due to advances in information technology and the decentring of accounting knowledge, such roles now occupy less of the management accountant's time.

Thus, in many organisations time has been freed up for management accountants, with many moving into new business areas (including the marketing and IT departments), or engaging in new advisory roles as described above. The latter work occurs 'out-in-the-field' (Scapens *et al.*, 2003), alongside different business groups and units situated along the value chain – for instance, operations, engineering, sales and marketing, and product development. They are integral members of process-oriented management teams and must understand the complexities of, and linkages across, entire business processes. Hence, they require a broad grasp of business and management issues and must utilise their technical accounting skills across different organisational foci and orientations.

An interesting issue concerns the extent to which today's advisory role of management accountants can be formally integrated into new, process-oriented organisational structures. Pharmaceuticals elected to retain a centralised accounting department, so all the accountants remained functionally attached to that department and accounting departmental costs (including time spent in business streams by consulting accountants) were charged as an overhead to product streams. Other organisations, however, could formally integrate their consulting accountants into the business streams, thus leaving only small and specialist accounting departments.

Nowadays, the management accountant's utilisation of accounting information is more proactive, strategy-oriented and interwoven with non-financial performance measurement, and is directed at business improvement and increasing efficiencies and value creation (IMA, 1999). The role thus embraces the knowledge and expertise of both traditional and new management accounting techniques. Such technical expertise, however, is not necessarily the dominant part of the management accountant's contemporary role.

Increased use of non-financial information in businesses has had a significant impact upon management accountants' roles. A related change in the focus of management accountants is a shift from 'feed-backward' orientation (e.g. comparing actual results to budgeted results) to a feed-forward orientation (e.g. projecting from actual results to predicted results), as discussed by Scapens *et al.* (2003). Nowadays, for business managers in particular, forecasts can be more important than the comparison of actuals against budgets – that is, there is a leaning towards less 'rear-view analysis' and more real-time, forward-looking orientation (Granlund and Lukka, 1997).

Much of the data, both financial and non-financial, used by hybrid accountants in Pharmaceuticals was produced and held in the product streams. One of their primary tasks was to collate such data in a form that satisfied business managers' information needs. Particular emphasis was given to rolling forecasts and 'feed-forward' information. Budgets remained important as an overall guide for the year, but the rolling forecast, generated within product streams, received most management attention. Further, as the forecasts were generated internally rather than imposed from outside, there was a greater feeling of ownership of this information and a stronger commitment to its achievement.

Financial measures, including cost-related measures, are no less important. Indeed, profit is the ultimate goal for all private and commercial enterprises, but is increasingly viewed as part of a broader set of performance measures aligned to corporate strategy and business value creation (IMA, 1999; May, 2002; Scapens *et al.*, 2003). Moreover, causal links between non-financial and financial performance are being explored and exploited through holistic and strategically focused measurement systems like the balanced scorecard.

An important role for management accountants is to link the monthly management accounts to the wider set of information now available to the management team. This information includes financial and non-financial measures, as well as both long-term and short-term performance indicators. The management accountant has to reconcile this broader perspective of a business (expressed in the various performance measures) with the narrower financial view shown in the management accounts. To do this, the management accountant needs a broad-based understanding of the business and its operations.

This implies a management accounting role different to the traditional controllership role described at the outset. A traditional role involved management accountants being independent and objective monitors of the financial performance of various business sections, normally within a system of responsibility accounting and with a focus on cost control. But today, the management accountant is usually more concerned with integrating different sources of information and explaining interconnections between non-financial performance measures and management accounting information. This is important because it enables individual managers to see the linkages between their day-to-day operations, how these are represented in monthly management accounts, and their relation to the broader strategy of the business (as reflected in non-financial measures). Thus, integration is now a key task for the management accountant, but still requires 'technical' expertise to integrate financial and non-financial performance measures into a coherent and comprehensive picture of the business (Scapens *et al.*, 2003).

Within this new role, management accountants now engage in multiple new tasks. Scapens *et al.* (2003) provide a by no means exhaustive list that includes: assessing the financial implications of operational decisions, risk assessment, strategy formulation, change management, systems design and implementation, and customer relationship management. The future role of management accountants is likely to comprise a combination of these (and other) tasks: it is not confined to an accounting or finance silo. The increase in process/horizontal forms of organisation has broken management accountants' functional embeddedness because they must re-orient themselves across (ex-)functions. However, the evidence suggests that the primary task of these consulting accountants is still analysing the financial implications of operational decisions (Burns and Yazdifar, 2001).

New accountants' roles and tasks are not necessarily planned but can emerge, for example from new organisational forms (Burns and Baldvinsdottir, 2005). In other words, today's management accountants use their skills to assist business managers to manage the business process. This was the case in Pharmaceuticals. Accountants were perceived as working 'out-in-the-field' to increase the efficiency of the business processes by supporting business process managers. They had to be cross-functional team players able to work with different people from various functional and discipline backgrounds. Their main task was to integrate operational performance, accounting information and the strategic context of the business, and to enable process managers to take informed decisions in the light of the circumstances confronting them. Thus, this new accountant is more of an all-rounder, very different to the traditional scorekeeper/controllership role.

Finally, management accountants are becoming key players in business strategy formulation, business value-creation, and instilling an ethos of efficiency and continuous improvement. They are experiencing (and in some instances driving) a shift from routine accounting to more proactive roles within the broader management process. They are no longer merely support staff. Jablonsky *et al.* (1993) summarised the 'core values' of a consulting accountant (or, in their terms, a 'business advocate') as follows:

- *Shared control* – i.e. team-playing, shared understandings of strategic issues, educating managers in their use of financial-oriented concepts and techniques.
- *Service to customers* – i.e. leadership and support to business units, broad knowledge about the business, active involvement in the business.
- *Analytical capabilities* – i.e. sophisticated analysis support to business managers, financial models to support business units, focus on strategic management issues.
- *Seamless systems and communication* – i.e. horizontal communication within business units, integrated reporting systems, encouraging wider use of financial information.

New skills requirements

Although traditional accounting skills pertaining to stewardship and control remain important for today's management accountants (as highlighted above), they are no longer dominant. Rather, such skills are an assumed and taken for granted part of a management accountant's present day expertise.

However, the emergence of broader roles, described above, has presented new 'hard' and 'soft' skills requirements (Yasin *et al.*, 2005). Hard skills include proficiency in information technology and a broad business understanding. A management accountant should understand, design and communicate new systems using the latest technologies, including new and advanced accounting systems and techniques, and increasingly integrated information systems such as enterprise resource planning systems. Management accountants will need a good understanding of information technology but need not necessarily be an 'IT expert' because most businesses will retain their computing technicians, programmers and the like. However, management accountants will need to be willing to embrace new technology and identify new ways of applying it to their businesses. In addition, management accountants must have a grasp of, and be able to integrate, their organisations' strategic objectives, key operational drivers of success, market dynamics and new product development initiatives.

Soft skills, on the other hand, comprise attributes that commentators have claimed were lacking amongst management accountants 10–15 years ago (IFAC, 2002). For instance, several commentators have cited the importance of excellent communication skills (IMA, 1999). More specifically, management accountants must be able to frame their accounting reports to business managers 'through the eyes of the user', using various means such as presentations, written reports and video-conferencing. Another frequently cited new skill is an ability to recognise and cope with different organisational perspectives and viewpoints, especially when engaged in roles that involve personal leadership, drive and conviction – i.e. finding creative solutions that integrate conflicting views (Granlund and Lukka, 1998).

Interpersonal skills are also important for today's management accountants, particularly in their 'integrating' role, to augment their ability to interact and build trustworthy relationships with colleagues across different business areas and different levels of seniority. This integrating role has recast today's consulting accountants from an isolated accounting department and into situations where relationship building, teamwork, interpersonal skills and trust building have become essential elements of the management accounting process. In Pharmaceuticals a product stream leader illustrated this when describing her relationship with her senior management accountant:

> If I've got something bothering me, I pop my head round, or vice versa. If we see anything changing in the business, or we pick up anything on the grapevine, we talk very quickly. He understands my reasoning for the business and why I feel we need to do things in certain ways. We sing from the same hymn sheet. (Burns and Baldvinsdottir, 2005)

Here trust has built up between the product stream leader and the accountant. Honest and open discussion is facilitated by integrating the accountant into the business process-oriented team.

Finally, professional status and awareness remains important. Arguably, management accounting is optional and 'works from a blank sheet' in any organisation. Consequently, management accountants must make judgements and decisions in an ethical manner. Most international professional accounting bodies prescribe ethical guidelines for their members, although such codes are likely to be modified to incorporate organisational and possibly cultural characteristics.

Discussion

Opportunities

The traditional 'controllership' role of management accountants monitored the performance of responsibility units, and produced financial reports that were transmitted up the organisational hierarchy and ultimately consolidated for the business as a whole. Nowadays, however, management accounting is also concerned with decision support and teamwork, whereby management accountants work alongside the business managers to integrate operations, financial performance and strategy. New perspectives on 'control' are thus needed to recognise these developments in management accounting practice (Scapens *et al.*, 2003; Nixon and Burns, 2005). When an organisation is business process-oriented, responsibility for the performance of each process may cut across traditional functional areas of, say, procurement, design, operations and sales. Managers and other workers in those functional areas will be jointly responsible for the performance of the entire business process. This is intertwined with issues of empowerment and lays significant weight on 'new' notions of trust, teamwork and cooperation rather than dividing the business into functional areas of responsibility for monitoring and control purposes.

For effective empowerment, managers and other employees need to receive the information and other resources they require. But, above all, they must be trusted to perform their tasks effectively. However, this does not imply an absence of control. Senior management must be in control of their company – they cannot just delegate responsibility to suitably empowered employees and expect the entire business to function efficiently. Controls will be exercised at different levels compared to traditional systems of responsibility accounting. For example, cross-functional teams, rather than individuals, must be controlled. This can create problems, particularly for traditional control systems grounded in 'narrow' assumptions of individual responsibility. Thus, more team-based performance measures might be needed, along with accounting information that encourages cooperation rather than competition.

This requires broader-based knowledge of the business and how various processes and functions interact, and an emphasis on integration rather than individualisation. It will require an understanding of all functions, from day-to-day operations to corporate strategy. Furthermore, it requires that incentive systems be redesigned from individual-based to team-based reward schemes.

Accompanying such changes, we are beginning to see redesigns of the accounting department. On the one hand, there is the increasing centralisation of routine accounting tasks into 'Centres of Excellence', with the possibility of some being outsourced (Moore and Birkinshaw, 1998; Mirchbandani and Ligget, 2002). On the other hand, management accounting is becoming increasingly decentralised as business managers undertake more tasks themselves (Scapens *et al.*, 2003). Thus, we see management accountants situated within the business processes, working alongside managers, and possibly only occasionally meeting their accounting colleagues who work in other processes. The decentring of accounting knowledge, and the increasing recognition of the financial consequences of management actions at all levels, has made such change broadly acceptable. In the Pharmaceuticals case, for example, locating the consulting accountants within the business processes was generally regarded as desirable by business process managers (although this was not unanimous, see below).

Management accountants who fulfil the consulting role (as undertaken by hybrid accountants in Pharmaceuticals) can help managers to interpret financial and non-financial information and to evaluate the operating and strategic consequences of alternative courses of action. A broad-based knowledge of the business, reinforced through interactions with accounting colleagues in other areas, enables the management accountant to recognise the wider impact of decisions. This is vital for management accountants as it integrates the activities of the business in a seamless information and communication system.

Significant areas of accounting work, including some traditional roles of management accountants, have already disappeared or are reduced in scale and require fewer qualified accountants. For example, the spread of integrated information systems has made it easier to centralise routine accounting tasks such as transaction processing, clerical forms of financial control and, to some extent, external financial reporting. For instance, in the BM Inc. study of Scapens *et al.* (2003), the European division of a US multinational, with plants in various European countries, used SAP to centralise all transaction processing in one location. Such trends will continue to drive reductions in personnel employed in accounting departments, and may entice some accountants to transfer to other business areas to employ their relatively broad skills.

The computerisation and centralisation of routine tasks does, however, enable management accountants who wish to undertake broader consulting roles to do so. Since this normally requires the accountant to be a member of management teams rather than a functionally separated accounting group, this significantly decentralises management accounting. Indeed, it has been suggested that by 2010 the 'finance [or accounting] department will no longer exist' (KPMG, 1998, p. 4). Instead, there will be small, centralised and specialist groups dealing with routine accounting tasks and maintaining associated computer systems, with accounting experts within individual management teams. It is the latter (i.e. consulting) role that will attract more qualified management accountants in the future (IMA, 1999).

Tomorrow's roles, however, should not be taken for granted. Seizing and sustaining opportunities will require proactive rather than static perspectives on role development. The changes in Pharmaceuticals were influenced by the proactivity and vision of one senior accountant in particular (see Burns and Baldvinsdottir, 2005). As Scapens *et al.* (2003) suggested, tomorrow's management accountants must be able to adapt to fluid business demands, extend their input to business managers, continue to broaden their business acumen while maintaining their financial expertise, recognise the limitations of accounting, be alert to negative perceptions, and pre-empt potential and actual resistance.

Challenges

There are potentially significant challenges ahead. For example, managers with formal management training, including financial literacy through (say) an MBA degree, represent a threat to management accountants. A financially literate engineer or production manager may also fill the consulting-type role that we have elucidated. IT specialists also pose a threat to management accountants, as they could become the information specialists of the future. New integrated information systems such as enterprise resource planning systems (ERPs) provide accounting information alongside other forms of management information. For many management accountants, designing and implementing these new information systems is daunting. However, at least in the immediate future, a management accountant's ability to link accounting information to operational performance measures, and to relate financial and non-financial information to corporate strategy, offers some advantage over potential professional competition.

Despite the substantial change in the role of accountants within Pharmaceuticals, there was actually little change in the management accounting systems and techniques used. Management accounting systems were described by some as 'antiquated', despite innovations elsewhere (including implementing MRPII and data warehousing). There was discussion of implementing a new (activity-based) cost system in the early 1990s, but it was not introduced, despite support from some business managers who wished to reduce overheads. One operations manager remarked that he would welcome such an 'advanced and sophisticated' cost system, as it would provide 'ammunition' to challenge the overhead charges to his business segment for services rendered by accountants. He confessed to valuing the (hybrid) accountants' support, and he regarded them as integral members of the process-oriented managerial teams, but he objected to the magnitude of the accounting charge in his manufacturing profit statement.

Nevertheless, activity-based costing was not considered a priority in Pharmaceuticals; many other changes were taking place which senior company decision-makers regarded as potentially more beneficial. Despite this the case also suggested that management accountants must provide value for money in the services they offer to their businesses – whether in transaction processing, financial control, business consulting support or external financial reporting. Importantly, this may not be achieved simply by redesigning the accounting department. As information becomes more accessible at all levels of the organisation, and as business managers develop greater personal financial knowledge, they are increasingly likely to question the cost of management accountants working in their area. Accounting is becoming increasingly transparent and, hence, more accountable as it becomes dispersed within organisations.

Within Pharmaceuticals, the hybrid accountants were perceived as a 'different' accountant: they were officially titled 'finance analysts', rather than 'accountants', for they were expected to provide a service for product stream managers and were an integral part of the process team. Furthermore, the demand for information they provided came from the business process managers themselves, not merely from the accountants or senior managers.

However, the physical locations of hybrid accountants differed. At one site they spent at least three days working within the product streams, in offices next to the product stream leaders, but they also had an office/desk in the accounting department. Nevertheless, their office within the product streams was regarded as their 'home'. This was typical of the approach across the UK operations sites. However, at a second site, the hybrid accountants were centrally located (and only) alongside other finance staff. Hence, if the accountants wanted to talk to product stream managers, they had to walk for ten minutes to the plant. Importantly, this decision on proximity (or lack of it) was perpetuated by the desire of a more elderly and senior accounting manager at that site for 'his accountants' to 'remain independent from the business units'.

Within Pharmaceuticals, the hybrid accountants had direct (functional) responsibility to their senior accounting managers, and only indirect responsibility to product stream managers. Typical of most UK manufacturing sites, however, the hybrid accountants' day-to-day responsibilities were commonly deemed as being 'direct' to the product stream leaders. At the second site, the senior accountant considered personal relationships were more important than physical location and felt that good relationships were not dependent on being physically located in the same building.

Conclusion

This chapter has investigated recent (and growing) claims that management accountants are experiencing significant role changes – i.e. from 'scorekeeping' roles to proactive 'consultancy' roles. The evidence suggests that significant shifts are under way, particularly in large commercial organisations. Further investigation is warranted, however, especially regarding why and how such role changes emerge and unravel in different organisational settings (Burns and Baldvinsdottir, 2005). Opportunities and challenges abound for tomorrow's management accountants, but the nature and speed of such developments remain hard to predict.

References

Anthony, R.N. and Govindarajan, V. (1998) *Management Control Systems,* 9th edn, Boston, MA: Irwin McGraw-Hill.

Burns, J. and Baldvinsdottir, G. (2005) 'An institutional perspective of accountants' new roles – the interplay of contradictions and praxis', *European Accounting Review,* **14**(4), 725–57.

Burns, J. and Yazdifar, H. (2001) 'Trick or treats', *Financial Management* (CIMA), March, 33–5.

Copeland, J.E. (2005) 'Ethics as an imperative', *Accounting Horizons,* **19**(1), 35–43.

Dimnic, T. and Felton, S. (2006) 'Accountant stereotypes in movies distributed in North America in the twentieth century', *Accounting, Organizations and Society,* **31**, 129–55.

Granlund, M. and Lukka, K. (1997) 'From bean-counters to change agents: the Finnish management accounting culture in transition', *The Finnish Journal of Business Economics,* **46**(3), 213–55.

Granlund, M. and Lukka, K. (1998) 'Towards increasing business orientation: Finnish management accountants in a changing cultural context', *Management Accounting Research,* **9**(2), 185–211.

Hopper, T. (1980) 'Role conflicts of management accountants and their position within organisation structures', *Accounting, Organizations and Society,* **5**(4), 401–11.

Institute of Management Accountants (IMA) (1999) *Counting More, Counting Less: Transformations in the Management Accounting Profession (Executive Summary),* Montvale, NJ: Institute of Management Accountants (IMA) Publishing.

International Federation of Accountants (IFAC) (2001) *A Profession Transforming from Accounting to Management,* New York: IFAC Publications.

International Federation of Accountants (IFAC) (2002) *CFO 2010 – The Role of the Chief Financial Officer in 2010.* New York: IFAC Publications.

Jablonsky, F.S., Keating, P.J. and Heian, J.B. (1993) *Business Advocate or Corporate Policeman,* New York: Financial Research Foundation.

Johnson, H.T. and Kaplan, R.S. (1987) *Relevance Lost: The Rise and Fall of Management Accounting,* Boston, MA: Harvard University Press.

KPMG Management Consulting (1998) *Finance of the Future: A Guide for Business Users,* London: KPMG Publications.

May, M. (2002) *Transforming the Finance Function: Adding Company Wide Value in a Technology-based Environment,* 2nd edn, London: Pearson.

Mirchandani, K. and Liggett, J. (2002) 'Using outsourcing to stay on top', *The CPA Journal,* June, p. 18.

Moore, K. and Birkinshaw, J. (1998) 'Managing knowledge in global service firms: centers of excellence', *Academy of Management Executive,* **12**(4), 81–92.

Nixon, W.A.N. and Burns, J. (2005) 'Management control in the 21st century', *Management Accounting Research,* **16**, 260–8.

Scapens, R.W., Ezzamel, M., Burns, J. and Baldvinsdottir, G. (2003) *The Future Direction of UK Management Accounting Practice,* London: CIMA/Elsevier.

Smith, M. and Briggs, S. (1999) 'From bean-counter to action hero: changing the image of the accountant', *Management Accounting,* January, 28–30.

Yasin, M.M., Bayes, P.E. and Czuchry, A.J. (2005) 'The changing role of accounting in supporting the quality and customer goals of organizations: an open system perspective', *International Journal of Management,* **22**(3), 323–31.

Further reading

Burns, J. and Baldvinsdottir, G. (2005) 'An institutional perspective of accountants' new roles – the interplay of contradictions and praxis', *European Accounting Review,* **14**(4), 725–757. A more detailed discussion of the UK pharmaceuticals manufacturer case study that features in this chapter. It adopts institutional theory to assist in the interpretation of the case findings.

Granlund, M. and Lukka, K. (1998) 'Towards increasing business orientation: Finnish management accountants in a changing cultural context', *Management Accounting Research,* **9**(2), 185–211. An excellent study of changes in the roles of management accountants in Finland, towards business-oriented/consultancy roles. This paper also adopts institutional theory to assist the interpretation of the case findings.

May, M. (2002) 'Generation next', *Financial Management,* September, 28–29. Another short article from CIMA's journal. It explains how and why world-class organisations are increasingly expecting their finance or accounting departments to do less number crunching and begin to create corporate value. It also considers what accounting professionals might do to meet the challenges ahead.

Mouritsen, J. (1996) 'Five aspects of accounting departments' work', *Management Accounting Research,* **7**(3), 283–303. An insightful examination of the traditional and modern-day roles of management accountants.

Parker, L. (2002) 'Advance and be recognised', *Financial Management,* April, 32–33. A short article, published in the journal of the Chartered Institute of Management Accountants (CIMA), which explains how and why the role of management accountants has changed and why professional accountants need to take on the mantle of a strategic business partner or face extinction.

Scapens, R.W., Ezzamel, M., Burns, J. and Baldvinsdottir, G. (2003) *The Future Direction of UK Management Accounting Practice,* London: CIMA/Elsevier. A CIMA research monograph that documents the findings of a study of changing UK management accounting practices, incorporating surveys and case studies.

Part 2

'New' management accounting techniques

7

Strategic management accounting

Beverley R. Lord

Introduction

The concept of business strategy was borrowed from the military. The *Concise Oxford Dictionary* (1982) defines strategy as the 'art of so moving or disposing troops or ships or aircraft as to impose upon the enemy the place and time and conditions for fighting preferred by oneself'. Similarly, business strategy produces long-term plans for the business, taking into consideration plans and possible actions of competitors, the main objective being to position the firm so it has a competitive advantage. Note that strategy is more than just long-term plans: as competitors act and react, the firm will have to modify its plans in order to maintain competitive advantage.

Continuing the military analogy, Tricker (1989) compares the relationship between business strategy and management accounting to the relationship between military strategy and military intelligence. If management accounting is to play this role in strategic management, it must provide managers not only with internal, financial information, but also with information, both financial and non-financial, about the environment in which the firm is operating: *strategic* management accounting.

This chapter will first describe business strategy and show why traditional management accounting is not sufficient to provide information for strategic decisions. Then the various components of strategic management accounting will be described along with examples of their implementation taken from research. Finally critiques of strategic management accounting will be reviewed.

Strategy and information needs

Bowman (1990) traced the development of strategic planning from its internal focus on budgeting, forecasting and portfolio analysis, to its external focus. From the 1970s onwards, firms began to focus on their place in their industry. An economic orientation was taken, in which external 'actors were considered adversaries who tended to drive profits toward zero' (Bowman, 1990, p. 13). Later this developed into strategic management, characterised by the following: planning at different levels of the business, cutting across organisational boundaries; an emphasis on entrepreneurial thinking, flexibility and creativity; and managers' commitment to corporate strategy, reinforced by teamwork, commitment to making things happen, open communication and a shared belief that ambitious goals can be achieved. In this orientation, competitive forces are not necessarily considered to be enemies: there is the possibility of partnership with suppliers, competitors and customers, with benefit to all.

In his 1980 book, Porter listed several disadvantages posed by competitors: the threat of new competitors entering the market; the intensity of rivalry among existing competitors; the pressure from substitute products; and the bargaining power of buyers and suppliers. These forces influence the prices, costs and investment of firms in an industry and hence determine their profitability. However, in his 1985 book Porter listed some advantages of competitors. For example, competitors already in the market can help increase competitive advantage by absorbing demand fluctuations, enhancing the ability to differentiate by establishing standards of comparison, and serving unattractive segments that the firm does not want to deal with. They can share the costs of market development, and help block new entrants, for example by blocking the channels of distribution.

A range of relationships between competitors has been found in research in organisations. For example, Bengtsson and Kock (1999) analysed the relationships between competitors in two Swedish industries. Sometimes competitor companies merely coexisted – they knew about each other but had no mutual interactions. This was the relationship, for example, between a large manufacturer and its two very small competitors, who were not considered a threat because of their size. At other times companies cooperated, with frequent business, information and social interactions. For example, one company marketed the product made by another company. However, at times these two companies were competitive, in an action–reaction pattern, where one of the companies would launch a new product and the competitor would quickly follow. Sometimes companies simultaneously cooperated and competed. For example, two companies competing in the same market also cooperated by combining their research and development operations. As each company brought their own areas of competence to the development, they could develop products more cost-effectively and offer new and innovative solutions to their customers.

As views on competitive forces have changed, the concept of strategic management accounting as providing 'intelligence' about the 'enemy', i.e. competitors, has also broadened and changed over time. The relationship with competitors can be cooperative as well as confrontational, with information sharing between competitors.

Also a company needs external information about more than just competitors. Gordon *et al.* (1978) were among the first to link accounting information to strategic decision-making, pointing out that different information was needed at each phase of the strategic decision process. They claimed that the strategic problem identification phase requires primarily non-financial, qualitative information about external issues such as competitors' actions and changes in demand, technology and governmental regulations. When strategic alternatives are being generated, both financial and non-financial quantitative data is needed about both internal and external issues such as 'resources, skills, time availability, lines of credit, geographical sites and characteristics, [and] demand forecasts' (Gordon *et al.*, 1978, p. 210). When strategic actions are being selected, primarily quantitative, financial, internal information is needed about costs, payoffs, and probabilities of the possible actions. Note that non-financial as well as financial, and both qualitative and quantitative information is needed. Thus traditional management accounting information is insufficient for strategic decision-making.

Traditional management accounting and strategy

There are several problems with trying to use traditional management accounting information for strategic management. Traditional management accounting is too short-term, and emphasises profit for artificial accounting periods (such as the financial year or operating months). Strategic management accounting, on the other hand, has a long-term focus, viewing profit in the context of the firm's competitive position over time. Most traditional management accounting is backward-looking, focusing on past results, whereas strategic management accounting is forward-looking. Traditional management accounting is inward-looking, focusing on costs within the firm and particularly emphasising precise product costs and manufacturing activities. Strategic management needs internal information about marketing, other support costs and linkages between activities, and external information on customers, suppliers and competitors. Strategic management also requires non-financial as well as financial information and approximations may be sufficient. Finally, traditional management accounting systems tend to be programmed or reactive, dealing with regular events (such as the preparation of budgets) or one-off decisions (such as the choice between making or buying a component). Strategic management accounting needs to be proactive and able to contribute to all stages of strategic decision-making, which is usually un-programmed. See Table 7.1 for a comparison of traditional and strategic management accounting characteristics.

Given that traditional management accounting does not provide the sort of information needed for strategic management, several authors have discussed what should be used instead. These components of strategic management accounting are detailed next.

Table 7.1 Characteristics of traditional and strategic management accounting

Traditional management accounting	Strategic management accounting
Historical	Forward-looking
Introspective	Outward-looking
Narrow scope	Broad scope
Internal performance	Performance relative to competitors
Single period	Multiple periods
Manufacturing focus	Competitive focus
Existing activities	Possibilities
Reactive	Proactive
Programmed (often)	Un-programmed
Overlooks linkages	Exploits linkages
Based on existing systems	Unconstrained by existing systems
Built on conventions	Ignores conventions
Financial measures	Financial and non-financial measures
Exact figures	Approximations

Source: adapted from Wilson (1995).

Components of strategic management accounting

There are several views on the relationship between strategy and management accounting. The first view emphasises information about competitors. The second view expects different aspects of the management accounting system to be emphasised depending on the strategic position chosen by the firm. The third view takes a value chain perspective, looking at ways of achieving competitive advantage by exploiting linkages in the value chain and optimising cost drivers. A fourth view takes a product focus and looks at market-oriented information. Each of these views will be briefly described, along with particular techniques one would expect to see in a strategic management accounting system and examples taken from current research in organisations.

Competitor information

Early advocates of strategic management accounting emphasised the need to collect information that would enable comparisons between the firm and its competitors. Simmonds (1981), who coined the name 'strategic management accounting', saw profit arising not from how efficiently the firm operated internally, but from the firm's competitive position over time. Thus he advocated the following processes: collecting and estimating cost, volume and price data on competitors; determining whether competitors' products are in the build, maintain or harvest phase of their life cycles; and calculating market share in order to assess the strategic position of one's own firm in relation to its competitors.

Knowledge of a competitor's costs enables a firm to detect when the competitor is trying to change relative competitive position, for example by manipulating prices. Knowledge of cost structure, position in the life cycle, and relative market share enables decisions to be evaluated in the light of possible competitor reactions. Much of this competitor information can be collected from existing sources. For example, production people and equipment suppliers know a lot about competitors' plants. Other sources include published accounts, brokers' and analysts' reports, trade magazines, advertisements, newspaper articles, industry surveys and government departments.

Simmonds suggested several ways in which competitor information could be reported. Market share could be simply incorporated into management reports. Budgets could be prepared which compared one's own cost, volume and profit information with that of important competitors. Any information about buyer response to the costs of various inputs would enable management to identify actions that would increase competitive advantage. Simmonds also highlighted the importance of considering strategic change when evaluating investment opportunities. He encouraged not only evaluating projected profits if the strategic investment were taken up, but also estimating the change in market share and flow-on effects of that change.

Bromwich (1990) suggested that management accountants gather information about the costs of barriers to entry such as economies of scale, product differentiation, cost advantages, capital requirements, strategic pricing by incumbents, intensive research and development, excess capacity, vertical integration and existing sales networks. Bromwich pointed out that established firms in an industry have already incurred these costs, so do not need to consider them when making strategic decisions, whereas newcomers must incur these costs to enter the industry.

Coad (1996) gave a detailed description of the collection and use of competitor information by a service department in a city council. Information was obtained in a number of ways: via the 'grapevine'; from former employees, suppliers and customers of the competitors; from publicly available information such as company accounts, news releases, promotional material, trade journals, commercial analysts' reports and databases; and from council records of previous tenders. The information was used to estimate the tender price a major competitor would submit. The service department then bid lower than the estimate and successfully undercut their competitor, winning the contract.

Collier and Gregory (1995) provided some examples of strategic management accounting being used in the hotel sector. Accountants were involved in several processes: analysing strengths, weaknesses, opportunities and threats (SWOT analysis); monitoring cost structures and pricing policies of competitors; and comparing the performance of the company against its competitors. In some cases, the marketing function undertook these analyses. One use of the analyses was the evaluation of strategic alternatives, including joint ventures with, or acquisitions of, competitors. Similarly, Guilding *et al.*'s (2000) survey of large companies in New Zealand (NZ), the United Kingdom (UK) and the United States of America (USA) found a high use of competitive position monitoring, competitor performance appraisal based on published financial statements, and competitor cost assessment.

These researchers have all taken the perspective that strategic management accounting emphasises information about competitors, including costs, volumes, prices, life cycles, market share, barriers to entry and threats. Another perspective is that the components of strategic management accounting will depend on the strategic position taken by the firm.

Strategic position and management accounting emphasis

Porter (1980, 1985) outlined two main ways in which managers can position their firms to gain a strategic advantage over their competitors: firms need to either differentiate their product(s) or be cost leaders. To differentiate its product, a firm must provide something unique that is of value to the purchaser, for example better quality, or features that are not included in the competitors' products. Competitive advantage can then be attained by being able to ask a higher price, by being able to sell more at the given price, or by increased customer loyalty. However, superior performance can only be achieved if costs are kept as low as possible, especially the costs of differentiation. Cost leadership involves not just lowering costs, but having costs lower than all competitors. A firm can employ cost leadership or differentiation strategies that target the entire market, or just a segment of the market.

Shank (1989) expected that firms would have different management accounting emphases depending on which of these strategic positions was taken (see Table 7.2). For product differentiators marketing is very important – they have to let the market

Table 7.2 **Different management accounting emphases**

	Primary strategic emphasis	
	Product differentiation	Cost leadership
Role of standard costs in assessing performance	Not very important	Very important
Importance of such concepts as flexible budgeting for manufacturing cost control	Moderate to low	High to very high
Perceived importance of meeting budgets	Moderate to low	High to very high
Importance of marketing cost analysis	Critical to success	Often not done at all on a formal basis
Importance of product cost as an input to pricing decisions	Low	High
Importance of competitor cost analysis	Low	High

Source: Shank (1989, p. 55, Table 1).

know how their product is differentiated. Therefore product differentiators could be expected to place a great deal of importance on marketing cost, but little emphasis on product cost. On the other hand, cost leaders want to have the lowest cost so will place high importance on cost control and comparisons with competitors' costs.

Chenhall and Langfield-Smith (1998a) hypothesised that differentiators would strongly emphasise and benefit from the following: balanced performance measures; employee-based measures; benchmarking of products and operational and management processes; and strategic planning techniques, such as formal strategic planning, long-range planning, benchmarking strategic priorities and benchmarking with outside organisations. They hypothesised that firms focusing on low costs would benefit most from traditional accounting and activity-based techniques. In their survey of 78 manufacturing firms, Chenhall and Langfield-Smith found the expected relationship between firms selecting differentiation positions and the management accounting techniques of benchmarking (both internally and with outside organisations), employee-based measures and strategic planning techniques. However, they were surprised to find that traditional accounting techniques also provided high benefits to these firms. Of the firms with a low-cost strategy, activity-based techniques were associated with higher performance, as expected by the authors. However, some of these firms also derived benefits from techniques such as benchmarking and strategic planning. Similarly, Lord's (1996) case study of a bicycle manufacturer with differentiated products found the expected lack of emphasis on budgets and variance analysis, but instead of emphasising marketing costs, the firm collected and analysed information on competitors.

Cooper (1996) claimed that lean enterprises do not compete on either differentiation or cost leadership; instead they 'collide'. That is, they 'introduce products that match their competitors' offerings so rapidly that it makes it virtually impossible for any firm to sustain a competitive advantage . . . they are forced to compete by repeatedly creating temporary [advantages]' (Cooper, 1996, p. 219). This 'confrontation' strategy entails a trade-off between cost, quality and functionality. Firms using this strategy will place heavy reliance on their suppliers and will have relationships with suppliers that include information sharing, even perhaps combining their research and development, product innovation and cost-reduction ideas. Cooper claimed that 'firms adopting the confrontation strategy must develop integrated quality, functionality, and cost management systems' (p. 228) which enable them to have low-cost products.

In his research in Japanese firms following a confrontational strategy, Cooper (1996) identified six cost management practices. Feed-forward controls included target costing, value engineering and inter-organisational systems (with suppliers). Feedback systems included product costing focusing on product lines and interdependencies between products, operational control through variance analysis, and kaizen (continuous improvement) costing. Cooper claimed that the feed-forward techniques were effective when firms were competing on functionality, that feedback techniques were effective for those competing on price, and that integration of kaizen costing and TQM would benefit firms competing on quality.

Another typology for strategic positioning is that of Miles and Snow (1978), who classified three successful strategies – Prospector, Defender and Analyser – and an unsuccessful strategic position – Reactor. The Prospector firm is an innovator, always searching for market opportunities and experimenting with ways to respond to potential trends. 'The Prospector's prime capability is that of finding and exploiting new product and market opportunities' (p. 55). The Defender firm, in contrast, is a stable organisation focused on a healthy but narrow product-market domain. The Defender searches for ways of improving the efficiency of its existing operations, 'reducing manufacturing and distribution costs while simultaneously maintaining or improving product quality' (p. 37). The Analyser firm is a combination of the Prospector and the Defender, operating in both stable and changing product-market domains. The Analyser is concerned with 'how to locate and exploit new product and market opportunities while simultaneously maintaining a firm core of traditional products and customers' (p. 70). The Reactor firm does not respond effectively to change and uncertainty in its environment, because it lacks a viable strategy, or its strategy, structure and processes are not linked appropriately, or because it has not changed its strategy to remain relevant to changed environmental conditions.

Using Miles and Snow's classification, Simons (1987) divided his sample of 171 firms into Prospectors and Defenders in order to determine the kinds of control systems expected in each type of firm. He hypothesised that Prospectors would emphasise individual creativity and innovation rather than accounting controls. He found that forecasting, especially qualitatively, setting tight budget goals and carefully monitoring outputs were important for high-performing Prospector firms. Large Prospector firms emphasised frequent reporting and used customised control systems. Cost control did not seem to be important for Prospectors. Prospector firms were aggressive in obtaining informal information about competitor activities through, for example, photographing equipment at trade shows, tracking government legislation and even using spies.

Simons hypothesised that Defenders would emphasise formal accounting procedures, especially cost control. He found, as expected, that Defenders paid bonuses based on achievement of budget targets and had stable control systems. Large Defenders placed little importance on tight budget goals and output monitoring. Unexpectedly, however, Defenders did not appear to emphasise cost control.

Anderson and Lanen (1999) also investigated the relationship between Prospector and Defender strategies and management accounting emphases. They found that Prospectors placed greater importance on long-range plans. Defenders placed greater importance on cost data when preparing budgets and made more intensive use of these data, made more effort to measure both their own and their suppliers' quality, and assessed their on-time delivery to customers. They were surprised to discover that Prospectors claimed greater success in meeting their budgets and that there was no difference in the extent of collection of cost data between the two groups.

This section has shown that there are some differences between the theoretical emphases of strategic management accounting and emphases in practice. Even if the strategic position of firms can be classified as cost leadership, differentiation, focus or confrontation, or if the firms can be categorised as Prospectors, Defenders, Analysers or Reactors, the consequent emphases of their management accounting systems cannot be predicted. There is scope for further research on the relationship between firms' strategic positions and management accounting systems in practice.

The value chain perspective

The value chain perspective on strategic management accounting includes value chain analysis, cost driver analysis and competitive advantage analysis. Each is now covered in turn.

Value chain analysis

The value chain is 'the linked set of value-creating activities all the way from basic raw material sources for component suppliers through to the ultimate end-use product delivered into the final consumers' hands' (Shank, 1989, p. 50). Porter (1985) suggested that firms should analyse their own value chain, identifying activities which add value within the firm and their associated cost. Linkages, or 'relationships between the way one value activity is performed and the cost of performance of another' (Porter, 1985, p. 48) could then be identified, providing opportunities for optimising, coordinating and reconfiguring these activities.

Illustrating this point, Lord (1996) described how a small cycle manufacturer made cost savings by exploiting linkages within the company. For example, cost savings were made by working with employees to design an acceptable employment contract and involving them in innovations in design and set-ups.

The firm's value chain is joined to the value chains of suppliers and customers. Thus linkages are not only to be found within the value chain of a firm, but also between firms and their suppliers and customers. For example, Lord (1996) found that the cycle manufacturer achieved cost savings on freight by arranging with overseas suppliers in the same country to consolidate their orders into one shipping container, and by positioning its after-sales warehouse where it could obtain cheaper air freight rates. The cycle manufacturer also enhanced its desirability to customers and its points of differentiation by offering customised products, high quality and fast delivery.

Exploiting linkages, within the firm's own value chain and between the value chains of the firm, its suppliers and its customers, can result in lower costs and therefore a competitive advantage. Also most value chain activities are potential sources of differentiation, as they affect the specifications, quality and performance of the product.

Shank and Govindarajan (1992a) compared value chain analysis with traditional net present value analysis for a major forest products firm. The firm was vertically integrated, from research on trees through to distribution of paper and wood products. However, the logging operations were carried out by private contractors. The forest products firm was evaluating whether or not to introduce another technology for felling trees. Using a traditional investment appraisal tool, net present value (NPV), showed that the returns to the logger from the present technology and the new technology were virtually identical. Therefore there was no incentive for the logger to make a change. However, using value chain analysis, it became evident that major savings for the forest products firm could be made from the change, but in parts of the value chain other than the logging operations. Value chain analysis, with its broader perspective, revealed aspects relevant to the decision that were ignored by NPV.

Shank and Govindarajan (1992b) also evaluated a strategic positioning choice by a packaging company. The company was considering whether to continue emphasising a commodity product with a declining market, or whether to build market share with a differentiated product in a growing market that demanded high quality. Traditional analyses, such as calculating internal rate of return and carrying out portfolio analysis, were compared to value chain analysis. The portfolio analysis implied that the company should 'harvest' in the commodity market and build market share in the differentiated product market, with an internal rate of return predicted at 13 per cent. Value chain analysis included the value created by both markets: supermarkets and convenience stores which took the commodity product, and processors which demanded high quality because the packaging was an important part of their marketing strategy. Value chain analysis, because it included the market structure, provided 'dramatically different strategic insights' (Shank and Govindarajan, 1992b, p. 193), showing that the company lacked the product quality to compete in the differentiated market, and that it needed to find ways of reducing cost to effectively compete in the commodity market.

Cooper and Slagmulder (2004) showed how some Japanese firms exploit linkages between suppliers and buyers with cost savings to both parties. Collaborations range from limited interactions, in which trade-offs between functionality, price and quality are negotiated, through to cost investigations, in which significant changes may be made to the design of the purchased item and the specification of the product in which it is to be used. Also, interactions between the buyers' and the suppliers' design engineers may lead to major changes in both the components being purchased and the product in which they are being used. Cost-saving trade-offs may arise from relaxing specifications for the purchased item, or inter-organisational cost investigations may result in the redesign of components or end products so that some activities are performed more efficiently or avoided altogether. Occasionally suppliers' and buyers' engineers may spend time at each other's premises, so they can provide input at the design stage of both components and end products which will result in overall cost reductions.

Activity-based costing could be used to analyse linkages with suppliers. Costs of batch activities to do with processing orders (such as ordering, receiving, inspecting, returning, moving, paying and storing) could be determined using activity-based costing. Similarly, product-related costs (such as maintaining specifications) and vendor-sustaining costs (such as negotiating with suppliers, maintaining files, and evaluating potential new suppliers) could be determined. If these costs were then added to the purchase price, the analysis would reveal which suppliers are worth dealing with. As a result of the analysis, firms could develop long-term relationships with a reduced number of suppliers who have contracts that guarantee specified levels of quality, delivery times and price.

Dekker (2003) analysed the value chain between suppliers and a UK supermarket chain, Sainsbury. The logistics department at Sainsbury developed an activity-based costing model. First, they determined both Sainsbury's and their major suppliers' activities in supplying products to the store shelves. Then they identified the cost drivers for the activities. Participating suppliers gave Sainsbury cost data and cost driver quantities. Analyses of the activity-based costing model outputs were discussed with suppliers in order to generate cost-reduction ideas. If improvements had unequal benefits for suppliers and Sainsbury, allocation of the benefits was negotiated. Sainsbury added to the value chain approach by benchmarking individual suppliers against the whole supplier network; that is, 'a number of value chains . . . were compared with each other within and across different supplier networks . . . [enabling] Sainsbury to manage not only the supply chains with individual suppliers, but also to manage the efficiency of the larger supplier network' (p. 20).

Similarly, techniques such as activity-based costing could be applied to activities between customers and the firm. The revenues from customers and the costs incurred in dealing with them could be calculated to determine whether particular customers are profitable or not. The firm could then work with unprofitable customers to find ways of reducing costs so the customers become profitable. For example, the Harvard Business School Kanthal case reports how a Swedish company analysed their customers' profitability using activity-based costing to find that only 40 per cent of their customers were profitable. By raising prices and imposing surcharges and handling charges, the company induced its customers to order customised products in larger volumes. Other cost-saving changes included replacing sales representative visits by on-line ordering and converting a customer who made many small orders into a distributor.

Life-cycle costing, that is, the determination of total costs from the time a product idea is conceived, through design, manufacture and use, to its disposal at the end of its life, could be used to determine the value chain costs. However, Shields and Young (1991) found that although managing the product's life cycle is important for competitive success, the nine aerospace and electronics firms they studied emphasised costs at the manufacturing stage of the life cycle rather than during the pre-manufacturing and post-manufacturing stages. Guilding *et al.* (2000) also found little usage of life-cycle costing by large NZ, UK and US firms.

Of the above examples of value chain analysis, it is unclear whether Shank and Govindarajan's were actually used for the decision-making process of the firms or if they were applied by the authors after the event to show how value chain analysis would have helped managers make a better decision. Nevertheless, several research studies have found value chain linkages being exploited in practice, thus extending management accounting information to consider the firm's involvement in the whole life cycle of the product, giving a strategic context.

Cost driver analysis

Both Porter (1985) and Shank (1989) advocated determining the causes ('drivers') of costs for each value activity. Shank (1989) divided his list of cost drivers into structural drivers, to do with the underlying economic structure of the firm, and executional drivers, to do with the firm's ability to 'execute' or carry out its business. (See Table 7.3: note that each of Porter's drivers is listed alongside the comparable Shank driver, but Porter

Table 7.3 **Cost drivers**

Porter (1985)	Shank (1989)
Structural cost drivers	
Scale	Scale
Integration	Scope
Learning	Experience
	Technology
	Complexity
Timing ('first-mover' or 'follower')	
Location	
Discretionary policies (e.g. product mix, delivery time, production scheduling)	
Institutional factors (e.g. government regulation, unionisation, tariffs)	
Executional cost drivers	
	Workforce commitment
	Total quality management
Capacity utilisation	Capacity utilisation
	Plant layout efficiency
Linkages	Exploiting linkages
Interrelationships	

did not divide drivers into executional and structural.) Shank claimed that an improvement in executional drivers will always result in lower costs; i.e. they are drivers of cost *reduction* rather than of cost incidence. An increase in structural drivers, however, could result in either increases or decreases in costs. For example, costs may decrease as the scale or scope of the business increases but at some point there are diseconomies of scale and scope. The choices the firm makes about the levels of each of the cost drivers and their relative importance determine the firm's cost position, and therefore its competitive position.

In Shank and Govindarajan's (1992a) example of a forest products company's choice of logging technology, cost drivers also provided insight into making the strategic choice. Technology was the critical structural cost driver. Shank and Govindarajan decided that other structural drivers were of minor importance in this context. They then compared the critical structural driver with the executional drivers, 'to see if they offset or reinforce[d] the structural impact of the technology factor' (p. 48). They decided that participative management, a philosophy of continuous improvement, and total quality management were all important, and that they all supported the new technology being considered. Linkages between the firm and the contract loggers were equally important. Shank and Govindarajan suggested that the firm should look at ways to share the potential benefits (identified in the value chain analysis) to induce the logger to accept the new technology. Another option was for the firm to vertically integrate and re-enter the logging business. However, diseconomies of vertical scope seemed to rule out this option, unless the logger demanded a disproportionate share of the potential benefits.

Porter, Shank and Govindarajan all claim that analysis and comparison of the relative importance of structural and executional cost drivers can be a useful and important addition to traditional management accounting information, enabling better strategic decision-making.

Competitive advantage analysis

Value chain analysis can be extended to the analysis of competitors' value chains. Porter (1985) suggested collecting as much information as possible about competitors so their value chains can be estimated, including both activities performed and their costs. The total costs of competitors' value chains can then be compared. If the total cost of performing all the value activities in the firm's value chain is lower than that of its competitors, the firm has a cost advantage. This cost advantage is sustainable if the firm's sources of cost advantage are difficult for competitors to copy. If the firm does not have a cost advantage, they may achieve it by reducing costs through controlling cost drivers of value chain activities, or by reconfiguring the value chain, for example by adopting a more efficient way to design, produce, distribute and/or market the product.

The section on the value chain perspective has shown that there is ample evidence of value chain and cost driver analyses being carried out in practice. However, the extension of competitive advantage analysis does not yet appear to be researched or documented.

Market-oriented information

Another perspective on strategic management accounting is customer-oriented: collecting market information on product attributes desired by the customer, and then producing the product at a price the customer will pay.

Bromwich (1990) claimed that competitive advantage is achieved in the market. He suggested analysing the attributes of products and what differentiates them and makes them desirable to customers. These attributes include operating performance, reliability, warranty arrangements, the degree of finish and trim, assurance of supply, and after-sales service. Once the attributes desired by customers have been determined, the firm needs to produce products with those attributes at a competitive cost level.

One tool to enable this is target costing. The marketing department determines the price the market will pay and likely sales volumes. The target cost is determined by subtracting the desired profit margin from the selling price. Then a team made up from many functions in the firm, such as designers, production supervisors, engineers, marketing personnel and finance people, carries out an iterative process of designing the product and production process so that the product can be made for the target cost.

This focus on the price the market will pay was included in Guilding *et al.*'s (2000) term 'strategic pricing'. In their questionnaire, they defined strategic pricing as the analysis of such factors as 'competitor price reaction; price elasticity; market growth; economies of scale; and experience' (p. 132) in the process of deciding on prices. They found that strategic pricing was used by large NZ, UK and US firms, but target costing was little used.

Although it is some time since Bromwich advocated a market focus, there is little evidence of management accounting explicitly including market-related aspects. Nor does practice reveal expected differences in management accounting emphasis for particular strategic positions. However, as shown above, the strategic management accounting elements of competitor information and value chain and cost driver analysis can be observed in use.

Criticisms of strategic management accounting

The previous sections have described how the concept of strategic management accounting has arisen and what components it might have. Examples from research show that there is some use of these components in practice. However, since its inception, strategic management accounting has had its critics. Some of the criticisms of strategic management and strategic management accounting are reviewed next.

The strategic planning process

Nyamori *et al.* (2001, p. 63) criticised the literature on strategic management accounting for not questioning 'what strategy is, how it is formed, how it comes to change, and how strategic change constitutes and is constituted by accounting'. They argued that there is a considerable body of literature on strategy and strategic management, but only parts of it are cited in papers on strategic management accounting.

For example, Mintzberg (1978) pointed out that strategies are not always a result of strategic planning. The types of organisation in which strategic plans are likely to be achieved as planned are those with highly ordered, neatly integrated processes, or entrepreneurial firms where a powerful leader makes bold, risky decisions to implement his or her vision. However, in other firms strategies may fall out of a process of conflict and bargaining between many decision-makers, or may emerge from interactions between management, employees and the environment. Sometimes a series of decisions may show some consistency or a pattern, which is then called a strategy in hindsight. But, this strategy was not necessarily deliberate. Also some planned strategies may never be achieved.

Dermer (1990) labelled the strategic planning/positioning school 'teleological', that is, 'predicated on the assumption that organizations are purposeful cohesive systems and that issues and support are controlled by management' (p. 68). Under the teleological view, the success of the system is measured by managerial effectiveness in coping with external events. Dermer advocated consideration of the ecological viewpoint as well, which starts from the assumption that any organisation has multiple stakeholders who are all trying to satisfy themselves. Each stakeholder will present his or her point of view, supported with relevant data, and the resulting 'emergent' strategy will depend on the strength of each stakeholder's case. That is, strategy is not always planned; it often just happens. Emergent strategies arise from decisions on separate issues dealt with singly: the pattern that emerges can only be seen in retrospect.

Dermer (1990) claimed that, taking a view of strategic change as an unplanned result of conflicting stakeholders contending for control, protagonists may be using accounting 'in ways not anticipated by accountants' (p. 75). Accounting could be used as a language of discourse, as a powerful way of establishing and maintaining the credibility of those using it, and as a way of providing a history 'establishing the context of agenda setting' (p. 74).

The descriptions of the components of strategic management accounting in the previous section are based on the assumption that strategies are planned and then achieved as planned. Strategic management accounting is seen as providing information to help with making strategic decisions. If, however, the deliberateness of strategy formation is questioned, the usefulness or even the very existence of something called strategic management accounting is also questioned.

Even if one accepts that there are deliberate strategies that are achieved, the usefulness and validity of the components of strategic management accounting can also be questioned, as outlined next.

Competitor analysis

Harari (1994, p. 38) warns against becoming too focused on competitor analysis: 'conventional competitive analysis is . . . tantamount to driving a car on the highway looking side to side at "competitor" cars while ignoring the road ahead'. Firms that concentrate too much on competitors tend to just match competitors action by action. Instead, firms can compete and gain an advantage by being innovative and doing something completely different to competitors.

The promoters of competitor analysis also do not seem to recognise the possibility of alliances with competitors – the benefits of competitors stated by Porter (1985), and the opportunities for cooperation illustrated by Bengtsson and Kock (1999). Competitor analysis still has military overtones of enmity.

Carr and Tomkins (1996) found that strategically oriented German companies analysed strategic considerations thoroughly, but were critical of formal strategic planning techniques such as SWOT, value chain, competitor and market analyses. Instead they used intuition, a feeling for the product and the market, and a knowledge of customer needs based on close relationships with customers. German companies examined value chain issues and ensured that their investments secured competitive advantages, but without emphasising financial calculations. That is, there is a role for intuition or managerial judgement in strategic decision-making – decisions are not always made based on financial analysis.

These authors are warning that competitor analysis, a proposed component of strategic management accounting, may not be a good thing if carried out too often or relied on exclusively without consideration of intuitive, immeasurable aspects.

The value chain perspective

Lord (1996) showed how a small cycle manufacturer exploited linkages in the value chain without the need for financial analysis. She claimed that firms with effective operational management processes would already be finding cost-saving opportunities, and firms with a focus on customer and supplier relationships would automatically be exploiting linkages without formal analyses, such as those demonstrated by Shank and Govindarajan (1992a, 1992b). In other words, value chain linkages and cost-saving opportunities may be being recognised and acted upon without accounting analyses being carried out, that is, without the need for strategic management accounting.

The role of the accountant

Whether there is a role for the accountant in strategic decision-making has been questioned. There are a few cases of strategic management accounting highlighting a role for accountants. Rickwood et al. (1990) presented an example of strategic management accounting led by a management accountant who, because of his position of authority in the organisation, was able to pressure the marketing department into giving him the competitor information they held. He used this information for strategic decision-making when the firm was threatened by a competitor's action. Collier and Gregory (1995) also gave examples of accountants being involved in collecting competitor information.

On the other hand, several cases studies report the use of techniques like strategic management accounting, but not by accountants. Lord (1996) described a firm that was using many of the components of strategic management accounting. However, the techniques were employed by production, marketing and management personnel, with no input from the management accountant. Cunningham's (1992) field study of three transportation companies found that marketing had an extensive influence on the management accounting systems, and that 'accounting-type activities take place outside the accounting function and are performed by persons who do not consider themselves to be accountants' (pp. 94–5). Indeed, interviewees claimed that the influence of marketing rather than accounting was a major contributor to the success of their competitive strategy.

Kawada and Johnson (1993) reported that at Teijin Seiki 'it is an ironclad rule to start . . . with a complete . . . survey of changes in the external business environment, including regulation, the economy, resource availability, technology, competition, the market, and so on' (p. 37). However, they argued that production, sales and engineering personnel, not accounting people, should carry out strategic management accounting.

Chenhall and Langfield-Smith (1998b) examined a company, Cleanco, that had identified strategic priorities of enhancing customer satisfaction and reducing costs in order to sustain their competitive advantage. Measures were developed on the shop-floor by team members and manufacturing managers. Although these measures did not always support strategic priorities, the management accountants were not interested in being involved in the development of more strategically driven performance measures. Chenhall and Langfield-Smith found a similar lack of involvement at two further firms, Containers and Coalcorp. This contrasted strongly with the other two firms in their study, Chemco and FoodInc, in which management accountants were closely involved in the development of performance measures to support changes in strategy. Chenhall and Langfield-Smith concluded that 'in organizations that have adopted team-based structures, accountants who continue to derive their authority from their position in a formal hierarchy are likely to have difficulty being accepted by teams' (p. 382). These findings imply that if strategic management accounting is to be useful in supplying information for strategic decisions, it needs to be developed by management accountants in a team context, with input and involvement from a range of disciplines, such as marketing, production and design personnel, as well as accountants.

Coad (1996) claimed that strategic management accountants need to be oriented towards learning new skills and mastering tasks. They will prefer challenges, and consider errors and mistakes to be part of the learning process. Strategic management accountants also need 'good communication skills and an ability to empathize with others both within and outside the organization' (p. 404). Coad's case illustrated how a small part of a larger organisation could carry out strategic management accounting without the need for the whole organisation to be committed to it.

The debate about the role of the accountant in providing information that will be useful in strategic decision-making is a warning to management accountants. Unless they can learn to work in teams, contributing their strengths in data collection and analysis to the strengths of other team members, it is possible that something like strategic management accounting may develop without any involvement of accountants.

Conclusion

This chapter has traced the developments in strategic management, and deficiencies in traditional management accounting, that have given rise to strategic management accounting. The literature and research on strategic management accounting indicate that it comprises: the collection of information about competitors; a matching of accounting emphases with the strategic position chosen by the firm; exploitation of cost-reduction opportunities shown by value chain, cost driver and competitive advantage analyses; and the use of customer/marketing information.

However, except for competitor pricing and competitor accounting, Guilding *et al.* (2000) found little use of strategic management accounting. Although there are examples of aspects of strategic management accounting in use, there is scope for more research, particularly on the relationship between strategic positioning and management accounting techniques, on the relationship between marketing and management accounting, and seeking to find out whether firms compare their value chains with their competitors'.

The concept of strategic management accounting may need to be further developed to show its role in emergent strategy and its benefits in strategy formulation. Also the applicability of strategic management accounting in global markets might be explored. For example, is it even feasible to carry out competitor analyses when competitors are in differing economic, political and cultural settings? Can value chains be compared across countries?

Although the topic of strategic management accounting is now included in many management accounting courses and professional bodies' requirements, Guilding *et al.* (2000) found that the term 'strategic management accounting' is rarely used in organisations and that appreciation of its meaning is limited. Also, the research examples in this chapter indicate that if accountants want to be involved with strategic management accounting they will need to work together with other functions, such as marketing and production, in the collection and analysis of data. Perhaps today's students, who have been exposed to both the debate over strategic management accounting and the need to be a team player, will be the ones to disseminate the concept of strategic management accounting in their workplaces when they finish their education and are involved in its implementation.

References

Anderson, S.W. and Lanen, W.N. (1999) 'Economic transition, strategy and the evolution of management accounting practices: the case of India', *Accounting, Organizations and Society,* **24,** 379–412.

Bengtsson, M. and Kock, S. (1999) 'Cooperation and competition in relationships between competitors in business networks', *Journal of Business & Industrial Marketing,* **14,** 178–94.

Bowman, E.H. (1990) 'Strategy changes: possible worlds and actual minds', in J.W. Fredrickson (ed.), *Perspectives on Strategic Management,* New York: Harper Business, pp. 9–37.

Bromwich, M. (1990) 'The case for strategic management accounting: the role of accounting information for strategy in competitive markets', *Accounting, Organizations and Society,* **15,** 27–46.

Carr, C. and Tomkins, C. (1996) 'Strategic investment decisions: the importance of SCM. A comparative analysis of 51 case studies in U.K., U.S. and German companies', *Management Accounting Research,* **7,** 199–217.

Chenhall, R.H. and Langfield-Smith, K. (1998a) 'The relationship between strategic priorities, management techniques and management accounting: an empirical investigation using a systems approach', *Accounting, Organizations and Society, 23*, 243–64.

Chenhall, R.H. and Langfield-Smith, K. (1998b) 'Factors influencing the role of management accounting in the development of performance measures within organizational change programs', *Management Accounting Research, 9*, 361–86.

Coad, A. (1996) 'Smart work and hard work: explicating a learning orientation in strategic management accounting', *Management Accounting Research, 7*, 387–408.

Collier, P. and Gregory, A. (1995) 'Strategic management accounting: a UK hotel sector case study', *International Journal of Contemporary Hospitality Management, 7*, 16–21.

Cooper, R. (1996) 'Costing techniques to support corporate strategy: evidence from Japan', *Management Accounting Research, 7*, 219–46.

Cooper, R. and Slagmulder, R. (2004) 'Interorganizational cost management and relational context', *Accounting, Organizations and Society, 29*, 1–26.

Cunningham, G.M. (1992) 'Management control and accounting systems under a competitive strategy', *Accounting, Auditing & Accountability Journal, 5*, 85–102.

Dekker, H.C. (2003) 'Value chain analysis in interfirm relationships: a field study', *Management Accounting Research, 14*, 1–23.

Dermer, J. (1990) 'The strategic agenda: accounting for issues and support', *Accounting, Organizations and Society, 15*, 67–76.

Gordon, L.A., Larcker, D.F. and Tuggle, F.D. (1978) 'Strategic decision processes and the design of accounting information systems: conceptual linkages', *Accounting, Organizations and Society, 3*, 203–13.

Guilding, C., Cravens, K.S. and Tayles, M. (2000) 'An international comparison of strategic management accounting practices', *Management Accounting Research, 11*, 113–35.

Harari, O. (1994) 'The hypnotic danger of competitive analysis', *Management Review, 83*, 36–8.

Kawada, M. and Johnson, D. (1993) 'Strategic management accounting: why and how', *Management Accounting (NAA), 75*, 32–8.

Lord, B.R. (1996) 'Strategic management accounting: the emperor's new clothes?' *Management Accounting Research, 7*, 347–66.

Miles, R.E. and Snow, C.G. (1978) *Organizational Strategy, Structure, and Process*, New York: McGraw-Hill.

Mintzberg, H. (1978) 'Patterns in strategy formulation', *Management Science, 24*, 934–48.

Nyamori, R.O., Perera, M.H.B. and Lawrence, S.R. (2001) 'The concept of strategic change and implications for management accounting research', *Journal of Accounting Literature, 20*, 62–83.

Porter, M.E. (1980) *Competitive Strategy: Techniques for Analyzing Industries and Competitors*, New York: The Free Press.

Porter, M.E. (1985) *Competitive Advantage: Creating and Sustaining Superior Performance*, New York: The Free Press.

Rickwood, C.P., Coates, J.B. and Stacey, R.J. (1990) 'Stapylton: strategic management accounting to gain competitive advantage', *Management Accounting Research, 1*, 37–49.

Shank, J.K. (1989) 'Strategic cost management: new wine, or just new bottles?' *Journal of Management Accounting Research, 1*, 47–65.

Shank, J.K. and Govindarajan, V. (1992a) 'Strategic cost analysis of technological investments', *Sloan Management Review, 34*, 39–51.

Shank, J.K. and Govindarajan, V. (1992b) 'Strategic cost management: the value chain perspective', *Journal of Management Accounting Research, 4*, 179–97.

Shields, M.D. and Young, S.M. (1991) 'Managing product life cycle costs: an organizational model', *Journal of Cost Management,* **5**, 39–52.

Simmonds, K. (1981) 'Strategic management accounting', *Management Accounting (CIMA),* **59**, 26–9.

Simons, R. (1987) 'Accounting control systems and business strategy: an empirical analysis', *Accounting, Organizations and Society,* **12**, 357–74.

Tricker, R.I. (1989) 'The management accountant as strategist', *Management Accounting (CIMA),* **67**, 26–8.

Wilson, R.M.S. (1995) 'Strategic management accounting', in D. Ashton, T. Hopper and R. Scapens (eds), *Issues in Management Accounting,* 2nd edn, London: Prentice Hall, pp. 163–4.

Further reading

The following four articles provide examples of strategic management accounting in use:

Coad, A. (1996) 'Smart work and hard work: explicating a learning orientation in strategic management accounting', *Management Accounting Research,* **7**, 387–408.

Collier, P. and Gregory, A. (1995) 'Strategic management accounting: a UK hotel sector case study', *International Journal of Contemporary Hospitality Management,* **7**, 16–21.

Dekker, H.C. (2003) 'Value chain analysis in interfirm relationships: a field study', *Management Accounting Research,* **14**, 1–23.

Rickwood, C.P., Coates, J.B. and Stacey, R.J. (1990) 'Stapylton: strategic management accounting to gain competitive advantage', *Management Accounting Research,* **1**, 37–49.

The following paper provides an example of value chain, cost driver and competitive advantage analysis:

Shank, J.K. and Govindarajan, V. (1992) 'Strategic cost analysis of technological investments', *Sloan Management Review,* **34**, 39–51.

8

Activity-based costing and management: a critical review

Maria Major

Introduction

In the late 1980s, following the publication by the Harvard Business School of several case studies on 'innovative' costing practices by American firms, a 'new' cost accounting approach was advanced by Cooper and Kaplan. This was initially called 'transaction costing' (Johnson and Kaplan, 1987) but soon became known as 'activity-based costing' (ABC).

The Harvard case studies were based on practical experiments by Cooper, Kaplan and colleagues in firms such as Schrader Bellows and John Deere Component Works. Together with Johnson's 1986 Weyerhaeuser Corporation study, they were milestones in the development of ABC as they were the first cases to illustrate how it would aid management (Jones and Dugdale, 2002).

The development of ABC has been described as associated with two important networks (Jones and Dugdale, 2002): the 'Harvard network', led by Kaplan and Cooper and later joined by Johnson; and the 'Computer-Aided Manufacturing, International (CAM-I) network', later entitled 'Consortium for Advanced Manufacturing, International' (see Jones and Dugdale, 2002). The sponsors of CAM-I were organisations concerned to improve cost management practices, including the largest USA manufacturing firms, big professional accountancy firms and government agencies. Both the Harvard and CAM-I networks described conventional management accounting systems as obsolete and inadequate, claiming they prevented organisations from enhancing efficiency and profitability and impeded the ability of American firms to compete successfully (Johnson, 1992; Jones and Dugdale, 2002). Traditional management accounting was described as being in a major 'crisis' because it could not provide managers with relevant information. ABC systems were advocated as the solution for restoring the relevance of accounting. ABC was described as a 'revolutionary' cost management system that, if appropriately implemented, would enable American firms to recover their competitiveness and profitability.

Since its inception in the 1980s, ABC has received considerable attention from consultants, business schools and the business media (Innes and Mitchell, 1998; Jones and Dugdale, 2002). It has increased in popularity and attracted new adherents by changing its features and core arguments in response to its opponents' criticisms. Two main phases of ABC development have been identified (Jones and Dugdale, 2002): first, until the late 1980s ABC was applied mainly to product costing, that is to obtain unitary product costs;

second, from the 1990s until today it has been used to provide managers with a better understanding of costs through the identification of activities, hence aiding managers in managing their organisations' activities. ABC has thus evolved from a simple cost accounting approach into a management approach labelled 'activity-based management' (ABM); to reflect this change its acronym has shifted from ABC to ABC/M (activity-based costing/management) (Jones and Dugdale, 2002).

This chapter provides a critical review of the ABC/M approach that incorporates technical, historical, economic and behavioural aspects of its emergence, implementation and operation. The chapter begins by exploring the circumstances in which ABC/M emerged; to this end, Johnson and Kaplan's (1987) perspective on the historical development of management accounting is reviewed and the new competitive corporate environment is described. The chapter continues with a discussion of how ABC/M is not entirely new, then its main features and mechanics are described. The next section analyses how ABC evolved into ABC/M, then reviews studies on ABC/M implementation. The chapter ends with an evaluation of ABC/M and conclusions.

The emergence of ABC/M

Conventional management accounting was criticised by ABC/M advocates as giving inadequate support to managerial decision-making as it had not altered since the early twentieth century, despite the business environment having undergone radical changes since the 1960s. This is discussed below, initially with a review of Johnson and Kaplan's (1987) account of USA management accounting history and how cost management had stagnated, and then with a description of the main changes in the corporate environment after the 1960s and their effects on management accounting.

Management accounting in the 1980s according to Johnson and Kaplan

Johnson and Kaplan (1987) outlined their claims about the obsolescence of management accounting in a controversial book *Relevance Lost: The Rise and Fall of Management Accounting*, which reviewed USA management accounting practices over the last century from the perspective of transaction cost economics. According to the authors, all management accounting techniques used in the 1980s, such as budgeting, standard costing, variance analysis, transfer pricing and divisional performance measures, had been developed in American firms by 1925. The emergence of large hierarchical organisations in the mid nineteenth century, in textile and steel manufacturing and in transportation and distribution, partly explains why management accounting developed in the late nineteenth and early twentieth centuries. These organisations became too complex to manage without regular and relevant management accounting information. Developments in management accounting were fuelled by the Scientific Management movement of the late nineteenth and early twentieth centuries. Standards for material and labour costs were devised from physical standards (material quantities per unit, labour hours per unit), which were used to improve internal efficiency. The growth of multi-activity and diversi-fied organisations (like DuPont Powder Company) in the early twentieth century demanded further developments in management accounting. Innovations such as budgeting and the return on investment (ROI) measure were conceived to enhance internal motivation and to evaluate the performance of operating units and entire organisations.

Johnson and Kaplan argued that management accounting failed to keep pace with the evolution of technology and business after 1925. One of the main reasons they gave to explain the decline of management accounting was its subservience to financial accounting. They claimed that, subsequent to the growth of firms and their dispersion of capital, stock markets acquired an important role in sustaining eco-nomic activity. Financial statements – namely the balance sheet and profit and loss statement – had to be prepared regularly to report the financial and economic position of firms. Auditors and regulators became key actors in assuring firms' stakeholders that financial reports were based on objective, verifiable and realised financial transactions. They preferred conservative accounting practices when auditing external financial reports. Auditors were not primarily concerned with whether overheads were being traced to their cause or whether 'adequate' alloca-tion procedures were followed in product costing, since their main objective was to derive inventory values from the historical transactions recorded in a firm's ledger. As a result, simple methods of indirect cost allocation based on direct labour hours or direct labour costs were adopted, and the main role of management accounting became the provision of data for inventory valuation. However, empirical studies of UK firms conducted in the early 1980s found no evidence that management accounting was subservient to financial accounting (see Hopper et al., 1992). This suggests that more studies are needed to investigate the reliability of Johnson and Kaplan's claim.

Johnson and Kaplan further claimed that early in the twentieth century the use of allocation bases related to volume (such as direct labour hours or direct labour cost) was not problematic, since firms' products were not diversified and direct costs formed the bulk of the cost structure. Volume bases were simpler to install, operate and comprehend than other methods. Moreover, the poor state of prevailing information technology prohibited the adoption of complex cost allocation meth-ods. The combination of poor information technology and the dominance of finan-cial accounting explain, in Johnson and Kaplan's view, why separate systems for management and financial reporting did not emerge until the 1980s, when cost management problems intensified due to drastic changes in the competitive envi-ronment and good information technology became more widely adopted.

The new competitive business environment

Business environment changes in the last decades of the twentieth century includ-ed the deregulation of markets, increased global competition, shortened product life cycles, and increased product lines (Innes and Mitchell, 1993, 1998). Firms responded to these changes by adopting new philosophies of production management and implementing automated information systems and manufacturing technologies.

Researchers have noted that although new automated technologies and production techniques – such as computer-aided design (CAD), computer-aided manufacturing (CAM), flexible manufacturing systems (FMS) and materials requirements planning (MRP) – were adopted in USA industry from the 1970s onwards, the 'old' management accounting systems developed in the early twentieth century continued to be used into the 1980s (Johnson and Kaplan, 1987; Cokins *et al.*, 1993). Furthermore, automated manufacturing technology increasingly affected how firms operated and placed new demands on information systems, while management accounting systems remained unchanged. Critics argued that traditional management accounting practices failed to support the demands of the new production environment, especially in the areas of product costing, investment appraisal and performance evaluation. Management accounting systems were accused of providing insufficient information for managers making these decisions.

For example, modern firms are undertaking new, more complex activities to enhance their competitiveness (Miller and Vollman, 1985). Product quality and variety have become critical factors in business success. Also, studies have indicated that in many industries overhead costs have significantly increased in absolute and relative terms, accompanied by a decrease in the proportion of direct labour costs (Innes and Mitchell, 1993, 1998). Moreover, overhead costs tend to vary less with production and sales volume, and more with the complexity of firms' activities (Cooper, 1990a). Miller and Vollman (1985) argued that overheads have risen dramatically because of the growing number of 'transactions' within firms (exchanges of information and materials needed to assist production).

The traditional use of product volume-related bases to allocate overheads to products was criticised for inadequately identifying the consumption of overheads by products (Cooper, 1990a; Innes and Mitchell, 1993, 1998). ABC/M advocates claimed that direct labour hours and direct labour costs, the most popular cost allocation bases, were designed for times when product volume was the most important determinant of overhead costs. Since modern overheads are mainly driven by complexity, they advocate alternative bases as more appropriate (Miller and Vollman, 1985; Johnson and Kaplan, 1987).

Origins of ABC/M systems

The origins of the ABC/M approach are commonly associated with Cooper and Kaplan and the Harvard Business School (and to a lesser degree CAM-I), but several researchers claim that ABC/M's basic concepts existed in accounting much earlier (Innes and Mitchell, 1998). For example, Drucker (1963), in writing 'Managing for Business Effectiveness' for the *Harvard Business Review*, referred to some of ABC/M's basic concepts. He alleged that cost accounting, which he described as intending 'to direct the resources and the efforts of the business toward opportunities for economically significant results' (p. 54), had been ineffective in helping managers do their jobs. To improve efficiency, Drucker suggested that managers should review how resources have been allocated and how they should be allocated in future to support the activities of greatest opportunity.

In his 1971 book *Activity Costing and Input–Output Accounting* (reprinted as part of Staubus, 1988), Staubus demonstrated similarities with Cooper and Kaplan's understanding of costing. Staubus claimed that 'decisions are made to do things' and that 'objectively measuring the economic effects of doing things are [sic] among the most valuable of accounting operations' (p. 23). Twenty years before ABC/M, Staubus defined the concepts of cost, objects of cost and costing in a similar way to ABC/M proponents. He suggested a conceptual framework for cost accounting, defining activities as the objects of costing. His framework was based on the principle that each major resource used should be identified and measured, and then traced to the objects of costing – activities.

Other developments were akin to ABC/M also. For instance, in the early 1960s General Electric (GE) developed an 'activity cost analysis' system, based on concepts analogous to ABC/M, to improve the quality of information about indirect costs. In 1963, a team appointed to reduce GE's indirect costs decided to analyse the firm's activities to determine their costs. They concluded that most indirect costs were triggered by upstream decisions not controllable in the departments where the costs were incurred. The GE team called the causes of activities, known in the ABC/M approach as 'cost drivers', 'key controlling parameters'. GE also developed advanced interviewing techniques to collect information about activities and cost drivers, and prepared a dictionary of activities (Johnson, 1992).

The activity-based cost management techniques developed by GE were subsequently licensed and developed by the Arthur Andersen & Co. consulting practice during the 1970s (Johnson, 1992). Arthur Andersen described the technique as 'cross-functional cost analysis' and replaced the term 'key controlling parameter' with 'cost generator'. Johnson, who in the 1990s recanted his belief in ABC/M, claims that 'GE's technique for activity-based cost analysis anticipates virtually everything that is claimed for present-day activity cost management systems' (Johnson, 1992, p. 137).

The development of planning-programming-budgeting systems (PPBS) in the USA Department of Defence may have been directly related to GE's development of activity cost analysis. PPBS was implemented in 1961 to improve resource allocation, cost control and the pricing of defence contracts. It was then adopted by GE's Research and Development unit in the 1960s, as a result of GE's contracts to provide equipment to the USA Department of Defence. Hence, there may have been a direct relationship between PPBS and GE's activity cost analysis practices in the 1960s (Scapens, 1991).

Considering all of these earlier developments, it may be that ABC/M is not as innovative as Cooper and Kaplan suggested. Indeed, several researchers have referred to it as 'old wine in new bottles' (Scapens, 1991; Jones and Dugdale, 2002). Various researchers and practitioners were already preoccupied with explaining cost causality before the emergence of ABC/M in the late 1980s.

Having discussed the origins of ABC/M, its main features and related concepts are presented next.

Features of ABC/M

Basic concepts

CAM-I, in its glossary of activity-based management (CAM-I, 1990), defined ABC as a method that assigns cost activities to cost objects such as products, services and customers, based on two main stages. The first stage pools costs to activities according to each activity's consumption of resources. The second stage assigns costs to cost objects based on their use of activities. The glossary described ABC/M as an approach that draws on ABC for key data and information for managing activities. Identifying activities (actions by firms to achieve their goals and objectives) plays a central role in both ABC and ABC/M. It may be possible to identify hundreds of activities in a large complex firm. These activities are usually described by a verb – examples include ordering raw materials, receiving materials, planning production, and setting up machines. Often firms identify activities using 'dictionaries of activities' that contain standard definitions (Cokins *et al.*, 1993). Four categories of activities can be defined according to their cost behaviour in an ABC system (Cooper, 1990a): (i) unit-level, which are directly related to the volume of production; (ii) batch-level, which vary by each production batch; (iii) product-sustaining, which are related to the production of each type of product; and (iv) facility-level, which support the entire process.

ABC makes two major assumptions: activities consume resources and cost objects consume activities (Cokins *et al.*, 1993). ABC emphasises understanding which factors drive activities, and how activities relate to products. Resource costs are assigned to activities using resource cost drivers (or first-stage allocation bases). Then, activity costs are traced to cost objects using activity cost drivers (or second-stage allocation bases). Cost drivers are the factors that determine the volume of work associated with each activity and its distribution across cost objects. There are unit, batch and product level cost drivers and, in a well-designed ABC system, these cost drivers should match activities (Cooper, 1990a). For example, when tracing unit-level activity costs to products, volume-sensitive bases (i.e. unit-level cost drivers) should be adopted. However, for batch-level or product-sustaining activities non-volume-related bases (i.e. batch-level or product-level cost drivers) should be used. If cost drivers fail to match activities product costs may be distorted, as the allocation basis will not link an activity's costs directly to the products that consume that activity.

Differentiating between ABC and traditioFnal cost accounting

Conventional cost accounting systems and ABC have some similarities (Innes and Mitchell, 1993). For instance, both have two stages whereby resource costs are pooled before being assigned to cost objects. The first stage pools indirect costs in production cost centres (in conventional systems) or in activity centres (in ABC systems). The second stage allocates overheads to cost objects using volume-related bases (in conventional systems) – usually direct-labour hours, direct-labour costs or machine-hours, or a mixture of both volume and non-volume-related bases (in ABC systems). However, despite these similarities several features differentiate the two systems. First, in traditional costing systems only manufacturing overheads are normally allocated to cost objects, whereas manufacturing and non-manufacturing overheads are assigned in ABC systems (Innes and Mitchell, 1993, 1998). The inclusion of non-production overheads in ABC is particularly useful for analysing product profitability by distribution channel, customer or market segment. Second, an ABC system usually has considerably more cost pools (based on activity centres) than a traditional system (based on production departments). Third, ABC uses more 'sophisticated' and complex allocation bases, particularly during the second stage of tracing costs to products. In an ABC system, batch-level and product-sustaining activity costs are allocated to cost objects using cost drivers other than unit-level ones (Cooper, 1990a). ABC advocates argue that these differences make ABC systems superior, as they provide managers with more reliable information about product costs. Conventional cost accounting practices are accused of frequently overestimating the costs of high-volume products and underestimating those of low-volume ones, especially when overheads are less related to volume – a characteristic of modern manufacturing (Miller and Vollman, 1985; Innes and Mitchell, 1998).

The mechanics of ABC

There are several steps in developing activity-based costing systems (Innes and Mitchell, 1993, 1998): (i) identifying activities; (ii) costing activities; (iii) selecting activity cost drivers; and (iv) allocating costs of activities to products. Each step is described below.

Identifying activities carried out within the organisation can be difficult, particularly because most organisations are used to¡ identifying functions rather than activities (Innes and Mitchell, 1993, 1998). An activity analysis may prove useful in profiling both mainstream and support activities. Interviews are often conducted with managers and employees to prepare an inventory of activities. Management accountants should be able to distinguish activities from actions or tasks conducted in the organisation, as an activity may be comprised of several actions and tasks. This stage is usually the most time-consuming, but also the most enlightening for managers as they can discover ways of eliminating waste and making improvements. According to Eiler and Ball (1993) interviews should focus on the following: listing activities in each area, concentrating on the most important and time-consuming; estimating the percentage of total time spent on each activity; discussing interviewees' opinions about which events trigger activities; obtaining information on volumes of transactions, runs and set-ups; and determining who and what are the major consumers of each area's activities (products, other departments or external customers).

The second step of ABC assigns resource costs to each activity according to the activities' consumption of resources. Often the costs of resources cannot be traced directly to activities because some resources (e.g. staff, equipment, buildings) are consumed by several activities (Innes and Mitchell, 1993). Collecting data on staff time involved in each activity can help assign labour costs to activities. Accountants should attempt to find ways of identifying causal relationships between activities and resources.

Activities' cost drivers are chosen in the third step. The system should accurately measure the various products' consumption of activities, though ideal cost drivers may not be available. Since activities usually cut across traditional departmental boundaries, flowcharts of the paths of costs and processes can help to provide a clear understanding of costs and their behaviour. Often alternative cost drivers emerge. In this case, management accountants should consider the costs associated with measuring costs drivers and use the cost–benefit criterion when choosing cost drivers (Innes and Mitchell, 1993, 1998).

Finally, activity costs are attributed to cost objects based on cost driver rates, which are calculated by dividing a period's activity costs by the period's cost driver volumes. A four-stage process is followed to assign activity costs to cost objects, namely: the computation of activity costs; the measurement of activity volume based on appropriate cost drivers (e.g. the number of purchase orders, hours of test time, number of component insertions, or number of customer calls); the calculation of activity cost driver rates; and the attribution of activity costs to cost objects by multiplying activity cost driver rates by cost driver volumes. Obtaining the costs per unit is facilitated if a bill of activities is prepared for each cost object. Final product costs are obtained by totalling the activity costs (both manufacturing and non-manufacturing) of each of the firm's products. The following example illustrates how ABC works.

Example: Comparison of traditional and activity-based costing systems

XYZ Ltd is a UK based firm established in 1995 to manufacture products X and Y. Details of the two products and relevant information for one period are given in Table 8.1.

Product X is produced in runs of 1,000 units and product Y in runs of 10 units. The total manufacturing overhead for the period is £135,450. Traditionally the firm has used a direct labour rate to allocate manufacturing overhead. Table 8.2 presents the resultant full costs of products X and Y.

Recently, XYZ Ltd decided to adopt an activity-based costing system to refine product costing. After conducting interviews with relevant personnel the steering committee, aided by consultants, identified five activity cost pools and corresponding cost drivers. This information and the associated activity costs are shown in Table 8.3.

Activity cost driver volumes are presented in Table 8.4, and Table 8.5 shows how cost driver rates were calculated.

Table 8.1 **Production, sales and costs**

	Product X	Product Y
Production and sales	15,000 units	500 units
Selling price (per unit)	£70	£100
Direct material cost (per unit)	£10	£20
Direct labour cost (per unit)	£20	£30

Table 8.2 **Full costs using traditional cost accounting**

Cost	Product X	Product Y
Direct material costs	£150,000[1]	£10,000[2]
Direct labour costs	£300,000[3]	£15,000[4]
Manufacturing overhead costs	£129,000[5]	£6,450[6]
Total manufacturing costs	**£579,000**	**£31,450**
Product cost per unit	**£38.60**	**£62.90**

Notes:

[1] £10 × 15,000 units
[2] £20 × 500 units
[3] £20 × 15,000 units
[4] £30 × 500 units
[5] [£135,450 / (£300,000 + £15,000)] × £300,000
[6] [£135,450 / (£300,000 + £15,000)] × £15,000

After calculating cost driver rates by dividing activity costs by cost driver volumes, overheads were assigned to products X and Y. The activity costs assigned to each product were calculated by multiplying the cost driver rates by the cost driver volumes for each product. These are shown in Table 8.6, and unit product costs under ABC are computed in Table 8.7.

This example shows that there was cross-subsidisation between products X and Y under traditional costing; product X was over-costed and Product Y was under-costed. This is because traditional cost accounting did not consider the differing complexities of products X and Y – it allocated production overheads using only a volume-based allocation (labour costs). Thus, a high volume product like X tends

Table 8.3 **Activities and cost drivers**

Activities	Activity costs	Activity cost drivers
Materials handling	£15,050	Component parts
Setting-up	£21,000	Set-up time
Machining	£49,600	Machine hours
Assembly	£30,000	Assembly-line hours
Inspection	£19,800	Inspection hours

Table 8.4 **Activity cost driver volumes**

Activity cost driver	Product X	Product Y	Total
Materials handling	1800 parts	200 parts	2000 parts
Set-up	5 hours per production run	6.5 hours per production run	
Machining	1000 hours	550 hours	1550 hours
Assembly	1200 hours	300 hours	1500 hours
Inspection	4500 hours	1500 hours	6000 hours

Table 8.5 Activity cost driver rates

Activity cost driver	Activity cost a	Cost driver volume b	Cost driver rate c = a / b
Materials handling	£15,050	2000 parts	£7.525 per part
Set-up	£21,000	400 hours*	£52.5 per hour
Machining	£49,600	1550 hours	£32 per hour
Assembly	£30,000	1500 hours	£20 per hour
Inspection	£19,800	6000 hours	£3.3 per hour

*Product X consumes 75 hours of set-up time, as each production run requires 5 hours of set-up and there are 15 production runs (15,000 units / 1000 units = 15 production runs; 15 production runs × 5 hours = 75 hours set-up).
Product Y consumes 325 hours of set-up time, as each production run requires 6.5 hours of set-up and there are 50 production runs (500 units / 10 units = 50 production runs; 50 production runs × 6.5 hours = 325 hours set-up).
Total set-up time for products X and Y is, therefore, 400 hours (75 hours + 325 hours).

to subsidise a low volume product like Y. ABC seeks to overcome this problem of cost distortion by capturing the 'real' consumption of overhead resources, attributing costs to products based on the activities they require.

Table 8.6 Activity cost assignment

Activity cost driver	Cost driver rate	Product X	Product Y
Materials handling	£7.525 per part	£13,545[1]	£1,505[2]
Set-up	£52.5 per hour	£3,937.5[3]	£17,062.5[4]
Machining	£32 per hour	£32,000[5]	£17,600[6]
Assembly	£20 per hour	£24,000[7]	£6,000[8]
Inspection	£3.3 per hour	£14,850[9]	£4,950[10]
Total		**£88,332.5**	**£47,117.5**

Notes:
[1] £7.525 × 1800 parts
[2] £7.525 × 200 parts
[3] £52.5 × 75 hours
[4] £52.5 × 325 hours
[5] £32 × 1000 hours
[6] £32 × 550 hours
[7] £20 × 1200 hours
[8] £20 × 300 hours
[9] £3.3 × 4500 hours
[10] £3.3 × 1500 hours

Table 8.7 Full unit cost by ABC

Cost	Product X	Product Y
Direct material costs	£150,000	£10,000
Direct labour costs	£300,000	£15,000
Manufacturing overhead costs	£88,332.5	£47,117.5
Total manufacturing costs	**£538,332.5**	**£72,117.5**
Product cost per unit	**£35.89**	**£144.24**

From ABC to ABC/M

Originally ABC/M focused on product costing for valuing stocks and setting prices, but nowadays its scope is wider (Innes and Mitchell, 1993, 1998; Jones and Dugdale, 2002). Criticisms of the shortfalls of ABC for product costing stimulated its evolution into ABC/M in the early 1990s. Jones and Dugdale (2002) argued that activity-based costing transformed itself from an ('accurate') costing technique into a management tool – ABC/M – that can help managers understand costs in organisations, and thus improve decision-making. ABC/M evolved from a fully allocated costing system, in which product costing was the central objective, to a system that is primarily concerned with the management of activities (Jones and Dugdale, 2002). This 'new' emphasis on cost management has attracted new allies, such as KPMG, to this approach (Jones and Dugdale, 2002).

ABC/M advocates contended that cost management was the key to improving firm efficiency and competitiveness (Innes and Mitchell, 1993, 1998) and promoted it as a means to help managers use ABC information to enhance their competitive position (Jones and Dugdale, 2002). The usefulness of ABC/M therefore stems from its use of ABC information to support efficiency improvements. ABC information (Innes and Mitchell, 1993) is useful in cost reduction, cost modelling, analysis of customer profitability, performance measurement, the design of new products and services, and the construction of activity-based budgets.

It is claimed that ABC makes overhead costs more visible to managers, hence providing more relevant information on the use of resources (Cokins *et al.*, 1993; Innes and Mitchell, 1993). Overhead cost analysis enables managers to control resources by tracing their consumption to activities and outputs. Anecdotal accounts claim such analysis has generated major cost savings, and ABC/M advocates argue that it can help eliminate activities that do not add value to the organisation.

Several researchers have argued that accounting research made simplistic assumptions about cost behaviour (Scapens, 1991; Innes and Mitchell, 1993). Traditionally costs are 'fixed' if they do not vary with short-term production volumes, or 'variable' if they change with volume. This categorisation of costs, which has dominated accounting theory until recently, is challenged by ABC/M. Advocates of ABC/M argue that most 'fixed costs' are actually variable (even if production volumes are constant), as many costs vary with the volume of *activities* (Miller and Vollman, 1985; Cooper, 1990a). Costs do not vary exclusively with the volume of production, but also according to the number of batches or product lines (Cooper, 1990a). Thus, it is argued that ABC/M provides managers with a new perspective on cost behaviour as it makes them aware that costs are not just related to output volume, but also to batch volumes and the number of product lines offered. ABC/M provides managers with different cost assumptions and aids cost modelling and 'what if' exercises. Hence, according to its proponents, it is valuable tool in managing costs (Innes and Mitchell, 1993).

Furthermore, it is claimed that ABC/M facilitates customer profitability analysis by identifying the activities needed to sell products to each customer. Here the cost objects are not products, but the customers. ABC is thought to reveal that, even if the sales value of customers are similar, their profitability can differ because it depends on the costs incurred to meet their demands – information that should be helpful to managers in formulating market strategies and promotional activities (Innes and Mitchell, 1993). ABC/M promoters also claim it provides information for performance measurement. Cost driver rates link overhead costs to cost objects and thereby reveal opportunities for improvement. Cost driver rates can be regarded as the unit cost of activity outputs, and they report important information about the efficiency and productivity of activities. It is also contended that ABC/M provides managers with information that improves their ability to design cost-effective products. Finally, ABC/M outputs may be used for budgeting and control, since estimates of future expenditure can be derived from analyses of current and historic costs of activities and cost driver rates (Cokins *et al.*, 1993).

It is claimed that, by focussing on the analysis of activities and drivers and thereby helping managers to understand production processes, ABC/M is more relevant than ABC, which simply calculates product costs (Innes and Mitchell, 1993, 1998).

ABC/M implementation

Studies on ABC/M implementation are relatively scarce (Anderson, 1995; Major and Hopper, 2005). Furthermore, ABC/M implementation has been approached mainly from a technical perspective whereas the behavioural, social, political and organisational effects of ABC/M implementation have received less attention (Shields, 1995; Major and Hopper, 2005). This section examines ABC/M implementation from both a technical and non-technical perspective. It reviews ABC/M advocates' prescriptions for implementing ABC/M and also some studies of ABC/M implementation.

Prescriptions for a 'successful' ABC/M implementation

Despite the ABC/M implementation literature widely using the term 'success', there is little consensus on what constitutes a 'successful' ABC/M implementation. Foster and Swenson (1997) identify four sets of measures that have been used to assess ABC/M success: (i) the extent to which it is used in decision-making processes; (ii) its affect on managers' actions and decisions; (iii) its financial impact upon the firm; and (iv) managers' satisfaction with it. However, there are other possible meanings of 'success'. For example, Anderson's (1995) study of ABC implementation in General Motors regarded success as the 'use of ABC data in the manner intended by the firm prior to implementation' (p. 3). Several measures of success have been proposed by CAM-I: the ease and practicality of data collection; the ease of implementation; financial benefits; acceptance by users; and the completeness and accuracy of its outputs. 'Success', it seems, means different things to different authors.

Cooper (1990b) advocates a two-phase structured approach to 'successfully' implementing an activity-based costing system. The first phase involves prior decisions about ABC/M system characteristics. The second involves following specific 'steps' throughout the ABC/M implementation. Cooper argues that managers should answer six questions before beginning an ABC/M implementation process:

1 Should the ABC/M system be integrated with the existing system or kept separate?
2 Should managers approve the formal ABC/M design before implementing it?

3 Who will assume 'ownership' of the final system?
4 How precise should the ABC/M system be?
5 Should it report historical or future costs?
6 Should the initial design be complex or simple?

Cooper (1990b) argues that initial agreement over these issues by managers will ease ABC/M implementation. Then user and resource needs should be identified from interviews along with an assessment of the current information systems. A multidisciplinary team, embracing people from functional areas other than the finance department, should be constituted to foster commitment. ABC/M promoters argue that a full-time steering group should be involved during implementation, except possibly when the project is still exploratory (Cooper, 1990b; Eiler and Ball, 1993). Cooper's (1990b) structured plan for a 'successful' ABC implementation has seven major phases:

1 Seminar on ABC
2 Design seminar
3 Design and data gathering
4 Progress meeting
5 Executive seminar
6 Results meeting
7 Interpretation meetings

The seminars on ABC and systems design seek to educate managers about ABC/M and its benefits and help develop a strong team identity. Issues that should be covered in the seminars are as follows: how to identify activity centres; methods of assigning costs in the first and second stages; and data collection. The design and data gathering stage should identify major activities performed in the organisation, determine activity costs, identify what drives activity consumption, determine cost driver volumes demanded by each product, and compute activity-based product costs. Interviews with functional managers and workers are extremely important at this stage as they reveal what activties are conducted in the organisation, how much time is spent on each activity, and how often activities are performed. In addition, the interviews provide an excellent opportunity to continue education on the merits of ABC/M (Cooper, 1990b; Eiler and Ball, 1993). The progress meetings should inform managers about progress made and ensure that all organisational members accept the design of the new system and that users' needs are met. The executive seminars are to discuss other aspects of ABC/M implementation. These discussions should enhance managers' commitment to ABC/M and inform them what to do once the system is running. The last two types of meetings are intended to discuss results by comparing product costs generated by the firm's previous cost accounting system with those generated by ABC/M, to investigate why these product costs vary, and to decide how to improve efficiency.

Three distinct approaches to implementing ABC/M can be followed (Eiler and Ball, 1993): the prototype, pilot and staged approaches. The prototype approach consists of demonstrating ABC/M concepts and principles using examples. Its scope for analysis is narrow and thus its value is limited. The pilot approach implements ABC/M at specific organisational points (e.g. departments or business units). A well-designed pilot study should reveal whether ABC/M should be adopted throughout the firm. In the staged approach, ABC/M is implemented gradually in each main area of the organisation. Pilot implementation, followed by a staged implementation before full implementation of ABC/M, has been recommended. A first-off full ABC implementation is risky and consumes substantial resources and time. The following steps are advised in both pilot and staged implementations (Eiler and Ball, 1993):

1 Identify user needs and the system's objectives.
2 Flowchart processes to aid documentation and understanding.
3 Identify firm activities, cost objects (e.g. products, customers, and business segments) and cost drivers.
4 Determine activity cost driver volumes, activity costs and the activity cost driver rates.
5 Create a bill of activities for products or processes, including sales, general and administrative activities, and examine and revise it (as necessary).
6 Validate the model by reconciling ABC/M information with outputs of the traditional cost accounting system.
7 Examine results to discover opportunities for improvement and to determine which products need their prices adjusting or re-negotiating with customers.
8 Proceed with further pilot studies or staged installations.

It is contended that ABC/M systems should be flexible, amenable to change, responsive to users' information needs, user-friendly and simple to understand and use (Cooper, 1990b; Eiler and Ball, 1993). In order to make ABC/M an effective tool, firms should revise its design frequently and update cost drivers at least every six months based on interviews with employees. Similarly, the system software should be re-evaluated regularly (annually if possible). This will help those responsible for the system to identify changes in cost drivers and the frequency of activities, and provide users with feedback when using ABC/M (Eiler and Ball, 1993).

Research on ABC/M implementation

It has been argued that the scope of ABC/M implementation extends beyond its purely technical aspects (Major and Hopper, 2005). Research indicates that firms often experience problems because they over-emphasise technical issues (such as software architecture and design) and neglect behavioural, cultural, organisational and political aspects of the new system (Shields, 1995). Recognising this, CAM-I recommends substantial investment in education as a means to implement successfully a new cost management system. Adequate education programmes overcome employees' fears of the unknown and ensure that the need for change is properly understood and accepted. Also, Shields and Young's (1989) behavioural model for implementing cost management systems and Argyris and Kaplan's (1994) approach to implementing new knowledge both highlight the value of behavioural and organisational factors in achieving a successful implementation. Shields and Young (1989) developed the 'Seven Cs Model' (champion, controls, compensation, change process, continuous education, commitment and culture), which emphasises the importance of developing an organisational culture based on the commitment of all employees to continuous improvement for successfully implementing cost management systems. Change is more easily achieved if there is a person ('champion') who fosters the new system and is accountable for securing the organisation's commitment to the project. Appropriate organisational controls, compensation programmes and continuous education are also seen as fundamental for successful implementation.

Also, Argyris and Kaplan (1994) advocate implementing ABC/M via education and sponsorship programmes to stimulate organisation members' capacity to accept new ideas. Key individuals should be identified, both to champion the process of change and to persuade top managers about the benefits of implementing ABC/M. Moreover, Argyris and Kaplan argue that the creation of internal commitment and the alignment of incentives are essential to successfully implement ABC/M. They claim that internal commitment, which exists 'when individuals assign the causal reasons for their energy and attention to themselves' (Argyris and Kaplan, 1994, p. 103), leads to the best implementations.

ABC/M, like other cost management techniques, may be more an administrative than a technical innovation, its success depending on 'how well it matches the preferences, goals, strategies, agendas, skills and resources of dominant or powerful coalitions of employees, particularly top management' (Shields, 1995, p. 149). Like other administrative innovations, top management support is crucial for successful ABC/M implementation, as top management has the power to allocate the resources needed to operate the new management accounting system (e.g. money, personnel, time and equipment). Also, top management's long-term commitment to ABC/M and its incorporation into the goals and strategies of the organisation play a decisive role in promoting it throughout the organisation. Shields (1995) studied which factors were associated with ABC/M success and concluded that the degree of top management support was one of the most important variables affecting ABC/M implementation. Similarly, McGowan and Klammer (1997) found that top management support was an important variable when analysing how employees' satisfaction levels are associated with successful ABC/M implementations. Behavioural, cultural and organisational issues thus play an important role in ABC/M implementation and should not be ignored.

Much of the literature on ABC/M implementation has been accused of being too prescriptive, managerial and naïve as it assumes that senior managers can manage change smoothly if they follow the 'correct' process (Major and Hopper, 2005). This means that unsuccessful ABC/M implementations are often attributed to inadequate participation and involvement on the part of managers and employees. However, success or failure may not be as dependent on adopting the right user-involvement strategies as the ABC/M implementation literature implies. Moreover, research on ABC/M implementation has been criticised for seeking to investigate which factors explain ABC/M success or failure, and for aiming to produce statistically testable theories of the success of ABC/M implementations. It is alleged that statistical analysis of factors affecting ABC/M implementation provides only a limited view of the issues firms face (Major and Hopper, 2005). ABC/M literature has also been accused of ignoring issues of power and conflict. It is argued that resistance to ABC/M is often structural, and hence power and political issues should be considered when implementing ABC/M. It is claimed that how managers perceive ABC/M to affect the distribution of power in the organisation often affects its implementation, and that ABC/M is unlikely to succeed if dominant organisational actors perceive it as a threat to their power. Pursuing case studies may help researchers gain deeper insights into the difficulties and problems encountered during ABC/M implementations (Major and Hopper, 2005).

An evaluation of ABC/M

Most researchers concur that ABC/M represents a conceptual advance on traditional management accounting systems. If product ranges are diversified and non-volume-related overheads are significant, traditional cost management may lead to the subsidisation of small-batch, specialty products by large-batch, generic products. ABC/M recognises that products with varying complexity make dissimilar demands on resources, so overheads should not be allocated to all products at the same rate (Innes and Mitchell, 1993, 1998). In traditional cost management systems cost allocations are volume-based, but in ABC/M both volume-based and non-volume-based allocations are used (Cooper, 1990a; Cokins *et al.*, 1993). The use of different cost drivers within the ABC/M approach may provide a better measure of resource consumption than traditional alloca-tion bases. ABC/M contests traditional notions of short-term and variable costs as it treats all costs as ultimately variable and identifiable with cost objects (Cooper, 1990a; Innes and Mitchell, 1993). ABC/M focuses on both production and non-production overheads – sales, distribution, administration and other non-manufacturing overheads are traced to cost objects together with manufacturing overheads. Furthermore, its advocates have argued that ABC/M can be usefully implemented in all types of organisation, be they profit or non-profit, manufacturing or non-manufacturing, service organisations or gov-ernment entities. ABC/M proponents claim that its focus on activities and cost drivers helps managers to monitor and control production and service department costs (Cokins *et al.*, 1993). ABC/M may provide new insights into which factors cause overhead costs and reveal that it is not production volume that triggers costs, but complexity expressed by transaction volume (Miller and Vollman, 1985). Also, cost driver analysis can provide useful information about activity performance, which can help managers to enhance effi-ciency and improve organisational performance (Innes and Mitchell, 1993). Better com-prehension of cost drivers should also facilitate planning and budgeting (Cokins *et al.*, 1993; Innes & Mitchell, 1993).

However, despite its merits, ABC/M has been criticised for being only a marginal refinement of traditional management accounting techniques. Although ABC/M usually has a larger number of cost pools and its allocation bases are more diversified, the simi-larities between ABC and conventional cost management systems, as outlined earlier, exceed the differences. Furthermore, ABC/M assumptions about the reality of the world in many ways reflect conventional management accounting wisdom (Scapens, 1991).

Several researchers have disputed the accuracy of ABC calculations – a core argument for ABC, particularly in its early years (Jones and Dugdale, 2002). Economics based research demonstrates that ABC provides relevant costs for product discontinuation and design decisions only under certain rigorous conditions, namely: linear cost functions, zero fixed costs at the level of the cost pool, and no joint processes (Noreen, 1991). In practice, these conditions are seldom met. Moreover, some indirect costs cannot be allocated in ABC/M systems. ABC may capture causal relationships between unit-level, batch-level and product-sustaining costs and cost objects, but it cannot assign facility-level costs in a non-arbitrary way (Cooper, 1990a). In an optimal system, activity cost pools should be homogeneous and causal relationships between activities and cost drivers should be respected when choosing drivers. The selection of cost drivers and the definition of activities have been major difficulties in ABC/M implementation, and some degree of estimation remains necessary. Also, assumptions about cost causality have been criticised and the relevance of unit costs obtained through ABC questioned, since decisions or even the passage of time may explain costs better than activities do (Piper and Walley, 1990). Increasing awareness of ABC's technical deficiencies may explain why ABC moved from a product costing to a cost management emphasis. Jones and Dugdale (2002) note that, as 'ABC-builders' experienced external challenges and internal reflections concerning the accuracy of ABC costing, important transformations occurred in the way ABC was 'sold'. This explains why 'allocation' was replaced by 'estimation' and 'accuracy' was redefined as subjective judgement rather than objective fact (Jones and Dugdale, 2002).

Other management accounting researchers have observed problems with ABC/M implementation. It can be costly in terms of human and physical resources and can cause significant disruption in organisations (Innes and Mitchell, 1998). The selection of drivers and activities is a complex and time-consuming process (*ibid.*). Also, employees often experience difficulties in understanding and categorising activities when supplying data for the ABC/M system (Major and Hopper, 2005). The accurate recording of time spent on activities is crucial to ABC/M's operation, but employees may resist disclosing this information. Also, ABC/M has been accused of provoking managerial resistance and bias. Managers may manipulate data if they believe the use of ABC/M threatens their power or position in the organisation, hence rendering ABC/M unworkable. The complicity of employees in ABC/M implementation is vital since ABC 'success' depends on employees' willingness to use it (*ibid.*). Nonetheless, it is difficult to devise a system that satisfies everyone, as managers' information needs can differ according to their function (*ibid.*). Hence perceptions of ABC/M effectiveness can vary and it is unlikely that ABC/M will always succeed, even if its implementation is skilfully managed.

ABC/M critics have also questioned the need to replace traditional management accounting with new cost management techniques. They argue that ABC/M has not resolved the poor competitiveness of Western industry as promised (Johnson, 1992), and contest the claim that management and cost accounting practices have stagnated since the early twentieth century and hence need reform. Critics have argued that improving competitiveness lies not in 'sophisticated' cost accounting techniques, but rather in improving the behavioural and organisational contexts in which management and cost accounting systems operate. Also, despite its alleged benefits and the promotion it has received, ABC/M has not been widely adopted. Surveys conducted in several countries show that only a small proportion of firms (usually large firms) have adopted ABC/M (Innes *et al.*, 2000). Many firms continue to use traditional systems, perhaps supplemented with other non-financial information, rather than adopting 'revolutionary' management accounting approaches. This may be because some stability is needed to cope with the recent major changes in the business environment. Such observations have led researchers to question whether ABC/M represents an advance or whether it is just a bandwagon effect (Innes *et al.*, 2000; Jones and Dugdale, 2002). Critics claim that a 'rhetorical fashion-setting community' comprised of consultants, business media and business schools have shaped collective beliefs that ABC/M is rational and at the forefront of management progress (Jones and Dugdale, 2002), whereas it is no more than a reinvention of old business practices ('old wine in new bottles'). This argument has credence, particularly if criticisms of Johnson and Kaplan's (1987) historical account of management accounting development and Johnson's (1992) recantation of present-day ABC/M are accepted. The rhetoric of ABC/M aims to convince fashion followers that it is the right way to pursue efficiency goals. For instance, Kaplan and Cooper's ABC/M case studies conducted in the 1980s were used to illustrate how ABC/M brought new managerial possibilities to managers, and proved to be an important means of popularising ABC/M amongst practitioners and academics (Jones and Dugdale, 2002). More research is needed to determine whether ABC/M is merely a management fashion or offers real benefits to managers (Innes *et al.*, 2000). Nevertheless, some researchers are already concerned about the complexities of ABC/M models in practice, the behavioural problems associated with their implementation, large implementation costs, and the managerial resistance they can invoke (Major and Hopper, 2005). These issues have given rise to concerns that ABC/M may fail to meet expectations, just as other approaches like zero-based budgeting (ZBB) and PPBS have failed before it.

Conclusion

This chapter has described the main features of the ABC/M approach. Harvard and CAM-I networks, like other ABC/M advocates, depict it as an innovative approach that can enhance the efficiency and competitiveness of firms within the new business environment. It is relatively well accepted that ABC/M can offer important benefits and provide relevant information for management. However, after some years of enthusiasm for this approach, several case studies of ABC/M implementation have reported difficulties and failures. Three main criticisms have been levelled at ABC/M. First, it may be only a refinement of traditional management accounting rather than an original approach. Second, there are technical pitfalls and limitations and ABC/M is unable to compute accurately full product costs. Third, ABC/M is costly to implement and operate and often generates resistance and conflict. More research is needed to reveal whether ABC is merely the result of a bandwagon effect or if, on the contrary, it represents an effective alternative to traditional management accounting.

References

Anderson, S.W. (1995) 'A framework for assessing cost management system changes: the case of activity based costing implementation at General Motors, 1986–1993', *Journal of Management Accounting Research*, **7**, Fall, 1–51.

Argyris, C. and Kaplan, R.S. (1994) 'Implementing new knowledge: the case of activity-based costing', *Accounting Horizons*, **8**(3), 83–105.

CAM-I (1990) *Activity-accounting Project Guide,* August, CAM-I.

Cokins, G., Stratton, A. and Helbling, J. (1993) *An ABC Manager's Primer,* Montvale, NJ: Institute of Management Accountants.

Cooper, R. (1990a) 'Cost classification in unit-based and activity-based manufacturing cost systems', *Journal of Cost Management,* Fall, 4–14.

Cooper, R. (1990b) 'Implementing an activity-based cost system', *Journal of Cost Management,* Spring, 33–42.

Drucker, P.F. (1963) 'Managing for business effectiveness', *Harvard Business Review,* May–June, 53–60.

Eiler, R.G. and Ball, C. (1993) 'Implementing activity-based costing', in B.J. Brinker (ed.), *Handbook of Cost Management,* New York: Warren Gorham Lamont.

Foster, G. and Swenson, D.W. (1997) 'Measuring the success of activity-based cost management and its determinants', *Journal of Management Accounting Research,* **9,** 109–41.

Hopper, T., Kirkham, L., Scapens, R. and Turley, S. (1992) 'Does financial accounting dominate management accounting – a research note', *Management Accounting Research,* **3,** 307–11.

Innes, J. and Mitchell, F. (1993) *Overhead Cost,* London: CIMA.

Innes, J. and Mitchell, F. (1998) *A Practical Guide to Activity-based Costing,* London: Kogan Page.

Innes, J., Mitchell, F. and Sinclair, D. (2000) 'Activity-based costing in the UK's largest companies: a comparison of 1994 and 1999 survey results', *Management Accounting Research,* **11,** 349–62.

Johnson, H.T. (1992) *Relevance Regained,* New York: Free Press.

Johnson, H.T. and Kaplan, R.S. (1987) *Relevance Lost: The Rise and Fall of Management Accounting,* Cambridge, MA: Harvard Business School Press.

Jones, T.C. and Dugdale, D. (2002) 'The ABC bandwagon and the juggernaut of modernity', *Accounting, Organizations and Society,* **27,** 121–63.

Major, M. and Hopper, T. (2005) 'Managers divided: implementing ABC in a Portuguese telecommunications company', *Management Accounting Research,* **16,** 205–29.

McGowan, A.S. and Klammer, T.P. (1997) 'Satisfaction with activity-based cost management implementation', *Journal of Management Accounting Research,* **9,** 217–37.

Miller, J.G. and Vollman, T.E. (1985) 'The hidden factory', *Harvard Business Review,* September–October, 142–50.

Noreen, E. (1991) 'Conditions under which activity-based cost systems provide relevant costs', *Journal of Management Accounting Research,* Fall, 159–68.

Piper, J.A. and Walley, P. (1990) 'Testing ABC logic', *Management Accounting* (UK), September, 37 & 42.

Scapens, R.W. (1991) M*anagement Accounting: A Review of Recent Developments,* 2nd edn, London: Macmillan.

Shields, M.D. (1995) 'An empirical analysis of firms' implementation experiences with activity-based costing', *Journal of Management Accounting Research,* Fall, 148–65.

Shields, M.D. and Young, S.M. (1989) 'A behavioral model for implementing cost management systems', *Journal of Cost Management,* Winter, 17–27.

Staubus, G.J. (1988) *Activity Costing for Decisions: Cost Accounting in the Decision Usefulness Framework,* New York: Garland Publishing.

Further reading

Brimson, J.A. (1991) *Activity Accounting: An Activity-based Costing Approach,* New York: John Wiley & Sons. A comprehensive guide to activity-based costing implementation.

Cooper, R. (1988a) 'The rise of activity-based costing – part one: what is an activity-based cost system?' *Journal of Cost Management for the Manufacturing Industry,* Summer, 45–54.

Cooper, R. (1988b) 'The rise of activity-based costing – part two: when do I need an activity-based cost system?' *Journal of Cost Management for the Manufacturing Industry,* Fall, 41–48. In these articles Cooper describes some of the most important aspects of the ABC approach.

Friedman, A.L. and Lyne, S.R. (1999) *Success and Failure of Activity-based Techniques: A Long-term Perspective,* London: CIMA. This research monograph explores the long-term organisational consequences of implementing activity-based techniques and the causes of their success and failure.

Granlund, M. (2001) 'Towards explaining stability in and around management accounting systems', *Management Accounting Research,* **12,** 141–66. A longitudinal case study in a Finnish food manufacturing firm that faced difficulties in an ABC project implementation.

Lukka, K. and Granlund, M. (2002), 'The fragmented communication structure within the accounting academia: the case of activity-based costing research genres', *Accounting, Organizations and Society,* **27,** 165–90. A study of the main features of ABC research genres (consulting research, basic research and critical research) and their influence on management accounting academia.

Malmi, T. (1999) 'Activity-based costing diffusion across organizations: an exploratory empirical analysis of Finnish firms', *Accounting, Organizations and Society,* **24,** 649–72. An interesting investigation of how and why management accounting innovations, such as ABC, diffuse among organisations.

9

The balanced scorecard

Hanne Nørreklit and Falconer Mitchell

Introduction

Management accounting has been defined as a discipline whose purpose is to:

> create, preserve and increase value so as to deliver that value to the stakeholders of profit and not for profit organisations both public and private. (CIMA, 2000, p. 3)

Central to the supply of information for this purpose is the measurement of organisational performance. Not only is this a major part of the substance of management accounting, but it also provides a considerable design challenge for management accountants since they must exercise professional judgement to create a system that suits the situation for which it is intended. The challenge in this task is great because individual, or indeed even sets of, performance measures are unlikely to capture the full complexity of organisational reality. At best, they provide a model of actuality that is partial in nature and often involves the use of surrogate indicators for the complex principal of organisational performance (Ijiri, 1978). Consequently, the outputs from performance measurement systems are notorious for their capacity to mislead and confuse the user and to produce unintended and often dysfunctional consequences through their effects on those preparing them and those subject to them (Ridgeway, 1956).

In the early 1990s the balanced scorecard (BSC) was proposed as a framework to provide a structure for related sets of organisational performance measures (Kaplan and Norton, 1996a). Its designers have claimed that it addresses many of the shortcomings of the more traditional accounting approaches to performance measurement (Kaplan and Norton, 1996a). It provides a standard approach for categorising performance measures (see 'Structure', below) on an interrelated, quadruple set basis. Within its general framework specific measures can be selected to suit the nature and circumstances of the organisation adopting it. Thus, while the BSC specifies the classes of measure to be used, it also has the flexibility to customise its design to user requirements through the selection of individual measures within each class or category. These attributes have enabled the BSC to quickly achieve a high degree of prominence in practice as one of the most widely used recent innovations in management accounting (Cobbald and Lawrie, 2002, p. 4).

This chapter first describes, explains and exemplifies the BSC solution to the challenge of organisational performance measurement. Research on the BSC and its strengths and weaknesses are then reviewed. In addition, the manner of its textbook presentation is subjected to a short literary analysis to uncover how the technique has been promoted in print. Finally some conclusions are drawn on this new and innovative method.

The nature of the BSC

The BSC was first presented in published form in 1992 (Kaplan and Norton, 1992). Since then, its two creators have outlined and developed its conceptual and practical characteristics in a series of books (1996a, 2000) and articles (1993, 1996b, 2001, 2004). Their text entitled *The Balanced Scorecard* (Kaplan and Norton, 1996a) provides their most comprehensive exposition. In a subsequent book they illustrated, through a series of case studies, how a number of companies have actually implemented the BSC and how it can be integrated with strategy maps. Researchers have subsequently reported on the diversity of performance measurement systems labelled BSCs (e.g. Butler *et al.*, 1997; Mooraj *et al.*, 1999; Ahn, 2001). However, Kaplan and Norton consider that a 'true' BSC possesses the features outlined below (Kaplan and Norton, 1996a).

Structure

The BSC is a component of an organisation's strategic management system. It is based on an ordered, rational view of organisational strategy and its main purpose is to translate that vision and strategy into measurable objectives with a practical meaning for management. Thus, the BSC provides a quantitative representation of key variables and a financial perspective on outcomes. Thereby, it takes a primarily accounting-influenced perspective on organisational performance. Its structure is based on a quadruple categorisation of performance measures comprising the financial, customer, internal business process and learning and growth perspectives on organisational performance (see Figure 9.1). To some extent this may be viewed as a move towards a stakeholder perspective on performance, especially in some applications

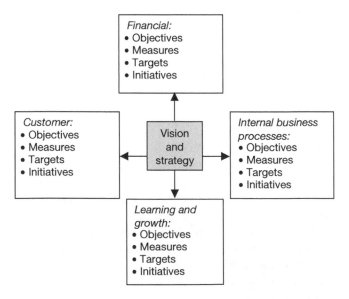

Figure 9.1 The BSC framework

Source: Adapted from Kaplan and Norton, 1996a, p. 9.

that have incorporated a separate employee category (Ax and Bjornenak, 2005). In corporate terms the financial perspective identifies how a company wishes to be viewed by its shareholders. The customer perspective reflects how it wishes to be viewed by its customers. The internal business process perspective indicates the areas where the company has to be particularly adept in order to satisfy its customers and shareholders. The organisational learning and growth perspective involves the improving developments that the company needs to realise if its strategy and vision are to be achieved (Kaplan and Norton, 1996a, pp. 30–1).

Some variation to and within this BSC framework is possible. Kaplan and Norton recognise that sometimes the nature of corporate vision and strategy may require further perspectives (Kaplan and Norton, 1996a, p. 34). For example, alternative perspectives focusing on organisational problems and human elements have been suggested by Olve *et al.* (1997) and Maisel (1992) respectively. Within the suggested framework, the selected measures representing each perspective may differ across organisations. The appendix to this chapter illustrates this variation by showing the BSCs in two different types of entity.

Cause and effect distinctiveness

The BSC is designed to measure and thereby facilitate the monitoring of the drivers of future long-term success, and capture outcome measures that demonstrate the extent to which success has been achieved. The 'balance' it incorporates is tri-dimensional consisting of (i) these driver and outcome measures, (ii) external measures relating to shareholders and customers and internal measures relating to organisational operations, and (iii) the level of objectivity of measurement usually found in outcome measures and the measurement subjectivity, which is often a characteristic of the driver measures (Kaplan and Norton, 1996a, pp. 8–10). The main differentiating feature of the BSC is the linking together of the four perspectives' measurements in a causal chain. Without this characteristic a 'true' BSC does not exist. Kaplan and Norton observe that:

> Many managers believe they are using a BSC when they supplement traditional financial measures with generic, non-financial measures about customers, processes and employees . . . [But] A scorecard should contain outcome measures and the performance drivers of those outcomes, linked together in cause and effect relationships. (Kaplan and Norton, 1996a, p. 53)

The causal relationship or chain among the four perspectives that is assumed to underpin the BSC is shown in Figure 9.2. The measures of learning and growth therefore drive the measures of the internal business processes. These latter measures then drive the measures of the customer perspective and, in turn, the customer measures drive the financial outcome measures.

A well-designed BSC should therefore comprise a mix of outcome measures (lag indicators) and performance drivers (lead indicators). An example of a lag indicator is *increase in turnover,* while *order execution time* would be a lead indicator for it. Each perspective should have lead and lag indicators, yielding two-directional cause and effect chains. Lead and lag indicators apply horizontally within the areas and vertically between areas. The causal paths from the scorecard variables should be linked to the financial targets of the organisation. This procedure implies that strategy is translated into a set of hypotheses about cause and effect (Kaplan and Norton, 1996a, p. 30).

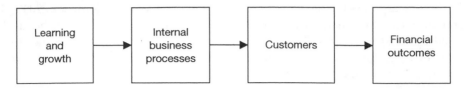

Figure 9.2 **The assumed causal relationship in the BSC**

Multiple purposes

A BSC constructed in this way is not simply a strategic measurement system, but is also a strategic control system that can be used to (i) clarify and gain consensus about strategy, (ii) align departmental and personal goals to strategy, (iii) link strategic objectives to long-term targets and annual budgets, (iv) identify and align strategic initiatives, and (v) obtain feedback to learn about and improve strategy (Kaplan and Norton, 1996a, p. 19). The mix of financial and non-financial measures and their cause–effect relationships is designed to combat the short-termism fostered by traditional accounting measures. Kaplan and Norton (1993, p. 142) also specifically identify the BSC as a tool that can be employed to help drive the process of organisational change by clarifying the objectives and critical success factors of those involved in delivering the change.

To use the BSC to achieve these purposes, the organisation must start by clarifying and translating its vision and strategy into specific strategic objectives and measures that can represent them. The next step is to communicate the vision and strategy to teams and employees. This requires translating the overall strategic objectives and measures into objectives and measures appropriate for the teams and employees who represent key segments of the organisation. Eventually, rewards will be linked to these performance measures. The communication of strategy and vision is achieved through executive announcements, plant meetings, videos, brochures and newsletters. The deployment of the objectives upon which the scorecard is based occurs through a type of atomic, analytic process whereby top management objectives cascade to the lower levels (Kaplan and Norton, 1996a, p. 213). It is then necessary to set targets for the selected measures, align strategic initiatives to objectives, and link budgets with long-term plans. The final step involves obtaining strategic feedback and learning from it.

Research on the BSC

Researchers and commentators have identified widespread satisfaction with the BSC as a tool for implementing and communicating strategy. For example, the following benefits have been recognised: the clarity of focus which it brings to the critical factors determining performance (Kanji and Sa, 2002; Ritter, 2003); its value as an information system for diagnosis and control (Pandey, 2005); its contribution to the effectiveness of strategy implementation through the translation and communication of strategy in the form of tangible measures (Brabazon, 1999; Kanji and Sa, 2002); its use as a substitute for traditional budgeting (Ax and Bjornenak, 2005); and its flexibility and fit to different organisations (Kanji and Sa, 2002). However, research has also shown that BSC users are not very knowledgeable about the cause and effect relationships that should govern the selection of performance measures. In practice, users simply have a belief in the relationship between measures rather than testing and identifying the nature of actual relationships. Implementations have met a series of practical problems (Ahn, 2001). Organisations have focused on building an operational tool that apparently works at a technical level, rather than following the conceptual blueprint of Kaplan and Norton. As with many novel developments linked to control and remuneration, resistance to change has been apparent. Kasurinen (2002), for example, found that three different types of barriers to BSC implementation exist, which he terms 'confusers' (uncertainty about the role for the BSC), 'frustrators' (the existence of an antagonistic engineering culture), and 'delayers' (difficulty in specifying strategies). Consequently the process of implementation requires careful attention if the BSC is to be adopted successfully. This view is confirmed by Ax and Bjornenak (2005), whose study of BSC diffusion in Sweden showed that its original framework had to be amended during implementation to suit 'local' culture and conditions. This was achieved by including an employee perspective, a link to an intellectual capital model, and the use of non-budgetary control systems.

The nature of linkages

Crucial to the successful functioning of the BSC is the validity of the linkages among the measurements. This section examines this validity, first for the measures contained in the individual BSC that applies to the overall organisation, and second for the relationship between the measures of various BSCs used at different levels in the organisational hierarchy. The examination starts with a brief introduction to three possible, though not exclusive, linkages – causality, logic and finality.

Possible linkages

Cause and effect

According to Kaplan and Norton (1996a, 1996b) the cause and effect chain is a central feature of the BSC. Indeed, this distinguishes the BSC from other performance measurement models. However, Kaplan and Norton (1996a) do not clearly define the cause and effect relationship they used.

Hume's criteria for a cause and effect relationship are commonly adopted within the theory of science (Føllesdal *et al.*, 1997, p. 155) and are used here. These criteria are: (i) X precedes Y in time; (ii) the observation of an event X necessarily implies the subsequent observation of another event Y; and (iii) the two events can be observed close to each other in time and space. Within a business context, the assumption of cause and effect relationships is essential because it allows non-financial measurements of events to be used as predictors of future financial outcomes. Thus, the implicit assumption of the BSC approach to performance measurement is that non-financial measures indicate the drivers of financial outcomes (Kaplan and Norton, 1996a, p. 8). The validity of this assumption (and thus of the BSC) depends on the existence of a specified set of cause and effect relationships across the four areas of measurement that give the BSC its structure.

Does such a relationship exist? An answer is important because, to the individual firm, the BSC is a risky model, since any proof or testing of cause and effect relationships can only be demonstrated after the fact, i.e. once (non-)achievement of the financial result has occurred (Haas and Kleingeld, 1999, p. 244). It is also important because, as will be seen, it determines managerial response to performance variation as it indicates which actions are deemed to be drivers of future financial performance.

Logical relationships

In a cause and effect relationship, events X and Y are logically independent (Føllesdal *et al.*, 1997, p. 155). This means we cannot rationally infer Y from X, but can only do so empirically. In this sense there is *a logical relationship* between a cost decrease and (other factors held constant) a profit increase. In contrast, there can be a cause and effect relationship between machine speed and resource consumption. Logical relationships are concepts within a language, in this case the accounting language. They are verified by the reasoning underlying them. In contrast, cause and effect relationships are part of the operation of real world events and are susceptible to verification through empirical testing.

Accounting models, such as net present value or profit calculations, are logical in nature, serving the purpose of creating financial rationality in an organisation. They are based on logical arguments and not on empirical observations of company structures and relationships. As companies in western societies are evaluated on financial results, accounting models are a priori requirements for the measurement of profitability, cash flow and financial position in organisations. Accounting models can only be logically proved or rejected. Thus, the correctness of financial results can only be argued and proved by reference to the appropriate accounting methods.

The relationship between two phenomena cannot be both logical and causal. Consequently, it is important for the management of a company to know the type of relationship that exists among events because this determines whether the effect of an action will be inevitable or probable. Indeed, the relationship determines whether decisions about which action will be most financially successful should be based on statistical analysis or on an accounting calculus. For example, it determines whether we should use statistics or accounting calculus to determine whether customer satisfaction drives ROCE.

Finality relationships

A third relationship possibility is a finality-type relationship between the suggested measurements. A finality relationship occurs when human actions, wishes and views relate to each other. It exists where a relationship involves (i) someone who believes a given action to be the best means to an end, and (ii) the end and this view actually cause the action (Føllesdal *et al.*, 1997, pp. 170–1). Actions are performed because they are adapted to the views and wishes of a person. Thus, there is a reciprocal relationship between ends and means. The action is not a reflex, but is due to human volition. For example, the implementation of a quality control programme can be seen as a means to increase profit.

Finality relationships may be more complex than logical or causal ones because to reach an end, it may be necessary to move away from it at first. For example, a satisfactory financial result may be obtained by first supplying a good product at low prices, making customers very satisfied and gaining a market share and an image, and then later reducing the level of satisfaction by raising prices. Any means is one of several for reaching the end, and each means may have numerous other effects. Consequently, unlike for causal relationships, no general law exists to show the sources of actions.

Claiming finality is therefore more ambiguous than invoking causality. A finality relationship does not assume the existence of a general law that presumes that certain actions will bring good financial results. Assessing the financial consequences of an action requires a financial calculus. Also, to obtain good control practice it is important that a person's belief in a given action as a means to an end is valid, i.e. the means should work not only in thought, but also in practical acts.

Linkages and the BSC

This section discusses Kaplan and Norton's (1996a, 1996b) description of cause and effect relationships among measures from the four perspectives and their suggestions for linking the various hierarchical levels within the BSC. The discussion makes suggestions for improving the validity of the linkages.

What are the linkages among the BSC measurements at the overall level?

The relationship between BSC measures is ambiguously described by Kaplan and Norton (1996a). On the one hand, the authors claim causality: a financial result will necessarily, or highly probably, occur if a given cause exists (ibid. p. 70). On the other hand, their description relies on arguments and concepts that assess actions on the basis of financial reasoning. For example, the use of activity-based costing ensuring that specified activities are financially profitable (ibid. p. 71). This raises questions about the types of linkages used to represent actual relationships between the sections of the BSC.

Causal relationships?

First, we consider whether a cause and effect chain occurs across the dimensions of learning and growth → efficient internal business processes → a high level of customer satisfaction → good financial results. For example, does X (say, the institution of total quality management) precede Y (say, a rise in profits) in time? Are X and Y logically independent? Does the observation of X necessarily entail the observation of Y? To illustrate the analysis, we will focus on the last two links of the BSC model. Here Kaplan and Norton (1996a, p. 67) suggest that *generic* relationships are involved between measures of the two areas. We may therefore question Kaplan and Norton's assertion that if a company delivers high value and quality to its customers, then the customers will be loyal and profits will necessarily, or very probably, be generated. Kaplan and Norton base their claim on Jones and Sasser (1995), who write: 'This high level of satisfaction will lead to greatly increased customer loyalty. And increased customer loyalty is the single most important driver of long term financial performance. Separate research has validated these beliefs' (p. 90).

The assumption of a causal relationship between customer satisfaction and loyalty (Jones and Sasser, 1995; Kaplan and Norton, 1996a) is based on the Jones and Sasser (1995) finding of considerable co-variation between high levels of customer satisfaction and loyalty. This is not surprising, however, as these concepts are expressions of a similar customer characteristic. Customer satisfaction reflects the intent of the customer to be loyal, so customer loyalty is logically linked to their level of satisfaction. As the two concepts are so logically similar, their measurements are inevitably linked. The relationship is, in essence, part of the same concept and therefore it has to be a logical one.

An investigation by Reichheld and Sasser (1990) supports the assumed causal relationship between customer loyalty and profitability. Using four case studies, they found the profit each customer generated had increased over the five-year period investigated. This trend was found in over a hundred companies (Reichheld and Sasser, 1990), hence their claim that loyal customers are the most profitable ones. The explanation was that attracting new customers involves initial costs whereas loyal customers involve less marketing and are willing to pay more for a product they have confidence in. However, Reichheld and Sasser (1990) ignore the customer who is loyal and satisfied, but only places small orders and/or buys customised products at low prices. This is exactly the type of customer who is not profitable according to Kaplan and Cooper (1998, p. 191). If a company has only profitable and loyal customers, it may be that its management control system works well and that the company does not sell to unprofitable but satisfied and loyal customers. Reichheld and Sasser (1990) defined loyal customers as those who generate low costs and accept high prices. Therefore, a priori, they equate loyal (and therefore probably) satisfied customers with profitable customers. Logically, the relationship they hypothesise is inevitable. Similarly, when Kaplan and Norton point out that a large market share combined with highly profitable customers drives good financial results, the relationship they identify is logical. Their claim is inherent in the concepts they use: a large volume of profitable sales will produce a good financial profit. Viewing the relationship as causal, as Kaplan and Norton (1996a, p. 70) do, is therefore misleading.

Other empirical investigations demonstrate a positive relationship between a high level of customer satisfaction and financial returns. Buzzell and Gale (1987, pp. 103–35), for example, show that the profitability of a company improves with increasingly positive customer assessment of the company's products and services relative to those of competitors. Their results, however, are based on statements made by companies and only occasionally tested on customers (Buzzell and Gale, 1987, p. 105). It is a reasonable and logical assumption that a company with good earnings believes its customers view its products as better than those of competitors. However, the direction of the causality is questionable: good results could cause company employees to make positive statements about their customers' views.

Logical fallacy

The following quotation from the manager of a strategic business unit illustrates some problems related to satisfaction analyses:

> I don't believe in customer satisfaction analyses. We would be told that our prices are too high and our quality too low. It is important to keep an eye on customers which disappear,

of course, but there may be a reason for it. For example, we will not try to keep a customer which squeezes us too hard. (An anonymous group manager, quoted in Nørreklit, 2000)

Furthermore, it is a tenet of statistics that one cannot conclude a causal relationship exists where an association is found between two variables. Profitability derived from customer satisfaction or customer loyalty is neither an inevitable nor a highly probable outcome. Of course a firm with loyal and profitable customers will necessarily show an overall profit. However, while we may claim that customers who are not loyal are costly, it does not follow that loyal customers are always inexpensive. Similarly, we know if it is raining the streets will be wet, but we cannot conclude the converse that if the streets are wet it has been raining. Drawing such conclusions would be a logical fallacy and the reasoning underpinning the operation of the BSC suffers from this limitation. This could lead to the selection of anticipatory performance indicators that are faulty, with the consequences of dysfunctional organisational behaviour and sub-optimised performance (Haas and Kleingeld, 1999).

Time lags

Finally, if a cause and effect relationship requires a time lag between cause and effect, then it is problematic that time is not part of the scorecard. The effect of the measures will occur at different times as different areas of performance involve different time scales. For example, the introduction of more efficient processes may yield more satisfied customers within months, while major product innovation may take much longer to implement and therefore not affect the financial results until a year or more later. Since the effect of some efforts will be almost immediate and that of others very slow, and numerous factors influence the financial results, it becomes difficult to determine when the financial effect of an action will occur or its scale. The financial effect of internal business process improvement, for example, may depend on the prior amount of slack in the company. Quality, for instance, could be a slack-creating mechanism if quality improvements are at the expense of volume or even productivity, and so any cost advantage would be reduced. If there is excess demand, a minor cut in quality performance may permit additional workload. If a temporal database of performance measures was established on a balanced scorecard then, after a while, it would identify relationships between actions and their effects over time on factors such as cost, output quantity and quality.

Measuring the effects of actions for new and complex activities is particularly problematic, since it is difficult and often impossible to establish performance measures for activities with which the organisation has little or no experience. Therefore, measuring effects is particularly difficult in companies that must constantly adapt to new situations and where innovation is important to competitiveness. The time lag and complexities between drivers and outcomes obscure the relationship between operations and end performance – i.e. exactly the relationship upon whose clarity the BSC depends.

Accounting methods

Abandoning the assumption that cause and effect forms the basis of the relationships between the four measurement sections of the BSC has major deleterious consequences for the BSC. First, accounting methods, in one form or another, are necessary within organisational life, but are insufficient for assessing the various acts and activities in which a company engages. Accounting methods are necessary when financial measures are central to constituting the reality of companies. Accounting is likewise required for assessing the financial consequences of factors such as increased customer satisfaction or quality improvements. Accounting information may show, amongst other things, which products or customers will be profitable and which input factors and processes generate costs of corresponding products or services. Activity-based costing analyses may help identify which products and customers are most profitable and guide managerial selection, pricing and resource consumption policies in relation to them (cf. Kaplan and Cooper, 1998). Such analyses may be used to define the firm's strategy and policies, which may subsequently be translated into financial and non-financial measures using the BSC. Case studies of firms may illustrate the cost impacts of strategies and policies in the individual firm. Other firms may learn from them, but it should be noted that no policy or strategy guarantees profit in all circumstances. Many of the factors determining profitability are firm specific. Fulfilling certain non-financial objectives such as those used in the BSC may be necessary, but they are also insufficient conditions for financial success. At best they are indicators of the likelihood that success will ultimately be achieved rather than a completely reliable predictor of it.

Finality

Finality can be another basis for the relationship between measures. Finality is fundamentally different from a cause and effect relationship. The consequence of assuming finality is that relationships among the various performance measures become more ambiguous and complex. (For example, profits may fall in the short run where loss leaders are used to gain operational scale; only in the longer term will positive profit effects emerge and the full relationship become apparent.) As a result, many of the benefits suggested for the BSC will be impracticable and its ability to inform and facilitate management control will be greatly reduced. If finality is involved, then other tools must be employed to report and analyse performance prior to making decisions.

Strategic coherence

When viewing a relationship between performance measures as one based on finality, it is important to establish coherence (Nørreklit and Schoenfeld, 1996; Haas and Kleingeld, 1999). Given the aim of obtaining certain results, coherence focuses on whether the relevant phenomena match or complement each other. For example, action is coherent if the actions taken (i.e. the means) are appropriate for the intended end. One condition for obtaining an end (e.g. profit improvement) is having access to input factors (e.g. appropriate human and technological resources) with the potential to realise the end. For managers or employees, it is a condition that they can access methods (e.g. motivational remuneration incentives) that allow them to control the input factors and, in turn, obtain the end intended. If there is lack of coherence (i.e. suitable resources and motivational techniques), then the conditions for reaching the targets are insufficient, sub-optimal, or even unobtainable. Our ability to judge coherence and so predict results requires sufficient knowledge of both the means and the ends. Insufficient knowledge (of means and ends) reduces the possibility of predicting and safeguarding results and brings greater uncertainty.

A coherent strategy requires the properties of the different areas of strategic focus (finance, market requirements, technology, internal business processes, etc.) to be integrated and harmonised, so allowing planned ends to be achieved. If any dissonance or imbalance is too marked, the financial results will fall short of expectations. Coherence evaluation involves constant monitoring of the relationships between the firm's resources. Coherence control at the strategic level needs to address both the present situation, to ensure that finances, market requirements, technology and internal business processes are coherent, and the future situation in which these same areas of strategic focus have to be coherent over time. Any imbalance must be identified through continual monitoring and then rebalanced. Strategic coherence therefore needs performance measurement support that integrates and coordinates the components of the firm across functional specialisms and over time.

Subjective judgements

Finally, it should be noted that predicting future performance is often complex. An evaluation system that does not coherently integrate all significant and relevant variables cannot show consistently valid results. As argued above, the causal relationship that Kaplan and Norton (1996a) suggest underpins the BSC lacks validity. Instead of the BSC, models that validly increase understanding of how business performance is created would be of greater practical benefit. However, this does not mean that measurement systems will have to be objective. Performance measurement and evaluation will always be partly subjective and to some extent depend on the intuition of the top management, because both past results and the impact of future opportunities should form part of the performance picture. Uncertainty about the future means that the most appropriate systems will involve subjective assumptions and judgements.

What are the linkages across the BSCs in use at different hierarchical levels?

Analytical linking

As mentioned previously, the method that Kaplan and Norton (1996a, pp. 8–15 and 199–223) advocate for implementing the BSC is hierarchical and top-down. Interrelated BSCs will be produced at each level in the organisation. The measurements used in BSCs for the bottom levels are derived from a deductive analytical process and the linkages between the BSC measurements at each level are therefore based on logical relationships. The BSC goes beyond mere accounting logic by assuming a logical relationship at a physical level. For example, it posits a logical relationship between aspects of operator ability and fuel consumption (Kaplan and Norton, 1996a, p. 214). However, at lower levels in the organisational hierarchy some relationships may actually be causal while other relationships may reflect a finality nature (see above).

The assumed measurement links at lower levels disregard any implementation problems and winning support for the system developed is considered unproblematic. Local conditions are defined by top management and local units are assumed unable to act on their own. They are reactive and never proactive.

Linking to commitment and realisable procedure

In order to make employees proactive, it is important to foster their *internal commitment* and not just their *external commitment* (Argyris and Kaplan, 1994, p. 91). Individuals with external commitment are primarily motivated by variables outside themselves (such as managers' instructions, organisational incentives and rewards) while individuals with internal commitment are motivated by variables within themselves (such as their own values and beliefs). External commitment is important for establishing organisational rules and communicating behaviour that is desirable and worthy of reward, but it is insufficient for developing individuals who are active and creative problem-solvers, since they are likely to act from internal commitment, i.e. they see themselves as responsible, self-motivating individuals.

Due to their top-down approach, BSCs for lower hierarchical levels are designed to relate to external commitment. This results in an added danger since, where the focus on external commitment is high, employees focus their attention only on what is measured. Employees will try to achieve good results in the areas measured, but this may be to the detriment of other important elements of performance.

Kaplan and Norton (1996a) assume goal congruence in organisations and that top management defines these goals. Research has, however, consistently shown that firms are a coalition in which top management is merely one party and many parties' aspirations must be juggled and balanced (Parker, 1979). It is not the firm but employees who act. The behaviour of employees is complex, determined by environmental and personal factors, and is a function of cognition, perception, beliefs, knowledge, rewards and goals (Parker, 1979). A different solution, therefore, might be to build the BSC so it is rooted in employees' internal commitment (Nørreklit and Schoenfeld, 1996), which may help ensure that measures are realisable. Apart from the input resources needed, the method needs to show which actions will enable employees to attain the results envisaged. Just describing the specifications of a new house and placing the materials and resources needed at the disposal of employees is not sufficient. An operational guide or manual is also needed (Nørreklit and Schoenfeld, 1996). Performance measures should reflect this and therefore they need to be organisationally rooted in a realisable way. If not, it is unlikely that the BSC will be successful.

Linking to language

The BSC also needs to be rooted in the language of employees. A key objective of the balanced scorecard is to communicate strategy throughout the organisation. The extent to which this succeeds will depend on whether the performance measures reflect the strategy and how performance measures are understood and interpreted by employees. The advantage of the strategic performance measures is that they are concrete. The disadvantage is that they are inevitably a simplified depiction of any strategy. If a given measurement is used, lower-level employees will not necessarily attribute it the same meaning as managers do (Føllesdal *et al.*, 1997). The meaning of a measure may differ with the social or cultural group in which the language game takes place, hence the importance of using an interactive method for building the BSC to develop both language and comprehension.

Coherence control

Coherence control links the goals and resources of each process to the overall company goals (Nørreklit and Schoenfeld, 1996). This must be coherent from several perspectives: (i) vertically/hierarchically – i.e. goals must match the view of top management; (ii) vertically/organisationally – i.e. the goal system must incorporate the views of employees; (iii) horizontally/organisationally – i.e. the goal systems of employees in interdependent positions must be constructed so that they support each other. Achieving coherence in measurement systems is unlikely if the system is designed and imposed by top management; interaction between the managerial and employee constituencies is more likely to produce a successful system.

Linking through strategic dialogue

A strategic dialogue (Simons, 1995; Nørreklit and Schoenfeld, 1996; Haas and Kleingeld, 1999) can be important for uncovering or influencing perceptions or actions when strategy and performance measurements are formulated. The dialogue is a dialectic process between two or more parties, during which both pose questions and receive answers. The aim is to increase each party's awareness and understanding. This may help bridge differences of perception and comprehension, so goal congruence increases. Communication through language provides opportunities for this to happen. Thus, management can use dialogue to encourage employees to continuously search for external problems and opportunities, while creating a network whereby internal commitments can be discovered. The dialogue should be part of a management style that allows top managers to continuously gather information relevant to strategic control of the company and influence the employees in the direction intended.

The strategic dialogue is important for formulating performance measures linked to the resources and internal commitments of organisational groups (Haas and Kleingeld, 1999). It helps ensure that employees have the internal commitment to reach the ends by the given means. If problems or opportunities are uncovered during performance measurement, this may contribute to strategy formulation.

Financial measurements

Finally, it should be noted that strategic dialogue and coherence control do not, of themselves, secure profit. Accounting systems to guide and monitor managerial efforts also have to be involved. However, a dialogue may contribute to the efforts of accountants to move away from a pure scorekeeper role towards a new, more integrative, role as business analysts and strategic management accountants.

Promoting the BSC

The preceding discussion has cast a measure of doubt on the reliability of some of the key conceptual foundations of the BSC. Given these limitations, how has the BSC achieved its popularity? One answer lies in the style of its advocacy and promotion. In this section, the main presentational text for the BSC (Kaplan and Norton, 1996a) is subjected to a literary and argumentation analysis. The results suggest that the book belongs to the genre of the management guru text, where sound argumentation is not a prevalent feature (Nørreklit, 2003). Instead it employs stylistic devices and argumentation that appeal to an audience's emotions as a means of persuasion.

Some rhetorical devices

The author of a text may attempt to gain reader approval in three different ways: through ethos, pathos or logos (Aristotle, 1996). Ethos is concerned with the reader's trust in the author; the credibility or authority of the author generates reader approval. Pathos appeals to the reader's emotions and mood, while logos appeals to the reader's rationality. Logos covers everything that humans can establish through reason and includes both logical and empirical argumentation. A scholarly text by a reputable researcher is expected to appeal primarily to a reader's ethos and logos, but not to their pathos (Aristotle, 1996). It is expected to be logical, direct and unequivocal. In contrast, poetry or adverts are expected to win approval by appealing to their readers' pathos.

Tropes is a stylistic device which includes the use of figurative language in the form of, for example, analogies and metaphors (Corbett and Connors, 1999). These figures of speech can be used to develop either pathos or logos in a text. They can clarify scholarly argument but they can also be used, without sound logos, for propaganda. They cause a reader to transfer qualities from one object to another by virtue of similarities between them (Bonet, 1994). Such associations influence the reader's judgement. Thus it is important to recognise that comparisons by analogy and metaphor have limitations. First, they are partial as they emphasise only certain aspects of the objects they employ. Second, aspects that count for little in one context may be extremely important in another. Third, due to their ambiguities they may create the idea of similarity where none actually exists.

Consequently, in scholarly texts these devices should be used only where the similarities are reasonable (Aristotle, 1996) and they can contribute to new scientific insights (Arbib and Hesse, 1986). Scientific metaphors must be internally tightly knit by logical and causal interrelations. Moreover, they only become explanatory when extended and developed by logic and analogy rather than by mere association (Arbib and Hesse, 1986). In non-scholarly works their use may be less rigorous and they can be used to develop pathos rather than logos.

The BSC literary style and argumentation

The pilot analogy

The BSC text begins with an analogy that likens the management of a company to piloting a plane. This is evident in the following quotations:

> Yet navigating today's organizations through complex competitive environments is at least as complicated as flying a jet. (Kaplan and Norton, 1996a, p. 2)

Managers, like pilots, need instrumentation about many aspects of their environment and performance to monitor the journey toward excellent future outcomes. (Kaplan and Norton, 1996a, p. 2)

Kaplan and Norton (1996a) also use the following aviation metaphors: *cockpit, jet airplane, pilot, airspeed, altitude, altimeter, fuel, fuel gauge, mountains, airspace and navigate.*

The *jet airplane* is the modern, faster version of the company-as-a-machine metaphor. The jet airplane belongs in the information age while the machine lies in the industrial age. Comparing jet plane navigation to managing a peopled organisation operating in a complex competitive environment is, however, problematic. People are equated to mechanical components in an airplane that react when the pilot pushes the control stick. Furthermore, the image of organisations as machines characterises entities that operate bureaucratically, routinely, predictably and in specialised ways. These are not attributes normally associated with large, contemporary organisations operating in complex competitive environments.

By contrast, personal enrichment occurs when the manager is compared to a pilot who (as the term suggests) is in control. Furthermore, the pilot metaphor gives the manager the aura of an international globetrotter – an image with which the reader is pleased to identify. The pilot metaphor thus enhances the recipient's perception of his own *ethos*. It is problematic, however, for a pilot does not practise management but uses mechanical control. The pilot metaphor creates a highly simplified image of management. The jet airplane argument gives rise to an invalid *argument from analogy* as it assumes that the similarities between the items under comparison are numerous. However, this is a problem since the phenomena the authors compare are not very alike. Overall, the aviation metaphor appeals primarily to readers' emotions (*pathos*) and less to their rational commitment (*logos*). The logos of the analogy is not valid.

The natural science analogy

The text (Kaplan and Norton, 1996a) also uses metaphors, concepts and quotations well established in the area of natural science: *drivers* (p. 2), *physical* (p. 1), *battery of instrumentation* (p. 2), *force* (p. 7), *collision* (p. 7), *synthesis* (p. 7), *cause and effect* (p. 15), *hypothesis test* (p. 17) and *valid and disconfirming evidence* (p. 17). Moreover, within the BSC text scientific usage occurs in several of the postulates:

The collision between the irresistible force to build long-range competitive capabilities and the immovable object of the historical-cost financial accounting model has created a new synthesis: the Balanced Scorecard. (Kaplan and Norton, 1996a, p. 7)

Through a series of cause-and-effect relationships embodied in the Balanced Scorecard, these capabilities eventually become translated into superior financial performance. (Kaplan and Norton, 1996a, p. 14)

In the natural sciences, the meaning of these words is fairly unequivocal but this is often not so when they are used in other fields. *Force*, for example, is a clearly defined concept in physics but is more vague when used elsewhere. Furthermore, *hypothesis tests* of causal relationships are well established within natural science while their appropriateness in social science is more debatable. Any reader who is inattentive to the differences runs the risk of attaching qualities to the concepts that they only hold in natural science. Using metaphors from physics and aviation, the authors imply that the issue under consideration belongs in an unequivocal scientific universe.

The problem of the authors' use of these scientific concepts is that they are not expressions of the reality in which companies operate. As shown earlier, the causal relationships to which Kaplan and Norton allude do not exist. Employees do not necessarily react when managers push the control stick and, if they do, their reaction may be dysfunctional. Metaphors may appeal to intellect (*logos*), but in the case under consideration the metaphors employed appeal to emotions, while creating the illusion that companies operate in a context subject to scientific laws.

Contradictions

Sometimes Kaplan and Norton use concepts from the realm of science with concepts from other branches of knowledge, which results in mutually contradictory concepts. For example, the claim: 'The emphasis on cause and effect in constructing a scorecard introduces dynamic systems thinking' (Kaplan and Norton, 1996a, p. 15) is contradictory because a cause and effect relationship is most likely to exist where variables exhibit stable patterns while dynamism destroys the ability to discern cause and effect. The authors may have goals and means in mind rather than cause and effect, but this is not explicitly stated.

Elsewhere, when the BSC technique is described, the authors' claim that both a cause and effect relationship and a logical relationship hold between, for example, satisfied customers and profitability (Kaplan and Norton 1996a, pp. 71–2) But, again, this is confusing because both relationships cannot hold simultaneously. Thus, the *logos* is unclear and open to misinterpretation.

Ethos

The text contains a large number of postulates or claims, such as those given above, that lack explanation or evidence supporting their truth. Thus the readers' belief in the postulates rests on the authority of the text's source, i.e. its ethos. The authors' intention may have been to use *analysis*-backed claims, meaning they are true or false as a consequence of the definition of the expressions used. But, if so, they fail, as the claims are not self-evident and require some explanation. Alternatively, the claims may be *synthetic* (also known as *empirical* claims), meaning that their truth or falsehood cannot be established merely on the basis of the definition of the expressions used. But, if so, the authors ought to demonstrate their truth or show they are common knowledge. However, as many claims relate to what the BSC can accomplish, they cannot be common knowledge. The few references in the text are mainly related to the Harvard Business School, the lead author is professor there and the publisher is the Harvard Business School Press. So the argumentation is: if Harvard says P, P is true.

This argument appeals to the authority of Harvard. The text (Kaplan and Norton, 1996a) also includes arguments that rest on the authority of the authors, which is evident through the use of first person personal pronouns as in *our experience* (pp. 12 and 18) and *we consider* (p. 15).

190

In order to evaluate the validity and nature of arguments appealing to authority, it is important to determine whether they draw on the expertise of the Harvard Business School or merely its prestige. The analysis here encourages scepticism of arguments appealing to the expertise of Harvard as, for example, significant claims regarding the BSC are not valid. They rely on the reader's conception of the Harvard Business School as an institution whose researchers are highly qualified and gifted. The appeal is to ethos. It is, however, also emotional (pathos) rather than intellectual (logos) because it requires the reader to believe the authors and accept their claims without explanation.

The management guru genre

The literary style of the BSC text matches that in the work of other management gurus (Huczynski, 1993; Boje *et al.*, 1997; Alvarez, 1998). Many of these publications are characterised by unclear and loaded concepts, analogies and metaphors as well as contradictions, jargon, banal and optimistic claims and an absence of critical apprais-al of their theories. Management authors often refer to their own experience, and arguments appealing to their own authority are common. Their attitude to academic traditions is rather lax (Alvarez, 1998).

One reason why management guru concepts have become popular is their useful-ness for creating social order and legitimacy. Storytelling is a powerful device where-by managers and consultants may challenge old stories or ways of doing things to justify change (Boje *et al.*, 1997). Thus, BPR (business process re-engineering), for example, may help to justify firing employees (Boje *et al.*, 1997), while the BSC may justify cost reductions and make employees increase customer service.

However, hierarchical top-down systems suffer from employees trying to bypass and undermine them. What employees say they will do differs from their actions (Argyris and Schon, 1978). Employees often do not do what managers expect them to do, which is why rational order is undermined. To retain the focus of the organisation and keep it together, managers must 'restory' (or resell) the bureaucratic model. The new story draws renewed attention throughout the organisation, which may lead to more efficient actions, as the Hawthorne experiments indicated (Mayo, 1933). Hence, the need for new theories (or new stories) such as the BSC is constant.

Furthermore, organisational employees need to show that they can control the uncertainty involved in their jobs. One way they can do this is by becoming iso-morphic, i.e. copying others whom they consider good exemplars (Meyer and Rowan, 1977). Thus the motivation for adopting tools such as the BSC does not lie exclusively in the wish to introduce more rational techniques and processes. A 'bandwagon' based on mimicry can occur and this can enhance the personal kudos accorded to the managers responsible rather than deliver any economic benefits to the firm.

This legitimacy-providing, but not necessarily efficiency-enhancing, effect (Meyer and Rowan, 1977) of management theories is supported by Staw and Epstein (2000). They show that companies associated with popular management techniques (relative to those which have no such association) are more admired, perceived as more innovative and are rated higher in management quality.

However, their financial performance is not better. Staw and Epstein (2000) also show that popular management techniques endow the management profession with legitimacy and further the interests of chief executives in companies associated with these techniques as they receive higher remuneration.

If the intention is to restory as justification for new administrative method adoption, then a lack of clarity, superficiality and undefined content may be an advantage. Theories with these characteristics are easier to adapt to the needs and convictions found in various organisations and groups. The fact that the concepts are open to interpretation may be a precondition of their successful adaptation to the local culture (Alvarez, 1998), as readers can interpret the theory to suit their own ends. This flexibility also has the attraction of making it easier for adopters to evade the issue of mistakes and to explain away problems.

Finally, it should be noted that theories of management gurus may further the interests and legitimise the social existence and roles not only of companies and their managers, but also of consultants, the academic community, intellectuals, governmental groups and granting bodies (Alvarez, 1998). The motives of these groups create an institutional network in which theories of management gurus play an important role in keeping everybody within the network in check (Latour, 1987). Politicians and funding bodies may want business schools to research and teach subjects relevant to the business community so that their allocation of resources to such schools appears justified in the eyes of the business community and the public. In urging practitioners to act in accordance with the models offered by the management gurus, the gurus imply that they *know how* to act as practitioners (Alvarez, 1998).

The business community's preferences for models offered by gurus are reinforced by supportive writings by intellectuals in popularised business media. Given the inherent forces of the network, academics in business schools may promote the models of management gurus to legitimise their own profession and further their own interests. They become disciples of the management gurus, who apparently link academia and practice. Furthermore, scientific journals can reinforce the promotion of such theories as they tend to look for research on topics of current interest. Thus, the academic community contributes to the legitimising and restorying syndrome (Straw and Epstein, 2000). Moreover, the long acceptance processes of recognised academic journals may lead to critical perspectives on such models not being publicly available until the widespread interest in the models has faded (Straw and Epstein, 2000).

The world of organisational management is not a well-ordered, rational world. Managerial actions such as introducing new techniques like the BSC may be motivated by more than just the immediate search for profit. They may reflect managers' personal needs to be seen to be changing things, to resemble admirable others, to acquire legitimacy by employing the latest techniques, and to retain flexibility in the ways information is used within their organisations. Moreover, the impetus to use these techniques may be reinforced by the educational environment and by the consultancy profession whose prosperity partly depends on maintaining a supply of novelties for management.

Conclusion

It is not uncommon for management models to be heuristic – payback period and break-even analyses are two long-standing examples of this type of management tool. The BSC falls into this category, as it is a simplistic representation of the highly complex phenomena that is organisational performance. Judging a heuristic can be undertaken on both an empirical and a conceptual basis as both its practical and theoretical benefits and limitations will be relevant to its assessment.

The practical popularity of the BSC provides *prima facie* empirical evidence of its positive assessment. The BSC offers a clear and simple framework that can be customised through the selection of measures for each of its four components. It allows financial and non-financial measures to be put together as a package. Underlying its design is an alleged cause and effect relationship across its parts that directs improved performance and facilitates feedforward control actions.

It is possible to challenge the validity of the central cause and effect model upon which the BSC is based. The complexities of organisational performance are unlikely to be accurately represented by such a simple linear model and the relationships it suggests may be of a logical or finality, as opposed to cause and effect, nature. Consequently, the BSC may motivate inappropriate action by managers based on the information fed to them. However, it is too early to make definite conclusions about its use in practice. Its relative novelty in many organisations makes difficult any reliable determination of whether the BSC has become a long-term addition to the established portfolio of management techniques, or whether it makes a significant economic contribution for its users. It may be one of the many management technique fads, of relatively short duration, that are temporarily driven to popularity by the neo-institutional forces described above involving isomorphism, legitimacy and social order.

Our conclusion, therefore, is that the evidence available on the BSC is currently quite ambiguous. Its origins are related to academia, but its documentary presentation does not explicitly contain a high standard of argumentation. It has a strong ethos derived from its Harvard Business School connections, but relies on the reader bringing their own intentionality to bear on interpreting much of the BSC text's content. However, the case for the BSC is based on extensive use of arguments and literary devices which lack internal validity and consistency, but which strongly appeal to source authority. Hence it allows power to take precedence over reason. In summary, empirical research as yet precludes drawing firm conclusions on the practical worth of the BSC. At a conceptual level there are several significant reasons to treat with some caution claims for its value as a management accounting tool.

References

Ahn, H. (2001) 'Applying the balanced scorecard concept: an experience report', *Long Range Planning*, 34, 441–61.

Alvarez, J.E. (1998) *The Diffusion and Consumption of Business Knowledge*, London: Macmillan Press.

Arbib, M.A. and Hesse, M. (1986) *The Construction of Reality*, Cambridge: Cambridge University Press.

Argyris, C. and Kaplan, R.S. (1994) 'Implementing new knowledge: the case of activity-based costing', *Accounting Horizons*, 8(3), 83–105.

Argyris, C. and Schon, D. (1978) *Organizational Learning: A Theory of Action Perspective*, Boston, MA: Addison-Wesley.

Aristotle (1996) *Retorik*, Copenhagen: Museum Tusculanums Forlag, The University of Copenhagen.

Ax, C. and Bjornenak, T. (2005) 'Bundling and diffusion of management accounting innovations: the case of the balanced scorecard in Sweden', *Management Accounting Research*, **16**(1), 1–20.

Boje, D.M., Rosile, G.A., Dennehy, R. and Summers, D.J. (1997) 'Restorying reengineering: some deconstructions and postmodern alternatives', *Communication Research*, **24**(6), 631–68.

Bonet, E. (1994) *From Reality to Metaphor: An Introduction to Analysis and Creation of Language*, Barcelona: Fundacio Catalancia per a la Recerca.

Brabazon, T. (1999) *The Balanced Scorecard*, London: The Association of Chartered Certified Accountants.

Butler, A., Letza, S. and Neale, B. (1997) 'Linking the balanced scorecard to strategy', *Long Range Planning*, **30**(2), 242–53.

Buzzell, R.D. and Gale, B.T. (1987) *The PIMS Principles: Linking Strategy to Performance*, New York: New York Press.

CIMA (2000) *Official Terminology*, London: Chartered Institute of Management Accountants.

Cobbald, I. and Lawrie, G. (2002) *Classification of Balanced Scorecards Based on Their Intended Use*, 2GC Active Management. Available online at: www.2gc.co.uk/pdf/2GC-PMA02-3f.pdf.

Corbett, E.P.J. and Connors, R.J. (1999) *Classical Rhetoric for the Modern Student*, Oxford: Oxford University Press.

Føllesdal, D., Walløe, L. and Elster, J. (1997) *Argumentasjonsteori, Språk og Vitenskapsfilosofi*, Oslo: Universitetsforlaget.

Haas, M. de and Kleingeld, A. (1999) 'Multilevel design of performance measurement systems: enhancing strategic dialogue throughout the organization', *Management Accounting Research*, **10**(3), 233–61.

Huczynski, A. (1993) *Management Gurus: What Makes Them and How to Become One*, London: Routledge.

Ijiri, Y. (1978) *The Foundations of Accounting Measurement*, Houston, TX: Scholars Book Co.

Jones, T.O. and Sasser, W.E. (1995) 'Why satisfied customers defect', *Harvard Business Review*, November/December, 88–99.

Kanji, G.K. and Sa, P.M. (2002) 'Kanji's business scorecard', *Total Quality Management*, **13**(1), 13–27.

Kasurinen, T. (2002) 'Exploring management accounting change: the case of the balanced scorecard implementation', *Management Accounting Research*, **13**(3), 323–44.

Kaplan, R.S. and Cooper, R. (1998) *Cost and Effect: Using Integrated Cost Systems to Drive Profitability and Performance*, Boston, MA: Harvard Business School Press.

Kaplan, R.S. and Norton, D.P. (1992) 'The balanced scorecard: measures that drive performance', *Harvard Business Review*, **70**(1), 61–6.

Kaplan, R.S. and Norton, D.P. (1993) 'Putting the balanced scorecard to work', *Harvard Business Review*, **71**(3), 134–47.

Kaplan, R.S. and Norton, D.P. (1996a) *The Balanced Scorecard*, Boston, MA: Harvard Business School Press.

Kaplan, R.S. and Norton, D.P. (1996b) 'Linking the balanced scorecard to strategy', *California Management Review*, Fall, 53–79.

Kaplan, R.S. and Norton, D.P. (2000) *The Strategy Focused Organisation*, Boston, MA: Harvard Business School Press.

Kaplan, R.S. and Norton, D.P. (2001) 'Transforming the balanced scorecard from performance measurement to strategic management', *Accounting Horizons,* 15, 87–104.

Kaplan, R.S. and Norton, D.P. (2004) 'How strategy maps frame an organisation's objectives', *Financial Executive,* **20**(2), 40–5.

Latour, B. (1987) *Science in Action – How to Follow Scientists and Engineers Through Society,* Cambridge, MA: Harvard University Press.

Maisel, L.S. (1992) 'Performance measurement: the balanced scorecard approach', *Journal of Cost Management,* Summer, 47–52.

Mayo, E. (1933) *The Human Problems of Industrial Civilization,* New York: Viking Press.

Meyer, J. and Rowan, B. (1977) 'Institutionalized organizations: formal structure of myth and ceremony', *American Journal of Sociology,* 83, 340–63.

Mooraj, S., Oyon, D. and Hostettler, D. (1999) 'The balanced scorecard: a necessary good or an unnecessary evil?' *European Management Journal,* **17**(5), 481–91.

Nørreklit, H. (2000) 'The balance on the balanced scorecard: a critical analysis of some of its assumptions', *Management Accounting Research,* **11**(1), 65–88.

Nørreklit, H. (2003) 'The balanced scorecard: what is the score?' *Accounting, Organizations and Society,* **28**(6), 591–619.

Nørreklit, L. and Schoenfeld, H.M. (1996) *Resources of the Firm: Creating, Controlling and Accounting,* Copenhagen: DJØF Publishing.

Olve, N.G., Roy, J. and Wetter, M. (1997) *Balanced Scorecard. Svensk Praktik,* Sweden: Liber AB.

Pandey, I.M. (2005) 'Balanced scorecard: myth and reality', *Vikalpa: The Journal for Decision Makers,* **30**(1), 85–102.

Parker, L.D. (1979) 'Divisional performance measurement: beyond an exclusive profit test', *Accounting and Business Research,* Autumn, 309–19.

Reichheld, F.F. and Sasser, W.E. (1990) 'Zero defections: quality comes to services', *Harvard Business Review,* September/October, 105–11.

Ridgeway, V.F. (1956) 'Dysfunctional consequences of performance measurements', *Administrative Science Quarterly,* 1, 240–7.

Ritter, M. (2003) 'The use of balanced scorecards in the strategic management of corporate communication', *Corporate Communications: An International Journal,* **8**(1), 44–59.

Simons, R. (1995) *Levers of Control,* Boston, MA: Harvard Business School Press.

Staw, B.M and Epstein, L.D. (2000) 'What bandwagons bring: effects of popular management techniques on corporate performance, reputation and CEO pay', *Administrative Science Quarterly,* **45**, 523–56.

Further reading

Kaplan, R.S. and Norton, D.P. (1992) 'The balanced scorecard: measures that drive performance', *Harvard Business Review,* **70**(1), 61–6. This paper provides a short, readable description of the BSC by its creators.

Kaplan, R.S. and Norton, D.P. (1996) *The Balanced Scorecard,* Boston, MA: Harvard Business School Press. This text contains an extensive description of the BSC and how it is designed and used. It highlights its many advantages and provides numerous illustrative examples.

Kaplan, R.S. and Norton, D.P. (2000) *The Strategy Focused Organisation,* Boston, MA: Harvard Business School Press. This text extends previous work on the BSC by focusing on its role in strategy creation, communication and implementation.

Kaplan, R.S. and Norton, D.P. (2001) 'Transforming the balanced scorecard from performance measurement to strategic management', *Accounting Horizons,* **15**, 87–104. This paper provides a short, readable exposition of how the BSC supports the business strategy process.

Nørreklit, H. (2000) 'The balance on the balanced scorecard: a critical analysis of some of its assumptions', *Management Accounting Research,* **11**(1), 65–88. This paper contains a critique of the BSC which highlights its technical limitations as a performance measurement tool.

Nørreklit, H. (2003) 'The balanced scorecard: what is the score?' *Accounting, Organizations and Society,* **28**(6), 591–619. This paper examines how the BSC has been promoted by its creators through a series of literary techniques.

Appendix: Examples of the balanced scorecard

(1) Bank: Metro Bank

Strategic objectives	Strategic measurements (Lag indicators)	Strategic measurements (Lead indicators)
Financial		
Improve returns	Return on investment	
Broaden revenue mix	Revenue growth	Revenue mix
Reduce cost structure	Deposit service cost change	
Customer		
Increase customer satisfaction with our products and people	Share of segment	Depth of relationship
Increase satisfaction after the sale	Customer retention	Satisfaction survey
Internal		
Understand our customers		
Creative innovative products	New product revenue	Product development cycle
Cross-sell products	Cross-sell ratio	Hours with customer
Shift customers to cost-effective channels	Channel mix change	
Minimise operational problems		
Responsive	Service error rate	
	Request fulfilment time	
Learning		
Develop strategic skills		Strategic job coverage ratio
Provide strategic information	Employee satisfaction	Strategic information availability ratio
Align personal goals	Revenue per employee	Personal goals alignment

Source: Kaplan and Norton (1996a, p. 155).

(2) University: The University of Edinburgh BSC 2004/05 (see www.ed.ac.uk)

Organisational development perspective *Sustaining a dynamic institutional profile*		Financial perspective *Use of resources in a cost-effective manner to further strategic aims*	
Performance indicator name	Value	Performance indicator Name	Value
Shape of student population • Proportion of full-time undergraduates from Scotland	52.2%	% of total income from non-formulaic funding sources	66.0%
• No. of research postgraduate students	2,874		
• Fee income from taught postgraduate students	£10,808k		
• Lifelong learning registrations	17,026		
Flexibility of curriculum	17.7%	Historic cost surplus as % of turnover	2.3%
Research grant applications submitted p.a. per member of academic staff (AT and AC)	1.22	Administrative operating costs as % of academic operating costs	9.9%
Proportion of new appointments to Chairs who are women	19.0%	Research indirect cost recovery contribution as % of total research income	10.9%
Headcount of staff development attendees	3,574	Commercialisation of research (licences signed)	34
Number of staff on fixed-term contracts as % of all staff employed	30%	Fundraising	£9.13M
–	–	Ratio current assets: current liabilities	1.56:1
–	–	Average annual cost of a full-time equivalent staff member	£36.3k
–	–	Utilities, maintenance and servicing costs per square metre	£53 psm
Stakeholder perspective *Attraction of high calibre students from a broad range of backgrounds to an institution nationally and internationally respected by peers staff and the public*		Internal business perspective *Consistent support to the university in achieving its mission and strategy*	
International student headcounts	2,939	Number of full-time students per open access computing seat	6.2
Proportion of students achieving a first or upper second class degree	74.9%	% of library stock issued by self-service	52.6%
Widening participation: proportion of students from state schools/colleges	65.7%	Proportion of central committees with an online service for members and the proportion of papers available online from these committees	73% provided 94% online
Intake of home/EU students from ethnic minorities as % of total intake of home/EU students	4.9%	Total income per square metre of gross internal area	£666 psm
Newspaper cuttings analysis: % of column centimetres positive	98%	Capital expenditure and planned maintenance as % of estate value	5.9%

(Continued)

% of academic staff in 5 and 5* RAE units of assessment	74.4%	Total property cost as % of university total income	7.9%
–	–	Backlog maintenance spend required for the university to comply with the Disability Discrimination Act	circa £5.5M
–	–	Room utilisation	42.3%

10

Strategic investment appraisal

Deryl Northcott and Fadi Alkaraan

Introduction

Mergers and acquisitions, expansions into new lines of business, advanced manufacturing technology initiatives and e-business developments. These strategic investments, and others like them, have a major impact on the future direction of organisations, so it is important that they are made carefully. This is not easy, however. Strategic investments involve significant long-term financial commitments, slow-to-materialise benefits and high levels of uncertainty, all of which makes them difficult to evaluate.

As we will outline in this chapter, strategic investment appraisal calls for a variety of decision-making approaches – from 'rational economic' to 'incremental-adaptive' – and a variety of analysis tools. Some of these tools, such as internal rate of return (IRR), net present value (NPV) and many risk analysis techniques, are well established and firmly rooted in rational economic principles. The calculation, relative merits and shortcomings of these analyses are outlined in many textbooks, so are not the focus here. (Interested readers would benefit from reviewing Dugdale and Jones's discussion of investment appraisal techniques in Chapter 9 of the second edition of this book.) Other analysis tools are relatively new and less well structured, but are thought to have the potential to address shortcomings in the scope and flexibility of established tools. Finding the right combination of appropriate and helpful analysis tools is a key challenge for managers involved in strategic investment appraisal.

In this chapter we first explain why 'strategic' investment decisions are different from everyday, operational capital investment choices – i.e. what makes them difficult and complex? We then outline various conceptual models of investment decision-making, and consider how established analysis tools fit (or do not fit) within these models. At the limits of established analysis tools, new, more 'strategic' approaches are emerging – we identify five such approaches and outline why they are considered promising for strategic investment appraisal. Then, we review the evidence from practice. What do practitioners tell us about the tools they use for strategic investment appraisal? Are they content with the established analysis techniques, or are they now looking to emergent 'strategic' approaches? Finally, we reflect on ways forward in dealing with the complexities of strategic investment analysis, and suggest some guidelines for the development and adoption of appropriate analysis approaches.

What are strategic investment decisions?

The capital investment literature distinguishes between investment decisions that are *operational* in nature and those which are *strategic*. Operational decisions are more 'everyday'. They can be readily conceptualised by managers, since the risk and likely outcomes are well understood, and can usually be executed via routine (or 'programmed') decision-making protocols and procedures. Examples of operational investment decisions include the replacement or expansion of existing assets, or investments in activities, products or markets that are close to the organisation's current operations. Such decisions focus on sustaining current or 'normal' activities rather than initiating new, more innovative and risky endeavours.

In contrast, strategic investment decisions commit an organisation to a new strategic direction. Various characteristics have been associated with strategic investment decisions (see, for example, Mintzberg et al., 1976; Butler et al., 1993). They can be summarised as follows:

1 *Non-programmed and unusual* – strategic investment projects present a challenge to managers because there are no obvious exemplars to follow.
2 *Substantial* – they require a significant commitment of resources.
3 *Complex* – they tend to impact multiple operational areas (e.g. research and development, production, marketing) and require diverse expertise.
4 *Long-term* – they have a profound impact on the firm's long-term activities and performance and are intended to help a firm achieve its long-term goals.
5 *Competitively orientated* – they are intended to maintain or enhance the firm's competitive position by developing new product or market opportunities, exploiting technology developments, or enhancing production flexibility and/or efficiency.
6 *Uncertain* – their costs and benefits can be difficult to determine, so decision-makers' knowledge of the possible outcomes is often incomplete.
7 *Subjective* – they are influenced by the values and expectations of those who determine the organisation's strategy.

Typical examples of strategic investment decisions include: company acquisitions and mergers, the introduction of major new product lines, investments in long-term marketing initiatives, the installation of new manufacturing processes, the introduction of advanced manufacturing and information technologies, and substantial shifts in production capability (Mintzberg et al., 1976; Van Cauwenbergh et al., 1996; Slagmulder, 1997).

To understand the significance of strategic investment decisions, we need to understand the concept of business strategy. A strategy is a long-term plan for how an organisation intends to compete in its environment and what sorts of structures, resources and actions are required to achieve these intentions. The concept of business strategy was discussed in Chapter 7, but it is sufficient for our purposes to note that capital investment decisions both *shape* strategy (by dictating the assets that are at the organisation's future disposal) and *reflect* strategy (since the outcomes of investment decision-making are guided by strategic goals). Strategic investment decision-making cannot be seen as a separate, independent activity, therefore. It is an integral part of strategy formulation and occurs alongside it rather than following it.

Models of strategic decision-making

Given the close alignment between strategy formulation and strategic investment appraisal, various conceptual models of strategic decision-making are helpful in understanding the complexities of these decisions. In this section we outline five models of decision-making that illuminate different aspects of investment decision-making.

The *rational* model derives from neo-classical economic assumptions. It takes a classic view of decision-making as an orderly and rational process aimed at wealth maximisation. A problem is defined and isolated, information is gathered, alternatives are identified, and outcomes are rationally analysed. The assumptions underpinning this model, and their abstraction from the realities of organisational decision-making, are well known. Decision-makers are assumed to have known, unambiguous objectives, full information (i.e. no uncertainty) about the consequences of different alternatives, and the ability to consistently evaluate the relative advantages of each option and select the optimal alternative. This model leaves no room for emotions, inconsistent values, sub-optimal cognitive capabilities, politics, persuasion or negotiation.

The *bounded-rationality* model has its roots in the work of Simon (1957) and Cyert and March (1963) in particular. These writers challenged the validity of the neo-classical economic viewpoint by rejecting the notion of human decision-makers as value-maximising calculators. Simon (1957) introduced the concept of decision-makers as *satisficers* who use their imperfect cognitive abilities to make satisfactory (albeit sub-optimal) decisions under conditions of incomplete information, time limits and political pressures. The rationality of these decisions is, therefore, 'bounded' by these constraints. As a consequence, intuition and judgement rather than rational computation may form the basis for making a decision (Butler *et al.*, 1993).

The *political/bureaucratic* model acknowledges the further complications of self-interest, competing goals and political behaviour. Organisations are seen as political systems within which individuals and groups bargain, beguile, contest and coalesce to advance their own self-interests (Pettigrew, 1973). Decision-making therefore becomes a power game between interest groups competing for control of organisational resources. Like the bounded-rationality model, this perspective is a reaction to economic assumptions that organisations possess a single, superordinate goal. Instead, decision-making is seen as highly dynamic and only partially predicated on rational economic analysis.

Cohen *et al.* (1972) proposed the *garbage can model* to describe decision-making in organisations characterised by ambiguous, ill-defined or inconsistent goals. It provides a stark contrast to the rational economic model of decision-making, since it suggests that decisions result from the random union of people, problems, solutions and choice opportunities – i.e. a form of 'organised anarchy'. Decision-makers are thought to discover their goals as they act, rather than having predetermined goals that direct their action. In comparison to the preceding models, the garbage can model draws attention to the impact of chance on fuzzy decisions that lack clear beginning and end points.

The fifth model describes *incremental-adaptive* decision-making. It combines elements of the previous models to recognise that decision-making draws on a set of techniques that have both rational/analytical and power/behavioural aspects. The cognitive limitations of decision-makers are recognised, as are the variety of values, attitudes and interests amongst those involved. The outcomes of the decision-making process are thus seen as a mixture of both incremental and rational elements whereby objectives are reconsidered and sometimes reformulated as the decision progresses.

The various decision-making assumptions and depictions represented in these five models capture differing aspects of investment appraisal. On the face of it, the rational model seems to fit best with straightforward operational investment decisions, where information and likely outcomes are clear and goals and interests are less contested. Certainly, where there is low environmental uncertainty and high consensus among decision participants as to goals, alternatives and likely outcomes, rational economic analyses such as internal rate of return (IRR) and net present value (NPV) offer unambiguous, transparent and persuasive means of appraising investment options.

However, these established economic analysis tools are also applied to *strategic* investment decisions, even though these decisions rarely match the rational model's assumptions. Strategic investment decisions are, as we have noted, characterised by incomplete knowledge, making it impossible to identify and quantify all the relevant decision parameters, variables and possible states of nature. Uncertainty, and the challenge it presents to financial analysis, is endemic in strategic investment decision-making. Also, managers are human beings whose cognitive limitations prevent them from following a completely rational-analytic approach and so, as per Simon's (1957) bounded-rationality model, they satisfice rather than optimise in their decision-making behaviour. They also face political complexities where goals and interests are contested and negotiated, and where the political/bureaucratic and incremental-adaptive models best describe their decision-making practices. In some instances, ill-defined or ambiguous goals lead to the sort of fuzzy and random decision-making described in the garbage can model, meaning that decision-makers have to navigate an inconsistent and messy choice pathway, relying on their own judgement to guide them. How can rational economic analysis tools possibly support such inconsistent modes of investment decision-making?

Here we come to a central theme of this chapter. Given the complexities of strategic investment appraisal, how can managers combine the strengths of different decision-making approaches across the gamut of rational to garbage can? What, if any, analysis tools can support decisions that are so multifarious? Is greater economic rationality to be preferred, or are strategic decisions better served by informed (though subjective) managerial judgement?

A growing appreciation of the cognitive psychology and organisational behaviour literatures has guided us to an understanding that judgement, rather than being an *irrational* process, complements analytical methods. As the product of experience and learning, judgement skills are particularly important to strategic investment analysis because they create a capacity for decision-making where no obviously correct model or rule is available or when relevant data is unreliable or incomplete. Indeed, Butler *et al.* (1993, p. 92) noted that for some companies 'judgement is the dominant strategy of the decision strategies (rating even slightly above the computation strategy)'. It is apparent that judgement can play a major and justifiable role in decision-making, particularly within firms that operate in high-tech, dynamic and/or highly competitive environments. Thus, strategic investment appraisal cannot be based entirely on financial analysis; informed judgement is also crucial. Ignoring either aspect will render decision-making less effective.

The key to developing improved techniques for strategic investment decision-making therefore lies in coupling rational economic analysis with strategic thinking and judgement. In the next section, we outline five emergent analysis approaches that have been promoted as useful for strategic investment appraisal, before turning to empirical evidence to examine whether practitioners see value in these more 'strategic' approaches.

Developing strategic appraisal approaches

In recognition of the limitations of established investment analysis techniques, numer-ous calls have issued for more sophisticated approaches that integrate strategic and financial considerations (e.g. Slagmulder *et al.,* 1995; Shank, 1996).

Broadly, there are two avenues for developing alternative strategic investment appraisal techniques. The first involves modifying established approaches to correct their technical shortcomings and expand their capacity to incorporate neglected 'strategic' project benefits. *Real options analysis* (ROA) and *fuzzy set theory* (FST) fit into this category (these approaches are explained later). The second avenue involves drawing on analytical frameworks that represent significant departures from conven-tional financial and risk analyses. Often, suggestions for these latter approaches come from outside the management accounting literature, appearing instead in project management, strategy and technology journals, for example. In the remainder of this section we outline five approaches that have been linked with strategic investment decision-making, yet which remain largely absent from textbook prescriptions on capital investment analysis.

The balanced scorecard

Kaplan and Norton devised the popular 'balanced scorecard' as a framework for link-ing financial measures of performance with non-financial measures (focused on cus-tomers, internal business processes, and innovation and learning), to give managers an integrated framework for managing and evaluating their businesses. Kaplan and Norton (2001) advocated the balanced scorecard as a strategic management and decision-making tool, leading others to suggest that a balanced scorecard approach could be usefully applied to strategic investment decision-making (Lyons *et al.,* 2003; Milis and Mercken, 2003).

The balanced scorecard provides a framework within which financial analysis tools (such as NPV) can be engaged alongside non-financial considerations of cus-tomer/user outcomes, internal business impacts and innovation and learning out-comes. Milis and Mercken (2003) illustrate the application of a balanced scorecard framework to information technology investments, mixing established financial analysis techniques with other metrics that evaluate the project's strategic fit. They note that this multi-dimensional appraisal requires significantly more input from top management than traditional capital investment analysis, thus compelling top management to take a broad, strategic view of investment projects rather than leaving their assessment to financial experts. Lyons *et al.* (2003) described how a hospital applied the balanced scorecard to their capital investment decision-making by developing investment criteria based on balanced scorecard goals. Projects were then evaluated on their ability to promote the achievement of key strategic goals as well as their financial viability. While noting practical difficulties in determining the relative weights of various goals and interpreting the final project 'score', Lyons *et al.* stress that the process of negotiating through these issues itself has some benefits. It forces managers to consider how the capital budget aligns to strategic goals, and it requires consensus building that focuses on the entire organisation rather than departmental concerns.

As a framework for aligning financial and strategic project considerations, the balanced scorecard appears to have some potential, therefore. The challenge in applying it relates to the usual practical considerations of implementing balanced scorecards – how to select the key indicators and operationalise the 'balancing' that must be achieved between them. But, if these issues can be managed in other applications of the balanced scorecard, they should present no special challenge in capital investment decision-making.

Value chain/strategic cost management analysis

It is more than a decade since Shank brought the idea of a strategic cost management (SCM) framework for analysing technology investments to the attention of management accountants (see Shank, 1996). Noting the need to evaluate projects' strategic aspects as explicitly as their cash flows, he suggested that the SCM approach ought to replace NPV, which acted 'more as a constraint than a decision tool' (Shank, 1996, p. 196). In an earlier paper, Shank and Govindarajan (1992) described SCM as an appropriate framework for giving strategic issues much more explicit attention in the investment decision-making process.

Shank and Govindarajan's SCM framework comprises three related elements: value chain analysis, cost driver analysis and competitive advantage analysis. These three themes can readily be discerned in practitioners' concerns with the quality and reliability of outputs, the requirements of customers, greater manufacturing flexibility, and keeping up with the competition (Carr and Tomkins, 1996). The first element, value chain analysis, is proposed as a useful tool for identifying strategically important, value-creating activities and developing appropriate competitive strategies (Porter, 1985). The value chain is 'the linked set of value-creating activities all the way from basic raw materials through to component suppliers, to the ultimate end-use product delivered into the final consumers' hands' (Shank and Govindarajan, 1992, p. 40). Its analysis focuses on finding opportunities, within the firm's segment of the value chain, to enhance customer value or lower costs.

Strategic cost management blends value chain analysis with cost driver and competitive advantage analyses. The first of these requires that cost drivers are carefully analysed so that their impact on the firm's cost structure and competitive position are understood. In regard to capital investment decisions, *structural* cost drivers (i.e. those relating to the firm's explicit strategic choices) will flow from an investment decision, so their impact on future cash flows must be appropriately identified. Competitive advantage analysis completes the SCM picture with an evaluation of whether a project's achievable benefits are consistent with the firm's competitive positioning strategy. Shank and Govindarajan refer to Porter's broad distinction between a *low-cost* strategy and a *differentiation* strategy. Using an SCM approach to project appraisal ensures that a project's contribution to the chosen strategy, through either enhancing differentiation or lowering costs, is explicitly considered.

Although they stop short of providing a step-by-step guide for performing SCM analyses of strategic investment projects, Shank and Govindarajan (1992) illustrate how value chain analysis produces different decisions to those obtained using established project analysis techniques, particularly where impacts on upstream and downstream value chain linkages are an important aspect of the decision. Shank (1996) also uses an illustrative case study of a US logging company to highlight the limitations of traditional financial analysis and to show that a systematic analysis of strategic implications can offer a broader view of a project's outcomes.

Technology roadmapping

Since new technology projects comprise a substantial portion of strategic capital investments, developments in technology planning and appraisal offer insights for strategic project analysis. One such recent development is 'technology roadmapping', a planning process whereby a team of experts develops a framework for organising and presenting the information needed to make technology investment decisions. As part of the roadmapping process, this team attempts to predict the needs of tomorrow's markets, and produces charts and graphs that identify the links between technology and business needs. This process is said to contribute to the definition of technology strategy by assisting managers to identify, select and develop technology alternatives to satisfy future service, product or operational needs (Groenveld, 1997, p. 48).

The concept of technology roadmapping has gained widespread recognition, particularly in US firms. The American firm Motorola, for example, led the way in technology roadmapping in the late 1980s. According to its proponents, technology roadmapping: (i) helps an industry predict the market's future technology and product needs, (ii) defines the 'road' that industry must take to compete successfully in tomorrow's markets, (iii) guides technology research and development decisions, (iv) increases collaboration, shared knowledge and new partnerships, (v) reduces the risk of costly investment in technology, and (vi) helps the industry seize future marketing opportunities (see, for example, Banigan, 2000).

Since a key aim of technology roadmapping is to look within and beyond the firm to ensure that the right capabilities are in place to achieve strategic objectives, it has clear potential application to strategic investment decision-making. The use of this approach for strategic investment analysis may help to balance long-term strategic issues alongside near-term financial performance and, as Miller and O'Leary (forth-coming) note:

> The requirement that investments be consistent with a technology roadmap means that pro-ponents of individual investments have to ensure that their proposals synchronize and fit with related investments taking place within and beyond the firm in a manner that enhances value.

While Miller and O'Leary have documented extensive use of technology roadmaps in their Intel Corporation case study, its use in capital investment decision-making prac-tice is still in its infancy. Despite its recognised potential for supporting strategic investment decision-making, this strategic analysis tool has yet to make its way into mainstream capital investment textbooks.

Fuzzy set theory

The three approaches outlined so far all shy away from modifying the numerical cal-culations that support strategic project appraisal. Abdel-Kader and Dugdale's (2001) *fuzzy set theory* (FST) is very different. It is a mathematical approach that combines ele-ments of the *analytical hierarchy process* (AHP) framework (Saaty, 1980) with the math-ematical concept of FST to propose a model for evaluating advanced manufacturing technology investments.

A number of writers have proposed the AHP decision model as a means of struc-turing and systematising the evaluation of non-quantifiable project attributes. The AHP approach requires that decision-makers formulate a decision problem as a hier-archical structure, breaking down the overall objective (the investment decision) into its key attributes and sub-attributes. They must then assign subjective weights to the various project attributes. Finally, they calculate an overall rating for each project alter-native by adding up the weighted scores for each of the project's attributes. Angelis and Lee (1996) suggest that AHP allows decision-makers to focus on those project attributes most important to achieving the organisation's strategic goals. The approach cannot eliminate subjectivity from decision-making (it is inherent in the identification and weighting of project attributes), but it does promote the identification of both financial and non-financial project outcomes and provides a structured framework for evaluating and communicating their impact.

Fuzzy set theory allows ambiguous variables to be represented by a range of inexact, 'fuzzy' numbers. Combining it with the AHP approach, Abdel-Kader and Dugdale propose a model for integrating the financial and non-financial elements of strategic project appraisal. A project's expected performance is evaluated in terms of three measures: financial return, intangible (strategic) benefits, and risk (Abdel-Kader and Dugdale, 2001, p. 43). While NPV is still recommended as an appropriate technique for determining financial returns, the model uses a *fuzzy* NPV to recognise that cash flow estimates are uncertain. Strategic and risk factors, which cannot be translated into cash flows, are given a similar treatment. The model employs a 'fuzzy linguistic scale' to evaluate the 'fuzzy importance' of non-financial investment criteria and risk factors, and to assign 'fuzzy ratings' to the alternative projects. Abdel-Kader and Dugdale

(2001) give a comprehensive illustration of how this 'fuzzy linguistic scale' and other FST calculations work, so interested readers should refer to their paper for more details of this method. For our purposes, it is sufficient to note their claim that the FST approach permits the assessment of non-financial and risk factors without the pressure or expectation of being precise. And, while FST provides a mechanism for modelling and comparing the financial, strategic and risk attributes of investment projects, its architects note that it does not provide a single measure of project desirability. Rather, the final accept-or-reject decision depends on decision-makers' preferences. So, despite the mathematical complexity of the FST method, the pervasive necessity for subjective judgement remains critical to the decision-making process.

Real options analysis

A second calculative analysis development, which emerged from the finance literature, has already made its way into capital investment textbooks. Real options analysis (ROA) attempts to address the inability of established financial analysis techniques (e.g. NPV and IRR) to recognise the value of having flexibility (i.e. 'options') within investment projects. This value was previously considered non-quantifiable and ignored in established appraisal methods like NPV. Since strategic decisions are inherently uncertain, flexible projects are less risky and have greater value to the firm, because they allow it to respond to strategic and competitive opportunities rather than remaining locked into a fixed course of action. For example, a project that can be deferred, expanded, contracted, suspended or abandoned, or which offers follow-on investment opportunities, presents the firm with future options that it may, or may not, choose to exercise as more information becomes available. MacDougall and Pike (2003, p. 2) define such real options as 'the opportunities latent in an investment, which, if exercised, enhance competitive advantage'. They offer as examples options to 'take advantage of changes in consumer demand, respond to or curtail competitors' actions, or to make subsequent, contingent investments which add potential and value to the initial investment'. Since the potential to change a project's direction, rather than remaining locked into a particular course of action, is particularly relevant for strategic investment projects with high levels of uncertainty, ROA has been seen as a useful technique for appraising strategic capital investments.

Real options analysis extends financial options theory to the valuation of options on real capital assets. The ROA approach considers any investment opportunity as a 'growth option', analogous to a call option on securities. As for financial options, real options relate to an underlying asset (the capital investment). But, while financial options are specified in a contract, real options are embedded within strategic investments and are typically not traded. The underlying models and information requirements are much the same, however. Various different ROA valuation formulae exist, all derived from models developed to value financial options. The most common are the Black–Scholes formula and the binomial model. While the mathematical details of the ROA model are beyond the scope of this discussion, interested readers should refer to Trigeorgis (1999) for a comprehensive discussion of ROA models and Busby and Pitts (1998) for a user-friendly guide to applying real options principles in investment appraisal.

Research and development (R&D) project appraisal is one area where ROA has seen increased use. Established analysis techniques, such as NPV, are not suited to the valuation of R&D projects because the total economic value of these projects includes an option value associated with future opportunities. Like many other strategic investments, R&D projects typically involve high levels of uncertainty and are intended to create future profitable investment opportunities rather than to generate short-term returns. Although the cost of an R&D investment may be relatively well known, the benefits are highly uncertain and cannot be measured simply in terms of the cash flows directly connected with the project. Real options analysis provides a formal means of calculating the value of future options embedded in an investment project. Since it is clear that financial analyses are an important part of the strategic investment decision-making activity, the inclusion of ROA may avoid the error of rejecting a project because its direct cash flows produce an unfavourable NPV outcome, when its long-term, strategic benefits justify the initial investment.

The ROA approach does not provide a complete solution for the challenges that face strategic investment decision-making, however. Although it promotes the consideration of project flexibility, it is far from easy to calculate. In particular, where an investment project entails multiple, related flexibilities, it is difficult to value these compound options. The mathematical complexity of ROA means that the typical firm will need to access specialist help, so it is likely to be used only for evaluating large investments where this cost can be justified. Alternatively, using ROA without specialist assistance requires a number of simplifying assumptions that may not be realistic. As for fuzzy set theory, mathematical elegance is both ROA's main theoretical strength and its greatest practical challenge.

All five emergent analysis techniques outlined in this section have been suggested to have utility for strategic investment appraisal. In their various ways, they acknowledge that investment decisions do not fit well within the rational decision-making model, but also require judgement and the consideration of a project's strategic 'fit' within the organisation. Their strength lies in their ability to support decision-making that occurs *outside* the rational economic model, where satisficing, bargaining, compromise and judgement are called for. Might we therefore expect these strategically oriented tools to find favour as alternatives to established economic analysis tools? In the next section, we review the empirical evidence. What do practitioners tell us about the tools they use for strategic investment appraisal and their preferences for economic versus strategic approaches?

Evidence from practice

Several surveys have examined the use of various investment appraisal techniques over the past three decades. In general, they have focused on the relative popularity of discounted cashflow techniques (e.g. IRR and NPV) compared to simpler, but less rigorous, approaches such as payback period (PP) and accounting rate of return (ARR). Many have also enquired about the use of risk analysis techniques as a particular aspect of investment appraisal. Key techniques included here are sensitivity analysis, hurdle rate adjustments (e.g. revising the required rate of return or target payback period), probability analysis, and the capital asset pricing model approach (which draws on portfolio theory to assess project volatility – i.e. 'systematic risk' – relative to a diversified market portfolio of assets). While varying in their degree of sophistication, all of these financial and risk analysis methods are grounded in the rational economic model described earlier.

The findings of the various surveys often seem contradictory, although they are hard to compare due to variations in the samples, locations and questions asked. We will draw on several UK studies to illustrate the diversity of findings within this one country.

Use of established analysis techniques

In 1994, Lefley observed secondary use of the more sophisticated analysis methods by UK manufacturing firms. While 94 per cent of firms used the simplistic payback period analysis, only 69 per cent used IRR or NPV, the recommended discounted cash flow techniques. Later studies by Pike (1996), Abdel-Kader and Dugdale (1998) and Arnold and Hatzopoulos (2000) found that most companies used multiple financial analysis techniques. While these combination approaches often went against textbook prescriptions by including payback period and accounting rate of return (ARR), they also signalled the wide use of the NPV and IRR techniques, with IRR more popular than NPV in the earlier two studies and NPV more popular in later studies (Arnold and Hatzopoulos, 2000; Alkaraan and Northcott, 2006). Figure 10.1 illustrates the frequency of use of analysis methods in the UK according to various surveys, including our own 2002 survey of UK manufacturing companies. These surveys report the use of techniques for *any* type of capital project, not just strategic investments. Note that only those techniques surveyed by Pike (1996) and Arnold and Hatzopoulos (2000) are included to facilitate longitudinal comparison, and that reported aggregate percentages exceed 100 per cent because many companies use more than one technique.

While these studies agree that larger UK firms generally use multiple financial analysis techniques (98 per cent of firms did so in our 2002 study), findings are contradictory regarding which techniques are attributed the highest importance by practitioners. Abdel-Kader and Dugdale found that the less sophisticated techniques (payback and ARR) were rated marginally more important, while Arnold and Hatzopoulos found greatest emphasis on NPV and IRR (Pike is silent on this issue). As Figure 10.1 shows, the two main themes to emerge from survey findings are that (i) practitioners continue to use simple financial analyses even though more rigorous alternatives are available and (ii) most firms use multiple techniques.

One explanation suggested for the continued use of simplistic analysis techniques is that practitioners recognise the shortcomings of NPV and IRR in capturing strategic and non-financial aspects of projects. They therefore feel that simple financial analyses, coupled with subjective evaluation of other project dimensions, will suffice since more complex economic analyses add little to their decision-making. Other explanations have been offered for the trend towards the use of multiple techniques. Some authors suggest that payback period is included as a screening tool, to check on the liquidity effects of a project, rather than a principal decision criterion. Similarly, ARR

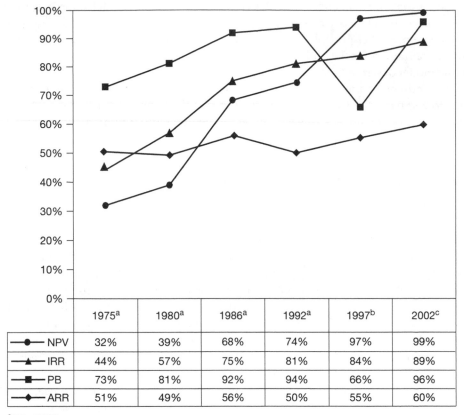

	1975[a]	1980[a]	1986[a]	1992[a]	1997[b]	2002[c]
●— NPV	32%	39%	68%	74%	97%	99%
▲— IRR	44%	57%	75%	81%	84%	89%
■— PB	73%	81%	92%	94%	66%	96%
◆— ARR	51%	49%	56%	50%	55%	60%

[a] Pike (1996)
[b] Arnold and Hatzopoulos (2000)
[c] Alkaraan and Northcott (2006)

Figure 10.1 Financial analysis techniques used to evaluate capital investment projects in large UK companies (1975–2002)

Source: Alkaraan and Northcott, 2006, p. 160.

is thought to remain part of the mix because it parallels other accounting-based measures, such as return on assets/equity/investment, which managers are keen to monitor because these measures are linked to their performance appraisal and rewards. Pike noted that the widespread availability of computers makes it easier for firms to use multiple evaluations, leading to a 'more the merrier' approach to financial appraisal (Pike, 1996, p. 84). More recently, Arnold and Hatzopoulos (2000, p. 609) raised the interesting suggestion that using multiple criteria might be seen as a way of overcoming the limiting assumptions of the NPV model by 'evaluating the project from different perspectives'.

For strategic investments, these 'different perspectives' would seem particularly relevant. Since the NPV model cannot incorporate vital, non-quantifiable factors (such as improved quality, flexibility, lead times, customer satisfaction and consistency with corporate strategy), it has been noted that financial appraisals are usually supplemented by less well-defined strategic evaluations and investment criteria

(Abdel-Kader and Dugdale, 1998). This reliance on strategic appraisal does not seem to lessen the use of financial analyses, however. Our own study (Alkaraan and Northcott, 2006) analysed for any differences in the use of established financial analysis techniques for operational and strategic investment projects. No statistically significant differences were found. (This also accords with Abdel-Kader and Dugdale's findings in regard to AMT investments.) These findings and our follow-up interviews suggest that managers see financial evaluation as a key part of the assessment of strategic investment proposals. Indeed, projects without a clear financial rationale are unlikely to be accepted, even where they have acknowledged 'strategic' benefits and high levels of uncertainty.

What does this tell us? Despite the challenges presented by strategic project appraisal, firms make no discernable adjustment to their use of financial analyses when faced with such projects. Rather, they continue to rely on financial analyses while attempting to balance them against a project's strategic dimensions. Managers continue to be attracted to 'rational' economic decision-making tools, even though they may be ill-suited to the uncertain and complex strategic decisions that are best described by political, garbage can or incremental-adaptive decision-making models.

The survey findings on project risk analysis tell a similar story. Figure 10.2 presents the overall levels of use (across both strategic and non-strategic projects) for each of the techniques outlined earlier. Again, only those techniques surveyed by Pike (1996) and Arnold and Hatzopoulos (2000) are included in this longitudinal comparison.

Notwithstanding the apparent inconsistency of the 1997 results (from Arnold and Hatzopoulos, 2000), most of the risk appraisal methods appear to be growing in popularity. Strong upward trends can be observed in the use of adjusted required rates of return, shortened payback periods and probability analysis. The most widely used risk technique – sensitivity/scenario analysis – has dominated since the 1980s, with our own recent study confirming its position as the most widely used risk assessment technique, apparently due to its perceived simplicity and intuitive appeal.

The capital asset pricing model (CAPM) approach, although gaining in popularity over the past decade, continues to lag significantly behind. This confirms Abdel-Kader and Dugdale's (1998) observation that theoretically preferred methods can be perceived as less useful, even for high-risk strategic projects, despite their apparent 'scientific' rigour. Our follow-up interviews revealed little enthusiasm for this sophisticated analysis tool, with one finance director calling it 'a tool in the textbooks, but not something you'd necessarily use from a business perspective'.

When we analysed our 2002 survey findings to distinguish between risk analysis of strategic and non-strategic investments, the less sophisticated techniques (adjusting required rate of return or payback hurdle rates) achieved significantly higher usage scores for strategic projects. However, use of the more sophisticated risk analysis techniques (probability, CAPM and sensitivity analyses) did *not* differ significantly between strategic and non-strategic projects. This surprised us, since we expected complex strategic investments to prompt greater use of sophisticated risk analysis methods. Persistent themes to emerge from the follow-up interviews were the intractability of risk, particularly for strategic investment projects, and the need to accept risk-taking as an inherent part of being innovative and responsive to customer and market

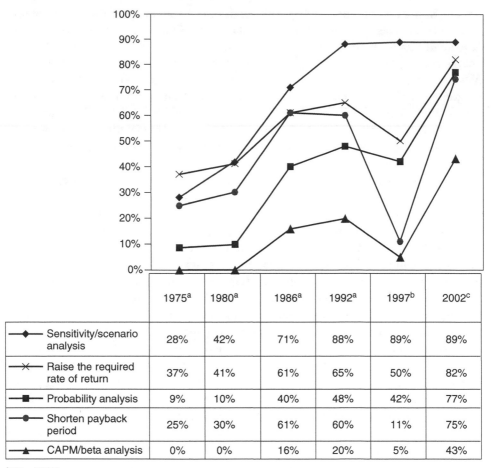

	1975[a]	1980[a]	1986[a]	1992[a]	1997[b]	2002[c]
◆ Sensitivity/scenario analysis	28%	42%	71%	88%	89%	89%
✕ Raise the required rate of return	37%	41%	61%	65%	50%	82%
■ Probability analysis	9%	10%	40%	48%	42%	77%
● Shorten payback period	25%	30%	61%	60%	11%	75%
▲ CAPM/beta analysis	0%	0%	16%	20%	5%	43%

[a] Pike (1996)
[b] Arnold and Hatzopoulos (2000)
[c] Alkaraan and Northcott (2006)

Figure 10.2 Risk analysis techniques used to evaluate capital investment projects in large UK companies (1975–2002)

Source: Alkaraan and Northcott, 2006, p. 163.

opportunities. One finance director warned that by conducting detailed risk analyses 'you might considerably minimise the risk, but it's likely that you'll miss the opportunity because you spend so much time gathering the information'. Our findings, together with those of prior studies, suggest that although increasing use is made of the more sophisticated risk appraisal methods, the important task of assessing which forms and levels of risk are palatable still falls to the subjective judgement of decision-makers.

To summarise on the use of established financial and risk analysis techniques, several key findings seem to point to a need for alternative approaches to strategic investment analysis. Managers look for ways to make their decision-making processes structured, transparent and defensible. Consequently, they are attracted to analysis tools that are perceived as 'rational'. In the absence of alternatives, managers have continued to rely on established financial and risk analysis tools, even for strategic projects where they fail to capture many relevant decision factors. In an effort to address the shortcomings of these tools and to evaluate projects from different perspectives, managers have combined more rigorous analyses with simple and intuitively appealing approaches such as payback period and sensitivity analysis. In theory, this analytical doubling-up adds nothing to a rational economic project appraisal. But in practice, it seems to signal managers' efforts to supplement rational economic analysis with some recognition of other decision dimensions and the need to exercise judgement in considering projects from different perspectives.

These findings echo our earlier discussion of emergent strategic analysis approaches and their claimed usefulness for appraising strategic investment projects. There *does* seem to be a need for innovative strategic analysis tools that help managers appraise all relevant aspects of investment projects. So, are practitioners starting to pick up on emergent analysis tools? When faced with incomplete, uncertain information and the need to bargain, compromise and exercise judgement, are they seeing value in alternative 'strategic' analysis approaches? We examine the evidence next.

Use of emergent strategic analysis techniques

The five emergent appraisal approaches we have outlined are all thought to have potential to support investment decision-making by bringing together financial and strategic aspects of project appraisal. Some have been around in the management accounting literature for a while now (the balanced scorecard, strategic cost management and real options analysis), whereas others are more recent arrivals (technology roadmapping and fuzzy set theory).

To date there has been little empirical examination of whether these strategic appraisal tools are being adopted in practice. Real options analysis (ROA) is the one we know most about from surveys (Busby and Pitts, 1998; MacDougall and Pike, 2003; Alkaraan and Northcott, 2006). These studies reveal that ROA is not well known amongst practitioners and is little used in practice. However, it has been suggested that the use of differential discount rates for different project types may be a surrogate for ROA, since it can be a way of acknowledging that flexible projects are less risky and therefore more valuable. While our own survey revealed that 26 per cent of respondents used a higher discount/hurdle rate for investment projects they considered 'strategic', we consider it somewhat optimistic to assume this reflects any practical engagement with real options analysis! In fact, our survey results dispel any inkling that ROA might be impacting strategic investment analysis. Around 80 per cent of respondents indicated that ROA was of 'below average' or 'no importance' to their strategic investment analysis practices. Only 4 per cent rated it 'important', while none rated it 'very important'. This disinclination to use ROA was confirmed in follow-up interviews. Managers commented on ROA's practical infeasibility due to the lack of reliable input data and the problem of managers not understanding the workings or results of this 'black box' analysis.

Since the application of ROA to capital investment appraisal has been on the academic agenda since the late 1980s, the fact that it has made few inroads into practice is perhaps puzzling. It seems that its mathematical complexity counts against it. Fuzzy set theory approaches to capital investment appraisal are much more recent and have not yet been empirically examined, but the findings related to ROA do not bode well for the uptake of this similarly mathematical and complex approach.

The use of the other strategic analysis approaches we have outlined has been examined only in our own 2002 survey. Strategic cost management/value chain approaches and the balanced scorecard framework do seem to be finding a place in strategic investment decision-making. Around 19 per cent of respondents rated SCM as 'important' or 'very important', while only 10 per cent rated it 'not important'. Its mean usage rating was slightly above that for the balanced scorecard, which achieved a similar spread of popularity. Technology roadmapping produced interesting results. While a huge 54 per cent of respondents rated it completely unimportant, perhaps because they were unaware of this approach, it was rated 'very important' by around 4 per cent of respondents (the same result achieved by SCM) and was of average or greater importance to more than 20 per cent. Technology roadmapping is a very new tool in the capital investment context, but it does appear to be gaining a foothold in practice. Interestingly, its mean usage rating exceeded that of the more established ROA. This suggests that qualitative approaches, which embrace the need for judgement in investment decision-making, may be more appealing to practitioners than complex approaches that attempt to quantify and calculate the strategic impacts of investment projects.

To summarise, the limited empirical evidence on the uptake of these five strategic analysis approaches suggests they are little used compared to established analysis techniques, despite their espoused benefits for strategic investment appraisal. Of course, these techniques are relatively new and their practical potential may not yet have emerged. Reflecting on the various models of strategic decision-making outlined earlier, these strategic analysis approaches do seem promising because they offer support to decisions that fall outside the 'rational model'. All five approaches recognise the need to give strategic issues, such as competitor analysis, technology advances and project flexibility, much more explicit analytic attention even though they are difficult to quantify. Most allow for negotiated decision criteria, where key indicators are mutually agreed (balanced scorecard), based on managerial judgements about strategic aims (value chain analysis and technology roadmapping) and/or subjectively evaluated (fuzzy set theory). All acknowledge uncertainty in the decision-making environment and provide a framework for managing it by drawing on informed managerial judgement, rather than relying on traditional economic analyses that capture only risk and assume away uncertainty.

Given the potentially promising characteristics of these five emergent analysis techniques, what will determine whether they develop a significant role in practice? In the next section we reflect on ways forward in dealing with the complexities of strategic investment appraisal and suggest some guidelines for the development and adoption of appropriate analysis approaches.

Strategic appraisal and the investment decision-making process

In these final reflections, we concentrate on two challenges in advancing the theory and practice of strategic investment decision-making. First, we suggest some guidelines for evaluating the likely contribution of emergent analysis techniques. Since empirical research has shown new techniques often struggle to displace established (though less sophisticated) approaches, what are the characteristics that might distinguish those developments that *are* likely to connect with practice? Second, we suggest a broadening of the research agenda to include those aspects of the investment decision-making activity that are often overlooked in empirical studies. Specifically, we reflect on pre- and post-analysis decision stages, which have a significant impact on strategic investment outcomes, yet are often excluded from research that focuses on investment appraisal.

Criteria for the contribution of new techniques

We have suggested that the development of useful analysis tools depends on finding new ways to couple economic analysis with managerial judgement, since both are key to strategic investment decision-making. Since judgement is enhanced through learning, it follows that any new technique should enhance analysis, promote learning, or (preferably) do both. Some recently advocated approaches, such as real options analysis and fuzzy set theory, focus on enhancing the rigour and comprehensiveness of economic analysis. They present decision-makers with sophisticated new tools that, if used well, have the potential to overcome theoretical shortcomings in the currently prevailing techniques. Yet, they cannot stand alone. While there is always merit in enhancing the rigour of calculative analyses, these approaches are only ever as good as the managerial judgement that underpins the input to these analyses. Real options analysis is helpful only after managers have made judgements about possible future developments and directions. Similarly, in advancing fuzzy set theory Abdel-Kader and Dugdale (2001, p. 484) note that some project elements can only ever be subjectively assessed and final decisions are subject to decision-makers' preferences. Furthermore, approaches that enhance calculative rigour are not guaranteed a place in practice, as witnessed by the continued invisibility of real options analysis.

Other approaches, such as balanced scorecard, strategic cost management and technology roadmapping, provide attractive frameworks for collecting and organising information to inform strategic investment decisions, but they cannot mitigate risk, they are inexact, and their effectiveness inherently depends on managerial judgement. So if they do not provide 'the answers', what can these emergent strategic analysis tools offer to practice? In our view, the answer lies in the promotion of managerial experience and judgement through *learning*.

There are several ways in which strategic analysis techniques can support learning:

1 *Promoting broad thinking*. The generation of innovative investment ideas will be promoted by analysis approaches that stimulate broad thinking about opportunities that arise both inside and outside the organisation, along the entire value

chain, across diverse markets, and in response to changes in competition and technology.

2 *Guiding the search for information.* No analysis method can provide the necessary information – research and judgement are required for that. But, where they provide a structured framework for considering an investment project from all appropriate angles, analysis techniques can help guide the search for information so that relevant variables and choices are recognised, uncertainty is reduced, and no foreseeable risks are overlooked.

3 *Valuing flexibility.* Analysis approaches that recognise the value of project flexibility in reducing risk will encourage decision-makers to seek out alternatives that can accommodate strategic responses to new information and environmental change.

4 *Giving expression to key variables.* Judgements about the nature and magnitude of key decision variables (such as operating costs or revenue increases) are a key part of investment decision-making. Approaches that require decision-makers to reach a consensus on the scope and measurement of such variables provide a basis for the discussion and analysis necessary for a thoughtful consideration of important project elements.

5 *Clearly communicating decision processes and outcomes.* Transparent, understandable and inclusive analysis approaches are more likely to facilitate participation and discussion in the decision-making process. This will enhance the sharing of organisational knowledge and learning, and improve the acceptability of decision outcomes to organisational actors.

6 *Providing a framework for monitoring and review.* Systematic reviews of past decision processes can help to improve procedures, information and analysis tools for future investment decisions. Analysis approaches that provide a clear framework for conducting such reviews will, therefore, support organisational learning and build a knowledge base to underpin managerial judgement.

Each of the strategic analysis tools outlined in this chapter has at least some of these characteristics, which may explain their nascent use in practice. However, complex quantitative approaches seem to score less well on criterion 5, presenting a potential obstacle to their use. The continued unpopularity of real options analysis illustrates this point (although its singular emphasis on flexibility means that shortcomings in relation to criteria 1 and 2 may also limit its appeal). Only time and further research will reveal whether practitioners are becoming sufficiently comfortable with the technical aspects of advanced quantitative approaches, such as real options analysis, to consider them understandable and useful. Meanwhile, we believe that the above criteria form a helpful 'checklist' for evaluating new strategic analysis approaches. If new techniques fail to support decision-making in these key areas, then their potential to inform strategic investment practice seems limited.

Locating analysis techniques in the investment decision-making process

It is also important to recognise the roles of various analysis approaches at different stages of the decision-making process. More than 30 years ago, King (1975) suggested that an overly narrow view of capital investment decision-making may lead to a theoretical and empirical over-emphasis on refining appraisal techniques at the expense of developing other stages of the decision-making process. This concern has strong parallels with the dominance of the 'rational' decision-making model and the relative neglect of other models that depict limited, political, messy and incremental decision-making approaches. Consider King's model of the investment decision-making process in Figure 10.3.

This model, along with more recent empirical studies, characterises investment decision-making as a process with several stages. The *evaluation* stage is where investment options are formally appraised and it is here that the dominant concerns with financial analysis, risk analysis and economic decision criteria are centred. But, by the time an investment decision gets to this stage, most of the strategic thinking has already occurred. The project has been conceived, identified as fitting the organisation's aims, and judged worthy of evaluation. It has also been scoped, defined, and framed as a decision alternative, meaning that its relevant features and expected outcomes have been conceptualised and captured. It is hardly surprising, therefore, that the *evaluation* stage has focused on rational economic tools – the complex strategic analysis has already been done.

The key to understanding the complementary needs for rational economic analysis, strategic evaluation and managerial judgement lies in broadening our conception of the investment decision-making process to include its pre- and post-analysis stages. It has been noted that, although analysis techniques constitute a framework within

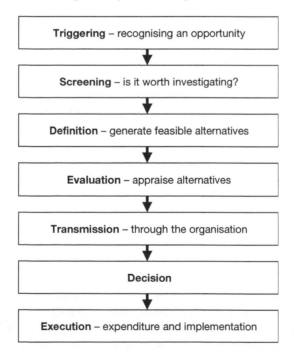

Figure 10.3 King's model of the investment decision-making process
Source: Adapted from King, 1975, p. 72.

which to formalise investment decisions, they are not the sole determinants of decision outcomes, particularly for strategic projects (Butler *et al.*, 1993; Carr and Tomkins, 1996; Shank, 1996). The dimensions of capital investment decision-making that lie outside the 'analysis' phase have a significant role in shaping the outcome of strategic investments, yet they are often overlooked by textbooks and by researchers.

For example, the influence of pre-decision controls (such as strategic plans, application and approval procedures, expenditure authorisation levels, predetermined hurdle rates and preliminary screening exercises) means that strategic investment decisions are in part already shaped even before they enter the formal evaluation stage. Managers draw on pre-decision controls when soliciting and screening project ideas for 'strategic fit', therefore limiting the types of projects that are considered. Similarly, capital investment policies and procedures set the parameters against which investment projects are evaluated, dictating the scope and detail of the information included in their evaluation and the criteria they must meet. These important decisions made *before* the formal analysis stage can play a part in shaping strategic investment outcomes, and it may be here that emergent strategic analysis tools can have their greatest impact. If we are to better understand decision-making practice and develop appropriate means of supporting it, more attention is required in the design and choice of pre-decision controls.

Other insights may emerge from further examination of post-decision project performance review (or 'post audit'). This fits with our earlier theme of learning as a key factor in developing the judgement that underpins effective decision-making. Project performance review is an essential part of the feedback loop that informs managers' experiences of capital investment outcomes and supports their learning. Although surveys of practice report that project performance reviews are widely undertaken (e.g. Arnold and Hatzopoulos, 2000), little is known about the impact this activity has on strategic investment practice. What do managers learn from project reviews? How are analysis approaches modified in the light of project review results? Do some analysis frameworks provide better bases for evaluating project outcomes? Do post-decision reviews impact on strategic goal setting and the design of pre-decision controls? And, in regard to the theme of this chapter, do emergent strategic analysis tools have a role to play in supporting this feedback and learning activity? Locating analysis techniques within the broader capital investment decision-making activity will be an important step in identifying their potential utility *beyond* the narrow confines of a rational model of project analysis.

Conclusion

This chapter reviewed the research findings on how complex and uncertain strategic investment projects are analysed. When it comes to financial analysis, well-established techniques remain firmly entrenched and differ little from those used for routine, non-strategic projects. Established financial analyses remain important in appraising investment choices, despite their limiting assumptions and their recognised shortcomings in capturing strategic project dimensions. However, managers balance these economic analyses with less-structured, strategic analyses underpinned by informed judgement. Similarly, sophisticated risk analysis techniques have failed to overtake more rudimentary and subjective approaches, reflecting the prevalence of judgement over calculative rigour in managers' assessments of strategic project risk. And, when it comes to developing new approaches, it seems that mathematically elegant decision-making models are eschewed in favour of those that acknowledge the important role of managerial judgement.

The fact that empirical studies reveal a continued reliance on judgement by investment decision-makers does not mean that rational economic analysis is a futile exercise. Indeed, such analyses are useful and important tools in strategic investment decision-making, as witnessed by their continued use in practice. What studies of practice *do* seem to suggest is that the theory and practice of strategic investment decision-making need to take into account *both* economically rational and intuitive decision processes.

Reflecting on the research evidence, we conclude that strategic investment appraisal will be best supported by approaches that (i) couple sound economic analysis with the development of managerial judgement, and (ii) take account of the broader decision-making context within which both economic and strategic analyses are used. Tools developed for practice must move beyond the constraints of the rational economic model and support decisions that are by nature uncertain, political, messy and incremental. Just as financial and strategic analyses must go hand-in-hand, so too must theory development and enhanced understandings of practice. There remains much scope for work on both fronts.

References

Abdel-Kader, M.G. and Dugdale, D. (1998) 'Investment in advanced manufacturing technology: a study of practice in large U.K. companies', *Management Accounting Research,* 9(3), 261–84.

Abdel-Kader, M.G. and Dugdale, D. (2001) 'Evaluating investments in advanced manufacturing technology: a fuzzy set theory approach', *British Accounting Review,* 33(4), 445–89.

Alkaraan, F. and Northcott, D. (2006) 'Strategic capital investment decision-making: a role for emergent analysis tools?' *British Accounting Review,* 38(2), 149–73.

Angelis, D.I. and Lee, C.Y. (1996) 'Strategic investment analysis using activity based costing concepts and analytical hierarchy process techniques', *International Journal of Production Research,* 34(5), 1331–45.

Arnold, G.C. and Hatzopoulos, P.D. (2000) 'The theory–practice gap in capital budgeting: evidence from the United Kingdom', *Journal of Business Finance and Accounting,* 27(5/6), 603–26.

Banigan, J.M. (2000) *Technology roadmapping: a strategy for success,* Ottawa: Industry Canada.

Busby, J.S. and Pitts, C.G.C. (1998) *Assessing Flexibility in Capital Investment,* London: The Chartered Institute of Management Accountants.

Butler, R., Davies, L. Pike, R. and Sharp, J. (1993) *Strategic Investment Decision-making: Theory, Practice and Process,* London: Routledge.

Carr, C. and Tomkins, C. (1996) 'Strategic investment decisions: the importance of SCM. A comparative analysis of 51 case studies in UK, US and German companies', *Management Accounting Research,* 7(2), 199–217.

Cohen, M.D., March, J.G. and Olsen, J.P. (1972) 'A garbage can model of organizational choice,' *Administrative Science Quarterly,* 17(1), 1–25.

Cyert, R. and March, J. (1963) *A Behavioral Theory of the Firm,* Englewood Cliffs, NJ: Prentice-Hall.

Groenveld, P. (1997) 'Roadmapping integrates business and technology', *Research Technology Management,* 40(5), 48–55.

Kaplan, R.S. and Norton, D.P. (2001) 'Transforming the balanced scorecard from performance measurement to strategic management: part 1', *Accounting Horizons,* **15**(1), 87–104.

King, P. (1975) 'Is the emphasis of capital budgeting theory misplaced?' *Journal of Business Finance and Accounting,* **2**(1), 69–82.

Lefley, F. (1994) 'Capital investment appraisal of advanced manufacturing technology', *International Journal of Production Research,* **32**(12), 2571–776.

Lyons, B., Gumbus, A. and Bellhouse, D.E. (2003) 'Aligning capital investment decisions with the balanced scorecard', *Journal of Cost Management,* March/April, 34–8.

MacDougall, S.L. and Pike, R.H. (2003) 'Consider your options: changes to strategic value during implementation of advanced manufacturing technology', *International Journal of Management Science,* **31**, 1–15.

Milis, K. and Mercken, R. (2003) 'The use of the balanced scorecard for the evaluation of information and communication technology projects,' *International Journal of Project Management,* **22**(2), 87–97.

Miller, P. and O'Leary, T. (forthcoming) 'Flexibility, complementarity relations, and mechanisms of investment appraisal', in L. Trigeorgis (ed.) *Innovation, Organization and Strategy,* Oxford: Oxford University Press.

Mintzberg, H., Raisinghani, D. and Theoret, A. (1976) 'The structure of "unstructured" decision processes', *Administrative Science Quarterly,* **21**(2), 247–75.

Pettigrew, A. (1973) *The Politics of Organizational Decision Making,* London: Tavistock.

Pike, R. (1996) 'A longitudinal survey on capital budgeting practices', *Journal of Business Finance and Accounting,* **23**(1), 79–92.

Porter, M. (1985) 'Technology and competitive advantage', *Journal of Business Strategy,* **5**(3), 60–78.

Saaty, T. (1980) *The Analytic Hierarchy Process,* New York: McGraw Hill.

Simon, H.A. (1957) *Models of Man,* New York: Wiley.

Shank, J.K. (1996) 'Analysing technology investments: from NPV to strategic cost management (SCM)', *Management Accounting Research,* **7**(2), 185–97.

Shank, J.K. and Govindarajan, V. (1992) 'Strategic cost analysis of technological investments', *Sloan Management Review,* **34**(1), 39–51.

Slagmulder, R., Bruggeman, W. and Wassenhove, L.V. (1995) 'An empirical study of capital budgeting practices for strategic investments in CIM technologies', *International Journal of Production Economics,* **40**(2/3), 121–52.

Slagmulder, R. (1997) 'Using management control systems to achieve alignment between strategy and strategic investment decisions', *Management Accounting Research,* **8**(1), 103–39.

Trigeorgis. L. (ed.) (1999) *Real Options and Business Strategy: Applications to Decision-making,* London: Risk Books.

Van Cauwenbergh, A., Durinck, E., Martens, R., Laveren, E. and Bogaert, I. (1996) 'On the role and function of formal analysis in strategic investment decision processes', *Management Accounting Research,* **7**(2), 169–84.

Further reading

Abdel-Kader, M.G. and Dugdale, D. (1998) 'Investment in advanced manufacturing technology: a study of practice in large U.K. companies', *Management Accounting Research,* **9**(3), 261–84. A well-crafted study that examines decision-making practice in regard to a specific type of strategic investment (advanced manufacturing technology).

Abdel-Kader, M.G. and Dugdale, D. (2001) 'Evaluating investments in advanced manufacturing technology: a fuzzy set theory approach', *British Accounting Review,* **33**, 445–89. The key paper on fuzzy set theory as a potential tool for strategic investment appraisal.

Busby, J.S. and Pitts, C.G.C. (1998) *Assessing Flexibility in Capital Investment,* London: The Chartered Institute of Management Accountants. A user-friendly guide to applying real options analysis in investment appraisal.

Milis, K. and Mercken, R. (2003) 'The use of the balanced scorecard for the evaluation of information and communication technology projects', *International Journal of Project Management,* **22**(2), 87–97. Proposes balanced scorecard as a useful tool for evaluating strategic-type investment projects.

Miller, P. and O'Leary, T. (forthcoming) 'Flexibility, complementarity relations, and mechanisms of investment appraisal', in L. Trigeorgis (ed.) *Innovation, Organization and Strategy,* Oxford: Oxford University Press. Illustrates how technology roadmapping can support investment decision-making.

Pike, R. (1996) 'A longitudinal survey on capital budgeting practices', *Journal of Business Finance and Accounting,* **23**(1), 79–92. A good example of survey research that has traced the adoption of well-established investment appraisal techniques.

Shank, J.K. (1996) 'Analysing technology investments: from NPV to strategic cost management (SCM)', *Management Accounting Research,* **7**(2), 185–97. Outlines the potential for strategic cost management analysis to inform investment decision-making.

measurement. Although there are numerous frameworks for each approach, the main focus will be on the most popular examples of each, *the balanced scorecard* (BSC) for the stakeholder school and *economic value added* (EVA) for the shareholder school (EVA is the registered trademark of Stern Stewart). Research evidence is then used to compare theory with practice.

The measurement metrics

Stakeholder perspectives

Stakeholder perspectives argue that companies compete on many dimensions whose evaluation cannot be confined to narrow financial indicators. Simply focusing on financial performance can give misleading signals for the continuous improvement demanded by today's competitive environment. Important issues of customer satisfaction and establishing good employee relations would be missed by such a system. The challenge then becomes to develop non-financial performance measures that capture the quality, service and flexibility issues of today's customer-oriented competitive strategies. A number of frameworks have been proposed to help organisations define a set of measures which reflect their objectives and assess their performance. They include the SMART pyramid (Lynch and Cross, 1991), the results and determinants framework (Fitzgerald, *et al.*, 1991), the balanced scorecard (Kaplan and Norton, 1992) and the performance prism (Neely and Adams, 2001). Common threads emerging from these multidimensional frameworks are that performance measures should:

- be linked to corporate strategy;
- include external (customer service type) as well as internal measures;
- include financial and non-financial measures;
- make explicit the trade-offs between the various measures of performance.

An important feature of these frameworks is their prescriptive nature, in that the generic dimensions of performance are specified – such as flexibility and customer satisfaction. The actual measures of these dimensions will depend on the business type and, importantly, on the specific competitive strategy adopted by the organisation. So, the types of measures used need to reflect, either directly or indirectly, success factors critical to the achievement of corporate strategy.

The balanced scorecard (BSC) is probably the most widely known multidimensional framework adopted by organisations in the quest for improved corporate performance. The BSC concept is built on the premise that what is measured motivates organisational stakeholders to act. The original model proposed that performance should be measured from four perspectives: *the financial perspective* (how do we look to our shareholders?), *the customer perspective* (how do we look to our customers?), *the business process perspective* (what must we excel at?) and *the innovation and learning perspective* (how can we continue to improve and create value?). It was suggested that up to four measures should be developed for each dimension (Kaplan and Norton, 1992). The contention was that the non-financial measures would be leading indicators of future success, that is, future financial performance would be determined by the current non-financial measures. However, limited guidance is given on the nature of the measures to be placed in the BSC boxes.

A number of advantages have been claimed for this stakeholder approach to performance measurement. Providing information on the four perspectives helps to combine the disparate elements of a company's competitive agenda in one report. The number of measures is limited, encouraging focus on the few critical success factors. It attempts to address the sub-optimisation problem by forcing managers to consider all the key operating measures together and how improvements in one area may be at the expense of another. Critics have argued that the framework takes no account of the external environment beyond the direct customers of the business, and that it is incomplete because it ignores other stakeholders such as employees and suppliers.

Shareholder perspectives

The guiding principle underlying shareholder perspectives of measurement is that measuring and rewarding activities that create shareholder value will ultimately lead to shareholder wealth. These approaches form part of the value-based management agenda summarised by Cooper *et al.* (2001). All value-based management programmes share the basic premise that profit measurement needs to take into account the cost of capital employed to generate it. Theoretically they involve just two steps: first, adopt a residual income type metric as a key performance measure and, second, tie compensation to the achievement of the targeted metric. This seems disarmingly easy and widely attractive. The concept of residual income is not new; it has been advocated by accountants and economists for many years on the premise that for a company to create wealth, its earnings on its total invested capital should exceed the cost of that capital. The calculation of residual income is relatively straightforward – the cost of capital is subtracted from accounting profit to determine how much is left over for reinvestment or distribution to owners. The argument runs that using traditional accounting 'profit' to measure performance reflects only the cost of debt capital, whereas residual income includes the costs of both debt and equity capital.

Despite its alleged superiority as a performance measurement tool grounded in economic theory, survey evidence in the late 1980s and early 1990s suggests limited use of the residual income measure in practice. Managers are often more preoccupied with other measures such as growth in turnover and market share. However, the pursuit of growth objectives rather than value objectives may actually destroy shareholder value. More recently, several consultants have developed the concept of residual income into various value metrics that have generated considerable publicity. Performance measures marketed by consulting firms include: discounted economic profits (EP) by Marakon Associates; economic value management (EVM) by KPMG Peat Marwick; economic value added (EVA) by Stern Stewart; and cash flow return on investment (CFROI) by Boston Consulting Group's HOLT Value Associates. There has been intense competition between the advocates of various measures, which has been referred to as the 'metric wars' in the financial press. The claimed advantage of these value-based metrics is that they ensure a business has a single financial objective that can be used to drive all its decisions. This contrasts with stakeholder metrics, which tend to have multiple measures stemming from multiple objectives requiring managers to make trade-offs. In this chapter we will focus on the widest known and used of these value-based metrics – economic value added (EVA), proposed and marketed by Stern Stewart.

The calculations of residual income and EVA are outlined below:

Residual income

Residual income (RI) can be calculated in two ways:

$$RI = \text{operating profits after tax} - \text{capital charge} \qquad (1)$$

where the capital charge is defined as:

Invested capital $\times$ the weighted average cost of debt and equity capital (WACC)

or

$$RI = \text{invested capital} \times (\text{return on capital} - \text{WACC}) \qquad (2)$$

Equation (2) demonstrates that RI is defined as the amount of capital invested in the business multiplied by the 'performance spread', which represents the difference between the return achieved on the invested capital and the weighted average cost of capital (see Arnold, 2005, for a discussion on the calculation of WACC). A positive RI indicates that the company has invested in value-increasing projects, whereas a negative RI means the projects did not cover the cost of capital.

Residual income can be used to value a business, measure and evaluate performance, and fulfil a more strategic role in evaluating investment opportunities. Focusing on the equations we can see there are three main opportunities, other things being equal, to increase RI:

● Increase operating profit after tax.
● Decrease the weighted average cost of capital.
● Reallocate capital away from negative-spread to positive-spread investments.

These value drivers can be used to develop more detailed performance targets and indicators.

Use of RI as a managerial performance measure solves the sub-optimisation problem associated with ROI; managers are motivated to invest in all projects that promise returns higher than, or at least equal to, the cost of capital. It also addresses the financing sub-optimisation problem. By considering the costs of both debt and equity financing, RI removes the manager's temptation to increase leverage through excessive debt financing (Merchant and Van der Stede, 2003).

Economic value added

The residual income concept was refined by US consultants Stern Stewart to produce the economic value added metric.[1] The EVA concept extends the traditional RI measure

---

[1]See also Chapter 12 for a critical evaluation of EVA.

by adjusting the financial performance measure for distortions introduced by GAAP (generally accepted accounting principles). It is calculated as follows:

$$\text{EVA} = \text{adjusted operating profits after tax} \\ - (\text{adjusted invested capital} \times \text{WACC}) \quad\quad (3)$$

or

$$\text{EVA} = \text{adjusted invested capital} \times (\text{ROI} - \text{WACC}) \quad\quad (4)$$

Adjustments are made to the operating profit measure in order to replace historic accounting data with a measure that approximates to economic profit and asset values. Stern Stewart advocate up to 164 possible adjustments to accounting profits and capital. These result in the capitalisation of discretionary expenditures such as research and development, marketing and advertising by spreading these costs over the periods in which the benefits are received. The adjustments raise a number of difficulties in practice and involve subjective adjustments. Should assets for research and development expenditure be added back for 5 years, 10 years or 20 years? Over what period should the benefits be allocated?

Having to make 164 adjustments would seem both costly and time consuming and it could involve arbitrary judgements that are as subjective as the original accounting numbers. In practice, however, Stern Stewart claim most organisations will need to make only about ten adjustments. They recommend that adjustments are made only in cases that pass the following four tests:

- Is it likely to have a material impact on EVA?
- Can the managers influence the outcome?
- Can the operating people readily grasp it?
- Is the required information relatively easy to track or derive?

(Stewart, 1994: quoted in Cooper and Davies, 2004)

One additional benefit of using EVA rather than traditional RI to measure managerial performance is that it capitalises some of the most important types of discretionary expenditures that managers may be tempted to cut if they were pressured for profits. The EVA system is designed to provide a single value-based measure that can be used to evaluate business strategies, value acquisitions, evaluate investment projects, set managerial performance targets, measure performance and pay bonuses.

Merchant and Van der Stede (2003) issue a warning on the interpretation of EVA. They point out that, despite its name, EVA is not economic income and does not address all the problems that differentiate accounting income from economic income:

> In particular EVA still reflects primarily the results of a summation of transactions completed during the period and importantly EVA still focuses on the past, whilst economic income reflects changes in *future* cash flow potentials. Thus EVA will be a particularly poor indicator of value changes for organizations that derive a significant proportion of their value from future growth. (Merchant and Van der Stede, 2003, p. 422)

The implementation of *stakeholder* and *shareholder* metrics places differing demands on managers. An early problem with balanced scorecards was that many organisations used existing financial and non-financial performance measures of performance, which were combined within a scorecard framework without questioning whether they were the right measures to drive the organisation forward. Existing information was merely rearranged, with little attempt to identify linkages between the measures. The adoption of a shareholder perspective was rather more demanding. As can be seen above, the calculations for the advocated financial performance metrics can be complex and require that the weighted cost of capital is calculated and some subjective adjustments are made.

Performance measurement to management

We have discussed the measurement of performance, but this is not an end in itself. Measuring performance will have no impact unless action is taken as a consequence of that performance measure. There is general agreement that performance measurement plays a critical role in organisations, both revealing how well an organisation achieves its corporate objectives (evaluation and accountability) and identifying required improvements (planning and control). For evaluation and accountability we need, prior to measurement, to understand the company's strategy, organisation and processes. This requires the identification of objectives and the provision of relevant information for monitoring them. Whether adopting a stakeholder or shareholder approach, the chosen strategy must be translated into a set of objectives. The dimensions of performance used to monitor that strategy will be defined in financial and non-financial terms in a stakeholder approach, and as a single financial metric in a shareholder approach.

Research shows that measuring managers' performance changes their behaviour. This is intuitively appealing and we have all seen illustrations of such behaviour. For example, water companies in the UK were required to reduce leakage from pipes and targets were set for this. The intention was to encourage the companies to improve their pipe network. An easier way of achieving the target, adopted by some companies, was to reduce the pressure of the water passing through the pipes. The target was met, but the water pressure was so low that some fire hydrants would not work. The message is clear – performance measurement is a powerful tool, particularly when rewards are linked to targets, and interdependencies between the measures need to be considered. This powerful tool needs to be used with caution because managers may deliver on the performance measure, but not always as intended. This begins the transition from measurement to management. Measurement is not an end in itself. To be effective it must be part of a feedback control system where corrective action is taken within the process (single-loop learning) and results are fed back into a consideration of future strategy (double-loop learning). These processes involve linking performance specification and evaluation to an organisation's practices for establishing and evaluating strategy, and also instilling practices that are iterative and responsive to systematic process feedback.

A prerequisite is the articulation of company strategy into a set of objectives. Three generic questions must then be addressed to operationalise the chosen strategy:

- What *dimensions* of performance does the organisation seek to develop?
- How will appropriate *targets* be set?
- What *rewards* and/or penalties will be associated with achievement of performance standards?

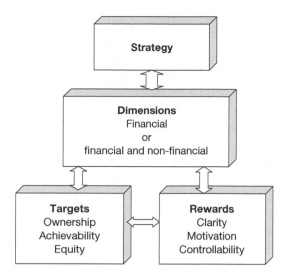

Figure 11.1 The building blocks of performance management
Source: Adapted from Fitzgerald and Moon, 1996.

These questions form the building blocks of a performance management system (Fitzgerald and Moon, 1996), as shown in Figure 11.1.

The main difference between stakeholder and shareholder dimensions of performance is that stakeholder approaches involve a number of measures, both financial and non-financial, whereas shareholder approaches focus on one financial metric. Within the stakeholder approach there are several performance measurement frameworks that could be adopted. Common to all will be financial measures (results) combined with leading indicators of future performance related to stakeholder interests.

Having decided what to measure, the dimensions, the second building block for performance measurement systems entails setting appropriate targets for these measures. This involves consideration of who sets the targets (*ownership*), at what level the targets are set (*achievability*) and whether the targets facilitate comparison across the business units (*equity*).

First, the issue of *ownership* requires consideration of whether senior management should impose the targets or whether managers responsible for delivering the performance should participate in the target setting process. Generally, participation is considered to be beneficial as it alleviates, or at least reduces, many dysfunctional consequences associated with traditional control models. In particular, managers who participate in the standard setting process are more likely to accept the standards and work towards achieving them. Participation does, however, provide opportunities for introducing 'slack' targets.

Second, there is the issue of *achievability*. Research findings indicate that defined quantitative targets motivate higher levels of performance than if no targets are set. Providing the target is not perceived as impossible, the more demanding the target the better the resulting performance. Thus, the target level that motivates the best performance is unlikely to be achieved all of the time and adverse variances will occur.

Targets need to be realistic enough to encourage employees to perform, but not set at levels so high they become totally demotivated. Actually finding the balance between what the company views as achievable and what the individual being measured views as achievable is a frequent source of conflict within organisations. A starting point would be to look at what has been achieved in the past. This historical information needs to be supplemented with what is being achieved elsewhere. One mechanism for developing this is through benchmarking, both internal and external. Internal benchmarking works well if there are similar business units within the organisation. External benchmarking tends to focus on competitors and information is sometimes obtained through formal collaboration between companies. This is common in the hotel industry for example, where information on occupancy figures and achieved room rates is shared.

The third factor of concern is *equity*. Are the targets comparable across similar business units, or do some have an inherent advantage? Consider a parcel delivery service organised by geographical region. An urban region is likely to generate more business than a rural region, so setting the same revenue target would be inequitable. Some business units may be subject to higher degrees of environmental uncertainty than others. There is empirical evidence to suggest the higher the level of uncertainty, the greater the reliance placed on subjective judgement in appraising performance, with less reliance on objective, financial data.

The reward structure is concerned with motivating individuals towards achieving the performance targets set. It means posing three questions: first, does the system exhibit *clarity* to all those whom it affects? Second, if it is clear what is expected of individuals, how are they *motivated* to achieve that performance? Third, what level of *controllability* do individuals have over areas they are responsible for?

Regarding *clarity*, if a major purpose of the performance measurement system is to successfully implement company strategy, then this should be understood by employees. Research indicates that most managers react well to clear, unambiguous targets and acceptance of targets is facilitated by good upward communication. People should know what the organisation is trying to do, what is expected of them, and exactly how and why their contribution to the organisation's performance in meeting its objectives will be appraised.

The second factor concerns *motivation*. In principle, employees may be motivated to work together to achieve strategic objectives if performance is tied to rewards, for example through bonuses. Goal clarity and participation contribute to higher motivation to meet targets, providing managers accept those targets. The reward system and how it is used complicate the effects of targets on motivation. Is the system used positively to encourage, or negatively to condemn, or both? When properly used, a responsibility accounting system does not emphasise blame. If managers feel they are excessively criticised when unfavourable variances occur, they are unlikely to respond positively. Instead, they will tend to undermine the system and view it with scepticism.

The third and final factor is *controllability*. The traditional view in responsibility accounting is that people should only be responsible for what they can control (i.e. have some influence over) and they should be rewarded only for the results of their efforts. The implication is that managers would lose interest in cost control if their performance were judged on events outside their control. From the viewpoint of the organisation as a whole, all costs are controllable and need to be controlled. The problem here lies in pinpointing responsibility, particularly regarding the allocation of common costs.

We have discussed stakeholder and shareholder approaches to performance measurement. In moving from measurement to management, we have identified the need to consider targets and rewards associated with achieving those targets. The next section considers the management aspects of stakeholder and shareholder approaches.

Developments in balanced scorecard thinking

Two major developments in the BSC have transformed the concept from a measurement system to a management system. These are the development of strategy maps and the linking of incentive compensation to achievement of BSC targets.

Though intuitively appealing, the causal linkage between the BSC's four areas of measurement has been questioned (Nørreklit, 2000). A recent development in scorecard thinking has been the idea of strategy mapping (Kaplan and Norton, 2001). Each measure within the scorecard is embedded in a chain of cause-and-effect logic that connects outcomes from the desired strategy with the drivers of that strategy. A prerequisite for this analysis is that strategy needs to be translated into operational terms. This identification of causality moves the BSC from a framework for measuring organisational performance towards a framework for strategy management.

Linking incentive compensation to BSCs is acknowledged as important for two reasons. First, it focuses employees' attention on measures that are most critical for strategy. Second, it provides extrinsic motivation by rewarding employees when they and the organisation succeed in reaching targets (Kaplan and Norton, 2001). However, Kaplan and Norton conclude that 'the only generalisable finding from all of the company experiences in linking compensation and reward to Balanced Scorecards is that they do it' (p. 265). Some used team and organisational-unit rewards only, others used a mixture of individual and organisational rewards. As with developing the measures, little guidance is given on compensation packages other than to say that they are important.

Shareholder approaches to rewards

Whatever value-based metric is adopted, the intention is to use the measure to motivate managers to increase shareholder value. Whether or not compensation packages are tied to the attainment of targets depends on which consultancy firm, and hence which metric, is considered. Holt Associates adopt a prudent position and suggest waiting some time before linking rewards to the outcomes of the CFROI (cash flow return on investment) model. This is consistent with the work of Rappaport (1998) who suggests managers must be given sufficient time to understand and accept the measures they will be accountable for, otherwise the shareholder value programme could be compromised.

The reward system is central to the Stern Stewart model, beginning with rewarding top management and gradually extending this throughout business units. They propose using EVA as the single financial objective to measure and reward managerial

Table 11.1 Comparison of balanced scorecard and economic value added approaches to performance management

	Balanced scorecard	Economic value added
Dimensions of performance measured	Multiple objectives based on strategy.	Single financial objective.
		Other measures abandoned.
Target setting	Limited advice.	Zero EVA as the minimum acceptable target.
	Claims that the 'employees are more willing to sign up to the stretch targets because they see the linkages, integration and initiatives that make achievement possible'. (Kaplan and Norton, 2001, p. 336)	EVA goals as a basis for stretch targets.
Rewards	Acknowledged as important but limited guidance on compensation packages.	Appropriate incentive schemes a central part of the methodology. Features of the schemes: • Unambiguous single target • Uncapped bonuses • Use of a bonus bank to stretch the horizon from short term to long term.

performance, using predetermined EVA benchmarks derived from objective models rather than budget negotiations. Otley (1999) suggests two reasons for this: Stern Stewart's history as a compensation consultant, and a recognition that, even after all the accounting adjustments have been made, EVA remains an imperfect measure. The problem of short-termism, in regard to rewards, remains. To overcome this, the suggestion is that although bonus calculations should be based on the attainment of target levels of EVA, the bonus would not be paid immediately. Normally, one-third of the bonus earned in a year is paid in that year, while the remainder is added to the bonus bank and paid over the next two years. Whilst advocating a bonus bank to smooth peaks and troughs in the business cycle, the recommendation is that bonuses should be uncapped. The argument runs that EVA makes managers act as though they are shareholders of the firm. If the manager acts in his or her own self-interest, the firm as a whole will benefit.

Table 11.1 Compares BSC and EVA approaches to performance management.

Empirical evidence

Research is emerging on the efficacy of stakeholder and shareholder approaches to performance management. The results are mixed and often contradictory. As with much management accounting research, there is a wide diversity in samples used, research methods applied and theoretical perspectives used to interpret the data. The results must be interpreted with caution, therefore. The following presentation of these research findings has been organised to answer three key questions:

- What metrics are companies using?
- Is performance improved by adopting a formal business performance management programme?
- How is the performance measurement system used in the firm?

This is followed by a focus on the successful adoption of value-based management at Lloyds TSB.

What metrics are companies using?

Recent survey data from large organisations in the United States revealed that 46 per cent (359 of the 780 organisations that participated) use formal performance measurement in their business performance management. Of these 359 organisations, three-quarters use the BSC as their main methodology, a small minority rely on EVA, and there was no mention of CFROI (Marr, 2004). Focusing on the US financial services industry, Ittner and Larcker (2003) identified an adoption rate of 20 per cent for the BSC and 36 per cent for EVA. One of the reported problems with EVA is that managers, particularly non-financial managers, find it difficult to understand. This may partly explain its greater adoption in the financial services industry, which is likely to have a higher proportion of financially aware managers. Take up of the BSC is similar in German-speaking countries with a 24 per cent of adoption rate (Speckbacher, et al., 2003). Given the publicity surrounding EVA, particularly in the United States, it seems surprising that its adoption hardly registered in the Marr (2004) study.

There is evidence that a firm's strategy influences the measurement metric adopted. Prospector firms follow innovation and differentiation strategies and have a higher research and development spend than defender firms adopting a defender (cost leadership) strategy. Capitalisation of research and development expenditure is one of the key accounting adjustments made in the EVA calculation. Stewart (1991) argues that companies with large research and development costs benefit more by using EVA over traditional accounting measures. This would suggest that firms who have implemented EVA have higher levels of research and development costs. This was not supported by the Lovata and Costigan (2002) study, which found that firms using a *defender* strategy were more likely to use EVA than those adopting a *prospector* strategy. This needs further research.

Is performance improved by adopting a formal business performance management programme?

Organisations with formal business performance management believe they out-perform organisations without it. This perceived superiority applies to overall performance and drivers of that performance, including higher quality data, more consistent measurement, improved interpretation of performance information, better communication and building of business models (Marr, 2004). Notice that the claim is 'perceived'

233

superiority. Few companies have quantified the benefit, which is surprising given the cost of implementing these performance measurement systems.

Several research studies have reported on BSC applications in the US and Europe. Answers are mixed to the basic question *does the adoption of a BSC lead to improved performance?* Davis and Albright (2004) compared the financial performance of bank branches that had implemented the BSC with a control group of branches that had not. Their findings indicated that branches in the BSC group outperformed the others. Here, performance was improved. In contrast, Ittner and Larcker (2003) found a negative association between BSC adoption and return on assets. Closer analysis by Ittner and Larcker (2003) revealed that of their sample of 157 adopters of BSC only 23 per cent consistently built and verified causal models, but these had, on average, a 2.95 per cent higher return on assets and a 5.14 per cent higher return on equity than companies that did not use causal models. Clearly we have a definition problem – what constitutes a BSC? Is it a measurement system or a management system?

The first generation BSCs were focused on measurement, combining financial and non-financial strategic measures. The second generation developed linkages between the dimensions by using cause-and-effect chains to link strategic objectives to drivers. The third generation completes the transformation to a strategic management system by linking incentives to the achievement of BSC targets (Speckbacher, *et al.*, 2003). It may be that performance improvement benefits will not be achieved until the organisation moves towards a second or third generation system. This remains unknown, although the Ittner and Larcker (2003) research suggests benefits accrue from the introduction of causal maps (second generation). An interesting feature of the Speckbacher *et al.* study was that, irrespective of the type of BSC in use, all the companies using them intended to continue. Furthermore, the more developed the scorecard the greater the commitment to future development. Recent studies have reported that about half of the organisations adopting stakeholder models of performance had built business models (Marr, 2004). There seems to be a dynamic at work here with companies initially using the BSC for measurement (first generation), then developing it using strategy maps (second generation), and finally transforming to a management system by including incentive structures (third generation).

Academic researchers are beginning to focus on EVA measures of performance. Two key claims have been made about using EVA as a performance measure:

- EVA is a better predictor of stock market returns than traditional accounting earnings.
- A performance measurement and reward scheme based on EVA will provide higher rates of return for shareholders than conventional reward systems based on earnings per share and other popular financial measures.

The first claim is questioned by Biddle *et al.* (1999). They found that traditional accounting measures were more closely associated with stock returns and firm values than EVA, RI and cash flows from operations; i.e. traditional accounting measures outperform the new metrics in explaining stock market returns. The second claim is supported by two studies. Kleiman (1999) compared 70 adopters of EVA with non-adopters from the same industry. In the three-year period prior to adoption there was no distinguishable difference between the stock market performance of EVA companies and their industry competitors. Following adoption of EVA, the EVA companies outperformed their median competitors by 28.8 per cent over four years. The Wallace (1997) study demonstrated that companies adopting EVA and RI in compensation schemes tended to generate higher levels of residual income than control companies by improving operating efficiency, disposing of selected assets, and repurchasing more shares. All these actions are consistent with shareholder wealth creation.

It would seem that the market does not yet recognise the information content of EVA for firm valuations and stock returns. When used as an internal control and performance measure, EVA appears to motivate managers to take actions consistent with shareholder wealth creation. These findings need further consideration.

A problem in interpreting such findings is that the sample data comes from publicly available sources – typically published EVA data from Stern Stewart. Although this contains some of the standard accounting adjustments proposed in EVA analysis, it excludes firm-specific adjustments made for corporate clients and thus may distort the findings. A further complication arises in interpreting what constitutes an EVA company. The adoption of an EVA-based compensation scheme is often taken to mean a company that has adopted EVA, but this could be only a partial adoption. If we compare this with the development of the BSC from first to third generation, we may be looking at 'first generation' EVA systems where only senior executive pay is linked to EVA rather than it having been adopted throughout the organisation.

There are gaps in our understanding of stakeholder and shareholder approaches to performance management. The approaches are developing. The four generic categories of BSC measures are being supplemented by a fifth category to include an employee perspective. The learning and growth dimension continues to cause problems in specifying measures. The measurement metrics for shareholder approaches are well defined, although the debate continues over which metric is superior. We have definition problems that affect our understanding of some of the research findings. What constitutes a BSC approach and what constitutes an EVA approach? We have limited insights into the processes of target setting, though this is an important element of performance management. Executive reward systems are an important component of performance improvement, but actual schemes vary significantly from one company to another.

How is the performance measurement system used in the firm?

Research studies to date suggest a variety of uses of stakeholder and shareholder management in practice. Earlier in this chapter it was proposed that all performance measurement systems need to define strategy in operational terms. This will inform the *dimensions* of performance that need to be measured, the *targets* to be set and the *rewards/penalties* associated with the achievement of performance standards. For stakeholder perspectives we would expect to see a range of performance measures, both financial and non-financial, reflecting the interests of the various stakeholder groups. In contrast, the value-based management literature suggests the use of a single value-based measurement metric of performance. No systematic differences would be expected in target setting approaches. In terms of reward structures, we would expect some alignment between the performance measures and the reward structures, so would expect to see a broader base of indicators used in stakeholder approaches compared to shareholder approaches.

Results from a study of UK firms reveal considerable overlap between the two approaches (Cooper *et al.*, 2001). In stakeholder firms the three most important stakeholders were shareholders, customers and employees. They used a wide range of measures, 5.5 on average. All used traditional profit-based measures and most supplemented these with customer and employee measures. Around one-third of this group also used value-based measures. These were being used to augment, not replace, traditional profit-based measures. Regarding reward systems, all companies used a financial measure of performance, with 80 per cent citing this as the most important measure. In addition to financial measures, one-third of companies included personal performance as part of the reward package. The broader stakeholder approach did not form part of the reward base for 70 per cent of the companies. This could be interpreted as prejudicial to their wider stakeholder-oriented corporate strategy, or it could be argued that the other objectives were implicit (Cooper *et al.*, 2001; Fitzgerald and Moon, 1996).

Adopters of value-based measures identified shareholders, customers, employees and suppliers as their most important stakeholder groups. Whilst every company considered shareholders to be important stakeholders, less than half considered them to be the most important. This is surprising given value-based management is predicated on the primacy of shareholders. Although value-based measures dominated, most companies supplemented these with profit, ROCE and stakeholder measures. When rewarding performance, only 20 per cent of companies relied solely on value-based measures; for some, profit and/or earnings per share remained paramount. In practice we can see overlaps between stakeholder and shareholder approaches to measuring and managing performance. Companies are using metrics that suit their needs rather than following a particular method. Some stakeholder approaches incorporate value-based metrics within their financial perspective. Shareholder value-based measures rarely replace financial measures; rather they supplement them.

Several studies address the implementation problems faced by value-based management companies. The difficulties can be divided into technical, behavioural and organisational. Technical difficulties include: getting the data to calculate the value-based metric, estimating the weighted cost of capital, the volatility of the weighted cost of capital calculation, and problems in translating value-based financial measures into meaningful operational measures. Data problems forced one company to stop using EVA at the business unit level and return to using it only at the firm level. The major problem was establishing asset registers at the business unit level owing to the network nature of the business. Behavioural difficulties centred on getting managers to understand the new measures and to adopt them, particularly when the new metrics exposed previously good performers as 'poor' performers. Several companies reported communication problems, chiefly if senior management were not fully committed to the new system. Other organisational difficulties include the time and effort required for implementation and ensuring that it proceeds sufficiently quickly to maintain momentum.

We have presented an overview of research findings from a number of studies drawn from the accounting and finance literature. The next section focuses on making value-based management work. The case of Lloyds TSB is presented with findings on the five elements common in successful value-based management implementations.

Case study: Lloyds TSB

In 1983 Lloyds bank appointed a new CEO, Brian Pitman, who remained with the company until his retirement in 2001. During that period the company's market capitalisation moved from £1 billion to £40 billion and the compound shareholder return averaged 26 per cent annually. In financial performance terms, it was a success story. He embraced a value-based management philosophy recognising that this 'involves much more than putting in place some faddish new performance metric or accounting method' (Pitman, 2003, p. 4).

The first priority was to get some agreement on what constituted success for Lloyds. This was easy – they wanted to be the best financial services company. Then the problems started. What did that mean? To some people it meant being the biggest; for others it was about having the highest levels of customer satisfaction. After some debate the board agreed that the single governing objective would be improving shareholder value. The agreed metric for measuring this was return on equity (ROE), with an initial target set at 10 per cent above the rate of inflation (5 per cent at the time). One board member argued that, whilst the measure was right, the target was wrong and ROE should be compared to the cost of equity. At the time no one in the organisation had calculated the cost of equity. When they calculated it at between 17 per cent and 19 per cent this was something of a shock, as hardly a business in the company was producing those levels of return.

In pursuit of shareholder value, a number of difficult divestment decisions led to the reformulation of strategy to concentrate on unglamorous products like mortgages and insurance. The focus moved from generating *profit* to generating *value*. The target for every business was to achieve a return above its cost of equity and executive compensation was based on ROE. The measure was refined over the years but maintained the single objective – increasing value for shareholders. Brian Pitman was totally committed to a single overarching objective: 'Systems like those (BSC) rely on multiple objectives, which set up competing claims on people's time and send confusing signals about what you are trying to accomplish' (Pitman, 2003, p. 4).

As the system developed, target setting moved towards using external process benchmarks and the targets became more challenging. The reward system extended throughout the organisation. Performance targets were set for all employees and rewards were based on achieving them. It is not evident whether bonuses were capped, but they were significant. The performance management system was driven from the top, senior managers used the system, targets and goals were explicit, and rewards reinforced motivation.

The success of this programme was not just about changing metrics; it was about changing the organisational culture. The key issue was the involvement and commitment of staff to the overarching objective. This involved a learning process that promoted heated debate culminating in a shared vision. As with many change initiatives, senior management commitment was vital.

The Lloyds TSB case study supports findings from a global survey on value-based management implementation (Haspeslagh *et al.*, 2001). Their view was that a successful value-based management programme is about changing company culture, not just changing measurement metrics. Changing culture is difficult and the main reason why many value-based management initiatives fail. The survey suggests five common elements in successful programmes:

- *An explicit commitment to shareholder value at board level.* Many managers are focused on growth or becoming the biggest organisation in their market, but the focus needs changing from growth to profitability. A public statement of commitment to shareholder value signals a change of culture to both external and internal constituencies.
- *A training programme that encourages thinking in terms of generating shareholder value.* Successful value-based management companies invest a great deal of time, effort and money in training large numbers of employees, since everyone needs to believe that managing for value is the way the company should be developing. Not everyone will be convinced of this and some managers may leave.
- *Reinforcing training with broad-based incentive schemes closely tied to value-based performance measures, thus giving employees a sense of ownership.* The key factor here was including a large number of employees in the reward schemes.
- *Being prepared to make major organisational changes through divestment, investment and structural change within the company.* Organising for value often makes the company's cost structure more transparent. Fewer costs are allocated and more are directly traceable, which has the potential to reduce the noise around the politics of cost allocations.
- *Broad and inclusive changes to company processes.* This affects the management accounting function. The survey suggests that unsuccessful companies tend to focus on changing their accounting and control systems, typically investing considerable time in developing and applying complex measures of performance. Successful companies take a broader approach and follow four rules when changing their systems:
  - avoid accounting complexity
  - identify value drivers
  - integrate budgeting with strategic planning
  - invest heavily in information systems

Managers need to understand the metric they are being measured by. Earlier we considered problems in calculating value-based metrics, noting their complexity and subjectivity. The proposal here is for 'good enough' accounting, keeping the calculation simple since technical refinement can undermine the measure and bring rejection of the whole system by operating managers. Economic profit needs translating into something measurable for managers. This requires considerable time and effort in identifying and assessing value drivers with the greatest influence on economic profit. Successful companies are more likely to tightly integrate their budgeting with their strategic planning processes. It is unlikely that existing information systems will have the breadth and depth of data required for value-based management initiatives, so investment in information systems is one way that companies can demonstrate their commitment to the value-based management programmes.

Conclusion

From the research it appears that organisations with formal performance management out-perform organisations without it. Beyond this, things become more confused. Some studies show adopters of balanced scorecards and EVA outperform control groups of non-adopters. However, there are definition problems. In particular what do we mean by BSC? Is it a generation type one, two or three? How do we define an EVA organisation? Is it sufficient to use EVA as a reported performance measure and for executive compensation, or should the EVA philosophy permeate all decision-making and management within the company? More research is needed on these issues, especially the cultural dimension. Many reported studies have been conducted in the USA, which has a long tradition of executive compensation packages being based on performance. Formulae that are successful in the USA may not translate to a different cultural setting, which has implications for multinational organisations.

Reflecting on the uptake of stakeholder and shareholder performance management systems, one of the surprising features is that around 60 per cent of survey respondents continue to manage within the traditional accounting framework. The picture emerging from a recent study of UK management accountants is that whilst budgeting – the cornerstone of traditional management control – continues to be important, business performance evaluation will remain a key task. How to measure that performance remains an open question. Understanding the interplay between financial and non-financial indicators together with systems knowledge to structure data would seem to be key skills required to support the analytical and interpretive roles of management accountants.

When looking at performance management within the firm, the stylised theoretical approaches of stakeholder and shareholder approaches illustrated in Table 11.1 seem to break down in the UK context. BSC adopters use a wide range of performance measures and are including some value-based measures. Reward structures concentrate on financial dimensions of performance; few applications incorporate the wider stakeholder view. Value-based management adopters continue to use traditional performance measures of profit and ROCE alongside their value-based metrics. Few companies rely solely on a value-based metric in their reward systems. Rather, companies appear to mix and match the methodologies.

It may be that EVA works at the company level, but translating this to business unit levels and down to operational managers is problematic. The idea of translating EVA into measurable value drivers sounds similar to the strategy mapping proposals of the BSC. Undoubtedly there are some successes in using value-based methods – the Lloyds TSB case, Coca-Cola and Cadbury for example. But these are not just about the metric adopted; they are also about how it is managed. Key features of successful implementations are:

- an explicit commitment to shareholder value at board level;
- a training programme that encourages thinking in terms of generating shareholder value;

- reinforcing training with broad-based incentive schemes closely tied to value-based performance measures, thus giving employees a sense of ownership;
- being prepared to make major organisational changes through divestment, investment and structural change within the company;
- broad and inclusive changes to company processes.

These elements require a fundamental change in orientation, are beset with technical, behavioural and organisational difficulties, and require significant investment in support systems. Some companies clearly feel the effort is worthwhile; others remain to be convinced. With 60 per cent of companies operating traditional frameworks to measure performance and management accountants rating business performance evaluation as their key future task, the multi-million pound performance measurement industry looks set to flourish.

References

Arnold, G. (2005) *Corporate Financial Management,* Harlow: Prentice Hall.

Ashton, C. (1997) *Strategic Performance Measurement: Transforming Corporate Performance by Measuring and Managing the Drivers of Business Success,* London: Business Intelligence Ltd. London.

Biddle, G.C., Bowen, R.M. and Wallace, J.S. (1999) 'Evidence on EVA', *Journal of Applied Corporate Finance,* **12**, 69–79.

Cooper, S., Crowther, D., Davies, M. and Davis, E.W. (2001) *Shareholder or Stakeholder Value: The Development of Indicators for the Control and Measurement of Performance,* London: CIMA.

Cooper, S. and Davies, M. (2004) 'Measuring shareholder value – the metrics', in D. Starovic, S. Cooper and M. Davies (eds), *Maximising Shareholder Value: Achieving Clarity in Decision Making – Technical Report,* London: CIMA, pp. 10–15.

Davis, S. and Albright, T. (2004) 'An investigation of the effect of balanced scorecard implementation on financial performance', *Management Accounting Research,* **15**, 135–53.

Fitzgerald, L., Johnston, R., Brignall, S., Silvestro, R. and Voss, C. (1991) *Performance Measurement in Service Businesses,* London: CIMA.

Fitzgerald, L. and Moon, P. (1996) *Performance Measurement in Service Industries: Making it Work,* London: CIMA.

Haspeslagh, P., Noda, T. and Boulos, F. (2001) 'Managing for value: it's not just about the numbers', *Harvard Business Review,* **79**, 65–73.

Ittner, C.D. and Larcker, D.F. (2003) 'Coming up short on non-financial performance measurement', *Harvard Business Review,* **81**, 88–95.

Kaplan, R.S. and Norton, D.P. (1992) 'The balanced scorecard – measures that drive performance', *Harvard Business Review,* **70**, 71–9.

Kaplan, R.S. and Norton, D.P. (2001) *The Strategy Focused Organization,* Boston, MA: Harvard Business School Press.

Kleiman, R. (1999) 'Some new evidence on EVA companies', *Journal of Applied Corporate Finance,* **12**, 80–91.

Lingle, J.H. and Schiermann, W.A. (1996) 'From balanced scorecard to strategic gauges: is measurement worth it?' *Management Review* (New York), March, **85**, 56–62.

Lovata, L.M. and Costigan, M.L. (2002) 'Empirical analysis of adopters of economic value added', *Management Accounting Research,* **13**, 215–28.

Lynch, R.L. and Cross, K.F. (1991) *Measure Up! Yardsticks for Continuous Improvements,* Oxford: Blackwell.

Marr, B. (2004) *Business Performance Management: The Current State of the Art,* Cranfield: Cranfield School of Management.

Merchant, K.A. and Van der Stede, W.A. (2003) *Management Control Systems,* Harlow, Essex: Prentice Hall.

Neely, A. and Adams, C. (2001) 'The performance prism perspective', *Journal of Cost Management,* **15,** 7–15.

Nørreklit, H. (2000) 'The balance on the balanced scorecard: a critical analysis of some of its assumptions', *Management Accounting Research,* **11,** 65–88.

Otley, D.T. (1999) 'Performance management: a framework for management control systems research', *Management Accounting Research,* **10,** 363–82.

Pitman, B. (2003) 'Leading for value', *Harvard Business Review,* **81,** 41–6.

Rappaport, A. (1998) *Creating Shareholder Value,* New York: The Free Press.

Speckbacher, G., Bischof, J. and Pfeiffer, T. (2003) 'A descriptive analysis of balanced scorecards in German-speaking countries', *Management Accounting Research,* **14,** 361–87.

Stewart, G.B. (1991) *The Quest for Value,* New York: Harper Business.

Wallace, J.S (1997) 'Adopting income-based compensation plans: do you get what you pay for?' *Journal of Accounting and Economics,* **24,** 275–300.

Further reading

Cooper, S., Crowther, D., Davies, M. and Davis, E.W. (2001) *Shareholder or Stakeholder Value: The Development of Indicators for the Control and Measurement of Performance,* London: CIMA. Reports on performance measurement in practice.

Fitzgerald, L. and Moon, P. (1996) *Performance Measurement in Service Industries: Making it Work,* London: CIMA. Stakeholder approaches to performance management are explored in four service organisations.

O'Hanlon, J. and Peasnell, K. (1998) 'Wall Street's contribution to management accounting: the Stern Stewart EVA financial management system', *Management Accounting Research,* **9,** 421–44. A thorough review of the theoretical underpinning of EVA.

Otley, D. (2001) 'Extending the boundaries of management accounting research: developing systems for performance management', *British Accounting Review,* **33,** 243–61. Stresses the need to study accounting techniques within their management context.

Starovic, D., Cooper, S. and Davies, M. (2004) *Maximising Shareholder Value: Achieving Clarity in Decision Making – Technical Report,* London: CIMA. A comprehensive overview of value-based management.

Part 3

'New' applications of management accounting

12

Does EVA add value?

Jan Bouwens and Roland F. Speklé

Introduction

In this chapter we investigate the use of economic value added (EVA) for purposes of performance evaluation, management compensation and – more generally – management control. As management control is concerned with influencing managerial behaviour in the pursuit of organisational effectiveness, we will discuss EVA in the context of decision support (does EVA help managers to select 'correct' courses of action that take into account the influence on organisational performance?) and in the context of motivation (does EVA provide incentives to increase managerial interest in improving performance?).

Our discussion proceeds as follows. First, we discuss performance measurement issues in general, introducing some useful notions underlying our examination of EVA as a performance metric. After exploring the technicalities of EVA's computation and its relation to traditional residual income, we begin our analysis with an evaluation of a fundamental claim made by EVA proponents, i.e. that EVA is the best proxy for value creation. If this claim is valid, there may be economic benefits in linking managerial compensation to realised EVA, because such a compensation scheme would help to align the goals of the manager with those of the shareholders. We demonstrate analytically that EVA is indeed compatible with a value orientation. However, this result is insufficient to support a preference for EVA as the ultimate measure for management control since other accounting measures may also be compatible with a value orientation. In addition, even if EVA and value creation are strongly correlated, firms (and their shareholders) may have perfectly good reasons not to use EVA for performance evaluation and compensation. One such reason is that the positive association between EVA and the focal measure (i.e. value creation) may disappear once the firm starts to use EVA as a measure of performance. A second, related reason is that it may not be possible to observe the association within a reasonable timeframe. Finally, EVA tends to induce parochial behaviour, which is problematic when organisational goal achievement requires cooperation between sub-units. We address these issues in our discussion. However, even though EVA may not be the perfect performance measure, the key question is whether organisations that use EVA for purposes of management control achieve superior performance. This being an empirical question, we turn to the academic literature to discuss the evidence on EVA's effect on performance. The final section summarises our argument and presents the conclusions.

Performance measurement and decentralisation

In the realm of business and organisation, performance measurement is closely linked to decentralisation or delegation of decision rights. Decentralisation occurs when an agent acquires the right to make decisions and to act on behalf of someone else (the principal), while the consequences of the agent's decisions and actions are borne (at least partly) by the principal. Decentralisation is endemic within organisations. Thus, we observe shareholders delegating the management of 'their' companies to a CEO. Likewise, we see CEOs delegating part of their authority to managers of divisions and business units, who in turn assign specific decisions to managers lower in the hierarchy. In this section, we discuss how decentralisation and performance measurement are related. Although the ideas in our discussion apply to agency relations in general, we shall develop them – for ease of exposition – in the specific context of the relationship between a profit centre manager and the organisation's senior management.

Decentralisation and the distribution of knowledge

Probably the most fundamental reason to decentralise has to do with knowledge (e.g. Jensen and Meckling, 1992). As organisations grow in size and complexity, organisational actors must specialise in particular areas of knowledge. As a result of this specialisation, information asymmetries arise. Usually, a production manager has superior knowledge of the production technology and its operation. Similarly, a sales manager is better informed about customers' preferences and how these can be met. These different and dispersed repositories of knowledge are valuable in that they have the potential to contribute to the success of the organisation. In order to realise that potential, the organisation must somehow tap these repositories to ensure that its decisions and actions capture valuable knowledge. This requires a 'collocation of knowledge and decision rights' (Jensen and Meckling, 1992) or, to put it in more mundane terms, it requires that the decision-maker has access to the relevant knowledge.

One way to do this is to centralise decision rights and to transfer the information to some central decision-making authority. This is not always efficient, however. Centralisation requires local managers to communicate their knowledge upwards so that their supervisor takes the best decision. But collecting, transferring and processing information is costly and is bound to affect the quality of information in several ways. For one, it takes time to communicate, decreasing the organisation's responsiveness to changing circumstances. Also, it may be very difficult to decide what knowledge to communicate. Local agents may not fully be aware of the information needs at higher hierarchical levels and cannot be expected perfectly to anticipate these needs. And vice versa, central managers may have a hard time identifying the right questions to ask. Furthermore, human cognitive abilities are limited (indeed, that is why specialisation arises in the first place). Centralisation may easily overburden the information handling capacity of the central decision-maker. For these reasons, it is inevitable that at least some valuable knowledge gets lost in the process of communication.

If the transfer of knowledge to a central decision-making authority is problematic, the alternative is to decentralise, i.e. to grant decision rights to those individuals that possess the best information to make decisions. Effectively, decentralisation implies assigning local managers to the job of taking initiatives to exploit their local knowledge in profitable ways. Decentralising decision rights, however, has problems of its own. Though it promotes local initiative, it is less helpful in supporting cooperation (Roberts, 2004). Local managers may not fully understand how their actions and choices affect the performance of other organisational units and the firm as a whole. Additionally, the goals of local managers may differ from those of the organisation, and these managers may seek to exploit organisational resources to their own advantage rather than for the firm. Therefore, unit level decision-making tends to focus on how action alternatives impact on local performance, ignoring (inadvertently or deliberately) their effect on other parts of the organisation.

This discussion suggests that organisations face a trade-off in deciding on the allocation of decision rights. Centralisation enhances coordination, but is fraught with communication costs and losses of local knowledge. Decentralisation, on the other hand, is valuable in that it supports local knowledge capturing, but it comes at the price of coordination problems and private goal pursuit. The costs of decentralisation, however, are not exogenously determined, but can be influenced by the organisation through its management control structure, especially through its performance measurement and incentive system. The next section examines the issues that arise here.

Performance measurement

In decentralised organisations, senior management needs to create conditions that motivate profit centre managers to use the decision rights granted to them in ways that contribute to organisational goal achievement. The performance measurement system is an important instrument in this context. Performance standards communicate what the organisation expects from local agents, providing guidance to profit centre managers as to how they can contribute to the organisation. If the same measures are also used for performance evaluation and managerial compensation, they provide an incentive that helps to align individual goals with the objectives of the organisation. In addition, measuring performance produces feedback to both local managers and their supervisors on how action choices affect local performance, and how this relates to overall firm performance. Thus, the performance measurement system alleviates the problems associated with decentralisation. Or rather, it does so on the condition that the system has been designed appropriately. That, however, is problematic. Both the literature and the business press are full of stories illustrating 'the folly of rewarding A while hoping for B' (Kerr, 1975). What, then, is an appropriate performance measurement system, and why is it apparently so difficult to design one? The following discussion introduces several notions that help to address the issues involved.

Sensitivity

One problem in designing appropriate performance measurement structures is that, in many practical organisational settings, the role of the performance measure places conflicting demands on its properties. In a decentralised organisation, a performance measure should help the manager to select correct courses of action, and it should help to identify how a manager's actions affect performance. This requires the performance

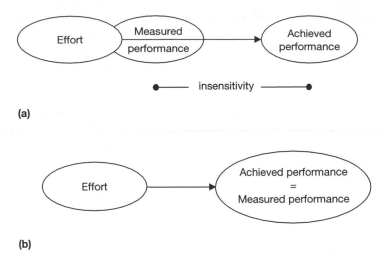

Figure 12.1 Sensitivity: (a) insensitive measure of performance; (b) fully sensitive measure of performance

measure to be responsive to managerial action, i.e. the score on the measure must be affected by the managers' decisions and effort. This notion of *sensitivity* is important for several reasons. If the measure is not sensitive to managerial behaviour, it does not allow inferences about the quality of the manager's efforts and fails to provide information relevant for evaluation purposes. Neither is an insensitive measure useful in guiding action choices, for if the score on the measure does not depend on the manager's decisions, it cannot help to discriminate between decision alternatives and does not provide meaningful feedback.

Figure 12.1 illustrates the problem of insensitive performance measures. Consider a manager exerting effort. This effort results in achieved performance. However, the firm does not observe achieved performance directly, but uses its measurement system to assess the outcome of the manager's efforts. Thus, the firm observes measured performance rather than achieved performance. These two performance figures need not be identical. If the measure is insensitive, measured performance hardly responds to effort, while achieved performance does. Figure 12.1(a) reflects this situation. Ideally, the measured performance oval covers the achieved performance oval (Figure 12.1(b)). However, the more the ovals are separated, the less sensitive the measure. For an example of an insensitive measure, consider a housekeeping team servicing hotel rooms. Assume team effort is assessed with sales volume. Is this measure sensitive to the efforts of the team? The team's actions probably affect customer satisfaction. However, additional effort will not increase hotel occupancy directly. Though room cleanliness is an important factor for hotel guests, they are unlikely to respond to small differences in cleanliness – provided that the quality of cleaning remains above some threshold level. Guests will reconsider their patronage only when room cleanliness drops below that level. Thus, sales volume is only sensitive in the extremes and does not register the nuances of guests' satisfaction with the quality of the services provided.

Noise in the measure

A second problem of performance measurement is that factors other than effort affect measured performance. It is often the case that the score on the measure depends on both the effort of the manager and on uncertain, uncontrollable events. Then, the measure contains *noise,* and reflects the performance of the manager inaccurately. Even if a manager achieves the desired purpose, it is entirely possible that this result is concealed because of noisy measurement. Several examples spring to mind. Consider a manager who does in fact achieve some desired cost reduction. If profitability is the performance metric, it is possible that this success will not surface in the measure, because other factors (e.g. soaring oil prices that negatively affect profitability) mask the positive cost effects. In that case, the measure signals that profit is lower than expected, concealing the cost-reduction achievements of the manager. As another example, consider a sales manager who has been able to secure a full quota of orders. However, because the production department did not maintain its machines well, production comes to a standstill. The sales department cannot deliver the products in time and clients cancel their orders. As a consequence of the interdependence between production and sales, the sales manager underperforms in terms of profitability, despite doing his utmost to increase profit. We illustrate this phenomenon in Figure 12.2. The arrow pointing to achieved performance represents the effect of effort, while the arrow pointing to measured performance deviates from achieved performance. The steepness of the slope represents the level of noise.

Distortion

Another issue to consider is whether the performance measure supports *congruity* between the objectives of the firm and those of the agent (Feltham and Xie, 1994). If not, performance measures are *distorted* (Baker, 2002). A performance measure is congruent or undistorted to the extent that it provides incentives that are systematically aligned with the organisation's objective. As performance measures induce managers to engage in behaviours that positively affect the score on the performance measure, it is important to ensure that positive (negative) scores on the measures actually reflect a positive (negative) contribution to ultimate goal achievement. Distortion implies that

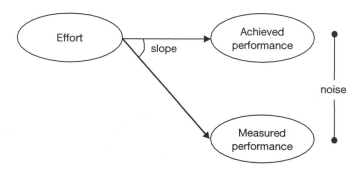

Figure 12.2 **Measurement noise**

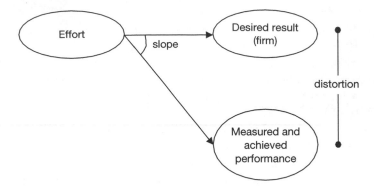

Figure 12.3 **Distortion**

managers can choose actions that make them look good on the measure, without actually enhancing goal achievement. It also implies that there may be actions that do in fact contribute to the ultimate objective, but that will not be picked up by the measure. Thus, whereas noise and sensitivity refer to differences between measured and achieved performance, distortion refers to a discrepancy between measured and desired results. We illustrate distortion in Figure 12.3. Assume that achieved performance is equal to measured performance, so the measure is not noisy or insensitive. Suppose the measure considered is customer satisfaction. If we use this measure for evaluation purposes, managers are stimulated to improve customer satisfaction. However, at some point the cost incurred to improve customer satisfaction will exceed the benefits. This is where we should stop creating more satisfied customers. But if the measure does not tell us that we should cease our efforts, it gives a distorted signal to the manager. Achieved performance and desired performance will start to diverge. In Figure 12.3, the steepness of the slope between the arrows represents the degree of distortion. Ideally, the effort–achieved result arrow covers the effort–desired result arrow completely. In that case, any action that positively affects measured performance brings about desired improvements in the firm's results. The more the two arrows deviate, the more distorted the measure.

Causes of distortion: timeliness and completeness

Distortion appears in many guises. Two characteristics are especially important when considering the degree of incentive distortion: the measure's *timeliness* and its *completeness*. The performance measure should convey the results of managerial behaviour in a timely way. If a long period of time elapses between the moment a decision is taken and the point at which the results of this decision surface in the measure, that measure is likely to result in dysfunctional behaviour. This problem is known as the horizon problem and can be thought of as an instance of insensitivity, leading to incentive distortion. A common manifestation of this occurs when the time necessary for the effects of a decision to surface in the performance measure exceeds the expected tenure of the manager. Suppose a manager expects to remain in office for another two years and the firm uses profitability as the main performance metric. Will this manager be prepared to invest in, say, an R&D project that will bear fruit only in the long term?

Probably not, for this investment will negatively affect current profitability, while the future proceeds will be harvested by the manager's successor.

In addition, a performance measure must be complete. That is, an ideal measure must summarise fully the effects of all decisions for which the manager is responsible. Incomplete measures lead to management myopia as they prompt managers to pay unbalanced attention to results that are being measured, while unduly neglecting areas for which performance is not assessed. For instance, a firm pursuing a strategy of cost leadership is likely to place strong emphasis on efficiency measures. Nevertheless, the firm also expects its managers to care about product quality, even though this is much harder to assess. But if performance evaluation does not incorporate quality measures, the firm runs the risk that cost savings will be realised at the expense of product quality.

The tension between sensitivity, noise and distortion

If possible, organisations want to use performance measures that are sensitive, noise-less and undistorted. In the real world, however, these desirable properties cannot usually be achieved simultaneously and firms must make a trade-off. This can be illustrated with an example. Consider a large, diversified company in the petrochemical industry. Suppose this firm has embraced value creation as its ultimate goal. The firm is publicly traded and measures its performance in terms of the firm's market value of equity. This measure is undistorted, i.e. it measures performance in a way that is perfectly aligned with the organisation's true objective. However, although the measure is appropriate for assessing firm performance, it is less informative about managerial performance. Equity value will be influenced by a variety of factors that have little to do with managerial accomplishments. For instance, the market value of an oil company depends to a large extent on the price of crude oil on the world market; a factor that is clearly beyond the control of the firm's managers. Hence, equity market value is a noisy indicator of managerial performance, which limits its usefulness for motivational and monitoring purposes. Also, the measure's sensitivity is questionable, especially at lower levels in the managerial hierarchy. In this large, diversified organisation, it is doubtful that the actions of individual sub-unit managers are readily visible in the measure, and that these managers are able to relate to the measure and frame their decisions in terms of their effects on the market value of the firm's equity. In our oil company example, it is unlikely that the manager of, say, the retail division has a clear notion of how his or her actions will impact the market value of the company's equity. Then, the measure is of limited value as an instrument to stimulate managers to make decisions that are good for the firm. Also, it has limited meaning in the context of decentralised decision evaluation. Therefore, the firm may want to consider using an alternative measure of performance that more directly captures the performance of the retail division, such as the centre's profitability or its return on investment. The problem with such measures at the profit centre level, however, is that they tend to be distorted, i.e. they are not perfectly aligned with the ultimate objective of the organisation. It is entirely conceivable that actions that improve (worsen) the centre's profitability do not simultaneously increase (decrease) the firm's market value of equity. For instance, if local profitability is used, the manager is less likely to consider how his

251

or her actions affect other parts of the firm, leading to problems of sub-optimisation. So, this local measure cannot guarantee goal-consistent behaviour.

Incentive degeneration

Although in practice most measures are distorted, some are more distorted than others. Thus, organisations face the challenge of selecting those performance measures that are sufficiently sensitive and informative, while at the same time not too distorted. Intuitively, one might expect that this implies that firms look for performance indicators that are strongly correlated with the ultimate goal of the organisation. In fact, there is a large literature that seeks to measure the correlation between various accounting metrics of performance and firm value to determine whether firms should include these metrics in their incentive contracts. However, the correlation between a proxy for performance and the organisation's ultimate objective should not be the major concern. Rather, the crucial issue is whether or not the actions managers choose affect the performance measure and the organisation's goal in the same way (Ittner and Larcker, 1998; Baker, 2002). This an important point, because the correlation between a performance indicator and the ultimate goal depends on whether or not the indicator is being used for incentive purposes (cf. Baker, 2002). A measure that seems perfectly aligned with the firm's objective may lose this desirable quality once the firm starts using it as a performance target, thus degenerating incentives.

An example might illustrate this point. Suppose a firm has access to a large-sample empirical study reporting a strong and positive correlation between customer satisfaction and firm profitability. Based on this study, the firm decides that it makes good sense to include measures of customer satisfaction in its incentive system. The problem with this system, however, is that there are many ways to increase customer satisfaction that do not also increase firm performance. For instance, granting additional discounts might positively affect customer satisfaction. Increasing the level of after-sales services might have a similar effect. Such actions, however, do not necessarily pay off in terms of firm performance. In fact, they may erode profitability. In that case, introducing customer satisfaction into the reward structure creates incentives for managers to engage in actions that make them look good on the measure used to assess their performance, while simultaneously jeopardising ultimate goal attainment. Then, the customer satisfaction measure distorts incentives. Obviously, if this problem of behavioural displacement exists, it should have manifested itself in the empirical study on which the company based its decision, but only if a significant proportion of the firms in the sample actually rewarded their managers on the basis of customer satisfaction. If this condition is not met, it is entirely possible that the correlation disappears as soon as larger numbers of firms start to base managerial compensation on customer satisfaction scores.

The properties of EVA

Proponents of EVA build the case in favour of their preferred performance measure on the claim that EVA is the best proxy for value creation. They argue that the use of EVA maintains the systematic link between various value-affecting decisions (i.e. finance, investment and operational decisions). The effects of operational decisions surface in the profit part of the measure. The effects of investment and finance decisions also come to light because profit is evaluated against the product of assets and cost of capital. From a managerial point of view, this feature of EVA is desirable because it directs managerial attention to asset deployment (i.e. increasing profit) and asset commitment (the size and timing of the investments, and the risk associated with assets in place). If this claim is valid, there may be good reasons to give EVA a prominent place in the management control structure, for it would help to align managerial goals with the objective of shareholder value creation. This section examines a number of important issues associated with this claim.

Our argument proceeds as follows. First, we define EVA and address its relationship with traditional residual income. Then, starting from the notion commonly accepted in the finance literature that the value of a project (or a firm as a set of projects) is equal to the net present value of the associated cash flows, we demonstrate that EVA-based valuation yields exactly the same outcome as discounted cash flow valuation. Assuming that the market also bases its value judgements on expected cash flows – which it does according to a huge literature in finance – this result suggests that EVA must be strongly correlated with stock returns. However, more traditional accounting measures are also correlated with stock returns (Easton, *et al.*, 1992). Therefore, the mere existence of a correlation cannot support a preference for EVA. At the least, EVA should be a better predictor of stock returns, and the incentives it provides should compare favourably to those of alternative accounting measures. We continue our discussion with a review of the relevant empirical literature and a comparative analysis of EVA's incentive properties.

EVA defined

EVA is a specific profit measure. However, while traditionally profit is regarded as earnings after interest and tax, EVA also subtracts the costs of equity capital. Although EVA has been included in management accounting handbooks for quite some time, it is useful to review the steps involved in its calculation. In essence, EVA starts from traditional residual income:

	Sales revenues
minus	Costs of operational activities (including taxes)
minus	Financing costs (= cost of capital × capital employed)
=	Residual income

EVA, however, differs from residual income in that it adjusts for 'arbitrary' accounting rules. Stern Stewart uses a list of 164 possible adjustments. According to this consulting firm, most clients consider using 20 to 25 of these adjustments, but actually apply between 5 and 10. So, in a sense, there is no unequivocal definition of EVA. Specific 'accounting distortions' are eliminated by each company to the extent that it is practical to do so. Stern Stewart has never published all 164 adjustments, although the most important ones have appeared in print. Table 12.1

Table 12.1 **Examples of accounting adjustments according to Stern Stewart**

Accounting item	Conventional treatment	EVA adjustment
Marketing and R&D costs	Deduct directly from earnings; capitalisation of development costs, depreciation over limited number of years. At the same time establishment of a statutory reserve equal to the amount capitalised.	Record as asset and amortise over the expected economic lifespan.
Deferred taxes	Record as asset and/or liability.	Reverse recording of asset and/or liability to reflect cash basis reporting.
Purchased goodwill	Record as asset; amortise over the expected duration, then deduct directly from earnings or reserves.	Reverse amortisation to reflect original asset amount.
Operating leases	Deduct directly from earnings.	Record asset and amortise; record liability and related interest.
Bad debts and warranty costs	Estimate accruals: amount to be written-off (bad debts) or provision (warranty costs).	Reverse accruals to reflect cash basis reporting.
LIFO inventory evaluation	LIFO permitted.	Convert into FIFO.
Construction in progress	Record as asset.	Remove from assets.
Discontinued operations	Include in assets and in earnings.	Remove from assets and earnings.

Source: Biddle *et al.* (1999).

gives an overview (taken from Biddle, *et al.*, 1999). It is interesting that the adjustments, although presented as corrections for arbitrary accounting rules, may actually introduce new arbitrary elements to the performance measure. Take for instance the case of marketing costs. In conventional accounting, these costs are expensed when incurred. For purposes of EVA calculation, some of these costs are treated as an investment that should be capitalised. However, how is one to decide which marketing costs to capitalise? And how is one to pick the appropriate amortisation policy?

Stern Stewart suggests using the capital asset pricing model (CAPM) to assess the specific market-based risk for the company and its individual divisions. This assessment underlies the determination of the cost of capital, which should compensate for investing in the company.

The main idea behind the accounting adjustments and the inclusion of the cost of capital is that EVA should approximate the economic concept of profit, as opposed to the traditional accounting notion of profit. Compared to traditional profit, EVA (and residual income) has the distinguishing feature of measuring asset proceeds, asset usage and capital costs. It is this difference that we emphasise in this chapter. Hence, we treat EVA as a specific residual income measure.

The relationship between EVA, cash flow and value

Valuation according to the EVA model can be shown to yield exactly the same outcome as the discounted cash flow model. Our reasoning here builds on an argument originally developed by Peter Easton; we are grateful for his permission to reproduce his argument.

For a single forecast period, the discounted cash flow value of a project can be calculated as:

$$V_0 = \frac{FCF_1}{1 + r} + \frac{V_1}{1 + r} \qquad (1)$$

where V_t is the intrinsic value of the operations of the firm at time t, FCF_t is the expected free cash flow for the period t and r is the expected rate of return (also referred to as the discount rate or the cost of capital).

Over the period t, FCF is equal to operating income (profit) minus investments in additional assets. Hence, FCF is equal to:

$$FCF_1 = OI_1 - (NOA_1 - NOA_0) \qquad (2)$$

where OI_t is operating income for the period t, and NOA_t refers to net operating assets at time t. Notice that if operating income and net operating assets do not reflect true income or value, the difference will net to zero in the calculation of free cash flow. For example, if an asset is over-depreciated in the calculation of operating income, net operating assets will be valued too low by exactly the amount of the over-depreciation.

Substituting equation (2) into (1) yields:

$$V_0 = \frac{OI_1 - NOA_1 + NOA_0}{1 + r} + \frac{V_1}{1 + r} \qquad (3)$$

We can now rearrange equation (3) into:

$$V_0 = NOA_0 + \frac{OI_1 - rNOA_0}{1 + r} + \frac{V_1 - NOA_1}{1 + r} \qquad (4)$$

Note that the term $(OI_1 - rNOA_0)$ is known as residual income or EVA. It is the income in excess of the required rate of return on the book value of the net investment in operations.

Similarly to equation (4), the value at time $t = 1$ (V_1) can be expressed as:

$$V_1 = NOA_1 + \frac{OI_2 - rNOA_1}{1 + r} + \frac{V_2 - NOA_2}{1 + r} \qquad (5)$$

and this applies to all future periods 1, 2, 3,. . ., n. If we observe an n-year horizon, value at $t = 0$ (substituting recursively for V_1, V_2,. . ., V_n) can be expressed as:

$$V_0 = NOA_0 + \sum_{t=1}^{n} \left\{ \frac{OI_t - rNOA_{t-1}}{(1 + r)^t} \right\} + \frac{V_n - NOA_n}{(1 + r)^n} \qquad (6)$$

If we substitute back FCF for $OI_t - (NOA_t - NOA_{t-1})$ we get:

$$V_0 = \sum_{t=1}^{n} \left\{ \frac{FCF_t}{(1 + r)^t} \right\} + \frac{V_n}{(1 + r)^n} \tag{7}$$

Notice that equations (6) and (7) yield the same V_0. This shows that EVA is fully compatible with a value orientation. The economic value of a project (or a firm) – defined as the present value of future cash flows – can also be modelled as the present value of future EVAs, with identical results. Thus, the proponents of EVA are right in claiming that EVA is a good measure for capturing value creation. For a more extensive discussion of the formal relation between EVA and value, see O'Hanlon and Peasnell (1998).

EVA versus cash flow accounting and stock market performance

Having established that EVA-based valuation yields the same outcome as discounted cash flow valuation, there is strong reason to believe that EVA and the stock market value of the firm will be closely related. After all, a huge finance literature suggests that the stock market bases its value judgements on expected cash flows. At this point, one might begin to wonder why firms would want to use EVA for management control. If EVA's claimed superiority is based on its association with cash flows and stock market returns, why don't firms rely on cash flow or, even better, stock return measures instead? Surely, no measure can reflect stock returns better than stock return itself (Garvey and Milbourn, 2000). The answer to this question resides in the fact that EVA is a less noisy metric of managerial achievement than stock market performance, and in the fact that EVA (or accrual accounting more generally) is more informative than cash flow measures. Both reasons will be developed below.

Cash flows

Although realised cash flow in a specific period is closely related to project or firm value, a single period's cash flow (when observed in isolation) is meaningless in evaluating performance. Cash flow based assessment of project or firm performance requires a focus not on individual cash flows within a period, but on changes in the net present value over a period. Consider a business unit experiencing a negative cash flow in a specific year. Does this imply weak performance? Not necessarily, for the negative cashflow may result from significant investments in highly valuable projects, the benefits of which will surface in future periods. In the discounted cash flow model of value, net operating assets (NOA) do not play a role in establishing value (see equation (7)). Each cash outflow is treated as a cost, while each inflow is considered income. An investment in assets is treated as if it were written off at the time of investment. The disadvantage of this approach is that one can only establish how well a project develops if one is prepared to take future cash flows into account. In the absence of perfect foresight, this implies that performance evaluation will be influenced by estimates and expectations. This is particularly problematic if the individual best equipped to make the projections is the manager in charge of the project. This situation arises quite frequently, for typically the project manager has superior knowledge of the project and its potential. But this manager will be evaluated on the project's performance. Hence, he or she cannot be expected to report unbiased projections. In the event that project expenses and proceeds are volatile over time, evaluation based on EVA at least provides a closer approximation of value created. Consequently, managers are more likely to make accurate forecasts of future profitability under EVA than under cash flow performance assessment. To conclude, relative to discounted cash flow, EVA is the less distorted measure.

Stock returns

For publicly traded firms, stock market return has obvious appeal as a measure of performance. However, using stock returns as the main performance measure has some limitations. One problem is that stock market returns also reflect general, market-wide sentiments, macro-economic shocks, industry-wide factors, regulatory actions, etc. Such factors have little to do with firm performance and even less to do with managerial accomplishments. Thus, although stock return may be appropriate for assessing organisational performance, it is less informative about managerial performance, limiting its value in monitoring the behaviour of managers. Specifically, if a firm's stock returns do not match expectations, that observation alone does not warrant the conclusion that its managers have failed. Moreover, as stock market performance is influenced by many factors outside the control of the manager, it is of limited value in guiding action choices. As managers may only have a partial understanding of how their decisions and actions influence stock market performance, they are unable systematically to select the alternative that best contributes to the measure. This is especially true at managerial levels below the firm's top management team. Stock market performance can only be assessed for the firm as a whole, not for business units and divisions of the firm. Also, it is unlikely that actions of individual managers will have a clear effect on stock market performance, raising issues of sensitivity. The further one moves down the organisational hierarchy, the greater the disjunction between managerial action and stock returns, and the less meaningful stock market performance is in guiding and evaluating behaviour. When stock performance is a noisy, insensitive measure of managerial effort, firms may prefer to use EVA instead.

EVA versus alternative accounting measures

EVA has the advantage that – unlike stock market return – it can be applied in all firms and at all levels within the firm. Additionally, unlike cash flow measures, EVA does not require predictions. These advantages are not specific to EVA, however, but accrue to more traditional accounting metrics as well (e.g. net income or return on investment). What, then, is the possible edge EVA has over alternative accounting measures?

One answer could be that, unlike traditional accounting measures, EVA is related to value. This answer, however, is clearly false. Easton *et al.* (1992), for instance, provide conclusive evidence that accounting earnings and market value are related, at least over longer time windows. They show that over a return period of ten years, earnings explain more than 60 per cent of the variance in market returns. Given this empirical result, an alternative answer could be that EVA is a *better* predictor of stock returns than more traditional accounting measures like earnings and operating income. This claim has been examined intensively in the empirical literature (see Ittner and Larcker, 2001, for an overview). The results, however, are inconclusive. While this literature documents a correlation between EVA and stock market performance, there is no strong evidence that EVA outperforms alternative accounting measures in predicting stock returns. Some studies actually find that traditional measures are better in explaining stock prices (e.g. Biddle *et al.*, 1997).

From a management control perspective, however, this literature measures the wrong thing. The existence of a correlation between EVA and market value does not imply that organisations should use EVA in their performance management systems. The key problem is how the use of EVA as a performance measure affects managerial behaviour. In this context, the issue is not whether EVA correlates to stock returns. Rather, the question is whether the actions managers choose affect EVA and the market value of the organisation in the same way. Consistent with our earlier argument, the correlation between EVA and firm value may depend on the fact that not many firms actually use EVA to motivate their managers, and it is entirely possible that this correlation disappears as soon as larger numbers of firms start to base managerial compensation on EVA scores. This is not just a hypothetical point. Ittner and Larcker (1998), for instance, reproduce evidence that the majority of firms adopting economic value measures do not use the measures in their incentive plans. The next step, then, is to examine the extent to which EVA is vulnerable to distortion.

EVA and investment incentives

One important characteristic of EVA is that it summarises the effects of a broad set of managerial action choices in one performance metric – a broader set than net income, for instance, is able to capture. Whereas net income incorporates the effects of operating decisions on revenues and expenses, it captures only part of the investment and financing choices. At the level of the firm in its entirety, net income includes interest on debt used to finance the asset base, but does not include any charge for equity financing. At the divisional level, net income may not include any financing charge at all. EVA, on the other hand, measures the total return after deducting the cost of all capital employed by the firm (or, for sub-unit EVA, the cost of all capital employed by the sub-unit). Thus, EVA is more complete in this respect. This is important from a management control perspective, because EVA leaves less room for dysfunctional behaviour, i.e. behaviour that improves the score achieved on a performance measure without simultaneously improving the value of the firm. For example, managers who can influence the asset base of their business units, but whose performance is measured by net income, have an incentive to over-invest. Any investment that generates a return in excess of operating cost and depreciation (and hence increases net income) is worth making from their perspective, even if the excess is insufficient to cover the opportunity cost of capital. Such an investment, however, would decrease the value of the firm. Had the firm used EVA, the investment would have yielded a negative EVA and would not have been undertaken.

EVA is not the only measure to capture the effect of investment and financing decisions. Return on investment (ROI) and conceptually similar measures like RONA (return on net assets) also relate net income to the investment base that generates the income. However, ROI does this in a way that is not necessarily consistent with the aim of value creation. For example, suppose a division currently yields an average ROI of 20 per cent, while the required return is equal to 15 per cent. The division manager identifies a new investment opportunity with a ROI of 18 per cent. This new project's ROI is well above the cost of capital, so investing would increase the value of the division. But, accepting the project reduces the division's ROI (to a figure somewhere in the range of 18 to 20 per cent, depending on the size of the new project relative to the existing asset base). If the manager is evaluated on ROI, he or she will be inclined to reject any project that reduces average ROI, because the new project would reduce slack. In an EVA environment (or, more generally, in a residual income environment), the project would have been accepted, enhancing the value of the division.

EVA and decision rights: formal versus real authority

Typically, profit centre managers do not have the right to decide on investments. So, it might appear perfectly sensible to base their performance evaluation on net income. Net income at the profit centre level incorporates the effects of operating decisions on revenues and expenses, but it excludes the cost of capital associated with the investment base from which the income is earned. However, even if profit centre managers have no formal rights allowing them to commit resources, they may affect the assets in place – albeit in subtler, less visible ways (cf. Aghion and Tirole, 1997). Suppose that a profit centre has many clients, including a small number of very large customers. These large customers account for a significant proportion of sales, but tend to pay relatively slowly. Serving these clients therefore increases working capital requirements. Typically, decision rights on which customers to serve and applicable sales conditions reside with the profit centre manager. This is because the manager tends to be better informed about client preferences and market opportunities than his or her superior and, consequently, is better equipped to make appropriate decisions. Even though the manager does not have formal asset commitment rights, his or her choices as to how to treat these customers do affect the asset base of the profit centre in a very real way. However, if the performance metric does not capture these working capital ramifications, it is likely the manager will ignore the associated costs. One could argue that this problem is easily solved by installing capital restrictions and requiring the manager to file an investment proposal each time additional working capital is needed. But, this solution is intensely bureaucratic. Also, it effectively transfers decision-making authority from the profit centre manager to higher levels of management, which may be inconsistent with the distribution of knowledge and the associated level of decentralisation (cf. Abernethy *et al.*, 2004). Alternatively, the organisation could include a charge for working capital employed in the net income measure, i.e. it could decide to adopt EVA. EVA is more complete and less distorted than the original measure, and provides an incentive to the manager to pay attention to the working capital effects associated with serving large but slow-paying clients.

EVA in the context of interdependence

The foregoing discussion suggests that EVA is the most complete value consistent summary measure currently available. However, performance measures that summarise asset use at the local profit centre level become increasingly problematic at lower firm levels as interdependencies between profit centres increase (Abernethy *et al.*, 2004). Interdependencies are present when the organisation's sub-units are not completely self-contained, but when decisions taken in one sub-unit affect the performance of other units. Familiar examples include situations in which different organisational units share a common resource, such as funds available for investments. Interdependence also occurs when one organisational unit's output becomes the input of another, or when for instance one unit's marketing success spills over to other units that benefit from an increased market franchise. Interdependence creates externalities within the firm, i.e. costs or benefits imposed on other units without their consent and without compensation.

The existence of externalities implies that a profit centre's EVA is a noisy measure of the centre's performance and of its manager's accomplishments, decreasing its usefulness for performance evaluation. But interdependencies also affect EVA's completeness. Because EVA at the profit centre level does not capture externalities, it no longer expresses fully the effects of decisions for which the manager is responsible. In this case, EVA distorts incentives and cannot guarantee goal-consistent behaviour. When interdependencies are important, the firm wants managers to coordinate their decisions and seek cooperation whenever this increases firm value more than any local initiative would. However, because the value created in such joint projects will only partially be reflected in the EVA measures of individual units, the incentives to explore joint efforts are typically weak, and managers are more likely to seek projects that benefit primarily their own unit.

It should be emphasised that this incentive distortion in the presence of interdependence is not unique to EVA. Profitability measures also tend to induce parochial behaviour. How, then, do firms encourage cooperative behaviour? One approach is to hold managers responsible not for the EVA of their own individual unit, but for the joint EVA. The disadvantage of this approach is that although it encourages cooperation, this shift in attention may come at the expense of managers' motivation to explore opportunities at their own level. Also, this approach increases the noisiness of the performance measure. An alternative would be to appoint a higher-level manager to decide on joint projects and to pursue synergies. This, however, involves centralisation, with the associated costs of processing information and capturing local knowledge.

Additional notes on EVA and distortion

The issue of incentive distortion is not confined to the case of interdependence. For instance, EVA-based performance appraisal provides incentives to reduce excess capacity. As asset disposal decreases the asset base, this leads to an increase in reported EVA. However, some excess capacity may well be valuable to the firm (and its shareholders) as it affords a flexible response to new market opportunities. Thus, EVA-induced divestment may come at the expense of diminished value capturing ability in future periods. As another example, think of the case of a manager considering a strategic investment opportunity with a positive net present value, but with negative profitability in the first years of its life. Because EVA is a backward-looking measure and the manager will not be credited with the anticipated future benefits until they materialise, EVA-based performance measurement may discourage the manager from investing in the project. Conversely, managers may be lured into investing in riskier projects, particularly if they are under severe pressure to improve EVA. Although such investment behaviour should lead to a higher cost of capital, it is unlikely that firms can continuously adjust the cost of capital to reflect the true risk profile of their project portfolio. In that situation, managers are able to show a higher EVA, even when the returns from the new projects are insufficient to compensate for the higher risk.

These examples suggest that EVA is susceptible to myopia problems and that managers under an EVA regime may experience incentives to choose actions that are inconsistent with long-term value creation. It should, however, be emphasised that EVA as a financial management system anticipates such problems, and provides several suggestions to resolve them. For example, promoters of EVA have proposed a number of accounting adjustments that must be made in calculating EVA (see Table 12.1). Some of these, such as capitalisation of investments in R&D and marketing, are designed to avoid penalising managers for investing in intangible assets. Also, the frequently recommended 'bonus bank' concept helps to mitigate horizon problems (O'Hanlon and Peasnell, 1998). In a bonus bank system, awarded bonuses are not immediately paid out, but are added to a bonus bank with their subsequent payment dependent on continued good performance. Such a system allows organisations to award high bonuses based on a single year's performance, because if subsequent events show the performance to have been illusory, much of the bonus will be eliminated before it is paid out (O'Hanlon and Peasnell, 1998). However, although these added features of EVA might help to alleviate dysfunctional consequences, they do not entirely solve the associated problems. Therefore, EVA is not the perfect performance measure.

Performance consequences of EVA: empirical evidence

The previous section concluded that EVA is not the perfect performance measure. But then again, perfection is not a relevant yardstick by which to evaluate the quality of performance metrics. What matters is not technical perfection, but the impact on organisational performance. Even though EVA is imperfect, it may still perform better than other performance metrics. So, the relevant question is this: do organisations that use EVA as their primary performance measure for purposes of management control achieve superior performance? This section reviews the – still fairly scarce – evidence. But first, we provide some details on the incidence of EVA use.

Diffusion of EVA

Over the last decade, EVA has attracted significant attention, both in the business press and in the professional and academic journals. This coverage in the literature suggests that EVA has gained considerable popularity among firms. This impression, however, must be qualified. Although we do not have clear data, an examination of the empirical literature reveals that the diffusion of EVA is actually fairly limited. Hogan and Lewis

(1999) identified only 51 US firms in the LEXIS/NEXIS database adopting EVA-like measures during the 1988–94 period. This number is biased downwards because of industry and data restrictions, but it is clear that few firms actually use EVA. Within the population of all publicly traded US companies, Kleiman (1999) found 71 firms adopting EVA during the period 1987–96. More recently, Lovata and Costigan (2002) found 135 US firms in the LEXIS/NEXIS database that explicitly used EVA for compensation purposes as of June 1998. The size of their control sample totalled almost 2,000 non-EVA firms. Again, this suggests that only a minority of firms have actually implemented EVA. Finally, Bouwens and Van Lent (2005) report in a cross-section of 140 Dutch firms that only 23 of these firms use EVA/residual income-type measures.

The limited diffusion of EVA suggests that its potential benefits cannot be enjoyed universally, and that EVA is only appropriate in specific conditions. Although very little research has been done to identify if and how EVA adopters differ from non-adopters, a few studies offer some valuable clues. Kleiman (1999) found that EVA-adopting firms are heavily concentrated in the manufacturing industries, this industry accounting for roughly two-thirds of the total number of EVA-using firms. This suggests that capital intensity is associated with the adoption decision, an indication for which Garvey and Milbourn (2000) provide additional support. Lovata and Costigan (2002) examined whether strategy affects the use of EVA. Their argument is that firms adopting a defender strategy (i.e. a cost leadership focus) are more likely to benefit from EVA use than firms with a prospector or differentiation strategy. The intuition behind this argument is that, as prospectors focus on developing new products and adapting to a changing environment, financial measures such as EVA are less important than non-financial metrics such as new product developments and time-to-market. Defenders on the other hand emphasise efficiency and, therefore, are more likely benefit from EVA. Lovata and Costigan (2002) also investigated whether ownership factors influence EVA adoption. Specifically, they hypothesised that insider ownership negatively affects EVA use, because owner/managers do not need a sophisticated system to assess performance. They also suggest that a high degree of institutional ownership positively impacts EVA adoption. In support of their expectations, they found that EVA-based incentive structures are significantly more prevalent among defender firms, and that ownership structure is significantly associated with EVA use, in the hypothesised directions.

Bouwens and Van Lent (2005) found evidence that the weight put on residual income measures like EVA in the periodic assessment, bonus determination and career-related decisions of profit centre managers is related to the span of their decision rights. This is consistent with the idea that firms want managers to consider the full consequences of their initiatives; an aim that is more likely to be achieved with EVA-like metrics than with a less complete measure of performance like profit, revenue or cost. These authors also found evidence that interdependencies affect the use of EVA-like measures. The relationship is not direct, however. The presence of interdependencies appeared to reduce decentralisation, while greater centralisation reduced the use of EVA-like measures. Hence, when coordination is important, firms tend to centralise decision-making to ensure that coordination occurs. This supports our earlier argument that EVA is unable to solve problems of coordination.

The effects of EVA on performance

Does EVA improve performance?

One of the first studies to examine the effects of EVA adoption on firm performance was by Wallace (1997). Wallace investigated whether managers of firms adopting compensation contracts with EVA-like performance measures take actions consistent with the incentives from these measures. He found that, relative to control firms using more traditional accounting metrics, firms that adopted an EVA-like performance metric (i) increased their disposal of assets and decreased new investment, (ii) increased their payouts to shareholders through share repurchases and (iii) used their assets more intensively. Although these actions are not necessarily good for value creation, they are consistent with a strong focus on rate of return. Overall, firms using EVA-like measures reported a significantly larger change in residual income than the firms in the control group, suggesting that firms do in fact get what they measure and reward. Wallace (1997) also found weak evidence that stock markets respond favourably to the adoption of residual income-based compensation plans, leading to increased stock returns.

However, Wallace's (1997) study examined changes in performance rather than performance levels, and examined such changes only over a one-year period. Hogan and Lewis (1999) argue that, if plans that compensate managers on the basis of economic profits (including EVA) provide incentives to make better investment decisions, firms that adopt such plans should experience improved long-run stock price and operating performance. In their study, they looked at performance data of firms adopting EVA-type measures in the four year period prior to and following plan adoption. They found that the operating performance of adopting companies increased dramatically in the year the plan was adopted and the subsequent four years. However, closer examination of the adopting firms revealed that they were relatively poor performers prior to adopting EVA-type plans, and that the dramatic improvements may not be unique to EVA adopters. When investigating the operating performance of a sample of comparable non-adopting firms, they found similar performance patterns. Hogan and Lewis (1999) propose and test two different explanations for this similarity in performance between adopters and non-adopters. One explanation holds that the improvements may reflect a return to historical performance levels (i.e. that the observed improvements are instances of mean reversion), and have nothing to do with managerial action. In this explanation, the fact that this return coincides with EVA plan adoption is taken to indicate that managers may have introduced the new compensation plan just to cash in on anticipated increases in EVA (see also Wallace, 1997, note 14). The second possible explanation is that the performance improvements are in fact the result of improved incentive alignment. Hogan and Lewis (1999) found no support for their first explanation. Although they did observe a strong increase in bonus payments in the adoption year for firms changing to EVA-related systems, they found an equally large increase in payments in control firms. These results suggest that firms respond to poor recent performance by strengthening the link between bonuses and performance, but that the basis for calculating bonus payments has little impact. This leaves us with the second explanation, which attributes the observed performance improvements to enhanced goal alignment. However, Hogan and Lewis (1999) found no indication that EVA does a better job in improving goal alignment than more traditional incentive plans. Thus, they conclude that 'the recent popularity of products like Stern Stewart's EVA simply reflects impressive marketing, rather than a new and different way to motivate managers' (Hogan and Lewis, 1999, p. 3).

Another study investigating operating changes following EVA implementation is by Kleiman (1999). His results are broadly consistent with Wallace (1997). Like Wallace, Kleiman found that EVA adopters improve their monitoring of working capital, intensify asset dispositions, and increase financial leverage. However, a closer look at his results indicates that these EVA-consistent actions are not caused by EVA adoption, but were already part of the firms' endeavours in the years prior to EVA implementation. Only asset disposal shows a marked increase following EVA adoption. In addition, when compared to the median S&P 500, EVA adopters appear no different from non-adopters, except for their propensity to dispose of assets. This propensity was already larger for EVA-using firms prior to adoption, but increases further after adoption.

Kleiman (1999) also examined the effect of EVA adoption on stock returns. For the three years following the adoption decision, he compared the stock returns of EVA adopters to the median stock market performance of firms in their industry that have not adopted EVA, and to their closest-matched competitor in the industry (based on four-digit SIC codes and volumes of sales). His findings indicate that, as a group, EVA companies outperform both their closest-matched peers and their median competitor by a significant margin, and that this effect appears to persist – at least over the period of his study. These 'abnormal results' can probably not be attributed to mean reversion, because EVA adopters performed no worse than their competitors in the years prior to implementing EVA. In contrast to these results, Ittner et al. (2003) found no association between EVA use and one-year or three-year stock returns. They did, however, find that firms using EVA intensively are more likely to intensify their use of non-financial performance measures that are associated with improved share price. This suggests a more complex relationship between EVA and stock return. Finally, a recent study by Griffith (2004) found that EVA adopters significantly underperform both their peers and the market for periods of up to five years after EVA adoption.

A cautionary note: limitations of the performance studies

The studies discussed above provide mixed evidence on EVA's effects on performance. To help understand why, it is important to emphasise the limitations of these studies. For instance, Wallace (1997) compared the change in residual income reported by EVA adopters to that of non-adopting firms. The residual income change of non-adopting firms is computed using publicly available financial data and does not contain the accounting adjustments advocated by EVA's proponents (cf. Ittner and Larcker, 2001). Also, Wallace's computations are based on a hypothetical cost of capital that may not be realistic. Thus, his findings may misstate the effects of EVA adoption, which may drive the performance differences he found.

In a similar vein, Hogan and Lewis (1999) rely on operating performance data to measure performance effects. Such data need not be an accurate reflection of value creation, which presumably is the ultimate goal of EVA adopters. In this respect, the

Kleiman (1999) study appears more relevant, because it focuses on stock market return. However, the superior stock market performance of EVA adopters he observed does not imply that EVA adoption is always a good idea. Kleiman's results indicate that for nearly one-quarter of the sample EVA did not result in superior performance, suggesting that EVA is not universally beneficial. Also, Kleiman does not address the distribution of the 'abnormal' stock market results. Although he does report that about 73 per cent of the firms had higher stock market returns than their median peer, the results may be influenced by a few outliers, with the general EVA effect being insignificant. This might help to reconcile his findings with those of Ittner *et al.* (2003) and Griffith (2004).

In addition, all studies (with the possible exception of Griffith, 2004) focus exclusively on EVA-based compensation for executives. The problem with this focus is that the positive effects of EVA may only emerge if – as Stern Stewart suggests – EVA has been made the cornerstone of financial management. Then, the studies may underestimate the potential of EVA (if implemented fully) to contribute to business success. And there is evidence that EVA implementation differs widely across firms. In their field study of six organisations that announced their intention to apply value-based management practices, Malmi and Ikäheimo (2003) found a large diversity in the actual use of such practices, ranging from an almost comprehensive implementation to a merely rhetorical reference to EVA concepts with no real meaning for decision-making or management. Similarly, Griffith (2004) reports that only about half of his sample of EVA adopters has implemented the complete EVA incentive system.

Complexity of EVA

One potential explanation for the limited evidence for any positive effects of EVA on firm performance (and for its limited diffusion as discussed earlier) may involve the measure's complexity. Ittner and Larcker (1998) provide some evidence on a large firm that was among the first to adopt EVA for decision-making and compensation purposes (this firm's EVA-based bonus plan once covered approximately 110,000 employees), but that abandoned the EVA system within five years of its introduction. They report that one of the primary reasons for this demise was that, despite extensive training, the EVA measure was too complex for most employees to understand and to act upon.

This theme has been taken up in a study by Riceman *et al.* (2002). They examined the effect of EVA on the performance of individual mid-level managers. The primary focus of their paper is on whether or not managers on EVA bonus plans outperform managers on traditional accounting-based incentive plans. Their research setting is an EVA-focused company that has managers on both EVA and traditional bonus plans (52 managers were on pure EVA schemes; 65 managers were on more traditional plans that included only a small EVA element). Although Riceman *et al.* (2002) found no significant differences in performance between these groups, their results suggest that managers on EVA plans *who understand the concept of EVA* outperform managers on traditional bonus plans. However, further analysis of their data revealed that this interaction effect is only significant for the subset of managers whose direct superiors show an interest in EVA. This additional finding may suggest that the observed performance increase is driven by improved consistency in the manager's evaluation–reward system (i.e. the manager can be confident that his or her interests are closely aligned with those of his or her superior), rather than by some intrinsic superiority of EVA as a performance measure. In addition, Riceman *et al.* (2002) provide preliminary evidence to suggest that the effects of EVA on middle managers' performance depend on the managers' areas of employment. Specifically, their finding that managers on EVA schemes who understand the concept of EVA outperform managers on traditional compensation plans applies only to managers working in an operations-related function. For managers in customer support functions or in new business development, they found no effect (or even a significant negative effect). The authors argue that these findings suggest that EVA – emphasising capital employed – may work in capital-intensive environments, but is less effective in service areas where it is more difficult to identify and operationalise EVA drivers.

Conclusions

In this chapter, we examined the value of EVA for purposes of management control. We argued that, ideally, performance measures should be simultaneously (i) undistorted, (ii) sensitive and (iii) noiseless, and we used these three criteria to evaluate the usefulness of EVA. Perhaps unsurprisingly, we found that EVA is not universally superior to alternative performance measures and that EVA's value depends on the specific circumstances in which it is used.

We argued that EVA provides a relatively undistorted signal of performance, i.e. EVA captures value creation better than alternative (accounting) metrics. EVA is algebraically equivalent to the discounted cash flow model of value, but EVA is to be preferred over cash flows for performance evaluation because cash flows provide a more volatile and distant approximation of value than EVA. We also demonstrated that EVA is more complete than traditional accounting measures like earnings. Firms that decentralise decision rights over asset levels (formally or informally) may benefit from using EVA, because EVA motivates managers to consider not only revenues and costs, but also the opportunity cost of capital associated with initiatives to increase profitability. Certainly, EVA is not the only metric to provide a relatively undistorted signal of performance. Stock return measures are even better in this respect. These measures tend to be noisier than EVA, however. Also, stock return measures are less sensitive than EVA, especially at lower hierarchical levels.

But then again, EVA is no panacea. If profit centre managers lack influence over the asset base of their unit, they will have only limited possibilities to affect EVA. Then, EVA may be insensitive to managers' action choices, and less comprehensive measures are required. Moreover, there are circumstances in which even EVA is an incomplete representation of performance. When interdependencies between a firm's units are significant, the use of EVA may distort incentives. Because unit-level EVA does not incorporate the impact of the unit manager's decisions on other units, EVA provides no incentive to consider these effects. Moreover, unit level EVA is a noisy metric when the focal manager's EVA is affected by the performance of other managers. Consequently, EVA is not particularly good at supporting inter-unit cooperation. For these reasons, firms need to take into account levels of decentralisation and issues of interdependencies when deciding on the appropriate measure of performance.

Empirically, there is little solid evidence to suggest that EVA actually works. The number of studies addressing the antecedents and consequences of EVA use is still limited, and their results are mixed. Studies that investigated the diffusion of EVA show that only relatively few firms have implemented EVA. Although some studies found that these EVA adopters outperform their peers, other studies found either no performance effect, or even a negative effect. These studies are, however, rather coarse in that they focus on performance differences between groups of EVA adopters and groups of non-adopters. By their nature, such studies cannot address the heterogeneity within groups and, consequently, are unable to capture subtler details. Overall, our conclusion is that EVA is not universally beneficial, and that much more work is needed to understand precisely if and when EVA adds value.

References

Abernethy, M.A., Bouwens, J. and Van Lent, L. (2004) 'Determinants of control systems design in divisionalized firms', *The Accounting Review, 79*, 545–70.

Aghion, P. and Tirole, J. (1997) 'Formal and real authority in organizations', *Journal of Political Economy, 105*, 1–29.

Baker, G. (2002) 'Distortion and risk in optimal incentive contracts', *Journal of Human Resources, 37*, 728–51.

Biddle, G.C., Bowen, R.M. and Wallace, J.S. (1997) 'Does EVA beat earnings? Evidence on associations with stock returns and firm values', *Journal of Accounting and Economics, 24*, 301–36.

Biddle, G.C., Bowen, R.M. and Wallace, J.S. (1999) 'Evidence on EVA', *Journal of Applied Corparate Finance, 12*, 69–79.

Bouwens, J. and Van Lent, L. (2005) 'Assessing the performance of profit centre managers', Working paper, Tilburg University.

Easton, P.D., Harris, T.S. and Ohlson, J.A. (1992) 'Aggregate accounting earnings can explain most of security returns', *Journal of Accounting & Economics, 15*, 119–42.

Feltham, G.A. and Xie, J. (1994) 'Performance measure congruity and diversity in multi-task principal/agent relations', *The Accounting Review, 69*, 429–53.

Garvey, G.T. and Milbourn, T.T. (2000) 'EVA versus earnings: does it matter which is more highly correlated with stock returns?' *Journal of Accounting Research, 38*, 209–45.

Griffith, J.M. (2004) 'The true value of EVA', *Journal of Applied Finance, 14*, 25–9.

Hogan, C. and Lewis, C. (1999) 'The long-run performance of firms adopting compensation plans based on economic profits', working paper Southern Methodist University and Over Graduate School of Management. Available online at: http://ssrn.com/abstract=191551.

Ittner, C.D. and Larcker, D.F. (1998) 'Innovations in performance measurement: trends and research implications', *Journal of Management Accounting Research, 10*, 205–38.

Ittner, C.D. and Larcker, D.F. (2001) 'Assessing empirical research in managerial accounting: a value-based management perspective', *Journal of Accounting and Economics, 32*, 349–410.

Ittner, C.D., Larcker, D.F. and Randall, T. (2003) 'Performance implications of strategic performance measurement in financial services firms', *Accounting, Organizations and Society, 28*, 715–41.

Jensen, M.C. and Meckling, W.H. (1992) 'Specific and general knowledge, and organization structure', in L. Werin and H. Wijkander (eds), *Contract Economics*, Oxford: Basil Blackwell, pp. 251–74.

Kerr, S. (1975) 'On the folly of rewarding A, while hoping for B', *Academy of Management Journal, 18*, 769–83.

Kleiman, R.T. (1999) 'Some new evidence on EVA companies', *Journal of Applied Corporate Finance, 12*, 80–91.

Lovata, L.M. and Costigan, M.L. (2002) 'Empirical analysis of adopters of economic value added', *Management Accounting Research,* **13,** 215–28.

Malmi, T. and Ikäheimo, S. (2003) 'Value based management practices: some evidence from the field', *Management Accounting Research,* **14,** 235–54.

O'Hanlon, J. and Peasnell, K. (1998) 'Wall Street's contribution to management accounting: the Stern Stewart EVA financial management system', *Management Accounting Research,* **9,** 421–44.

Riceman, S.S., Cahan, S.F. and Lal, M. (2002) 'Do managers perform better under EVA bonus schemes?' *European Accounting Review,* **11,** 537–72.

Roberts, J. (2004) *The Modern Firm: Organizational Design for Performance and Growth,* Oxford: Oxford University Press.

Wallace, J.S. (1997) 'Adopting residual income-based compensation plans: do you get what you pay for?' *Journal of Accounting and Economics,* **24,** 275–300.

Further reading

Baker, G. (2002) 'Distortion and risk in optimal incentive contracts', *Journal of Human Resources,* **37,** 728–51. Formal yet accessible treatment of incentive distortion.

Kerr, S. (1975) 'On the folly of rewarding A, while hoping for B', *Academy of Management Journal,* **18,** 769–83. Classic and sometimes hilarious paper on incentive distortion.

O'Hanlon, J. and Peasnell, K. (1998) 'Wall Street's contribution to management accounting: the Stern Stewart EVA financial management system', *Management Accounting Research,* **9,** 421–44. A careful study of the formal properties of EVA.

Solomons, D. (1965) *Divisional Performance: Measurement and Control,* Illinois: Irwin. One of the first studies to introduce the concept of residual income. Still relevant today.

Stewart, G. (1991) *The Quest for Value,* New York: Harper Business. All one needs to know about managing for value – at least according to one consultant.

13

Management control in inter-organisational relationships

Kalle Kraus and Johnny Lind

Introduction

Inter-organisational relationships, defined as various forms of cooperation between independent organisations, seem to have been on the increase during recent decades. When companies cooperate and, consequently, to some extent adapt their activities and resources to suit each other, they become more closely tied to one another. Thus, interdependence is a central ingredient in inter-organisational relationships. Inter-organisational relationships are characterised by being both closer and more long-term than the relationships between companies involved in occasional buying and selling. Companies find that collaborative efforts made in conjunction with other companies are likely to produce benefits which are not realisable in arm's-length transactions through the market or within the company. Frances and Garnsey (1996), for example, argue that the success of British supermarkets is due to the development of close inter-organisational relationships with their suppliers.

Inter-organisational relationships are heterogeneous and involve several different forms of cooperation, which take place under names such as joint ventures, strategic alliances, technology licensing, research consortia, strategic partnerships, supply chain relationships, business relationships, and outsourcing relationships. The increased emphasis on inter-organisational relationships can arise as ongoing customer/supplier relationships evolve to become closer and more long-term in their nature. But, this emphasis can also originate from the formation of new inter-organisational units, such as joint ventures, and the establishment of new inter-organisational relationships through outsourcing.

The increase in the number and importance of inter-organisational relationships imposes new demands on managers and will have an impact on management control. It will affect the management control conducted, who conducts it and how the control is implemented. Traditionally, management control has been focused on activities and resources within the company, and the boundary between the company and its environment has been viewed as the line dividing what can be influenced and what is considered to be given. This recent emphasis on inter-organisational relationships and the significance that they have taken on have made it necessary for managers to extend management control beyond the company's borders. This is not only necessary when managers want to assess the company's performance, but also concerns what they should try to control and influence. Thus, managers must consider activities and resources belonging to counterparts such as suppliers and customers, as well as the activities and resources within their own company. In addition, the managers need to consider how these activities and resources are related to one another. Naturally, the converse is true for the company's suppliers and customers, who must extend their management control to include activities and resources beyond their own company borders and analyse how they are to be used in relation to their own operations.

Managers also need to handle a mixture of inter-organisational relationships, some closer than others. For this purpose it is useful to perceive the company as a part of a larger network of interconnected inter-organisational relationships in which it is embedded. The embeddedness and the interdependencies of inter-organisational relationships lead to network effects, meaning that changes in the relationship between a company and, for example, one of its suppliers can also affect the company's other relationships with suppliers and customers. The opposite is also the case, so that any one of the company's inter-organisational relationships may be affected by events taking place within the interconnected network of relationships. These interconnections impose new demands on management control. One consequence is that activities and resources can no longer be considered in isolation, and this must be considered in the design and use of management controls.

This chapter starts by introducing and explaining the main drivers behind the increased formation of inter-organisational relationships and describing two general development trends that have increased inter-organisational relationships. Thereafter, specific forms of inter-organisational relationships are described. A discussion of inter-organisational control in dyadic settings and in network settings follows, and a number of management control techniques that can be used for inter-organisational control are outlined. This is then complemented by a discussion of some common theories used in the literature on inter-organisational control. Finally, some issues of importance for future research on inter-organisational control are discussed.

Inter-organisational relationships – drivers and trends

No consensus has been reached on which are the main drivers behind the development and increased importance of inter-organisational relationships. Some researchers talk about important environmental shifts, while others argue that there has been a more gradual change. There are, however, a number of explanations, in terms of 'drivers', which are frequently put forward. These are described below.

Main drivers

Increased *globalisation* is one factor often used to explain the increased formation of inter-organisational relationships. Globalisation initiates fierce competition on a worldwide basis, and facilitates rapid transformation of existing customer structures and the emergence of new business opportunities. Companies operating in the global market need to have fast and efficient access to customers and to be able to develop new products quickly. Collaboration with other companies, through the formation of different kinds of inter-organisational relationships, has become an important tool for achieving success.

Another important factor is the *rapid technological transformation* that has been taking place. When the pace of technological change was relatively slow, vertical integration was a successful strategy. But today's companies are facing rapid technological change, making it difficult for them to maintain in-house expertise in every potentially relevant technical area. Thus, it makes sense for a company to outsource some, often non-core, activities to other companies who are experts in the area concerned, thereby avoiding the risks, costs and probable lengthening of lead-times associated with in-house development in an unfamiliar field.

The significance of the speed of technological change is further reinforced by the fact that the *technical complexity of the products* has increased. Companies often have products in which many technologies need to be coordinated, with the result that hardly any companies can rely solely on their own research and development (R&D) function. A company cannot be on the technological forefront in every area, and needs to use its suppliers' knowledge to develop its products.

To sum up, it can be said that companies today need to handle globalisation, worldwide competition, rapid technological development and more complex products. The formation of inter-organisational relationships is considered important in enabling companies to share the fixed costs and risks associated with technological and product development, to enhance their core competencies, to gain access to complementary competencies, and to increase the speed of market entry. So, both revenues and costs can provide the motives for forming inter-organisational relationships. Some companies enter into inter-organisational relationships in an attempt to increase revenue by gaining access to complementary resources, to improve product development, and to get better access to customers. Other companies attempt to decrease costs by achieving economies of scale by engaging in joint research projects and/or joint marketing or production activities. The formation of inter-organisational relationships also creates barriers to entry for competition, by securing long-term relationships with key suppliers in order to exchange knowledge and to cooperate in technological development.

Having described some of the drivers most commonly put forward as explanations for the increased formation of inter-organisational relationships, we can now identify two general trends through which the increased number of inter-organisational relationships has come about. These are: (i) the development of closer business relationships between companies buying from and selling to each other and (ii) the break-up of large hierarchically controlled companies into independent units through outsourcing. These two trends are described below.

Two general trends

One obvious difference between the two trends is that, in the first one, existing relationships are being developed to form close, long-term inter-organisational relationships, whereas in the second, new inter-organisational relationships with suppliers are being formed through the outsourcing of activities that were previously performed in-house. Both of these trends reflect attempts to remain competitive in a globalised world where rapid technological transformation occurs and where the products incorporate many different kinds of technology.

Closer business relationships between buyers and sellers indicate that buyers and sellers are working more closely together over longer periods of time than was the case in the past. This change has been illustrated by Cooper and Slagmulder (2004) in their study of buyer–supplier relationships in Japan, where the authors found, for example, that the relationship between the buyer (Komatsu) and its supplier (Toyo Radiator) had become much closer over time. The inter-organisational relationship was characterised by high design dependence. The companies established joint product specifications and actively integrated their product development processes.

Cooper and Slagmulder (2004) described how the companies dedicated engineers to work closely together in order to develop each other's products. They also invested in specific product lines and machinery that was earmarked for dedicated use by the other company. In addition to these more tangible aspects of the integration, information sharing was a central issue within the relationship and supported the integrated development process. For example, the companies shared a considerable amount of information about future products early in the product development process, which made it possible for both companies to adapt their products and methods of working to each other.

This kind of close and long-term business relationship between companies buying and selling from/to each other has probably always existed, but it has become more apparent in recent decades. Managerial tools such as CRM (customer relationship management) and KAM (key account management) have been developed to support the seller's wish to create more value for, and loyalty from, its customers. Managerial tools can also operate the other way around; for example, supply chain models have been developed to support the buyer in creating efficient and innovative supply chains.

The introduction of more general managerial tools such as JIT management (just in time management), TBM (time-based management) and TQM (total quality management) are closely related to the development of closer business relationships. These managerial tools decrease the buffers required in terms of, for example, inventory, spare time and idle capacity. This fosters a closer and longer-term relationship between units within and outside the company, enabling the company to handle the increased interdependence.

The second general trend is *outsourcing* of units that previously formed part of hierarchically controlled firms. Over the last decade, outsourcing has become a popular activity within large companies. A recent Swedish survey conducted in the engineering industry showed that more than 65 per cent of the production units with more than 500 employees had outsourced the production of a product or component during the last three years (Bengtsson *et al.*, 2005). However, it is increasingly common to outsource functions other than production – for example IT, maintenance, development and internal auditing. Another indication of the popularity of outsourcing is that companies' purchasing costs have increased as a proportion of total costs within western companies.

Outsourcing is often seen as a way to reduce costs and to improve the development of new products by collaborating with suppliers. Its use is often justified by the need for companies to focus on their core competencies, but it is increasingly apparent that companies perceive outsourcing as a means of gaining access to a supplier's know-how with the intention of improving product quality.

Mouritsen *et al.* (2001) showed how a small Danish electronics company manufacturing alarm systems outsourced its development processes. Before the decision to outsource had been taken, the processes involved in product development were considered to be some of the company's key strengths. The company was known to introduce new products regularly and it constantly developed and redesigned its existing products. Thus, it was important for the company to be always at the forefront of technology in its field. However, it was increasingly difficult for it to remain at this forefront because of the increasing complexity of the technologies used in the alarm systems and the speed of change in the technologies concerned. This was further complicated by the need to meet the requirements of specific customers.

The company did not have sufficient resources to handle the demands imposed on it by its customers and to keep up with the rapid developments within the different technologies. As a consequence, the firm outsourced its development activities to external suppliers who were responsible for particular technologies. After the changes had been implemented, the development department consisted of just a few employees. This example clearly illustrates a general reason why firms might outsource. The Danish company perceived outsourcing as part of its strategy to create a leaner company and to reduce costs. More importantly, outsourcing was necessary for the company to maintain its competitiveness by taking advantage of the supplier's technical know-how.

To sum up, it has been shown that the increased formation of inter-organisational relationships, either through the development of existing relationships to make them closer and longer-term, or through the formation of new relationships via the outsourcing of activities, are ways for companies to stay competitive in a rapidly changing world. This is of importance for understanding why inter-organisational relationships have moved up the company agenda and are perceived as important concerns for managers. In the next section, some common forms of inter-organisational relationships are described.

Inter-organisational relationships – dyads and networks

Inter-organisational relationships have been discussed in two settings. The first is dyadic relationships between collaborating companies. These relationships may take the form of vertical collaboration between a company and its customers and suppliers in the supply chain, or horizontal collaboration between companies targeting the same customers. In the second setting, networks, the various inter-organisational relationships cannot be considered in isolation of each other, as they are all interdependent. Thus, this setting consists of networks of interconnected inter-organisational relationships. The two settings are described in more detail below.

Dyadic relationships

Companies engage in a variety of vertical and horizontal inter-organisational relationships. The most common are vertical collaborations between companies in the supply chain. These vertical relationships are usually long-term and involve a large number of individuals with different functional specialities, adaptations in product features and production processes, and adaptations in administrative and logistical activities.

Some common forms of these inter-organisational relationships are technology licensing, research consortia, joint ventures and strategic alliances. *Technology licensing* is seen as a way of getting rapid access to technology at a low cost, and it offers the opportunity for a company to exploit the know-how of another firm by paying a fee or royalty based on sales. It can be argued that technology licensing lowers development costs, reduces both technology and market risk, speeds up product development times, and results in a faster market entry compared to in-house development. On the negative side there is often a loss of control over operational issues, such as pricing and product quality.

A *bi-lateral research consortium* consists of two companies working together on a relatively well-specified project. Forming a consortium provides an opportunity to share the costs of research and the inherent risks, as well as allowing the companies involved to learn from each other. *Strategic alliances* are voluntary, cooperative arrangements between two separate organisations. Typically, they take the form of an agreement between the two organisations to co-develop a new technology, product or service with specified goals and to a predetermined timetable. Whereas research consortia tend to focus on basic research, strategic alliances involve more complex development projects. An alliance can be viewed as a long-term relationship that does not have an ultimate (individual) decision-making authority and that aims to improve the competitive position and performance of the companies involved through the sharing of resources.

Joint ventures are more formal than strategic alliances. They straddle the gap between full integration and remaining totally separate. Joint ventures involve setting up a new firm with (at least) two parent companies as its owners. An important difference between a strategic alliance and a joint venture is that the latter involves a distinct operating entity with an authority structure deriving from the combination of resources provided by two companies, which then share the ownership and control. There are two forms of joint venture, one in which a new company is formed by its parent companies and its ownership is defined by the shares that they each control (this is known as an equity joint venture), and one that is formed on a more simple contractual basis for the distinct purpose of collaboration (known as a non-equity joint venture).

The inter-organisational relationships described above, i.e. technology licensing, research consortia, joint ventures and strategic alliances, can also be established within horizontal inter-organisational relationships between potential competitors. An example of this is the collaboration between Volvo and Mitsubishi in forming NedCar, the Dutch car manufacturing company.

Networks

A central issue when attempting to examine inter-organisational relationships is how a relationship can be conceptualised. An inter-organisational relationship can be viewed as a dyadic relationship and treated as an isolated 'island'. However, inter-organisational relationships can also be seen as an element within a network of relationships. This is a setting that involves the simultaneous handling of a set of interconnected relationships that are interdependent. Thus, the network setting is characterised by the embeddedness of the actors. This means that interactions between companies A and B can have an influence through network effects on company C. This embeddedness can even connect competitors to each other, even though they do not have any direct interactions. This can arise because of the interdependence created through the adaptation of activities and resources within the individual business relationships.

The embeddedness of relationships between companies within networks is mentioned by most researchers who write about networks (see, for example, Lind and Thrane, 2005). However, networks have been defined in many ways and have been given different meanings. Lind and Thrane (2005) identified the setting of boundaries as a central issue in differentiating the network definitions in the inter-organisational control literature. Networks can be seen either as bounded, with a clear boundary that is apparent to other companies outside the network, or unbounded, without any clear formal or legal boundaries.

The bounded network is a distinct organisational entity in itself with a network centre. This type of network is described by Mouritsen and Thrane (2005) in their study of Consult.Net, a Danish consulting network comprising nine small consulting firms. It is a bounded network with its own goals and its own centre, and the companies within the network cooperate to achieve the network's common goals. Accounting controls were installed to support the network entity. Thus, this type of network can to some extent be seen as a distinct hierarchy.

The unbounded network does not form such a distinct organisational entity. This type of network can differ depending on the chosen focal point. Håkansson and Lind (2004) described an unbounded network in their study of a telecom network, in which the relationship between Ericsson and Telia acted as the point of departure. The authors showed how Ericsson was embedded in a complex network of relationships with customers such as Telia and Mannesman, suppliers like Flextronics, and competitors such as Nokia. In a similar way, Telia was found to be embedded in a complex network of relationships with customers, suppliers and competitors. An unbounded network does not have a network centre and no common goals exist for the network as a whole.

Irrespective of whether one views inter-organisational relationships as dyads or networks, these novel settings pose unique control problems as compared to the classic control system within organisations. In such inter-organisational relationships, control encompasses the separately owned companies and, thus, there is no longer a superior authority with the right to impose hierarchical control. Inter-organisational control takes different forms and will have a different focus depending on the inter-organisational setting (see Håkansson and Lind, 2006, for a more thorough literature review). In the following two sections, inter-organisational control in dyadic settings is described and the theories used in this type of setting are outlined. Later, inter-organisational control in network settings and the corresponding theories will be described.

Inter-organisational control in dyadic settings

Collaboration in dyadic relationships may be in the form of relationships between suppliers and customers, as well as relationships between companies targeting the same customers. The most common dyadic setting, in practice as well as in the inter-organisational control literature, is ongoing business relationships within a supply chain. Another area of interest is newly established alliances or newly established outsourcing relationships. Management controls are described as the specific mechanisms used in the control process to influence the behaviour of people to work towards the goals of the inter-organisational relationship. In the inter-organisational control literature there is often a distinction between three different types of management controls: outcome controls, behaviour controls and social controls.

Outcome controls

Outcome controls measure, evaluate and reward the outcome or results of the inter-organisational relationship. The outcome to be measured should reflect whether the goals of the relationship are being achieved or not, so it is important to decide which outcomes to measure and how this can best be done. Accounting measures are an important part of outcome controls. Dekker (2004) identified a number of inter-organisational outcome controls in his study of a newly established alliance between a supplier of railway safety systems and the company responsible for the rail infrastructure in the Netherlands. Some examples were goal setting, measurement of cost reductions and ordering quantities, and financial reward systems. He showed that accounting measures gave the companies a feeling that they were receiving a fair share of the benefits of the relationship, motivating both companies to cooperate and to put greater effort into the relationship. The two companies developed a financial incentive system to ensure that the financial results from the inter-organisational relationship were fairly shared between them.

Outcome controls need not only be financial measures; often there is a mix of financial and non-financial measures. Van der Meer-Kooistra and Vosselman (2000), in their study of outsourcing relationships, described such a mixture. In that inter-organisational relationship quality and cost were both traced over time. Productivity was measured on a monthly basis by a third party. Other non-financial measures, such as client satisfaction and the ratio of indirect and direct supporting hours, were also measured. These measures helped the two companies develop a well-functioning inter-organisational relationship by facilitating the coordination of interdependent tasks and guiding the people in the companies towards what were perceived to be important goals for the collaboration.

Thus, outcome control is a central part of inter-organisational control practice. A number of techniques, most of which are accounting based, can be used to control inter-organisational outcomes and to assist the two companies to achieve an efficient and effective cooperation. Some of the most common techniques will be described below. They are open-book accounting, the use of integrated information systems, target costing, inter-organisational cost management, value chain analysis and rank-based rewards.

Open-book accounting was initially associated with Japanese companies, but the technique has recently spread throughout the world. It builds on the simple logic that one or both of the companies in a relationship 'open their books' to their counterpart(s) and disclose data that had previously been kept within the company. This increased transparency and the extensive flow of information between the companies enables them to develop each other's operations. However, in practice, open-book accounting is often one-sided, with a strong customer requiring its supplier to give it access to financial and non-financial information, thereby enabling it to become actively involved in improving its supplier's operations. It is important that the customer does not misuse this financial and non-financial transparency. In a sense, the system of open-book accounting can be self-regulating, as a customer that misuses such transparency will have problems establishing new open-book accounting arrangements with other suppliers.

Carr and Ng (1995) described how a Nissan factory in the UK was granted access to cost information about material, labour and other costs, as well as non-financial information about quality, lead times and productivity, by some of its suppliers. Nissan thereafter set up cross-functional groups that used the information and were dedicated to the collaboration with those suppliers. These cross-functional groups consisted of staff from various functions, such as purchasing, production, accounting and engineering, who identified interdependencies between the companies. The groups also helped suppliers to improve their activities and to adapt them to Nissan's operations. In addition, the groups had the task of reviewing the suppliers' costing models and suggesting new allocation bases for overhead costs. In order to increase trust in the inter-organisational relationships, each supplier interacted with only one cross-functional group.

A more formalised way of exchanging information within an inter-organisational relationship is through the use of *integrated information systems*. Frances and Garnsey (1996) illustrated how British supermarkets use integrated information systems to coordinate operations across company boundaries. The supermarkets transmit real-time sales information to their suppliers using electronic point-of-sale scanners and EDI (electronic data interchange). The real-time sales information goes straight into the suppliers' production planning systems and the suppliers can adapt their supply to the final customer demand.

Target costing, and the closely related 'functional analysis', are other techniques used in inter-organisational relationships. Target costing is a tool for reducing the overall cost of a product with the help of all the company's departments and suppliers. It was originally developed in Japan and has been diffused to companies around the world. Car manufacturers with high demands for continuous cost reductions were the early adopters.

Target costing focuses on the period *before* the product is produced, and two important aspects are functionality and cost. The cost is always compared to what it is expected to add in terms of value for the customer. The basic idea is to reduce the life-cycle costs of new products, while ensuring that quality, reliability and other customer requirements are met. This is done by examining all possible ideas that might bring about cost reductions in the product's planning, research and development, and prototyping phases. The involvement of suppliers is crucial because supplier costs are a large part of the total product cost.

Carr and Ng (1995) showed how closely Nissan was related to its suppliers. This was essential because supplier costs represented more than 80 per cent of the total vehicle cost. Nissan identified a vehicle target cost based on the target profit for that vehicle and the overall business plan. The vehicle target cost was then split into its smallest elements, with each part and each component having specific objectives for functionality and allowed cost. Nissan integrated its suppliers in this planning and objective-setting process. As a result, the target costing process affected the cost consciousness of both Nissan and its suppliers. In this way, Nissan coordinated its efforts at costs reduction within its own departments and with its suppliers through target costing processes.

Inter-organisational cost management is described as management by means of formalised buyer–supplier interactions aimed at identifying opportunities for joint cost reduction. It extends beyond other cost management techniques by actively involving the buyer's and the supplier's design teams in the joint management of costs (Cooper and Slagmulder, 2004). Target costing is one important element of inter-organisational cost management, but there are other elements as well. On the basis of empirical studies conducted in Japanese manufacturing companies, Cooper and Slagmulder (2004) identified three approaches: functionality–price–quality trade-offs; inter-organisational cost investigations; and concurrent cost management.

Functionality–price–quality trade-offs were used to resolve relatively minor cost overrun problems, where small specification changes and limited interactions between the companies' design engineers were sufficient to resolve the problems. Such trade-offs were initiated when the manufacturing cost exceeded its target cost and the only way to reduce costs to the target level was to relax functionality and/or quality specifications in ways that would be acceptable to the buyer. The estimated savings obtained in this way were in the range 0–5 per cent.

When more significant changes to the product design and, occasionally, to the end product specifications were required, *inter-organisational cost investigations* were used. More intense interactions between the design engineers were then needed, and parts often had to be redesigned so that all the steps from raw material to finished product were more cost-efficient. The cost savings from this technique were estimated to be in the range 5–10 per cent.

Finally, *concurrent cost management* was used when fundamental changes in both the buyer's product and the supplier's component were needed. In this case there were frequent meetings between the two design teams to discuss the design changes that the supplier could make. This technique required the early involvement of the supplier in the design process, and was estimated to generate cost savings in the range 10–15 per cent.

A further approach, *value chain analysis*, can be used to analyse, coordinate and optimise linkages between interdependent activities in the value chain. In such a process the whole value chain, from raw materials to end product, is broken down into strategically relevant segments, enabling the managers to gain a better understanding of cost behaviour and the sources of differentiation.

Value chain analysis was illustrated by Dekker (2003), who described how the UK retailer Sainsbury used an ABC (activity-based costing) model based on the logic of value chain analysis. The cost model only considered 'moving' activities – i.e. activities related to moving the products from the suppliers to the stores. The primary focus of the value chain accounting model was to reduce the cost of each stage in the value chain. The model gave suppliers' cost information to Sainsbury, which it used to benchmark the suppliers and to monitor costs. The activity costs of each supplier were benchmarked against the average of all of the suppliers so that potential areas for improvement could be targeted. The cost model was also used in strategic 'what-if' analyses and in trend analyses. The strategic what-if analyses identified possible changes in the supply chain and their related costs, while the trend analyses were used to monitor the long-term development of the supply chain costs.

Another way of motivating suppliers to produce cost savings and quality improvements is to use *rank-based rewards*. Gietzmann (1996) described how Japanese assemblers ranked their suppliers into categories: A, B, C or D. Rank A and B suppliers were considered to be excellent suppliers and, therefore, the assembler engaged in close and long-term relationships with them. Inter-organisational relationships with rank D suppliers, on the other hand, were not expected to endure and would be terminated unless considerable improvements became evident. Rank C suppliers were used as capacity buffers. The logic was that suppliers who achieved relatively high performance increased their chances of being awarded a more profitable assignment in the future.

Summing up, when it comes to outcome control in an inter-organisational relationship, the focus lies on measuring, evaluating and rewarding outcomes. Accounting measures are an important part of outcome control. Open-book accounting, integrated information systems, target costing, inter-organisational cost management, value chain analysis and rank-based rewards are all examples of inter-organisational outcome control techniques that help companies to achieve successful inter-organisational relationships. However, it is often difficult to identify the desired outcomes, especially in the early stages of an inter-organisational relationship. It can also be hard to agree on the measures to be used. Fortunately, however, other ways of exercising inter-organisational control exist; for example behaviour control. This is described next.

Behaviour controls

Behaviour controls first specify how the parties should act and then evaluate whether the specifications have been followed. Common behaviour controls in inter-organisational relationships are policy documents, procedures, and the structures set up for regulating employment and training. Policy documents and procedures set out what is considered acceptable behaviour, while the structures specify the roles of the different actors in the relationship. Dekker (2004) identified several different forms of inter-organisational behaviour controls, such as ordering and supply procedures, functional specifications, programmes of innovation, quality plans, task groups and board monitoring. He found that specifying rules for programmes of innovation helped to coordinate the necessary tasks. A planning scheme was introduced that specified five activities considered to be of importance for successful innovation in the inter-organisational relationship. This scheme included details of the routines to be used for defining functional requirements and for undertaking attainability studies. Quality plans, following an ISO-9001 quality procedure, were used to ensure that quality was high in the innovation process. These plans described the agreements made and the methods that had to be followed throughout the innovation process.

The importance of meetings is often stressed when discussing behaviour controls. People from both companies in the inter-organisational relationship should meet regularly to develop and discuss guidelines for joint projects and the routines to be used to reduce costs. There is often a need to clarify how everyone should behave as well as having a forum for communication; meetings provide an ideal opportunity for both clarification and communication.

Dekker (2004) described a very formalised way of deciding on appropriate behaviour controls. In the alliance he studied an 'alliance board' was formed, with members representing both companies, and it decided on the rules to be followed and the routines to be established.

However, it can sometimes be difficult to specify either the outcomes to be achieved or the behaviour guidelines to be followed, especially at the beginning of an inter-organisational relationship. In such cases, social controls can also be important; these are described below.

Social controls

Social controls relate to the values, norms and culture that influence the behaviour of the people in the companies. Research on inter-organisational control has shown that values, norms and culture are also important influences on behaviour in inter-organisational relationships. To establish long-term business relationships, it is important to create trans-organisational work groups and these groups are often controlled by social controls.

Social controls cannot be explicitly designed, but can be influenced through the choice of partner, through activities such as meetings and ceremonies, and by conducting negotiations. Because of this, the selection of a partner is important if a successful relationship is to be achieved. Prior experience of working together and evidence of 'matching' cultures are important criteria when choosing a partner for an inter-organisational relationship.

Dekker (2004) described how having a prior history and compatible cultures were important considerations when two companies decided to form an alliance. Both companies believed it was important to put a great deal of effort into selecting a suitable partner. Furthermore, when they made joint decisions, the preferences of both companies were considered and this led to the creation of shared meaning and visions that were integrated into common goals and plans. As it takes time to build a common culture, it is important that managers are dedicated to the task and that they initiate activities with this aim in mind. Without such support and involvement it is difficult to have a successful cooperation.

Trust can be an important means of maintaining social control in inter-organisational relationships (c.f. Dekker, 2004). Trust is a difficult concept to tie down and there are a variety of definitions of trust in the literature on inter-organisational control. A useful starting point is to note that trust is closely associated with expectations. Trust is often regarded as a 'state of mind'. One might ask whether trust can exist at an organisational level, as trust is in a person's mind and organisations do not have a mind. It can, however, be seen that organisations act as if they had trust (Tomkins, 2001), and an organisation is essentially a number of people acting as a group, and the group (the organisation) can agree to trust things, persons or other organisations. At an organisational level, therefore, trust is the expectation by one organisation in a relationship that the other(s) will behave in a predictable and acceptable way (Sako, 1992). Trust may stem from previous experiences, or it may gradually develop in a relationship through learning and adaptation. Unless a certain level of trust is established, it will be difficult for those involved in the relationship to agree on goals, to create rules, or to work together in teams. It has also been claimed that trust can strengthen a relationship as it simplifies the information exchange and the process of building an understanding of the other company's interests. Trust also improves the sharing of information and makes it easier to have common development projects, which can be advantageous in inter-organisational relationships.

It is often argued that a high level of trust in an inter-organisational relationship decreases the need for extensive use of the more expensive outcome and behaviour controls. A high level of trust also makes it easier to agree on the measures to be taken and the procedures to be adopted in a relationship, thereby facilitating the process of finding acceptable outcome and behaviour controls. It is believed that companies should invest in trust-building activities to consolidate inter-organisational relationships and, if trust is to be built up, it is important that a common understanding is reached about the issues of interest to both companies. This can be done by holding regular meetings, establishing performance measures that can be used to divide the benefits of the relationship between the companies, and establishing a joint means of resolving disputes to ensure that any conflicts that arise in the inter-organisational relationship are sorted out quickly. Other ways of building trust include ensuring that there are open communication channels between the individuals in the respective companies and focusing on developing personal relationships between key people in each company.

A combination of outcome, behaviour and social controls

The three types of controls were described separately above, but this was done merely for illustrative purposes. There is a general consensus in the literature on inter-organisational control that control is achieved through a combination of these different types. Thus, inter-organisational control in practice consists of a mixture of outcome, behaviour and social controls.

Outcome controls are argued to be especially suitable for handling appropriation concerns, while outcome, behaviour and social controls all are thought to be useful for coordinating interdependent tasks. In the empirical investigation mentioned above, Dekker (2004) showed that many different controls are used in combination in an inter-organisational relationship. The outcome controls used were, to a large extent, based on accounting information (such as financial reward systems, budgeting and cost estimations), which was made transparent through open-book agreements. These means of gaining information about the operations and of governing the inter-organisational relationship were complemented by behaviour controls, which took the form of quality plans, innovation programmes, functional specifications and setting up a board to monitor progress. Social controls – stemming from shared history, as the companies had known each other before the relationship was formed – were also important. Dekker identified various activities that were used to establish social controls, such as shared decision-making, goal setting through joint task groups, and activities aimed at creating a high level of trust. He also described how, by putting considerable effort into selecting a good partner with a compatible culture, the need for outcome controls could be reduced.

At this point, the dynamic aspects of inter-organisational management control need to be mentioned. Often the relative importance of the three different forms of management control can change over time. For example, outcome controls tend to become more important as the companies learn about the processes and activities, as they enable them to specify outcome measures and standards for those measures. Similarly, behaviour controls can become more useful with the passage of time, while social controls are most valuable early in an inter-organisational relationship when there is insufficient knowledge to design detailed outcome and behaviour controls.

To recap, the above sections have described a palette of controls that managers can use in inter-organisational relationships, and the need to combine the different types of control at the various stages of the relationship was also identified. However, a question still remains: how should managers decide the most appropriate combination of controls? Should the emphasis be on outcome, behaviour, or social controls? Transaction cost theory provides criteria for making such decisions and, together with agency theory, is reviewed in the next section.

Management control issues and theories in dyadic settings

For dyadic settings, theoretical frameworks based on transaction cost economics (TCE) and agency theory have frequently been used in the literature on inter-organisational control (Håkansson and Lind, 2006). TCE and agency theory have many similarities because both approaches are built on neoclassical micro-economic theory. Their origins can be traced to Coase's (1937) seminal paper on the theory of the firm. TCE and agency theory both assume that human beings are characterised by bounded rationality and opportunism.

Transaction cost economics

The majority of articles published on inter-organisational control have used TCE as their theoretical framework (Håkansson and Lind, 2006). TCE provides criteria for answering two questions concerning inter-organisational relationships and inter-organisational control. First, under what circumstances should an inter-organisational relationship be chosen as the most suitable governance form? Second, what control mix should be chosen for the inter-organisational relationship?

The first question concerns why some transactions are more likely to be executed within a particular form of governance. From a management point of view, this can provide insights into the most appropriate form of governance for particular types of transactions. The question for managers is whether particular transactions should be executed within the company (in the hierarchy), through the market, or somewhere in between (e.g. through an inter-organisational relationship). In other words, under what circumstances should managers choose to form inter-organisational relationships? The second question is related to how management control can support the three governance forms. From a management point of view, the question to be addressed after choosing an inter-organisational relationship as the form of governance is: how should this inter-organisational relationship be structured, managed and controlled?

The first question has long been seen as the classical make-or-buy decision, which has traditionally been viewed as a competition between the company and an arm's length supplier. In other words, the company compares the purchasing prices available from possible suppliers through short-term price bidding, then takes the lowest purchasing price and compares it with the internal production cost to choose the most efficient form of governance. But, more recently, closer and longer-term relationships with individual suppliers have been seen as another alterative. This situation imposes new demands on accounting, as it is not enough to focus narrowly on supply prices and production costs to make sourcing decisions. The analysis must be extended to include the efficiency and effectiveness of the entire value chain and now the focus of sourcing decisions is on minimising the entire cost of ownership, i.e. the life-cycle cost of the item to be purchased.

Writers who have used TCE link the three forms of governance (market, hierarchy and inter-organisational relationship) to characteristics of the transactions. Two important characteristics are the degree of asset specificity and the uncertainty of the transactions. Asset specificity relates to the possibility that opportunity losses could arise if the investment made to support the transactions has to be put to an alternative use or given away to other users. It is usually defined in relation to a specific customer or supplier. High asset specificity means that the asset can be used in no more than a few other relationships and hence the opportunity loss arising from the termination of the inter-organisational relationship is potentially high. Uncertainty refers to the degree to which the intended performance can be specified and to the predictability of the environment within which the transactions are to be executed.

The choice of governance form depends on the character of the transactions. By choosing the most suitable form of governance, transaction costs can be minimised. Market governance can be expected for transactions that have little uncertainty and low asset specificity; here the market functions smoothly and at low cost. When asset specificity and uncertainty increase an inter-organisational relationship can be anticipated, as alternative controls are needed to protect the transaction from an opportunistic breach of contract. When asset specificity and uncertainty are both high, the hierarchy is usually the most appropriate form of governance.

The second question concerns the role that management controls can play within the different forms of governance. The three forms of governance differ in the controls they employ. The use of management controls based on authority, incentive structures and monitoring – for example measuring the direct cost of labour and materials, and using standard costs, break-even charts, budgets, responsibility accounting and transfer prices – are usually associated with hierarchical governance. Market governance is controlled through free competition, and market prices are the central source of information for decision-making. Management control is critical to ensure reciprocity in exchange relationships. A management control system is needed to collect market prices, oversee the implementation of contracts, and estimate market opportunities and threats. In this way it is possible for companies to compare costs and benefits for any given market exchange. However, in inter-organisational relationships long-term contracts and additional safeguards are used to assure compliance, and the management controls focus on relational cooperation between the buyer and supplier. This is further described below.

When designing inter-organisational control systems it is important for managers to decide on the most suitable combination of outcome, behaviour and social controls. TCE provides criteria that could assist in making these decisions. Van der Meer-Kooistra and Vosselman (2000), for example, used TCE to study how firms can structure the management control of inter-organisational relationships. They identified three different control patterns: (i) market-based, (ii) bureaucracy-based and (iii) trust-based. Within each control pattern, different controls are at work. The market-based pattern is associated with competitive bidding and no special management controls are needed. The bureaucracy-based pattern is linked to specified norms, standards and rules, and the measurement and evaluation of performance. Here outcome and behaviour controls are needed. The trust-based pattern is associated with personal consultation and coordination and, in this instance, outcome and social controls are needed.

Managers should choose the market-based pattern when few investments in specific assets are needed in the inter-organisational relationship, the transactions are characterised by high repetition, and the environment is characterised by low levels of uncertainty about future circumstances. Managers should choose a bureaucracy-based pattern when investments in specific assets can be protected by contractual rules, the transactions are characterised by low to medium repetition and, although there are medium to high market risks, future contingencies are more or less known. Finally, managers should choose a trust-based pattern when there is high asset specificity, transactions are characterised by low repetition, and the high market risks and future contingencies are unknown.

Agency theory

Agency theory is the second most popular theory used in the inter-organisational control literature (Håkansson and Lind, 2006). The notion of incomplete contracting is important from an agency theory perspective (Baiman and Rajan, 2002). Incomplete contracting means that it is impossible to incorporate all the information required to cover future contingencies in a final contract. Potential inefficiencies in the buyer–supplier relationship are consequences of at least the following two characteristics: information asymmetry and opportunism. Information asymmetry means that one company is in possession of information that can be used 'against' the other company in the relationship. Given these assumptions, one important role of inter-organisational controls is to encourage information sharing between the companies in order to reduce the information asymmetry. Another important role is to provide incentives to discipline and motivate the companies so that they do not behave opportunistically.

Increasing the exchange of information leads to greater effectiveness in the supply chain, as the supplier and/or customer can more easily identify improvements and cost reductions. Information can be exchanged through, for example, open-book accounting, target costing, performance measurement, meetings and conversations. They should all be encouraged, although in so doing, the potential for misuse of information increases. For example, greater access to information might lead to a company trying to increase its bargaining power and exploiting the additional information it has received when it comes to the renegotiation of the contract. Companies need to safeguard themselves against this eventuality.

If one company makes an investment, there is a risk that other companies in the supply chain will free-ride on the back of that investment, thereby capturing benefits without incurring any of the associated costs. As a result, investments that are beneficial to the value chain as a whole may not be carried out because each firm will consider only its own interests. This raises the problem of risk and profit sharing. Thus, a central issue from an agency theory perspective is to design inter-organisational control systems which mitigate these incentive problems. Rank-based rewards and information sharing through open-book accounting, described in the section on outcome controls, are ways of mitigating some of these incentive problems.

Inter-organisational relationships can be considered as dyadic relationships when inter-organisational control is described and analysed. However, inter-organisational relationships can also be viewed as an element within a network of relationships. This topic is discussed below.

Inter-organisational control in network settings

If particular inter-organisational relationships are considered to be embedded within a network of interconnected relationships, it is not enough to focus separately on each inter-organisational relationship when discussing the design and operation of inter-organisational control systems. Instead, consideration must be given to how control operates in the whole interconnected set of inter-organisational relationships (Lind and Thrane, 2005).

A network dimension of inter-organisational control

The importance of embeddedness was shown by Mahama and Chua (2005) in their study of inter-organisational control in the Australian telecommunication industry. The buying company together with its suppliers established inter-organisational control through various forms of financial and non-financial measurement, incentive schemes with a fixed-price agreement for a range of services, and open-book accounting arrangements. However, the suppliers did not act as the buyer had expected; they overpriced all supplementary services not included in the fixed price agreement.

The content of the ongoing relationships changed after the buying company recruited two new suppliers to deliver the extra services. This changed how the existing suppliers acted, as they faced the competition from the two new suppliers. This is a clear example of how a company can change the nature and content of one inter-organisational relationship by actions taken outside that particular relationship. Thus, the content and control of an inter-organisational relationship are dependent on the other relationships in which that relationship is embedded.

Håkansson and Lind (2004) analysed the role of control in the formation of embedded inter-organisational relationships. They studied the inter-organisational relationship between the Swedish cellular telecommunication company Ericsson and the Swedish telecommunication operator Telia. Ericsson had many vertical inter-organisational relationships with different customers, such as Vodafone, Telia, Orange and France Telecom, and with different suppliers, such as Flextronics and Hewlett Packard. But, Ericsson also had several horizontal relationships with Nokia, Sony and Microsoft, for example. Ericsson was interwoven in a complex network where there were interdependencies between the different relationships.

With this in mind, when trying to understand inter-organisational control in a particular inter-organisational relationship, it becomes important to include the interconnected relationships in the analysis. From Ericsson's perspective, inter-organisational control was about handling the interdependencies between multiple inter-organisational relationships, both vertical and horizontal. The use of outcome controls, such as responsibility accounting, budgets, reward schemes and profit measures, was vital to enable Ericsson to handle this complexity.

The inter-organisational relationship between Ericsson and Telia consisted of a complex mixture of hierarchies, relationships between sub-units, and market elements. Ericsson systematically used outcome controls to create units with partially overlapping accountabilities. This enabled it to manage the interconnected inter-organisational relationships. Furthermore, Ericsson evaluated the individual units on actions and measures that could not necessarily be controlled by the unit. For example, Ericsson's customer units had goals that related to their particular customer. As such, the customer units were, to some extent, evaluated and rewarded as a result of their customer's actions. One manager within the customer unit responsible for Telia Mobile, for example, was evaluated on how successful he had been in persuading Telia Mobile to use a new software feature in its operations. Each customer unit handled one customer and the customer unit acted as its customer's voice in Ericsson. Each customer unit tried to influence Ericsson's development units to meet its customer's needs.

The overlapping accountabilities were also used for the technical units within Ericsson, which were responsible for the development, supply and support of hardware and software for parts of the cellular system. Examples of technical units were switching systems, base transceiver systems and base station systems. The technical units were financially accountable for the consolidated return on sales for their subsystem. They were also accountable for worldwide revenue, but they did not have any direct customer contacts because the customer units 'owned' the customers.

The financial performance of the base station systems unit, for example, depended on the performance of the customer units and the other technical units. The above examples show how Ericsson used outcome controls to coordinate different interconnected relationships by creating a structure that forced units to interact with each other.

Telia had inter-organisational relationships with Ericsson, as discussed above, and also with Nokia. Telia had to coordinate these two inter-organisational relationships, as it could not entirely adapt its operations to either one of them because they were both suppliers for Telia Mobile's cellular system. It was, therefore, important that both Ericsson and Nokia developed the same software features and that they delivered them at almost the same time. Similarly, from Telia's point of view, inter-organisational control also needed to consider competitors, as they tried to influence Ericsson and Nokia and persuade them to adapt to their cellular systems.

Tomkins (2001) described ways of designing inter-organisational controls when inter-organisational relationships are embedded in a complex network of interconnected horizontal and vertical relationships. He argued that any company will be restricted to some degree, and will have to take as given many aspects of the network. However, he argued that managers still have a key role to play in manoeuvring their company vis-à-vis the other companies in the network. With the help of bilateral negotiations, managers can change some of their company's relationships, thereby influencing the network. When engaged in bilateral negotiations, it is important that managers do not forget the other interconnected inter-organisational relationships, as these might be indirectly affected by any changes that are brought about.

Tomkins claimed that there are two important questions for managers to consider. The first is whether the company has a suitable information system. As the company functions within a network of interconnected relationships, the information system needs to capture both the direct effects on the other company in the inter-organisational relationship, and also the effects on the third and fourth parties in the network. The company has to make choices about what to include in the analyses and must consider some parts of the network as exogenous. Tomkins claimed that there is little need for new accounting techniques, but instead there is 'a need to consider how to use them [the existing techniques] in negotiation processes when there are more complex interactions across organisational boundaries' (Tomkins, 2001, p. 183). Ericsson's system of overlapping accountabilities is an example of how management controls can be used in a relative way, i.e. recognising that the inter-organisational relationship in question is embedded in a network of interconnected relationships.

The second question for managers to consider is whether the company's portfolio of inter-organisational relationships is appropriate for achieving its goals. As the company is likely to be involved in a mixture of arm's length as well as inter-organisational relationships, it will not be possible to have close relationships with all its suppliers and customers. Hence, managers need to choose which relationships should be prioritised. To be able to make these choices, managers need to assess the entire mix of their business relationships, as changes in one relationship can affect others due to the aforementioned network effects. Such choices can be made by mapping the network in which the company currently operates along various dimensions. Tomkins suggested four dimensions: 'the transactions needed, the degree of economic interdependence and value of the relationship, the current trust intensity, and the current information' (Tomkins, 2001, p. 184). Managers can use other dimensions as well; the important thing is to have a network view in the analysis. Based on such an analysis, managers can decide what changes are needed in specific inter-organisational relationships and in the portfolio of relationships.

Open-book accounting, self-regulation and orchestration mechanisms

Kajüter and Kulmala (2005) described a German car manufacturer which has a network of inter-organisational relationships with its suppliers. Open-book accounting is used to enable the manufacturer to control this network. Using information about each individual relationship, the company tries to understand the interconnections between them. The company uses worksheets to formalise the disclosure of the costs within different parts of the supplier network. It also uses a value flow chart to obtain transparency within the network and to provide a picture of the interconnections between the different relationships. For example, the names and locations of upstream suppliers are shown on the value flow chart, along with the connections between the suppliers, the flow of materials, and each supplier's added cost.

In addition, the manufacturer delegates the collection of information to some of its suppliers. For example, first-tier suppliers are responsible for collecting information about upstream suppliers and providing a detailed breakdown of the costs for its subsystem. Open-book accounting is supported by ongoing work in cross-functional and cross-company teams and technical support is provided free of charge by the manufacturer. Open-book accounting is used by the manufacturer to manage the network of interconnected relationships and to increase its knowledge of the interconnections so that it can manoeuvre within the network.

Other researchers have focused on formalised horizontal networks; that is, networks in which companies target the same customers. Mouritsen and Thrane (2005) studied networks formed by potential competitors who cooperated to develop new knowledge and new brand assets. Here the focus was not on each dyadic relationship in isolation; instead, the network of interconnected inter-organisational relationships was of interest. In these networks there were two types of control mechanisms aimed at handling the multiple relationships in order to maintain and develop the network.

First, there were self-regulating mechanisms that stabilised the flow of interactions in the network. An important ingredient was to make the calculation of financial flows more predictable. Examples of self-regulating mechanisms were transfer prices and systems of fees that distributed the financial gains arising from each relationship according to rules laid down at the outset. This made the financial gains of the cooperation more predictable.

Second, there were orchestration mechanisms aimed at giving the network an identity and a common objective, even though it comprised a number of separate companies. One example was the development of a network strategy. Other examples were fairs, meetings and events that made the various companies visible to each other.

Summing up, management control in network settings seems to consist of traditional accounting techniques and control mechanisms such as incentive schemes, responsibility accounting, open-book accounting, transfer pricing, rules and meetings. However, the accounting techniques and control mechanisms are used to handle the embedded inter-organisational relationships. In the bounded networks with a network centre, management control is used to influence the separate companies to work for the goals of the network as a whole. Here managers can use self-regulation and orchestration mechanisms. In the unbounded network, management control is used to support the interaction processes between the interdependent companies, and managers can use overlapping accountabilities.

Management control issues and applied theories in network settings

Theoretical frameworks derived from actor network theory and the industrial network approach have been used to study control issues in a network setting. However, only a limited number of published papers currently exist (e.g. Håkansson and Lind, 2006).

Actor network theory

A central aim of the studies that have applied a framework based on actor network theory is to understand how relationships work and how control functions within these relationships. The focus is on the processes of interaction between heterogeneous actors, and how management controls are involved in constituting the actions in inter-organisational relationships. Thus, these studies adopt a process approach, which can be contrasted with TCE studies. TCE normally adopts a structural approach to explaining forms of governance and management controls.

In an actor network theory approach, inter-organisational relationships are conceptualised as 'action nets'. The underlying concept recognises that changes in the relationship between actor A and actor B can also change the relationship between actor B and actor C. Thus, actor B and its relationships are embedded in a larger action net. An interesting aspect of actor network theory is that management controls are often viewed as 'actors' in their own right. Consequently, the management control system plays an active part in the shaping of the inter-organisational relationships. Thus, the management control system constructs a particular reality within the inter-organisational relationships and, as such, can be mobilised and used to shape the relationships.

Research based on actor network theory investigates how management control systems acquire their nature, existence and influence in the network. Management control is not regarded as a set of techniques, but instead is viewed as one element that influences heterogeneous actors within a network of embedded relationships. Finally, it should be noted that actor network studies are concerned with understanding processes of management control, rather than prescribing how management controls should be used.

Industrial network approach

The industrial network approach is another network theory used in the literature. This approach considers relationships to be important for company performance, but does not assume that actors behave opportunistically. Interdependence and the embeddedness of actors, activities and resources are central ingredients of the industrial network approach, which has implications for management control. In a network setting, the assessment of resources and activities needs to take these interdependencies into consideration. Therefore, a central concern for management control is to provide information about both the direct and indirect effects of changes in the individual inter-organisational relationships.

For example, when a company evaluates customer profitability it must apply a mixture of customer accounting techniques. Some customers may seem 'unprofitable' when a yearly customer profitability analysis is prepared. But, the same customers could appear profitable if evaluated through customer valuations, in which the time period is extended and the indirect benefits of network effects are measured.

A closely related concern is the mix of customer and supplier relationships that the company should have to fulfil its goals and the role management control can play when the company prioritises its inter-organisational relationships. From a network perspective it is often impossible for a company to adapt its operation to the satisfaction of all its customers and suppliers. Instead, the company must choose which of its inter-organisational relationships it wants to be close and intensive, and which inter-organisational relationships should be more arm's length. This will affect the information exchange, as the amount of information divulged to customers and suppliers will differ depending on the nature of the inter-organisational relationship. Similarly, different amounts of information will be expected from the customers and suppliers. The prioritised inter-organisational relationships will involve more information exchange about operations and financial situations, and these customer and suppliers will have greater potential influence over the company's future choices.

Another important role for management control is in creating a dynamic network structure. As Håkansson and Lind (2004) showed in their study of Ericsson and its inter-organisational relationships, management control, with its overlapping accountabilities, created contradictions and an unstable business network in which actors continuously needed to find provisional solutions. As a result, problems, conflicts and contradictions were distributed across the various interfaces between the companies, instead of all being focused at a single interface. Management control created a network structure that could develop and change through co-evolution despite the complexity produced by the interdependence and embeddedness of actors, activities and resources.

To sum up, actor network theory and industrial network approach focus on the role management controls have in interaction processes between actors within a network of embedded relationships. Studies which have applied a framework derived from TCE identify suitable forms of management control to use within particular inter-organisational relationships – based on asset specificity and transaction characteristics. But this is a rather stable and very static view of the relationship between management control and inter-organisational relationships, as each dyadic inter-organisational relationship is analysed in isolation without reference to the wider network of interconnected relationships. In contrast, actor network theory and the industrial network approach afford management control a more dynamic role. Different forms of management control are suitable within different inter-organisational relationships and the management controls also work to change these relationships. Furthermore, inter-organisational relationships are analysed as part of the wider network of interconnected relationships, thereby giving a network dimension to the analysis.

Future prospects

Having reviewed inter-organisational relationships and inter-organisational control, we can now turn to future prospects and point to areas where there is potential for further contributions to be made.

Control of and in inter-organisational relationships

It is important to be clear about the distinction between control *of* and control *in* an inter-organisational relationship. This distinction is rarely made in the literature. Who is controlling whom? From which company's perspective is the analysis made and what consequences does this have? Control is often viewed from the perspective of one particular company, and the controls discussed are the controls imposed on the others. But an alternative approach would be to discuss controls that are agreed by companies in an inter-organisational relationship, such as joint reward schemes. Inter-organisational control is best considered as a mixture of controls agreed upon by the companies concerned and the controls through which one company tries to control the other. The connections between these different controls warrant greater clarification and focus in future research. It is also important for managers to reflect on the roles they can serve in the relationship, and not to focus entirely on controlling the other company, but instead discuss and agree forms of joint control.

One way of studying these connections is to focus on the processes that shape the control mechanisms observed in inter-organisational relationships. This calls for attention to the role of negotiations between the companies and their use of management controls. This means we need to understand the processes that have led to the control practices we observe. Such a perspective requires a more dynamic approach to inter-organisational control; bringing to the fore the processes of negotiation and renegotiation in which control plays an important role.

The conceptualisation of inter-organisational relationships

We have stressed that inter-organisational control is viewed in different ways depending on whether inter-organisational relationships are conceptualised as isolated dyads or as relationships embedded in a network of interconnected relationships. There are, however, also other important dimensions regarding the conceptualisation of inter-organisational relationships. One dimension is the connection between inter-organisational control and internal control within the companies. Little progress has been made in studying the simultaneous operation of internal and inter-organisational control systems. Another dimension is the conceptualisation of actors within the inter-organisational relationship; for example the importance of interest groups with divergent goals. These two dimensions are described in turn below.

Discussions of inter-organisational control are often divorced from the internal control processes in the companies concerned. It is important to note, however, that the companies involved in an inter-organisational relationship will also have an internal agenda that exists apart from that relationship. There will be important things going on that have nothing to do with the inter-organisational relationship, and there will be important control processes within each company that will continue whether or not the company has inter-organisational relationships. This raises questions about connections between the internal control processes within each company and the control of the inter-organisational relationship. Should inter-organisational control be conceptualised as an isolated process, disconnected from the internal control processes within each company? Or should inter-organisational control be considered in an integrated analysis that also considers internal control processes?

This is an issue that has received little explicit attention in the literature. The studies by Mouritsen *et al.* (2001) and Håkansson and Lind (2004) are exceptions. Mouritsen *et al.* (2001) investigated the effects of introducing inter-organisational control techniques, such as open-book accounting and target costing, in inter-organisational relationships. As expected, the first effect they noted was that these techniques were important in the inter-organisational control process, closing the perceived knowledge gap in the development and production processes by sharing information about the activities and operations. There was also a second effect that had not previously been described in the literature. The inter-organisational control techniques also had internal effects, as the information thereby obtained prompted changes in company's perception of technology, organisation and strategy, and led to changes in the identity and core competence of the company. In the other study, Håkansson and Lind (2004) showed that Ericsson handled the tension between internal goals and inter-organisational goals by forming units with overlapping accountabilities, and by including some of their customers' most important goals in the reward system they set up for their units.

The conclusion to be drawn from these studies is that inter-organisational control processes have connections with the control processes within the companies concerned, and these connections need to be included in the analysis. Thus, there is a need for more research into the connections and interdependencies between internal and inter-organisational control processes. Such research will need to map the internal control processes and plot the interdependencies with the inter-organisational control process. This is also important for managers when deciding on their control strategies.

The second important dimension concerns the conceptualisation of the actors within and between companies. Inherent in most previous research on inter-organisational control is the belief that the managers of the companies intervene directly (with outcome or behaviour controls) or indirectly (through activities intended to increase the sense a common culture and/or activities aimed at increasing trust) and thereby successfully effect change. As such, by changing the mix of the existing controls, managers are supposed to be responding to internal and/or external change. Thus, management is portrayed as the sole interest group and the degree to which non-managerial interest groups can genuinely influence outcomes tends to be ignored.

Håkansson and Lind (2004) argued that it is necessary to analyse the individual *sub-units* within each of the companies in the inter-organisational relationship, as they did not consider it sufficient to analyse each of these companies as a whole. Different sub-units have their own agenda and goals, and sub-units within the individual companies can have conflicting goals, which may correspond more closely to the goals of sub-units within their counterpart business units than to their own company's goals. In this way, a more detailed conceptualisation of inter-organisational relationships could produce interesting results that differ from those obtained by considering the relationship as a homogeneous whole.

In future studies of inter-organisational control there is a need to conceptualise companies in terms of multiple interest groups within the companies and between the companies in inter-organisational relationships. Each interest group is presumed to have its own perspective and rationality, and to act consistently (Hopper and Powell, 1985). When this perspective is adopted there can be no presumption of a unity of (inter-)organisational goals; companies comprise interest groups with divergent and often mutually inconsistent goals and interests. How these interest groups are formed and interact in an inter-organisational relationship, and how inter-organisational controls can be applied, are interesting avenues to explore.

Conclusion

This chapter has considered inter-organisational relationships and inter-organisational control. It is clear that inter-organisational relationships have proliferated in recent years. Many researchers consider this to be the result of increased globalisation, rapid technological transformation, and the increasing technical complexity of products. The formation of inter-organisational relationships is one way for companies to stay competitive in the complex and rapidly changing world they inhabit.

These inter-organisational relationships have emerged through the coming together of two separate trends. First, companies are developing their existing relationships into closer and longer lasting relationships. Second, companies are outsourcing activities that were previously performed in-house and as a result they are entering into new inter-organisational relationships.

Different labels are given to inter-organisational relationships, and their description and understanding differs depending on how the relationships are conceptualised. Inter-organisational relationships can be conceptualised as dyadic relationships and come under names such as strategic alliances and joint ventures, and they are analysed in isolation. Alternatively, inter-organisational relationships can also be conceptualised as part of a bounded or unbounded network and analysed relative to one another, stressing the interconnections between the different relationships.

We have also observed the need for managers to find ways of managing and controlling their inter-organisational relationships. This chapter has indicated some of the tools that can be used for inter-organisational control. It has been stressed that inter-organisational control has different meanings and focus depending on the perceived setting of the relationship, i.e. a dyadic or a network setting.

Within dyadic settings, the focus is on choosing an appropriate blend of controls for each inter-organisational relationship. We have provided examples of outcome controls, behaviour controls and social controls. Open-book accounting, target costing, value chain analysis, alliance boards, choosing a partner with matching culture, and investing in trust-building activities have all been discussed. Each inter-organisational relationship is evaluated separately when designing and making decisions concerning inter-organisational controls.

Within network settings, inter-organisational control needs to recognise that each company is embedded in a network of interconnected relationships. Controls should be used in a way that enables the company to handle the interconnections between different inter-organisational relationships. The network effects of decisions have to be considered, as what happens in one inter-organisational relationship can affect other interconnected relationships. Tools, such as overlapping accountabilities, developing information systems that take network effects into consideration, mapping the network of interconnected relationships, open-book accounting, and developing self-regulation and orchestration mechanisms, have been discussed.

The different focus in each of the two settings can be illustrated through the use of open-book accounting. When adopting a dyadic view, as much information as possible should be provided, assuming safeguards against opportunism are in place. This applies to each inter-organisational relationship that a company is involved in, and information sharing within one relationship is treated as unrelated to information sharing within other relationships. With a network view, each inter-organisational relationship has to be seen in relation to the other inter-organisational relationships that the company is involved in either directly or indirectly. Thus, information sharing within one relationship is treated as related to the information sharing within other relationships. In this case there is a need to use information from open-book accounting agreements to increase the company's knowledge of the interconnections between the different relationships, as well as to increase the knowledge of each individual relationship. However, the interdependencies between the relationships could mean that more information sharing and closer adaptations in one relationship could create problems in other relationships. Therefore, the company needs to prioritise and the extent of information sharing may differ between the inter-organisational relationships.

This chapter has also provided a review of the theories used in the literature on inter-organisational control. It has been shown that, from a theoretical point of view, inter-organisational relationships primarily encompass two different sets of control issues. First, there is the issue of governance; an agreement between the companies in a relationship, specifying how monetary gains or losses are to be divided, is required. Using the metaphor of baking a cake, this issue concerns how the resulting cake is to be divided. Second, there is the issue of how the inter-organisational relationship develops. Here, the focus is on the process of baking the cake: the existence of the cake is not taken for granted. We have argued that these two issues are stressed to a greater or lesser extent depending on the theoretical underpinnings of the study. In TCE and agency theory, appropriation concerns are the most important issue; thus, dividing the cake comes to the fore and the analysis is rather static. But in actor network theory and the industrial network approach it is the development of relationships and the processes of interaction that are the primary concerns and the analysis is more dynamic. As companies are not assumed to act opportunistically, there is no need to focus excessively on how the cake is divided; the cake itself is seen as something that can be influenced by the companies involved.

Finally some interesting areas for future research were identified. First, there is a need for a clearer distinction between control *of* and control *in* an inter-organisational relationship. The connections between the controls through which one company tries to control the other company and the controls that are agreed by both companies need to be clarified and better analysed in future research. Second, there is a need to increase our understanding of the interdependencies between internal control and inter-organisational control. Inter-organisational control systems do not operate in a vacuum; the two companies have their own internal operations and their own internal control systems, which must be taken into account. Third, more research is needed on how non-managerial interest groups influence inter-organisational relationships and inter-organisational controls.

References

Baiman, S. and Rajan, M.V. (2002) 'Incentive issues in inter-firm relationships', *Accounting, Organizations and Society*, **27**, 213–38.

Bengtsson, L., Berggren, C. and Lind, J. (eds) (2005) *Alternativ till Outsourcing*, Malmö: Liber (in Swedish).

Carr, C. and Ng, J. (1995) 'Total cost control: Nissan and its U.K. supplier partnerships', *Management Accounting Research*, **6**, 347–65.

Coase, R. (1937) 'The nature of the firm', *Economica*, **4**, 386–404.

Cooper, R. and Slagmulder, R. (2004) 'Interorganizational cost management and relational context', *Accounting, Organizations and Society*, **29**, 1–26.

Dekker, H.C. (2003) 'Value chain analysis in interfirm relationships: a field study', *Management Accounting Research*, **14**, 1–23.

Dekker, H.C. (2004) 'Control of inter-organizational relationships: evidence on appropriation concerns and coordination requirements', *Accounting, Organizations and Society*, **29**, 27–49.

Frances, J. and Garnsey, E. (1996) 'Supermarkets and suppliers in the United Kingdom: system integration, information and control', *Accounting, Organizations and Society*, **21**, 591–610.

Gietzmann, M.B. (1996) 'Incomplete contracts and the make or buy decisions: governance design and attainable flexibility', *Accounting, Organizations and Society*, **21**, 611–26.

Håkansson, H. and Lind, J. (2004) 'Accounting and network coordination', *Accounting, Organizations and Society*, **29**, 51–72.

Håkansson, H. and Lind, J. (2006) 'Accounting in an interorganizational setting', in C.S. Chapman, A.G. Hopwood and M.D. Shields (eds), *Handbook of Management Accounting Research*, vol. 2, Oxford: Elsevier, pp. 885–902.

Hopper, T. and Powell, A. (1985) 'Making sense of research into the organizational and social aspects of management accounting: a review of its underlying assumptions', *Journal of Management Studies*, **22**, 429–466.

Kajüter, P. and Kulmala, H.I. (2005) 'Open-book accounting in networks. Potential achievements and reasons for failures', *Management Accounting Research*, **16**, 179–204.

Lind, J. and Thrane, S. (2005) 'Network accounting', in S. Jönsson and J. Mouritsen (eds), *Accounting in Scandinavia – The Northern Lights*, Malmö: Liber and Copenhagen Business School Press, pp. 115–37.

Mahama, H. and Chua, W.F. (2005) *Making Strategic Supply Relationships Work: Struggling with Accounting Numbers,* Working paper, University of New South Wales, Sydney.

Mouritsen, J., Hansen, A. and Hansen, C.Ø. (2001) 'Inter-organizational controls and organizational competencies: episodes around target cost management/functional analysis and open book accounting', *Management Accounting Research,* **12,** 221–44.

Mouritsen, J. and Thrane, S. (2005) 'Accounting, network complementarities and the development of inter-organizational relations', *Accounting, Organizations and Society,* **31,** 241–75.

Sako, M. (1992) *Prices, Quality and Trust: Interfirm Relations in Britain and Japan,* Cambridge: Cambridge University Press.

Tomkins, C. (2001) 'Interdependencies, trust and information in relationships, alliances and networks', *Accounting, Organizations and Society,* **26,** 161–91.

Van der Meer-Kooistra, J. and Vosselman, E.G.J. (2000) 'Management control of interfirm transactional relationships: the case of industrial renovation and maintenance', *Accounting, Organizations and Society,* **25,** 51–77.

Further reading

Inter-organisational relationships in general

Ford, D., Gadde, L.-E., Håkansson, H. and Snehota, I. (2003) *Managing Business Relationships,* 2nd edn, Chichester: John Wiley & Sons. This book gives a thorough introduction to inter-organisational relationships and discusses the importance of such relationships for the competitiveness of companies.

Specific outcome control techniques

Cooper, R. and Slagmulder, R. (2004) 'Interorganizational cost management and relational context', *Accounting, Organizations and Society,* **29,** 1–26. Discusses the importance of inter-organisational relationships for developing and producing products at a low cost and gives detailed examples of the use of inter-organisational cost management techniques.

Dekker, H.C. (2003) 'Value chain analysis in interfirm relationships: a field study', *Management Accounting Research,* **14,** 1–23. Illustrates the use and effects of value chain analysis in inter-organisational relationships.

Kajüter, P. and Kulmala, H.I. (2005) 'Open-book accounting in networks. Potential achievements and reasons for failures', *Management Accounting Research,* **16,** 179–204. Provides a detailed example of the use of open-book accounting in inter-organisational relationships.

Specific theoretical applications

Baiman, S. and Rajan, M.V. (2002) 'Incentive issues in inter-firm relationships', *Accounting, Organizations and Society,* **27,** 213–38. Reviews the assumptions and main arguments of agency theory and discusses central issues in inter-organisational relationships from an agency theory point of view.

Håkansson, H. and Lind, J. (2004) 'Accounting and network coordination', *Accounting, Organizations and Society,* **29,** 51–72. This article outlines central themes in the industrial network approach and discusses control in an unbounded network setting.

Mouritsen, J. and Thrane, S. (2005) 'Accounting, network complementarities and the development of inter-organizational relations', *Accounting, Organizations and Society,* **31,** 241–75. Discusses inter-organisational control from an actor network theory point of view and illustrates how companies are embedded in a bounded network.

Van der Meer-Kooistra, J. and Vosselman, E.G.J. (2000) 'Management control of interfirm transactional relationships: the case of industrial renovation and maintenance', *Accounting, Organizations and Society,* **25,** 51–77. This article outlines the main assumptions and concepts of transaction cost theory and develops a model of the design of inter-organisational control systems.

14

Management accounting and accountants in the public sector: the challenges presented by public–private partnerships

Jodie Moll and Christopher Humphrey

Introduction

Since the late 1970s, public sectors around the world have been subjected to wide-ranging reforms in response to growing pressures and constraints on resources and changing demands and expectations about the delivery of services, all of which have challenged the way that public services are managed and controlled (see Olson *et al.*, 1998; Guthrie *et al.*, 2005). Under the broad label of new public management (NPM) reforms, various market mechanisms have been introduced as public organisations have been pressured to import managerial processes from the private sector. At the same time, major investments have been made in operational performance measurement and monitoring systems to analyse the efficiency and effectiveness of public service delivery. In recent years, the private finance initiative/public–private partnerships (PFI/PPP) approach has sought to expand such initiatives. This approach seeks improvement in the procurement and management of public sector capital assets, so as to ensure the maintenance of a long-term asset base capable of supporting and sustaining the government's commitments to the provision of public services. This reform initiative is premised on the assumption that the public sector can benefit from private sector project management and fund raising expertise.

As Burns and Baldvinsdottir have demonstrated in Chapter 6 of this book, the roles of management accountants and management accounting systems have changed significantly over recent years in the private sector – moving from basic scorekeeping activities to functions of a more strategic or consulting orientation, with management accountants playing key roles in process-oriented management teams. According to Burns and Baldvinsdottir, management accountants have to understand the complexities of, and connections between, business processes. They need a broad knowledge of business and management issues and routinely have to apply their technical accounting knowledge in different organisational contexts and settings. In short, management accountants are becoming more proactive and strategic, concerned with both financial and non-financial performance measurement and seeking to contribute towards ongoing business development and value-creation.

The changes in resource management processes advocated and generated by new public management (NPM) reforms have significant implications for management accounting and the role of management accountants working in public sector organisations. Accounting systems and processes are being assigned a more prominent role in the management of public services, both in short-term operational and longer-term capital investment decision-making. According to Coombs and Jenkins (2002) such a change has presented both challenges and opportunities for public sector accountants (who must be able to provide financial advice to service providers) and for public service managers (who are increasingly required to make financial decisions regarding the services for which they are responsible). Much of the existing literature on NPM reforms has focused on performance measurement and the monitoring of the day-to-day provision of public services, while studies of public sector capital investment have concentrated on overall questions of value-for-money, risk-transfer and the political influences on the financial accounting treatment of expenditure incurred through such schemes (see Broadbent and Laughlin, 2004; Edwards *et al.*, 2004). Research has generally highlighted the unintended consequences and contradictions of public sector financial management initiatives and the need for public sector managers, politicians and other stakeholders to use public sector performance information with care and discretion (for an international review, see Guthrie *et al.*, 2005). However, there has been relatively little analysis of the organisational implications of PPP reforms for public sector management accountants. This is a surprising omission given the large-scale capital investment commitments being made through such initiatives and the significant consequences for the reputation of public sector organisations if such investment projects are mismanaged.

This chapter provides such an analysis and, in the process, highlights the important role of the management accountant in contemporary public sector organisations. It also emphasises several key issues about which public sector management accountants and students need to be suitably informed. In the next section we provide a brief overview of the NPM reform movement and the growing international scale and significance of PPP arrangements. Sections three and four focus on the PPP procurement process and the associated involvement of, and challenges for, public sector management accountants. The chapter closes with some reflections on the nature of PPPs and their potential implications for the future role and status of the public sector management accounting function.

New public management and the development of PPPs

The changes witnessed in the public sector over the past three decades are commonly referred to as new public management (NPM). This umbrella term is used to describe a set of reforms undertaken by various governments across the world to shift the focus of public management away from legalistic concerns with stewardship and towards efficient and effective service delivery. While definitions of what NPM entails differ, according to Hood (1995) it can be distinguished by the following doctrines: (i) hands-on professional management, (ii) explicit standards and measures of performance, (iii) emphasising output controls, (iv) shifting to disaggregated operating units, (v) greater competition in the public sector, (vi) promoting private sector styles of management practice, and (vii) stressing greater discipline and parsimony in resource use. Some authors have highlighted the financial emphasis within NPM. Olson *et al.* (1998), for instance, identified five specific forms of new public financial management (or NPFM) reform, including the introduction of new financial reporting systems, the development of commercially minded, market-oriented management systems, the development of performance measurement systems, the promotion of devolved budgets, and changes to both internal and external public audits (p. 18). The importation of commercially based accounting practices and the use of key performance indicators has also led to such reforms being described as the 'accountingization' of the public sector (Hood, 1995), reflecting an era of governmental management rooted in financial technologies (Humphrey *et al.*, 2005).

Historically, public administrative traditions (rooted in a culture of compliance with the administrative rules and procedures that govern the commitment and authorisation of public sector funds) meant that government departments had relatively basic management accounting systems and were consequently not well placed to keep up with the pace of NPM reforms (Funnell and Cooper, 1998). Such reforms have necessitated the provision of more accounting information for planning and control purposes, in turn generating significant increases in the number of accountants employed in the public sector. Internationally, Australia, New Zealand, Sweden and the UK have generally been considered to be in the vanguard of new public management developments, although they do exhibit different tendencies in terms of the promotion of particular reforms and their commitments to notions of a welfare state (see Guthrie *et al.*, 2005). Other countries including France, the Netherlands and Canada have also witnessed significant change in processes of public sector management.

There are problems and dangers in ranking countries in terms of levels of development, or in assuming that those in the 'vanguard' of NPM developments have the most 'advanced' public sector management systems (Olson *et al.*, 1998). Nevertheless, it is fair to say that in most countries where NPM reforms have gained a foothold, the development path has tended to focus initially on the management and control of operational expenditure and the daily provision of public services. Accordingly, the NPM mantra has been very much about setting organisational objectives and targets, measuring and monitoring performance in accordance with key indicators, and taking corrective action where necessary. The related financial management processes have focused on cost-improvement programmes, efficiency scrutiny, competitive tendering for public service contracts, value-for-money and best value audits, service inspections, financial and non-financial performance indicators or even 'comprehensive' performance assessment schemes, resource or accrual accounting, devolved planning and budgeting, and delegated management systems. Academically, such developments have been accompanied by a growing public sector management literature. This literature has either encouraged and promoted NPM/NPFM developments in countries yet to apply them or, in contrast, been very critical of such developments. Generally, critics have highlighted the evident tensions in NPM/NPFM reforms. These include the degree to which the reforms are: enabling or controlling; devolving or centralising; under- or over-auditing; delivering on their promises or dominated by unintended consequences; and/or aided by a privileged status through which implementation problems are assumed away as teething troubles, rather than being acknowledged as fundamental problems of design (for reviews, see Humphrey *et al.*, 1993; Guthrie *et al.*, 2005).

The above literature has tended to focus on the implications of NPM/NPFM reforms for public sector managers rather than public sector management accountants. For example, critiques have sought to ensure that public sector officials coming fresh to accounting-based reforms are sufficiently sensitive to the sheer power, subjectivity and contextually dependent nature of accounting practice and the dysfunctional consequences that can arise if accounting information is relied on excessively. Empirical evidence has also reported instances of qualified public sector accountants challenging the growing managerial reliance on particular forms of accounting information, and emphasised how easy it is to misinterpret and misuse such information (Guthrie *et al.*, 2005).

In this chapter, we use the vehicle of PPPs to reflect on the changing role of the public sector management accountant. While PPPs are a relatively new venture, significant capital expenditure is being committed to such projects. For instance, work published by PricewaterhouseCoopers (2005) found that internationally 206 PPP projects were contractually finalised during 2004 and 2005 (to a value of US$52bn); with 152 of them being in Europe (totalling US$21bn). Many countries develop PPPs in the transport sector and later extend their use to other sectors such as education, health, energy, water and waste treatment (PricewaterhouseCoopers, 2005, p. 35). While there is international diversity in the form and operation of PPPs (Abadie and Howcroft, 2004, pp. 11–12), it is clear that the UK is developing them at a rate unrivalled by other countries (HM Treasury, 2000a; OECD, 2002). It is estimated that from January 1994 to September 2005, of the US$120bn invested worldwide in PPPs, two-thirds related to UK deals (PricewaterhouseCoopers, 2005, p. 37). Although, the empirical focus of this chapter is on the development of PPPs in the UK, the messages for public sector management accountants are of international relevance, particularly given the growing international interest in PPPs. HM Treasury (2000a, p. 9), for instance, has suggested that more than 50 countries have consulted them to learn from the UK experience with PPPs.

Launched in the UK by the Chancellor of the Exchequer in 1992, PPPs (then referred to more specifically as the PFI) were heralded by the government as a new way of delivering and paying for high quality, but cost-effective, public services. As part of the government's modernisation programme, PPPs have been promoted as an important way of addressing the claimed deterioration and disinvestment in infrastructure assets (evidenced by run-down schools, hospitals, motorway, etc.) and countering rising public borrowing levels and cash accounting problems (OECD, 2002). English (2004, p. 2) states that 'the term PPP refers to a complex long-term contractual arrangement involving the provision of services that require the construction of infrastructure assets'. PPPs differ from conventional contracts, wherein the private sector is paid to construct an asset while separate contracts are undertaken for its ongoing maintenance and operation (see Select Committee on Public Accounts, 2003). PPPs usually involve the private sector providing a 'bundle' of services such as designing, building and operating a prison or a hospital for a contractual period, after which certain assets and the provision of certain services are handed over to the public sector (Webb and Pulle, 2002). Broadbent and Laughlin (2004) identified four main forms of PPPs: build-own-transfer (BOT), build-own-operate (BOO), build-own-operate-transfer (BOOT) and design-build-finance-operate (DBFO). The form of a PPP depends on several factors including the government's objectives and its desired balance of public–private control, the nature of the project, the availability of public finance, and the expertise and skills transferable from the private sector (Webb and Pulle, 2002). In the UK, DBFO schemes are said to be the most common form of PPPs (Broadbent and Laughlin, 2004).

PPP projects are supposed to overcome many of the weaknesses of previous infrastructure projects (wherein new assets were delivered late and often over budget) by increasing competition and sharing the risk between the public and private sectors – with contractual arrangements designed to offer the potential for long-term value for money (VFM) and gains from innovation (see Froud, 2003). Private sector competition, for instance, is said to enhance incentives for delivering high quality services, with PPPs reported to deliver savings of 17 per cent compared with traditional procurement routes (HM Treasury, 2000a). PPPs also enable government projects to be brought forward, because they require less up-front borrowing. Instead, the private sector, as a minimum, finances the initial cost of infrastructure, with the public sector making agreed payments (or 'unitary charges') to the contractors over the life of the contract. These can be likened to lease payments. The typical PPP arrangement is designed so that the private sector bears the costs of developing the assets and the public sector begins to pay only when the asset is operational. Such annual payments or charges will be higher than would be expected under an equivalent (traditionally public sector) procured project, but the avoidance of the capital construction costs is, in theory, supposed to make the PPP option less expensive.

Since the PPP's inception, the UK government has committed itself to 677 projects valued at £ 42.7bn. These projects include prisons, hospitals, sports and leisure facilities, transport assets and urban regeneration schemes. For 2005/06, the total PPP investment was set to rise to 2.1 per cent of GDP (HM Treasury, 2003a). PPPs follow the spirit of other NPM reforms, which assume that the private sector can provide the most efficient and effective services in the form of capital construction projects and/or the operation of public services. Starting from this premise, one could expect the 'ideal' PPP arrangement to be one that maximises the role of the private sector provider, with the public sector specifying the expected outputs and the private sector operating without further interference and free from traditional public sector problems and constraints. However, since the risks associated with the delivery of such services ultimately remains with the public sector, procurers are required to ensure that the private sector contractors focus on service quality. Failure to meet the required governmental PPP standards results in a range of penalties, including payment deductions or even termination of the contract.

It is often said in UK governmental and public service circles that, when it comes to public sector capital investment programmes, PPPs are really the 'only show in town' (Maltby, 2003). Given the political overtones associated with PPPs (evident in both professional and academic reports – see ACCA, 2002; Edwards *et al.*, 2004; Flinders, 2005) and the long-term financial commitments in such ventures, public sector management accountants need to be fully aware of the nature of PPP projects and the demands placed on them. For instance, if PPP schemes are described by vocal critics as 'expensive, inflexible and . . . adding to the current financial burdens (of public sector organisations)' (Blitz, 2006, p. 3), questions are likely to be asked of the public sector management accountants contracting and working with such project partners. The remainder of this chapter addresses these matters. It focuses first on the procurement of PPPs and then explores the implications that procurement, project management and evaluation processes present for public sector management accountants.

PPP investment appraisal

The official overriding procurement rule for a PPP project is that it should be pursued only when it is likely to offer better VFM. VFM is the term that describes 'the optimum combination of whole-life cost and quality (or fitness for purpose) to meet the user's requirement' (HM Treasury, 2000b, Annex 22.1, para. 2). This optimum is said rarely to equate to the lowest-priced project (Office of Government and Commerce, 2002). HM Treasury's VFM assessment guidance suggests that a PPP should be considered only in cases where the following criteria have been met (adapted from HM Treasury, 2004a, section 1.17, p. 7):

- the project is a major capital investment programme, requiring the effective management of risks associated with construction and delivery;
- the private sector has the expertise to deliver and there is good reason to think it will offer VFM;
- the structure of the service is appropriate, allowing the public sector to define its needs as service outputs that can be adequately contracted for in a way that ensures effective, equitable, and accountable delivery of public services into the long term, and where risk allocation sharing between public and private sectors can be clearly made and enforced;
- the nature of the assets and services identified as part of the PFI scheme are capable of being costed on a long term, whole-of-life basis;
- the value of the project is sufficiently large to ensure that procurement costs are not disproportionate;
- the technology and other aspects of the sector are stable, and not susceptible to fast-paced change;
- planning horizons are long term, with assets intended to be used over long periods into the future; and
- there are robust incentives for the private sector to perform.

In the UK, VFM analysis is conducted in three stages: the investment programme level assessment, the project level assessment, and the procurement level assessment.

Stage 1: the investment programme level assessment

The starting point in the procurement process involves identifying those services that may be supplied using a PPP. Specific consideration should be given to whether a PPP is likely to produce the requisite outcomes and offer VFM, or whether alternative procurement routes will offer better VFM. According to Watson (2004) this can include construction, maintenance and provision of a service or the ongoing provision of a service using existing infrastructure. In the UK, IT/ICT procurements and individually procured projects valued at under £20m are deemed unsuitable for a PPP (HM Treasury, 2004a). The government recommends a combination of qualitative and quantitative approaches for the investment programme level assessment. The recommended qualitative assessment guidelines focus on the viability, desirability and achievability of a PPP compared with alternative procurement routes (section 3.11). Viability, as defined in this context, requires an assessment of PPP bids to determine whether there are any efficiency, accountability or equity issues that necessitate government (i.e. non-private sector) delivery. Assessments should also include non-financial factors, including the impact of each project on different individuals or societal groups based on income, gender, ethnicity, age, geographic location or disability (HM Treasury Taskforce, undated). Assessments of desirability require a consideration of the benefits and disadvantages of the various procurement alternatives, including traditional procurement methods. Achievability is measured through an investigation of the level of likely market interest and the management capabilities of the respective bidders (including their ability to design quality infrastructure and to deliver long-term quality services).

For the quantitative assessment, accountants are asked to prepare high-level estimates for the procurement programme including estimates of the values for the capital and operating costs, adjusted for 'optimism bias' and/or specific risks. Optimism bias is the term used to describe the risk that cost and benefit estimates are over-optimistic. These estimates should be based, as far as possible, on the evidence of past procurements. It should be noted, however, that the reliability of PPP outcome assessments has been questioned, with attention drawn to the pressures on politicians to show they are improving public services and the obvious short-term attractiveness of commission now–pay later capital investment projects (for further discussion, see Webb and Pulle, 2002).

Stage 2: the project level assessment

The second step in the procurement process is to confirm that the projects pursued under an investment programme meet VFM criteria and that sufficient market conditions (i.e. quality bidders) exist for the submission of VFM bids. This stage also provides advice on which project procurement route, including traditional ones, offers the best VFM. The project level assessment, like the investment programme level assessment, comprises both quantitative and qualitative elements. The qualitative element assesses each project's ability to meet the criteria of viability, desirability and achievability. For the quantitative assessment, accountants are asked to calculate more specific estimates of the capital and operating costs of each project using the public sector comparator (PSC). The PSC utilises net present value (NPV) methodology to determine the proposed project's likely cost if it was undertaken in the public sector, based on the type of delivery and best practice. This cost normally comprises four components: (i) the raw PSC, (ii) the transferable risk, (iii) the retained risk, and (iv) the competitive neutrality adjustment. The raw PSC incorporates the capital expenditure (e.g. preliminary costs, material and labour costs, professional costs, a contingency fund and any taxes), life cycle and operating costs (e.g. cleaning and catering, insurance costs) expected if the public sector constructed, owned, maintained and delivered the service over the contractual period. Transferable risk refers to risks that the government would typically bear under the traditional approach, but which are likely to be transferred to the private sector under a PPP. Retained risk refers to the risk that the government will sustain under a PPP contract. Finally, the competitive neutrality adjustment recognises any competitive advantage the government may benefit from through (existing) government ownership (such as cheaper finance). When the net discounted cost saving of the PSC exceeds the net discounted cost of the PPP option, the PPP alternative is said to offer VFM (National Audit Office, 1999). It is particularly important that such decision-making processes give sufficient consideration to whole-life values and sustainability issues. Indeed, the Office of Government and Commerce (see www.ogc.gov.uk) emphasises that initial construction costs will usually only represent 2–3 per cent of a project's total life cycle cost.

Stage 3: procurement level assessment

The final stage in the PPP procurement process is for contractors to be invited to submit an expression of interest. The submissions are shortlisted based on their ability to deliver the proposed facility/service and a VFM analysis is then conducted on each bid. Here, consideration should be given to the financial viability of each bid, the capability of the bidders to deliver the tendered facility/service and the appropriate sharing of risk. Since 2004, to simplify the process the UK government has mandated the use of a quantitative evaluation tool (in the form of a spreadsheet) for testing VFM procurement alternatives (HM Treasury, 2004a). In making a final decision, the procuring department will usually ask why any one bid is preferred, what the options are for allocating risk, how continued VFM can be demonstrated in the absence of periodic re-tendering of the service, and whether the project will be able to continue to demonstrate VFM should changes be made in the contract (e.g. the delivery of new buildings or the closure of buildings over the life of the contract).

Key issues for public sector management accountants in the procurement, management and evaluation of PPPs

The contractual basis of PPP arrangements has introduced new dimensions and relationships into the delivery of public services and has important implications for processes of public sector management and management accounting. The scale and complexity of PPPs as a form of service delivery provides both challenges and opportunities for how management accounting information is used in public sector organisations, including how it can help to improve the efficiency and effectiveness of service delivery.

For instance, capital investment appraisal techniques that may seem relatively straightforward in a private sector context are made more complex because they have to consider potentially wide-ranging public sector VFM criteria. Performance measurement is complicated by the imprecise objectives emanating from multiple public sector stakeholders. Despite such complexity and challenges, the impact of PPP contracts on the design of management accounting systems remains under researched. The work that does exist routinely highlights issues that public sector management accountants need to debate. For instance, Broadbent *et al.* (2004), in work commissioned by CIMA, argued for the development of more proactive post-project evaluation (PPE) systems, focusing on a clear quantification of costs and transferred risk and the management of such matters over the life of the project. In other work, they have highlighted the need to assess what the terms VFM and risk represent and how they are operationalised in the context of PPPs across different parts of the public sector (see Broadbent and Laughlin, 2004, 2005). Froud and Shaoul (2001) noted significant problems in the appraisal and evaluation of PPPs. Using *ex post facto* evaluations of two case studies of failed information technology PPPs, Edwards and Shaoul (2003) called into question how project risk was shared between contracting parties. Similarly, a briefing report by the ACCA (2002) identified a number of PPPs where risk transfer may have been questionable, while Froud (2003) highlighted the limits of management by contract; in particular regarding the government's ability to 'risk manage' the provision of public services over the medium term.

In the UK, the accounting officer is formally responsible for compliance with VFM guidance provided by HM Treasury (2004a, section 2.9). Other Treasury guidance on how best to manage PPP contracts notes that a typical contract management team should possess knowledge of the following areas: the supply conditions and developments in relevant markets; pricing mechanisms; risk management techniques and contingency planning; benchmarking techniques and their application; performance management techniques; quality assurance techniques; and how to forecast future demand (see HM Treasury Taskforce, undated). The ability to identify the principal demand and cost drivers for each service, to analyse contract risks, and to control expenditure are also considered useful. Public sector management accountants are evidently assumed by the government to possess this basic knowledge and the requisite technical and analytical skills. As such, they need to minimise the chances that PPP contracts leave the public sector with deteriorating infrastructure and failing services. It is likely that public sector management accountants will need to develop their technical and analytical skills, including working more closely with engineers to review the relative costs and benefits of PPP tenders, such as the quality of proposed asset design, construction and maintenance. The remainder of this section picks up on this theme by addressing practical management accounting issues associated with PPP projects, such as how to assess the affordability of PPPs, what is involved in the bidding process, and how such new types of business arrangement affect the role of the public sector management accountant.

Assessing the affordability of PPPs

Determining whether a project proceeds is an issue of affordability. Affordability is the term used to describe a department's ability to pay for a project over its life, taking into consideration future income and liabilities. Inaccurate affordability projections increase both the likelihood that new transaction costs will be incurred and the risk that public and private resources will be wasted as a result of poorly maintained assets and inefficient service provision. This is likely to mean that the public sector will be no better off than when it used traditional procurement methods, and when a lack of government commitment to future spending on maintenance supposedly resulted in poorly preserved fixed assets and inefficient service provision. Budgetary constraints faced by public sector departments could pressure managers into making suboptimal budget decisions, including accepting PPP projects that are unlikely to deliver VFM over the life of the contract. It is surprising, therefore, that issues of affordability have been rarely debated in the PPP literature. Public sector management accountants need to be sensitive to the fact that their organisation may take a sub-optimal short-term perspective – choosing a project that will meet immediate service demands but ultimately lead to higher project maintenance costs. Strict tests are required to ensure that the PPP is an affordable option over the total life of the project (i.e. including operating and maintenance costs), taking into consideration its impact on the provision of other services and the likely availability of sufficient budgetary funds.

Managing the bidding process

Public sector management accountants involved with PPP bidding processes need to recognise that enough quality bidders must be attracted to ensure the chosen bid will be competitive and deliver VFM. PPP tendering processes can be notoriously lengthy, tying up government resources and delaying the implementation and provision of services. Delays in decision-making and preparing the contractual documentation, and a lack of standardisation may increase the transaction costs for private enterprises wishing to engage in the tendering process. For instance, bidding for a £ 350 million PPP hospital in East London collapsed because of the high costs involved with preparing the bid (Gates, 2005). Howard (2002) also explains that when bidding, firms should consider incorporating the cost of preparing contracts that they have not been awarded. Such costs can be substantial – in 2004, for example, the cost of design, planning, legal and financial work undertaken during the bidding process was estimated to be £ 400m (Gates, 2004). In response to these problems, the UK's Private Finance Panel has recently attempted to reduce such transaction costs by developing standard contractual templates for PPP agreements.

Measuring VFM

The introduction of PPP is based on the premise that such schemes will achieve VFM through (i) competition, (ii) more innovative design solutions, (iii) new ways of providing services and (iv) reducing the cost of service delivery by allocating risk to the party best able to bear it. Since bad procurement decisions could have far-reaching implications for the future provision of public sector infrastructure and services, public sector management accountants need to do their best to ensure that VFM assessments are accurate, particularly given that a National Audit Office (2001) report pinpointed cost estimation and control weaknesses as a significant problem in PPP processes.

That said, they should also be aware that VFM interpretation is subjective and continues to be a significant issue for governments and departments who promote and commission PPPs. This can be best illustrated by considering the 'public sector comparator' (PSC), a critical element in the assessment of PPP bids. The PSC is based on best practice assumptions, which can be particularly problematic for monopoly type assets or innovative investment programmes where best practice benchmarks are not available and cost profiles are unknown. Being based on NPV principles, the PSC is supposed to adjust the capital and operating costs of a proposed PPP for 'optimism bias' and any expected transaction costs. However, it has been hampered by inaccurate estimates of project costs and benefits and is said to depend heavily on the professional judgement/manipulation of those responsible for its preparation (Heald, 2003).

Contracts that have officially suffered from 'poor' VFM analysis include Dartford and Gravesham Hospital, Airwave, MOD Main Building and the West Middlesex Hospital (see House of Commons Committee of Public Accounts, 2002, p. 8). According to the Select Committee on Public Accounts, some PSCs:

> have contained material errors and omissions. Others have been given a spurious precision as a result of over-complexity, a preoccupation with financial modelling, and a failure to take account of uncertainties. Some PSCs have been manipulated to get the desired result. (Select Committee on Public Accounts, 2003, p. 19, pt. 3)

The Treasury has also stated that 'the PSC is focused only on the narrower benefits and disbenefits of the future project options and is often done at a stage where it is not possible to take sufficient account of the wider factors around pursuing a PPP procurement programme, such as pre-contract costs' (HM Treasury, 2003a, para. 7.8, p. 80). The National Audit Office has similarly noted that, in some cases, procuring authorities have treated the PSC too narrowly as a pass/fail test to justify their choice of PPP procurement option (see HM Treasury, 2003a, para. 7.9, p. 80).

With HM Treasury (2003b, p. 26) relying on the NPV as 'the primary criterion for deciding whether government action can be justified', it is also apparent that PPP procurement decisions can depend on chosen discount rates. As Broadbent and Laughlin (2005, note 10) emphasised, many existing PPP projects would not have been considered to offer VFM if they had been assessed on the post-2003 recommended discount rate of 3.5 per cent rather than the 6 per cent rate previously recommended by the Treasury (see HM Treasury, 1997). This is because the stream of payments to the PPP contractor would have been discounted at a lower rate, making the present value of these project costs higher and the NPV of the PPP correspondingly lower (and less attractive). Joe Grice, Chief Economist and Director, Public Services had argued that the 3.5 per cent rate provides a better reflection of the cost of a project because it 'unbundles the discount rate. . .based on the social time preference' (HM Treasury, 2003b, preface, p. v).

To demonstrate VFM, the total risk of each project must be identified and compared with traditional procurement methods. Ideally, the party bearing the risk should be the one that can best manage it at the least cost. The allocation of too much risk to the private sector, or inaccurate calculations of risk, can leave the public sector having to bear financial losses when the private partner goes out of business and cannot provide the required services. The nature of the PPP contract also implies a range of other risks beyond design and construction and operating risks, including demand (or volume/usage) risks, residual value risks, technology and obsolescence risks (including taxation and planning permission), optimum bias risks, and project financing risks. Public sector management accountants charged with risk management need to take a broad based perspective when constructing or assessing the respective costs and benefits of proposed capital investment projects.

HM Treasury (2003a) emphasised that public sector managers need to be aware of the qualitative and non-financial risks associated with a PPP project, commenting that: 'the financial appraisal is just one part of a project's VFM . . . public sector managers should in future ensure that VFM decisions are not based on one-dimensional comparisons of single figures' (para. 7.9, p. 80). To address this concern, guidance was recently provided on the evaluation of differences in the quality of construction or services (HM Treasury, 2004a).

In theory, PPPs are designed so that most of the project risk is transferred to the private sector. But in practice, many contract negotiations appear to struggle with the issue of risk transfer. For instance, in a survey of contractors and authorities engaged in PPP projects, the National Audit Office (2001) reported that only two-thirds of respondents believed risks had been transferred appropriately. Furthermore, it was reported that 79 per cent of authorities were totally satisfied with the risk allocation compared with just 53 per cent of contractors, suggesting that rather more risk is being allocated to contractors than some critics of PPP schemes have suggested (National Audit Office, 2001, p. 7, para. 1.13).

The length of most PPP contracts means they are likely to be varied in the future to address changed circumstance. For instance, the National Audit Office (2003, p. 12) suggests that such variations may involve commissioning extra building work or modifying how other assets are being used. Such contractual changes could reduce the VFM of the contract and need to be accounted for in any project evaluation. Presentation is also a crucial issue here. Whilst managers of PPP contracts may be responsible for deciding which project yields the highest VFM, they are less likely to be expert in assessing such information, so it is important that public sector management accountants present such information logically and clearly, detailing the relevant issues, costs and benefits of each option (for more guidance, see HM Treasury, 2004a). This is particularly pertinent given Froud and Shaoul's (2001) finding that renegotiation costs, which arise when contracts are changed, have been excluded from PPP cost calculations.

Managing PPP costs

Ideally, PPPs are designed to reduce the risk of capital investment cost overruns; however PPP projects in the UK have so far been largely unsuccessful in this respect. For instance, the Norfolk and Norwich NHS trust overran its budget by 60 per cent and the Jubilee line in London's underground exceeded its £ 2.1bn initial cost estimate by £ 1.4bn and was delivered 2 years late. Changes in the demands of public sector procurers are commonly blamed for such cost overruns (Allen, 2001), which points to the need for further assessment of the budgetary planning and implementation skills of the contract management team in the procurement process.

Poor designs and associated implementation problems have been held out as contributing to significant time and cost overruns, in turn creating negative perceptions of how PPPs are being managed. One lesson learned is that the risk sharing nature of the PPP agreement makes it essential that a joint consideration of the project outcomes supplants the standard dichotomised customer/supplier relationship (Comptroller and Auditor General, 2001). However, achieving a mutually consistent set of project outcomes can be problematic in practice. For instance, there is a considerable contrast between private sector contractors, who seek to achieve returns on invested funds and are used to operating in a competitive market, and public sector organisations. The latter are concerned with minimising risk in the realisation of social goals open to political opinion and political influence and, traditionally, working in arenas where competition has been restricted.

Open-book accounting systems have been advocated as a way of helping the procuring department understand and monitor the contractor's capability to provide the required services (National Audit Office, 2001). Open-book accounting describes the systematic disclosure of cost and performance information between contracting partners – something that requires sensitive handling on the part of public sector management accountants. For private contractors, who traditionally have not been required to divulge performance information beyond the external financial report, open-book accounting systems represent a new level of accountability. They will need to be assured they are not divulging performance information that competitors can access for their own competitive advantage. Caution will be required with respect to the level of detail sought from contractors; too much involvement in the management of a PPP project by the procuring department could transfer risk from the PPP contractor back to the public sector. Care is also needed regarding imposition of penalties when poor performance is revealed by open-book accounting practices, as the public sector organisation will risk destroying its working relationship with PPP contractors (although it clearly has a responsibility to respond to inadequate contractor performance).

A particular problem in managing the PPP relationship arises when multiple private contractors are involved, especially if consortia (also known as special purpose vehicles) are established. The question with such arrangements is: how far down the supply chain should open-book accounting systems operate for effective management of the PPP? As Brewer and Johnson (2004) point out, typical statutory company accounts do not provide the level of detail required for the project method of accounting traditionally used in the public sector. Therefore, consideration must be given to the appropriate level of reporting required for VFM assessments over the life of a PPP project. Experience to date suggests that such issues have received little attention and that, while open-book accounting systems can help, PPP project management has been quite limited.

PPP project performance measurement and evaluation

The economic case for using PPPs in the delivery of public services rests on whether they are delivering the promised VFM, so it is important that the analysis of VFM is both systematic and accurate. Failures here will increase the risk of the public sector entering into contracts where the project under-performs or, more seriously, collapses. Part of the VFM evaluation, therefore, has to involve assessing whether departmental requirements have been clearly specified and translated into measurable outcomes, and whether consideration has been given to the implications of delivery failure. To demonstrate accountability, the British government has emphasised that users of PPP-delivered services should be involved in contract specification, including performance measurement, to ensure that appropriate levels of customer satisfaction are agreed upon and tailored to the needs of users rather than providers (HM Treasury, 2000a).

Under PPP arrangements, the developer or private sector contractor has an incentive to minimise whole-of-life-costs by providing only minimum service standards in the contract. In cases where the PPP asset/infrastructure (e.g. a hospital) is to be transferred to the public sector at the end of the contract, the contract must adequately specify the conditions of transfer. If it doesn't, there is a further incentive to run down the asset in the later years of the contract, leaving future generations of taxpayers to bear a major residual cost from the PPP contract (Corry, 1997). PPP contracts can constrain public sector organisations from shifting funding to meet changes in government priorities, and can be difficult to cancel because of the likely financial penalties. It is, for instance, a concern that at least 1 in 5 authorities in the UK consider the value of PPP contracts to have diminished since their implementation (Select Committee on Public Accounts, 2004).

To achieve VFM, it is advocated that PPPs are subject to rigorous performance evaluation and management to determine whether they are meeting desired performance levels and to keep the project risk to a manageable level. Quantitative data should be available from the financial accounting system, but qualitative measures may require separate measurement and input into the accounting system. Such (internal control) performance measures may be reported externally (in organisational annual reports) in an attempt to satisfy the accountability demands of stakeholders. The collection and review of such performance information is a function that public sector management accountants should expect to perform. Indeed, HM Treasury (2004b) guidance requires the use of a system of performance points, with financial penalties imposed on contractors when points awarded (for poor performance) accumulate beyond a certain threshold. Designing and implementing appropriate key performance measurement systems to assess VFM is not straightforward, however – especially because of inconsistencies in the public/private objectives of PPP projects and the range of accountability demands. How might public sector management accountants rise to such performance management challenges?

Whilst significant efforts in the UK have been directed at establishing pre-decision criteria, it can be argued that far less attention has been directed at the evaluation and monitoring of established PPP projects. (Although the *Guardian* did report in July 2002 that 58 per cent of public bodies had penalised private sector contractors because of poor performance, and a notable recent case saw a fine of around £ 27m imposed on firms contracted to repair and improve the London Tube [BBC, 4 July 2005]). Broadbent *et al.* (2003, 2004) attempted to address this performance assessment gap by developing a proactive, post-project evaluation system to help ensure that projects continue to offer VFM once implemented. This evaluation system focuses particularly on risk allocation, financial management and non-financial features, including culturally related, operational aspects of the PPP project.

The designer of an *ex-post* PPP evaluation system has to consider how much information project managers need to make day-to-day decisions, including improvements in project performance and cost control, and manage the contractual relationship (particularly in cases involving PPP consortia and any associated string of subcontractors). Consideration must also be given to how much performance measurement is needed to hold managers accountable for the operations and outcomes of PPP projects. Contractual parties will have to agree key performance indicators (KPIs) and the financial penalties to be imposed should performance fall below agreed targets. Getting the performance measurement system right can bring important benefits. For example, emphasising the delivery of quality services in a timely fashion may reduce the risk of attracting contracting firms who seek to profit from PPPs by providing low-grade services at minimum cost. An effective performance measurement system can also provide information for learning about the practical benefits and disadvantages of PPPs and 'best-practice' that can be applied in the development and assessment of future PPP projects (HM Treasury, 2004a).

According to the HM Treasury Taskforce (undated, p. 5), the criterion for choosing performance measures is that they should be 'based on the potential significance of impact on the service and risk of occurrence of events'. Common performance targets in the private sector revolve around efficiency, outcomes and the citizen/customer experience. Assessing the 'customer' experience can clearly be difficult in the public sector. Are those receiving public services to be treated as 'customers', or as 'citizens' who receive the services by right? Is the focus on the end-user (e.g. a patient or student) or the person or organisation purchasing such services on their behalf (e.g. a health or local education authority)? One potential way of managing such a situation is to engage in systematic benchmarking – comparing and evaluating products, services and work processes against other businesses or departments. Benchmarking PPP projects could help to ensure that efforts are directed towards service-enhancement rather than cost-cutting strategies. Difficulties arise in identifying suitable benchmarks, however. This could be because such services have previously had no direct private sector comparator, or because visible outcomes do not arise until 10, 20 or 30 years in to the project.

Any PPP performance measurement systems need to be well documented and maintained, since the same contract management team is unlikely to monitor the entire project (HM Treasury Taskforce, undated). It is also likely that the procurement objectives will change over the course of the project, in accordance with shifts in political and social preferences/commitments. Changes in project expectations will mean that project performance indicators may need to be revised. This provides an opportunity for contractors to discard measures where performance is declining, or manipulate indicators to ensure they are seen to be offering the negotiated contract outcomes. The possibilities for such levels of change may, however, be limited, especially once the scope of a very long contractual period has been agreed. For instance, Froud (2003, p. 583) suggests that because of the contractual nature of PPPs, 'the starting position becomes one of what is possible within the existing contract (or what modification can be afforded) rather than how service provision should be reshaped to take advantage of new technology and possibilities and to respond to democratic and political demands'. Certainly, these are questions and concerns that today's active and informed public sector management accountant will have to ensure are addressed by his/her organisation.

Conclusion

This chapter has focused on PPPs to explore some of the important managerial and accountability issues expected to confront today's public sector management accountants. The analysis demonstrates that PPPs, and the need to ensure they deliver the promised VFM, present several important challenges to public sector management accountants. In particular, they need to develop appropriate ways of assessing the affordability of PPP arrangements, determining decision criteria for VFM assessments, developing effective performance measurement systems, and generally managing and evaluating PPP contracts.

The PPP contracting arena is highly political and public sector management accountants, whatever their personal political affiliations, must be sensitive to such a context. In their day-to-day work they are likely to encounter a range of views, from those who see PPPs as undoubtedly good developments to those who, pragmatically, see them as the only way for public sector organisations to secure funding for much needed capital investment projects. They may come across managers, contractors and politicians who are reluctant to measure PPP performance levels, on the basis that the 20–30 year duration of most ongoing PPPs makes it too difficult to determine the realisable benefits. They should also be aware that critics have labelled PPPs as overrated, both in terms of their financial and public service contributions. Indeed, even the Select Committee on Public Accounts (2003) has warned that government departments may enter into PPP contracts without full consideration of the alternatives.

Contractually, public sector management accountants need to be sensitive to the fact that private sector providers who are paid only when the asset is operational may be under pressure to employ methods that will deliver the asset quickly. This may lead to knock-on compromises in terms of design quality, innovation and subsequent asset maintenance costs. Long-term PPP contracts can also leave the public sector having to manage assets that, as a result of demographic changes, may not be best suited to the needs and demands of the local community. Environmentally or socially responsible management accountants need to remember that such 'local' concerns may be of remote interest to the private sector contractor – particularly if the contractor is part of an international corporate group with company headquarters located overseas.

As with their counterparts in the private sector, public sector management accountants have to become increasingly sensitive to commercial considerations and PPP contracts present them with a number of economic challenges and questions. The length of PPP contracts can undermine positive competitive influences in that, once secured, a PPP contract could be in place for up to 60 years before the competitive tendering process becomes available again. Thus, successful contractors know they do not have to maximise service performance, but just ensure that they do not breach their minimum PPP contractual service agreements. Another concern is that the costs involved with the bidding process may dissuade private contractors from entering future bidding processes, with existing tendering parties being assumed to have developed a powerful rapport with the relevant governmental contracting body/department. Public sector management accountants will be placing their organisation (and its associated budgetary and financial position) at considerable risk if they enter PPP negotiations without a considered awareness of the economic incentives and downsides associated with PPP contracts.

In an era where we talk increasingly about the interactions between management and financial accounting, PPPs provide a reminder that public sector management accountants also need to be aware of the financial accounting implications of such contracts. With the increasing promotion of accrual-based budgeting and accounting systems in the public sector, there can be serious knock-on effects (such as increased organisational debt) if PPP contracts have to be incorporated in the organisation's balance sheet. It is crucial that public sector management accountants understand the degree to which contractual risks are being transferred to the private contractor rather than being borne by the public sector.

Finally, given the concerns and controversies associated with PPPs, it is not surprising to find that complex procurement rules govern such projects. Any credible public sector management accountant involved with PPP contracting will need to know these rules and any associated recommendations thoroughly. However, they also need to be aware that PPPs, as with so many NPM or NPFM reforms over the last 20–30 years, can embody numerous contradictions and ambiguities. Any public sector management accountants lacking understanding of such tendencies and the context associated with the promotion of PPPs put themselves and their organisations in potentially exposed positions – particularly given the large scale of many PPP contracts. In the search for a prime example of the value of developing understanding of the theories and practices of management accounting, the case of PPPs has to be a short-priced favourite.

References

Abadie, R. and Howcroft, A. (2004) *Developing Public Private Partnerships in the New Europe,* London: PricewaterhouseCoopers. Available online at: www.pwc.com/Extweb/service.nsf/docid/ 6FDD654BE69A4B3385256BDC00527C30.

ACCA (2002) *The Private Finance Initiative: A Briefing,* London: The Association of Chartered Certified Accountants.

Allen, G. (2001) *The Private Finance Initiative,* House of Commons Library Research Paper 01/117. Available online at: www.Parliament.uk/commons/lib/research/rp2001/rp01-117.pdf.

BBC (2005) 'Tube PPP firms "fined millions"', 4 July. Available online at: http:/news.bbc.co.uk/1/hi/ england/london/4648545.stm.

Blitz, J. (2006) 'PFI deals on six hospitals reignite row', *Financial Times,* 19 August. Available online at: www.ft.com/cms/5/8f12af-11db-a973-0000779e2340.html.

Brewer, P.K. and Johnson, L. (2004) *Partnering in Practice: New Approaches to PPP Delivery,* London: PricewaterhouseCoopers. Available online at: www.pwc.com/extweb/service.nsf/docid/ B23A2E5A5C5DD64C85256F3500501406.

Broadbent, J. and Laughlin, R.C. (2004) 'PPPs: nature, development and unanswered questions', *Australian Accounting Review,* 14(2), 4–10.

Broadbent, J. and Laughlin, R. (2005) 'The role of PFI in the UK Government's modernisation agenda', *Financial Accountability and Management,* **21,** 75–97.

Broadbent, J., Gill, J. and Laughlin, R.C. (2003) 'Evaluating the private finance initiative in the national health service in the UK', *Accounting, Auditing and Accountability Journal,* **16,** 422–45.

Broadbent, J., Gill, J. and Laughlin, R. (2004) *The Private Finance Initiative in the National Health Service: Nature, Emergence and the Role of Management Accounting in Decision Making and Post-decision Project Evaluation,* London: CIMA Research Foundation.

Comptroller and Auditor General (2001) *PPP in Practice: National Savings and Investments Deal with Siemens Business Services, Four Years on,* HC 626, London: The Stationery Office.

Coombs, H.M. and Jenkins, D.E. (2002) *Public Sector Financial Management,* 3rd edn, London: Thomson Learning.

Corry, D. (ed.) (1997) *Public Expenditure: Effective Management and Control,* London: The Dryden Press.

Edwards, P. and Shaoul, J. (2003) 'Partnerships: for better, for worse?' *Accounting, Auditing and Accountability Journal,* **16,** 397–421.

Edwards, P., Shaoul, J., Stafford, A. and Arblaster, L. (2004) *Evaluating the Operation of PFI in Roads and Hospitals,* ACCA Research Report No. 84, London: Certified Accountants Educational Trust.

English, L. (2004) 'Public private partnerships', *Australian Accounting Review,* **14,** 2–3.

Flinders, M. (2005) 'The politics of public-private partnerships', *The British Journal of Politics and International Relations,* **7,** 215–39.

Froud, J. (2003) 'The private finance initiative: risk, uncertainty and the state', *Accounting, Organizations and Society,* **28,** 567–89.

Froud, J. and Shaoul, J. (2001) 'Appraising and evaluating PFI for NHS hospitals', *Financial Accountability and Management,* **17,** 247–70.

Funnell, W. and Cooper, K. (1998) *Public Sector Accounting and Accountability in Australia,* Sydney: University of New South Wales Press.

Gates, C. (2004) '£400m PFI waste', *Building Design,* 5 November. Available online at: www.bdonline.co.uk.

Gates, C. (2005) 'Compensate PFI bidders, urges report', *Building Design,* 22 April. Available online at: www.bdonline.co.uk.

Guardian (2004) 'PFI is a waste of money, say MPs', *Guardian,* 11 July. Available online at: http://society.guardian.co.uk/privatefinance/comment/0,8146,753563,00.html.

Guthrie, J., Humphrey, C., Jones, L.R. and Olson, O. (eds) (2005) *International Public Financial Management Reform: Progress, Contradictions and Challenges,* Greenwich, CT: Information Age Publishing.

Heald, D. (2003) 'Value for money tests and accounting treatment in PFI schemes', *Accounting, Auditing and Accountability Journal,* **16,** 342–71.

HM Treasury (1997) *Appraisal and Evaluation in Central Government: The Green Book,* London: The Stationery Office.

HM Treasury (2000a) *Public Private Partnerships: The Government's Approach,* London: The Stationery Office.

HM Treasury (2000b) *Government Accounting 2000.* Available online at: www.government-accounting.gov.uk.

HM Treasury (2003a) *Meeting the Investment Challenge,* London: The Stationery Office.

HM Treasury (2003b) *The Green Book: Appraisal and Evaluation in Central Government,* London: The Stationery Office.

HM Treasury (2004a) *Value for Money Assessment Guidance,* London: The Stationery Office.

HM Treasury (2004b) *Standardisation of PFI Contracts Version 3,* London: The Stationery Office.

HM Treasury Taskforce (undated) *How to Manage the Delivery of Long Term PFI Contracts,* London: Butterworths.

Hood, C. (1995) 'The "new public management" in the 1980s: variations on a theme', *Accounting, Organizations and Society,* **20**(2–3), 93–109.

House of Commons Committee of Public Accounts (2002) *Delivering Better Value for Money from the Private Finance Initiative,* London: The Stationery Office.

Howard, M. (2002) 'Losing the initiative', *Financial Management,* November, 26–7.

Humphrey, C., Miller, P. and Scapens, R. (1993) 'Accountability and accountable management in the UK public sector', *Accounting, Auditing and Accountability Journal,* **6**(3), 7–29.

Humphrey, C., Guthrie, J., Jones, L.W. and Olson, O. (2005) 'International developments in public sector financial management: a question of progress or a progression of questions, contradictions and challenges?' in J. Guthrie, C. Humphrey, L.R. Jones and O. Olson (eds) *International Public Financial Management Reform: Progress, Contradictions and Challenges,* Greenwich, CT: Information Age Publishing, pp. 1–22.

Maltby, P. (2003) 'PPPs: the only show in town?' *Public Money and Management,* 30, April. Available online at: www.publicnet.co.uk/publicnet/ffeatures.htm.

National Audit Office (1999) *Examining the Value for Money of Deals Under the PFI,* HC 739, Session 1998–99, London: The Stationery Office.

National Audit Office (2001) *Managing the Relationship to Secure a Successful Partnership in PFI Projects,* London: The Stationery Office.

National Audit Office (2003) *PFI: Construction Performance. Report by the Comptroller and Auditor General,* HC 371 Session 2002–2003, London: The Stationery Office.

OECD (2002) OECD Economic Surveys, United Kingdom.

Office of Government and Commerce (2002) *Best Practice: Value for Money Evaluation in Complex Procurements.* Available online at: www.ogc.gov.uk.

Olson, O., Guthrie, J. and Humphrey, C. (1998) *Global Warning: Debating International Developments in New Public Financial Management,* Oslo: Cappelen Akademisk Forlag.

PricewaterhouseCoopers (2005) *Delivering the PPP Promise: A Review of PPP Issues and Activity,* London: PricewaterhouseCoopers. Available online at: www.pwc.com/extweb/pwcpublications.nsf/docid/5D37E0E325CF5D71852570DC0009C39B.

Select Committee on Public Accounts (2003) *Thirty-fifth Report,* London: The Stationery Office.

Select Committee on Public Accounts (2004) *Forty-second Report,* London: The Stationery Office.

Watson, D. (2004) 'The challenge for public accounts committees in evaluating public private partnerships', *Australian Accounting Review,* **14**(2), 78–84.

Webb, R. and Pulle, B. (2002) *Public Private Partnerships: An Introduction,* Research Paper No. 1, 2002–2003, Canberra: Department of Parliamentary Library.

Further reading

Australian Accounting Review (2004), **14**(2) and *Accounting, Auditing and Accountability Journal* (2003), **16**(3). These journal issues are devoted to the accounting implications of PPP.

Guthrie, J., Humphrey, C., Jones, L.R. and Olson, O. (eds) (2005) *International Public Financial Management Reform: Progress, Contradictions and Challenges,* Greenwich, CT: Information Age Publishing. This book reviews international NPM developments.

PricewaterhouseCoopers (2005) *Delivering the PPP Promise: A Review of PPP Issues and Activity,* London: PricewaterhouseCoopers. Available online at: www.pwc.com/extweb/pwcpublications.nsf/docid/5D37E0E325CF5D71852570DC0009C39B. This monograph provides a review of PPP issues.

15

Knowledge resources and management accounting

Hanno Roberts

Introduction

This chapter explores the management accounting implications of the knowledge-based organisation. With many organisations around the world wishing to migrate from an industrial era to a knowledge ('new') economy form of organisation, existing management accounting systems are under scrutiny. The main question is whether we can continue to use our existing management accounting systems in knowledge-based organisations. Answering this question requires an understanding of what knowledge is, how it manifests itself in business activities, and the extent to which knowledge-based organisations actually differ from 'traditional' organisations. It is generally assumed that knowledge can be treated as a competitive resource for the organisation and, thus, accounted for in a comparable fashion to financial or human resources.

The first sections of this chapter examine the varieties of knowledge, asking the question 'what is knowledge?' and discussing knowledge as a resource and as a flow. This discussion leads us to consider knowledge as a possession to be accounted for, and also to consider knowledge as a practice with activities that have to be accounted for. The connection with existing concepts and models of management accounting systems is made in the last section, with special reference to the economic characteristics of knowledge as an organisational resource. We approach the consequences and implications for management accounting by first trying to understand knowledge as a resource and how it develops within the knowledge-based organisation. The various economic characteristics of knowledge as an organisational resource are discussed in terms of their increasing returns to scale, non-scarcity, externalities, incomplete property rights and high development uncertainties. We end with a series of clues about how management accounting concepts and information can support the knowledge-based organisation, concluding that existing tools continue to be useful.

What is knowledge?

The definition of knowledge, both in terms of what it is and how it functions, has been discussed for centuries. Here, we will draw on the Webster dictionary definition of knowledge as 'the act, fact or state of knowing, specifically the acquaintance or familiarity with a fact or a range of information' (1988, p. 748). As this definition implies, knowledge is multi-faceted as it can mean a state or condition, or a process.

This multiple meaning has resulted in many interpretations of the role of knowledge in organisations within the various disciplines. For example, for a pharmaceutical firm involved in new product development knowledge means scientific knowledge, while for a furniture manufacturing company it means the machine-operating experience of its shop floor workers. For the sake of this chapter, we will limit ourselves to interpretations provided by the business administration and management discipline, broadly defined.

Knowledge typologies

The management of knowledge tends to follow the above distinction between knowledge-as-a-state (a stock) and knowledge-as-a-process (a flow). Additionally, knowledge can be classified in terms of its explicit and tacit components, or in terms of individual versus collective carriers. Other classifications typify knowledge in terms of general versus specific, or possessed versus practiced. Each classification is related to a specific perspective on how to interpret and manage knowledge. Some of these classifications and their implications for management accounting are discussed below.

Knowledge as a resource: 'embodied' and 'embedded' knowledge

Knowledge can be embodied in individuals or embedded in the organisation (Blackler, 1995), as shown in Figure 15.1. That is, knowledge can be conceptualised as a stock that is located in the people (embodied) or in the organisation's operating procedures and routines (embedded). Management implications immediately follow from this distinction. The identification of key personnel holding relevant knowledge as, for example, in 'company yellow pages' or 'competence catalogues', or an emphasis on competencies and continuous development and training of personnel are typical manifestations of a focus on embodied knowledge. Similarly, a focus on embedded knowledge directs attention to the efficient storage, maintenance, updating and retrieval of work-related procedures, often with an intensive use of computerised work systems, such as 'best practice databases' or 'customer management protocols'.

The embodied–embedded distinction and the efficient use of an existing knowledge stock are aided by information and communication technologies (ICT). In fact, what is considered to be the 'first generation of knowledge management' originates from this focus on computerised efficiency in knowledge utilisation. Its value proposition is based on making past knowledge ('old learning') more available and reusable for employees throughout the organisation, thus avoiding 'reinventing the wheel'. The basic idea is to share existing knowledge better and thus improve performance.

Knowledge as a flow: 'encultured' and 'embrained' knowledge

Attending to the individual versus collective nature of knowledge, it is also useful to distinguish between 'encultured' and 'embrained' knowledge (Blackler, 1995). Encultured

Emphasis on **knowledge embedded** in technologies, rules and procedures	Emphasis on **encultured knowledge** and collective understanding
Emphasis on collective endeavour (ii) *Knowledge-routinised* organisations: • Typically labour, capital or technology-intensive • Hierarchical division of labour and control Tends to focus knowledge effort on: • Organisational competencies and corporate strategies • Development of computer-integrated work systems *Example:* 'Machine bureaucracy' such as a traditional factory	(iv) *Communication-intensive* organisations: • Communication and collaboration are key processes • Expertise is pervasive and distributed • Empowerment through integration in processes Tends to focus knowledge effort on: • 'Knowledge creation', dialogue, sense-making processes • Development of computer-supported collaborative work systems (CSCW) *Example:* 'Ad hocracy', innovation-oriented production, engineering or software firm
Emphasis on contributions of key individuals Emphasis on the **embodied knowledge** of key members (i) *Expert-dependent* organisation: • Performance of specialist experts is key • Status and power from professional reputation • Strong emphasis on training and qualifications Tends to focus knowledge on: • Development of individual competency • Computer displacement of action skills *Example:* 'Professional bureaucracy' such as a hospital	Emphasis on the **embrained knowledge** of key members (iii) *Symbolic-analyst-dependent* organisation: • Entrepreneurial problem-solving • Status and power from creative achievements • Manipulation of symbols is a key skill Tends to focus knowledge effort on: • Expert systems design and information support • Organisation of the firm, developing symbolic analysts *Example:* Software consultancy

Focus on familiar problems	*Focus on novel problems*

Figure 15.1 Knowledge typology, organisational interpretations and subsequent managerial areas for attention
Source: Adapted from Blackler, 1995, p. 53.

knowledge refers to a *collective* and shared understanding of what is important for the organisation, as well as how the organisation responds and reacts to emerging issues. Encultured knowledge is about communicating what an event actually means and how to create a response; its focus is on communication, stories ('debriefings'), language and continuous exchange.

Embrained knowledge refers to individual conceptual skills and abstract cognitive abilities. The embrained type of knowledge represents a higher level of abstraction than embodied knowledge. The difference between embodied and embrained knowledge lies in the latter's focus on cognitive abilities rather than on operating skills, competencies and other formalised learning.

With respect to encultured knowledge, the communication flow is concurrent with the collaborative flow of people talking and working alongside each other, creating meaning and taking action as two sides of the same coin. A typical ICT manifestation is the increasing popularity of so-called 'groupware' or 'collaborative works systems', which provide both synchronous (immediate) and asynchronous (delayed) communication and interaction facilities online. Continuous communication acts as a proxy for continuous interaction, where the expert knowledge of particular groups is contrasted with opinions and expertise of other groups. It is important to note that expertise in this respect can originate from formal training or experience; in other words, 'encultured' knowledge organisations are not necessarily made up of people with advanced degrees. People with decades of experience working in the industry or firm are equally able to provide alternative interpretations and make sense of their knowledge activities.

The 'brain' part of the term 'embrained knowledge' refers to individual cognitive ability to work with, manipulate and understand abstract symbols and artifacts. Workers with embrained knowledge possess difficult to imitate high-level skills such as problem solving, problem identification, and the ability to broker problems between different fields of expertise. For example, software development firms, accounting firms and management consulting firms all work with abstract expertise such as object-oriented programs, accounting for financial instruments or providing strategic consultancy. For the organisation, working with embrained knowledge (workers) implies a continuous focus on the configuration and integration of different sorts of abstract expertise in the workflow. This implies that the design, documentation and continuous review of work processes are at the core of knowledge management, with its accounting equivalent in the accentuation of activity analysis and costing.

The 'encultured' and 'embrained' knowledge typology addresses an important underlying issue – the different kinds of knowledge creation that can occur within organisations. In the 'embodied–embedded' knowledge typology, knowledge is assumed to be a *resource* that requires efficient utilisation ('exploitation'), with its value proposition being the efficient (re)use of the existing knowledge stock. In contrast, the encultured versus embrained typology refers to knowledge as a *flow*, a relational process that combines existing knowledge into new knowledge. Hence, it is not about better utilisation of inventories of existing knowledge, but about generating new knowledge outcomes. The underlying idea is that the organisation does not improve performance by using the existing stock better, but by delivering new knowledge outcomes (even though these outcomes may be simply new combinations of existing knowledge). In accounting terminology, the former's value proposition is to invest (in ICT and knowledge sharing) in order to eliminate (knowledge) waste and inefficiency – *a cost savings argument*. The latter's value proposition is to invest (in ICT and knowledge production) to produce (knowledge) returns and gains – *a revenue argument*. It connects knowledge and its management clearly to the issue of innovation and the management of the profit and loss statement's top-line.

Depending on what knowledge typology (embedded, embrained, embodied, encultered) and which interpretation (knowledge as possession, knowledge as practice) is used, one can have different opinions on what the knowledge-based organisation is (or ought to be) and how it (should) behave(s), with different implications for management accounting as a result. We now discuss two of these interpretations and their consequences for different aspects of management accounting.

Knowledge as a possession

When organisations consider knowledge as an asset, they tend to engage in the activities of identifying, visualising and measuring this 'invisible asset'. Typical questions are: what knowledge do we (the organisation) actually have, where is it located, and how can we show and measure what we have? Our first reflex is to argue that if knowledge is assumed to be an organisational asset – if not possessed then at least controlled by the organisation – then disciplinary frameworks from accounting and economics can be utilised.

Traditionally, accounting captures some knowledge assets (based on existing definitions and treatments of intangible assets), such as patents, trademarks and other intellectual property rights (IPRs). Typically, in this traditional view, knowledge is understood as an explicit, codified (in IPRs) and tradable object (Amin and Cohendet, 2004, pp. 14–35) to which market mechanisms and economic concepts can be applied. Knowledge can be priced, valued, accumulated and inventoried, processed, aggregated, allocated and costed. In short, knowledge can be treated as an economic good; hence, its quantity and value can be expressed in financial terms.

This line of argument reduces knowledge to information and considers all knowledge as a homogeneous, explicit and tradable good. As a result, knowledge-based organisations are managed and coordinated as knowledge markets. This approach implies the creation of an internal marketplace within the organisation, where all parties have access to full information on who knows what, making possible the exchange of knowledge between individual suppliers and users of knowledge across the organisation. The role of management is limited to setting up the market infrastructure (information access, parties involved, exchange mechanism) and acting as market regulator once the internal knowledge exchange has started. Creating a mechanism for knowledge exchange involves setting transaction standards, establishing an internal regime for intellectual property rights and replication, encouraging competition, setting appropriate pricing mechanisms, and providing a market facilitator or agency (e.g. professional staff that act as a clearing house for knowledge exchanges, (Teece, 1998; von Krogh and Grand, 2002).

The concept of 'knowledge as a possession' aligns well with an accounting perspective. Knowledge can be understood as an intangible asset close to, although not entirely the same as, intellectual property rights (IPRs) and goodwill. This conception triggers a reflex to account for knowledge in a similar manner. The assumption is made that if knowledge is under the control of the organisation, it can be valued as part of the organisation's wealth and priced for sale, and it follows that management accounting treatments can be used. For example, knowledge can be depreciated or costed for its consumption, and the fixed–variable and direct–indirect cost typologies apply, allowing for the computation of knowledge profitability margins and knowledge cost allocations. Moreover, understanding knowledge as an asset permits the use of International Accounting Standards (IAS) and International Financial Reporting Standards (IFRS) to resolve whatever definitional problems might arise. For example, IAS provides rules on when an asset is controlled by the organisation, rules for valuation ('fair value'), rules for measurement, and rules for defining the production or buying of knowledge. Hence, it is both logical and convenient to fall back on financial accounting principles and concepts when accounting for knowledge as a possession.

The problem is that not all knowledge assets of the organisation can be identified, priced and processed as easily as patents (IPRs) or trademarks. As an alternative to traditional accounting, some scholars have tried to capture other types of knowledge resources, which they have grouped into human, relational and structural capital (Bontis, 1999). The term 'capital' implies ownership by the organisation and triggers the use of accounting concepts and tools. Take, for example, the *human capital* component. Undoubtedly, people are the prime generators of new knowledge, as well as important 'carriers' of knowledge. However, people do not figure on the balance sheet, as the organisation does not own them (at least, not since the abolition of slavery). One can claim that the organisation owns their time in terms of yearly production capacity, approximated by wage expenses and labour costs, but, then again, these numbers show up on the profit and loss statement, not on the balance sheet.

Similarly, *relational capital* covers exchange and transactional relations both internally, between organisation members, and externally with suppliers and customers. Relations as such do not appear on the balance sheet as the focus is on economic transactions. However, relationships might have their approximation in the balance sheet item 'business combinations and (minority) interests', which reflects legally constituted bundles of formal relationships.

Structural capital consists of the formal systems (e.g. IT systems), procedures (e.g. purchasing and training procedures) and managerial technologies of the organisation (e.g. budgeting, teamwork, or activity-based costing). Thus, structural capital ties in with a series of costs and expenses that arise as an essential part of an organisation's existence. The items usually included in the structural capital component are best conceived as addressing the embeddedness characteristic of knowledge – i.e. the various procedures, methods and routines of working and communicating used by an organisation to provide the context in which its knowledge is deployed.

It could be concluded that the alternative approach to capturing knowledge as a resource, by decomposing it into human, structural and relational capital, is tied more closely to the concept of knowledge as a practice than to the concept of knowledge as a possession. Bringing the former closer to the latter by means of capitalising this mix of cost categories does not, however, fit well with existing financial accounting and rule-based conceptions of intangible assets. The main reason is the emphasis in the existing financial accounting rules on reliable measurement and unambiguous ownership of the resource, in contrast to the emphasis in the intellectual capital concept on relevance. In financial reporting the tension between the criteria of reliability and relevance is decided in favour of reliability.

The discussion above suggests that accounting for knowledge is perhaps best served by relying on the definition of knowledge as a practice of knowing. Instead of equating knowledge with knowledge as a possession – which in turn equates with conventional intangible assets and their financial accounting-dominated treatment – knowledge as a practice refers to activities and activity management. Accounting for knowledge as a practice implies focusing on what people and organisations actually do with what they have.

Knowledge as a practice

From a more management accounting-oriented perspective, being able to identify the elements that constitute the internal knowledge generation process and to put a financial number on each element, i.e. 'costing' the production of knowledge, would assist in managing it. This approach means adopting an *activity perspective*, with each activity being evaluated in terms of its knowledge generating aspects and elements. Activities can be conceived as 'ways of working', as practices, somewhat similar to the activity perspective adopted in activity-based costing. Adopting an activity perspective implies that doing and knowing are inseparable and that carrying out work activities equals the 'situated production of understanding' (Brown and Duguid, 1991, p. 44), simultaneously using existing knowledge and creating new knowledge. In contrast to the perspective of knowledge as a possession, a perspective of knowledge as a practice is adopted.

Knowing is complementary to, and enabled by, knowledge; we cannot do something without possessing some knowledge, while possessed knowledge needs practice to keep it up-to-date and relevant. Although apparently only of academic interest, the change of perspective from knowledge as a possession to knowledge as a practice has profound consequences for organisations, management and management accounting. By focusing on knowledge as a practice, attention is directed to the activity patterns of individuals and collectives.

The dynamic nature of knowledge is not limited to individuals only. Organisations also engage in continuously producing new knowledge while simultaneously using their existing knowledge. For example, there is knowledge embedded in physical output and in work routines and management procedures, with new knowledge being generated each time these are applied in changing conditions. Integrating both in doing, in 'practising', is of key relevance for the organisation because this approach taps into the organisation's capability to grow and innovate. In short, perceiving knowledge as a practice of knowing (how to work, interact, communicate, etc.) provides an approach to managing it – by focusing on its use.

To understand the role of daily work activities in relation to the dynamics of 'knowing', we can use the iceberg metaphor. Day-to-day work is the visible part of the iceberg above the waterline, subject to well-codified and explicit processes of melting and change. Under the waterline, however, the less well codified knowledge dynamics occur, with people in their everyday activities applying their existing knowledge, both tacit and explicit, while simultaneously creating new knowledge processes and new ways of knowing how to handle different circumstances and conditions. It is in regular work processes that knowledge unfolds itself, which is why the organisation, coordination and management of work are at the heart of the knowledge-based organisation (KBO). By acknowledging the large, underwater part of the iceberg, which every work organisation contains, the organisation undertakes a first step in transforming itself into a KBO. For example, the World Bank calls itself the 'knowledge bank', achieving its mission of alleviating poverty in the world by sharing knowledge and advancing learning, with money lending and project funding being a means to that end. Or, as Zack (2003, p. 69) puts it:

> The knowledge-based organization, regardless of whether its products are tangible, holds a knowledge-oriented image of itself. That is, it takes knowledge into account in every aspect of its operation and treats every activity as a potentially knowledge-enhancing act.

In other words, the management of work processes is not only about task assignment and the division of labour, but just as much about knowledge sharing and knowledge creation. Every organisation has some sort of work organisation, and knowledge activities can be framed as an integral part of day-to-day work activities. For example, knowledge-based practices can be identified by focusing on the moments when people collaborate and share and interpret knowledge.

The recognition that all work to some extent uses existing knowledge and creates new knowledge triggers a different perspective on the identity, means of production, and outputs of an organisation. Such a perspective usually implies a strong(er) service orientation and a redefinition of the organisation's core competencies and key products. Furthermore, customers are not merely perceived as parties in a financial transaction, but also as parties from whom to learn new ways of working and acquire inputs essential to generating new, knowledge-intensive products and services. In the next section, we discuss the implications for management accounting of the perspective of knowledge as a practice.

Accounting for knowledge as a practice

Management accounting is able to support the perspective of knowledge as a practice in several ways. First, it can provide information on the upstream and downstream work processes – for example the costs of purchasing and purchasing systems, and the costs of after-sales support and sales support systems. Scrutinising what knowledge drives these cost categories can open them up for discretionary decision-making. For instance, the repetitive elements of after-sales support constitute a codified knowledge base that could be made to stand alone as a support website. Conversely, the non-repetitive and usually more costly support problems might be handled interactively, involving internal sales or operational staff experts who help in solving the problem, usually creating new knowledge as a result. This new knowledge in itself can provide the basis for new features, knowledge-based services related to the existing product, or even entirely new products, each of which can create new revenue streams.

Second, the activities making up the existing workflow may be part of an activity-based cost system. Identifying which activities are most knowledge-intensive because of, for example, scarce and costly human expertise, allows us to combine accounting information with knowledge management. High salary expenses and high knowledge intensity overlap in directing attention to areas requiring closer monitoring and management intervention.

Third, cost drivers and cost allocation criteria can have a double role, assisting both management accounting and knowledge management. What drives cost can also drive knowledge and, vice versa, the basis for allocating cost can also provide the basis for allocating knowledge (to activities and processes). For example, an allocation criterion such as 'amount of time spent with the customer' can be used for allocating sales cost to cost objects. But it can also be used to distribute the scarce time of internal experts across customers or to suppliers from whom the organisation can learn and thereby enhance the knowledge base and practices of the organisation.

Fourth, management accounting systems can put monetary values on knowledge capacities by using time spent as a cost base. The deployment of different sorts of knowledge will take different amounts of time, as any lawyer or consultant can confirm. Analysing the various time consumption rates for the production of different sorts of knowledge, and assigning costs accordingly, results in different contribution margins for each knowledge 'product', helping to identify the primary kinds of knowledge that drive the organisation's profitability.

Finally, the awareness that the organisation is knowledge-based and shares a common knowledge base with its competitors will have an impact on its key products. Notably, the knowledge locked up in existing products and services becomes easier to identify and can be unbundled and offered as a separate service. This can reach such a scale that a classic product-oriented manufacturing firm could transform itself into a fully fledged service provider, including the accompanying shift in business model. A well-known example is IBM, which realised that its knowledge was not in manufacturing hardware but in how to use that hardware, thus turning itself into a service organisation that is presently the largest consultancy worldwide.

From a management accounting perspective, the impact of acknowledging that the organisation is actually knowledge-based and shares common knowledge with other firms, which are not necessarily in the same conventional industry classification, has two major implications.

First, the role of management accountants as guardians of the financial resources needs to be revised. One can argue that the knowledge base is the ultimate resource, with the financial and human resources as components of it. Expressing consumption and returns on the financial and human resources should ultimately lead to increases (or decreases) in the knowledge resources of the organisation. As a result it would make sense for an individual, who could be labelled the 'resource controller', to manage all three resources under the single heading of Resource Management. Competing on the basis of knowledge would imply managing knowledge in an integrated manner, and not splitting its coordination across functional areas such as finance, personnel and IT.

Second, the unifying element that allows all three resource areas to work together might not be the financial common denominator but, instead, the common denominator of time. Human resources and financial resources can already be well expressed in terms of time, for example duration of time consumption. Knowledge resources also can be expressed in terms of time, perhaps even better than they can be expressed in terms of money. For example, out-competing other firms on the basis of a continuous flow of new products exemplifies a fast-moving and accelerated pace of knowledge activities. Given that the proper use of knowledge often comes down to timing, i.e. choosing the right moment, management accountants can assist in preparing, for example, time-based budgets and suggesting activity-based cost drivers based on time consumption.

Additional considerations: the economic characteristics of knowledge

Any attempts to account for and manage knowledge have to consider the economic characteristics of knowledge:

- knowledge is a non-scarce (ubiquitous) resource;
- knowledge externalities exist;
- knowledge has incomplete property rights, resulting in spillovers and partial excludability;
- knowledge has high development uncertainty.

Following Lev (2001), the first two economic characteristics (non-scarcity and externalities) can be considered the two major drivers of benefits from knowledge, while the last two characteristics can be considered the major cost drivers of knowledge. Each of the above characteristics will be discussed below with respect to its management accounting implications.

The non-scarcity or ubiquity of knowledge is sometimes also understood as its non-rivalry. It means that knowledge can be used simultaneously for multiple purposes in contrast to, say, a physical or human resource. The time spent by an engineer or group of engineers, or the work done by a production facility, excludes simultaneous use for another purpose. Similarly, flying an airplane on a certain route, although it is a knowledge-intensive practice, excludes ('rivals') its use on another route. However, the reservation system of the airline, a knowledge-based asset of accumulated, codified and bundled practices, can be used at the same time and next to a number of appropriately trained reservation staff; the 'reservation knowledge resource' utilisation does not exclude one use from the other.

From a management accounting perspective, this kind of non-scarcity (or non-rivalry) has three implications. First, knowledge resources have high fixed, sunk costs for their initial investment, followed by zero (or very low) marginal cost. Once the airline reservation system is in place, usually at a substantial cost, the subsequent cost for each reservation is close to zero. As indicated above, the knowledge resource is not subject to diminishing returns to scale as traditional assets are. This is a major value driver for the individual organisation, as it means that knowledge returns are almost unlimitedly scalable; the only limit basically being the size of the market, not the asset's capacity. This cost behaviour of high fixed, sunk cost and zero incremental cost combines with the issue of knowledge investment appraisal. Typically, investment appraisal (capital budgeting) uses a discounted cash flow method to estimate future benefits, conventionally assuming that future benefits will decrease over time, whereas investments in knowledge assets have increasing cash flows over time with the increase based on estimates of the market size (and extent of use).

A second implication is that the revenue streams from non-scarce or non-rivalrous knowledge assets would benefit from being clearly separated out from revenue streams from conventional, scarce (rival) assets and resources (physical assets or human assets). These revenue streams can be separated by singling out the corresponding resources as standalone assets, either by unbundling them from the product or service they are sold with, or by placing them into separate organisational or accounting vehicles (e.g. organisational units or separate legal entities that can be securitised). An example of unbundling the knowledge resource and making its separate revenue streams identifiable can be found in after-sales service. Instead of selling access to after-sales engineers or specialist staff as part of the original purchase price (a bundled product including the scarce resource of human experts), after-sales service can be split into a separately priced access to human experts and an online, permanently accessible knowledge base of FAQs (frequently asked questions), the latter being a typical, non-rivalrous asset. Once customers are provided with the opportunity to input their experiences (knowledge), the knowledge resource of the organisation actually starts to grow autonomously.

This brings us to the third implication of the non-scarcity of knowledge resources, the unlimited scalability of the knowledge productivity contribution. The inputs by customers on an after-sales support website allow the organisation to learn and improve its original knowledge base. Even when the feedback is negative, the knowledge gained by the organisation enables it to improve and develop better services and products. In other words, the knowledge accumulation provided by the market drives the value creation of the individual organisation. In practical terms, this means that unbundling the non-rivalrous knowledge resource from the conventional resource in the product or service offered, needs to be followed up by combining the knowledge gained from the market with the internally accumulated knowledge. Thus, the increasing marginal productivity of every investment in the knowledge resource can be guaranteed, if the combinatory value of the knowledge investment is fully acknowledged.

Knowledge externalities are based on the network design of knowledge practices, particularly the networked flow of knowledge sharing. Externalities consist of benefits derived from being part of a network: the larger the network, the greater the benefit for the individual participant. In other words, bigger is better. Examples include the use of computer operating software such as MS-DOS or Windows, or the use of a particular mobile phone network: the more people who use the same system or telephone network, the more benefit there is for the individual consumer using that system or network, because there are more people to access or interact with. Similarly, increased network size leads to more applications, support services and additional functions being developed for it, thus further enhancing the benefits of becoming a member of that network. This form of accelerating positive feedback means that success leads to success, and revenue streams are almost guaranteed once the network has reached a certain size threshold.

From a management accounting perspective, the existence of network externalities of the knowledge resource implies that high upfront costs (in building the externalities around the knowledge resource) are a cost behaviour feature to be acknowledged, with most of these costs being sunk costs. This argument aligns with the high fixed cost and low marginal cost of the previously discussed non-scarcity characteristic. Moreover, the network externalities characteristic of the knowledge resource mean that costs of partnering and alliance building are to be conceived as investments in future value. The drivers of this value are the extent and speed of adding network participants/users to the existing network base. In other words, the cost of user acquisition equals the cost of getting a revenue stream out of the organisation's knowledge resource. A non-trivial aspect is the importance of the time dimension – gaining network externalities on the knowledge resource is a race against time. Having the funds, and acknowledging the heavy spending needed to accelerate market share gain over a set period of time, are both necessary conditions for reaping benefits from knowledge-based value creation.

The major cost drivers of knowledge

The two key economic characteristics that drive the value to be gained from the knowledge resource – non-scarcity/scalability and network effects/positive feedback – are one part of the cost–benefit trade-off in managing the knowledge resource. The management accounting implications basically play out in the revenue 'top-line' of the profit and loss statement, and in the cost behaviour patterns underlying knowledge-based value creation.

The cost side of the trade-off is more singularly focused on typical cost and expenditure categories that originate from deploying the knowledge resource – i.e. from doing something with what one knows. For many organisations, the cost side is the first issue they consider, mainly because the cost implications immediately follow from equating the knowledge resource with conventional intangible assets.

Managing conventional intangible (knowledge) assets is difficult and costly to begin with, due to the imperfect definitions and enforcement of existing intellectual property rights. Therefore, managing non-conventional (knowledge) assets can only be more difficult and expensive. Conventional intangible assets are hard to manage because, in economists' terms, investments in the knowledge resource are only partially excludable and have spillovers (Lev, 2001). That is, other people and organisations cannot be fully prevented from enjoying some of the benefits of investments in, say, specialist training or MBA education. Once a trained employee leaves the original organisation, such benefits can spill over from investments in knowledge assets to non-owners of the knowledge resource. Attempts by organisations to limit spillovers and exclude others from benefiting are already recognised as a major challenge in managing conventional intangible assets. For example, many organisations try to capture employee knowledge and experience by coding it into formal systems, manuals or procedures. These attempts to convert human and relational capital into organisationally owned structural capital are expensive in terms of both time and money. The upside is that an organisation can also benefit from spillovers from other organisations and people. However, this again requires specific attention to knowledge management, usually in the form of information technology-based efforts to capture, codify and transfer internal and external organisational knowledge.

Adding to the difficulty of managing conventional intangible assets is the fact that existing management accounting systems, notably costing systems, are skewed towards providing information on physical, industrial-type production processes (Johnson and Kaplan, 1987). Management information is captured in terms of materials, labour and overhead categories, relegating knowledge intangibles (such as customer acquisition, after-sales service or new market development) to period expenses. As a result, the production, utilisation and maintenance of knowledge within an organisation is under-identified and, consequently, under-represented in managerial decision-making. Somewhat surprisingly, even fully knowledge-based organisations (e.g. consultancies, education providers, laboratories) continue to use industrial era blueprints for capturing and representing their cost information.

Finally, the knowledge resources represented by human capital, specific organisational procedures or R&D investments are considered to be the key inputs for an organisation's innovation process, which in turn generates the basis for sustainable competitive advantage. However, as important as innovation processes are, the high level of uncertainty associated with innovation activities has to be acknowledged. For example, in technological innovation only a few products are commercially successful, while the majority are not. Although all investments carry an element of uncertainty, the uncertainty related to investments in knowledge is relatively higher.

From an accounting perspective, the uncertain prospects of knowledge investment provide the justification for expensing the outlays immediately. In the area of management accounting, uncertainty refers to the causal ambiguity (the unknown cause–effect relationship) regarding which knowledge elements and practices can be combined to create an innovation. Understanding the networked nature of innovation processes may help to resolve this causal ambiguity, and can be a first step towards allocating costs to the relevant stages in the innovation process – within the process of knowledge production. For example, identifying the various roles people hold in a networked production process can provide a cost allocation base, while the networks themselves can serve as responsibility centres for cost accumulation. Reducing causal ambiguity by mapping the knowledge production process might not in itself reduce overall uncertainty; however, it does go some way towards clarifying the locations (space) and moments (time) at which uncertainty arises. Corralling uncertainty in responsibility centres within knowledge-sharing, networked communities lifts the organisation's knowledge deployment above the non-financial waterline, allowing monetarisation of the practices and people associated with each responsibility centre. Stated differently, knowledge deployment (learning) can be situated in specific organisational vehicles that can be accounted for as separate entities or responsibility centres.

Management accounting and knowledge clues

As suggested by the above discussion of the economic characteristics of knowledge, there are both value drivers and cost drivers involved in accounting for knowledge, and the cost–benefit trade-off between them provides the impetus to start accounting for knowledge. The value drivers of knowledge resources are essentially based on its increasing returns to scale and network effects, while the cost drivers of knowledge resources are based on the partial excludability and spillover effects, as well as the relatively high uncertainty of investment outcomes and causal ambiguity in knowledge production processes. Does this mean that the organisation's knowledge base cannot be accounted for and should be left to its own (managerial) devices?

The present state of insight on what knowledge is (its different types, possession or practice aspects) and how it can be organised, visualised and coordinated has generated a growing body of managerial approaches, each of which can be verified against existing management accounting concepts and tools (Roberts, 2006). For example, the revenue drivers of knowledge resources can be acknowledged by filtering out the non-rivalrous/non-scarce assets from existing knowledge-intensive practices and unbundling them into distinct, standalone practices that have identifiable revenue streams. The online practices of e-business models can serve as exemplars in this respect. Also, various existing cost categories can be scrutinised to identify typical knowledge costs, such as certain communication and travel and entertainment (T&E) expenses necessary for knowledge sharing in time and space. For the typical period expenses that are related to knowledge provided for specific customer groups or market niches, a review of batch or product-line sustaining activity costs in an activity-based costing (ABC) system might act as an initial cue. Moreover, within an ABC or joint cost system, the various (common) knowledge resource pools a company has can be identified as either the main activity centre or as the process where joint costs arise.

The knowledge production process is not in itself a totally alien concept to management accounting. For example, the emphasis on information exchange, knowledge sharing and communication in knowledge production processes can be reflected in the existing cost categories. Notably, IT costs, travel and entertainment expenses, R&D expenses, after-sales support costs, purchasing/supplier selection costs, and training expenses all revolve around combining and bridging knowledge or experiences. Additionally, the knowledge production process can already be roughly outlined via the use of management control-oriented, non-financial performance indicators, such as are used in the balanced scorecard (Roberts, 2003). Taking a good look at which indicators are actually representative of the (non-financial) knowledge production process can provide further clues about what to account for.

Conclusion

This chapter has provided an initial knowledge typology (of *embedded* versus *embodied* knowledge) that is applicable to solving familiar problems and using existing knowledge at both individual and collective levels. This typology aligns well with conventional accounting perceptions of knowledge as a possession – an asset that needs to be used optimally in order to avoid wasting time and money by 'reinventing the wheel', and for which internal and external knowledge markets can be created and used for knowledge sharing.

A different perspective was provided in the alternative typology of *encultured* and *embrained* knowledge. This concerns solving unfamiliar (unknown) problems and generating new knowledge. This knowledge typology refers to knowledge as knowing – an activity of doing something with the knowledge one has. The activity of knowing (what to do) revolves around sense-making and negotiated meanings of what an event, situation or problem actually is and how it can be tackled. This is a social activity, which is based on connectivity and the work-related interdependence of people as key knowledge carriers.

Via 'cross-learning', groups and communities combine existing knowledge into new ways of problem solving. However, cross-learning is expensive in terms of time and money, pointing us to the economic characteristics of knowledge resources. Knowledge's increasing returns to scale (scalability) and its non-scarcity and non-rivalry set it apart from conventional assets. Together with the externalities or network effects that knowledge resources enable an organisation to develop, these three characteristics provide the key factors that can generate revenue on the basis of knowledge resources. However, the key cost drivers of knowledge as a resource are the difficulty of fully appropriating its benefits and the high uncertainty levels involved in commercialising knowledge. It could be that knowledge generated by one organisation spills over to other organisations, thereby reducing the incentive to invest in knowledge. Similarly, the high level of uncertainty in the early stages of generating new knowledge carries high costs. Nevertheless, management accounting information and systems can help the knowledge-based organisation to identify and manage the activity areas that are most knowledge-intensive, by identifying relevant cost drivers and cost allocation bases. Moreover, costs incurred in enabling knowledge sharing, such as time spent by employees, communication expenses, travel and entertainment expenses, and information and communication technology expenses, can assist in monetarising knowledge production.

The overall message about how management accounting tools can enable the management of knowledge resources is twofold. First, management accounting for knowledge resources does not require a radical overhaul of existing management accounting concepts, methods and tools. Rather, it requires a long and hard look at what can be used, taking into account the different characteristics and modes of organising and coordinating knowledge resources. Second, the criteria for reviewing, selecting and using existing management accounting information categories and concepts themselves originate from knowledge resources. That is, we must look from the knowledge management area towards the management accounting area in order to assemble the components of a relevant knowledge accounting system.

Acknowledgements

Helpful comments by Cristina Chaminade on an earlier version, and editing assistance provided by Leif Hommen and Trudy Berscheid are gratefully acknowledged.

References

Amin, A. and Cohendet, P. (2004) *Architectures of Knowledge: Firms, Capabilities, and Communities,* Oxford: Oxford University Press.

Blackler, F. (1995) 'Knowledge, knowledge work, and organizations: an overview and interpretation', *Organisation Studies,* **16**(6), 1021–46.

Bontis, N. (1999) 'Managing organizational knowledge by diagnosing intellectual capital: framing and advancing the state of the field', *International Journal of Technology Management,* **18**(5–8), 433–62.

Brown, J.S. and Duguid, P. (1991) 'Organizational learning and communities of practice: toward a unified view of working, learning, and innovation', *Organisation Science,* **2**, 40–57.

Johnson, H.T. and Kaplan, R.S. (1987) *Relevance Lost: The Rise and Fall of Management Accounting,* Boston, MA: Harvard Business School Press.

Lev, B. (2001) *Intangibles: Management, Measurement, and Reporting,* Washington, DC: Brookings Institution.

Roberts, H. (2003) 'Management accounting and the knowledge production process', in A. Bhimani (ed.), *Management Accounting in the Digital Economy,* Oxford: Oxford University Press, pp. 260–83.

Roberts, H. (2006) 'Making management accounting intelligible', in A. Bhimani (ed.), *Contemporary Issues in Management Accounting,* Oxford: Oxford University Press, pp. 308–28.

Teece, D.J. (1998) 'Capturing value from knowledge assets: the new economy, markets for know-how, and intangible assets', *California Management Review,* **40**(3), 55–79.

von Krogh, G. and Grand, S. (2002) 'From economic theory toward a knowledge-based theory of the firm', in C.W. Choo and N. Bontis (eds), *The Strategic Management of Intellectual Capital and Organizational Knowledge,* Oxford: Oxford University Press, pp. 163–84.

Webster's New World Dictionary (Third College Edition of American English) (1988), New York: Simon & Schuster.

Zack, M.H. (2003) 'Rethinking the knowledge-based organisation', *MIT Sloan Management Review,* Summer, 62–71.

Further reading

Amin, A. and P. Cohendet (2004) *Architectures of Knowledge: Firms, Capabilities, and Communities,* Oxford: Oxford University Press. A short and compact book, firmly grounded in the 'knowledge as practice' tradition, which provides rigorous theoretical arguments and empirical evidence on knowledge formation and governance, to produce a new conception of the firm.

Carlsen, A., Klev, R. and von Krogh, G. (eds) (2004) *Living Knowledge: The Dynamics of Professional Service Work,* London: Palgrave Macmillan. A concise series of empirical articles on the actual (European) practices of knowledge work processes. All contributions originate from ten years of Norwegian action research on knowledge in organisational activities.

Hislop, D. (2005) *Knowledge Management in Organizations: A Critical Introduction,* Oxford: Oxford University Press. A compact and highly readable book that addresses the management of knowledge from the dual perspectives of knowledge as an object and as a practice, while providing concise coverage of its coordination, organisation and competitive contexts.

Part 4

Understanding management accounting change

16

Managing accounting change

Sven Modell

Introduction

The emergence of novel management accounting techniques and the changing roles of management accountants in contemporary organisations, discussed in other chapters, have been accompanied by growing interest in the challenges involved in managing change. In particular, the implementation of techniques such as activity-based costing (ABC) and the balanced scorecard (BSC) has been the subject of considerable research since the early 1990s. Numerous theoretical approaches and frameworks geared towards understanding management accounting change more generally have also been advanced, notably by authors informed by institutional theories (e.g. Burns and Scapens, 2000). However, research on management accounting change has been guided by a very broad range of social theories. Some of these have a pronounced managerialist emphasis whilst others take a wider view of the organisation and the various stakeholders influencing change processes (Burns and Vaivio, 2001; Granlund and Modell, 2005).

This chapter reviews a number of influential strands within the growing literature on management accounting change and assesses their relative merits and limitations. The theoretical underpinnings of the various bodies of literature are explicated and some suggestions offered on how these might be integrated in future research. Although particular emphasis is placed on implications for research, attention is also paid to the managerial lessons that may be learnt from prior research. The chapter focuses on the non-technical aspects of implementing various management accounting techniques, rather than the design of such techniques. Emphasis is placed on the managerial challenges involved in implementation and change processes, although the theoretical approaches reviewed differ considerably in the depth with which such processes are analysed. Whilst the literature review is far from comprehensive, it aims to depict some broadly representative developments in recent research on how management accounting change may be managed.

I will start by outlining the background to the growing interest in managing accounting change over the past two decades, before reviewing several influential strands of research on this topic. These are broadly classified into two categories. First, a number of *factor studies* are reviewed. These seek to identify what drives and hampers successful implementation of management accounting techniques. Second, some *process-orientated approaches,* more concerned with the intricate social and political dynamics of implementation, are discussed. Recent advances in the latter vein raise the issues of the meaning of change (as opposed to stability) and implementation success (as opposed to failure) and how these might be researched. The significance of recognising these issues in management accounting research is discussed in some detail. I then outline how insights gleaned from factor studies and more process-orientated approaches based on institutional theories may be integrated in future research. Finally, some related managerial implications are noted and conclusions presented.

Studying management accounting change: a prelude

Concerted efforts to study the challenges involved in managing accounting change are a relatively new phenomenon in the accounting literature. Prior to the early 1980s, in-depth empirical studies of the social factors and processes involved in changing management accounting techniques and practices were rare as a result of the dominant position of economics-based 'mainstream' accounting thought. Most early theorising in this vein had a prescriptive and normative emphasis and was based on an essentially static approach predicated on the idea that optimal management accounting solutions would tend to reflect some economic equilibrium. The process of transition between such equilibria was of little interest to accounting scholars, so the problem of why theoretically optimal solutions often proved untenable in practice remained largely unexplored. A number of developments in management accounting thought have since altered the research agenda considerably to place a much heavier emphasis on change. Some of these developments will be described here.

At one level, the growing attention to management accounting change may be a side-effect of the establishment and entrenchment of interpretive and critical research traditions in accounting, which emerged as 'alternatives' to the predominantly North American 'mainstream'. Although research conducted within these emerging traditions did not always have a clearly articulated interest in theorising the process of change as such, it shifted the emphasis towards understanding the social and political processes involved in transforming management accounting practices. Also, within the critical vein the importance of questioning the status quo from a more ideological vantage point, fundamentally resting on a Marxist critique of history and society, prevailed. Most importantly, these advances in accounting thought introduced and legitimised research methods more conducive to the examination of organisational change processes, such as in-depth, longitudinal case studies.

Parallel to this development, scholars who have since taken a lead in studying management accounting change grew increasingly concerned with the obvious 'gap' between the 'conventional wisdom', as reflected by normative postulates in management accounting textbooks, and observations of management accounting practice (Scapens, 1984). Such concerns led to deeper examinations of evolving management accounting practices to explain the deviations between practice and received management accounting theory.

Similar critique and debate, grounded in observations of practical problems with established management accounting techniques, was triggered by the advent of *Relevance Lost* (Johnson and Kaplan, 1987). Johnson and Kaplan's critique pivoted around the obsolescence of established costing practices and the inability of traditional financial performance measurement techniques to provide useful information for managerial decision-making, especially from an operational perspective. Their call to radically rethink contemporary management accounting practices can be considered the starting point of a significant wave of innovation, first epitomised by the development of ABC and later the BSC. Whilst grounded in specific North American experiences and levelled at technical, rather than social and political issues of change, this critique provided management accounting scholars with new research opportunities and topics. An important reason for this was practitioners' increasing interest in experimenting with and implementing novel management accounting techniques.

The *Relevance Lost* critique and ensuing debate were paralleled by similar discussions in the United Kingdom (Bromwich and Bhimani, 1989). Whilst stressing the evolutionary rather than revolutionary nature of change in management accounting practices, this provided some additional, though somewhat more cautionary, notes on the need for change, especially in costing practices. Similarly, in Scandinavia important empirical advances examined the evolution of management accounting practices in their wider organisational and social context (Granlund and Modell, 2005). Particular interest was directed towards the ongoing experimentation with various performance measurement techniques and information systems at a relatively low (operating) level in the organisations examined. Echoing the arguments advanced in the *Relevance Lost* debate, such 'local' management accounting practices were often found to conflict with traditional accounting systems devised for more centralised financial control. Important insights were gained into theoretical issues such as organisational learning – that is, the ability of organisations to renew management accounting and operating practices and capitalise on the knowledge thus created.

These briefly sketched developments provide some clues to the impetus behind empirical examinations of management accounting change since the late 1980s. I now turn to reviewing several more recent streams of research on this topic and their achievements and limitations.

Factor studies

One stream of research into the growing use of novel management accounting techniques aimed to explain what organisational and contextual factors contribute to and hamper their effective implementation. Two particularly influential strands can be found within this category. The first series of studies concerned the implementation of ABC and mainly relied on survey-based inquiries. The second, case study-based strand of research established and refined a general framework for understanding management accounting change. Although the latter studies paid greater attention to the social processes involved in changing management accounting practices, they sought to abstract and categorise them into a generalisable framework. Hence, these studies share a concern with identifying the factors that explain management accounting change, or a lack thereof.

Implementation of ABC

Shields and Young (1989) presented an early conceptual framework that sought to explain the drivers of effective implementation of novel cost management systems, such as ABC. This model was later refined and tested by Shields (1995), who hypothesised that effective implementation of ABC systems was determined by seven organisational factors:

- top management support for the systems;
- the linkage of the systems to competitive (particularly quality and JIT) strategies;
- the linkage of the systems to performance evaluation and reward systems;
- sufficient internal resources (e.g. money and employee time) invested in the implementation of the systems;
- training in the design, use and implementation of the systems;
- non-accounting 'ownership' of the systems;
- consensus about, and clarity of, the objectives of the systems.

This framework positioned cost management in a wider organisational context and thus represents an early move away from the rather technical debate on how to design ABC systems. Rather than ABC being viewed in isolation, it was seen as intricately linked with other parts of the management control system with important behavioural implications in areas such as performance evaluation, reward systems and training. In addition, the importance of involving employees with wider, non-accounting expertise (e.g. engineers and operators), which has since been repeatedly emphasised in the literature, was highlighted. This foreshadowed recent debates concerning the need to transform the work roles of management accountants from the traditional 'bean-counter' image to more business-orientated roles as part of cross-functional teams. However, Shields and Young (1989) remained vague about the meaning of effective implementation. Similarly, Shields (1995) made loose reference to the 'success' of ABC and its perceived financial benefits as dependent variables. Subsequent surveys that built on these studies were more specific in this respect. McGowan and Klammer (1997) examined the impact of the seven factors identified by Shields (1995) on user satisfaction with ABC implementation. A broader approach was adopted by Foster and Swenson (1997), who investigated the impact of these factors on a range of overlapping success criteria, such as: the use of ABC for decision-making; operating-level actions taken based on ABC information; resulting financial improvements; and the perceived success of ABC implementation among managers.

These studies yielded some interesting results. Overall, Shields (1995) found that organisational factors like those outlined above were more important than technical aspects, such as having adequate information systems and expert support from consultants, in explaining the success of ABC implementation. This underscored the importance of connecting ABC implementation to wider managerial issues. In particular, top management support and links between ABC and other parts of the management control system (especially performance evaluation and reward systems) had a positive impact on the success of ABC implementation in the studies cited above. However, Foster and Swenson (1997) demonstrated that the explanatory power of models determining ABC success varied considerably with the choice of success criteria (i.e. the different dependent variables). This suggests that the success of management accounting change is a multifaceted phenomenon. This observation is further underlined by more recent process-orientated studies reviewed later in this chapter.

Insights such as these prompted other researchers to develop increasingly sophisticated models for examining ABC implementation. Krumwiede (1998) posited that the criticality of various organisational, environmental and task-related factors impinging on the implementation of ABC will vary across different implementation stages. Six key stages were identified:

- initiation
- adoption
- adaptation
- acceptance
- routinisation
- infusion

These stages represent an escalating organisational commitment to the use of ABC as part of the management control system. The framework allows us to differentiate between organisations that apply this technique in a relatively superficial and sporadic manner for limited purposes, and those that have wholeheartedly taken on the challenges of integrating ABC into a range of managerial tasks. This provides us with a more fine-grained model for determining whether and why ABC implementation has 'succeeded'. A key finding in Krumwiede's (1998) survey of organisations at different implementation stages is that, even though some factors tended to be important across several stages, other factors had a significant impact only at specific stages. For example, environmental disturbances resulting in cost distortions and the perceived usefulness of ABC information for decision-making were found to be important across several stages. However, organisational factors such as top management support, non-accounting ownership of ABC information and training, were found to be important mainly for organisations at advanced stages of ABC implementation. The important managerial lesson from this is the need for selectivity and flexibility in the choice of specific mechanisms in the implementation 'tool kit' as the organisation moves across different implementation stages. Managerial attention should be directed towards critical success factors, depending on the implementation stage the organisation is at. The problem, however, may be to realise exactly when the organisation moves to different implementation stages and requires a shift in managerial attention.

Recognising the importance of the implementation process, Anderson and Young (1999) distinguished between a range of contextual and process factors in their study of more than 20 ABC implementation projects in two US automobile manufacturers. Their results suggest that process factors, such as managerial support for and involvement in ABC implementation, interact with the organisational context in which the implementation takes place. Consistent with much prior research, reward systems (a contextual variable) were found to play a particularly important role in this respect. For example, stronger links between rewards and individual performance were found to have a positive influence on managerial support for the ABC implementation process. Respondents were also more likely to evaluate the outcome of ABC implementation positively under such reward conditions, irrespective of their level of involvement in the implementation process. The key managerial lesson here is that improvements of the implementation process may not resolve implementation problems. Attention to whether such improvements are supported by the wider organisational context may also be required.

Research on the implementation of ABC has thus progressed from relatively simple models, mainly ascribing implementation effectiveness to a range of contextual factors that may or may not be attributable to the implementation process, to increasingly elaborate analyses. As a result, the importance of examining the implementation processes associated with management accounting change was increasingly emphasised. As discussed later in this chapter, however, it may be argued that the survey-based literature on ABC implementation reveals relatively little of the complexity facing researchers and managers.

A framework for studying management accounting change

Parallel to the growing literature on ABC implementation, efforts were made to develop a theoretical understanding of what stimulates and hampers management accounting change more generally. Based on a series of case studies in the Scottish electronics industry, Innes and Mitchell (1990) concentrated on identifying factors that stimulated change in management accounting techniques. Drawing on their empirical findings, they identified three main categories of factors:

- *motivators* – general changes in the wider organisational context, especially those impinging on competitive market conditions, organisational structure, production technologies and product cost structures;
- *catalysts* – the more direct reasons for the initiation of change in management accounting practices, such as poor financial performance, loss of market share, the launch of competing products and other organisational changes;
- *facilitators* – organisational factors contributing to the realisation of change initiatives, such as staff and computing resources linked to the accounting function, organisational autonomy from the parent company and the authority of accountants.

These categories of factors were thought to be linked in the sense that motivators provided the impetus for the emergence of catalysts, whilst facilitators paved the way for subsequent change initiatives. Particular attention was paid to changes in product costing and performance measurement practices. Changes in such practices were mainly ascribed to technical factors, such as the needs for more accurate cost estimates and more timely and non-financial performance information in increasingly competitive and dynamic environments. In this respect, Innes and Mitchell's (1990) analysis resonates with the *Relevance Lost* critique. However, little attention was paid to the social and political processes involved in the choice of specific management accounting techniques in the organisations examined. One reason for this may have been that the case studies were mainly based on interviews with management accountants at various organisational levels, which reinforced the 'accounting centricity' of their analysis. The case studies were largely silent about the interactions between management accountants and other categories of staff in the production and use of accounting information. Hence, few insights were gained into the potential tensions between different functional areas involved in implementing novel management accounting techniques and the barriers to change these tensions created.

Whilst Innes and Mitchell's (1990) study drew on comparative case studies, their framework was further developed by Cobb et al.'s (1995) in-depth, longitudinal study of changes in a bank's management accounting system. Several of the changes initiated, such as the implementation of ABC, largely failed or encountered severe implementation problems. Such barriers to change were mainly of internal origin. Examples included changing priorities during the change process, accounting staff turnover and resistant attitudes to change. At the same time, Cobb et al. (1995) drew attention to the pivotal role of certain key individuals, or change agents, in overcoming such barriers and reinforcing the momentum for change over time. This resulted in a more refined model where motivators, catalysts and facilitating factors (seen as creating the potential for change) were supplemented by *leaders, barriers to change* and the *momentum for change*. The interplay between these factors was hypothesised to have an important influence on whether change initiatives materialise or not.

Kasurinen (2002) added a final refinement of the model developed by Innes and Mitchell (1990) and Cobb et al. (1995) based on his study of a BSC implementation in a Finnish manufacturing company. Whilst affirming the general relevance of distinguishing between factors triggering and creating a potential for change, Kasurinen's study also identified a broad range of barriers to change, which were classified as: *confusers*, including individual-level aspects such as diverging goals of key individuals; *frustrators*, referring to wider organisational phenomena such as cultural barriers suppressing change initiatives; and *delayers*, which were primarily issues of a more technical and temporary nature (e.g. information-processing difficulties) that slowed down the implementation of the BSC. The resulting framework is depicted in Figure 16.1.

This successively refined framework for studying management accounting change differs considerably from the simpler, normative 'checklist models' that describe how novel management accounting techniques, such as the BSC, should be implemented. The latter typically take the strategic dialogue initiated by top management as their point of departure, seeing it as a prerequisite for the gradual creation of consensus around the strategic vision and objectives of the organisation, which may become further specified within key performance indicators and targets. Changes in employee behaviour are then supposed to follow from linking strategic performance indicators to rewards and feedback systems. Kasurinen's (2002) study illustrates that such a linear view of how strategy is translated into action is oversimplified and unrealistic in the face of strong barriers to change. The implementation of the BSC was followed by unintended or unforeseen consequences partly attributable to a strong, engineering-based organisational culture bent on measuring a broad range of operating aspects. This weakened the link between the strategy set out by top management and the specific performance indicators that were developed. Although middle managers were involved in the implementation process and there was little active employee resistance to change, this culture obscured the overall purpose of adopting the BSC.

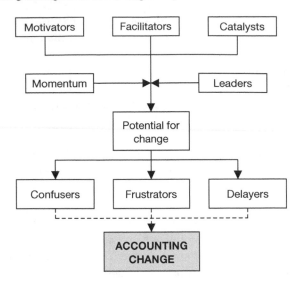

Figure 16.1 A framework for studying management accounting change
Source: Adapted from Kasurinen, 2002, p. 338.

Achievements and limitations

An important achievement of the literature on ABC implementation and the framework for studying management accounting change reviewed above is the emphasis placed on examining these phenomena in their broader organisational context. In contrast to most technical and normative literature on novel management accounting techniques such as ABC and the BSC, this better reflects the complexity involved in effecting management accounting change. Effective management of the implementation of such techniques depends on both the nature of the implementation process and a broad range of contextual factors, some of which are beyond the control of the organisation. Matching implementation tactics with particular environmental, technological, organisational and even individual-level characteristics thus becomes pivotal.

The studies reviewed here are similar to contingency theory research that seeks to explain what organisational, technological and environmental factors determine differences in the design and use of management accounting systems and subsequent implications for the effectiveness of such systems. But, in contrast to most contingency theory research on management accounting, the research reviewed here is more concerned with the dynamic aspects of implementation. Environmental factors extensively explored by contingency theorists, such as competitive conditions, may provide some general impetus for change in management accounting practices. But, whether such changes materialise and how deeply they penetrate the organisation depends on skilful management of a broad range of issues that may vary across different stages of the implementation process. In contrast to much contingency theory research, this highlights the role of individual actors, especially senior managers, as leaders or change agents who influence the choice and implementation of management accounting techniques. This is especially emphasised in some of the case study-based investigations of management accounting change (Cobb *et al.*, 1995; Kasurinen, 2002). However, the relatively consistent survey finding that top management support influences effective ABC implementation further underscores the importance of individual managers in the change process.

The two bodies of literature reviewed above also reflect an unusually pronounced concern with building a cumulative and coherent research agenda around specific management accounting issues. The theory-building efforts of the two strands of research are mutually supported by their consistent definition and use of theoretical concepts. Furthermore, the models explaining the implementation of ABC, as well as management accounting change more generally, were gradually refined with a view to corroborating and elaborating on the causal linkages between theoretical concepts. As indicated above, there is also some consistency of findings across the two streams of research even though their methodologies vary considerably. This is relatively rare in management accounting research and suggests some basis for drawing more generalisable conclusions. Nevertheless, there would seem to be scope for further refining the theoretical models advanced. For example, with some exceptions (Anderson and Young, 1999) researchers have not explored potential interaction effects between variables that influence effective implementation. In particular, the literature on ABC implementation has tended to produce extensive lists of factors independently influencing the effectiveness of implementation, whilst rarely clarifying how these determinants might impinge on each other. This would seem to be a natural step if research on management accounting change is to progress towards a systems perspective that recognises complex patterns of interaction between critical factors in the implementation processes.

The limitations of the two bodies of literature can largely be traced to their theoretical and methodological underpinnings. Theorising has mostly been informed by managerial perspectives on implementation and change. To the extent that social and political factors, such as employee involvement and resistance, were examined, these were mostly viewed as factors to be managed rather than as legitimate concerns and claims on the organisation (cf. Burns and Vaivio, 2001). Although some studies suggest that barriers to change can be deeply rooted in organisational cultures or diverging views of the purpose of specific management accounting techniques (Cobb *et al.*, 1995; Kasurinen, 2002), little attention was paid to the underlying conflicts of interests that might explain such phenomena. Similarly, effective implementation was typically defined in terms of the use of accounting information for managerial purposes and improved financial performance, without much critical analysis of whose interests are served by such success criteria. Hence, few insights were provided into potential power struggles between stakeholder groups with competing interests and the deeper political dynamics associated with management accounting change.

The impetus for change is usually attributed to economic or technical factors, such as growing market competition and changing production technologies, while the wider social processes involved in the diffusion of novel management accounting techniques across organisations is not discussed in any detail. Important actors who disseminate knowledge of novel management accounting techniques to practitioners (such as consultants) occasionally feature (e.g. Cobb *et al.*, 1995; Shields, 1995; Anderson and Young,

1999). However, they are treated as another factor impinging on implementation, whilst few details concerning their influence, involvement and interactions with other organisational actors in the change process are provided. This reinforces abstract depictions of change processes and detracts from deeper, process-orientated analyses, especially in survey-based research.

This managerialist emphasis and tendency to ascribe the sources of change in management accounting practices to economic and technical factors testify to an essentially functionalist methodology. Such research is typically based on a deterministic view that emphasises the structural prerequisites for change rather than the actions of individuals or groups in causing change processes to take unexpected or less malleable trajectories. Although the research reviewed above does pay some attention to the role of actors in the change process, it is not informed by theories which place the interplay between actors and structures centre stage. To gain deeper insights into this phenomenon we need to turn to more process-orientated approaches to studying management accounting change.

Process-orientated approaches

A broad range of theoretical approaches is available for examining change processes in greater detail. Occasionally lumped together under the banner of 'alternative' management accounting research, they include theories offering a radical critique concerned with the need for and desirability of change as well as drawing attention to obstacles to change of a predominantly non-technical nature (see Baxter and Chua, 2003, for a recent review). In contrast to the functionalist approach underpinning most factor studies, these theories share a concern with the wider social and political ramifications of change beyond merely managerial considerations. In particular, they question the possibility of purposeful and predictable change by drawing attention to how even concerted managerial change efforts may encounter resistance due to conflicting interests.

I will now focus on one increasingly influential strand of this 'alternative' research on management accounting change, namely that informed by various institutional theories. This research provides valuable insights into issues such as resistance and power struggles in organisations, and has important implications for the conceptualisation of change and stability and, ultimately, for the very meaning of 'successful implementation'.

Institutional research on management accounting change

Institutional research on management accounting change within the 'alternative' school of thought has primarily been inspired by a sociological branch labelled New Institutional Sociology (NIS) and, more recently, by more economics-centred perspectives, especially Old Institutional Economics (OIE). NIS-based research on management accounting change emerged in the 1980s and tended to emphasise the 'non-rational', symbolic nature and use of accounting information, especially in relation to budgetary control in public sector organisations. Change in management accounting practices was primarily ascribed to the need for external legitimisation and attempts by specific interest groups to pursue agenda other than strictly 'managerial' concerns with fiscal probity and accountability. According to this school of thought, management accounting techniques are not adopted so much as a result of rational choice processes, but rather due to the need for organisations to adhere to institutionalised (or taken-for-granted) rules that delineate socially legitimate practices. However, this need for external legitimisation often conflicts with internal, especially operating-level, requirements in organisations. Hence, institutionally induced accounting practices tend to be separated or decoupled from control systems used to manage operations (Baxter and Chua, 2003; Granlund and Modell, 2005).

Similar to NIS, OIE takes issue with the notion of change as a rationally planned and linear process unfolding without disruptions or unintended consequences. It also emphasises the rule-bound aspects of economic and organisational life and the cognitive and social processes whereby rules are translated into routines that regulate everyday actions. This explains how habitual patterns are formed in organisations. However, in contrast to much NIS research OIE is more explicit about how institutional rules, such as those embedded in new and existing management accounting techniques, come to permeate different parts of the organisation. Rather than assuming that such rules will invariably be decoupled from operating-level action and play a predominantly symbolic or ceremonial role, OIE recognises that these rules often have an important influence on the routinisation of everyday actions. However, through such actions individual or groups of organisational members may also transform rules in unintended ways. So while NIS has tended to treat institutions as largely 'given', OIE arguably provides deeper insights into how institutions are formed in organisations over time (Burns, 2000; Burns and Scapens, 2000).

Although these two perspectives evolved from distinctly different roots and emphasise different aspects of institutional processes, there is now some convergence between them in the management accounting literature. A first step towards this synthesis may be found in the framework elaborated by Burns and Scapens (2000). Even though they took OIE as a point of departure, important insights were also gleaned from more recent advances in NIS. In particular, Burns and Scapens (2000) recognised the importance of distinguishing between an *institutional realm* and the *realm of action* whilst arguing that these levels of analysis are intricately, though perhaps imperfectly, interlinked by the transmission and transformation of rules and routines (see Figure 16.2). Hence, whilst emphasising the interconnectedness of these levels, the possibility of at least partial decoupling of institutional rules from everyday action was acknowledged.

Burns and Scapens (2000) describe management accounting change as a more or less ongoing process occasionally energised or disrupted by discrete events in organisational life, such as the introduction of new management accounting techniques or acts of resistance among organisational members. Institutional rules prescribing, for example, how costs should be allocated and performance should be measured are embedded in management accounting techniques. However, for such rules to influence the evolution of organisational practices requires an element of routinisation. In other words, organisational members need to incorporate institutional rules into their cognitive frames of reference (or *scripts*) such that they come to shape their habitual action patterns. Burns and Scapens (2000) describe this as a process whereby rules and routines are first *encoded* within the institutional realm and then *enacted* by organisational members and gradually *reproduced* through their everyday actions

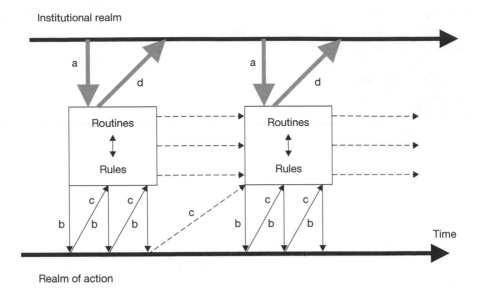

Key:
a = encoding
b = enacting
c = reproduction
d = institutionalisation

Figure 16.2 The process of institutionalisation

Source: Adapted from Burns and Scapens, 2000, p. 9.

and ultimately *institutionalised*, or taken for granted by some larger collective of actors (see Figure 16.2). The enactment and reproduction of rules and routines may imply that these undergo considerable transformations as they are interpreted in different ways by various actors. The cycle of encoding, enactment and reproduction may also be incomplete in that certain rules and routines are abandoned or ignored and thus have a marginal influence on everyday action. This gives rise to organisational phenomena akin to *decoupling* as described in NIS. Organisations may formally adhere to certain rules even though they have little influence on everyday actions. It is only when rules permeate actions and are widely recognised as the appropriate or legitimate way of 'doing things' that we may speak of more firmly institutionalised action patterns.

Burns and Scapens (2000) recognise that the transmission and transformation of rules and routines between the institutional realm and the realm of action requires an element of proactive agency. In contrast to much earlier NIS research, which tended to see institutions as 'given' structural properties that organisations adopt in a relatively unreflexive and slavish manner, their framework outlines the dynamic interplay between new and existing structures (e.g. rules) and the actions taken to transmit or transform them. However, existing structures are slow to loosen their grip on institutionalised action patterns. This gives rise to *path dependencies* in organisational change processes, i.e. the propensity of existing structures to influence and perhaps even amalgamate with newly introduced structures to form 'hybrids'. For example, the introduction of ABC as an alternative to traditional full-cost allocation models may result in ABC assuming a different meaning to conventional 'textbook' approaches so that the two models come to resemble each other and are used for similar purposes.

Institutional factors such as those outlined above often give rise to complex and multifaceted change processes. Burns and Scapens (2000) identify three dimensions along which such processes can be categorised, namely *formal/informal*, *revolutionary/evolutionary* and *progressive/regressive* change. Formal change refers to conscious, directed, and more easily observed kinds of design, whereas informal change refers to the tacit and unintentional aspects of organisational action. Revolutionary change refers to radical and fundamental disruption of rules and routines. This is contrasted with evolutionary change, which is incremental and emergent and causes only minor disruption of existing routines. Finally, progressive change is of an instrumental nature, implying that previously dominant values and practices are questioned and transformed with the aim of improving certain aspects of organisational life. In contrast, regressive change is predominantly ceremonial, preserving existing power structures and restricting institutional change.

Radical change initiatives in organisations, resulting from forceful managerial actions and/or externally induced 'shocks' or crises, often render formal change processes more revolutionary and are typically initiated to enhance progressive aspects of change (e.g. performance improvements). On the other hand, path dependencies often reinforce the informal, evolutionary and regressive nature of change processes. However, the three dimensions of change are continua and may coexist whilst being more or less pronounced at various stages of change processes. Granlund and Modell (2005) provide evidence of how the three dimensions may blend into each other and give rise to complex patterns of change in organisations. For example, radical change initiatives may turn into rather evolutionary processes as a result of clashes with firmly institutionalised value systems that breed employee resistance and confine new, formal control systems to a ceremonial role. By contrast, local, informal control systems may emerge and evolve in unexpected ways as a response to deficiencies in formal control systems, whilst still serving a progressive role as important means of managing certain operating activities. Both scenarios are consistent with the NIS and OIE arguments that structures are imperfectly linked to, or are decoupled from, each other and certain aspects of operating-level action. A few recent empirical studies are reviewed below to further illustrate how institutional research has contributed to our understanding of such issues as power and resistance in the process of changing management accounting practices.

Burns (2000) examined the introduction of new accounting rules aimed at enhancing financial accountability and awareness in a product development department of a chemicals manufacturer in response to deteriorating external business conditions. Stricter financial reporting routines were implemented to this end. To support these radical measures, top management mobilised various sources of power, some of which were embedded in the new accounting rules. For example, the traditional engineering-centered view of operations was challenged using the new accounting numbers. The new institutional accounting rules thereby played an enabling role as they enhanced top management's power over meanings. Despite these forceful measures, however, the research and engineering-based culture of the product development department proved remarkably resilient. Burns (2000) argues that the firmly institutionalised routines embedded in this culture enhanced the power of employees, enabling them to resist deeper change in their cognitive frames of reference. This accentuated intra-organisational conflicts. Nevertheless, the new accounting rules were mobilised to affect other aspects of product development work, such as the abandonment of certain development projects. Hence, whilst the change process may be described as revolutionary in some respects (i.e. the introduction of a more obvious accounting element in formal decision-making), it failed to impinge on firmly institutionalised action patterns involved in product development work. Change and stability may thus coexist as a result of some balancing of various sources of power in the organisation.

At one level, Burns' (2000) study is an illuminating example of how inconsistent institutional rules and routines, representing diverging financial and operating rationales, give rise to power struggles. More far-reaching and lasting institutional change, he argues, is probably only possible where attempts to exercise 'power over meanings' are supported by other sources of power, such as power over resources and decision-making. Without such mutually supporting mechanisms, new management accounting techniques can assume a largely ceremonial role, reinforcing the regressive aspects of change. However, this view of change emphasises the notion of power as something being imposed on resistant organisational members through accounting. As was the case for earlier institutional research on the role of accounting in organisational change processes, not least in the wake of public sector reforms, this emphasises the conflicting nature of institutional pressures, ultimately leading to some decoupling of institutional rules from the realm of action.

An interesting contrast to this view was provided by Collier (2001) in his study of the devolution of budgetary control in a local police force. The new budgetary control procedures accommodated both financial management and operating requirements. Prior to devolution, local police managers had little financial autonomy and influence over resource allocation. This limited their ability to meet non-financial performance requirements. By contrast, the new, devolved budgets were considered to have enabling powers, as managers were given greater discretion in balancing operational and financial concerns. Hence, little conflict arose between institutionally induced accounting changes, stemming from financial management reforms, and firmly institutionalised, operating-level action patterns. Financial concerns melded with operating-level decision-making, but without challenging the fundamental nature and purposes of police work. In other words, new institutional rules and routines embedded in formal control systems do not necessarily reinforce the regressive side of change. The accounting-led changes had some progressive, though perhaps not revolutionary, effects such as enhancing the ability of local police managers to deal with financial and operating matters within budgetary constraints. Yet, such changes may coexist with an element of stability, as evidenced by the preservation of the fundamental values guiding police work.

Similarly, Siti-Nabiha and Scapens (2005) illustrate how even unintended consequences of institutionally induced changes in formal control systems may produce progressive change. A new performance measurement system developed out of a gas processing company's efforts to implement value-based management principles. The formal performance indicators stemming from these changes failed to provide the intended, strategic direction for action. However, the changes triggered other developments in the organisation, leading to the evolution of a parallel set of performance indicators which were more consistent with the institutionalised values of operating-level managers and existing practices embedded in the control of production processes. Hence, even though the formal performance indicators linked to value-based management assumed a largely ceremonial role in the organisation, these were decoupled from other control practices that emerged from the same change initiative. Regressive and progressive aspects of the same underlying change process may thus coexist (cf. Granlund and Modell, 2005). Interestingly, this situation seems to have occurred without much overt resistance or struggle involving strongly conflicting sources of power. Again, this calls into question the notion that institutionally induced change fundamentally conflicts with operating-level action.

The advances reviewed above illustrate the close interweaving of dynamising and stabilising forces in management accounting change processes. Change may be energised by a range of factors, such as concerted managerial initiatives, the introduction of novel management accounting techniques, exertion of various forms of power, and processes to reduce conflicts of interest in organisations. On the other hand, existing and often firmly institutionalised values, operating-level practices and control systems play an important stabilising role by providing alternative sources of power to actors resisting change and giving rise to path dependencies. Management accounting may thus have both enabling and constraining roles in organisational change processes. However, exactly how the interweaving of dynamising and stabilising forces occurs remains an open question that can only be answered through close examinations based on qualitative and preferably longitudinal field research. In what follows, I offer a preliminary assessment of the achievements and limitations of institutional research on management accounting change.

Achievements and limitations

In contrast to most of the previously reviewed factor studies, the most important achievement of institutional research on management accounting change is its delineation of change as a continuous process rather than a series of discrete and identifiable events in organisational life (see also Burns and Vaivio, 2001). Rather than assuming that change processes have final outcomes which can be unambiguously labelled 'implementation success' or 'failure', institutional research emphasises the broad range of intended and unintended consequences of change initiatives. Although it is often possible to isolate those (relatively rare) points in organisational life at which new management accounting techniques are introduced, researchers focus on the complex social and political processes whereby these techniques become institutionalised rules and routines which influence parts of the organisation. This has two key implications for the notion of 'successful implementation'.

First, by examining how and why resistance to change occurs, institutional research directs our attention to the question of whose interests are being served by management accounting and how this impinges on change processes. Rather than assuming successful implementation reflects issues of instrumental or managerial concern (such as usefulness for decision-making, impact on operating-level actions and improved financial performance), this research considers whether such aspects are deemed appropriate or legitimate among a wider audience of stakeholders. Institutional research emphasises that what is deemed legitimate depends on some broader, collectively shared view of social realities rather than a few easily measurable criteria established by a managerial elite. In some circumstances, these aspects may overlap. However, where conflicting or inconsistent institutional logics prevail, the notion of successful implementation becomes problematic and must be assessed in relation to the goals of a range of opposing parties. Successful implementation could mean that the organisation has legitimised itself to external stakeholders (e.g. regulators, shareholders) and secured their support by adopting management accounting techniques that barely influence internal, operating-level practices. Such decoupling does not necessarily suggest that the management of implementation has been ineffective – it may be necessary for managing inconsistent institutional logics and avoiding disruptive organisational conflict. However, this requires that the quasi-consensual approach to implementation, in which resistance and conflict are seen as factors to be overcome rather than a natural part of organisational life, is relaxed.

Second, even where there is consensus concerning the legitimacy or desirability of various implementation outcomes in organisations, the determination of successful implementation may be complicated by unintended consequences that may be beneficial or detrimental to various stakeholders. The problem here lies in ascertaining what trajectory unintended developments will take and how soon they will be considered beneficial or detrimental. Examples of this can be found in the emergence of informal, 'local' control practices in response to managerial change initiatives. The evolution of such practices may be filled with tensions, although the emerging control systems eventually prove to be beneficial to certain actors (Siti-Nabiha and Scapens, 2005). Hence, there is a risk of short-term studies overemphasising the element of conflict and prematurely labelling such unintended consequences a sign of failed implementation. This risk is particularly pertinent in research that seeks to identify whether management accounting innovations (e.g. ABC) have 'survived' various implementation stages, whilst focusing only on how the formal control system is received in the organisation (e.g. Krumwiede, 1998).

Institutional research also examines the notion of power, which has been a neglected topic in the previously reviewed factor studies. Although power was not a central analytical category in much earlier institutional research on accounting (Dillard *et al.*, 2004), more recent studies have started to develop a deeper understanding of how power is implicated in management accounting change. These studies testify to the enabling as well as constraining roles of power embedded in the implementation of management accounting (Burns, 2000; Collier, 2001). They also illustrate how different sources of power may both support and conflict with each other, whilst emphasising that their exact manifestations and linkages are highly context-specific. Making strong a priori assumptions about the distribution of power in organisations is thus potentially fallacious. Certain actors (e.g. management) are not always powerful whilst others are relatively powerless. Power may shift as coalitions of interest form around specific issues in the implementation and change process. Hence, power should not be treated as a static property 'belonging' to certain actors, but as a dynamic force brought about by collective actions. A key issue here is how power is mobilised to reach (or hamper) agreements among actor collectives about the legitimacy of change initiatives. Institutional research has started to provide deeper insights into such issues although much empirical work remains to be done to enhance our understanding.

A number of limitations, which have only recently been addressed in institutional research on management accounting change, should be noted. First, although the dynamic interplay between institutionalised structures and agency forms a key element of Burns and Scapens' (2000) framework, it is conspicuously silent about *how* agency is exercised and *by whom*. Institutional change requires some shift in the collective consciousness and actions of a group of actors. However, it is less clear how such collective action patterns are mobilised and what role potential change agents, such as consultants and management, play. Empirical work building on Burns and Scapens' (2000) framework has started to address this issue (e.g. Burns, 2000; Siti-Nabiha and Scapens, 2005). Yet, a clearer conceptualisation is needed of how the actions of individual actors to transform rules and routines impinge on habitualised, collective action patterns.

Second, there is still a dearth of knowledge of how institutional processes at various levels of analysis influence each other. NIS research has primarily been conducted at the inter-organisational level, examining how innovations diffuse across and permeate larger populations of increasingly homogeneous organisations. On the other hand, Burns and Scapens (2000) primarily invoked OIE as a complementary perspective for examining management accounting change as an intra-organisational phenomenon. However, institutional processes around and within organisations interact. Further synthesis of insights from NIS and OIE thus requires more attention to the dynamics involved in this interplay (Dillard *et al.*, 2004). From a longitudinal perspective, this interplay often assumes an iterative and reciprocal character. The impetus for change may originate from the introduction of novel management accounting techniques, such as ABC and the BSC, at the organisational level. However, as individual organisations start to experiment with such innovations these may be modified through intra-organisational institutional processes. What eventually emerges as 'good practice' within an organisational field may then bear little resemblance to the original, 'archetypical' technique. Such inter-level dynamics have important implications for the distribution of power. As rules and routines are rarely fixed at the early stages of the institutionalisation process, early adopters can sometimes modify novel management accounting techniques to suit their interests and needs and thus enhance their power over what subsequently emerges as more firmly institutionalised standards. On the other hand, later adopters may be more constrained in their choice and implementation of management accounting techniques.

Finally, whilst emphasising the intricate social and political processes of management accounting change, institutional research has paid scant attention to the role of economic and technical factors, such as those examined in factor studies. Although this is probably a natural consequence of trying to provide an alternative to manage-rialist and efficiency-centred explanations of change, there is evidence that institu-tional, economic and technical factors interact in shaping power relationships and the trajectory of change processes (Malmi, 1997; Granlund, 2001). As discussed next, this observation provides a useful point of departure for assessing how insights from fac-tor studies and institutional research may be integrated in future research.

Towards a synthesis of perspectives

Whilst institutional theories have typically been seen as an alternative to functionalist explanations of change, such as those embedded in most factor studies, there may be scope for integrating these approaches in future research. The most obvious starting point for such research would be to pay equal attention to how institutional and eco-nomic and/or technical factors impinge on management accounting change. For example, Malmi (1997) illustrates how economic factors (e.g. seemingly efficient oper-ations) enhanced the power of actors to resist the implementation of ABC in a manu-facturing firm, and produced unintended consequences. Similarly, Granlund (2001) found that inertial forces of both an economic and technical nature (e.g. scarce resources, system complexity) and an institutional origin (e.g. existing routines, employee resistance and failure to legitimise change) gradually stabilised manage-ment accounting, despite radical change initiatives. Also, some factors facilitating or hampering implementation which have been extensively examined in factor studies, such as consensus about objectives, reflect issues of fundamental concern in works based on institutional theory. However, we still know very little about how economic, technical and institutional factors interact in the change process.

A more intricate issue is how the diverging methodological perspectives embedded in factor studies and institutional research may be reconciled to produce a genuine syn-thesis of insights from both research traditions. While factor studies have paid little attention to the meanings of such terms as 'change' (versus 'stability') and 'implemen-tation success' (versus 'failure'), institutional theories see these concepts as fundamen-tally context-bound and inherently ambiguous. One way of overcoming this divide may be to realise that even economic and technical factors need to be interpreted by organisational members to energise change efforts. Such factors do not exist as objectively verifiable elements 'out there'. Managers (and other organisational actors) interpret and try to make sense of the complex environment in which they work and then translate these interpretations into actions. These interpretations may diverge or converge across various groups of actors. The key insight from institutional theories is that convergence and the mobilisation of collective action depend on the processes involved in moulding consensus about the legitimacy of change. Managers may skil-fully construct accounts of economic developments or technical requirements based on their subjective interpretations of them to consciously legitimise the need for manage-ment accounting change. Similar accounts may be constructed concerning whether change implementation was successful, perhaps in some *ex post* rationalisation effort.

In keeping with such a perspective, it is important to realise that the search for legit-imacy may be tightly integrated with a desire to enhance organisational performance.

For example, Modell (2001) found legitimacy-seeking and efficiency-enhancing rationales to be closely interlinked in managerial efforts to change financial performance measurement practices in a large hospital. Moreover, some institutional research suggests that demands for external legitimisations are not necessarily inconsistent with the more technical requirements embedded in operating-level practices (e.g. Collier, 2001). Such variations are likely to impinge on the perceived need among managers and other actors to separate external legitimisation efforts from other spheres of organisational life. Modell (2001) found that although considerable managerial efforts were spent on linking financial performance measurement to operations, great care was taken to decouple these practices from other contentious performance aspects such as staff fatigue and discontent. In other words, decoupling is not the only possible response to institutional pressures. Whether it materialises or not partly depends on the perceived need for it among managers.

The discussion above indicates potential ways of 'bringing management back' into institutional analyses. Such analyses may add valuable insights into the role of management in gradually shifting collective consciousness and action patterns. This implies that the existence of collectively shared conceptions about what practices are legitimate is no longer taken for granted. On the other hand, management should not be viewed as some value-neutral category of actors who unreflectively comply with instrumental logic (an implicit assumption in some factor studies), but rather as a group of institutionally embedded agents with access to different strategies in managing accounting change.

A key implication of this discussion is that managers should not be viewed as omnipotent actors who rely only on rational analysis and decision-making when choosing and implementing management accounting systems. Influencing change processes requires skilful utilisation of different sources of power, among them the power over meanings achieved by translating economic and technical realities into legitimate arguments for change. However, managers also need to be aware of the boundaries inherent in institutionalised conceptions of what constitutes legitimate management accounting practices in a particular organisational context. Overstepping such boundaries may be an important explanation for difficulties in the implementation process. At the same time, windows of opportunity may open and close as institutionalised practices are questioned by other collectives of actors at different stages of the implementation process. Economic and technical factors (e.g. financial crises, system incompatibilities) may reinforce such opportunities and barriers as different actors use them to construct arguments for and against change.

Conclusion

This chapter has reviewed two influential strands in the management accounting change literature, namely factor studies focusing on the implementation of ABC, the BSC and management accounting change more generally, and more process-orientated research based on institutional theories. Some suggestions for how insights from these literatures may be integrated in future research have been offered. Given our relatively limited understanding of how economic, technical and institutional factors interact in change processes, in-depth, exploratory and preferably longitudinal case studies would seem an appropriate research strategy. However, there is also a need for comparative research examining how organisations subject to similar institutional pressures implement management accounting innovations under different economic and technical conditions. This is necessary to advance more general theorising about such interaction patterns. It is hoped that this chapter provides some inspiration for both these types of research into management accounting change.

References

Anderson, S.W. and Young, S.M. (1999) 'The impact of contextual and process factors on the evaluation of activity-based costing systems', *Accounting, Organizations and Society,* **24**, 525–59.

Baxter, J. and Chua, W.F. (2003) 'Alternative management accounting research – whence and whither', *Accounting, Organizations and Society,* **28**, 97–126.

Bromwich, M. and Bhimani, A. (1989) *Management Accounting: Evolution not Revolution,* London: CIMA.

Burns, J. **(2000)** 'The dynamics of accounting change: inter-play between new practices, routines, institutions, power and politics', *Accounting, Auditing and Accountability Journal,* **13**, 566–96.

Burns, J. and Scapens, R.W. (2000) 'Conceptualising management accounting change: an institutional framework', *Management Accounting Research,* **11**, 3–25.

Burns, J. and Vaivio, J. (2001) 'Management accounting change', *Management Accounting Research,* **12**, 389–402.

Cobb, I., Helliar, C. and Innes, J. (1995) 'Management accounting change in a bank', *Management Accounting Research,* **6**, 155–75.

Collier, P. **(2001)** 'The power of accounting: a field study of local financial management in a police force', *Management Accounting Research,* **12**, 465–86.

Dillard, J.F., Rigsby, J.T. and Goodman, C. (2004) 'The making and remaking of organization context: duality and the institutionalization process', *Accounting, Auditing and Accountability Journal,* **17**, 506–42.

Foster, G. and Swenson, D.W. (1997) 'Measuring the success of activity-based cost management and its determinants', *Journal of Management Accounting Research,* **9**, 109–41.

Granlund, M. (2001) 'Towards explaining stability in and around management accounting systems', *Management Accounting Research,* **12**, 141–66.

Granlund, M. and Modell, S. (2005) 'Nordic contributions to the management accounting change literature', in Jönsson, S. and Mouritsen, J. (eds), *Accounting in Scandinavia – The Northern Lights,* Malmö Sweden: Liber and Copenhagen Business School Press, pp. 159–92.

Innes, J. and Mitchell, F. (1990) 'The process of change in management accounting: some field study evidence', *Management Accounting Research,* **1**, 3–19.

Johnson H.T. and Kaplan R.S. (1987) *Relevance Lost: The Rise and Fall of Management Accounting,* Cambridge, MA: Harvard Business School Press.

Kasurinen, T. (2002) 'Exploring management accounting change: the case of balanced scorecard implementation', *Management Accounting Research,* **13**, 323–43.

Krumwiede, K.R. (1998) 'The implementation stages of activity-based costing and the impact of contextual and organizational factors', *Journal of Management Accounting Research,* **10**, 239–77.

Malmi, T. (1997) 'Towards explaining activity-based costing failure: accounting and control in a decentralized organization', *Management Accounting Research,* **8**, 459–80.

McGowan, A.S. and Klammer, T.P. (1997) 'Satisfaction with activity-based cost management implementation', *Journal of Management Accounting Research,* **9**, 217–37.

Modell, S. (2001) 'Performance measurement and institutional processes: a study of managerial responses to public sector reform', *Management Accounting Research,* **12**, 437–64.

Scapens, R.W. (1984) 'Management accounting: a survey', in R.W. Scapens, D.T. Otley and R.J. Lister (eds), *Management Accounting, Organizational Behaviour and Capital Budgeting,* London: Macmillan, pp. 15–95.

Shields, M. (1995) 'An empirical analysis of firms' implementation experiences with activity-based costing', *Journal of Management Accounting Research,* **7**, 148–66.

Shields, M. and Young, S.M. (1989) 'A behavioural model for implementing cost management systems', *Journal of Cost Management,* Winter, 17–27.

Siti-Nabiha, A.K. and Scapens, R.W. (2005) 'Stability and change: an institutionalist study of management accounting change', *Accounting, Auditing and Accountability Journal,* **18**, 44–73.

Further reading

Anderson, S.W. and Young, S.M. (2001) *Implementing Management Innovations. Lessons Learned from Activity Based Costing in the U.S. Automobile Industry,* Boston: Kluwer. This book provides a comparative analysis of the implementation of ABC in two automobile manufacturers, relying extensively on both qualitative and quantitative methods.

Brignall, S., Fitzgerald, L., Johnston, R. and Markou, E. (1999) *Improving Service Performance: A Study of Step-change Versus Continuous Improvement,* London: Chartered Institute of Management Accountants. This study contrasts two different strategies for performance improvement in a broad range of service-producing companies.

Jönsson, S. (1996) *Accounting for Improvement,* Oxford: Pergamon. This book details a range of empirical studies of how management accounting becomes implicated in everyday decision-making and operating-level actions in organisations.

Quattrone, P. and Hopper, T. (2001) 'What does organizational change mean? Speculations on a taken for granted category', *Management Accounting Research,* **12**, 403–35. This article discusses different conceptualisations of change and proposes an alternative conceptualisation, labelled 'drift', emphasising the evolutionary side of change.

Vaivio, J. (1999) 'Examining "the quantified customer"', *Accounting, Organizations and Society,* **24**, 689–715. This article examines the social and political processes involved in constructing non-financial performance measures to reflect a strategy of enhanced customer orientation in an organisation.

Vámosi, T.S. (2000) 'Continuity and change: management accounting during processes of transition', *Management Accounting Research,* **11**, 27–63. This article explores how management accounting is implicated in shaping new conceptions of economic realities in a previously government-owned company.

17

Management accounting innovations: origins and diffusion

Christian Ax and Trond Bjørnenak

Introduction

A large number of new management accounting models have been introduced in recent years. Innovations are often labelled with acronyms like ABC and EVA or they are given catchy names that attract attention, such as the balanced scorecard and intellectual capital. The introduction of these and other innovations certainly influences management accounting research, practice and teaching. In order to illustrate their impact, we compared the set of concepts listed in the glossaries of the 1982 and 2005 editions of the best-selling textbook *Cost Accounting: A Managerial Emphasis* by Horngren (1982) and Horngren *et al.* (2005). The comparison produced the statistics shown in Table 17.1.

As can be seen from the table, the number of concepts listed in the glossary is about the same in both editions. More interestingly, as many as 250 (59.2 per cent) of the concepts listed in the 2005 edition are new compared to the 1982 edition. It is also striking that 234 (57.6 per cent) of the concepts listed in the glossary of the 1982 edition are no longer found in the glossary of the 2005 edition. Thus, only 172 concepts are listed in both editions. A closer examination of the concepts listed only in the 2005 edition reveals that many of them can be directly linked to new management accounting models, for example activity-based costing and the balanced scorecard. Both the deletion and adoption of concepts can be seen as the effects of diffusion processes, and these diffusion processes are receiving increasing attention.

Traditionally, the diffusion of management accounting innovations has been seen as a consequence of economic imperatives. Companies search for, and find, new solutions to be used for planning, control and decision-making purposes. More recently, researchers have paid greater attention to the diffusion process *per se.* This includes focusing on how and why some innovations spread more successfully than others. Is it because they are more efficient, in the sense that they enhance the profitability of the adopters more than the alternatives do? Or, do the way they are presented and the role of propagators have an effect on the adoption rates?

This chapter deals with these questions. The purpose is to present alternative perspectives on how and why management accounting innovations spread to new locations. Note that these perspectives are not mutually exclusive. They interact and may have different amounts of explanatory power in different geographical areas and industrial sectors, and at different points in time.

The chapter is structured as follows. The next section discusses what is meant by an innovation and the origins of some popular modern management accounting innovations. The third section presents a demand perspective on the diffusion of innovations. Section

Table 17.1 **Comparison of concepts listed in two editions of** *Cost Accounting: A Managerial Emphasis*

	1982	2005
Number of concepts listed in the glossary*	406	422
Number of concepts listed not included in the other edition	234	250
Percentage of concepts not included in the other edition	57.6%	59.2%

* Abbreviations were excluded from the comparison when concepts were also listed in full.

four introduces an active supply side to the understanding of why some management accounting innovations are more successful than others. In the fifth section, the two perspectives are combined in a more dynamic perspective on innovations and how they may be formed and reformed during diffusion processes.

Management accounting innovations and their origins

An innovation is the successful introduction of an idea or a phenomenon, perceived as new, into a given social system. It may have existed earlier in another form or in another setting, but as long as the idea is perceived as new in the group or location, it may be viewed as an innovation. Concepts like activity-based costing (ABC) may thus have existed in other forms earlier, or at least contained some of the same characteristics, but the combination of new elements and the way ABC is presented to potential adopters makes it an innovation.

In this section, we adopt a technical and conceptual approach to analysing management accounting innovations. Specifically, we see management accounting innovations as a set of design characteristics, such as the type of cost objects (e.g. products, customers), allocation bases (e.g. non-volume related cost drivers), or data (financial or non-financial). An innovation is defined by its set of design characteristics. For example, ABC can be seen as a combination of a set of cost objects and allocation bases.

Some examples of recent innovations and their origins are presented below. These examples are not meant to give a full account of the historical development of the innovations, but rather to contrast design characteristics of new concepts with more traditional concepts and to illustrate some changes in the design characteristics of the innovations through time.

Activity-based costing (ABC)

Activity-based costing was introduced as a new concept in the late 1980s. Initially, the idea was to introduce new allocation bases for the allocation of indirect costs, including bases not directly proportional to volume (non-volume related cost drivers). The rhetoric was aimed at contrasting these allocation bases with traditional allocation methods that typically used direct labour and direct material as allocation bases. This idea was later concretised in the form of cost hierarchies. Hence, the selection of allocation bases was the key design characteristic in the initial phase.

Later, however, the concept was further developed into a form of multidimensional profitability analysis. More descriptive objects were introduced, such as customers, market segments and distribution channels – a process which in itself can be regarded as a continuation of the cost hierarchy. Another development feature was the initiative to separate the cost of unused capacity from activities, i.e. ABC as a resource usage model. In a traditional sense, the result was a mix between contribution margin and full costing.

The ABC literature often uses the term 'traditional costing' to describe an unsophisticated absorption costing system, thus depicting ABC as an innovation. This is indeed correct, when comparing it to the descriptions given in textbooks. However, comparing component by component reveals that most of the design characteristics were previously discussed in the literature. Non-volume allocation bases are widespread in German and Scandinavian literature and have been since the 1920s. This may explain why costing practices in these countries appear to be more complex than what is described as traditional costing methods in the ABC literature. The cost of unused capacity was addressed in the early 1900s. The concept of cost hierarchy is more recent, although it was discussed in both American and German writings in the 1960s. Even the term activity costing existed in the literature of that time. These factors all contribute to the claim that, component by component, the ABC literature does not represent anything new. Nevertheless, ABC is still an innovation in several respects. First, the combination of different design characteristics is new. Second, several of these characteristics are perceived as new in various settings. As an example, complex allocation bases were less widespread in the USA than in Germany and Sweden. Third, the design characteristics are incorporated in new concepts, such as cost drivers. The result is a management accounting innovation.

The balanced scorecard (BSC)

The balanced scorecard was first introduced in the early 1990s. Similarly to activity-based costing, Harvard Business School and Professor Robert S. Kaplan played important roles in the initial phase. The development of the BSC was based on the perceived need to supplement financial indicators with other types of performance indicators, particularly non-financial indicators, which were better suited for measuring the performance and value creation of businesses. Another similarity to the introduction of activity-based costing is that the BSC concept is based on visits to, and descriptions of, a number of individual companies. Furthermore, as new experience is gained, the concept is redesigned concurrently. The most significant development of the BSC concept has been the focus on causality between different strategic objectives and what today are referred to as strategy maps.

The BSC has also been much discussed and analysed in comparison with earlier work. In Europe, great emphasis has been put on the comparison with the French *tableau de bord*, a concept that has existed for more than 50 years. This concept has many of the same design characteristics as the BSC, including a strong focus on non-financial indicators. However, the structure is far more flexible in *tableau de bord*, and this may be perceived as making it more suitable to the French ideology (see Bourguignon *et al.*, 2004).

Economic value added (EVA®)

Economic value added is the first management accounting innovation to be registered as a trademark. The concept was introduced at the same time as the balanced scorecard and, like the other two innovations mentioned above, originates from the United States. However, unlike the other two innovations, which were introduced by well-known academics, this innovation was spearheaded by a consulting company (Stern Stewart & Co.). EVA is based on a model in which the company's cost of capital (debt and equity) is deducted from the operating profit. EVA is what remains after this calculation. This way of thinking can be found both among practitioners (such as General Electric in the 1950s) and academics. EVA can also be seen as a continuance and special version of the traditional concept of residual income. In the German tradition, imputed interest has been regarded as a cost for more than 100 years. Hence, this part of EVA can be seen as new only to a limited extent.

Once again, it is the bundle of different elements that defines the innovation. First, Stern Stewart uses financial theory in its arguments for introducing division-specific costs of capital based on industry-specific factors and risk assessment. Second, a number of adjustments are made to what is known as 'distortions introduced by generally accepted accounting principles (GAAP)'. The complete list of such adjustments is a kind of Stern Stewart company secret.

This brief review of three of the most successful modern management accounting innovations shows that:

- they all consist of design characteristics that existed in previous models;
- they all originate from the United States, two from the academic community and one from the consulting community;
- the perception of whether each is something new varies from country to country, as does the way the innovation is related to traditional concepts;
- each is the combination of design characteristics and rhetorical elements that define the innovation;
- the innovations and the manner in which they are presented are deeply rooted in examples and cases.

We have now reviewed the concept of innovation as well as the characteristics of some successful management accounting innovations. In the following sections, we take a closer look at the reasons why innovations spread to new businesses.

Why do innovations diffuse? A demand-side perspective

Diffusion is the process by which an innovation is spread or disseminated. The major point of interest in diffusion theory is how specific agents adopt particular ideas or phenomena, and why they do it (or not). Diffusion theory has multidisciplinary characteristics and explores matters such as the diffusion of diseases, rumours, economic developments and management accounting innovations. Traditionally, most diffusion research has emphasised the demand side of the process; i.e. an adopter perspective. Later, we will extend this perspective to include the supply side and look at how agents actively propagate innovations.

A demand-side perspective is based on an efficient choice criterion. Innovations are adopted in order to help an organisation attain its goals. The perspective relies on a model of (efficient) choice in which adopters make independent, rational choices guided by the goals of technical efficiency (Abrahamson, 1991). If we return to the previous three examples, Table 17.2 illustrates the link between company characteristics and three popular innovations.

There is limited support in empirical research for the notion that company characteristics actually explain the adoption of innovations. This, of course, could be explained by the fact that it is impossible to capture all relevant factors in 'effective choice' models. It could also be caused by influences from the supply side of the diffusion process, which will be further explained in the next section. A third explanation is that there may be barriers facing potential adopters of new solutions, such as lack of time or other resources.

Diffusion of innovation can take on different forms. It can be a process of relocation, where the innovator transports the innovation into new groups. An alternative and more common form, though, is where more and more players adopt the innovation over time. The spread of management accounting innovations, in particular, is generally a process of expansion, in which the number of adopters increases over time. However, it is also possible to observe a form of relocation where players (e.g. managers who change jobs) bring their ideas from one organisation to another. Nevertheless, in this case the outcome is also a process of expansion.

Within the area of expansion diffusion (the innovation is adopted by more and more companies, so that the total number of adopters is growing over time), two subgroups are often mentioned – contamination diffusion and hierarchical diffusion. Both of these are relevant when describing the spread of ABC or BSC, for example. First of all, it is possible that interaction with sources of 'infection', such as consultants, has a major impact on how the innovation is perceived, and thus affects its probability of adoption. It is also possible that the spread takes on a hierarchical form, where the innovation is first adopted by the largest and most influential business organisations.

The system of concepts within the area of expansion diffusion is to a large extent based on the work of the Swedish geographer Torsten Hagerstrand. In his book *Innovation Diffusion as a Spatial Process* (1967), Hagerstrand developed a series of models to describe how innovations spread over time. The models were tested to a large extent

Table 17.2 **Management accounting innovations and examples of company characteristics**

Innovation	Examples of company characteristics
ABC	Large proportion of overhead costs Many products High product diversity Intense competition Simple existing costing systems
BSC	Large amount of intangible assets Lower relevance of traditional performance measures High environmental uncertainty
EVA	High importance of capital cost High variances in cost of capital between business units High distortions from GAAP

on the spread of agricultural innovations in southern Sweden. The conclusion of his work was that the diffusion process can be divided into the following stages:

1 The primary stage – the first leading adopters have adopted the innovation.
2 The diffusion stage – this is the period with rapid growth. The innovation is introduced in ever new areas.
3 The condensing stage – the last areas are penetrated.
4 The saturation stage – the diffusion processes diminish and are replaced by new innovations.

This process is illustrated in Figure 17.1.

One important independent variable that may be used to explain diffusion patterns is the number of contacts potential adopters have made among other adopters. An information field characterises the extent of a potential adopter's contacts at a given point in time. This may vary substantially between potential adopters.

Barriers and resistance to change are other important factors from a demand perspective. Barriers may be physical (distance), but cultural barriers are perhaps more relevant and important in the modern world. In this respect, language, profession and institutional factors tend to play central roles. The limited spread of the BSC in France illustrates barriers and resistance. The lack of interest in the BSC here can be ascribed to cultural differences and the existence of the French *tableau de bord*.

In early studies little attention was given to the supply side of diffusion processes. In more recent studies, however, the supply side has been used more actively to explain the dissemination and adoption of management accounting innovations. This is discussed next.

Why do innovations diffuse? A supply-side perspective

The success of management accounting innovations can be measured in different ways. An important measure of success is, of course, the degree to which innovations are adopted in practice. Other measures of success might be the number of books and

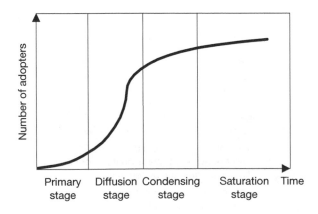

Figure 17.1 **Number of adopters over time**

journal/magazine articles devoted to innovations, and the number of people attending conferences, seminars, courses and workshops on innovations. All management accounting innovations are not equally successful. Different degrees of success might be understood from a demand-side perspective (see above). In addition, differences might also be addressed from a supply-side perspective. From this perspective, innovations do not diffuse by popular demand; they need propagators or entrepreneurs as proponents to diffuse them successfully. In the management accounting literature, two perspectives have been considered to direct attention to the role of the supply side in diffusion processes. They are:

● the management fashion perspective;
● the market and infrastructure perspective.

These perspectives are described below and research on the diffusion of management accounting innovations adopting the two perspectives is reviewed.

The management fashion perspective

Eric Abrahamson has presented the most comprehensive and influential framework on the role of the supply side in the diffusion of management fashion (he uses the label management fashion instead of management innovation). In his article 'Managerial fads and fashion: the diffusion and rejection of innovations' (1991), he questioned the dominant perspective in the diffusion of innovations literature, which reinforced pro-innovation biases because it relied on a model of adoption in which adopters make independent, rational choices guided by goals of technical efficiency. He proposed counter-assumptions and presented three additional perspectives on the adoption and rejection of administrative innovations – the forced-selection perspective, the fad perspective and the fashion perspective. Of these, the fashion perspective focuses on the supply side of the diffusion process and explores the role of fashion setters.

In his article 'Management fashion' (1996), Abrahamson developed the fashion perspective into a theory of management fashion. To him, a management fashion constitutes 'a relatively transitory collective belief, disseminated by management fashion setters, that a management technique leads rational management progress' (p. 257). From this perspective, management fashion setters – management gurus, consultancy firms, business schools/universities and others – pursue purposeful and active plans in order to achieve widespread diffusion of management fashions. Fashion setters have self-interest in a widespread diffusion of management fashions since their own success in terms of, for example profitability, status, legitimacy, public image and career, depends on the outcome. A key ingredient for management fashion setters is the development of norms of rationality and progress, which are used to influence managerial choices about which techniques and ideas to use. Managers will, it is argued, favour techniques and ideas that appear the most rational and progressive.

In Abrahamson's framework, the supply of management fashions is conceptualised as a four-stage process whereby fashion setters create, select, process and disseminate fashion propositions to fashion followers. In the *creation* stage, management fashion setters invent or reinvent (cf. 'old wine in new bottles') management techniques, which they present as innovative and superior to the state of the art. The techniques do not have to be more technically efficient than already available techniques; they just have to be significantly different from them. In the *selection* stage, fashion setters decide which techniques to process further. Here, techniques invented or reinvented by fashion setters, or the practising managers with whom fashion setters have come into contact, may be selected. The techniques that fashion setters perceive will satisfy an incipient demand from fashion users are selected over other techniques. In the *processing* stage, fashion setters develop 'a rhetoric that can convince fashion followers that a management technique is both rational and at the forefront of management progress' (Abrahamson, 1996, p. 267). To construct such a belief, the rhetoric must express both why it is essential that managers pursue certain organisational goals and why a particular technique offers the best means to achieve these goals. This includes presenting, for example, organisational performance gaps that managers need to narrow, stories about how successfully companies have increased their performance by adopting the technique, and evidence that the technique is superior to existing techniques as judged by a set of selected criteria. In the *dissemination* stage, the rhetoric developed is transferred back to the managerial audience. A range of actors are involved in this process. They typically include: management gurus, consultancy firms, professional associations, trade associations, the mass media, business schools/universities (including individual academics), institutions of management education, publishers, software vendors and successful companies (the early adopters). There are a number of channels that fashion setters use to communicate their rhetoric to managers. Among these are: books, brochures, newsletters, articles (and occasionally interviews) in research journals, business journals, management magazines, business newspapers and general newspapers with business pages or supplements, presentations at conferences, seminars, workshops and formal and informal meetings, videotapes, DVDs, CD-ROMs, websites, Internet forums and advertisements in the mass media.

Research on the diffusion of management accounting innovations adopting a management fashion perspective

Malmi (1999) investigated the diffusion of ABC across Finnish companies in several industries by means of four postal surveys sent to demand-side companies, interviews with consultants, academics and software vendors, and books and articles on ABC. The study aimed specifically at explaining what drives the diffusion of ABC during various phases. The following phases were used: the initial phase (1986–90), the take-off phase (1991–92) and later phases (1993–95). Malmi used Abrahamson's four perspectives – the efficient-choice perspective, the forced-selection perspective, the fashion perspective and the fad perspective – to assist data collection on, and interpretation of, the diffusion of ABC. The study explored several aspects of the diffusion of ABC, of which one in particular focused on the role of the supply side.

In the initial phase, efficient-choice motives for adopting ABC were the most frequently reported, particularly: 'we did not trust the information from the old system' and 'the old system did not meet the needs of management'. Concerning the role of the supply side, there were few indications that consultancy firms or other actors had an impact on the diffusion of ABC in this phase. Only a few ABC adopters had actually used consultancy services. In the take-off phase, motives for adoption related in part to the efficient-choice perspective, while the fashion and fad perspectives also were frequently mentioned. The fashion and fad motives stated by the companies were related to 'a wish to try a new tool' and to 'auditor/consultant advice'. The first motive may involve either fashion or fad as a motive for adoption, while the second motive refers to fashion alone. An analysis of the changes in the pattern of answers compared to the initial phase and other data seemed, according to Malmi, to provide support for the fashion or fad perspective in explaining the diffusion of ABC in this phase. The analysis of the supply-side actors showed that their activities had dramatically increased over time. First, the use of consultants in companies adopting ABC had increased noticeably compared to the initial phase. Secondly, consultancy firms, academics, a professional association (FINET), organisers of seminars, and software vendors were all very active in selling ABC at the time. Furthermore, the number of books and articles on ABC had increased considerably since 1990. Taking all the empirical data into consideration, Malmi suggested that the efficient-choice perspective and the fashion perspective both describe the adoption of ABC in the take-off phase. However, the driving force for the diffusion of ABC in this phase came from outside the group of adopting companies, i.e. from supply-side activities.

In the later phases, the motives for adoption centred on both the efficient-choice perspective and the fashion and fad perspectives. Based on an examination of the types of companies citing fashion and fad motives for adoption and the limited use of consultants among adopters, Malmi suggested that the fad perspective, rather than the fashion perspective, best explains diffusion in the later phases. Thus, the influence from supply-side actors in the diffusion of ABC seemed to have decreased compared to the take-off stage. In conclusion, the study suggests that the driving force behind the diffusion of ABC varied over time, with the impact of the supply side most evident in the take-off phase.

Ask *et al.* (1996) described the diffusion of activity-based costing (ABC) in Sweden. On the basis of documentation from seminars and conferences, advertisements from professional journals, marketing pamphlets for seminars, conferences, books and courses, and articles and books (all collected during the period 1988–94), they reported that four important groups of supply-side actors were members of an influential inter-organisational fashion setting network that sold ABC to potential adopters. The actors were the Association of Swedish Engineering Industries (ASEI), the early adopters of ABC, a small number of consultancy firms, and a few highly respected international academics. The actors were described as intertwined in a web of mutual relations, and formed a complex pattern of interaction that made it difficult to separate each actor's individual contribution in the diffusion process. However, the contributions of some distinct actors were identified. The ASEI, a professional/trade association for manufacturing companies, organised and coordinated the network. It was involved in different types of activities. For example, it collected information on current business problems and information needs from its member companies and passed this information to members of the network. It also arranged seminars and conferences (open to the public) and membership meetings on ABC. The contents of these seminars, conferences, and meetings were developed in collaboration with the early adopters of ABC and the leading consultancy firm on ABC. Also, five out of nine members of the Management Control Committee of the ASEI have been actively involved in ABC projects at their companies, and the leading ABC consultancy firm had also been involved in most of these projects.

The early adopters of ABC were typically large, well known multinational companies, of which all were members of the ASEI. The most active members in the network were Volvo, Ericsson and ABB. These companies frequently presented their ABC projects at seminars, conferences and meetings. The Volvo and Ericsson projects on ABC were also included in three practice-oriented books on ABC, one published by the ASEI and two by the leading ABC consultancy firm. Only a few consultancy firms were members of the ABC network. Particularly energetic in making contributions was Samarbetande Konsulter AB, the leading ABC consultancy firm in Sweden at that time. They were involved in most projects on ABC and have, as previously mentioned, published two books on the subject. Also, they regularly made presentations at seminars, conferences and meetings organised by themselves, the ASEI and others. A few highly respected international academics were also important members of the ABC network; among these were Robert S. Kaplan, Robin Cooper and H. Thomas Johnson. Their contribution to the network was primarily made through presentations at seminars, conferences and courses on ABC arranged by, for example, the ASEI and the leading consultancy firm. This study showed that different categories of management fashion setters collaborated in spreading the ABC idea in Sweden. The key actor in this collaboration was the ASEI. The role of professional/trade associations in diffusion processes has been recognised in fields outside management accounting. Newell *et al.* (1997, p. 311) argued that such associations are particularly important supply-side institutions as they bring together suppliers, users and potential adopters, thereby providing a forum for dissemination of fashionable management ideas. The Ax, Ask and Jönsson study provides support for this brokerage role of professional/trade associations in diffusion processes.

In an interview-based study of 17 Finnish companies, in several industries, which were using the balanced scorecard (BSC), Malmi (2001) examined how the BSC was applied and discussed the motives for adopting the technique. Concerning the application of the BSC, the study found variations in the contents, use, application practicalities, and effects of using the BSC. The study identified five distinct groups of motives for adopting the BSC. Four of them are related to the efficient-choice perspective and derive from the following proclaimed characteristics of the BSC: the BSC translates strategy into action; the BSC supports quality programmes and quality awards; the BSC supports other ongoing change programmes; and the BSC replaces or complements existing budgeting practices. The fifth group of motives relates to the supply side of the diffusion of the BSC.

According to this study, fashion setters seem to have had an influence on companies' decisions to adopt the BSC. First, half of the interviewed companies stated that they received information about the BSC from consultancy firms. Some respondents provided detailed information about the role of consultancy firms in BSC projects. For example, one said, 'the BSC was marketed to us during an activity-based costing project. The involved consultant "sold" the idea to us' (Malmi, 2001, p. 214). Another respondent said, 'a consultant was originally involved in a self-assessment. That is where the BSC originated. In the beginning of the project, the consultant was actually involved too much' (ibid.). According to a third respondent, 'there was a foreign consultant as project manager. He represented a consulting organization closely connected to Kaplan and Norton' (ibid.). Second, the interviews suggested that public seminars were an important source of information about the BSC. Third, a large number of seminars, articles and books contributed to making the BSC into a management fashion in Finland.

As mentioned previously, the BSC was applied in different ways in the surveyed companies. The study set out to explain this diversity using demand-side variables related to organisational type, strategy and structure. However, the study failed to identify any consistent pattern in this analysis. This caused the author to question whether the identified diversity in use reflects 'the development and dissemination of new ideas, suggesting a supply-side explanation for the observed phenomena' (Malmi, 2001, p. 216). In the concluding section of the article, Malmi provided two explanations for the popularity of the BSC in Finland and why many companies decided to adopt the technique. 'First, the logic of the BSC is certainly appealing to many in Finland. Second, and perhaps more interestingly, preliminary insight derived from this study suggests that supply-side organizations of the BSC have a significant effect on the decisions of organisations to adopt' (Malmi, 2001, p. 218).

In another study, Ax and Bjørnenak (2005) looked at the specific characteristics of how the BSC idea has been communicated by supply-side actors to potential adopters in Sweden. They reported that the BSC, as propagated in Sweden, frequently and conspicuously both extended and diverged from how it was presented in the original BSC literature. The study found that the original BSC presented by Kaplan and Norton has been supplemented with other administrative innovations and adapted for the prevailing business culture in Sweden, to make it more attractive to potential Swedish adopters. Using three data sources – conference invitations, the best-selling book on the BSC in Sweden, and articles in the country's leading professional journal devoted to management accounting issues – the study identified three elements, not found in the original version of the BSC, which the propagators of the BSC included in their Swedish BSC package. The three elements were: non-budget management, the intellectual capital (IC) model, and the employee perspective (the stakeholder model). The framework for the study started from the proposition that in order to popularise administrative innovations, it is important that supply-side actors make those innovations compatible with the society into which they are being diffused, and that cultural discourses and legitimacy are the main resources needed to enable the popularisation of the innovations. One way in which the supply side can popularise an innovation in a specific location, the authors argued, is by matching the design elements (the technical specification of the innovation) and rhetorical elements (the 'theory' of the usefulness of the design elements) to the preferences and knowledge of the potential adopters. The process of changing or adding design elements or rhetorical elements to innovations was referred to as the *bundling* process. Such changes/additions are made possible because administrative innovations are characterised by a certain degree of conceptual ambiguity that opens up the concepts

367

to different interpretations and uses. This ambiguity can potentially increase the supply-side influence on the diffusion process, for example by including elements in the bundling process that reduce barriers and resistance to change by aligning the innovation to the preferences and knowledge of potential adopters. A degree of ambiguity in its content endows an innovation with interpretative viability. A high level of interpretative viability can make the innovation compatible in new social settings. This study shows how supply-side actors used the interpretative viability of the BSC opportunistically to increase the size of the potential adopter market in Sweden.

The market and infrastructure perspective

The market and infrastructure perspective is primarily associated with Laurence Brown (1975, 1981). This perspective is based on systematic research, which has found that many diffused phenomena require propagators to maximise the pace and spread of the innovations in order to be considered successful. Being a geographer, Brown views diffusion primarily from a spatial perspective, which is concerned with how distance between adopters and propagators affects the relative time of adoption. This might explain why the centre of attention is mainly on issues related to physical distribution, logistics and marketing of innovations. According to the market and infrastructure perspective, the diffusion of an innovation can be constrained by its *availability* to potential adopters. It then becomes important to stimulate the demand for innovations and to make them available to potential adopters.

Within this perspective, the diffusion process is conceptualised as a process that involves three main activities. The first two activities, which together comprise the elements of the market and infrastructure perspective, represent the supply side of diffusion and shape its route. These factors affect the third activity by placing constraints on adoption. The three activities are as follows:

1 *The establishment of diffusion agencies.* Propagators have to decide when and where to establish a diffusion agency; this is an entity, such as retail and wholesale entities, government agencies or non-profit organisations, through which both information about an innovation and the innovation itself will be distributed or made available to the population at large. The agency decision is part of the broader market penetration strategy of the propagator, which also comprises decisions on the locus of decision-making with respect to the setting up of the diffusion agency, and whether to create a new network of diffusion agencies or to utilise an existing one.
2 *The establishment of the innovation in the service area of each diffusion agency.* To effectively induce the diffusion of the innovation, each diffusion agency has to decide on an inducement strategy. Such a strategy often includes the setting up of an infrastructure (e.g. distribution channels, service stations, and inventory and retail facilities), the development of organisational capabilities (e.g. sales, market research, and management and control systems), establishing a pricing policy, the selection and segmentation of markets, and the creation of promotional communication programmes.
3 *The adoption of the innovation.* Here, Brown agrees with the traditional adoption (demand) perspective. However, an important difference from this perspective is that the diffusion agency strategy interfaces directly with adopter behaviour.

Research on the diffusion of management accounting innovations adopting a market and infrastructure perspective

Bjørnenak (1997) studied the diffusion of ABC among Norwegian manufacturing firms from both a demand and a supply perspective by means of a postal survey. The demand-side perspective tested whether the ABC literature's propositions about when companies need an ABC system were related to the adoption of ABC. Specifically, the following factors were tested:

- cost structure measured by overhead cost as a percentage of total value added costs (direct labour costs + overhead costs);
- characteristics of the existing cost system measured by the number of cost pools and the number of allocation bases;
- product diversity measured by the number of product variants and the degree of customised production;
- competition measured by the percentage of annual sales exported and the number of competitors.

The only factor tested that agreed with the propositions was cost structure. ABC adopters have a larger proportion of overhead costs than non-adopters. Interestingly, in contrast to the propositions, the study found that ABC non-adopters make significantly more customised products (product diversity) and export a higher percentage of sales (competition). Overall, from a demand perspective the findings were disappointing. This prompted Bjørnenak to adopt a supply-side perspective on the diffusion of ABC. He then looked at two factors, namely company size and information sources. Company size represented the information field of potential adopters, i.e. the infrastructure of contacts and communication channels. The study found that company size (number of employees) significantly discriminates between adopters and non-adopters concerning knowledge of ABC. The interpretation of this finding was that larger companies have a bigger network of communication channels and the infrastructure necessary to adopt ABC. Next, the study tested whether size differentiated between adopters and non-adopters with knowledge of ABC. The test produced no significant result. The information sources included in the study were magazines, courses, and internal information (e.g. from other plants, divisions etc., within the same company). Adopters were, not surprisingly, found to have more information sources than non-adopters. More interesting, though, is the distribution of information sources. ABC adopters were found to more frequently obtain their information from courses and from other plants, divisions, etc., within the same company group (i.e. personal and internal information sources). Non-adopters were found to use magazines more as their source of information (i.e. a non-personal source of information). These findings indicate that information sources may affect the adoption of ABC.

Bjørnenak and Mitchell (2002) analysed the activity-based costing/cost management (ABC/M) literature that had been gathered in the UK and the USA in 17 academic/practitioner magazines and academic accounting research journals. The study looked at five dimensions of the ABC/M literature. In their study, one dimension (the content and role dimension) was linked to the supply side of ABC/M diffusion. Authors were seen as agents who take an active role in the diffusion process.

A distinction was made between two categories of authors, namely propagators and moderators. An article that propagates ABC/M was classified as a propagator. Articles classified as moderators were assumed to have a moderating effect on the diffusion process. The majority of articles identified in this latter category were critical of ABC/M. Articles that were neither propagators nor moderators were classified as neutral. Articles classified as propagators were given the value 1 and moderators were given the value −1. Articles classified as neutral were given the value 0. The values −0.5 and 0.5 were used for articles where the assessment was marginal. A propagator/moderator (P/M) index was calculated to analyse the differences in attitude towards ABC/M apparent in the journals. The P/M index is the average value within a group of articles. Bjørnenak and Mitchell performed three analyses using the index. First, they looked at P/M values for different journals for the 14 years covered by the study. They found that three practitioner journals were the most positive to ABC/M. These were the *Journal of Cost Management*, *Management Accounting* (UK) and *Management Accounting* (USA). General US academic journals and the specialist management accounting research journal *Management Accounting Research* were identified as being the most critical of ABC/M. No significant changes emerged over time. Second, Bjørnenak and Mitchell analysed P/M values for the combination of authorship and practitioner journal. Three categories were used for authors: academics, consultants and practitioners. Articles written by authors who fell into different categories were also included. The study found that academics in general, and particularly UK academics, are less positive to ABC/M than both consultants and practitioners. This applies for all the journals analysed. Third, the study looked at P/M values for different methods used in research on ABC/M published in academic research journals. The research methods analysed were: technical development, econometric analysis, survey, review, case/field study and mathematical modelling. The research that focused on the technical development of ABC/M was, not surprisingly, the most positive. There was a clear moderator dominance in the mathematical modelling and the case/field study-based research. On the whole, the picture that emerged from the study was that the literature is basically positive towards ABC/M, and that the key propagators of ABC/M are articles published in practitioner journals written by consultants/practitioners. Moderators of ABC/M were primarily identified in the academic journals, and particularly in UK case/field-based research and US quantitatively oriented research. Thus, in the case of diffusion of ABC/M, there seems to be obvious differences in both the contents of the messages produced by consultants/practitioners and academics respectively and the types of communication channels (journals) they use.

The two studies reviewed in this section indicate the importance of a supply-side perspective on diffusion process. The second study does not look into diffusion *per se*, but shows that different authors play different roles in the diffusion process by communicating the ABC/M message differently. In the study, consultants and academics are seen as diffusion agencies that distribute the innovation (ABC) and information about the usefulness of the innovation through various journals. The readers are potential adopters or redistributors of the innovation. Thus, the study offers insight into the first of the three elements of the market and infrastructure perspective. The first study (Bjørnenak, 1997) complements this by indicating that the success of the innovation diffusion may be affected by the choice of distribution channels. Personal and internal information sources seem to be more important than journals. However, journals may have an indirect effect through redistributors of innovations. This two-step model of the diffusion of innovation has not been given much attention in management accounting research.

A dynamic perspective on the diffusion of management accounting innovations

Traditionally, management accounting innovations have been viewed as discrete, uniform and static 'objects', which remain unchanged as they diffuse. However, this perspective can be challenged as overly simplistic. It is more realistic to adopt a dynamic perspective on the process of diffusion. This perspective views both suppliers and users of innovations as active groups of actors, which are either intentionally or unintentionally involved in changing the content and uses of innovations as they diffuse. Such changes are made possible because administrative innovations are not physical objects with fixed and definite components. They are intangible objects lacking a material component. Benders and van Veen (2001) claim that administrative innovations do not consist of clear-cut recipes, but are characterised by a certain degree of conceptual ambiguity, which contributes to their interpretative viability. This interpretative viability opens up a space for different interpretations and uses of innovations, making it possible for suppliers and users to recognise their own versions of the innovations. They 'can eclectically select those elements that appeal to them, or that they interpret as the fashion's core idea, or that they opportunistically select as suitable for their purposes' (ibid, pp. 37–8).

This section presents a conceptual framework for a dynamic perspective on the diffusion of management accounting innovations. In the framework, management accounting innovations are seen as models that consist of two elements, namely design characteristics and rhetorical elements. Both are basic components of all management accounting innovations. Design characteristics describe the 'hard' side and the rhetorical elements the 'soft' side of innovations.

Design characteristics represent the technical specifications of an innovation. All innovations have certain design elements. Viewed in this way, it is the package of design elements that defines the technical aspects of an innovation. Examples of design elements in the case of ABC are cost objects, activity hierarchies and cost drivers, and in the case of BSC strategy maps, scorecard perspectives and cause–effect linkages.

Rhetorical elements represent the alleged benefits of an innovation. Rhetorical elements are used to persuade an audience of managers about the value of an innovation to their organisations. Here, it is essential to persuade managers that an innovation is the most rational and modern approach to managing contemporary organisations. Rhetoric can focus on various aspects of the innovation; for example its benefits (often compared to existing techniques), areas of use and the problems it can solve. Also, stories about companies that successfully use the innovation represent an important rhetorical element.

Design characteristics and rhetorical elements can be changed, added, combined, etc. 'Redesigned' innovations can thus differ from what their originators had in mind. The degree of redesign is a function of a number of factors. The degree of ambiguity in the definition of the innovation is one important variable. Even though there is room for alternative interpretations in the ABC concept, the interpretative viability of the BSC concept seems to be higher. Another important factor is the role of propagators in the diffusion process. Propagators may try to adjust the innovation for the context into which it is being introduced. An example is the introduction of ABC as a full costing method in those countries which have a full costing tradition, for example by allocating facility sustaining costs to cost objects.

A model of the different degrees or levels of innovation viability is shown in Table 17.3. Different types of dynamic processes are described whereby changes are made in the design or the rhetoric of an innovation. The levels are examples of possible dynamic effects, and do not include all possible changes. The higher levels are typically consistent with a higher degree of change in the innovation.

Naming

In *naming,* a label (such as ABC or the BSC) is simply taken and applied to an existing idea. The whole content of ABC or the BSC is not diffused, only the name. This might be called a quasi-diffusion since the content of the idea is not adopted. A company that uses a set of financial and non-financial performance indicators might, for example, introduce the term 'the BSC' to describe its existing performance measurement system, without making any other changes or even without knowing much about the BSC. Naming is normally a demand side driven process, although it can also be a supply side driven process.

Selecting

Selecting is a partial use of the innovation where certain design elements or rhetorical elements of an innovation are adopted by an actor. An example of diffusion of design

Table 17.3 Levels of innovation variability in the diffusion process

Level and type	Characteristics
Level 1 – Naming	The name of an existing idea/technique is replaced by an innovation's name.
Level 2 – Selecting	Design elements or rhetorical elements of an innovation are selected for diffusion/adoption.
Level 3 – Relocating and reframing	The scope of the innovation is changed without changing design elements and, as a result, the applicability of the innovation is typically widened.
Level 4 – Linking	An innovation is entirely or partially linked to other innovations or existing ideas/techniques.
Level 5 – Bundling	The innovation is bundled with other innovations or existing ideas/techniques. This bundling results in a new 'innovation package'.
Level 6 – Housing	An unclear set of design elements and rhetorical elements from different innovations is combined in a new 'housing' concept, such as beyond budgeting or strategic cost management.

elements is where an organisation adopts the BSC perspectives for organising its performance indicators without using the label BSC or adopting the BSC in its entirety. Another example is when the concept of 'cost of unused capacity' from the ABC literature is adopted without implementing or using ABC.

The diffusion of rhetorical elements is not as obvious, however. The introduction of ABC included a strong rhetoric about deficiencies within existing costing systems. This critique can be accepted without adopting the innovation as such. Likewise, the rhetoric surrounding intangible assets in the BSC can be adopted without actually adopting the BSC.

Relocating and reframing

Relocating is when an idea is introduced into new contexts. ABC started out as a product costing idea, mainly with examples from the manufacturing industry. Later, the method was extended to service industries and the non-profit sector. It is also used in many different functions of the firm, such as supply and distribution, not only in production.

Reframing is when the idea is entirely or partially applied to new uses/problems. Two examples are the use of ABC re-engineering and activity-based budgeting. Another example is the use of the BSC for strategic communication.

Linking

In this process the innovation is expanded by *linking* some of its design elements to those of other innovations or existing ideas/techniques. One example is linking ABC with target costing. This process is typically supply side driven. The two (or more) innovations are still treated separately and both names are used. However, the synergies of the two innovations are emphasised, for example ABC can be used to support the introduction of target costing.

Bundling

Bundling is the process of packing new elements into an existing innovation. The BSC concept in Sweden is such an example. When introduced to potential adopters, the BSC concept was bundled with design characteristics of the Swedish intellectual capital model and with the rhetoric of non-budget management. However, the label BSC was still used. Another form of bundling is when an innovation is bundled (merged) with another innovation. Both innovations can be individually identified and their individual names used. Bundling is typically a supply side driven process and its purpose is often to reduce resistance and barriers for potential adopters.

Housing

In recent years we have seen the introduction of a new type of management accounting innovation, in which the content of the innovation is somewhat unclear. Often the innovation is a combination of other innovations or elements from other innovations. This process is called *housing* because the new innovation is based on, or is housing, elements from other innovations. Beyond budgeting is one example. It is not a management accounting innovation *per se*. However, it is a concept that is housing both rhetorical and design elements from, for example, the BSC literature. Another example is strategic management accounting, which is often described as a new combination and use of other ideas, including ABC.

This section has offered a new and dynamic view of the diffusion of management accounting innovations. The dynamics may be both demand side and supply side driven. The lower levels are often used by adopters (demand side) to signal change and indicate that the organisation is 'trendy'. The higher levels are more likely to be driven by propagators such as consultants and academic institutions. The dynamic perspective is potentially important in understanding how and why some innovations are more successful then others. So far, little research has been done in this area.

Conclusion

Many new concepts have been introduced in management accounting in recent years. Some have been more successful than others. Why? This chapter has discussed different perspectives on the diffusion of innovations. One important observation is that an innovation may have existed earlier in another form or another setting. As long as it is perceived as new in a particular social setting, it may still be considered an innovation. Some innovations are seen as new in some contexts or cultures, but not in others.

From the demand-side perspective, adopters are continuously looking for new ideas to develop and change their management accounting systems. Adopters may have different reasons for adopting or rejecting innovations. However, the role of propagators is increasingly important for our understanding of how and why any particular innovation is adopted or not. Two particular perspectives presented in this chapter, the management fashion perspective and the market and infrastructure perspective, both emphasise the importance of communication between adopters and propagators in the diffusion process.

The interaction between the demand side and the supply side of diffusion processes is important in a dynamic perspective on the diffusion of management accounting innovations. In this perspective, the innovation is seen as flexible and not a fixed technical solution. Both potential adopters and propagators may intentionally or unintentionally change the design characteristics or rhetorical elements of an innovation to make the innovation more attractive. Accordingly, the interpretative viability of many management accounting innovations may be an important factor in explaining the success of their diffusion processes.

References

Abrahamson, E. (1991) 'Managerial fads and fashion: the diffusion and rejection of innovations', *Academy of Management Review*, **16**, 586–612.

Abrahamson, E. (1996) 'Management fashion', *Academy of Management Review*, **21**, 254–85.

Ask, U., Ax, C. and Jönsson, S. (1996) 'Cost management in Sweden: from modern to post-modern', in A. Bhimani (ed.), *Management accounting: European perspectives* (pp. 199–217), Oxford: Oxford University Press.

Ax, C. and Bjørnenak, T. (2005) 'Bundling and diffusion of management accounting innovations: the case of the balanced scorecard in Sweden', *Management Accounting Research*, **16**, 1–20.

Benders, J. and van Veen, K. (2001) 'What's in a fashion? Interpretative viability and management fashions', *Organization,* **8,** 33–53.

Bjørnenak, T. (1997) 'Diffusion and accounting: the case of ABC in Norway', *Management Accounting Research,* **8,** 3–17.

Bjørnenak, T. and Mitchell, F. (2002) 'The development of activity-based costing journal literature, 1987–2000', *European Accounting Review,* **11,** 481–508.

Brown, L.A. (1975) 'The market and infrastructure context of adoption: a spatial perspective on the diffusion of innovation', *Economic Geography,* **51,** 185–216.

Brown, L.A. (1981) *Innovation Diffusion: A New Perspective,* London: Methuen.

Bourguignon, A., Malleret, V. and Nørreklit, H. (2004) 'The American balanced scorecard versus the French tableau de bord: the ideological dimension', *Management Accounting Research,* **15,** 107–34.

Haegerstrand, T. (1967) *Innovation as a Spatial Process,* Chicago, IL: The University of Chicago Press.

Horngren, C.T. (1982) *Cost Accounting: A Managerial Emphasis,* Englewood Cliffs, NJ: Prentice-Hall.

Horngren, C.T., Foster, G.M. and Datar, S.M. (2005) *Cost Accounting: A Managerial Emphasis,* 12th edn, Englewood Cliffs, NJ: Prentice-Hall.

Malmi, T. (1999) 'Activity-based costing diffusion across organizations: an exploratory empirical analysis of Finnish firms', *Accounting, Organizations and Society,* **24,** 649–72.

Malmi, T. (2001) 'Balanced scorecards in Finnish companies: a research note', *Management Accounting Research,* **12,** 207–20.

Newell, S., Robertson, M. and Swan, J. (1997) 'Professional associations as "brokers", facilitating networking and the diffusion of new ideas: advantages and disadvantages', in J.L. Alvarez (ed.), *The Diffusion and Consumption of Business Knowledge,* London: Macmillan Press, pp. 182–200.

Further reading

Bjørnenak, T. and Olson, O. (1999) 'Unbundling management accounting innovations', *Management Accounting Research,* **10,** 325–38. This article presents a framework in which management accounting innovations are seen as packages of design characteristics.

Carmona, S. and Gutiérrez, I. (2003) 'Vogues in management accounting research', *Scandinavian Journal of Management,* **19,** 213–31. Drawing on the literature of institutional sociology and management fashion, this article addresses the ebb and flow of research fashions in management accounting among national groups of accounting scholars.

Drury, C. and Tayles, M. (2005) 'Explicating the design of overhead absorption procedures in UK organizations', *The British Accounting Review,* **37,** 47–84. This article reviews empirical studies that have adopted a demand-side perspective on the diffusion of activity-based costing systems.

Gosselin, M. (1997) 'The effects of strategy and organizational structure on the adoption and implementation of activity-based costing', *Accounting, Organizations and Society,* **22,** 105–22. This article presents findings from a study on the effects of strategic posture and organisational structure on the adoption of activity-based approaches.

Lapsley, I. and Wright, E. (2004) 'The diffusion of management accounting innovations in the public sector: a research agenda', *Management Accounting Research,* **15,** 355–74. This article focuses on the dissemination and adoption of management accounting practices within the public sector.

Lukka, K. and Granlund, M. (2002) 'The fragmented communication structure within the accounting academia: the case of activity-based costing research genres', *Accounting, Organizations and Society,*

27, 165–90. This article examines the communication structures within management accounting academia, with a view to illustrating and thereby alleviating the difficulties of dialogue between different discussion circles within the field.

Perera, S., McKinnon, J.L. and Harrison, G.L. (2003) 'Diffusion of transfer pricing innovation in the context of commercialization – a longitudinal case study of a government trading enterprise', *Management Accounting Research,* **14**, 140–64. This article analyses and explains events surrounding the introduction, abandonment and reintroduction of transfer pricing in a government trading enterprise over a ten-year period.

Rogers, E.M. (2003) *Diffusion of Innovations,* 5th edn, New York: The Free Press. A classic in the field of innovation diffusion. A comprehensive review of several decades of traditional diffusion research and literature.

18

The relevance of the past

Richard Fleischman and Warwick Funnell

Introduction

In the first two editions of this book, Anne Loft (1991, 1995) approached the chapter on management accounting history by focusing upon the particular directions that research has taken and the paradigmatic grounding of the scholars who have undertaken these investigations of our discipline's past. Whilst this chapter will necessarily touch, albeit more briefly, upon issues that Loft's narratives covered in perceptive detail, this chapter instead will seek to emphasise the relevance of the history of management accounting to contemporary practice. A similar task confronted Bernard Crick when, in his book *In Defence of Politics* (1962), he sought to defend the art (and/or science) of politics against its persistent, cynical and vigorous critics. Fortunately, it is far easier to provide a believable, albeit partisan, defence of history than to undertake the arduous task Crick faced in spinning a good case for politics. The scepticism underlying questions about the relevance of the study of history and the value of politics can be appreciated by substituting, in three phrases from Crick's book, the word 'history' for 'politics':

> Politics [history] is too often regarded as a poor relation, inherently dependent and subsidiary; it is rarely praised as something with a life and character of its own. (p. 11)

> Politics [history] itself is attacked for dividing communities, for being inefficient, for being inconclusive and . . . for being unscientific. (p. 139)

> Politics [history] should be praised for doing what it can do, but also praised for not attempting what it cannot do. (p. 146)

It is not an easy task to convince practical-minded management accountants, who question the relevance of what has gone before, of the contemporary importance of management accounting history. In 1959, for example, the reports of two influential US funding agencies, the Carnegie and Ford Foundations, advanced the position that business research was only valuable to the degree that it directly impacted business practice. According to this view of history, the past, rather than providing a beneficial legacy to the present, was instead more likely to be a deceptive impediment to improvement in the present. This has been especially evident in management accounting, as argued by H. Thomas Johnson and Robert Kaplan (1987) in *Relevance Lost: The Rise and Fall of Management Accounting*. They discovered from their study of a half-century of costing history in the USA that 'the management accounting system not only fails to provide relevant information to managers, but also distracts their attention from factors that are critical for production efficiencies'.

The fact that history is a set of antecedent, completed and, therefore, certain events would suggest that the past be accorded pre-eminence over the present. The attention of management accountants, however, is necessarily on the future, concentrating on what will move the enterprise forward rather than on reporting the past (income statements) and present (balance sheets). According to Johnson and Kaplan, management accounting reports should provide managers with the means to reduce costs and assist them to improve productivity. While these are primarily activities looking to the future, they rely on the intimate dependence between the past and the future. The complexity of managing, arising out of the nature of an organisation's activities and the hostility and uncertainty of its commercial environment, ensures that managing is a difficult task that must rely heavily on information that will allow managers to influence the future. Deregulation of world markets with the removal or lowering of trade barriers through the auspices of world trade organisations has increased the complexity of managing by forcing more and more producers to compete in a world market. Technological change derived from advances in computerisation has also added to the difficulties by changing how products are manufactured and by accelerating the pace at which business is conducted. Products are now moved more efficiently to their destinations; financial transactions are concluded almost instantaneously and the management information systems of manufacturers and suppliers are increasingly integrated. Thus, at first glance, there would appear to be a tension between the practical, immediate needs of management accountants and the preoccupation of history with a concluded, superseded past as its defining feature. This chapter, however, will endeavour to demonstrate to students and practitioners of management accounting that a study of its history has much to offer in understanding and critiquing the contributions of current practice, in identifying new directions for practice, and also in exposing the moral culpability of management accounting and management accountants.

Current management accounting principles and practices, like all contemporary disciplines, form but the latest stage in an evolutionary process in which intimations of the impending stages are to be found. Few, if any, management accounting practices have arisen spontaneously from the present. Instead, most are but modifications of, and extensions to, long-standing management accounting techniques. Thus, activity-based costing (ABC) is just a more sophisticated and refined form of accounting for overheads by allocating these costs based on a greater variety of drivers than the traditional one or two. A century ago when labour costs were a major component of total product cost, it was an immaterial distortion of reality for overhead to be applied on the basis of the more easily measured direct labour cost or hours. In today's world where overhead has come to dwarf labour as the predominant conversion cost at many global enterprises (e.g. labour cost accounted for only 2.8 per cent of total product cost at Hewlett Packard in the early 1990s), ABC is a natural refinement of a process with a long history – it is not particularly new. General Electric was employing a prototype in the 1960s and George Staubus has been writing about it for a quarter of a century. Similarly, strategic management accounting has its origins in management accounting's previously peripheral consideration of the financial characteristics of competitors. Neither are competitors a new phenomenon, only the manner and degree to which their actions are now recognised by management accounting is new. Accordingly, whilst the practices, materials and processes of business served by management accounting may change greatly in terms of detail, the essential principles and motives of business have remained remarkably stable since the Industrial Revolution, and even before. Their debt to the past is undiminished; the present contains the residue of the past. Management is confronted with essentially the same problems arising from the need to achieve organisational goals with the scarce resources available, to satisfy the expectations of customers, and to be more successful than competitors. It matters little whether these goals are derived from the need to make a profit or to manage within a fixed, government budget allocation. Thus, as Johnson and Kaplan so dramatically demonstrated, an understanding of the past based on a study of the history of management accounting is essential to appreciating the motivations and relevance of present practices. It is also essential to comprehending the societal and economic impacts of the wide range of decisions that may be informed by data generated by management accountants. Decisions that may appear to meet the requirements of rational, economic decision-making may yet fail to meet the standards of ethical behaviour that society expects of its institutions.

This chapter is divided into three main sections that take us from the general to the more specific. We will consider initially what has been written about the intrinsic value of historical investigation. Here the focus will be on the erudition of historians and philosophers rather than that of accounting history practitioners *per se*. We will then concentrate on a discussion of the greater and lesser tangible benefits a managerial accountant, whether in the public or private sector, might derive from studying the past of his/her chosen discipline and craft. In the final sections of the chapter, the contributions of accounting to ethical business practice are examined.

History: what is past is prologue

The past can be studied for itself, for the pleasure provided from knowing about the lives of others and the events that have led to the present. In this way, the study of history has the ability to enrich our lives by, if nothing else, making the past accessible to us today and thereby enhancing our understanding of how institutions and practices developed and why they continue to be relevant. A study of history also can have a far more practical aspect by providing each generation with the ability to understand the political and social tensions of the present. Frequently, the progress of seemingly isolated events coalesces to create unpredictable crises and responses that become embodied in contemporary institutions and practices. In accounting history, this serendipitous nexus between historical events and institutionalised practices and beliefs has been particularly prominent in the rise of modern government accounting and accountability practices in Britain. This was obvious in the latter decades of the eighteenth century, when the military humiliations suffered by the English in the American War of Independence (1776–1783), and the rising indebtedness of England as a consequence of the war, unexpectedly awoke Parliament to serious flaws in government accounts. Parliament came to realise that most of the accounts of the civil departments of state were many years in arrears, thereby denying Parliament the opportunity to monitor closely the actions of the Crown. These deficiencies in the accountability of the Crown to Parliament had allowed the Crown to abuse its patronage rights to influence and corrupt members of Parliament and, thereby, to threaten the liberty of all. Ultimately, the political and economic crisis engendered by the American War of Independence prompted government accounting and audit reforms, which laid the foundations for British public sector audit reforms in the mid nineteenth century. The most important of these was the annual audit and presentation of all executive accounts to Parliament.

Many claims have been advanced either overstating or under-valuing the importance and relevance of history to our contemporary lives. Loft commenced this chapter in earlier editions with a quote from the noted historian E.H. Carr: 'We can fully understand the present only in light of the past' (Loft, 1995, p. 21). Similarly, fronting the National Archives of the United States is the statue of an elegant woman, dressed in classical garb, who could well be Clio, the muse of history. At the base of the statue the inscription reads, 'What is Past is Prologue', words from Shakespeare's *Tempest*. This faith in the didactic nature of history can be contrasted with the frequently heard quote from historian George Santayana whose belief that 'those who cannot learn from history are doomed to repeat it' echoes the less famous remark from the more renowned George Bernard Shaw: 'We learn from history that we learn nothing from history'. Needless to say, the conventional wisdom suggests that history's contribution to our learning is somewhere between these two extremes. Keith Windschuttle, whose 1994 book *The Killing of History* is one of the most perceptive and thought-provoking pieces of historiography that we have read, suggests something in between: 'What happens in history is by no means random or chaotic. Any major change in history is dependent on, that is, contingent upon, everything that came before' (p. 217). This is particularly apposite for management accounting, where novel practices rarely arise spontaneously from practice.

For the practicing management accountant, Marc Bloch's appreciation of the value of history is especially pertinent. Bloch, a noted French historian, wrote in *The Historian's Craft*: 'History is a continuum. Events of the past and present are intimately linked – impossible to isolate, separate, or treat separately'. The relationship was even more strongly expressed by Herbert Muller, in *The Uses of the Past*, for whom 'the past has no meaningful existence except as it exists for us, as it is given meaning by us'. A dean of American historians, Henry Steele Commager, wrote in *The Nature and Study of History* how history enlarges our experience and thus 'provides great examples and companions to the problems and concerns of the present'. Extending these past/present linkages to accounting, noted accounting historians Gary Previts and Rob Bricker observed perceptively: 'One benefit of conducting historical research is the development of perspectives about current problems; that is, simply to learn about the past as background to present day issues' (Previts and Bricker, 1994, p. 626). Allan Nevins took the argument one step further in *The Gateway to History*: '[History is] more than a guide for men in their daily round; it is a creator of their future' (Nevins, 1962, p. 18).

Henry Hallam and Thomas Babington Macaulay, both early nineteenth century historians, believed that not only was there a close association between the present and the past, but that this association betrayed a beneficial inheritance. This 'Whig interpretation of history' views history as a process of continuous improvement from past to present. The Whig interpretation has fallen into disrepute in today's world, largely the result of Herbert Butterfield's book of 1931 that exposed some of the theory's fallacies. Indeed, the pendulum has swung back strongly against an idealised appreciation of history. Thomas Kuhn, one of the most famous names in the history of science, has theorised that even science is a series of revolutionary dis-continuities rather than a seamless transition to greater understanding as one might expect. The French postmodernist philosopher Michel Foucault was so convinced of history's discontinuities that he urged his adherents to abandon the fruitless search for origins of contemporary practice, a pastime that occupies the attention of many historians. Windschuttle has written that one age is no better than another in terms of its practices, only different.

Accounting historians, whether 'new' or more traditional, believe their work has the ability to make a difference to our lived experience today. They have identified accounting as a moral practice with contributions to entrenched understandings of distributive justice and the intractability of racism, amongst others. Thus, Warwick Funnell's recounting of the importance of accounting to the 'efficiency' of the Nazis' implementation of the Holocaust is a particularly disturbing example of the possibili-ties for the use of accounting information; in particular, the information produced by management accounting for decision-making. The enduring metaphor for the Holocaust is that of the operation of an efficient machine with the sole objective of pro-cessing millions of people as quickly and cost-effectively as possible into corpses (see, e.g. Hilberg, 1985). In similar vein, Funnell and Stephen Walker have exposed the contributions of accountants and auditors to the misdistribution of relief during the Irish Potato Famine and the early years of the New Poor Law respectively. Richard Fleischman, Thomas Tyson and David Oldroyd have studied the complicity of accountants in perpetuating the horrors of slavery in the USA and the British Caribbean. In particular, accountants participated in the dehumanising activity of valuing slaves as chattels. Marcia Annisette, Owolabi Bakre, Charles Elad and Dean Neu, as well as Fleischman and Tyson, have critically examined the racism implicit in imperialist and post-colonial regimes. Theresa Hammond has chronicled the racism reflected in the denial of access to minority people, African Americans specifically, into the accounting profession.

Aside from the historical lessons to be learned or ignored as the case may be, the study of history does provide tangible benefits for the educational process. History affords a fas-cinating database for studying cause and effect relationships. It is food for thought for the honing of critical-thinking and problem-solving skills, attributes that are now highly val-ued by the accounting profession in entry-level recruits, rather than traditional technical knowledge (see, for example, the 1989 'white paper' of the then 'Big Eight' international public accounting firms – Arther Anderson *et al.*, 1989). In today's world of big interna-tional accounting and globally competitive industrial/service sector enterprises, success-ful business people need to be aware of the cultural mores of other societies. Business is conducted differently around the globe with a variety of conventions, customs and ethi-cal understandings. It is difficult to think of a resource more valuable to understanding the whys and wherefores of a foreign culture than the national history of its people.

Does history inform the management accountant?

Johnson and Kaplan's writing on the history of management accounting has been especially influential in establishing the importance of an understanding of the past to ensuring that, in circumstances of constant and rapid change, management accounting retains its relevance. They did not believe that all management accounting practiced before the 1980s was a historical irrelevancy or, worse, a deceptive irrelevancy. Rather, Johnson and Kaplan (1987) argued that a study of the past provided the means to expose the weaknesses or failings of management accounting in the late twentieth century. They sought to demonstrate, by tracing the events and forces that shaped management accounting practices, especially until the 1920s, how these were very different from the present. On the basis of their historical survey of business and the management accounting practices, Johnson and Kaplan were able to demonstrate that most of these practices were responses to outdated needs that consequently had themselves become outmoded.

Traditional forms of management accounting have been heavily influenced by the accounting demands of mass production. The ultimate goal of producing large quantities of similar products from a continuous, uninterrupted production process was to achieve economies of scale as measured by a reduction in costs per unit of finished product. The presumption was that cost reductions would arise from a number of sources. First, overhead costs would be distributed over more units of product, thus lowering the overhead cost component in successive units of output. Second, producing more of the same thing in comparatively labour-intensive industries encourages learning which has a favourable impact on costs due to the more efficient and effective utilisation of resources. Finally, the costs of continuous, large-scale production were preferable to the higher costs incurred when production was interrupted.

A study of the history of firms reveals that a major shortcoming of traditional mass production is that the pursuit of economies of scale condemns the firms to rigid production, cost and management structures. The regime of mass production dictates that production must not be interrupted and that product changes should be avoided. The extensive introduction of advanced manufacturing techniques in recent decades, with the associated decline in the importance of traditional forms of direct labour, has challenged management and management accountants to examine and overhaul long-held and almost sacred practices. The remarkable worldwide changes in manufacturing and service industries have involved far more than just new machines. For the firm to get the greatest return from its typically substantial investment in new technology, the entire organisation of production, especially its managerial practices and operating philosophies, must be questioned. Management accountants are expected to facilitate these attitudinal and infrastructure changes through the information they collect and how it is used, especially for performance evaluation. Without appropriate, that is relevant, complementary information, the impending metamorphosis to a more efficient and profitable organisation will be realised only partially, if at all. Knowledge of the history of management accounting and the decision needs that its practices were originally meant to serve can, in part, provide the means to expose practices that deny management the ability to see that it may be seeking the wrong information for the wrong decisions. Consequently, management may be unaware that its information needs have changed. A timely realisation of this reality has been especially critical in the history of the mega-corporation.

History has much to tell us about the developmental process of the mega-corporation, a business structure that has come to dominate the global economy, and its management practices. Alfred Chandler (1977), a renowned economic historian, and Johnson (1980), an equally noted accounting historian, have studied the rise of the diversified corporation, with particular emphasis on two of the earliest – DuPont and General Motors, business entities that rose to prominence in the early 1920s. Large corporations predated these enterprises to be sure; the difference between them and earlier giants such as Carnegie Steel, the American Tobacco Company and Standard Oil was the advent of a professional managerial corps charged with substantial responsibility in decentralised structures. The replacement of top-down, centralised control with modern managerialism created an agency relationship between these managers and their principals, the owners of the enterprises. The trade-offs between the satisficing behaviour of managers (the consumption of perquisites) and the enhancement of shareholder wealth has been one of the two major themes of academic business research for the past two decades. Managerial accountants, as the watchdogs of the corporation, need to deal with these issues and would do well to consult the historical and contemporary research that has used agency theory to gain valuable insights. Agency theory suggests that the activities of managers must be carefully monitored to guarantee that the well-being of the enterprise is not sub-optimised by their pursuit of wealth and power enhancement. However, important as theoretical insights are to understanding management accounting, the conclusions they might promote are not necessarily isomorphic substantiations of situations encountered in practice. Reality and individuals are far more complex and unpredictable than the prescriptions and proscriptions that might be allowed by neat theoretical propositions. Thus, whilst the fraudulent actions of Kenneth Lay at Enron may have vindicated the pessimism and cautions of agency theory, the selfless actions of accounting whistleblowers such as Sherron Watkins at Enron equally underline its limitations.

One of the dangers occasioned by American accountancy's disdain for history generally, and the positivistic linking of education and practice in particular, lies in the assumption that accounting theory and accounting practice operate in tandem. For example, cutting-edge business practices such as ABC and total quality management did not find their way into managerial accounting textbooks for nearly a decade after their inception in practice. These so-called 'schisms' between accounting theory and practice were even more pronounced in a historical context. For instance, one compelling reason why accounting historians of the mid twentieth century felt that sophisticated managerial accounting had its origins in the US scientific management movement early in the century was because there was no literature that suggested an earlier origin. Hence, David Solomons proclaimed a 'costing renaissance' only for that very late date. However, if these historians had done archival research, they would have found purposeful costing as early as the British Industrial Revolution. It was just that no one at the time was writing industrial accounting manuals and nobody was teaching the techniques in the schools of commerce. It is now fairly clear that practice was running far ahead of theory and education. Likewise, if those historians who have written extensively about scientific management in the USA from the vantage point of their respective paradigms (Johnson and Kaplan (1987) for economic rationalism; Peter Miller and Ted

383

O'Leary (1987) from a Foucauldian perspective; and Trevor Hopper and Peter Armstrong (1991) espousing a Marxist/labour-process analysis) had done archival research and had not accepted the judgements of their historical predecessors at face value, they would have discovered that the new methods suggested by Frederick Taylor and other consultants of the time (standard costing, variance analysis, time-and-motion studies, etc.) were rarely seen in practice. Here the 'schism' was the reverse of the British Industrial Revolution in that theory was far in the vanguard of practice. In fact, it took practice over 40 years to reach a stage in the utilisation of scientific management that the vast outpouring of theoretical literature suggested was present earlier.

Cost accounting and management accounting as practised today are the products of a series of industrial revolutions that extended from the late eighteenth century to the nineteenth century, first in Great Britain and subsequently in western Europe and the USA. It was a period when previously unknown industries were founded and when existing, simple forms of production were moved from cottages and concentrated in factories near sources of power needed to drive new machinery. The new industries (including textiles, iron and steel, and railways) were on a scale never before envisaged. They involved new risks and often required large quantities of capital that were beyond the capacity of one individual owner to provide. This led to the formation of limited liability companies in mid nineteenth century Britain and the onset of modern capitalism as we know it today, where corporations are managed by individuals employed by shareholding owners who contribute the capital but otherwise exercise no direct influence in the management of the firm. Thus, with the new industries and new forms of business organisations came demands for new types of information to meet the needs of both managers and absentee owners (the shareholders). The information needs of these earliest process-type industries, according to Johnson and Kaplan (1987), were to evaluate internal processes, not to measure profitability. This changed with the appearance and development of the multi-activity, diversified corporations of the early twentieth century.

Historians have been obsessed with the project of identifying the origins of purposeful cost accounting. According to accounting historians, large manufacturing firms were using very basic cost accounting systems well before the late nineteenth century, mainly to control labour costs. Early traditionalists such as A.C. Littleton, Paul Garner, Solomons and Murray Wells date the rise of sophisticated costing from the scientific management movement in the USA at the turn of the twentieth century. Chandler (1977) opted for an earlier origin, citing the accounting methods in evidence on the transcontinental railroads, particularly the development of a standardised unit referred to as cost-per-ton mile. Keith Hoskin and Richard Macve (1988, 1994) found what they called the genesis of modern management in the labour control mechanisms in evidence at a US munitions manufactory, the Springfield Armory, in the 1830s and 1840s. Here, the defining discontinuity was the imposition of labour discipline through techniques that had been developed at West Point. Johnson (1972) and Tyson (1992) have argued that the New England textiles industry was the true source, with the development of integrated processes and the accounting necessary to track the movement of product. Dick Edwards, Trevor Boyns and their collaborators, as well as Fleischman and Lee

Parker, have built a strong case for the British Industrial Revolution as cost accounting's seedbed (see, e.g., Edwards, 1989; Boyns and Edwards, 1996).

With the turn of the twentieth century, more sophisticated methodologies appeared which were designed, implemented and administered by engineers rather than accountants. The *Journal of Accountancy* in the 1910s featured a very interesting power struggle between the two professional groups as managerial accountants endeavoured to seize power from the engineers who had been in the vanguard of the scientific management movement. The Americans were well ahead of the British in most cost accounting practices until the First World War. Indeed, there is little evidence of cost accounting innovations being transplanted across the Atlantic prior to the first decade of the twentieth century. Although early manufacturers such as Josiah Wedgwood, the pottery king, and James Watt, the steam engine innovator, were confronted with costing problems not previously encountered, formal cost accounting systems were still rare in most businesses until the early twentieth century. Garcke and Fells' book on factory accounts, published in England in 1887, was the first to marshal and publicise manufacturing cost accounting practices which previously had been zealously guarded by firms as trade secrets. Certainly there is little evidence of any attempts by the British government to introduce cost accounting prior to the First World War.

During the First World War, the cost accounting reticence of British manufacturers began to disappear when the British government forced manufacturers supplying armaments to the British army under cost-plus contracting to justify their costings. The result was a rapid spread of cost accounting throughout most industries and the maturation by 1925 of most traditional cost accounting practices. Subsequently, the increasing sophistication of management and organisational structures after the Second World War precipitated the entrenchment of a management accounting function in larger firms. Despite unprecedented changes in manufacturing processes and products, according to Johnson and Kaplan, writing in the mid 1980s, little changed in management accounting from the 1920s. Accordingly, management accounting was in danger of losing all relevance in the modern, technologically driven manufacturing environment. Since the 1980s, however, the criticisms voiced by Johnson and Kaplan (1987) in *Relevance Lost*, perhaps the most influential book in management accounting history's history (certainly in terms of sales), have added a new array of contemporary techniques to the traditional forms of management accounting.

Although Johnson and Kaplan are regarded as pre-eminent economic rationalists, leading Foucauldian scholars Mahmoud Ezzamel, Hoskin and Macve (Ezzamel *et al*, 1990) conceded that *Relevance Lost* 'moved accounting's history centre-stage', despite their fundamental disagreement with its conclusions. Johnson and Kaplan were so impressed by the innovations made at DuPont and General Motors in the immediate aftermath of the First World War (e.g. return on investment, decentralisation, business forecasting, market-based transfer pricing, flexible budgeting) that they launched the outrageous claim that everything of importance in American managerial accounting as of the late 1980s was known by 1925. This analysis fails to account for such advances as the wide diffusion of budgeting, direct costing, mathematical variance analysis, accounting for uncertainty, linear programming, project management, etc. However, the point remains that some of the most valuable knowledge relevant to successful managerialism does lie in the past. Only a study of history can expose what is hidden from contemporary eyes.

The bottom-line message of *Relevance Lost* was the indictment of American managerial accounting for the loss of global industrial hegemony in the 1980s, mainly to Japan; hence, the loss of the discipline's relevance. At the time *Relevance Lost* appeared, the inadequacy of American managerial accounting was in sharp contrast to the just-in-time methods developed at Toyota and reflective of Japanese management more broadly. The bill of particulars included a number of items justified by recourse to history. Johnson and Kaplan argued that throughout much of the twentieth century, innovation in management accounting practices was impeded, even thwarted, by the increasing information demands of external parties, especially regulatory bodies, that had too much influence over the practices and products of cost and management accounting. So much so, they averred, that management accounting was drained of much of its usefulness by the insistent demands of financial accounting. In particular, Johnson and Kaplan alleged that inventory valuations required for financial accounting stunted the development of management accounting and diminished its relevance. The traditional cost accounting aims of inventory valuation and profit determination for external reporting had deflected management's attention from active involvement in the control of costs. Thus, according to Johnson and Kaplan, for too long cost accounting has been directed by the needs of financial accounting and not those of management. Management accounting can only be as good as the material with which it works, most of which comes from cost accounting. If cost accounting is captured to serve the financial reporting interests of external groups, then management accounting will almost certainly suffer. Two obsolete vestiges demonstrate the point clearly. Is it not ironic that many US institutions of higher education require their undergraduate accounting majors to take a course called 'cost accounting', whilst the course mandated for MBA aspirants is almost universally designated 'managerial accounting'? Thus, those students actually destined to practice accounting in the industrial sector take the course bearing a title that is both limiting and obsolete. Second, and vastly more damaging for the craft, is how the certifying examination for licensure in the USA dedicates only 10 per cent of one part (of four) to managerial accounting topics.

The charge was also made by Johnson and Kaplan that the limitations of discounted cash flow analysis meant that US firms were under-investing in computer-aided manufacturing. American academics also stood accused of teaching outmoded methods in managerial accounting courses, techniques more reflective of our fathers' cost accounting than what makes contemporary practice more competitive.

Johnson and Kaplan's book proved to be a very effective catalyst for change. Its conclusions and criticisms of management accounting not only exposed the possible servitude of management accounting to financial accounting and the consequent loss of relevance of management accounting, but the indignation shocked researchers and practitioners out of what Johnson and Kaplan saw as a state of indolence and acquiescence. The result was an avalanche of innovative renditions of management accounting practices. At first, Johnson and Kaplan's mission seemed to be accounting bashing, but within several years a solution was suggested – ABC, later broadened into activity-based management. Many of these re-evaluations of management accounting have proven to be transient in their impact, to be superseded by ever more innovative practices with catchy titles and even greater claims to success.

Management accounting and the challenge of history

Today's university-level managerial accounting courses resemble those of a generation ago only tangentially. It is still necessary to instruct some of the older methodologies because a substantial number of firms have not yet made the transition to today's conventional wisdom. If a young managerial accountant is asked to formulate a traditional production report, for example, by a superior schooled in the old ways, he/she must be so prepared. Notwithstanding the need to allocate some time to what is outmoded, the remainder of the course may be given over to the 'new management accounting', even if cutting-edge methods prove not to be best practice or become relegated to fad status in the fullness of time.

We do not wish to suggest that all of the methodologies taught decades ago in managerial accounting courses are irrelevant in today's world. Indeed, some writings of bygone years, which at the time of their appearance were cutting-edge approaches, have remained state of the art. Perhaps the best example is the Herbert Simon *et al.* 1954 classic work, which describes three essential components of the corporate controller's function – scorekeeping, attention directing and problem solving. This volume should remain on the bookshelf of every controller today and not just as a dust magnet. Other examples of studies just as pertinent today as they were years ago include Charter Harrison (1930) on standard costing, William Vatter (1950) on fund accounting and cost allocation, and Carl Devine on the behavioural aspects of accounting (Hendrickson and Williams, 2004).

To a great degree, 'cost accounting', as the title of the course so many of us teach, is a misnomer because what we are teaching transcends mere costing and is really no longer accounting; it is management pure and simple. Because it is management, it is more interdisciplinary than the old cost accounting. Managerial accountants in today's world need to be schooled in the application of sociology and psychology, as well as more traditional disciplines such as economics and mathematics. The historical literature in these fields is most helpful for developing a broader perspective and a deeper knowledge. For example, Miller and O'Leary's (1987) classic Foucauldian study of the history of the US labour movement from an accounting perspective draws heavily upon both psychology and sociology to describe how the American worker in the post First World War era was transformed into a 'governable person'.

A generation ago, descriptives such as 'bean counter' and 'number cruncher' accurately portrayed the managerial accountant. No longer is this the case! The phrase 'managing by the numbers' has been frequently bandied about in the historical literature of industrial enterprises. Johnson and Kaplan's indictment of US managerial accounting in the 1980s included the charge that the numbers supplied by the various accounting systems were so inaccurate that businesses were unable to distinguish those products which provided the bulk of their revenue (Johnson and Kaplan, 1987). The so-called 20/80 rule implies that 20 per cent of a diversified firm's product lines generate 80 per cent of its revenue, but that the accounting system cannot determine which the profitable ones are. Kaplan's suggested cure for this state of affairs was to improve the quality of the numbers through the introduction of new methods, such as ABC. Foucauldian historians have argued that the accounting numbers have always been highly suspect and, consequently, that any correct business decisions based upon them are fortunate happenstance. What is important within their frame of reference is not the accounting numbers, but the labour control mechanisms in place which track the efficiency of workers. We see value in both approaches. If the accounting numbers indicate the direction decision-making should take, pinpoint accuracy is not usually required. Vatter (1950) made the similar point that the timeliness of reports to management is more vital than absolute accuracy. Meanwhile, attention to labour efficiency, and its benefit for quality control and customer satisfaction, has become central to the craft today. Here again, history is valuable to us, not so much because it teaches us lessons on how to avoid the repetition of errors, but because of the concepts that can be drawn from the huge database we call the past. The richness of management accounting's past is especially impressive when compared to that of financial accounting.

Comparing managerial accounting history to that of financial reporting is akin to mixing apples and oranges. Financial reporting methodologies are dictated by standardised rules, necessarily so in order to guarantee comparability and consistency. Whilst mandated techniques vary from country to country and undergo revision with some regularity in many, the existence of standards is a fact of life. Managerial accounting, by contrast, suffers from no such constraints. There does exist a conventional wisdom, to be sure, but individual enterprises are free to devise whatever informational systems and formats seemingly benefit them the most. It is almost as if Adam Smith's 'invisible hand' functions at this level as well as at the level of the individual and the nation, both of which he discusses in *The Wealth of Nations*. It would seem that, within this context, history takes on greater importance for managerial accountants than for our colleagues in public accounting. It is helpful for managerial accountants to know what has worked and what has failed in the past. Financial accountants can depend upon regulators in either the public or private sector whose charge it is to track the verdicts of history and to legislate accordingly; managerial accountants do not have the luxury of such a standard-setting superstructure.

Managerial accounting has a longer, richer history to draw upon than does financial accounting. Historians, as we have seen, have been preoccupied with backdating the genesis of purposeful cost accounting from the scientific management era of the early twentieth century. Whilst sophisticated costing had to await large-scale industrial enterprise, it is more difficult to date corresponding developments in financial reporting. Historians here have relatively little to investigate before the advent of governmental regulation and professionalisation, commencing in the UK in the mid nineteenth century and significantly later in the USA where the first CPAs were not licensed until the 1890s and regulation did not commence until the 1930s. An overwhelming focus has been on the birth and subsequent expansion of double-entry bookkeeping. Subsequently, historians, both financial and managerial, came to concentrate on the processes by which costing and financial records were integrated into published financial statements.

Meanwhile, management accounting historians have had a much more attractive menu of management-related issues to investigate. These grander topics include the development of discounted cash flows, the coming of substantial industrial enterprises, the control of labour with various standard costing prototypes, a greater attention to costing for business decision-making, and the antecedents of budgeting and forecasting.

For students of management accounting's past, it is doubly important to avoid delusion by 'the Whig interpretation of history' (discussed earlier) – the notion that history moves progressively from past to present. Management accounting has changed remarkably in the past two decades with the introduction of a raft of method-ological innovations described in-depth elsewhere in this handbook. Three overarching manufacturing philosophies currently in evidence are just-in-time, activity-based management and, most recently, total quality management. The question is rightly asked, if these systems are of very recent origin and have come to dominate contem-porary management accounting, how will a study of history be helpful for under-standing and operationalising these methods? The typical, globally competitive firm does not introduce any of these methods in its purest form. Rather, bits and pieces of different approaches are integrated into a quilt-work of practices. History tells us this was the case with the coming of scientific management. When R.H. Hoxie investigat-ed the impact of the innovations proposed by consultants Taylor, Henry Gantt, and Harrington Emerson for the US Commission on Industrial Relations, he found that no single business enterprise had adopted lock, stock and barrel the entire system advanced by its hired consultant. History can provide clues and insights into combi-nations that might work and those with a greater likelihood of failing.

The Harvard Business School is in the vanguard of the growing number of institu-tions whose graduate instruction in business is built almost entirely around the case method. Managerial accounting lends itself particularly well to this form of pedagogy. History provides any number of good cases as to why enterprises have succeeded or failed in the past. However, the management accountant must be careful not to extrap-olate past episodes to contemporary situations too readily. What worked for a firm in the past may fail utterly in the present if the business climate or competitive realities change. Does this make the past too dangerous a reference point for the present? Not at all! Since every business enterprise is different, the value of historical knowledge lies at the level of broad concepts rather than particulars. In reality, the present does not serve us any better because variations in corporate, or even departmental, cultures limit the effective-ness of specific applications gleaned from the benchmarking processes currently in vogue.

Kaplan, as both a Harvard business professor and an advocate of the case study method, formulated his recommendations for ABC and the 'balanced scorecard' on the basis of consultancies he had undertaken with a number of businesses. He has been criticised for basing his suggestions for the recapture of American industrial hegemo-ny entirely on failed or failing enterprises. Despite this limited cross-section of busi-nesses, Kaplan represents his suggested remedies as examples of good management accounting practice. In this regard, his method parallels positivism, a natural sciences approach toward accounting research wherein the 'natural laws' of good business practice are discerned and described. Critics of Kaplan's case study approach iden-tify numerous factors that receive little or no attention in 'positivist framework' research – political aspects of management, power relationships, organisational past actions, alternative perspectives offered by social sciences research (Weberian and

Marxist), and the legitimacy, as distinct from the efficiency, of practices. The study of management accounting is thereby isolated from its broader social and moral context. These omitted attributes are those to which management accounting historians could furnish valuable insights.

Management accounting's ethics: the need to rethink

Too often history has shown that management accounting information has been used in a short-sighted, exclusionary fashion. Many firms let the figures provided by the management accountant blind them to other, possibly non-quantifiable and underlying, realities of what they are doing. Unfortunately, the past is strewn with commercially wrong decisions made on the basis of 'rational' management accounting numbers. (There is also, of course, the wreckage of firms that paid insufficient attention to the management accountants' numbers.) Overwhelmingly, the concern of management accounting practitioners, and many researchers, has been a preoccupation with the problems raised by capitalism, its need to promote an image of unproblematic operation, and its ability to harness accounting to ensure capitalism's continued existence. However, no matter how correct and convincing numbers appear to be, in particular the sacrosanct dollar numbers of management accounting, they are inherently fallible. The apparent objectivity and neutrality of management accounting numbers should not give them an unwarranted and undeserved level of acceptability and legitimacy and put them beyond appropriate critical examination. Probably, their apparent blandness and one-dimensional nature should put them more into question, given that they emanate from an extremely complex commercial and, ultimately, social base and seek to summarise this complexity, in all its forms, in one dimension of quantity. Management accounting should be open to the possibility that, whilst a decision heavily informed by accounting numbers may make economic sense, it may offend the basic tenets of ethical behaviour which society expects of organisations in return for the social legitimacy it bestows upon them.

Ethics is the study of the right and wrong of actions. It is also referred to as the study of the rights and duties of individuals who live together in a community of shared interest. Most often today's universities, instead of concentrating on accounting-related scenarios to demonstrate the profession's ethics, expose students to a great expanse of vignettes where ethics is taught as business ethics, often out of philosophy departments. Today's generation of accounting students are so isolated from the ethical failures of business to which management accounting contributed, or the ethical failures of management accounting itself, that their perception is that accountants' immoral actions commenced with Enron when, in reality, history is replete with instructive examples of situations which have tempted accountants into wrong paths. The celebrated McKesson & Robbins fraud of 1938–39, which featured a $37 million overstatement of inventory and fictitious sales to bogus customers, had so dramatic an impact on US accounting regulation that it led to the inauguration of financial reporting standard setting with the formation of the Committee on Accounting Procedure. At least the new, super-regulatory body created in the aftermath of the current American audit failures, the Public Company Accounting Oversight Board (PCAOB), has done its historical homework. This is evidenced by the fact that early PCAOB memoranda recognised Lawrence Dicksee and Robert Montgomery as authorities on auditors' responsibilities for fraud detection. The Gilbane Report Blog (http://gilbane.com/blog/archives/2005/05/pcaob_clarifies.html) recently reported that comments from the PCAOB were 'direct descendents' of the McKesson case in support of professional auditing standards and 'top-down' auditing. History is replete with many similar episodes, even if the repercussions have been less dramatic. Sometimes accountants have successfully resisted; far too often they have not, despite in more recent times the promulgation of codes of ethical conduct for management accountants by the professional accounting bodies in most developed countries.

When one thinks of ethics, one immediately focuses on prominent examples of frauds, defalcations, negligence, and activities that lead to well-publicised litigation, licence removal, and civil and criminal penalties. The concern predominantly is with the misdemeanours and more serious failings of the business world and their consequences for the owners of business, the shareholders. The plight of others whose well-being may also be significantly affected is rarely, and only then briefly, recognised to the same degree. It is these and other 'suppressed voices' that critical accounting scholars courageously and ceaselessly bring to our attention. Should not ethical management accountants be attentive to the plight of disadvantaged people whose handicaps may be accentuated and perpetuated by the decisions that management accounting serves – to minorities who suffer discrimination as they attempt entry into the profession, to women whose advancement is encumbered by the 'glass ceiling', to the working classes suffering alienation and deprivation in low-paying industrial jobs or sweatshops around the world? Here again, history provides the background knowledge of how these suppressions came to be and insights as to how past and current injustices might be righted.

The ability of accounting, with its aura of neutrality and objectivity, to privilege a limited set of interests and, thereby, to deny others a voice has been the means to discount the subjective, or that which is not easily quantifiable, as something necessarily inferior to the products of the rational logic of accounting. It has also been a convenient means of isolating accounting from ethical questioning. Johnson and Kaplan have also argued that overemphasis on rational, financial analysis can exclude qualitative consideration of elements important to any organisation's success and social legitimacy. In particular, managers may be induced to make decisions which are economically rational, but which may be unethical or dishonest. As a significant participant of history, accounting should not be allowed to escape consideration of its ethical dimensions and moral consequences. Jere Francis (1990) laments how 'all too often the accountant may imagine they are just reporting the facts' when accounting 'is also a moral practice'. Drawing on the work on 'virtue' by Alasdair MacIntyre, Francis condemns a 'rationality that naively presumes to stand outside of morality by not questioning ends on the grounds that they are subjective'. Recognition of the moral and discursive character of accounting, with its ability to cause things to happen, demands that management accountants desiring to be virtuous, in a moral sense as opposed to a purely professional interpretation, take more responsibility for their work by recognising its moral imperatives. Unlike appraisals of the results of accounting routines, morality judgements mean that something is either right or wrong according to criteria that transcend individual social and political contexts. There is an expectation that, irrespective of the context, there are standards of conduct that are invariable, trans-social and ahistorical. For the accountant, to behave in a moral way is, according to William Schweiker (1993, p. 233), to 'act on the principle of equal respect for others, to treat them as ends in themselves'.

Most human behaviour is unlikely to be motivated only by the desire for material gain, if necessarily at the expense of others. Instead, behaviour is a combination of self-interest and a respect for the norms of social behaviour. Indeed, adherence to acceptable standards of personal and social conduct may be a precondition for successful self-interested behaviour. As Charles Ryn (1978, pp. 82–3) writes:

> the intellectual, aesthetic, and economic life of a society may be said to be truly civilized to the degree that these activities serve the ethical goal . . . By this definition, a society which has reached a high level of efficiency in attaining its goals, but whose efficiency does not measurably serve the realization of moral ends, would not be civilized in the full sense of the word . . . The moral goal for society to which all other goals are subservient . . . we may call community . . . . Community can emerge only in a society where the forces of egotistical interests are tempered by concern for the common good.

Rather than accepting management accounting as a moral and social practice, our preoccupation with the processes which form the accounting function has made it easy to overlook its extended consequences beyond the quantifiable net of accounting. Accountants in history have been cast in the role of insignificant players who were to do the bidding of those who used the results of the accountants' work. The link was rarely made between broader social consequences and the role of accounting as a constituent element in engendering existing social and political arrangements. Accounting research over the past two decades has progressively exposed these perceptions of accounting as inadequate and deceptively favourable to the status quo. As a result, it has been established clearly by accounting researchers that accounting is an active agent in social processes, in the implementation of political programmes, and in the creation and maintenance of social structures. As a result of accounting historians and other critical accounting scholars, accounting is no longer able to hide behind a disguise of neutrality and disinterested objectivity; it is revealed as both technical and moral. A study of the history of management accounting establishes that accounting, as part of a structure of controls and practices designed to maximise the outcomes of policies contrived to deliver efficiency and effectiveness, can have effects which are momentous and which reach well beyond their historical setting to other periods in history. Thus, according to Peter Miller (1990, p. 334):

> political rationalities accord significances and meanings to quite mundane calculative routines, allowing their practitioners to articulate their potential contributions in terms that extend far beyond their operation within individual enterprises.

If management accounting is a moral practice, then history has shown that those who use it are moral agents. This was most clearly seen in the use of cost accounting information to enhance the efficiency with which the Nazis set about annihilating

European Jewry during the Holocaust. In terms of the Kohlbergian framework of morality adapted by Alan Lovell (1995) in his examination of the accounting profession, accounting practitioners who assisted the Nazis with their murderous undertaking operated at the 'conventional' level of morality where the most striking features were a desire to please superiors and to adhere strictly to laws, conventions and codes of practice. Overwhelming evidence indicates that movement to Lawrence Kohlberg's ultimate level of 'universalistic' or 'principled' moral reasoning, where individuals are prepared to stand against laws and orders that contravene natural justice, was not a feature of the practice of accounting in relation to the Jews throughout the Holocaust.

Dominick La Capra (1994, p. 90) describes the Holocaust as being 'calculated coldly and with the maximum efficiency and economy'. The killing of a very large number of people in a relatively short space of time, according to Raul Hilberg (1985, p. 9), was nothing more than 'an efficiency problem of the greatest dimensions . . . With an unfailing sense of direction . . . the German bureaucracy found the shortest road to the final goal'. Accounting, as an instrument of the German civil bureaucracy, provided at 'centres of calculation' new quantitative visibilities which were able to supplant the qualitative dimensions of the Jews as individuals by commodifying and dehumanising them and, thereby, for all intents make them invisible as people. Irrespective of the then-known ultimate fate of the Jews, the aggregation, reductionism and anonymity of accounting numbers allowed the forced movement of millions of people great distances from their homes to be drained of any consideration that the numbers and costings on the pieces of paper, passed from one bureaucrat to the next, related to prescient human beings. The Jews became just another cargo to be marshalled, costed and moved. Thus, management accounting in the service of the German civil and military bureaucracy, as it sought to implement the Nazis' Jewish extermination plans, was not only a means of expediting the annihilation of the Jews, but was also one of the means by which people who had no direct involvement in the murder of millions of Jews were able to divorce themselves from the objectives and consequences of their work. When it came time to dispose of the property taken from the Jews, the Nazis attempted to purify their actions and to sanctify their motives by insisting that there had to be a rigorous accounting before it was available to the state. In the process, the accounts were used as the symbolic means of spiritual cleansing for those directly engaged in the annihilation of the Jews.

Consideration of the ethical imperative in the practice of management accounting recognises that costs have a qualitative dimension. This is especially and increasingly of concern in the public sector. Whilst decisions by ministers and public servants should be heavily influenced by cost information, any effects of these decisions that are less easily measured by management accounting processes, such as equity and due process, must also be considered. Although these qualitative factors are often difficult to express in financial terms, it is unlikely that they will be costless. More importantly for governments intent on retaining office and implementing successful programmes, qualitative consequences invariably have political ramifications. A decision, for example, to close police stations to save money may prove to be politically costly should law and order on the streets deteriorate soon after. Thus, the realities of politics and social justice may dictate that a decision will be made for reasons other than cost considerations.

This is particularly apposite for government departments and budget dependent statutory bodies where there is the opportunity for considerable visibility and, therefore, political importance. As a consequence, public sector managers whose career prospects now depend on their ability to manage in a cost-efficient manner are often placed in a difficult situation. If they give precedence in their decision-making to costs rather than qualitative obligations, such as access to services and equity, they promote the goals of efficient, cost-effective government but risk embarrassing their political masters should circumstances subsequently show the error of a fixation on costs. The Bush Administration's decision to remove most funding for levee building and management in and around New Orleans prior to hurricane Katrina in 2005 subsequently had a heavy political cost. Democracy is qualitative in nature, not quantitative. Measures of its effectiveness should, therefore, acknowledge this relationship. Neo-liberal governments and their supporters, however, choose to argue that the monitoring costs in a democracy are examples of inefficiency. If markets are substituted for the hierarchical direction favoured by government bureaucracies, there will be no need for expensive monitoring mechanisms. If an activity is not being conducted efficiently, then competition may soon cause the demise of the inefficient service provider. This, of course, says nothing about the qualities of equity, fairness and justice in service delivery.

The spread of a corporatist culture in the public sector, in which accounting performance measurements figure prominently, has severely tested belief in a public service of high professional integrity, regulated by normative standards of conduct. A preference for using contracts to employ senior public servants, and for removing as many services as is economically and politically possible to the private sector, has seen the elevation of efficient management over a culture of ethical service. Contrary to the enthusiastic pledges of government commitment to traditional public service values of honesty, integrity and equitable service, qualitative dimensions of public sector performance have suffered from the competition of more efficiency-orientated, and measurable, accountabilities. From departmental secretaries down, public servants are expected to give priority to economic considerations as the only responsible way to husband scarce public resources in the presence of ever-rising demands for government services. Inefficient management is proclaimed as wasteful and leading to an inequitable distribution of increasingly scarce resources. Thus, as long as public servants adhere to the new priorities, reformist governments see little difficulty in melding performance accountabilities with traditional public service values.

Not everyone, however, is so easily convinced of a natural symbiosis between cultures of service and quantifiable performance. Indeed, so great can be the differences in objectives between concern for democratic values, such as justice and equity, and efficient management, that it has been described as possibly irresolvable. The result, observes John Saul (1993, p. 337), is that 'social morality is subordinated to the efficient functioning of the system . . . (and) the social contract is subordinated to the financial contract'. Ultimately, 'the public servant . . . who is paid by the citizen, now becomes the enemy of the citizen'.

For private sector firms, the tensions between costs and the qualitative dimensions of performance present themselves less often or less dramatically than in the public sector. The choice is usually very clearly in favour of immediate influences on profitability.

Qualitative considerations tend to be more long-term and less visible, although they may prove equally important to the organisation's long-term profitability. At great cost, American automobile manufacturers eventually learned that their Japanese competitors' emphasis on product quality and customer service had produced handsome dividends.

It is not difficult to appreciate how greater exposure to ethical dilemmas has the potential to improve the moral timbre of students training for practice. A heavy dose of ethics, particularly accounting-specific ethics that draws upon the great richness of historical record, could achieve much good both directly in the persons of new accountants and indirectly in their work. However, current management accounting ethics will not measurably improve unless there is a change to the mindset that first allegiance must be to the firm and its stockholders. Public accountants are charged to serve the public interest. Why should it not be the same for management accountants? Unfortunately, so long as managerial bonuses are tied into bottom-line net income, it is difficult to see how things will change voluntarily. What are the realistic chances, for example, that companies will undertake the moral actions necessary to protect the environment in the absence of either effective regulation or incentives to defray the high costs? We are sceptical in this instance that even knowledge of history can be of any help. Perhaps the hefty jail sentences meted out in 2004 and 2005 to prominent accountants and financial managers implicated in some of the largest corporate collapses in history may cause others to stop and think a little longer.

Ethical behaviour by management accountants could refer either to a set of fundamental principles of living, in which right and wrong have absolute or unchanging referents, or to codified expectations of professional behaviour. Thus, we expect people to tell the truth and not to defraud their employers. In addition, all professional accounting bodies to which a management accountant might belong have codes of ethics that they expect their members to adhere to in all circumstances. Each accountant, public or management, must re-examine his/her professional ethics in light of the rash of corporate failures and the subsequent overreaction that precipitated the demise of Arthur Andersen. All must share equally in the pain of the loss of public confidence. Some have said that ethics cannot be taught, that an individual's moral structure has been instilled long before he or she reaches business school. We, as accounting educators, can only hope this perception is untrue lest we be left powerless to influence our students' moral development.

Conclusion

In the 1991 edition of this handbook, Loft observed, citing *Relevance Lost,* that an important function of history is its use in attempting to justify change in the present. Management accounting since the British Industrial Revolution has been in a constant state of flux, with the most profound change occurring in the past two decades. Innovations have not always moved the craft forward to be sure. However, what has been most constant in the historical panorama is change itself.

History has much to offer management accountants. It tells us where our ethical code has come from, both in terms of past virtues and moral shortcomings. It speaks to the origins of the discipline's practices and how and why change has occurred in the past. Whilst history is not linearly progressive and its lessons are not universally helpful in application, there is a wealth of helpful insights, precedents and compelling examples to be found. To close somewhat as we began, as Crick wrote about politics, history should be appreciated and studied for what it can do for us but not vilified for what it cannot do.

References

Arthur Andersen & Co., Arthur Young, Coopers & Lybrand, Deloitte Haskins & Sells, Ernst & Whinney, Peat Marwick Main & Co., Price Waterhouse, Touche Ross (1989) 'Perspectives on education: capabilities for success in the accounting profession', white paper, no publisher given.

Boyns T. and Edwards, J.R. (1996) 'The development of accounting in mid-nineteenth century Britain: a non-disciplinary view', *Accounting, Auditing & Accountability Journal,* **9**(3), 40–60.

Butterfield, H. (1931) *The Whig Interpretation of History,* London: G. Bell, 1950 reprint.

Crick, B. (1962) *In Defence of Politics,* Chicago, IL: University of Chicago Press.

Edwards, J.R. (1989) 'Industrial cost accounting developments in Britain to 1830: a review article', *Accounting and Business Research,* **19**(76), 305–17.

Ezzamel, M., Hoskin, K. and Macve, R. (1990) 'Managing it all by numbers: a review of Johnson and Kaplan's *Relevance Lost'*, *Accounting and Business Research,* **20**(78), 153–66.

Francis, J. (1990) 'After virtue? Accounting as a moral and discursive practice', *Accounting, Auditing and Accountability Journal,* **3**(3), 5–17.

Garcke, E. and Fells, G. (1887) *Factory Accounts, Their Principle and Practice,* New York: Arno Press, 1976 reprint.

Harrison, G.C. (1930) *Standard Cost,* New York: Ronald Press Company.

Hendrickson, H. and Williams, P. (eds) (2004) *Accounting Theory: Essays by Carl Thomas Devine,* Routledge: London.

Hilberg, R. (1985) *The Destruction of the European Jews,* New York: Holmes and Meir.

Hopper, T. and Armstrong, P. (1991) 'Cost accounting, controlling labour and the rise of conglomerates', *Accounting, Organizations and Society,* **16**(5/6), 405–38.

Hoskin K.W. and Macve, R.H. (1988) 'The genesis of accountability: the West Point connections', *Accounting, Organizations and Society,* **13**(1), 37–73.

Hoskin, K.W. and Macve, R.H. (1994) 'Reappraising the genesis of managerialism: a re-examination of accounting at the Springfield Armory, 1815–1845', *Accounting, Auditing & Accountability Journal,* **7**(2), 4–29.

Johnson, H.T. (1972) 'Early cost accounting for internal management control: Lyman Millsin the 1850s', *Business History Review,* **45**(4), 466–74.

Johnson, H.T. (ed.) (1980) *System and Profits,* New York: Arno Press.

La Capra, D. (1994) *Representing the Holocaust: History, Theory, Trauma,* Ithaca, NY: Cornell University Press.

Loft, A. (1991) 'The history of management accounting: relevance found', in D. Ashton, T. Hopper and R. Scapens (eds), *Issues in Management Accounting,* New York: Prentice Hall, pp. 17–38.

Loft, A. (1995) 'The history of management accounting: relevance found', in D. Ashton, T. Hopper and R. Scapens (eds), *Issues in Management Accounting,* 2nd edn., New York: Prentice Hall, pp. 21–44.

Lovell, A. (1995) 'Moral reasoning and moral atmosphere in the domain of accounting', *Accounting, Auditing & Accountability Journal,* **8**(3), 60–80.

Miller, P. (1990) 'On the interrelationships between accounting and the state', *Accounting, Organizations and Society,* **15**(4), 315–38.

Miller, P. and O'Leary, T. (1987) 'Accounting and the construction of the governable person', *Accounting, Organizations and Society,* **12**(3), 235–65.

Previts G.J. and Bricker, R. (1994) 'Fact and theory in accounting history: presentmindedness and capital markets research', *Contemporary Accounting Research,* **10**(2), 625–41.

Nevins, A. (1962) *The Gateway to History,* Garden City, NY: Doubleday.

Ryn, C. (1978) *Democracy and the Ethical Life: A Philosophy of Politics and Community,* Baton Rouge, LA: Louisiana State University Press.

Saul, J. (1993) *Voltaire's Bastards: The Dictatorship of Reason in the West,* Toronto: Penguin Books.

Schweiker, W. (1993) 'Accounting for ourselves: accounting practice and the discourse of ethics', *Accounting, Organizations and Society,* **18**(2/3), 231–52.

Tyson T.N. (1992) 'The nature and environment of cost management among early nineteenth century U.S. textile manufacturers', *Accounting Historians Journal,* **19**(2), 1–24

Vatter, W. (1950) *Managerial Accounting,* New York: Garland Publishing, 1986 reprint.

Further reading

Chandler, A. (1977) *The Visible Hand: The Managerial Revolution in American Business,* Cambridge, MA: Harvard University Press. The classic history of the development of the US industrial sector and the coming of managerialism with all the accounting implications associated with those developments.

Edwards, J.R. (ed.) (2000) *The History of Accounting,* 4 vols, New York and London: Routledge. A mammoth collection of scholarly, accounting-history articles drawn equally from the financial and managerial branches of the discipline.

Fleischman, R.K. (ed.) (2006) *Accounting History,* 3 vols, London: Sage Publishing. A slightly smaller collection of academic articles than the above entry, with an emphasis on management accounting history and paradigmatic discourse.

Hilberg, R. (1985) *The Destruction of the European Jews,* New York: Holmes and Meir. The most detailed, authoritative examination of the role of civilian bureaucrats in ensuring that the Nazis' determination to kill all European Jews was carried out as efficiently as possible.

Johnson, H.T. and Kaplan, R. (1987) *Relevance Lost: The Rise and Fall of Management Accounting,* Boston, MA: Harvard Business School Press. The classic economic-rationalist study of the development of the American industrial sector and its accounting, with an indictment of it for the loss of global hegemony in the 1980s.

Lodh, S. and Gaffikin, M. (1997) 'Critical studies in accounting research, rationality and Habermas: a methodological reflection', *Critical Perspectives on Accounting,* **8**(5), 433–74. An excellent survey of the variety of paradigms reflected in 'critical' scholarship.

Napier, C. (1989) 'Research directions in accounting history', *British Accounting Review,* **21**(3), 237–54. A short, descriptive piece on the two primary functions of historical writing – 'discovery' and 'contextualisation', with a call for a synergistic relationship between the two.

Simon, H., Guetzkow, H., Kozmetsky, G. and Tyndall, G. (1954) *Centralization vs. Decentralization in Organizing the Controller's Department,* New York: Controllership Foundation. The classic description of the controller's function, featuring scorekeeping, attention directing and problem solving.

Windschuttle, K. (1994) *The Killing of History,* revised edition, Paddington, Australia: Macleay Press, 1996 reprint. A thought-provoking treatise on the travails facing history in the contemporary world with considerable attention given to the philosophy of history.

19

Economic research on management accounting

Robert F. Göx and Alfred Wagenhofer

Introduction

Under the perspective of economic research, management accounting provides information useful to decision-makers within the firm. The focus of interest is on the analysis of costs and benefits and on the design of information systems and their use in organisations. Economic research usually employs micro-economic models, mainly from information economics, such as agency theory or, more generally, game theory. We provide insights into typical management accounting issues studied, results obtained, and models employed in economic research and we discuss the achievements, strengths and weaknesses of economic research on management accounting.

From a normative point of view, economic research on management accounting helps to identify the role of management accounting in supporting decisions on the efficient use of resources within firms. Typical examples are decisions on the quantity and quality of inputs, product costing and pricing decisions, and decisions on the size and diversity of the product portfolio. From a positive point of view, economic research aims to explain the design and use of empirically observable accounting techniques and resource allocation mechanisms such as budgeting and transfer pricing procedures.

The use of management accounting information for decision-making helps to improve the resource allocation process within firms, but at the same time can be detrimental to other decisions. Moreover, the information provided by management accounting is a costly resource. Accordingly, the benefits of using the internal accounting system must be compared with the costs of providing this information. The cost–benefit approach is of particular importance for evaluating existing management accounting practices because the size and scope of internal accounting systems are largely at the discretion of their users. In contrast, the extent to which firms provide financial accounting information is determined mainly by legal requirements and other regulations.

A key ingredient of economic models in management accounting is the explicit consideration of uncertainty. If there were no uncertainty, the use of information systems would be pointless in a rational world. Information reduces uncertainty and potentially affects decisions within the firm. It is useful to distinguish between two roles for management accounting information:

- *Decision-facilitating role* – the information is used to improve decisions made by a single decision-maker (or unanimous group of decision-makers). Examples are the provision of product cost information for production quantity or pricing decisions, or the determination of divisional costs for cost management purposes.

- *Decision-influencing or stewardship role* – this role considers management accounting information in the context of an organisation of more than one decision-maker whose interests are not necessarily the same. Information is used to align the incentives of individual decision-makers with the objectives of the firm and to coordinate decentralised decision-making. Examples are the design of performance measures for division managers, or budgeting procedures to ensure the unbiased reporting of resource requirements by division managers.

In this chapter, we review major areas of research on each of these two roles in typical economic modelling frames. We use illustrative management accounting issues to provide a flavour of the analyses and results that are achieved by economic research. We also discuss key assumptions of economic models and evaluate the achievements of economic research for the further development of management accounting research.

Decision-facilitating role of management accounting information

Value of information

The value of management accounting information is determined in the context of a decision problem under uncertainty. A decision problem is described by the following elements:

- *Actions* – the task of the decision-maker is to pick exactly one action a_i from a set of feasible actions A.
- *States* – the states of nature capture all relevant factors affecting the outcome of the decision problem, which are beyond the control of the decision-maker. The possible states are denoted $s_j \in S$, where S is the set of possible states. Usually, the decision-maker can assign subjective or objective probabilities to the states. The probability π_j that state s_j occurs lies between 0 and 1, and the sum of all probabilities equals 1.
- *Outcomes* – the outcome $x_{ij} = x(a_i, s_j)$ is the direct consequence of choosing action a_i if state s_j occurs. Outcomes can consist of several dimensions, although economic research usually focuses on monetary payoffs.
- *Preferences* – preferences about outcomes are described by a utility function that aggregates multi-dimensional outcomes and the outcomes for a given action over possible states. Such aggregation is necessary for an ordering of the outcomes of an action and, therefore, for rational decision-making.

The following decision problem illustrates how these elements work together. A manager decides whether to introduce a new product. Of course, such a decision depends on many factors. Consider a firm that cannot exactly predict the production cost of the new product. Suppose, for example, that the production cost can take two values, high ('state' 1 (s_1) with $c_H = 300$) and low ('state' 2 (s_2) with $c_L = 100$), each occurring with an *a priori* probability of 0.5. The outcome for each state is computed as the difference between the price p and the state-contingent cost. Table 19.1 contains the outcome matrix for an assumed product price $p = 200$.

If the cost is actually low it is optimal to introduce the new product, otherwise the product should be rejected. Without additional information the expected cost equals

Table 19.1 Outcome matrix for new product example

	State	
	s_1	s_2
Action	(c_H = 300)	(c_L = 100)
a_1: accept	−100	100
a_2: reject	0	0

$E[c] = (0.5 \times 100) + (0.5 \times 300) = 200$ and the expected outcome is $p - E[c] = 0$, which equals the outcome from rejecting the product. $E[\cdot]$ denotes the expectation over the possible states. A risk neutral manager is indifferent between introducing and rejecting the new product. If he or she rejects it, nothing is received; if he or she accepts it, an expected profit of 0 results. Since risk does not matter, both alternatives are equivalent.

However, decision-makers are often considered to be risk averse. Risk aversion means that individuals do not like taking risks and attribute a cost to it. In the above example accepting the new product is risky but rejecting it is not. Since the expected profit is equal, the manager optimally rejects the product. Risk aversion is usually described by a utility function $U(x)$ that increases in x and is strictly concave. An example is the square root utility function $U(x) = \sqrt{100 + x}$. With this utility function, the manager receives a utility of $U(x = 0) = \sqrt{100} = 10$ for sure if the project is rejected. If the manager accepts the product, he or she makes either a loss of -100 or a profit of 100 with equal probability. Therefore, accepting the product yields an expected utility of $E[U(x(a_1, s_j)] = \left(0.5 \times \sqrt{0}\right) + \left(0.5 \times \sqrt{200}\right) = 7.07$, which is lower than the utility from rejecting the product.

A major use of management accounting information is the determination of product costs. Of course, producing such information can consume significant resources. The benefit is improved decision-making, because the decision-maker can avoid decisions that turn out to be 'mistakes' after the cost has been observed. In the example, the manager can make two types of mistakes. Rejecting the product when the cost is actually low, he or she forgoes profitable business. Accepting the product when the cost turns out to be high, he or she enters into an unprofitable business. Both mistakes can be avoided if the manager knows the actual cost before deciding on the new product. To illustrate this, assume that the accounting system provides perfect information about the cost (state) before the manager decides on the introduction of the new product. The decision-maker then picks the action that is optimal given this actual cost (state). If the cost is low, he or she introduces the product and makes a profit of 100. If the cost is high, he or she rejects the product and earns 0. Because the actual cost is not known *ex ante*, the expected outcome from optimally using the perfect cost information system equals

$$E[\max_{a_i}(x_{ij}|s_j)] = (0.5 \times 100) + (0.5 \times 0) = 50$$

The benefit is equal to the expected loss that can be avoided if the product was introduced (a_2) but the cost was high (s_1). The expected value of perfect information (EVPI) is the incremental benefit from optimally using the perfect information system relative to the no-information situation. In particular, the EVPI is the difference between the expected outcome with an optimal use of the cost information system (50), and the expected outcome for the optimal decision without precise cost information (0):

$$\text{EVPI} = \text{E}[\max_{a_i}(x_{ij}|s_j)] - \max_{a_i} \text{E}[x_{ij}|s_j] = 50 - 0 = 50$$

The EVPI cannot be negative. It is also the maximum price a risk neutral decision-maker would be willing to pay for a perfect information system.

The value of the information derives from the ability to change the decision-maker's action. If the information does not affect the decision, it provides no benefit and is not useful even if it is costless. For example, assume the cost in state s_1 is not $c_H = 300$, but only 150. Then, the manager would never make a loss. In state 1 the profit is still 100, and in state 2 the profit is now $200 - 150 = 50$. Therefore, the manager accepts the product whatever state occurs, which renders cost information of whatever quality useless.

To further illustrate the value of cost information, assume the cost is uniformly distributed between 100 and 300, i.e. the probability density function is $\phi = 1/200$. Consider the firm's profit for varying prices of p. As in the discrete example above, cost information is only valuable if the price lies between 100 and 300 because otherwise it does not affect the decision. If $p < 100$ (the price is lower than the lowest possible cost), the manager knows that he or she can never make a profit and rejects the product. For $p > 300$ (if the price is higher than the highest possible cost), he or she is sure that the new product is always profitable and introduces it. For $100 \le p \le 300$ the manager's decision is affected by the product cost information. If $p > c$, he or she introduces the new product and makes a profit of $p - c$. If $p < c$, the product is rejected and no profit is made. Therefore, the expected payoff with perfect cost information equals the expected profit, given that the product is actually introduced:

$$\text{E}[p - c \,|\, c \le p] = \int_{100}^{p} (p - c)\frac{1}{200}dc = \frac{(p - 100)^2}{400} \qquad (1)$$

Without information, the expected outcome equals $\max(0, p - 200)$ where 200 is the expected cost. The difference between these two expressions determines the EVPI as a function of the product price p. Figure 19.1 shows that the value of information increases in p up to the value of the expected cost, $\text{E}[c] = 200$, and then decreases again. At $p = 200$, the manager faces the highest risk of taking the 'wrong' decision. A slight increase of the price would cause the manager to accept the product, and a slight decrease of the price would cause him or her to reject it. Accordingly, precise cost information has a high likelihood of altering the manager's decision.

The EVPI also serves as an upper bound for the value of imperfect information. Because cost accounting systems determine the future cost from past cost observations and from technological conditions, imperfect information is the norm. The desirability of more or less precise information depends on its costs and benefits. For example, if the cost of more precise information increases exponentially, the optimal level of precision is somewhere between no information and perfect information. With risk aversion, the desirability of an information system must be determined by simultaneously incorporating the costs and benefits into the manager's utility function.

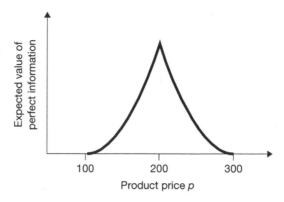

Figure 19.1 **Expected value of perfect information for different product prices**

The value of information concept helps us understand the cost–benefit trade-off in using more precise cost information, which underlies many of the economic models used in management accounting. It demonstrates that the value of information is heavily contingent on the decision problem at hand and on the preferences of the decision-maker. Its limited applicability in practice results from the fact that there are many different decision problems, many of them ill-defined, and many different decision-makers.

For example, activity-based costing aims to improve decision-making about products and processes. It introduces hierarchical cost pools and suggests that such a costing method is a better basis for managerial decisions. Economic research, however, shows that this need not result in better decision-making relative to using single-step costing (see Christensen and Demski, 1995). The reason, of course, is that different costing systems provide different information and their values depend on the decision problem at hand.

It is impossible to rank the value of information systems more generally. According to Blackwell's theorem, a finer information system can never be less valuable than a coarser system regardless of the decision problem and the decision-maker's preferences. Nevertheless, the value of information concept gives some generalisable insights. It makes precise the source of the value of information (i.e. to affect decisions), and it points to the circumstances under which a higher value is expected. For example, as shown above, perfect cost information has the greatest value if the expected profit margin is near zero. This will typically be the case in highly competitive industries, whereas in less competitive environments precise cost information is usually less important because the firm incurs a relatively low risk of accepting unprofitable orders. Similarly, if expected margins are highly negative, the risk of unintentionally rejecting a profitable order is small and, thus, a detailed cost analysis is less desirable.

Capacity cost and full cost pricing

It is a well documented empirical fact that firms often use full cost information for product pricing. Since this practice stands in sharp contrast with the usual textbook paradigm of product pricing, researchers have developed a number of potential explanations for this puzzling phenomenon. For example, it has been hypothesised that managers do not understand the economics of pricing, that they seek only satisfactory (but not maximum) profits, or that they simply do not have the time, resources and information to act in a profit-maximising fashion. All these explanations invoke some kind of bounded rationality. In the following, we demonstrate that full cost pricing can be the result of rational decision-making if the pricing problem is analysed as part of a multi-period planning procedure in which a firm sets production capacities first and then decides on product prices.

To illustrate the main insights of economic theory, we slightly modify our earlier example (more elaborate models are examined in Banker and Hughes, 1994, and Göx, 2002). Assume that a firm can sell q_s units of a standard product at a price of $p_s = 200$ (the index s indicates the standard product). The variable cost per unit is $c_s = 100$. The unit contribution of the standard product equals $p_s - c_s = 100$. Assume for now that the production capacity is already set. Capacity is measured in terms of the quantity of the standard product and is limited to producing up to 500 units of the standard product. However, unused capacity can also be used to produce customised versions of the standard product. Producing a customised product (indexed by n) incurs a variable unit cost of $c_n = 150$ and requires twice as much capacity per unit as a standard product. The question is how much the firm should charge a customer for one unit of the customised product. The answer depends on the existing capacity utilisation:

● If demand for the customised product can be fulfilled without affecting the standard production programme, the price must at least cover the variable cost of the customised product to make a profit. The minimum price equals $p_n = 150$.
● If all capacity is currently used by the standard production programme, the firm must reduce production of the standard product to satisfy the new customer's demand. Therefore, the price of the customised product must cover not only its variable cost, but also the forgone profits from the standard business. In the example, the minimum price increases to $p_n = 350$ because, in addition to the variable cost of 150, each unit of the new, customised product replaces two units of the standard product which results in a lost profit of $2(p_s - c_s) = 200$ per unit of the new product.

In general terms, the decision rule for accepting the special order can be expressed as follows (assuming arbitrarily divisible units):

$$p_n > c_n + 2\lambda \tag{2}$$

The special order must cover its variable cost, c_n, plus the opportunity cost of capacity, 2λ. If $q_s < 500$, the firm has slack capacity and $\lambda = 0$. If $q_s \geq 500$, the firm must forgo profitable business to accept the special order and $\lambda = (p_s - c_s)$. λ is determined solely by the current demand for the standard product, and is not related to the historical acquisition cost of the production capacity in place.

Such an analysis ignores the interrelationship between capacity planning and pricing. In particular, if the firm expects to have slack capacity it may decide to install less capacity in the first place. In addition, it is important to distinguish list prices from tactical prices when analysing the interrelationship between capacity planning and pricing.

Special order prices are tactical prices. They are set *after* capacity has been installed and the acquisition cost of capacity is already sunk. In contrast, list prices are long-term prices that are determined at an early stage of the product cycle, when the firm can still adjust production capacity.

Suppose the acquisition cost of capacity equals $r = 80$ per product unit. Since the list price of the standard product is set before the firm procures the capacity, the standard product can only be profitable if the list price satisfies the following condition:

$$p_s > c_s + r = 180 \tag{3}$$

That is, the list price covers the variable cost plus the capacity cost per unit. In other words, rational planning requires that list prices exceed the product's full manufacturing cost. If the firm believes that customers are not willing to accept this price, it is better to drop the product. Full cost pricing, thus, is a rational strategy for determining list prices of products.

Next we turn to the capacity planning stage and analyse its relationship to the tactical pricing problem. To start with, assume demand for the final product is known at the time of the capacity decision. With certain product demand, capacity planning is simple because profits are maximised by setting capacity equal to product demand. Hence, the firm has no slack capacity and the opportunity cost of capacity equals the contribution margin of the standard product, $p_s - c_s$. Further, we can conclude from equation (3) that the contribution margin of the standard product must exceed the capacity acquisition cost to assure a satisfactory list price. If we apply this logic to the tactical pricing formula in equation (2), we find that the tactical price must exceed the full cost of the customised product:

$$p_n > c_n + 2(p_s - c_s) > c_n + 2r = 310 \tag{4}$$

Thus, if capacity planning can be made under certainty, the full cost price is a lower bound for accepting special orders.

Next we extend the analysis to situations where capacity is determined before product demand is known. Assume demand for the standard product is uniformly distributed between 0 and 1000. The optimal capacity level takes into account the economic consequences of idle or full capacity. If capacity is set $k < q_s$, the opportunity loss is $(p_s - c_s)$ per lost demand unit. If the firm sets excess capacity $k > q_s$, the loss equals r for each unused capacity unit. At the optimal capacity k^*, marginal expected opportunity cost from forgone sales equals capacity acquisition cost:

$$(p_s - c_s)(1 - \Phi(k^*)) = r \tag{5}$$

where $\Phi(k) = k/1000$ denotes the probability that $q_s \leq k$. Rewriting (5) as $k^* = \Phi^{-1}(1 - r/(p_s - c_s))$ shows that the optimal capacity is determined by the ratio between the capacity acquisition cost and the contribution margin of the standard product. The two factors have countervailing effects on the optimal capacity. The higher the unit contribution margin of the standard product, the higher the optimal capacity level because the opportunity cost of lost sales is more severe. The higher the capacity acquisition cost, the lower the optimal capacity level because slack capacity becomes more costly. In the example, the ratio $r/(p_s - c_s)$ equals 0.8 and the optimal capacity is $k^* = 200$.

Optimal tactical pricing depends on the demand information available at the time the order comes in:

● If the special order arrives *before* the firm learns the demand for the standard product, the special order will only be accepted if it covers the expected loss from the forgone sales of the standard product, i.e. $\lambda = (p_s - c_s)(1 - \Phi(k^*))$. Thus, the firm accepts the order if and only if

$$p_n > c_n + 2\lambda = c_n + 2(p_s - c_s)(1 - \Phi(k)) = c_n + 2r = 310$$

where the last identity follows from the optimal capacity decision in equation (5). As for certain product demand, the price of the customised product must exceed its full cost.

● If the special order arrives *after* the firm learns the demand for the standard product, the situation is as described in equation (2). If there is slack capacity, the price of the customised product must exceed its variable cost of 150. If the capacity is fully utilised, the threshold for the tactical price becomes:

$$p_n > c_n + 2(p_s - c_s) = c_n + \frac{2r}{1 - \Phi(k)} \geq c_n + 2r$$

The first inequality follows from equation (2), the second from (5), and the last inequality from the fact that $\Phi(k) \leq 1$. In the example, $\Phi(k) = 0.8$ and, hence, $p_n > 350$. We conclude that, with full capacity utilisation, the special order will be rejected if the price of the customised product does not exceed its full cost, which is greater than the threshold derived before demand information is available.

To summarise, the full unit cost of customised products is an optimal threshold for accepting special orders in many cases. In particular, only if the firm knows for sure that spare capacity exists before deciding on the special order is it reasonable to lower the threshold to the customised product's variable cost. In all other scenarios the full unit cost of the customised product is a reasonable approximation for the minimum acceptable price.

This example shows that the economics of pricing is more complex than suggested by the simple marginal cost pricing rule. It demonstrates the interrelationship between pricing, capacity decisions, and the information available at the time the decision is made. The example also shows that the prevalent practice of setting prices at full cost can be an optimal policy under a broad set of circumstances. Economic research, thus, helps to formulate alternative hypotheses that may guide empirical research in this area.

Decision-influencing role of management accounting information

Performance measurement

In this section, we turn to the analysis of management accounting information in an organisation. The key characteristic is that there is more than one decision-maker with asymmetric information endowments and potentially conflicting interests. For example, a division manager typically has superior information about his or her area of responsibility and might also be more interested in the performance of his or her division than in the overall performance of the firm. In such a setting, the information may alter the decisions of both (or more) decision-makers with sometimes surprising results. In particular, research has identified conditions where the value of information is negative – a result that cannot occur in a single decision-maker setting. Such insights are important for the design of management accounting systems, as they alert management accountants to the limits of providing more and more precise information, aside from the direct cost of generating the information.

Agency models are typically employed to address management accounting issues because they focus on contracts between a principal (the firm, headquarters, or higher-level manager) and agents (division manager, lower-level manager), which suit a hierarchical organisation. Subsequently, we use the following basic model to discuss the research questions and insights in this area. The model builds on the situation described in earlier sections (see also Christensen and Demski, 2003).

A risk neutral principal owns a production technology that produces some output, denoted $x(a, s)$. The manager (agent) supplies action a, which is a productive effort and, together with the state s, determines the output level. The state s captures other input factors and process uncertainties that are beyond the control of the agent. Effort a is costly to the manager and incurs a personal disutility $v(a)$. For simplicity, we use a discrete setting with two actions, high (H) and low (L) with $a_H > a_L$, corresponding disutilities $v_H > v_L$, and two outcomes x_j, $j = 1, 2$, where $x_1 < x_2$. We assume incentives are provided via monetary compensation (alternatives would be job promotions, social status, or other non-pecuniary rewards). Compensation can be made contingent on the outcome x_j. We denote with w_j the compensation that is paid if result x_j is realised. The manager is risk averse in compensation, i.e. he or she strictly prefers a fixed salary over the same amount of expected variable pay. The manager's preferences are described by the following utility function:

$$U(w_j, a_i) = \sqrt{w_j} - v_i$$

High effort is more productive than low effort in that it increases the probability of a high outcome. Table 19.2 gives the probabilities of obtaining x_i given the manager chooses effort a_i. For example, if the manager chooses to make a low effort a_L, there is a higher probability that the low outcome results than if he or she chose to make a high effort. However, the disutility of providing high effort is also greater.

The underlying sequence is as follows. First, the principal proposes a compensation contract to the manager, who decides whether to accept or reject it. The manager has alternative employment opportunities that would provide a reservation utility $\underline{U}$. Therefore, he or she accepts the contract if the expected utility at least matches $\underline{U}$. Second, the manager exerts effort a_i. We assume the principal wants the manager to

Table 19.2 Outcome, probability structure and disutility

Action	Outcome		Disutility
	x_1	x_2	
a_L: (low effort)	0.6	0.4	0
a_H: (high effort)	0.2	0.8	4

exert high effort (otherwise, there is no incentive problem), but the principal cannot observe the effort (i.e. there is information asymmetry). The manager chooses a level of effort that maximises the expected utility, given the compensation contract. Third, the actual outcome x_i is observed, and the manager is paid according to the contract. Formally, the principal maximises the expected outcome given that the agent exerts high effort:

$$E[\Pi \mid a_H] = 0.2(x_1 - w_1) + 0.8(x_2 - w_2) \tag{6}$$

subject to the following constraints:

$$0.2\left(\sqrt{w_1}\right) + 0.8\left(\sqrt{w_2}\right) - v_H \geq \underline{U} \tag{7}$$

$$0.2\left(\sqrt{w_1}\right) + 0.8\left(\sqrt{w_2}\right) - v_H \geq 0.6\left(\sqrt{w_1}\right) + 0.4\left(\sqrt{w_2}\right) - v_L \tag{8}$$

Condition (7) is the participation constraint. It ensures that the manager accepts the contract. Condition (8) is the incentive compatibility constraint. It induces the manager to choose a_H because its expected utility is no less than from taking a_L. The principal anticipates the manager's effort choice and uses the probabilities for the outcomes (and compensation payments) resulting from the high effort when evaluating the manager's net utility.

The optimal contract satisfies (7) and (8) as equalities, because otherwise the principal would pay more than necessary to induce the manager to take the desired decisions. Given that, the optimal compensation can be stated in terms of utilities derived from monetary payments ('utils'), $u_j \equiv \sqrt{w_j}$, in the following manner:

$$u_1^* = \underline{U} + v_H - 0.8B, \quad u_2^* = u_1^* + B, \quad \text{where } B = \frac{v_H - v_L}{0.8 - 0.4} \tag{9}$$

The optimal compensation (measured in terms of 'utils') consists of the base salary u_1^* and the bonus B. The bonus is paid only if the high outcome is achieved. It is determined by the ratio between two differences: the incremental cost of providing high effort, $v_H - v_L$, and the incremental likelihood of obtaining the bonus after providing a high effort, which equals $0.8 - 0.4$ in the example. From (9), the base salary comprises the manager's reservation utility $\underline{U}$ and the disutility of the desired effort v_H minus the expected bonus payment $0.2u_1^* + 0.8u_2^* = 0.8B$. In expectation, the agent receives a utility $u_1^* + 0.8B = \underline{U} + v_H$. This compensation utility would also apply to a high effort level if the principal could observe the agent's action directly.

For the data in Table 19.2 and $\underline{U} = 20$ we calculate a numerical solution. From (9) the base salary equals 16, and the bonus equals 10. The outcome based compensation payments are $w_1 = 256$ and $w_2 = 676$, and the principal's expected compensation costs equal 592. If the principal could observe the effort, the payment would be $24^2 = 576$. The difference of 16 represents the agency costs. These costs are the upper bound for the price that the principal would pay for a perfect management accounting system that provides him or her with perfect information about the agent's effort.

The incentive component of the compensation is necessary to induce the manager to exert high effort. However, it comes at a cost. Since the manager is risk averse, he or she must be compensated for the compensation risk imposed for incentive purposes.

This reasoning is the source of the trade-off in the basic agency model. More incentive compensation motivates higher effort and, thus, higher expected outcome, but it increases the required risk premium. The optimal compensation scheme trades off these two effects. If risk allocation is considered of second-order importance, a similar agency problem can be formulated in which there are two types of managers, who differ in their productivity or other personal characteristics. If only the manager knows his or her type, the contract must motivate the more productive manager to choose a higher production level than the less productive manager. The trade-off then occurs between obtaining the manager's private information and the so-called 'information rent' that the more productive manager is able to elicit from the principal for revealing his or her superior information. This information rent compensates the more productive manager for the gain that he or she could have made from pretending to be less productive.

With such a structure, it is possible to explore a number of management accounting issues beside the factors that affect the shape of compensation functions. One theme is variance analysis in an agency setting. Managers are usually held responsible for variances between actual and budgeted performance. For example, if the budget equals the expected outcome, $E[x_j]$, a low outcome would result in an unfavourable variance and a high outcome in a favourable variance. Variance analysis investigates the causes of a variance. In the basic model, there are two possible causes: the manager did not provide the desired effort, or the state of nature was other than expected. In equilibrium, however, only the second possibility applies. The variance must have been caused by the state that occurred, which is by definition not controllable by the manager. The manager controls effort, but has no incentive to provide an effort different from the level desired by the principal because the optimal compensation contract is designed exactly that way, and both the manager and the principal know that. Nevertheless, the optimal contract holds the manager responsible for the variance and thereby imposes risk on the manager. This pay structure is *ex post* strictly inefficient because the principal must offer the risk averse manager a contract with risky compensation for providing appropriate effort incentives, which increases the expected cost of compensation as compared to a situation where the parties could write an enforceable contract on the agent's effort.

The above example does not suggest that a variance analysis is useless because the principal knows that the variance is attributable to the state of nature. Assume the variance analysis consists of an information system that provides perfect information about the manager's effort and the state of nature. Knowing *ex ante* that a variance analysis will reveal the effort and the state, the principal can simply force the manager to exert high effort and pay him or her a fixed compensation. The threat is that, if the variance analysis reveals that the manager deviated, he or she could be punished. Anticipating this consequence, the manager has no incentive to deviate. The fixed compensation shields the manager from any compensation risk, therefore, because another, more efficient incentive mechanism exists which relies on the variance analysis as a source of information. *Ex post*, however, the variance analysis is inefficient as its result can be readily anticipated. Nevertheless, the principal must commit to carrying it out since otherwise the incentive effect would vanish.

The possibility of renegotiating contracts can be detrimental in such a situation. But there exist some mechanisms that can substitute for a lack of commitment. An example would be to provide aggregate rather than line-item information. Aggregate information is less informative, but it avoids over-utilisation of the information and restricts the decision space of the principal.

The human resource and organisations literature often states a controllability principle, which says that a manager should not be held responsible for non-controllable events. The result of the economic analysis is in stark contrast to this principle because it evaluates the value of information sources on the basis of their information content. The information content of a particular information source depends on the inference that can be made about the agent's effort from observing it. Therefore, a performance measure can be valuable for contracting even if its outcome is beyond the manager's control. An example would be relative performance evaluation of two salespeople. Suppose they act in separate sales regions. The sales in each region depend on local sales effort and on factors common to both regions, such as economic conditions. In that case, the sales in one region are informative about the sales effort in the other region because both regions are to some extent affected by the same conditions. Evaluating one salesperson's performance on sales in their own region relative to sales in the other region filters out part of the common noise and reduces the risk in the salesperson's compensation. In essence, the firm benefits from holding the salesperson responsible for the other region's results (see also Antle and Demski, 1988). A similar logic applies to indexed stock options, which therefore can be superior to non-indexed stock options in executive compensation contracts.

A related theme is the value of additional accounting information. The above model assumes that only the outcome is used for compensation purposes. Usually, there are many other potential performance measures available in firms. Research has shown that additional performance measures cannot have a negative value if they are observed *after* the manager selects his or her level of effort. Although the additional measures may add uncertainty, they can be valuable if they are correlated with the effort or the state of nature. The risk is controlled by their weighting in the compensation function. The more informative such a performance measure is, the higher will be its weighting.

The interaction between different performance measures is subtle. To illustrate, suppose there are two performance measures, $y_k = s + \varepsilon_k$, $k = 1, 2$, where ε_1 and ε_2 are noise terms. Both measures are informative about the state of nature. If only one of them is used for contracting, its weight is clearly positive, but decreasing in the variance of ε_k because the variance determines the risk in the agent's compensation that it is borne by the principal. However, if both measures are used, depending on the parameter values one of them may receive a negative weight. A necessary condition is that the covariance between the noise terms ε_1 and ε_2 is strongly positive. Then the negative weight on one of the measures filters part of the total noise of the performance measures and, thus, enables the principal to reduce the manager's compensation risk for a given effort level.

If additional accounting information is provided *before* the manager selects his or her effort, it may have negative value. This is intuitive only if the manager gets to observe the additional information. While the manager can make a more informed effort selection, the principal loses some control over the manager, which may outweigh the productivity effect. A similar result can occur if both the principal and the manager receive pre-decision information. The reason here is that the additional information may make it more costly for the principal to enforce the desired effort. If additional information is costly to produce, such effects can occur even more often.

Management accounting research has taken much interest in the balanced scorecard and in non-financial performance measures. The balanced scorecard includes four perspectives – financial, customer, processes, and learning and growth – and attempts to measure them with several performance measures. In particular, it proposes both financial and non-financial measures. The balanced scorecard can be used as a decision-facilitating tool; in this role, it provides key performance measures to the manager to improve decision-making. It has also been proposed as a performance measurement system. Usually, weights are attached to each of the performance measures in the balanced scorecard, and an aggregate measure is calculated as the basis for incentive compensation. Agency theory guides the optimal determination of the weights and shows that an optimal aggregation depends on statistical characteristics, such as the sensitivity and precision of the signals rather than on their realisation (e.g. Banker and Datar, 1989). It also provides insights into situations in which the manager decides on his or her effort in a multi-task setting. Here, the weights depend on the precision and the congruence with the owners' outcome (e.g. Feltham and Xie, 1994). Likewise, performance measures may optimally be 'under-utilised' if a more intensive use for contracting purposes would shift the manager's attention away from other tasks that are more difficult to measure.

Most performance measures are short-term oriented. Long-term oriented measures are often very noisy and may be manipulated by the manager. Moreover, managers usually have short time horizons, for example because of short-term contracts or alternative employment opportunities within and outside the firm. Alternatively, managers may be 'impatient' in that they value current compensation much more than future compensation, an assumption which translates into a higher discount rate than that of the firm. Even if there are no other conflicts of interest (such as personally costly effort), such considerations create agency conflicts. Consider, for example, a manager who must make an investment decision two years before his or her retirement. A self-interested manager might only consider the monetary payoffs of the investment project for the next two years, but not for periods beyond this. If the firm must rely on short-term performance measures to motivate optimal investment decisions, these measures should incorporate as many of the monetary consequences as possible for the full planning horizon of the investment. Economic value added, a specific version of residual income, has been advanced by consultants and practitioners as such a measure. Agency research has generally supported this view and found that residual income is indeed a performance measure that is quite robust to changes in the underlying assumptions, but has also provided qualifying conditions for the measurement of profit used for residual-income-based performance measurement. These conditions mainly require adjustments to the measurement of book values and the calculation of income (e.g. Reichelstein, 1997; Rogerson, 1997).

This line of research contributes to our understanding of the popularity of economic value added measures and of the reasons for, and optimal choice of, adjustments to book values for incentive purposes.

Budgeting

Budgeting has been of continuing interest in management accounting research. From an economic perspective, budgeting is one means to influence decisions made on the divisional level and to coordinate them across the firm.

To give a flavour of the insights obtained from formal budgeting models, we extend our earlier decision-making example with the introduction of a new product under cost uncertainty. The actual cost c of the new product is uniformly distributed between 100 and 300. The price p also lies between the same bounds (to avoid trivial decisions). In contrast to our earlier scenario, we assume that the division manager has perfect information about the actual cost. The firm's headquarters holds only the a priori expectation, but is aware that the manager knows the true cost. Headquarters can either decide centrally on the introduction of the new product or delegate the decision to the manager and provide him or her with a cost budget b for producing the new product.

First, assume that headquarters decides centrally without using the manager's superior information. It accepts the new product if the price exceeds the expected costs (i.e. if $p > E[c] = 200$) and rejects it otherwise. The expected profit of centralised decision-making equals

$$E[\Pi^0] = \max(0, p - E[c]) = \max(0, p - 200) \tag{10}$$

Alternatively, headquarters may attempt to benefit from the manager's superior cost information by asking him or her to report the actual product cost. If the manager truthfully reports the cost, the product is introduced if $p > c$ and the expected profit equals (see equation (1) in the EVPI example)

$$E[\Pi^{FB}] = \frac{(p - 100)^2}{400} \tag{11}$$

This is the optimal outcome if headquarters had perfect cost information. It is also referred to as the 'first-best' or full information outcome. The same solution would be obtained if the manager reports the true cost and receives a budget of $b = c$. The two regimes replicate our earlier discussion of the value of information in the single decision-maker context.

However, the manager may have no incentive to communicate the actual cost truthfully. For example, a common observation is that managers tend to prefer budgetary slack because excess budgets allow for discretionary expenses. Assume, therefore, that the manager benefits by the difference between the budget and the actual cost, $b - c$. He or she then has an incentive to bias the reported cost upwards to receive the highest possible budget. In particular, if the manager proposes the budget and headquarters accepts all budget proposals for which $b \leq p$, the manager would demand a budget of $b = p$ because this budget maximises his or her budgetary slack. With this solution, the product would always be introduced if it is profitable, but at the same time the firm's profit is entirely consumed by the manager.

Being aware of these incentives, headquarters can design a more efficient budgeting procedure. It includes sacrificing some profitable projects to reduce budgetary slack. This trade-off is reflected in the two terms of the expected profit function:

$$E[\Pi] = (p - b) \times \Pr(b > c) = (p - b) \times \Phi(b)$$

the contribution margin $p - b$ and the probability that the budget covers the actual cost, $\Phi(b)$. If headquarters reduces the budget, the contribution margin increases, but the probability that the budget covers the actual cost goes down. For $b = p$ the contribution margin is zero but all profitable projects are accepted. On the other hand, if b is set to the lowest cost the contribution margin is maximised but there is zero probability that the budget is sufficient. The optimal budget balances both effects. It is determined by maximising $E[\Pi]$ with respect to b and solving the resulting first-order condition for b:

$$b^* = p - \frac{\Phi(b)}{\phi(b)} = \frac{p}{2} - 50$$

The solution implies that all projects with actual cost between b^* and p are not realised although they are profitable for the firm. The expected profit for headquarters becomes

$$E[\Pi^*] = \frac{(p - 100)^2}{800} \tag{12}$$

which is only half of the profit of solution in (11) for information symmetry. Figure 19.2 plots the firm's expected profit for all three regimes. The 'centralised decision' curve depicts the profit attainable with a centralised decision based on expected cost information (see equation 10). The 'information symmetry' curve shows the profit with a manager who reports truthfully (see equation (11)), and the curve labelled 'optimal budgeting' exhibits the expected profit with the optimal budgeting procedure.

This setting provides several insights. First, it shows that information asymmetry may be detrimental in that it can induce dishonest communication within the firm.

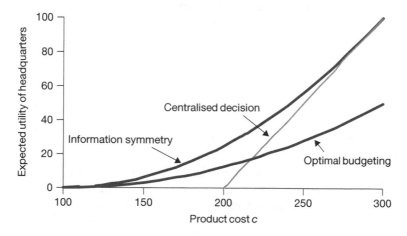

Figure 19.2 Expected profit for different organisational regimes

Headquarters cannot fully rely on the divisional report, but it is aware of that and reacts accordingly.

Second, the setting can explain the existence of budget rationing and profit targets, which induce suboptimal project decisions because not all potentially profitable projects are accepted. Due to this *ex post* inefficiency, the total profit (headquarters' profit and the manager's slack) is less than what could be achieved in an ideal world. However, headquarters deliberately commits to such a policy because it is optimal from an *ex ante* perspective (see Antle and Eppen, 1985).

Third, the setting shows that it might be preferable to decide centrally and ignore the superior cost information of the division manager. To see why, compare headquarters' expected profit under centralised decision-making with that for the optimal budgeting procedure in Figure 19.2. For $p < 217$ (rounded) headquarters benefits from the manager's information, whereas for $p > 217$ it does better by ignoring the information and deciding centrally because the agency cost exceeds the benefit of the cost information.

The setting examined above is simple and abstracts from a broad range of issues that arise in a realistic budgeting situation. However, there has been ample research into extensions and alternative models. For example, the division manager may be able to affect production cost by investment or managerial effort. Then, the budgeting mechanism must also provide sufficient incentives to the manager to do so. If a division manager has empire-building preferences, it can be optimal to increase the threshold for the required rate of return. Budgeting procedures are often categorised as top-down, bottom-up or both in an iterative process. Their respective usefulness depends on the information endowments of the manager and headquarters and the type of decisions made by each of them. In our model, the optimal budgeting procedure can be classified as top-down, whereas the procedure in which the manager proposes the budget can be classified as bottom-up. Usually, budgeting takes place in situations in which several divisions compete for scarce resources. In such a situation, headquarters must also consider the effects of the budgeting mechanism on the reporting behaviour of the other divisions. For example, a class of budgeting mechanisms, so-called 'Groves mechanisms' (Cohen and Loeb, 1984), can secure truthful reporting as the dominant strategy for all divisions, although this approach may have other shortcomings.

Transfer pricing

Transfer pricing is another theme that has received much attention in economics-based management accounting research. Cost allocations have similar economic effects and can be seen as a special case of transfer prices. As with budgeting, transfer pricing coordinates decentralised decision-making, albeit in an economically different way.

The typical transfer pricing model includes headquarters and two divisions. One division (upstream division) produces an intermediate good that is delivered to the other division (downstream division), which finalises the product and sells it to the market. Transfer prices coordinate the two divisions. They introduce a kind of 'controlled' market for the intermediate product, although a real market has been excluded by integrating the two divisions within the same firm. Thus, transfer prices are an alternative coordination device to budgets and, although their economic effects are different, their use is based on the same fundamental economic insights.

Where divisional profit is used as the performance measure, a conflict of interest is created by organising the two divisions as profit centres. Managers are incentivised to maximise divisional profit, no matter what negative effects this may have on the other division and on the firm as a whole. Of course, the usefulness of a profit centre structure is itself guided by an economic trade-off.

Many different models have been used to study transfer pricing issues in the economic management accounting literature. For the purposes of this discussion, we use only one of them. Division 1 produces an intermediate good with a variable unit cost of c_1. Division 2 finalises the good incurring a variable unit cost c_2 and sells it to the market. For simplicity, we normalise c_2 to zero. The market for the final product is assumed to be a monopoly with the unit price depending on quantity q supplied as follows: $p(q) = 10 - q$. Before production takes place, the manager of division 1 can reduce the unit cost c_1 by exerting effort a_1 at a personal cost of $v(a_1) = a_1^2$. At the time of the manager's effort decision, the success of the cost reduction measures is uncertain. In particular, we assume that $c_1 = 7 - (a_1 + \varepsilon)$, where ε is a noise term with mean zero and variance σ^2 and the support of its distribution is such that $c_1 > 0$ (i.e. the highest possible value satisfies $\varepsilon < 7 - a_1^*$). Both division managers can observe the effective cost reduction when deciding on the optimal production quantity, whereas headquarters cannot.

Before we analyse how alternative transfer pricing methods affect the manager's investment incentives, we consider the optimal solution that could be obtained if headquarters had all relevant information for deciding on q and a_1 (the so called first-best solution). The decision process has two steps. Working backward, we first determine the optimal production quantity q for a given value of c_1. Maximising the operating profit $\Pi_{op} = (p(q) - c_1)q = (10 - c_1)q - q^2$, and solving the resulting first-order condition for q yields an optimal quantity

$$q^* = \frac{10 - c_1}{2} = \frac{3 + a_1^* + \varepsilon}{2} \tag{13}$$

Substituting this solution into the profit function yields an expected operating profit of

$$E[\Pi_{op}^*] = \frac{(3 + a_1^*)^2}{4} + \frac{\sigma^2}{4} \tag{14}$$

The expected operating profit comprises two terms. The first term equals $E[q^*]^2$ and the second term represents the value of perfect cost information for the production decision. This variance appears in equation (14) because the firm knows ε when deciding on q. If the firm did not know ε when deciding on q, it would determine the optimal production quantity based on expected marginal cost and the expected operating profit would be equal to $E[q^*]^2$.

The optimal production quantity and the expected operating profit are increasing functions of the agent's effort. The higher a_1, the higher are the optimal quantity and the firm's overall profit. To determine the optimal (first-best) effort level that could be implemented if effort were contractible, the firm maximizes the total surplus of the agency with respect to a_1. The total surplus comprises the firm's expected operating profit from (14) and the agent's effort cost. The firm must compensate the manager for his or her effort cost, or the manager would refuse to work for the firm. Differentiating

$$\mathrm{E}[\Pi] = \mathrm{E}[\Pi^*_{op}] - v(a_1) = \frac{(3 + a_1)^2}{4} + \frac{\sigma^2}{4} - a_1^2 \tag{15}$$

with respect to a_1 and solving the first-order condition yields the solution $a_1^{FB} = 1$. Substituting the optimal effort level into (13) and (14) yields an optimal quantity $q^{FB} = 2 - \varepsilon/2$ and a total expected profit of $\mathrm{E}[\Pi^{FB}] = 3 + \sigma^2/4$. This profit serves as a benchmark for two decentralised settings, standard cost-based transfer pricing and negotiated transfer pricing.

Under standard cost-based transfer pricing, headquarters fixes a transfer price t before the manager of division 1 decides on his or her effort level and before the manager of division 2 determines the production quantity. Given the transfer price t, division 2 maximizes its divisional profit $\Pi_2 = (10 - t)q - q^2$ and sets a quantity $q^*(t) = (10 - t)/2$. The manager of division 1 anticipates the quantity decision of division 2 and chooses a_1 to maximize the division's expected profit $\mathrm{E}[\Pi_1] = (t - \mathrm{E}[c_1])q$, which results in an optimal effort level of $a_1^* = q^*(t)/2 = (10 - t)/4$.

Anticipating these decisions by the managers, headquarters can induce the manager of division 1 to choose the optimal effort level $a_1^* = a_1^{FB} = 1$ by setting $t = \mathrm{E}[c_1] - a_1^{FB} = 6$. This transfer price equals the expected (optimal) cost. This is the major advantage of standard cost-based transfer pricing. The disadvantage is that it induces a suboptimal quantity decision by division 2. Because the quantity is set on the basis of expected rather than actual cost (i.e. the firm cannot adjust its quantity policy to the actual value of ε), the optimal quantity differs from the (ex post) optimal quantity by $\Delta q = \mathrm{E}[q^{FB}] - q^{FB} = \varepsilon/2$. Ex ante, the quantity distortion results in a loss of $\sigma^2/4$, and the expected total profit with standard cost-based transfer pricing is $\mathrm{E}[\Pi^C] = 3$. We have seen that the optimal profit with contractible effort equals $\mathrm{E}[\Pi^{FB}] = 3 + \sigma^2/4$. The difference between the two profits is the expected value of perfect cost information with respect to the quantity decision.

Negotiated transfer prices occur in a setting in which headquarters does not administer transfer prices, but allows the two divisions to bargain over a mutually acceptable transfer price. In our model, the major advantage of negotiated transfer pricing over standard cost-based transfer pricing is that both divisions know the actual cost c_1 when they start bargaining. Thus, they can make an informed quantity decision. As a consequence, the quantity equals the (ex post) optimal quantity as described in equation (13).

The disadvantage of negotiated transfer pricing lies in its adverse investment incentives. At the time when divisions negotiate the transfer price and determine the quantity, the cost reduction effort by the manager of division 1 has already been taken and is a sunk cost. During negotiations, the manager has no credible threat to induce division 2 to share in the effort cost. Anticipating this situation, the manager under-invests relative to the optimal effort level with contractible effort. To illustrate, assume that the outcome of the negotiation is that division 1 receives a share $0 < \gamma < 1$ and division 2 a share of $1 - \gamma$ of the operating profit from their quantity decision. The expected profit of division 1 is:

$$E[\Pi_1] = \gamma E[\Pi_{op}^*] - v(a_1) = \gamma\left(\frac{(3 + a_1)^2}{4} + \frac{\sigma^2}{4}\right) - a_1^2 \qquad (16)$$

The manager receives only a fraction of the operating profit increase that results from his or her effort, but bears the full cost of that effort. As a consequence, he or she exerts an effort for cost reduction of $a_1^N = 3\gamma/(4 - \gamma)$, which is less than a_1^{FB}. This effect is the well-known hold-up problem (e.g. Edlin and Reichelstein, 1995).

With this inefficient effort, the total expected profit of the firm under negotiated transfer pricing becomes:

$$E[\Pi^N] = \frac{9 \times (4 - \gamma^2)}{(4 - \gamma)^2} + \frac{\sigma^2}{4}$$

This profit may be more or less than the profit attainable with standard cost-based transfer pricing. The result depends on the relative magnitudes of the effort distortion under negotiated transfer pricing and the quantity distortion with cost-based transfer pricing. The higher the anticipated profit share of division 1 in the bargaining solution, the lower the investment distortion and the more desirable is negotiated transfer pricing. The lower the cost variance, the lower the quantity distortion and the more desirable is standard cost-based transfer pricing.

Figure 19.3 depicts the expected total profits for the contractible-effort scenario and the two transfer pricing regimes for a cost variance of $\sigma^2 = 1$. It shows that cost-based transfer pricing is preferable if $\gamma < 0.5$ and vice versa. Negotiated transfer pricing replicates the optimal solution if division 1 has all the bargaining power. While this is true in the model examined here, giving division 1 all the bargaining power would not be optimal once both divisions exert effort or make specific investments.

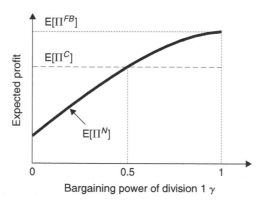

Π^{FB} is first-best profit,
Π^C profit under cost-based transfer price,
Π^N profit under negotiated transfer price.

Figure 19.3 Expected profit for different transfer pricing methods

One might wonder whether it is preferable to delegate the transfer price decision to division 1. However, this would worsen the result. The reason is that division 2 then acts as a price taker to division 1's monopoly pricing. The result is, again, an inefficient quantity decision. Indeed, under the conditions in the above example, only half the quantity under the negotiated transfer pricing method is transferred.

The above model illustrates the effects of different transfer pricing methods in a given organisational setting. Of course, the results depend on a number of assumptions. However, the model helps to identify the assumptions that drive preferences about transfer pricing methods. A common result is that it is impossible to identify a single transfer pricing method that dominates all other methods for a broad set of coordination problems (Wagenhofer, 1994; Göx and Schiller, 2007). This result is in line with surveys of company practice, which show that firms use very different transfer pricing methods. The research aims to identify conditions under which one transfer pricing method outperforms others.

Besides their coordinating role within the firm, transfer pricing methods can impact the competitive position (Alles and Datar, 1998; Göx, 2000). To illustrate, we modify the model and consider a symmetric duopoly with price competition. Ignoring the hold-up problem and cost uncertainty, we assume that division 1 has a marginal production cost of $c_1 = 7$. In addition, it has some sunk capacity cost that amounts to $r = 8.4$ per unit. Division 2 in firm i, $(i = 1, 2)$ sells the product on the final market where it faces the demand function $q_i(p_i, p_j) = 29 - p_i + 0.8p_j$.

We assume that both firms employ standard cost-based transfer pricing methods, but choose whether to use marginal unit cost $(t_i = c_1)$ or full unit cost $(t_i = c_1 + r)$ prices. Given the transfer price, the division managers determine the optimal prices by simultaneously maximising their profit functions $\Pi_{1i} = (p_i - t_i) \times (29 - p_i + 0.8p_j)$ with respect to p_i. The equilibrium prices are found by solving the resulting system of first-order conditions for p_1 and p_2. They are:

$$p_i = \frac{145}{6} + \frac{25}{42}t_i + \frac{5}{21}t_j \tag{17}$$

The equilibrium prices are increasing in both firms' transfer prices, i.e. the higher t_i and t_j, the higher are p_i and p_j. However, the positive effect of each firm's own transfer price is greater than that of the competitor's. If both firms transfer their intermediate product at marginal cost $(t_i = 7)$, the equilibrium prices are $p_i = 30$, and for symmetric full cost-based transfer pricing $(t_i = 15.4)$ the prices go up to $p_i = 65$. If only firm 1 bases its transfer prices on full cost, the equilibrium prices would be $p_1 = 35$ and $p_2 = 32$. Table 19.3 shows the resulting profits for both firms (the figures are obtained by substituting the appropriate transfer prices and product prices into the firms' profit functions, ignoring capacity cost).

The firms realise the largest profit if they both employ full cost-based transfer pricing. The reason is that the transfer pricing policy reduces the intensity of competition. By charging transfer prices above the marginal cost, both firms force their divisional managers to charge higher product prices than in the competitive price equilibrium between two centralised firms. Thus, the delegation of the pricing decision, paired with an appropriate transfer pricing policy, can have strategic value.

418

Table 19.3 Profits under different transfer pricing methods

Firm 1	Firm 2	
	$t_2 = 7$	$t_2 = 15.4$
$t_1 = 7$	529; 529	625; 549
$t_1 = 15.4$	549; 625	648; 648

It is well known that marginal cost-based transfer pricing replicates the optimal pricing policy of a centralised firm (under certainty). As seen in Table 19.3, both firms have strong incentives to decentralise their pricing decisions because they can increase their profits no matter what transfer pricing policy the competitor adopts. Thus, full cost-based transfer pricing is a dominant equilibrium strategy under this set of parameters. If the capacity cost becomes large, however, the induced price increase can become too large so that firms want to deviate from the full cost-based transfer pricing method. Effectively, the game would then revert to a symmetric marginal cost-based transfer pricing equilibrium.

It is also important that both firms know the other firm uses full cost-based transfer pricing, otherwise this policy is not an equilibrium even if the full cost mark-up is not too large. The firms don't have to know each other's transfer prices, but they must at least know the transfer pricing method used.

Key assumptions

The previous discussion shows several common characteristics of economic models in management accounting. By definition, models are simplifications of the real world, but even so they tend to become complex once assumptions are made more realistic. There is a trade-off between the realism of the model assumptions and mathematical tractability. However, reality is far more complex than any model (or other research method that attempts to explain an empirical phenomenon), so simplifying assumptions are a key ingredient for gaining specific insights. The true skill of good modelling then consists of selecting the relevant assumptions for a meaningful analysis of the underlying research question.

All the assumptions are stylised representations of practice. Management accounting occurs in firms, which are multi-person organisations with rules that allocate decision rights and responsibilities across the persons involved. The previous discussion emphasises the importance of the organisational form (e.g. the extent of delegation and responsibilities) for the design of management accounting and the results that can be achieved using it. This emphasis is in line with other research methods in management accounting, such as sociology-based research.

To reduce complexity, assumptions abstract from factors that are considered unimportant or second-order effects. This requires a value judgement because the research embodies the researcher's hypotheses about the major drivers for the result that he or she expects to obtain (so-called first-order effects). Examples of typical second-order effects include assumptions on the functional forms of cost, compensation, or utility functions. A popular version of the agency model, the LEN model, assumes compensation that is *linear* in the performance measures, an *exponential* utility (which serves to avoid wealth effects on risk attitudes), and a *normal* distribution of the random variables. Sometimes, such assumptions are not fully innocuous. For example, the LEN model cannot capture 'kinked' schemes such as employee stock options or conservative accounting norms. Results may be sensitive to such specifications, although they are not meant to be.

While earlier economic research emphasised the search for optimal solutions, for example optimal performance measures, more recent research compares a selected set of 'solutions' used in practice and identifies conditions under which one or the other performs best. Optimality is sacrificed to reduce complexity. Moreover, results that compare observed 'solutions' seem to speak to practice more than an optimal solution that may be sensitive to changes in minor assumptions.

Assumptions define the boundaries of what is exogenous or endogenous in the model. For example, the reservation utility of a manager is usually exogenously specified, although in practice it is likely that the manager's performance will have an effect on outside employment opportunities. A direct effect of this assumption is that firing the manager is not a penalty at all and, therefore, not an option in incentive contracting. Some assumptions may play a major role, but are outside the focus of the research, and are taken for granted. Examples are the potential for commitment and the enforcement of whatever contracts individuals agree upon. However, economic research is careful to distinguish between contractible (i.e. verifiable by, say, a court) information and information that is observable by the contracting parties but not by a court. Non-contractible information may nevertheless be useful for coordinating behaviour.

An important assumption is uncertainty. Without uncertainty management accounting cannot produce valuable information for rational decisions. It is important what information endowment a decision-maker has and when information is received. A related assumption is information asymmetry, which plays a key role in the decision-influencing use of management accounting information. Information asymmetry is usually introduced by assuming that all but a few variables are common knowledge. The focus is then on these few variables and their effect on decision-making. Conflict of interest is another essential theme in the analysis of decision-influencing uses of information. In conjunction with information asymmetry, it is a necessary condition for an agency problem to exist.

Of particular importance is the rationality assumption. Economic models assume rational players who are fully aware of the situation and maximise their expected utility using all the information available. Since analytical research is often difficult to read and comprehend, this assumption appears to be difficult to justify and has probably drawn the most criticism for economic research. The usual defence is that few people would intentionally deviate from rational behaviour. Therefore, it is a benchmark for describing behaviour.

The rationality assumption, however, is not a normative assumption about individuals' behaviour. While many models employ simple utility functions and appear to dismiss more complex theories of motivation, they are open to alternative specifications.

For example, slack preferences or empire building preferences can easily be incorporated into utility functions, although they are exogenous. Recent research in behavioural economics has looked for robust descriptions of actual individual behaviour and tried to modify utility functions to incorporate it. For example, fairness seems to be a robust property. Decision-makers may favour fair allocations over maximising their monetary payoff, and even accept a decrease in their own payoff to help implement a result they deem fair. Ethical behaviour is a similar issue. What matters for economic modelling, therefore, are not the arguments or the shape of the utility functions of individuals, but that individuals behave in a manner that is consistent with their objectives. Erratic behaviour is outside an economic analysis.

Another aspect of rational behaviour is the full understanding of the situation, including making the best use of available information, and considering the information other individuals have. This assumption is crucial because a major use of economic research lies in understanding strategic interactions among various actors. If the assumption is not included, there would be no real interaction and no clear solution to the coordination problem under consideration. It is possible to introduce costs of reasoning and understanding all aspects of a situation, but models have done poorly in formalising this idea. In a similar vein, economic models usually study optimal behaviour but do not reveal how decision-makers arrive at this behaviour.

Summary and potential for future research

Economic research in management accounting has been used to enhance our understanding of the role of management accounting information in supporting rational decision-making in organisations. It provides insights into, and guidance for organising and managing, resource allocation processes within firms under uncertainty. A key characteristic illustrated in this chapter is that it builds on a rigorous description of the structure of the issue that is analysed. A particular strength of the economic research approach is that the assumptions clearly define the boundaries of the research question. It also allows a critique of the assumptions. This characteristic makes the research highly consistent and objective so that other researchers will arrive at the same conclusions once they accept the assumptions underlying the model.

The discussion in this chapter has reviewed models and results that have been frequently used to address management accounting issues. A typical result is that features of a management accounting system and characteristics of individual information users, which include utility functions and information endowments, cannot be disentangled but interact in a specific way. Such a result makes it difficult to gain more general insights into management accounting systems. A related characteristic of modelling results is the statement 'it depends'. The statement is meant to indicate that model results are sensitive to changes in the parameter values or basic assumptions. This observation is often used to criticise economic research, and it is a valid criticism if one constructs assumptions so as to generate a certain result, whatever that may be. However, if the assumptions are 'realistic', the contingencies in the results can be used to sharpen the common understanding of management accounting by guiding other research. For example, empirical research can use the results to formulate refined hypotheses. The real world is not simple at all, and it would be surprising if simple solutions were found to be optimal in a broad set of circumstances. On the other hand, the search for robust results is appealing, and there are other results, for example, demonstrating the usefulness of residual income performance measures for aligning conflicts of interest in a decentralised firm.

Robust insights from economic research are the structures, economic effects and trade-offs involved in management accounting. One such insight discussed in this chapter is the importance of distinguishing between *ex ante* and *ex post* optimality. Contracting models typically involve activities that, from an *ex post* view, are inefficient. An example is a compensation contract that imposes risk on a manager, which is clearly inefficient after the manager has made the decision. However, it is optimal from an *ex ante* perspective, i.e. in regard to the incentives for a manager to make the decision. This insight is particularly important for understanding observed practice – many important aspects of control are not observable but still guide behaviour. For example, there has been much empirical research on the sensitivity of variable management compensation's impact on firm performance. This research sometimes finds the 'surprising' result that the sensitivity is low. A reason may be that variable compensation is but one way to motivate managers. Reconsider the earlier discussion on variance analysis, where we show that additional information generated by the variance analysis helps to provide incentives and shield the manager from compensation risk.

A particular strength of economic research lies in the analysis of interaction effects among various decisions made under different information endowments and at different stages, and of strategic interaction among various decision-makers. This would be much more difficult, or perhaps even impossible, without the strong formal apparatus of an economic model. As a consequence, economic research is most useful in situations where such interactions are symptomatic – in particular, management incentives and control issues in a decentralised organisation. The themes we consider in this chapter, such as precision of costs, pricing, performance measures, budgeting and transfer pricing, are typical of those well suited to the application of economic research.

In practice, management accounting information is often used in multiple, diffuse and innovative ways in organisations that rely on explicit and implicit coordinating devices. In such a setting, economic research is not much help, as it requires the *a priori* specification of the users' interests and environment. Thus, it is less helpful for exploring new and innovative themes, including management accounting change, knowledge diffusion and cultural effects, because they are hard to capture in a formalised structure and often contain many dimensions without any clear indication of which are most important.

Economic research on management accounting is probably most effective if it exploits the strength of this research approach, namely the analysis of interactions and the effects of differential management accounting information on its providers and users. We expect future economic research to focus on explicit and implicit incentives based on management accounting information in organisations, to better capture multi-period effects, and to use a broader set of assumptions than seem currently acceptable.

Economic research complements other research methods to better understand management accounting practice and better integrate insights generated using other research methods. After all, there are a plethora of issues that, as yet, are not sufficiently well understood.

References

Alles, M. and Datar, S. (1998) 'Strategic transfer pricing', *Management Science,* **44**, 451–61.

Antle, R. and Demski, J. (1988) 'The controllability principle in responsibility accounting', *The Accounting Review,* **63**, 700–18.

Antle, R. and Eppen, G.D. (1985) 'Capital rationing and organizational slack in capital budgeting', *Management Science,* **31**, 163–74.

Banker, R.D. and Datar, S.M. (1989) 'Sensitivity, precision, and linear aggregation of signals for performance evaluation', *Journal of Accounting Research,* **27**, 21–39.

Banker, R.D. and Hughes, J.S. (1994) 'Product costing and pricing', *The Accounting Review,* **69**, 479–94.

Christensen, J. and Demski, J.S. (1995) 'The classical foundation of modern costing', *Management Accounting Research,* **6**, 13–32.

Christensen, J.A. and Demski, J.S. (2003) *Accounting Theory: An Information Content Perspective,* New York: McGraw-Hill.

Cohen, S.I. and Loeb, M. (1984) 'The Groves scheme, profit sharing, and moral hazard', *Management Science,* **30**, 20–4.

Edlin, A. and Reichelstein, S. (1995) 'Specific investment under negotiated transfer pricing: an efficiency result', *The Accounting Review,* **70**, 275–92.

Feltham, G.A. and Xie, J. (1994) 'Performance measure congruity and diversity in multi-task principal/agent relations', *The Accounting Review,* **69**, 429–53.

Göx, R.F. (2000) 'Strategic transfer pricing, absorption costing, and observability', *Management Accounting Research,* **11**, 327–48.

Göx, R.F. (2002) 'Capacity planning and pricing under uncertainty', *Journal of Management Accounting Research,* **14**, 59–78.

Göx, R.F. and Schiller, U. (2007) 'An economic perspective on transfer pricing', in C.S. Chapman, A.G. Hopwood and M.D. Shields (eds), *Handbook of Management Accounting Research,* vol. 2, Oxford: Elsevier, pp. 673–95.

Reichelstein, S. (1997) 'Investment decisions and managerial performance evaluation', *Review of Accounting Studies,* **2**, 157–80.

Rogerson, W.P. (1997) 'Intertemporal cost allocation and managerial investment incentives', *Journal of Political Economy,* **105**, 770–95.

Wagenhofer, A. (1994) 'Transfer pricing under asymmetric information', *European Accounting Review,* **3**, 71–104.

Further reading

Christensen, J.A. and Demski, J.S. (2003) *Accounting Theory: An Information Content Perspective,* New York: McGraw-Hill. A comprehensive analysis of financial and management accounting information.

Christensen, P.O. and Feltham, G.A. (2005) *Economics of Accounting. Volume II – Performance Evaluation,* Secaucus, NJ: Springer. An advanced text with rigorous analysis of decision-influencing uses of accounting.

Demski, J.S. and Feltham G.A. (1976) *Cost Determination: A Conceptual Approach,* Ames: Iowa State University Press. A classical reference on the role of cost information in organisations.

Demski, J.S. (1994) *Managerial Uses of Accounting Information.* Boston, MA: Kluwer. Examines the value of information in different management accounting settings.

Ewert, R. and Wagenhofer, A. (2005) *Interne Unternehmensrechnung,* 5th edn., Berlin: Springer. This German-language advanced textbook covers the economics of management accounting.

Lambert, R.A. (2001) 'Contracting theory and accounting', *Journal of Accounting and Economics,* **32,** 3–87. A high-level survey and assessment of economic research in accounting.

Magee, R.P. (1986) *Advanced Managerial Accounting,* New York: HarperCollins. An early textbook with a strong economic focus.

20

Qualitative research on management accounting: achievements and potential

Juhani Vaivio

Introduction

This chapter provides an overview of (i) the rationale for qualitative research in management accounting, (ii) how qualitative research serves theory development, (iii) guiding principles for qualitative investigation, (iv) problems reflected in existing qualitative studies, and (v) the future potential of qualitative research efforts. The aim of the chapter is to build an understanding of qualitative research that enables the reader to appreciate the scientific purpose and theoretical significance of case and field studies. But, it also equips the reader with a critical lens through which to view the theoretical problems and methodological weaknesses of these studies. It gives a basis for evaluating qualitative studies and lays out stepping stones for designing, executing and reporting a qualitative study in management accounting. The chapter closes by identifying current research needs and proposing broad avenues of enquiry that the reader may later wish to follow.

Why do we need qualitative research on management accounting?

Qualitative research is a messy and time-consuming affair. Any academic who has been involved in the production of a case or field study would probably recall the difficulties: identifying relevant theory, formulating the research objectives, gaining access, finding the key people, getting your hands on documents, observing without disturbing, drowning in data, being puzzled by conflicting interpretations, trying to find theoretical sense, and writing an argument which is not only novel and intriguing, but also credible. After the intensive hours in the field, and the countless lonely hours in front of the computer screen, the 'qualitative' management accounting scholar inevitably faces a painful, almost existential question – does qualitative research in management accounting really matter?

It does, for three key reasons. First, qualitative research takes us beyond a narrow and functionalist view of the management accounting phenomenon, which I'll call here the *textbook view*. Second, qualitative research protects us against a scientific imperialism that reduces management accounting to an issue of mere economic choice; this I will call the *economics view*. Third, qualitative research critically scrutinises normative prescriptions for improving management accounting, which can be labelled the *consultancy view*. By qualitative research, we typically mean case-based research that relies on rich empirical material collected from a single target organisation or a handful of case-organisations and strives towards theoretically valuable interpretations. Qualitative research uses multiple sources of evidence, such as interviews, documents and other texts as well as forms of participant observation within the research site. Below, we discuss the achievements of qualitative research in 'saving' the management accounting phenomenon from being overwhelmed by the above three perspectives and in furthering our knowledge and understanding in this field of enquiry.

Beyond the *textbook view*

In the *textbook view*, management accounting is a practical technology – a collection of practical tools that practical people employ in practical situations, especially when they have business and money in mind. Cost allocations, profitability analyses of available options, long-run investment appraisals, traditional budgeting methods and non-financial performance measurements are all needed to manage the everyday life of the organisation. By applying management accounting tools, this everyday life becomes much more formalised and systematic. Managerial practices run beyond personal belief or emotion and are not at the mercy of mere speculation, whim and intuition. With the assistance of management accounting tools, the organisation thinks before it acts. It remains under coordinated control and heads steadily in the designated direction.

Many assumptions underlie the *textbook view*. The organisation is considered able to position itself in an 'environment' and identify its boundaries as an autonomous entity. It knows its preferences, and employs agents – responsible managers. It has specific goals, on which its participants broadly agree. It carefully plans its future before rushing into action, asking for 'hard' data and formally processed information. When the organisation acts, this action is coupled to routinised monitoring, documentation and follow-up. Hence, the organisation has two important, ongoing problems. The first is rational decision-making – how to choose the best available course of action as a result of a logical sequence of events that we know as the 'decision-making process'. The second is rational control – how to implement 'decisions' and steer the organisation by comparing specified outcomes with specified objectives.

Management accounting, as a functional technology that helps managers, is connected with both of these problems. It assists rational decision-making by providing quantitative information, economic analysis and financial evaluation that support informed, sound choices. It assists rational control by measuring and monitoring the organisation's progress towards specific, quantified financial and non-financial objectives, and allowing 'management by exception', which triggers immediate corrective action. Summing up, management accounting is seen as a practical medium that serves rational management purposes. It is a flexible and neutral technical instrument or formal system that can be moulded to the functional aims of its users.

One could almost wish this were the case. Everyday organisational life would be much more predictable! However, as qualitative research in management accounting continues to remind us, organisational reality does not match the implicit ontological simplifications of the *textbook view*. When we enter a real organisation, and a real business firm in particular, we soon realise that we are very far from the instructively appealing abstractions of textbooks. The organisation operates in multiple competitive and institutionalised environments. It faces conflicting demands. Sometimes the organisation is powerful enough to design and engineer its own 'environment'. For instance, a giant multinational enterprise is far from being a passive adaptor to imposed circumstances. The boundaries of many organisations are fuzzy, especially in the network economy of our times. Participation of organisational agents is fluid. Organisational agents and different coalitions within the firm may have contradictory goals. Often the organisation acts before it thinks; the cost of pausing to think may outweigh the benefits of planning and 'rational' decision-making since prompt action, without paralysing analysis, may be needed to secure the commitment of key agents. Alternatively, the organisation might act in order to discover its preferences, trying to learn what it actually wants in a highly ambiguous and dynamic situation.

Decision processes are rarely rational and linear. Rather, they are complex bundles of interconnected, loosely coupled events that bounce back and forth. They involve many actors who represent diverse opinions, interests, biases, hidden agendas and competencies. Decision-making often gets interrupted, marginalised, diverted, restarted or merged with another stream of urgent concerns. Moreover, rational control – on closer empirical examination – is also an illusion. What the 'official' decision in fact suggests in terms of concrete operational action cannot be articulated with precision. Targets are imperfect approximations of what the organisation seeks and are interpreted in different ways by biased local agents.

Consequently, those seeking a deeper understanding of the management accounting phenomenon 'from a distance', while avoiding the need for a direct involvement with the mundane practice of business, can learn a lot from the qualitative research literature and its documented illustrations of practice. Management accounting is not a compact 'toolbox' of functional techniques and neutral systems to assist rational choice and control. Rather, it is a loose assembly of calculative practices that are used selectively, in a bewildering variety of ways, by a multitude of agents within a broad range of organisational processes and situations. For instance, instead of serving internal decision or control needs, the numbers provided by management accountants may be used for merely cosmetic purposes, projecting an image of up-to-date management practice. Or they may be used as a substitute for action, to lure external parties into believing that a major transformation is occurring where none in fact exists. Furthermore, qualitative research has revealed that cost data may be used to gain a better negotiating position with a partner-supplier. Where cost data is used within the unstructured chaos of a decision process, it is often manipulated by key agents to serve local, perhaps sub-optimal, ends. Competing expert groups within a company can use management accounting information to gain the upper hand in internal battles for power and resources. Investment calculations might be used to legitimate *ex post* a large investment decision that was taken rather quickly, based on subjective but 'strategic' considerations. A bold market move, a 'shot in the dark', may be post-rationalised with management accounting figures to look like a premeditated, carefully analysed decision. Budgets and performance measurements can produce unintended consequences if they are misunderstood, fail to reflect real intentions, are subject to game-playing, or are deliberately manipulated. And management accounting professionals can take many different roles – they are not always boring 'bean counters' and may become powerful agents of strategic change.

Thus, qualitative research serves an important educational and pedagogic purpose by offering a deeper perspective into the subject of management accounting. It probes beyond textbook idealisations to expose management accounting as an imperfect practice, used in a variety of different ways to become the *de facto* organisational reality.

A counterweight to the *economics view*

The educational and pragmatic *textbook view* has borrowed much from the theoretical tradition underlying the *economics view* – a perspective that dominates important streams of academic enquiry in management accounting. With its roots in neoclassical economics, and the microeconomic theory of the firm in particular, the *economics view* offers an analytically powerful research perspective. The strength of this framework lies in its conceptual clarity, parsimony and elegance, as well as its universal character. It attempts to explain management accounting in abstract and often mathematically modelled terms that defy the constraints of time and place. This perspective offers, therefore, a 'general' theory.

Under this view, 'the firm' is an abstract productive entity, a 'black box' where input factors become efficiently transformed into an output to maximise profits. Management accounting is seen as a rational tool of self-interested economic agents of 'the firm', who operate under conditions of scarce resources and opportunity costs. These agents possess considerable computational skills and use them to maximise their utility. They operate in many different markets that tend, at least in the long run, towards equilibrium, and they can obtain reliable information about market prices. The preferences of these agents are exogenously given and known. Hence, management accounting becomes coupled to marginal decision-making – i.e. to the impartial weighing of marginal utility against marginal cost. Furthermore, the relationships between these rational agents are primarily transactional, but these transactions come at a cost. Recently, the *economics view* has drawn on concepts of the principal, the agent, contracting, moral hazard and asymmetric information to analyse management accounting techniques and economic incentives for the rational control of economic undertakings.

In management accounting research, the merits of the *economics view*, and its substantial impact on the North American theoretical tradition, are undeniable. It has allowed us to analyse problems of organisational control, i.e. the problems of evaluating the performance of different actors and tying suitable incentives to performance measurements. However, the limits of the somewhat imperialistic *economics view* need to be acknowledged (see Lazear, 2000; Luft and Shields, 2002). We should avoid closure in our theoretical paradigm and a premature shift into what Thomas Kuhn called 'normal science'. Here, qualitative research has served a remarkable role. In simple terms, it can be claimed that the largely European tradition of qualitative management accounting research has acted as a necessary counterweight to North American theoretical influences, preserving both theoretical and methodological pluralism.

The achievements of qualitative research are twofold. First, it has rejected the economist's notion of the organisation as a 'black box'. After all, the microeconomic theory of 'the firm' was never intended to become an accurate description of what happens *inside* firms. The theory of 'the firm', its rational agents and its *marginalism*, were meant to be the building blocks in a much wider macroeconomic theory, the general theory of market equilibrium, designed to explain vast classes of economic phenomena. 'The firm' was constructed as a *theoretical* firm – it was never meant to portray the *empirical* firm. Qualitative management accounting research has penetrated the economists' 'black box', seeking the *how* and *why* of organisational affairs, and discarding the stereotyped actors and their stylised economic transactions assumed in the *economics view*.

Qualitative studies have documented how management accounting instruments become intermingled with intricate political processes, in which the distribution of organisational power plays a central role. They have illustrated how budgeting procedures introduce organisational segmentation and tension. They have exposed how accounting measurements create disciplinary spaces for governing economic life. They have identified the ritualistic and symbolic value of financial controls in transforming an organisation's dominant culture. They have described how management accounting 'talk' becomes intertwined with other forms of organisational and managerial knowledge. They have identified the routinisation and institutionalisation of outdated management accounting techniques. They have reminded us that management accounting can be synonymous with exploitation (see for example Dent, 1991; Miller and O'Leary, 1994; Ahrens, 1997; Vaivio, 1999; Wickramasinghe and Hopper, 2005).

But the foremost message of these qualitative investigations is that management accounting does not reflect any single, given economic reality. And it is not the passive consequence of economic conditions. It is an active, constitutive phenomenon. With management accounting, we *make* reality (Hopwood, 1983). Management accounting calculations create urgency and relevance around particular issues whilst marginalising or discrediting others. They drive organisational initiatives into predefined alleys. Measurements determine what receives managerial attention, and so create a certain visibility within the organisation. For instance, cost and profit centres order and partition activity, thereby shaping actors' understandings of how operations are structured and how various elements are interlinked. Management accounting also maintains conformity in these perceptions, for example by standardising reporting formats.

Second, qualitative research has demonstrated that we need more than a 'general theory', based on economic analysis, if we want to understand the management accounting phenomenon. The universalism of the *economics view* must be complemented with a fundamentally different philosophy of what counts as legitimate 'theory' in management accounting research. In qualitative research, 'theory' is primarily a *local* description and explanation as well as a *temporal* creation. This suggests a different ontology and a different epistemology. 'Theory' emerges from a local context and is limited by the particular characteristics (in space and time) of this context. It is not supposed to be a universally valid construct, generalisable in a statistical sense from a sample to a wider population, across a broad range of empirical contexts, from one place to another. And it is not supposed to be an eternal construction that stands firm against the ravages of time. Instead, theories are born, have a lifespan and die.

429

Qualitative studies can be credited with introducing management accounting as a *context-bound* phenomenon. Empirically, management accounting is not a homogeneous set of calculative practices, but is highly contingent and situationally specific. Moreover, qualitative research provides evidence that management accounting is a dynamic, organisationally embedded *social* phenomenon. Organisational agents continually reinterpret management accounting in particular situations, creating meaning around specific forms of calculus and formal control. Thus, the shared making of this reality is in a constant state of flux. Management accounting instruments are not stable and fixed, but are often complex, temporary and fragile.

This is not to imply, however, that regularities, parallels and general tendencies between management accounting phenomena cannot be observed across contexts. Management accounting does not materialise 'case-by-case', as an entirely idiosyncratic, isolated and unique phenomenon, as shown by qualitative case and field studies. But an examination of qualitative research warns us against sweeping generalisations across contexts. Such 'general' theories, while empirically supported across a larger population of organisations, are often uninteresting and empty in substantive content. Such theories are 'general' because they tell us so little.

Problematising the *consultancy view*

A pragmatic perspective on management accounting is offered by what can broadly be described as the consulting industry. It is important to acknowledge that commercial interests are at play here, in a market where significant financial gains can be realised. Consulting agencies, multinational accounting firms, educational institutions with a consultancy orientation, and 'branded' academics operating as part-time consultants are the suppliers of progressive management products. Amongst other product offerings, these agencies include management accounting in their repertoire of fashionable 'packaged solutions'. They are rhetorically persuasive and logically appealing prescriptions of what *should be* done with 'new' management accounting technologies. Such normative statements should, however, be kept apart from scholarly research findings on how management accounting appears as an empirical phenomenon.

The *consultancy view* of management accounting draws on a vocabulary of reform and improvement coupled with illustrative examples, testimonies by leading authorities and selectively documented 'success stories'. Often, existing management accounting practice is portrayed as something orthodox and inadequate; something to be fundamentally questioned and reformed. For instance, *activity-based costing* (ABC) has been advanced as a remedy to the problems of conventional overhead allocation. Or a more compact set of *key figures* is marketed as a solution to the recognised problems of current, bureaucratic budgeting routines. Also, a 'new' management accounting technique may be put forward as a response to wider managerial concerns, just as *the balanced scorecard*, for example, has been proposed as a means of translating the organisation's strategic plans into grass-roots operational action. Hence, in the *consultancy view* management accounting is a practical technology that needs to be radically amended.

Qualitative research has traced the external origins and discursive underpinnings of organisational management accounting practices. It has linked the seemingly technical and impartial calls for management accounting reform with much wider societal programmes of efficiency and rationalisation. It reminds us of the big picture; for example, we should be aware of the often implicit societal ideals and political aspirations when the *consultancy view* comes into play. But, perhaps the most significant contribution of qualitative research has been to question the prescriptions of the *consultancy view*. It has brought these normative schemes under intensive, critical examination in various empirical settings. Their workings have been observed in real organisations and within the complex and shifting, socially constructed contexts in which 'new' management accounting technologies are implemented. It appears that these real-life contexts – where management accounting is redesigned, 'new' techniques are launched and the benefits of new calculations should materialise – are far removed from the idealised conditions assumed in the *consultancy view*. In reality, management accounting change progresses slowly. It takes unexpected turns and twists and it produces unintended consequences. Also management accounting change seems to be contextually limited. Success in one setting cannot be easily replicated in another setting (see Burns and Vaivio, 2001).

Management accounting change has been shown to be smaller and less significant than is presumed within the *consultancy view*. On closer examination, some organisations implementing 'new' calculative techniques make only marginal refinements in their practices or achieve only isolated, local changes (for instance, where only a minor unit in a larger organisation succeeds in implementing ABC). Also, change might remain at the level of top management intention, or people at the corporate centre and the organisational periphery may have different perceptions of the speed and impact of change. Many impediments to change have been identified, including the sedimentation of prevailing accounting routines, the lack of data systems support, and employee resistance in the lower echelons of the organisation.

Resistance to change has been identified as a considerable hindrance to the implementation of 'new' management accounting technologies. Resistance can take overt and articulated forms, or can dwell below the surface of organisational action – in silent, more subtle practices of non-compliance. New measurements may be rejected by a rebellious expert group that fears a violation of its decision rights. Or, a balanced scorecard, for example, can be pushed to the sidelines by a prolonged lack of real organisational commitment, for example when organisational members fear the prospect of detailed surveillance and newborn Taylorism through the use of nonfinancial measurements. Overall, qualitative research has contributed to our appreciation of management accounting change as a hazardous and non-linear process (Baxter and Chua, 2003), in which 'success' is a debatable and relative concept. Furthermore, change in management accounting must be contrasted with its stability. A new initiative can run into problems, coming eventually to a standstill. The remnants of an 'old' technology, after a long dormant period, can be rediscovered and reused. Key agents may leave, carrying the zeal of change with them, and focused change can be buried under more comprehensive reforms.

Besides critically examining the implementation of advocated 'new' management accounting techniques, qualitative research has uncovered an even more fundamental problem with the *consultancy view*. Taken together, qualitative studies have alerted us to the homogenising influence of normative prescriptions. While illustrating and explaining the adoption of fashionable management accounting techniques, qualitative research has revealed a tendency towards uniformity in contemporary practice. But, by embracing 'packaged solutions' organisations make themselves vulnerable. First, it is questionable whether proposed designs and templates offer genuine competitive advantage since these solutions are freely available in the market. Second, and more importantly, a packaged solution also contains a definition of what is to be reformed, i.e. it suggests a 'packaged problem'. Hence, adopting organisations may lean towards conformism as their understandings of what counts as an urgent managerial concern become more homogeneous. But are the deficiencies of cost accounting, or the imperfections of performance evaluation, really the organisation's most pressing issues? Or do more acute problems perhaps threaten the firm's survival? As will be discussed later, qualitative research offers opportunities to provide greater insights into the nature of such problems.

Qualitative research and theory development

Having summarised the achievements of qualitative research, we now turn to its epistemological foundations and methodological justification. How does qualitative research help to develop a theoretical body of knowledge in management accounting? And how can we distinguish between different kinds of qualitative studies in these terms? Of course, qualitative studies can be categorised in several ways. For instance, we can distinguish between descriptive, illustrative, experimental, exploratory and explanatory studies (Scapens, 1990). Alternatively, Keating (1995) suggests a framework that categorises case and field studies according to their different theoretical purposes. It is based on the notion of 'research scope', i.e. *what* the findings of a study suggest in theoretical terms. Keating differentiates between theory discovery, theory refinement and theory refutation studies.

A qualitative study aimed at theory *discovery* can be compared to an exploration of an unknown territory. The imagery of an eighteenth century explorer-adventurer, who sails off into uncharted waters, returning later to the Royal Society to report the first observations of previously unknown reptiles and exotic plants, captures the purpose of this genre of case or field study. The research seeks to explain a new phenomenon of interest, for which the boundaries may be unclear and only rudimentary patterns can be discerned. The study may be a revealing, rich description and first mapping of the research phenomenon, with little explanation of its connections with other known phenomena or of the more specific mechanisms operating within it. Where little prior theory exists, inductive and exploratory 'discovery studies' lead to preliminary theory that emerges from the empirical observations.

For example, the novel application of a management accounting technique, say a target costing system, is studied in a novel institutional and cultural setting which has had little contact with any management accounting practices. This kind of study leads to a preliminary interpretation of how the phenomenon of interest is shaped and behaves. It builds a set of concepts and informed descriptions, or perhaps advances more formal hypotheses of causal connections. Or, it may produce an illuminating, well-documented narrative that increases our understanding of the studied phenomenon.

The findings of theory discovery studies can be used as first building-blocks in further investigations, such as more focused qualitative studies, or survey studies that test the validity of preliminary hypotheses across a larger population.

Many other qualitative management accounting studies have sought theory *refinement*. While theory discovery studies proceed from a limited theoretical starting point and rely on emerging insights from field data, theory refinement studies start with a clear theoretical focus and objective. In a sense, before entering the field, the researcher has already decided which theoretical 'goggles' to wear in observing the phenomenon of interest. This does not suggest, however, that empirical observations are forced into a predetermined framework. Theory is being developed through novel, empirically embedded interpretations. Some theoretical elements are corroborated and strengthened; other elements become more clearly specified. As a consequence of this empirically substantiated refinement, theory may be partially rebuilt, as more appropriate constructs replace those with less explanatory power.

According to Keating (1995), this broad category of refinement studies can be further divided into studies that *illustrate* a particular theory, and those that *specify* an established theory. A case study that, for instance, uses a particular social theory to explain the power effects of management accounting systems may be viewed as an illustration of this wider theoretical perspective. It demonstrates the capacity of the social theory to explain phenomena in the management accounting domain, for instance when management accounting measurements and power considerations get intertwined. Such a study also reinforces the plausibility of the power-related social theory by showing that the generic theoretical framework applies in the investigation of accounting-related puzzles. Arguably, an illustrative study should also go a step a further and identify aspects of the adopted social theory that could be developed in the light of the empirical evidence.

Qualitative management accounting studies that specify (i.e. further develop) an existing theory can provide a theoretical starting point for empirical/critical research. The concepts and causal connections within the theoretical framework are partially revised to improve the theory's application within a specific organisational, social or institutional context. The theory can even be radically reformulated in light of the researcher's iterative interpretations of new field evidence. For instance, an initial theory about how senior managers use monitoring systems for strategic control might be further refined when applied within specific organisational contexts. Or, a theory that explains the mechanisms of management accounting change may be elaborated by applying it to a case study that reveals factors that inhibit or delay change.

Finally, the interpretation of evidence from a case or field study may reveal that practice does not match established management accounting theory. Rather than refining the theory, or illustrating how it works in a particular context, such an investigation contradicts the theoretical framework – as such, it is a theory *refutation* study. It should be noted that the refuted 'theory' might be a normative construction – a prescribed 'solution' which is based on certain premises and assumed causal relationships; for instance, between the adoption of a management accounting technique and specific financial or strategic benefits. This, of course, applies also to theory refinement studies, which may have a normative starting point. An example of a theory refutation study would be one that identifies dysfunctional consequences of 'strategic' non-financial measurement in an artistic organisation that shuns bureaucratic formalism, thereby contradicting a popular theory on the effects of a 'new' management accounting technology.

Doing qualitative research: some guiding principles

How should we proceed in actually *doing* qualitative research in management accounting? It is important to note that qualitative research is affected by unforeseen events and uncertain factors – it is a bold jump into the unknown. A study addressing a well focused, theoretically sound research question within an intriguing empirical site can suddenly run into problems and produce poor results. The phenomenon of interest may not be captured, being too tightly entangled with other organisational elements and dynamic social processes. The researcher may fail in data collection, gathering for instance only 'official' views about the role of a new accounting practice, or otherwise biased accounts. Access to critical locales may be denied. Or, the emerging interpretations can remain uninteresting and lacking in theoretical novelty. To minimise such problems, qualitative researchers need to follow some broad *guiding principles* about how to conduct successful case or field studies.

First, there is the question of *research design*. Is the research question relevant from theoretical and practical points of view, well formulated, and sufficiently focused? An overly pragmatic approach may result in findings that are deemed too technical or functional from an academic perspective. In contrast, an overly theoretical approach may produce findings that are welcomed by a small scientific community, but which have little practical value. A poorly articulated research question can lead to sloppy data collection, yielding very general and uninformative conclusions. A research objective that lacks focus may lead the researcher to observe 'the whole world' inside an organisation. But an overly focused research question may, in the worst-case scenario, leave the researcher empty-handed, wondering whether the phenomenon of interest exists at all (see Ferreira and Merchant, 1992).

A key decision in the design of a qualitative study concerns the extent to which prior theory should inform the research question and data collection. Some conceptualisation, and a clear a priori theoretical orientation, is needed to guide empirical observations to the right context and specific locales of interest. It assists in crafting interview themes and later in filtering the masses of research evidence. It should be noted that no researcher's mind is an empty canvas, a *tabula rasa*. We approach phenomena with some implicit assumptions about what we expect to see, casting a 'net' over the facts we wish to capture. A strong theoretical orientation and strict adherence to pre-specified constructs may, however, force preordained theoretical perspectives onto the observations, suffocating any innovative empirical insights. For instance, a researcher might perceive an organisation's performance appraisal practices solely in terms of the suggested dichotomy between diagnostic and interactive control systems. He or she may then fail to notice different local uses of accounting measurements that do not fit this categorisation, but which provide a better explanation of organisational practice. Hence, empirical sensitivity should not be sacrificed in the name of prior theoretical focus (see Ahrens and Dent, 1998).

Another key issue in qualitative research design concerns the dilemma of depth versus breadth. Should the study be a deep-probing investigation of a single organisation or other unit of analysis? Or, should it seek to theorise about a management accounting phenomenon that exists across multiple case study organisations? In the single case study, the phenomenon of interest is examined in its detailed context, against a rich background of organisational processes, tensions and competing sectional interests, which are reflected in management accounting calculations and practices. This contextual understanding, together with the contrasting observations *within* the case, allow for an appreciation of the social dynamics that surround the studied phenomenon. This provides a plausible, contextually rich explanation of the research phenomenon that has theoretical value.

In a multiple case study, comparisons *across* organisational contexts are sought, so each organisation can be studied less intensively. This approach usually draws on well-specified prior theoretical constructs, research instruments and protocols. Although the within-case analysis may be less detailed, visiting several empirical sites does provide an opportunity to examine cross-case patterns and search for similarities and differences in the studied phenomenon. The juxtaposition of the different case contexts can challenge simplistic a priori expectations and generate a more sophisticated theoretical understanding (Eisenhart, 1989). For example, this approach might reveal that dissimilar organisations experience similar difficulties in the implementation of a 'new' management accounting technique, indicating potential flaws in the normative design that has been applied.

Second, besides giving sufficient attention to research design, successful qualitative studies in the management accounting field have been built on reliable and valid empirical evidence obtained via professionally executed, meticulous *data collection* (McKinnon, 1988). Brief and superficial 'site visits', allowing for only one or two interviews, should be distinguished from genuine case or field studies. The latter involve the researcher for longer periods in the field. Generally, the longer the researcher spends in the studied context, the less vulnerable the study is to factors that jeopardise its reliability and validity. Some moderation is advisable, however. The notorious tale of the sociologist being finally rediscovered in a Borneo jungle wearing a hula skirt and with a ring through his nostril warns us about the threat of *going native*. Researchers undertaking qualitative studies must maintain an appropriate distance from the studied context.

Once in the field, even the best research design is unfortunately no protection against the obstacles the researcher faces within a real, working organisation. Typically, a good qualitative management accounting study, which succeeds in building a strong theoretical argument, is the product of careful underlying fieldwork. If interviews are the primary data source, they must be sufficiently extensive within the unit under study. They must be thoroughly prepared, and the researcher must try as far as possible to minimise respondent bias. It is not enough to interview only senior management about an ABC implementation, as people on the 'shop-floor' may have a totally different story to tell. The independent nature of the study must be explained to interviewees, to avoid any perception that the researcher is acting as a 'management spy'. The researcher must know the background of each interviewee and must address topics relevant to that person. She or he must avoid using scientific jargon and speak instead the 'language' of the interviewees. The researcher must not lead the discussion along preconceived paths, but must have the sensitivity and skill to steer the discussion away from clearly irrelevant topic areas, to maintain the focus on the phenomenon under study. At the same time, interesting leads should be followed with further probing questions. The researcher should not express his or her own opinions during the interview, or take sides in any way, otherwise the fieldwork may become 'politicised'.

Extensive interviews are often the primary, but not the only, source of data. A thorough qualitative study will complement interviews with other data sources. *Triangulation* between different empirical materials can increase the reliability of the evidence. For instance, a study examining non-financial management accounting measurement within an organisational improvement programme should seek critical documentary material, such as internal memos, reports, manuals, written instructions and official newsletters. Participant observation of critical management meetings provides another source of evidence to compare with interview transcripts and internal documents. Here again, the researcher must be very careful in the field, trying not to interfere in a way that alters the behaviour of organisational members, but also avoiding the threatening, mute behaviour of a police detective who sits in the corner and makes 'observations' (McKinnon, 1988).

Third, a successful qualitative study in management accounting can be distinguished by the theoretically oriented *interpretations* it produces. The investigation should have uncovered the intriguing organisational processes that are entwined with a particular management accounting phenomenon. Often, it will document a chain of interlocking events, and capture the multiple and shifting meanings that different actors give to uses of management accounting in specific contexts.

Even after all this empirical work to discover the 'reality' under investigation, the study is still only halfway to completion! What remains is to give theoretical sense to the masses of illuminating, perhaps even thrilling, evidence from the case or field study. We may have an intriguing narrative here, but why does it matter? What do we learn from it? Here, the role of interpretation is crucial.

Without bold interpretation and theorising, a qualitative study is just a collection of engaging field detail. In practice, theoretically valuable interpretation requires numerous iterations between theory and evidence. The layers of collected, often contradictory, pieces of field evidence gradually become more organised and things start to make sense. Some observations appear more important and more credible than others, and some pieces of evidence are pushed aside as irrelevant. A preliminary storyline takes shape. The first theoretically anchored patterns emerge. But the researcher must not jump to hasty conclusions. Maybe some additional evidence must be collected on curious empirical instances that stand out and require further explanation. And a new theoretical angle, perhaps from beyond the management accounting literature, might be discovered. It may develop the explanation of the observed instances and events, but without being harshly 'glued onto' the data. Alternative explanations and conflicting voices from the field should be considered, elaborating the study's logic. No story should be forced onto the evidence, however.

With patience, a documented and plausible *rich account* is constructed – not a sanitised, intellectually corrupt version of events that twists evidence into the simplistic formats of normative prescriptions (Ahrens and Dent, 1998). Finally, after multiple iterations between theory and data, a theoretically oriented interpretation can be extracted and reported.

Common problems in qualitative management accounting studies

Although the qualitative research tradition in management accounting has produced significant theoretical advances, some individual studies exhibit weaknesses. Of course, the same criticism can be leveled at any methodological approach and any research method. Still, a brief mapping of common weaknesses of qualitative research is worthwhile since, in any scientific domain, reasonable self-criticism promotes improvement.

Often, a disappointing qualitative study starts with a disappointing theoretical framework that fails to provide focus and guide the fieldwork. Instead, the theoretical framework might be a loose assemblage of reviewed literature that points at pieces of theory here and there. Some of its elements might be incompatible because they represent different streams of prior enquiry, proceeding from different ontological, epistemological and methodological assumptions. For instance, a study may try in vain to borrow both from economics-based agency theory and sociologically grounded interpretive ethnography. This can be thought of as the *'mixed salad'* problem of qualitative enquiry.

The digestion of such a disorientating theoretical mix can be difficult. The real disappointment, however, lies further ahead, when the study fails to fully utilise the theory it has introduced in its empirical and interpretive phases. 'Why this heavy theoretical "frontload"?' the reader grumbles. A meandering storyline and the absence of an explanatory backbone reflect the more fundamental problem: wearing too many theoretical 'goggles' may be no better than walking blind and may suggest to the reader that the empirical work was also muddled.

Another common problem arises when a study fails to reconnect with its theoretical starting point, even when this point is sufficiently clear and focused. The study may introduce an interesting narrative, interspersed with interview quotes and documentary material that give verisimilitude to the description of, for example, a management accounting change process. But, its theoretical interpretation and conclusions will fail to meet academic standards if they don't explain how the empirical evidence enriches our theoretical understanding of management accounting change. Since the phenomenon of interest is already theorised to some extent, how is this theory refined, specified or partially refuted by the interpretation of the field observations? If the study's empirical findings about the change process are not appropriately compared with previous theoretical contributions, its conclusions will be rather myopic. It may even claim to discover something that has already been demonstrated in other studies, thus falling victim to the *'rediscovering the wheel'* problem of qualitative investigation (Laughlin, 1995).

It is also common for qualitative management accounting studies to draw on social theory or socio-philosophical meta-frameworks. Such an approach explicitly acknowledges that management accounting is not just a universal, neutral and functional technology, but is a context-bound practice that has social, disciplinary and political dimensions. However, such studies often serve to illustrate only one particular social theory. A generic social theory, which was designed to explain a wide range of social phenomena and corresponding societal dynamics on a macro-scale, becomes empirically illustrated and verified in the context of a specific organisation's management accounting practices. This can lead to what I call the '*It fits, it fits!*' problem of qualitative studies.

When a novel social theory is first imported into the management accounting domain, such illustrative studies are well justified. But once the social theory has become established, the replication of purely illustrative studies becomes unhelpful. Instead, an attempt should soon be made to use the field or case study insights to challenge and refine the social theory, since – irrespective of their status and reputation – all theories should be treated as provisional and incomplete. Furthermore, qualitative studies that draw on a social theory should also examine the contingent nature of contemporary management accounting practice (Humphrey and Scapens, 1996; Malmi and Granlund, 2006). They should provide novel insight into specific applications of management accounting techniques.

The uncritical illustration of a theoretical starting point also occurs in another category of qualitative management accounting studies – those that seek empirical confirmation of a normative management accounting solution that has arisen from the *consultancy view.* The researcher, especially if inexperienced, may be unaware of this underlying motivation. Since popular normative arguments are generally easy to grasp, and since management accounting practice seems to follow the latest normative recommendations, an inexperienced researcher may be attracted to the *consultancy view* as a 'theoretical framework' to guide the study. In qualitative management accounting research, this may be termed the '*windsurfer problem*'.

Uncritical empirical illustrations of popular 'management products' often build on questionable fieldwork and fail to observe the *guiding principle* of professional data collection, discussed earlier. Convinced by the force of his/her popular 'wind', the researcher 'surfs' the field, collecting only superficial evidence. Those interviewees who freely speak out are often those agents who are promoting the new practice and who have an organisational interest in it. Their voices may come to dominate the interview data while the sceptics remain in the background, avoiding interview or daring only to relate a sanitised opinion to the researcher. Also, if the full impact of the new practice has not yet been felt, the views of many agents may be premature and may change later. Reliance on a *consultancy view* as a 'theoretical framework' can also result in observer bias, where the new management accounting technique is perceived to signify progress within the empirical site. The researcher may look for positive evidence of its implementation, ignoring or marginalising its more problematic aspects. Consequently, the findings of such studies tend to be unsurprising, uncritical and somewhat thin accounts of how, in yet another setting, a new approach (such as the balanced scorecard) has been adopted almost as its original blueprint would suggest.

Finally, qualitative management accounting researchers can be prone to over-generalising their findings. Having presented management accounting as a contextualised practice within a unique case study setting, some researchers then suddenly suggest that the findings can be generalised, in a statistical sense, to a larger organisational population. This inappropriate claim constitutes *'misplaced universalism'* – another problem of qualitative management accounting research, which stems from a positivist or modernist conception of science.

The desire to look beyond a particular study to discover something more general is to be applauded. But we have to be careful about what we mean by *generalisation*. The aim of qualitative management accounting research is not to produce generalisations of a statistical nature, or make inferences to a broader population. A single case study is not a statistical study with a sample of one, and it is a mistake to seek some kind of universal generalisation from it. Qualitative studies can, however, arrive at a different kind of generalisation – *theoretical generalisation* (Lukka and Kasanen, 1995). They can bring theories into contact with empirical reality, thus exposing their strengths and weaknesses, and modifying or even refuting them. In addition, exploratory qualitative studies can, as mentioned earlier, serve an important theory discovery role, building initial hypotheses for use in further studies that seek universal generalisations and higher external validity within larger populations.

The future potential of qualitative management accounting research

Qualitative research that pays attention to the above problems and strives towards high academic standards has a lot to offer to the further development of management accounting theory. At its best, a qualitative study is a theoretically informed, focused, intensive, well-documented and plausible analysis that increases our understanding of *how* management accounting operates in different societal, cultural, institutional and organisational settings. Because it explains management accounting practice as a context-bound and dynamic phenomenon, a qualitative study can probe beyond economic models and normative idealisations. It builds an understanding of management accounting as something very real – as something that affects the lives of countless individuals in their workplaces.

Hence, qualitative research has the potential to enhance our appreciation of how management accounting practices shape, and are shaped by, the unique contexts in which they are applied. Second, despite their contextual nature and historical specificity, management accounting practices do exhibit regularity and predictability across different contexts. Arguably, we can apply qualitative methods better, harnessing their full potential in building theories that connect with the actual challenges facing postmodern organisations and societies.

Qualitative studies can address fundamental, practical problems related to *how* management accounting is used and transformed in different settings. These studies should, however, draw rather more on existing management accounting theory, rather than seeking to illustrate a 'grand' social meta-theory. The findings of previous case studies in the same area can be a solid basis for the design of a new field study. Can we partly replicate this study in another empirical context, or partly refute it? Can we develop it further, perhaps adding some new explanatory dimensions, extending it to other organisational contexts, or learning something more specific about the conditions that must be met before a certain management accounting practice can be usefully deployed?

A well-positioned qualitative study can also take a recent survey study as a point of departure; for instance, a study could map current uses of different techniques. It could examine unexpected, inconclusive or oddly distributed survey results, or investigate an intriguing correlation that requires further explanation. For example, why is the adoption of formal controls so popular in a particular sub-category of enterprises? Can we explain the delayed implementation of management accounting reforms under certain strategic and organisational conditions? Can we explain dysfunctional practices that surprise us in a particular set of enterprises?

At a minimum, a qualitative study should contribute to coherent management accounting theory by comparing its *findings* with those of other relevant studies and looking for cross-case patterns. It should identify the theoretical dimensions that differentiate it from other studies that have examined similar management accounting practices. This promotes theoretical generalisation and may increase the external validity of the study's findings.

The external validity and theoretical insights of a qualitative study can be further improved by complementing it with a large-sample statistical study, using hypotheses that emerge from the qualitative study. Construct validity in such a survey is high, since the operational definitions of theoretical concepts, and the measurement instruments used in the survey, are based on the inductive empirical findings from the qualitative study. For example, it is easier to design a meaningful questionnaire about investment post-audit in the energy sector, if we can build on the findings of a case study that examined the detailed dynamics of post-audit processes in an oil company.

A qualitative study can also be complemented by a laboratory study that is designed to simulate the sort of 'natural setting' observed in the case or field study. Or, it can be followed by mathematical modelling that formalises key relationships uncovered in a field setting (Modell, 2005). The use of multiple methods, combined with tolerance and mutual respect within the research community, can help us to develop a less fragmented body of management accounting knowledge.

In particular, the potential of qualitative management accounting research should be applied to contemporary concerns of practice. Although we must guard against overly pragmatic and instrumentalist demands, qualitative research conducted in academic isolation may have little to contribute beyond a narrow scholarly debate. Thus, qualitative research should continue to question the emerging ideas that organisations embrace in the hope of improving their management practices. We must critically examine the latest *consultancy views*, probing their foundations and their implications, since their evaluation is too important an issue to be left to consultants! Qualitative research can caution managers and accounting practitioners against the deficiencies and dysfunctional consequences of normative schemes and identify the conditions under which these prescriptions are likely to work best. And, it can suggest how to modify and improve them. The tension between qualitative scholars and consultants should, therefore, fuel a constructive dialogue with current practice.

Important contemporary topics facing qualitative management accounting researchers include globalisation, hybridity and the network society (Baxter and Chua, 2003). Globalization often means that management accounting practices are uprooted from their original context, becoming diffused to other, remoter locations. Yet our knowledge of how these practices are transferred, and what problems arise, remains limited. Hybridity, a related concept, suggests that we have to examine the workings of management accounting in conditions that mix traditional and new elements, such as the local and the global, rivalry and partnership. How is management accounting used by organisations that combine, for example, the private and the public, as happens in educational institutions? Finally, it has been suggested that we now live in the network society; in other words, in a technologically advanced, digitised 'surveillance society', where management accounting can make visible almost any form of action. Using qualitative studies, we can ask whether management accounting is engaged in the creation of a 'superpanopticon' – i.e. an open space where there is someone watching our every move (Baxter and Chua, 2003).

This leads us to the question of how qualitative research can help us to examine the *quantification of organisational life*. As a consequence of normative prescriptions, such as the balanced scorecard and measurements of customer satisfaction and quality, and continual advances in information systems and data networks, organisational reality is increasingly dominated by both financial and non-financial measurements. This is fundamentally transforming how organisations perceive themselves and their environments, how they negotiate, and how they act upon issues and events. Recently, even the smallest aspects of organisational activity have become transparent and open to evaluation via management accounting measures. Organisational members can no longer escape ongoing surveillance as benchmarks and uniform standards are increasingly applied.

What are the implications of this increasing quantification within postmodern organisations? We know little about how it affects people in their jobs. Will they eventually become obedient, passive and risk-averse, instead of being creative actors who promote learning and innovation? Will increasing quantification change how decisions are made? Will it drive out the influences of intuition, practical experience and judgement? Will 'hard' numbers overwhelm 'soft' talk?

These questions should not be overlooked in qualitative management accounting research. They are important to the successful management of contemporary organisations, since they impact a range of issues, from the formulation of competitive strategy to organisational learning and operational flexibility. They are also important from a broader societal point of view. The quantification of organisational life is not only a narrow management concern; its implications run much deeper and concern how the everyday reality of the postmodern individual is being shaped. Qualitative research in management accounting must not lose sight of its societal duty. It should continue to provide theoretical and empirical insights that protect individuals against impersonal, institutionalised forces that go against their interests. Qualitative research needs to explore the social, the societal and the political in management accounting, reminding us of the larger picture and revealing the ideals and motivations that lie beneath the surface of contemporary practice.

Conclusion

This chapter has presented a broad panorama of ideas about qualitative research in management accounting. First, it emphasised the importance of qualitative research as a *counterweight* to textbook idealisations, formalised economic models and consultancy products. It examined how qualitative research contributes, in different ways, to the construction of management accounting theory. It then presented a practical 'road map' to guide the eager management accounting scholar who wants to use case or field study methods. The reader was then alerted to the common problems in existing qualitative research, in the hope that this will improve future studies. Finally, the potential of these future studies was illustrated across a number of possibilities, all of which could lead us towards a more coherent, valid, relevant and emancipating body of knowledge in management accounting.

References

Ahrens, T. (1997) 'Talking accounting: an ethnography of management knowledge in British and German brewers', *Accounting, Organizations and Society*, **22**, 617–36.

Ahrens, T. and Dent, J. (1998) 'Accounting and organizations: realizing the richness of field research', *Journal of Management Accounting Research*, **10**, 1–39.

Baxter, J. and Chua, W.F. (2003) 'Alternative management accounting research – whence and whither', *Accounting, Organizations and Society*, **28**, 97–126.

Burns, J. and Vaivio, J. (2001) 'Management accounting change', *Management Accounting Research*, **12**, 389–402.

Dent, J. (1991) 'Accounting and organizational cultures: a field study of the emergence of a new organizational reality', *Accounting, Organizations and Society*, **16**(8), 705–32.

Eisenhart, K. (1989) 'Building theories from case study research', *Academy of Management Review*, **14**, 532–50.

Ferreira, L. and Merchant, K. (1992) 'Field research in management accounting and control: a review and evaluation', *Accounting, Auditing and Accountability Journal*, **5**(4), 3–34.

Hopwood, A. (1983) 'On trying to study accounting in the contexts in which it operates', *Accounting, Organizations and Society*, **8**, 287–305.

Humphrey, C. and Scapens, R. (1996) 'Methodological themes – theories and case studies of organizational accounting practices: limitation or liberation?' *Accounting, Auditing and Accountability Journal*, **9**(4), 86–106.

Keating, P. (1995) 'A framework for classifying and evaluating the theoretical contributions of case research in management accounting', *Journal of Management Accounting Research*, Fall, 66–86.

Laughlin, R. (1995) 'Methodological themes – empirical research in accounting: alternative approaches and a case for "middle-range" thinking', *Accounting, Auditing and Accountability Journal*, **8**(1), 63–87.

Lazear, E.P. (2000) 'Economic imperialism', *The Quarterly Journal of Economics*, February, 99–146.

Luft, J. and Shields, M. (2002) 'Zimmerman's contentious conjectures: describing the present and prescribing the future of empirical management accounting research', *The European Accounting Review*, **11**(4), 795–803.

Lukka, K. and Kasanen, E. (1995) 'The problem of generalizability: anecdotes and evidence in accounting research', *Accounting, Auditing and Accountability Journal*, **8**(5), 71–90.

Malmi, T. and Granlund, M. (2006) 'In search of management accounting theory', paper presented at the Annual Conference of The European Accounting Association, Dublin, Ireland, March 2006.

McKinnon, J. (1988) 'Reliability and validity in field research: some strategies and tactics', *Accounting, Auditing and Accountability Journal*, **1**, 34–54.

Miller, P. and O'Leary, T. (1994) 'Accounting, "economic citizenship" and the spatial reordering of manufacture', *Accounting, Organizations and Society*, **19**, 15–43.

Modell, S. (2005) 'Triangulation between case study and survey methods in management accounting research: an assessment of validity implications', *Management Accounting Research*, **16**, 231–54.

Scapens, R. (1990) 'Researching management accounting practice: the role of case study methods', *British Accounting Review*, **22**, 259–281.

Vaivio, J. (1999) 'Examining "the quantified customer"', *Accounting, Organizations and Society*, **24**, 689–715.

Wickramasinghe, D. and Hopper, T. (2005) 'A cultural political economy of management accounting controls: a case study of a textile mill in a traditional *Sinhalese* village', *Critical Perspectives on Accounting*, **16**, 473–503.

Further reading

Birnberg, J., Shields, M. and Young, S. (1990) 'The case for multiple methods in empirical management accounting research (with an illustration from budget setting)', *Journal of Management Accounting Research*, Fall, 33–66. Outlines the strengths and weaknesses of different empirical research methods and how to combine them.

Dyer, W.G. and Wilkins, A.L. (1991) 'Better stories, not better constructs, to generate better theory: a rejoinder to Eishenhart', *Academy of Management Review*, **16**(3), 613–19. A sharp reply to Eisenhart's view that well-developed constructs should be applied whilst 'in the field'.

Kasurinen, T. (2002) 'Exploring management accounting change: the case of a balanced scorecard implementation', *Management Accounting Research*, **13**, 323–43. A good piece about the inhibitors of management accounting change.

Machlup, F. (1967) 'Theories of the firm: marginalist, behavioral, managerial', *American Economic Review*, March. Reprinted in E. Mansfield (ed.) (1982) *Microeconomics – Selected Readings*, 4th ed., New York: W.W. Norton & Company, pp. 93–108. A classic argument, from a brilliant thinker, on how 'the firm' can be conceived.

Malmi, T. (2001) 'Balanced Scorecards in Finnish companies: a research note', *Management Accounting Research*, **12**, 207–20. Points out that balanced scorecards, for instance, are often loosely coupled to competitive strategy.

Vaivio, J. (2005) '"Strategic" non-financial measurement in an organizational context: a critique', in S. Jönsson and J. Mouritsen (eds), *Accounting in Scandinavia – The Northern Lights*, Copenhagen: Liber & Copenhagen Business School Press, pp. 193–218. Provides a critical discussion of popular 'strategic' measurement.

Index